Japan in the World

Shidehara as a student at Tokyo Imperial University

Japan in the World

*Shidehara Kijūrō, Pacifism,
and the Abolition of War*

VOLUME I

Klaus Schlichtmann

LEXINGTON BOOKS
A division of

ROWMAN & LITTLEFIELD PUBLISHERS, INC.
Lanham • Boulder • New York • Toronto • Plymouth, UK

LEXINGTON BOOKS

A division of Rowman & Littlefield Publishers, Inc.
A wholly owned subsidiary of The Rowman & Littlefield Publishing Group, Inc.
4501 Forbes Boulevard, Suite 200
Lanham, MD 20706

Estover Road
Plymouth PL6 7PY
United Kingdom

British Library Cataloguing in Publication Information Available

Library of Congress Cataloging-in-Publication Data

Schlichtmann, Klaus, 1944–
  Japan in the world : Shidehara Kijuro, pacifism, and the abolition of war / by Klaus
Schlichtmann.
      p. cm. — (Asia world)
  Includes bibliographical references and index.
  ISBN 978-0-7391-2675-2 (cloth : alk. paper) — ISBN 978-0-7391-2676-9
(pbk. : alk. paper) — ISBN 978-0-7391-3269-2 (electronic)
  1. Shidehara, Kijuro, 1872–1951. 2. Prime ministers—Japan—Biography. 3.
  Diplomats—Japan—Biography. 4. Japan—Foreign relations—1912–1945. 5.
  Pacifism—Japan—History—20th century. I. Title.
  DS890.S4S357 2009
  952.04'4092—dc22   2008050754

Printed in the United States of America

⊗™ The paper used in this publication meets the minimum requirements of American
National Standard for Information Sciences—Permanence of Paper for Printed Library
Materials, ANSI/NISO Z39.48–1992.

Contents

Acknowledgments

My association with Japan started around 1960 with an interest in Buddhist literature and the East. After spending a couple of years in India I became active, in the 1970s, in the peace and environment movement, and eventually began a course of graduate studies at Kiel University, where I took up medieval and modern history as a major, and political science and public international law as my two minor subjects. When Hermann Kulke from the Heidelberg Institute of South-Asian Studies took over the chair for Asian history in Kiel, I switched to Asian history as my major. My master's thesis in 1990 already focused on Shidehara diplomacy. In early 1992 during three months of private research in Japan I followed up on my previous work to learn more through daily visits to the Shidehara Peace Collection (*Shidehara Heiwa Bunko*) in Japan's National Diet Library. My special thanks during this time go to Ms. Yasumoto Ken and her associates, who selflessly and energetically assisted me by providing accommodation and valuable material help and advice. Then, from September 1992 until August 1993, with a scholarship from the Japanese-German Center in Berlin (JGCB), it was possible to get my doctoral dissertation underway, again under the direction of Hermann Kulke at Kiel University. The insights that Professor Kulke shared with me, as well as his encouragement and countless suggestions, his criticism, and his humor and patience during my studies and as a doctoral candidate have been crucial and of lasting value.

My gratitude also goes to the coreaders of my dissertation, professors Wilfried Röhrich, Klaus Antoni, Ralph Uhlig, and Reinhard Zöllner, all of whom provided useful advice and active encouragement during my work on my dissertation in Germany and Japan.

I also received essential help during preparations for this work in Japan from Professor Kurino Ohtori, a longtime diplomat and peace activist, my personal advisor at Sophia University, Professor Miwa Kimitada (formerly Sophia University, Institute for International Relations), Professor Miyake Misaki (formerly at Meiji University), Professor Nakai Akio (formerly at Sophia University), Dr. Ulrich Pauly, Dr. Sebastian Frobenius, Aaron M. Cohen (formerly at Reitaku University), and Stefanie Kaufmann, the former head of the Goethe Institute's language department in Tokyo, who after the expiration of my scholarship opened for me the possibility to teach at the Goethe Institute in Tokyo. To all of these I owe special thanks. I am equally indebted to the former dean of the faculty of comparative culture at Sophia University, Professor William Currie, and the entire administrative and teaching staff of the faculty of comparative culture for having so long put up with me as a "guest scholar," as well as to Professors Fukase Tadakazu (Hokkaido University), Hata Ikuhiko, the late Father Heinrich Dumoulin at Sophia University who died suddenly in 1995, Dr. John Howes, Takemoto Tōru (Obirin University), Ian Nish, Ashok Sirkar (Sophia University), Urata Kenji (Waseda University), Rolf-Harald Wippich, the late Professor Katō Shunsaku, Thomas Burkman (University of Buffalo, New York), Joseph P. Baratta, Dr. Douglas Lummis, Mrs. Fukushima Chiyo, Father Neil Lawrence, the late Martin Knottenbelt, Dr. Reinhard Neumann, and Matthias K. Scheer (German-Japanese Jurists Association, Hamburg) who published the original German-language edition of my dissertation, which had been presented to the Philosophical Faculty of Kiel University in December 1996 and approved in February of 1997. I also thank the Jiji Tsūshinsha Publishing Company for their friendly permission to let me reproduce photos previously published in the 1955 Shidehara biography edited by Ujita Naoyoshi.

For this edition I owe special thanks to William R. Carter, who prepared a preliminary English transcript, and also Mark Selden, Aaron M. Cohen, John Howes, Ian Nish, Lawrence Wittner, and Joseph Baratta, who have made valuable suggestions or read through the document or parts of it. Their comments, discussions, and encouragement have made this English edition possible.

Remarks on Orthography

The transcription of Japanese words, including personal names, in the text follows the Hepburn System (but "Kinmochi" instead of "Kimmochi"!). Japanese personal names are given, as a rule, in the traditional Japanese sequence of family name first. Transcriptions of Chinese names and other terms follow the *pinyin* system, exceptions being personal or place names in quoted passages that may appear in the older Wade-Giles transcription. Korean names and other terms follow the McCune-Reischauer transcription system, except in the case of "Seoul" and certain cited authors who have established their own preferred spellings of their names.

Foreword

Ian Nish

It is a happy idea to use the figure of Shidehara Kijūrō to illustrate the book's theme, "Japan in the World," and at the same time cast a critical glance on the state of the world in general. Shidehara was a central figure in the history of international relations. In his long career as a diplomat, bureaucrat, and politician from 1896 when he entered the foreign ministry until his death in 1951, he had abundantly experienced how wars arise, how peace comes about, and, most elusive of all, how peace is kept.

Shidehara's first major post as envoy was to be minister to The Hague in 1914 as the lights were going out all over Europe. One wonders whether he had time to reflect on the success and failure of the two peace conferences at the Dutch capital in 1899 and 1907, which form an important part of this study, and with which he had been well acquainted as a diplomat.

His first ambassadorial role was at Washington between 1919 and 1922. At that time he served as Japan's delegate to the Washington Conference, where he played a pivotal role in forging a new order for the Pacific area that held good for a decade. He achieved excellence in conference diplomacy and the arts of conciliation, mediation, and arbitration. He knew the difficulty of achieving these goals instrumental to maintaining peace while upholding a country's national interest. Shidehara after all was the vice-minister of foreign affairs during the crisis brought about by the Twenty-One Demands, of which he disapproved, and had to work hard to outpoint the military during the Manchurian crisis of 1931.

Later, when Shidehara returned to politics after the war, he was confronted by the problem of the new constitution. Amid all the controversies about its origin, Klaus Schlichtmann makes a convincing case for Shidehara being the author of article 9, the critical article dealing with the abolition of war.

Schlichtmann has devoted his career to examining Shidehara as man as well as statesman. In assessing the man, he uses a wide range of sources that are a challenge to all writers in the field. His use of German in addition to the Japanese and other sources is refreshing and adds an extra dimension to American and British treatments of the subject. In assessing Shidehara as statesman, the author seeks to explore his pacifism and set it in the context of ideas of peace as they developed in the twentieth century and are held to be relevant by global scholars today. The light that the author sheds on Shidehara's insights will help man's eternal quest for the means of avoiding war.

Introduction to Volume I

Pacifist Thought in Japan

Peace studies and research in "peace history" are young disciplines. However, thinking about peace has been an important part of the Western political and philosophical tradition, which is rooted in the ancient Mediterranean civilizations. In the Hebrew peace tradition we find the Axial Age notion of a world without war. The Roman *pax* and the Greek *eirene* referred both to a divinity and a concept. After the advent of Christianity and of Christ as the Prince of Peace, in the Middle Ages numerous peace plans evolved, such as Pierre Dubois's *de recuperatione terrae sanctae* (1306), Desiderius Erasmus's *Complaint of Peace* (1521), Émeric Crucé's *New Cyneas* (1623), William Penn's *An Essay toward the present and future peace of Europe* (1693), and the Abbé de Saint-Pierre's *Project of perpetual peace in Europe* (1712), all of which had a strong Christian coloring. More recently, apart from such a well-known figure as Immanuel Kant (1724–1804), intellectuals and scholars, from Jeremy Bentham (1748–1832) to H. G. Wells (1866–1946), and neo-Kantians like Walter Schücking (1875–1935) in Germany have dedicated themselves to exploring the possibilities and establishing conditions for creating a peaceful international order.

Does a similar tradition of comparable depth and latitude exist in Japan? Or do we have to perceive the "opening" of Japan in 1853–1854 and the country's subsequent rapid development over the next fifty years only through the prism of the European Enlightenment, as a consequence and an offshoot of the European "discovery of the world"? In that case Japan, lacking a

1

corresponding tradition of its own, would have simply taken over European legal doctrines from France (and Germany after 1871), the philosophy of free trade and liberalism from Great Britain, and militarism and medical science from Germany. This, however, is not nearly an adequate description of the historical place of Japan's intellectual experience. To begin with, Buddhism has played a similar role in Asia as did Christianity in Europe. Buddhist tradition appears to have been even more peaceful and pacifist than its Christian counterpart. The more than two hundred years of "seclusion" in Japan had also been an opportunity for meditation and reflection, and indeed a process of maturation and preparation; at the same time, seclusion was seen as a strategy and an instrument of self-defense, to ensure the peace and security of the nation, which yet remained present as a trading partner in the Asian context. The tight control of Japan's external trade relations via the port city of Nagasaki and ensuring regional security through its seclusion policies were two sides of a coin.

To obtain a better understanding of Japan's foreign relations and place in the world, we therefore need to look at the traditions of Buddhism, Confucianism, Mohism, and Christianity in Japan, to the extent that they are relevant for establishing a Japanese ethics of peace. The following theses may also be useful to evaluate Japan's stance and its potential as an independent actor contributing to political world union and peaceful international cooperation—issues very much in line with Shidehara Kijūrō's political agenda and still relevant today:

- Japan is traditionally a place where diverse Asian traditions, including Christianity and Mohism, have converged (Japan being the final vantage point on the Silk Road, where all the essences accumulated in distilled and refined form) with a resultant strong cultural commitment (identity) and an assumed national mission;[1]
- Overseas trade has played a significant role through the seventh to thirteenth centuries—trade with the Asian continent intensified toward the end of the twelfth century—and continued in the Edo Period and up to the modern period and present day;[2]
- This (international) environment facilitated the development of a particular peace-and-security-oriented component of external affairs, which is at its core defensive and receptive.[3]

Japanese civilization had already developed and evolved an indigenous, distinct "ethics of peace" when the first Christians arrived in the sixteenth century. A historical inbred alertness and understanding of ancient traditions were seen as prerequisites for achieving a harmonious and peaceful world.

Early historical writings like the *Ōkagami* (ca. 1086),[4] the *Gukanshō* (1219)[5] and the *Jinnō shōtōki* (probably ca. 1339) are testimony to this.[6] Ogyū Sorai (1666–1728), the sublime enlightener of his time, remarked that a certain benign "ratio in the correlation between ethics and politics" comes—as Najita Tetsuo put it—*"only from the study of history,"* an idea that greatly influenced Maruyama Masao, the great educator in the postwar era after 1945. History can be either a part of and motivation for peace education or it can foster nationalism and promote militarism and chauvinism. Some of these early readings in Japan would seem to anticipate the political and ethical discourse of our own day.

Though the writing of history in Japan may not have enjoyed the prominence it held in Europe—the Wagaku Kōdansho School founded by Hanawa Hokiichi in 1793 being an exception perhaps—unquestionably, as in Europe, peace-and-justice-oriented concepts for realizing a political and social order had been firmly established early on. It was based on a system of education, law, and conventional ethics, enforced by a government bureaucracy with administrative organs, including, as in Europe, a characteristic military establishment with its own peculiar ethics, disciplines, training, and organization. The country's foreign trade was organized and controlled by government offices and commercial guilds with numerous trading posts throughout East and Southeast Asia, similar perhaps to the *Hanse* and the South Indian guilds.

There are in Japan interesting parallels to German and general European histories.[7] As Shmuel Eisenstadt phrased it: "Japan demonstrated in many spheres marked similarities with Western Europe, especially in the patterns of the organization of family relationships, in symbolisms, in the political field (feudalism and absolutism), and also in the relatively high level of urban development and organization. In both (these) centers of culture there were, especially in the Middle Ages, peasant uprisings, and social and economic modernization from the nineteenth century."[8] Thus Japan "shared with Europe not only the existence of such phenomena, but also their historical sequence (of events)."[9]

Diplomatic History

Shidehara must be seen within the overall context of Japanese diplomatic history. Ronald Toby described in 1984 for a Western readership, as Japanese scholars before him had shown for a Japanese readership (e.g., Asao Naohiro in 1975), that Japan during the "seclusion" (*sakoku*) period had not dropped out as a partner in Asian international relations and fallen into "a 250-year long sleep of the Sleeping Beauty," as the German ambassador in Tokyo Wilhelm Solf still believed in the 1920s (see volume II). Without this indigenous background, including Confucian- and Buddhist-inspired concepts of governance, the reception of the European "law of nations" (i.e., international law) would not have been so successful and borne fruit.

Reasons of state (*raison d'état*), the state's responsibility to protect prompted by the foreign impact, at the same time demanded the introduction of a nationwide military service (Imperial Edict of 28 November 1872). The overseas diplomatic missions of the 1860s and the "Iwakura Mission" (*Iwakura kengai shisetsu*) of 1871–1873 were meant to bring about Japan's revision of the "unequal treaties" that had been imposed by the foreign powers. The lack of success (in this regard) of the Iwakura Mission led to a change in Japan's attitude toward the notion of realizing guarantees in international law for national security and the country's full independence and equality. This can be clearly seen in Fukuzawa Yukichi's (1835–1901) about-turn; Fukuzawa was probably the most influential of the Meiji reformers and "popular educators," founder of Keiō University and author of numerous bestselling books on Western civilization at the time—a significant circumstance in a highly literate society.

Shidehara as Pacifist and Realist

The present work will show that it is precisely this possibility—not wholly lost with Fukuzawa's change of heart—of realizing a universal order and politically "organized peace" that motivated many in the 1920s—statesmen, intellectuals, and public alike. Foremost among those who shared this spirit in the foreign ministry were Shidehara and the "Shidehara clique," as it was known at the time.[10]

As Bamba Nobuya has pointed out, Shidehara was a pacifist and an internationalist. Concisely, using a definition from German historian Adolf Wild, pacifism may be said to be based on the premise of a "seriously taken appeal for human harmony, which condemns collective killing just as one condemns a single murder."[11] Related to this is the awareness of the "uselessness of misery and destruction" as well as the "moral conviction that might does not come before right, but that the latter has precedence." From this perspective, the object is "not to resolve conflicts militarily," since "military successes only bring with them new material for conflict."[12]

Shidehara's positive role in foreign policy until the early 1920s, which will be introduced in the final chapter of this volume, when as ambassador in Washington he actively participated in the Naval Disarmament Conference, enhanced Japan's status in relation to the other powers, establishing the island nation as a reliable, predictable, and equal partner among nations. Shidehara welcomed "the spirit of individualistic liberalism" and parliamentary democracy. He countered those who were opposed to a parliamentary system and who wished to expand their political power by favoring authoritarian measures and military force, and accepting the risk of war and "the glorification of one's own race and national spirit."[13] Shidehara believed strongly in the "Golden Rule" of reciprocity in international relations. We will see (in volume II) that at the end of his career, Shidehara placed the "dot on the i" when in January 1946 he suggested to MacArthur that the postwar Japanese constitution contain a stipulation, in keeping with the legal trends that had already become apparent in the interwar period, rejecting the institution of war as an instrument of national policy. It will become clear also that there is an obvious, meaningful, and logical link between the nuclear predicament and the abolition of war (as expressed in article 9) proposed by Shidehara.

OBJECTIVE AND STRUCTURE OF THE WORK

Chapter I gives an overall account of the history of "political" ideas and their spiritual background, which are relevant for arguing in favor of an indigenous Japanese ethics and tradition of peace. This seemed a necessary path to pursue in order to be able to develop the narrative and to understand how Japan's foreign policy developed until the 1920s. Against this background Shidehara's activities and commitment take on meaning and depth. Shidehara was a Buddhist, who applied Buddhist principles in his diplomacy,[14] while his wife was a Christian, "an exceptionally clever and accomplished woman," according to a secret 1945 U.S. report, who had "considerable influence with her husband." All these circumstances and traditional influences made it seem appropriate to look far back into history, and into the Asian spiritual foundations of peace.

Chapter II concerns itself with the origins of modern Japan, and especially the reception of international law, in which connection pacifism in international law is given a critical appraisal in the Japanese context. Modern Japan's foreign relations and the country's place in the international order of the League of Nations serve to introduce Shidehara in his role as a diplomat.[15]

The present work takes into account the new progressive internationalism that arose after 1900, assessing its effectiveness in Japan and elsewhere. It had set for itself, in light of the world's increasing economic and social interdependence, the task of finding appropriate ways and means to bring about "the all-embracing ideal of humanity" where, as Paul Reinsch said, "[e]very person is supposed to be inspired with a feeling of human brotherhood, and to strive for the abstract purposes of universality." Such an ideal was apt to "exercise a profound influence upon the attitude of mankind toward war."[16]

One such approach to outlaw war was the procedure under the Permanent Court of Arbitration in The Hague, which was established in 1900 and whose list of judges included Shidehara during the period 1918–1924. Authors who have underlined the important role of this judicial institution include Maruyama Masao (1914–1996), Fukase Tadakazu (b. 1927), Tabata Shinobu (1902–1994), Hata Ikuhiko (b. 1932), and Takemoto Tōru, all of whom, from their various vantage points, have also written about Shidehara in the context of the abolition or outlawing of war.

In spite of such rational and compelling principles and purposes, neither politicians in general nor the writers of history have so far paid sufficient attention to "those [social] . . . trends and practical beginnings which aimed at international harmony and the creation of a durable peaceful order."[17] It is not surprising that Shidehara, too, has generated little academic interest outside Japan, and even in Japan is today nearly forgotten.

Chapter III of volume I and chapters I, II, and III of volume II focus on Shidehara's life and work, in chronological sequence. Historical events are highlighted, in which Japan had a part, from the time of the first Sino-Japanese War (1894–1895) to the years immediately following the end of the Second World War. The concluding chapter IV of volume II analyzes Japanese pacifism and peace policies in the postwar era. The "conclusion" in volume II gives a summary and outlook into the future, with regard to peace in the Asia-Pacific region and the world, and international efforts to outlaw and abolish war as an institution. Since in this work Shidehara as a person, his pacifism, his "peace diplomacy," and article 9 of the Japanese constitution are brought together into a sort of organic whole, the last three chapters in volume II take up, in one way or another, practical and theoretical considerations having to do with the Japanese renunciation of war and the controversies (and possibilities) that have arisen out of this proposition. While not a comparative study throughout, a comparison with Germany is spotlighted at various points.

This volume and more significantly volume II offer a clear appreciation of the overall course of Shidehara's life and the events surrounding it, including the pacifist and war abolition movements. There emerges the perspective of a universal history of our modern age, from which definite conclusions can be drawn.

NOTES ON BIOGRAPHICAL RESEARCH AND SOURCES

General research on Shidehara has focused mainly on the so-called Shidehara diplomacy in the 1920s. Various authors have written after the Second World War about Shidehara in the context of the Washington and London naval disarmament conferences (1921–1922 and 1930) and in connection with the "Manchurian Incident." The works of Professor Kurihara Ken, the long-time director of the Ministry of Foreign Affairs Archives, and—for Japanese-Chinese relations in the 1920s—Professor Usui Katsumi, who published his comprehensive work in 1971, are exemplary for this period. However, there exist practically no works focusing on Shidehara's role and influence on Japanese foreign policy before 1919. This volume hopes to shed some light on this period. The "First Phase" (1924–1927) and the "Second Phase" (1929–1931) of Shidehara diplomacy will be dealt with in volume II (see the "Introduction for Notes on Biographical Research and Sources" there).

The status of much of the writing on Shidehara in Japan, and also in the United States and Europe, therefore gives (or gave) a rather partial and incomplete picture that seemed to argue that (1) since Shidehara was *partial to Western liberal ideas*, he was blind to the realities and too naïve and ill-equipped to prevent war; (2) he had difficulties dealing with the complicated political constellations in the interwar period, because *he was not enough of a realist* and rejected power politics; and/or (3) *he did not substantially differ in his goals from those who had all along sought a military solution*, only his choice of method was different. In such views Shidehara diplomacy was *no model* for a realistic alternative to a military "solution." These positions are, however, based on a rather limited perception of the actual historical configurations. My narrative, as it develops, will establish that Shidehara was at no stage an apologist for Japanese imperialism, and that he, and Japanese mainstream civilian politics in general, were on the contrary following a principled course to maintain international relations that aimed at peace, progress, and cooperation.

It is now possible to locate Shidehara in the larger context of the twentieth-century international peace movement in which, significantly, parliamentarians and diplomats actively participated, in addition to the "ordinary" pacifists. They endorsed an approach to world peace in consonance with the developing international and constitutional law and conscience. The core of this movement was made up of statesmen and pacifist academics and intellectuals who believed humanity's future and the progress of nations could only be secured by instituting "guarantees" into the system through treaty agreements and constitutional amendments, and a committed "peace diplomacy" that would eventually result, ideally, in a democratic world organized along federalist principles.

The main events in this volume, where Shidehara is portrayed, take place before and during the First World War as well as at the time of the creation of the *Berusaiyu-Washinton taisei*, or "Versailles-Washington system," which guaranteed Japan's security in the Pacific region. Shidehara's "inner emigration" (a term that so far has been used only in the German context) and position as prime minister after the Second World War are dealt with in volume II. There seems to be not much research published in languages other than Japanese on Shidehara's role as a diplomat and high-ranking foreign ministry official before and after the beginning of the First World War (the *Nichi-Doku sensō* or Japanese-German War in Japanese). The events surrounding the Hague Peace Conferences, the American "war outlawry" movement of the 1920s, and even, though only remotely related, the Korean independence movement initiated and led by Sŏ Chaep'il between 1896 and 1898, have received little attention in connection with Shidehara, although he was present when these events took place, and involved in varying degree. Since he was in Korea during Sŏ Chaep'il's time, and later, during the First World War in Tokyo, chief of the Japanese foreign ministry's information service, he is at the same time the person who in an exemplary way links these developments and events together—something that is in itself significant. If the sixteen volumes of the comprehensive diplomatic history that Shidehara had compiled for publication not long before the end of the Second World War had come down to us, and not been destroyed in one of the Tokyo fire-bombings, the details of matters referred to in the present work would come more clearly to light.

An important source has been the observations and reports of contemporaries as well as newspaper articles, official documents, and private papers of persons with whom Shidehara had dealings or maintained a correspondence because of his office or otherwise—for example, the papers of Dr. Wilhelm Solf, German ambassador in Tokyo between 1920 and 1926, which frequently mention Shidehara. In this way I have attempted to follow the thread of Shidehara's life and work, and to reconstruct his contributions in the context of the history of war and peace in the twentieth century.

Apart from the National Diet Library in Tokyo and the archives of the Japanese Ministry of Foreign Affairs (*Gaikō Shiryōkan*) in Tokyo, the Political Archive in Bonn, the Library of Congress in Washington, the Federal Archives (*Bundesarchiv*) in Koblenz and Bonn, Germany, the Netherlands State Archive (*Rijksarchiv*), and the Peace Palace (*Vredespalast*) in The Hague, the Library of the Inter-Parliamentary Union in Geneva, newspaper archives in Kolkata (Calcutta), and the Indian National Libraries in Delhi and Kolkata were consulted. In all of these collections, formerly unpublished documents that have a bearing on my subject were utilized. The original dissertation having been published in German in 1998, the present work has been updated to include recent research, literature, and developments, especially with regard to the issue of the revision of the "war-abolishing" article 9 of the Japanese constitution (see volume II).

NOTES

1. Thus some of the oldest Buddhist writings in the Chinese language—and even in Sanskrit—are preserved in Japan.

2. Copper, gold (since the end of the twelfth century), sulfur, mercury, fans, swords, and lacquer wares were exported and copper coins and luxury articles, including medicaments, were imported.

3. At least since the attempted Mongolian invasions (1274 and 1281), the vulnerability of the island nation appeared very real to the country's central administration.

4. *Ōkagami, The Great Mirror: Fujiwara Michinaga (966–1027) and His Times*, a study and translation by Helen Craig McCullough (Ann Arbor: The University of Michigan, Center for Japanese Studies, 1980).

5. *The Future and the Past: A Translation and Study of the Gukanshō, an interpretative History of Japan written in 1219*, trans. and ed. Delmer M. Brown and Ichirō Ishida (Berkeley, Los Angeles, and London: University of California Press, 1979).

6. *A Chronicle of Gods and Sovereigns: Jinnō Shōtōki of Kitabatake Chikafusa*, trans. H. Paul Varley (New York: Columbia University Press, 1980). For an assessment of the historical standpoints of the three above-named early historical works, see Miyake Masaki, "The Problem of Narrativity and Objectivity in Historical Writings, with Particular Reference to the Case of Japan," *The Bulletin of the Institute of Social Sciences*, Meiji University, vol. 18, no. 3 (1995), especially 13ff.

7. Among these are the spread and adoption of a universal religion around the sixth and seventh century AD—Buddhism in Japan and Christianity in Germany—the great cultural flourishing of the Heian Period (794–1192), which might to some extent be compared with the Omayyad period in Spain (755–1031) and the Pala Dynasty in Bengal (ca. 750–1120)—and also the religious zeal and expectations of an apocalyptic "end time" in the Middle Ages, especially after 1200. See Klaus Schlichtmann, "The West, Bengal Renaissance and Japanese Enlightenment: A Critical Inquiry into the History of the Organization of the World Around 1800," in Stephan Conermann and Jan Kusber (eds.), *Asien und Afrika* (Beiträge des Zentrums für Asiatische und Afrikanische Studien [ZAAS] der Christian-Albrechts-Universität zu Kiel, vol. 10), Studia Eurasiatica. Kieler Festschrift, Hermann Kulke for his 65th birthday, Schenefeld, EB-Verlag 2003, 411–40.

8. Shmuel N. Eisenstadt, "Die japanische Geschichtserfahrung (The Japanese historical experience)," in Eisenstadt (ed.), *Kulturen der Achsenzeit II* (Cultures of the Axial Age II), Part 1: *China, Japan* (Frankfurt: Suhrkamp, 1992), 236. See also, by the same author, *Japanese Civilization: A Comparative View* (Chicago and London: The University of Chicago Press, 1996). On the subject of Japanese peasants' uprisings, see Ulrich Pauly, *Ikkō-Ikki: Die Ikkō-Aufstände und ihre Entwicklung aus den Aufständen der bündischen Bauern und Provinzialen des japanischen Mittelalters* (Ikkō-Ikki: The Ikkō-uprisings and their development from the peasants' associations and provincials in the Japanese Middle Ages), dissertation, Bonn, Rhenische Friedrich-Wilhelms-Universität, 1985. Also compare the traumatic experiences of war during the "age of the warring states" (*sengoku jidai*, 1467–1573), which is similar to the traumatic experiences of the Thirty Years' War in Europe (1618–1648).

9. Eisenstadt, "Die japanische Geschichtserfahrung," 236. The catching-up as a "latecomer nation" in the second half of the nineteenth century, the militarist postures and aggressive forays in the twentieth century, and, finally, the adoption of a constitution with a pacifist orientation and the rebuilding of the nation after the Second World War testify to a type of development that, in its ensemble, underscores and explains Japanese historical identity and the phenomenon of rapid modernization—and with it an inherent interest in "scientific [organizational] pacifism."

10. See Doi Takeo, *The Anatomy of Dependence* (Tokyo: Kōdansha, 1973), 53, where the author discusses the "particular form of clique building (be it in school, in a clan, through marriage, financial interests or in military bodies). . . . These cliques always had within them the potential to become political forces and to assume administrative leadership." The "most important of all cliques" (*ōyake*) was the imperial family: "In reality it often happened that other cliques, in vying with one another, tried to attract this *ōyake*, the most important of all the cliques, to their side."

11. Adolf Wild, *Baron d'Estournelles de Constant (1852–1924), das Wirken eines Friedensnobelpreisträgers für die deutsch-französische Verständigung und europäische Einigung* (Baron d'Estournelles de Constant [1852–1924], activities of a Nobel peace laureate for German-French rapprochement and European union) (Hamburg: Stiftung Europa-Kolleg, Fundament-Verlag Dr. Sasse & Co., 1973), 4.

12. *Ibid.*, 4–5n11.

13. Tilemann Grimm, "Die weltpolitische Lage 1933–1935 (The world political situation 1933–1935)," in Oswald Hauser (ed.), *Weltpolitik 1933–1939, 13 Vorträge* (World politics 1933–1939, thirteen lectures) (Frankfurt and Zürich: Musterschmidt Göttingen, 1973), 205

14. E.g., the principle of cause and effect (*inga ōhō*).

15. See the pivotal work on Japan and the post–First World War international organization of peace by Thomas Burkman, *Japan and the League of Nations: Empire and World Order, 1914–1938* (Honolulu: University of Hawaii Press, 2007).

16. Paul Reinsch, *Public International Unions* (Boston: Ginn and Co., 1911), 141–42.

17. Wild, *Baron d'Estournelles de Constant*, 1.

I

The Historical Backgrounds of a Japanese Ethics of Peace— A General Justification

THE CHINESE TRADITION

"All men within the four seas are brothers."

Confucius, *Lunyu*, XII, 5[1]

The age of the so-called Axial Period discourse,[2] that of the Warring States (*zhanguo*) (453/403–221 BC), is a decisive one in China's intellectual history. The main figureheads were the Great Three of Chinese tradition: Laozi (Lao Tse, ca. sixth century BC), Kongzi (Confucius, 551–479 BC), and Mozi (Mo-tzu, ca. 480–381).[3] As in India, in Greece, and the Jewish tradition this discourse was also a *discourse about peace*, which defined the paradigms of war and peace, and whose dimensions extended into the future. In some way, though slightly later, this had an effect on Japan, too.

Out of the vicissitudes of the Period of the Warring States—the expansionist strivings of the Qin (318–210 BC) into the south (Korea, Vietnam) and the colonization in the north and northwest by the Earlier Han Dynasty between 136 and 56 BC—emerged a powerful unified China. Chinese garrisons were stationed from Korea to the "heart of Asia." The establishment of "diplomatic relations and the control of the important trade routes created a particularly favorable situation for the merchants."[4] To consolidate their gains and the resulting order, the Earlier Han Dynasty (206 BC–9 AD) and the Later Han Dynasty (25–220 AD) carried out a "policy of gifts . . . [distributed] among their neighbours," which led to the "integration" of the barbarians.[5]

Subsequently, with threats coming mostly from the outside, statecraft was "dominated and directed by the problems of the steppe."[6] China, being a bureaucratic state with a predominantly agrarian society, was quite naturally inclined toward pacifism. The veneration of ancestors was a religious or quasi-religious element in Confucian doctrine, a cultural tradition to which war was an abomination and the worship of heroes and warriors, so familiar to the West, quite alien.[7] The cult of the ancestors presupposes peace. Only on the frontiers of the empire did war appear, as confrontation with a potentially aggressive "outside world," the world of the barbarians, and therefore as war of defense.

Following the discourse of the Axial Period,[8] the School of Confucius became the dominant ideology, with an ethical setting that was decisive in molding the image of the state, even though the other schools, especially Mohism and Taoism, continued to thrive.[9]

Mozi, whose teachings were written down by his followers, was the most prominent rival of Confucius[10] and the founder of a genuine religion. He had condemned aggressive war in his teachings and on many occasions tried to prevent war among the Chinese warlords through his personal fiat. Mozi also concerned himself with technical questions.[11] His teachings, of a pacifist rhetoric and strongly ascetic character, influenced Taoism to an extent, which likewise has pacifist political connotations,[12] as in verse 31 of Laozi's *Daodejing*:

1. Now arms, however beautiful, are instruments of evil omen, hateful, it may be said, to all creatures. Therefore they who have the Tao do not like to employ them.
2. Those sharp weapons are instruments of evil omen, and not the instruments of the superior man—he uses them only on the compulsion of necessity . . . victory (by force of arms) is to him undesirable. To consider this desirable would be to delight in the slaughter of men; and he who delights in the slaughter of men cannot get his will in the kingdom.
3. He who has killed multitudes of men should weep for them with the bitterest grief.[13]

The teachings of Mozi decisively influenced the later School of Confucianism,[14] which took over from Mozi the method of dialectics. The dialecticians of the Mozi school,[15] all of them "convinced Pacifists," had also been gathering "the most accurate information on methods of waging war during the Warring States Period."[16]

Mozi's teachings as written down by his disciples were later received in Japan together with other Chinese scriptures and studied by a small number of scholars.[17] Mozi advocated a monotheistic religion, in which God reigned as King in Heaven, a universalism based on principles of equality and justice, as well as the concept of "unbound (i.e., undifferentiated) love" (*jian'ai*), which was also said to be of "mutual utility,"[18] quite similar to the Christian idea in many ways.

The Chinese scholar and reformer Hu Shi (1891–1962) remarked in 1919 that Mozi was "probably the only Chinese who had founded a religion" and "possibly one of the greatest spirits China ever produced."[19] Hu Shi came to the conclusion that "though it is to Confucius that his countrymen paid lip service it is Meh Tse [Mozi] who has—unknown to them—really molded their thought."[20] Mozi's practical philosophy contained elements of what one might call political science as well as fundamentals of a political and individual ethic. Among the main goals of his political ethic is the elevation of the welfare of the people and the general cultivation of law and good administration.[21] The utilitarianism of the Mozi school is everywhere emphasized in the literature as a main characteristic: "His aim is the mutual balancing of needs, based on equality. . . . The principle, however, that supports people's relations to each other is for Mozi not blood relationships and not ritual, but love."[22]

It was "that militant Confucian,"[23] Mengzi (Mencius, 372–289 BC), the follower of Confucius, and the main proponent of Confucianism, who sharply polemicized against other schools of thought and especially against the school of Mozi.[24] The result was that from that discourse a special "ethic of compassion" evolved, a positive contribution to the history of Chinese thought.[25] The *Book of Mencius* was "one of the basic texts of 'neo-Confucian' orthodoxy,"[26] belonging to the canon of neo-Confucian writings which were standard reading also, though somewhat later, in the Japanese centers of learning. This Confucian tradition "laid special emphasis on intuitive wisdom (*liangzhi*), an emotional intelligence in the sense of empathy or putting oneself in the place of others."[27] Mencius stressed, "Love overcomes what is set against it, like water overcomes fire." L. Tomkinson suggested that Mencius "borrowed [this] from the passage in his opponent's [Mozi's] work, in the chapter on 'Conversations with Keng Chu and Others.'"[28]

During Mencius's lifetime, the intellectual confrontation among the several schools of thought reached its peak. The flourishing and mutually contending Taoist and Mohist Schools went all out in their critique of Ruism (Confucianism),[29] launching, as Robert Eno remarked, "vigorous attacks upon the early established Ruist [Confucian] school," while seeking to integrate the contents of these "competing schools of Taoism and Mohism." It was the Mohists who "rested their case on their intuitive universality of the abstract utilitarian value of maximizing human welfare."[30] This discourse was fruitful. Chinese writers during these first two centuries BC referred to the "*ru-mo* teachings," combining the most common and basic elements of both Confucian and Mohist teachings.[31] Forke mentions the later Confucian scholar Han Yu (768–824), who presented himself as the "most illustrious defender" of Mozi and also sought to prove that both teachings "were in agreement on all essential points."[32] A Japanese bibliography of the ninth century, the *Nihonkoku genzaisho mokuroku*, edited by Fujiwara Sukeyo, a scholar of the time of Emperor Uda (reigned 888–897), mentions three contemporary titles of which at least one had to do with Mozi's philosophical system.[33] While Confucianism of course remained mainstream, this clearly shows the continued relevance of the teachings of Mohism.

The moral and social teachings of Confucius are said to have been brought to Japan by two Korean scholars, named (in Japanese orthography) Wani and Achi, perhaps as early as the year 285.[34] Wani founded the scholarly clan of the *fumi*, whose task was the compilation of royal edicts, and Achi founded the scholarly clan of the *fubito,* the official archivists and chroniclers.[35] Around 363 the Korean Kingdom of Shiragi (k. Shin-la) is said to have been occupied by the Japanese. It was subsequently controlled from a region that the Japanese called Mimana. During the reign of the Japanese Prince Shōtoku (572–621), interest in continental culture greatly increased. Japanese scholars visited the continent and on occasion Chinese "dissidents" found refuge in Japan. The blending of indigenous folk-Shintō beliefs and Confucianism with the newly arrived Buddhism promoted by Prince Shōtoku was a process that continued steadily over the next centuries.[36]

Another author who gives evidence of Chinese pacifist thinking is the eminent Confucian scholar and "chief ideologue" of the Earlier Han Period, Dong Zhongshu (ca. 175–105 BC), whose writings were also read in Japan. Dong based his teachings mostly on the Local Chronicle of Lu, the *Chunqiu*, which was highly valued by Confucius and formed one of the famous "Five Classics."[37] Dong Zhongshu described "the interplay of personal and social ethics" in this way: "The way of humanity consists in loving [other] people and not loving oneself; the way of duty consists in making oneself just and not making other people just. . . . Humanity emanates from myself, duty comes up to me [from outside]."[38] Such general principles were well matched to speak to popular sentiment. Accordingly, the *Zhongyong* (Doctrine of the Golden Mean), which is said to be written by Kong Ji, called Zisi (or Tsesse), grandson of Confucius, offers, in Lin Yutang's view, "the sanest ideal of life ever discovered by the Chinese."[39] In the opinion of a modern Chinese woman: "As far as world peace is concerned, Chinese pacifistic nature is perhaps related to the edification of such a nonaggressive philosophy."[40] Such ideas were also favorably received in Japan.

In the seventh century, reforms following the Chinese model were introduced in Japan. The Taika reforms (*Taika kaishin*) announced under Emperor Monmu (reigned 697–707) in 645 inaugurated a more centralized operation of the various ministries. The subsequent Taihō legal code of 702 furthermore provided a sort of constitution, whose nomenclature was used for government offices until the time of the Meiji constitution of 1889.

Neo-Confucian teachings of the Song Dynasty in China (960–1279) reached Japan toward the end of the Kamakura Period (1185–1333). The scholar Zhu Xi (1130–1200), "who perfected this intellectual structure of monolithic severity," is the chief representative of this school.[41] A predecessor of Zhu Xi, the philosopher Zhang Zai (1020–1077), coined this well-known phrase: "The main point is to direct one's mind to the whole universe, to open for the people the correct way, to revive the teachings of the *shengren*[42] of past times which have degenerated, and to bring about for all times the great peace."[43]

Among the Four Books (*Sishu*), the "Great Learning" (*Daxue*)[44] holds a special place, as it seeks to establish a relationship between individual and society, and even to the whole of mankind:[45]

In their desire to diffuse the shining virtue in all its clarity over the entire world, the ancients first sought to govern their countries well. In their desire to govern their countries well, they first ordered their families. In their desire to order their families, they first refined their own person. In their desire to refine their own person, they first rectified their mind. In the desire to rectify their mind, they first sought sincerity in thought. In the desire for sincerity in thought, they first increased their knowledge. . . . But only if things are examined [carefully] does knowledge grow. Only when knowledge grows does sincerity arise in thought. Only when sincerity in thought has been attained, is the mind rectified. Only when the mind is rectified does one's own person become refined. Only when one refines one's own person do the families become ordered. Only when the families are ordered are the countries well governed. And only when the countries are well governed is there peace in the world.[46]

This was the essence of the Confucian ethic, which even the common people could understand.[47] This applied similarly also to Japan. Toward the end of the twelfth century, an administrative system following Chinese patterns was set up, the *gozan* system of the Zen monks (Dhyana school), with its "five mountains" (*gozan*), each of which had its great temples and monasteries.[48] A small handful of learned monks of the "five mountains" studied Zhu Xi's teachings. At the same time foreign trade, carried on by the "bonzes"[49] of the *gozan*, came to be of growing importance.

The state-oriented religious ideology in the Muromachi Period (approximately 1336–1573) incorporated substantial elements of Buddhism and especially of Zen Buddhism. After 1473 Keian, a Buddhist monk who had studied in China, propagated the teachings, which had originated in the Song Dynasty, in Japan: "It was he who introduced into Japan and had printed at his patron's expense the Commentaries of Chu Hsi [Zhu Xi] upon the Great Learning and other works in the canon."[50] Eventually the so-called *Shushigaku* (i.e., the Song Dynasty neo-Confucianism of the Zhu Xi School) took root as the predominant state ideology during the Tokugawa Period (1603–1868, also called the Edo Period after the name of the Tokugawa shōguns' capital city, which is present-day Tokyo).[51] Wolfgang Bauer has called Zhu Xi "undoubtedly one of the greatest scholars of Chinese history."[52]

Eventually, Tokugawa Ieyasu (1542–1616), founder of the Tokugawa Shōgunate, furnished the country with a legal and social system that regulated all relations and public affairs, based on a corpus of one hundred laws.[53] This so-called Tokugawa constitution of the year 1615, which also contained the regulations of the military houses (*buke shohatto*), and complemented the Taihō code, stipulated in its first article that "the vassals and their men should devote themselves equally to learning and military exercises."[54] Apparently, the Tokugawa rulers saw the need to take precautions and demonstrate preparedness to counter possible attacks by foreign powers, like those of the Mongols in the thirteenth century.[55]

The canonical writings of the neo-Confucianist (*Shushigaku*) school now consisted of the New Commentary on the Four Classics (*Shisho shinchū*), written and compiled by Zhu Xi.[56] Fujiwara Seika (1561–1619), who was also a Buddhist priest and an advisor to Tokugawa Ieyasu, as well as the teacher of the famous historian Hayashi Razan (1583–1657), was pivotal in disseminating the teachings of Zhu Xi.[57] Even more consequential than in China, Japanese syncretism managed to set a common denominator for Buddhism and Confucianism. The School of Zhu Xi was taught as the "official state doctrine" in the Yushima Seidō—*seidō* meaning "holy" or "venerated" hall—which was erected by Hayashi Razan in 1630 in the Ueno district of Edo under the patronage of the third shōgun, Tokugawa Iemitsu. This establishment had an extensive library and, after 1632, a "shrine to Confucius." When it was moved to the nearby Kanda district in 1691, a school was set up with the name Shōheikō (also called the Shōheizaka Gakumonjo), taken from the place name Chang Ping (in China's Shandong Province), where Confucius was said to have been born. This school was the most significant establishment of learning in Edo, functioning as the official state university. There some of Japan's most distinguished Confucian scholars,[58] as well as many of the *Gokenin*[59] and *Hatamoto*,[60] were educated. In 1765 a medical faculty was added. Chinese studies continued in Japan in quite a similar fashion as Latin and Greek studies in Europe or Sanskrit studies in India.

Central to the Confucian social teachings stood the Five Virtues: benevolence (*jin*, ch. *ren*), performance of duty (*gi*, ch. *yi*), morality and etiquette (*rei*, ch. *li*), knowledge and wisdom (*chi*, ch. *zhi*), and reliability/sincerity (*shin*, ch. *xin*). These Five Virtues were to be put into practice in the five relationships (i.e., between lord-vassal-bureaucrat, father-son, elder brother-younger brother, husband-wife, and friend-friend). The doctrine of Zhu Xi was based on two conceptual pillars: "principle" (*ri*; ch. *li*) and "power" (*ki*; ch. *qi*), which are said to be in a relation of complementary interplay with one another.[61] Thus, "Confucianism provided most of the metaphysical and ethical categories and ideals by which Tokugawa thinkers interpreted the world."[62]

The four-class system (warrior-bureaucrats, farmers, craftsmen, merchants)[63] did not eliminate war or the warrior class, which secured the interests of the feudal lords (*daimyō*). Martial arts and contests, and a certain attachment to bravery and heroic virtue, demonstrated another side of this culture of literacy and learning. The ascetic lifestyle of the samurai, whose moderation, sobriety, self-discipline, and selfless dedication to the welfare of others could ideally come to the fore, justified their claim of legitimately maintaining order and peace.[64] No doubt, at the same time fierce determination and cruel persecutions could manifest themselves, if it was for a just cause believed to be worthy of pursuit.

Najita Tetsuo points out that toward the end of the seventeenth century Ogyū Sorai, the great reformer, saw and stressed pragmatically the significance of law, bureaucratic order, and political administration for human society, arguing that his theory about bureaucracy was grounded in their usefulness.[65]

> Ogyū's argument was provocative. Political institutions were not "fixed" according to timeless metaphysical norm. . . . Ethics were not abstract universals. . . . Ethics were rational, because they were used with practical intent. In the broadest sense, this intent meant providing peace and economic well-being for society (*anmin*).[66]

Reminiscent of contemporary discourse ethics, Ogyū's argumentation recognizes the necessity of achieving a sensible ratio in the relationship between ethics and politics: "The truth about the rationality of ethics and politics, Ogyū reasoned, could be understood through the study of history."[67] It is interesting that he took a similar view to that of a rational policy based on a modern, contemporary "moral conscience of law,"[68] which could be accomplished through the study of history—an indirect reference to the peace discourse with its history of over two thousand years in China, since the Axial Period, and its long history also in Japan.

Perhaps under Ogyū's influence, the shōgunate regime in 1720 cancelled to a large extent the prohibition against the import of Western books that had been applied in connection with the prohibition of Christianity (1637–1638) and the laws of 1639 which had mandated the closing of the country to trade with any of the Western powers except Holland. The government had no doubt recognized that "free" trade, free exchange, and communication with the Western powers could not be discontinued indefinitely. Although perhaps not averse to exploiting British-Dutch and Dutch-Portuguese rivalries, there was also the hope to ultimately be able to make use of European international law for the protection and furthering of Japanese interests as well as for the general regulation of the new international relations that were developing. Government and intellectuals used the political theories found in the Confucian tradition, of a common natural law and universally valid moral and legal principles, to come to an understanding of international law that would be attuned to their needs.

> Realizing the necessity of foreign intercourse, and placing great hope in the law of nations, the Shōgunate Government and intellectuals of Japan endeavoured to understand the law of nations through the political theories of natural law inherent in Confucianism and based on the natural principles which ruled the universe. Combining the knowledge of Confucianism with Western notions of international law, they interpreted the law of nations as a system of universal justice and righteousness which would eventually bring equal treatment of every nation without distinction between the strong and the weak, or even between European and Asian.[69]

While ordinary citizens were forbidden to meddle in political affairs,[70] the samurai warriors (*bushi*), versed in the *bushidō* code[71] and Confucian ethics, had the task of securing the peace by coercion or simply by their presence. Insofar as the duties of the "warrior" corresponded quite closely to the practices prevailing in Europe at the time, where armed militia preserved the peace, the ruler had to be at all times prepared to defend his interests and his people—essentially a medieval concept.[72]

An Asian ethics of a more peaceable direction is expressed by the Japanese scholar and would-be statesman Yoshida Shōin (1830–1859), written around the middle of the nineteenth century:

> The reason is that arms are dangerous instruments and not necessarily forces for good. How can we safely entrust them to any but those who have schooled themselves in the precepts of the classics and can use these weapons for the realization of Humanity and Righteousness? . . . If arms are taken up in a self-ish struggle to win land, goods, people, and the implements of war, is it not the worst of all evils, the most heinous of all offenses?[73]

Yoshida Shōin had read the Chinese, Buddhist, and Confucian classics and published his own books in Chinese. He was the teacher and one-time companion of two important Japanese statesmen, Itō Hirobumi (1841–1909) and Yamagata Aritomo (1838–1922). In 1859 the shōgunate government ex-ecuted Yoshida because of his all-too-liberal views.[74] Itō Hirobumi, between 1871 and 1873, visited the United States and Europe with the not-wholly-successful "Iwakura Mission" and later exercised great political influence as the first president of the privy council (founded in 1888/1889) and then as the sometime–prime minister between 1889 and 1901, when he was dealing among other things with the abolition of extraterritoriality. Yamagata, the "evil genius" (E. H. Norman), believing in military expansion beyond the Japanese archipelago, broke with Itō over the first Sino-Japanese War.[75]

An important matter was to perk up the general economic situation. While Japan already tried successfully to connect to the progressive West and was able at the end of the nineteenth century to practically revise its "unequal treaties" with the Western powers, China was still a long way from being able to do the same. Nonetheless, Chinese influence on Japanese political thought up until the First World War was in no way insignificant. One of the most notable Chinese political thinkers of the time, who had already advocated "disarmament and the outlawing of war" as the "initial step toward overcoming the first boundary, that of the sovereign state,"[76] was Kang Youwei (K'ang Yu-wei, 1858–1927).[77] From Kang, whom the German sinologist Wolfgang Bauer called "one of the most fascinating and influential figures on the borderline between the old and the new China," came "the most comprehensive plan for an ideal social system ever to have been produced in China,"[78] of global proportions and comparable to the best plans Europe ever produced for an ideal universal order.

> [T]he ancient ideal of "Ta T'ung," or universality, which Confucius envisioned as a harmonious Chinese social order . . . inspired the young Hung Hsiu-ch'uan [Hong Xiuquan], leader of the Taiping Rebellion, and provided the source for a conception of world government to the late Ch'ing reformer K'ang Yu-wei, author of the *Ta T'ung Shu, The Book of One World.*[79]

According to Kang, "humanity must experience in the course of its evolu-tion three stages, the last of which will see the disappearance of frontiers and social classes, the formation of a universal civilization, and the inauguration of a definitive peace. Modern institutions (constitutional monarchy, parlia-ment, and so on) and the development of commerce and industry respond to the needs of this process of evolution." These ideas, propounded in the Datongshu (*Ta-t'ung-shu*), which Kang Youwei wrote in 1897, were only published after his death, in 1935. In this "socialist utopia" the author antici-pates the establishment of a world government, and also the abolition of the nation state, and even of the family and of private property.[80]

The reformer Kang also reverted to the teachings of the Chinese pacifist Mozi: "It was no mere accident that these had been rediscovered during the second half of the Manchu Dynasty [1644–1912], for they had always been closely associated with socialist trends."[81] According to A. Forke, "the study of Mozi was newly popular since the end of the eighteenth century," including in Japan, where in any event the interest of the Japanese was "less in textual criticism than in the exposition and clarification of the teachings."[82] The (Chinese) publication by Bi Yuan (or Pi Yüan) of an edition of the *Mozi* in 1783, with which "a new era" in the study of Mozi is said to have begun, was followed in 1795 by a commentary on Bi Yuan's work by the Japanese Tozaki Inmei, written of course in scholarly Chinese.[83]

In Bi Yuan's own foreword to his 1783 work, he made the following remark, as translated by L. Tomkinson: "[T]he orthodoxy of Confucius cannot be properly appreciated without studying the heresy of Meh Tse [Mozi]."[84] For the modern political and intellectual history of Japan, Mozi has thus played a not insignificant role. Mozi's universalism found further followers in the 1930s and 1940s.

Sun Yirang (Sun I-jang, 1848–1908), who as a later biographer of Mozi attracted attention "for his search in Japan for extant Chinese works,"[85] around the turn of the twentieth century published a new edition of the work of Mozi, which Forke has called "a brilliant accomplishment of modern Chinese philology."[86] Progressive Chinese scholars cultivated contact with Japan. Sun Yirang's edition was published at the beginning of the twentieth century, together with Tozaki's commentary of 1795, in the fourteenth volume of an anthology of Chinese classics (with commentaries) edited by Koyanagi Shigeta, professor of Chinese philosophy at Kyoto Imperial University.[87]

Interest in "Bokushi" (the Japanese pronunciation of Mozi) continued into the interwar period. In 1921 Tsunashima Ryōsen published some very competent research on Mozi,[88] and Mozi's universalism found further cohorts in the 1930s and 1940s.[89] Shidehara was directly or indirectly involved in these cultural and academic pursuits, since he had been instrumental in returning the money from the Boxer indemnity, to be invested in setting up libraries, financing research, and promoting cultural cooperation, in the 1920s.

The potential for creating a just world order is evident in the diverse cultures of peace and the great civilizations that have come down to us from the Axial Period. It is significant that toward the end of the nineteenth century, in China and also in Japan, the political unification of the world, under the banner of universal peace, social justice, and the reciprocity of the interests of states, was already discussed as one of the goals to be pursued by progressive movements.

Until the beginning of the 1920s, among the Chinese and Japanese intelligentsia an intensive peace discourse, comparable to the Western deliberations on an all-embracing world peace, took place, although this was overshadowed by colonial and imperial predicaments. East and West seemed to be at cross-purposes when it came to implementing their designs. At the Hague peace conferences it was the Western countries that failed to achieve unanimity. Kang Youwei served for a short period as advisor to the Qing imperial court; his "Hundred Days Reform" (11 June–21 September 1898) was finally shattered by the reactionary forces, and he had to flee, first to Hong Kong[90] and then to Japan,[91] where he found for a time shelter in the home of the statesman and founder of the Progressive Party Ōkuma Shigenobu (1838–1922), who was prime minister in 1898. Ōkuma's "Pan-Asianism"—possibly inspired by Kang—became known as the "Ōkuma Doctrine."[92] In 1902 Kang Youwei completed his book, the *Datongshu*, in Darjeeling, India.[93]

On the other hand, numerous adherents of Kang came to study in Japan and learn Japanese, a language into which at the time a "great deal of western literature which had not yet reached China . . . had already been translated." Japan became "along with the United States the Mecca of all Chinese revolutionaries and modernists."[94] This encounter, which was fruitful for both sides, and should have complemented similar tendencies in the West, became markedly diminished and was eventually destroyed as a result of the various imperialist machinations of the great powers, climaxing in the disaster of the First World War.

Despite attempts by Ōkuma and others to act as go-betweens, it turned out to be impossible to move Kang Youwei and the great Chinese leader, Sun Yat-sen (Sun Wen, 1866–1925, known in Japan as "Son Bun"), to make common cause, something in which not only the Japanese had placed great hope. After vain attempts to arrange such a plan of common action, it was finally given up.[95]

Although Shidehara as foreign minister restored to China the "indemnity payments" stemming from the Boxer Uprising, and helped negotiate ways of using them to finance programs to promote Japanese-Chinese cultural exchanges—in 1923 already, the China Cultural Affairs Bureau had been established to make use of these funds[96]—China-Japan relations in the 1920s as a whole became increasingly problematic.[97] In May 1917 the last Qing emperor, Buyi (Pu-yi, 1906–1967), with the help of supporters of Kang Youwei, was again placed on the throne for two weeks in Beijing,[98] while in Russia the Communist Revolution was getting underway, facilitated by German imperial machinations. The same Buyi was once again enthroned in 1933, this time as a result of the Japanese attempt to establish an "independent" Manchukuo in northeastern China.

BUDDHISM AND PEACE

Since Shidehara occasionally used Buddhist terminology to explain his diplomatic philosophy—such as *inga ōhō*, the principle of cause and effect, or reciprocity, which he saw operating in diplomatic relations—it may be expedient to examine the Buddhist teachings, which also must be seen as a general source of Japanese pacifist thought.

The Buddhist doctrine[99] reached Japan via the Korean "bridge" in 538 or 552.[100] Early Buddhism was "universalistic," and had integrated the concept of the unity of the world.[101] Somewhat later, for many decades during the period between 750 and 1200 AD a kind of Buddhist ecumene existed in East Asia, including India and Japan, that might be seen as a precedent to an international political order, based on nonviolence, and the universalistic outlook of Buddhist Mahayana philosophy. The Buddhist "middle way" meant to give human life and sufferings a meaning and a purpose. Salvation and deliverance from suffering could be achieved in this lifetime, and even "in the world."[102] The concept of an all-embracing compassion comparable to the Christian love for one's fellowmen or to the Confucian "ethics of compassion" is evident in Buddhism from the earliest times:[103] "Moral cultivation rather than faith, worship, and sacrifice to a supreme being dictates human destiny . . . moral discipline and practice are at the core of Buddhism."[104] Buddhism teaches that one should "feel love for one's relatives and similarly also for enemies; and one should penetrate the whole wide world with a friendly heart. That is the teaching of all Buddhas."[105]

The late Buddhist scholar Nakamura Hajime notes, with reference to an important text of early Buddhism, the *Digha-Nikaya*: "The four states or conditions known as *Brahma*-abodes (*brahma-vihara*), are love, grief with the grief of others, joy with the joy of others, and indifference in regard to one's own joy or grief."[106] In meditation exercises benevolence or goodwill (*metta*), compassion (*karuna*), shared happiness (*mudita*), and equanimity (*upekha*) are "extended over the whole world."[107] This approach may be somewhat comparable to the more legalistic Western concepts of organized peace. Appealing "to the modern ethos . . . [and] the pragmatic tenor of our own Western culture" today, the Eastern approach may have "particular relevance for our own . . . period of transition and change."[108]

The Bodhisattva ideal of the "compassionate saint" perpetuates the concept of mercy in Buddhism, easing the all-too-rigid chain of causality.[109] One of them is Maitreya, the future Buddha of peace and justice, who is revered in the famous image of the Hōryūji temple at Nara, the ancient capital.

Soon after his enlightenment in Gaya and the subsequent sermon in the Deer Park at Benares, Gautama Buddha,[110] after the number of his disciples had grown to sixty-one, sent the monks to go out into all directions and spread the teaching (*dharma*) throughout the whole world. The "sixty-one" were to help bring about the establishment of a "kingdom of law" (*dharmarajya*). The Buddha instructed the monks:

> Therefore go out for the gain of many, for the welfare of many, out of compassion with the world, for the best, for winning, and for the benefit of gods and men! Go no two of you the same way! Preach the Teaching, which is excellent in the beginning, excellent in the middle and excellent at the end, in keeping with its spirit (*attha*) and with its written letters (*vyancana*)! Proclaim a perfect and pure life (*brahmachariya*)! There are creatures whose spiritual eyes are not much covered with dust; however if the Teaching is not preached unto them, they cannot reach liberation. They will understand the Teaching.[111]

The "victory of the good law" (*dharma-vijaya*) should ultimately bring liberation to all sentient beings. Ideally and ultimately, this strategy of a "spiritual" *dharma-vijaya* aimed at uniting the whole world and humanity "under one umbrella" (*Ekachattra*).[112] This completely revolutionized the Brahmanic concept of "world conquest" (*dig-vijaya*) through victory in war.

With King Ashoka (268–233) Buddhism became a powerful political and spiritual force, and advanced beyond the boundaries of India proper, after Ashoka had conquered the kingdom of Kalinga (today's state of Orissa) and brought the whole of India under his rule, and led him to eventually send missions to Sri Lanka and Burma. The bloody war against Kalinga had created an inner change in Ashoka, causing him to convert to Buddhism. From then on, he sought to further the ideal of peace, justice, and prosperity in human society, just as the Buddha himself had during his lifetime preached to reconcile with one another the contending kings in northern India's Ganges Basin.[113]

Max Weber, in his writings on the sociology of religion, emphasized Ashoka's pacifism: "The King declared that . . . forthwith it would not belong to the *dharma* of his descendants to conquer by the sword [but rather to conquer] by and for the power of true belief, and that more important to him than even these conquests was the salvation of the soul."[114] In the following centuries, Buddhism spread throughout the whole East Asian world,[115] making its influence felt even in Greece and Rome.[116] In the first half of the nineteenth century Ashoka's numerous inscriptions in diverse parts of India were successfully deciphered.[117] These inscriptions chiseled on pillars, stelae, and stones allow us to know more about Ashoka's "worldwide" mission, which was, as Hermann Kulke asserts, for that time (i.e., of the Hellenistic ecumene [*oikoumēnē*]) surely "a unique testimony to 'international' spiritual relations."[118] Although in India "soon forgotten after his death . . . his constant propaganda" did much to promote the "principles of nonviolence (*ahimsa*) and vegetarianism" in India and abroad.[119]

As a result of the missionary activities of Ashoka and his descendents, Indian Buddhists came into contact with Chinese traders.[120] During the Chinese Han Dynasty (206 BC—220 AD) Buddhism spread in China. In the first half of the fourth century AD, having been forgotten and abandoned in the meantime, Buddhist buildings and art were rediscovered by monks in various places in China; a number of holy places, which contained relics of the historical Buddha, were restored. According to some sources, nineteen "Ashoka monasteries" existed in various sites in China, and pagodas and so on were excavated. Sites are found in Pengcheng, a trade center in northern Jiangsu province, as well as in early Buddhist settlements in Loyang in the first centuries AD, and in the vicinity of the Ashoka Mountain, in Zhejiang Province near today's Ningbo.[121] Trade relations to these places, situated not far from the Japan archipelago, existed and Japanese monks frequently visited such Buddhist seats of learning in China. In 395 AD, the king of Sri Lanka, who had been converted to Buddhism centuries earlier by Ashoka's son Mahinda, sent a learned Buddhist monk to the court of the Chinese emperor.[122] Between the fourth and seventh centuries, in a second wave, Buddhism conquered not only all of China,[123] but also Southeast Asia, Tibet, and Japan.

The Ashoka legend played a significant role in China and all East Asia.[124] Knowledge of Ashoka, the founder of the welfare state, arrived in Japan no later than the seventh century, together with the early Buddhist writings.[125] In this context, the aforementioned concept of *dharma-vijaya*, the "victory of the [good] law," which should replace victory through armed aggression,[126] is significant.

Wilhelm E. Mühlmann makes an interesting comparison between King Ashoka and the Japanese Prince Shōtoku (574–622): "After many wars of conquest and annexations, Emperor Asoka announced numerous edicts of tolerance, by which he made use of the Buddhistic ethics as a means of domesticating [pacifying] robber castes and rebellious and uncertain tribes. The same was done by Prince Shōtoku of Japan in the sixth century; the universal ethics of Buddhism aided him in shattering the traditional clan units and welding together a centralized state."[127] Prince Shōtoku Taishi, who did much to establish Buddhism in Japan, and Ashoka are both referred to and related in the early literature on Buddhism in Japan.

The concept of peaceful cultural interaction and discourse that developed in India was, over many centuries, to show its effect in East Asia, too.[128] Through Buddhist pagoda and stupa architecture—according to the legend Ashoka himself is said to have commissioned the building of eighty-four thousand stupas (mounds bearing the Buddha's relics, i.e., pagodas) in Asia

(*Jambudvipa*)[129]—aspects of the *dharma-vijaya* concept came all the way to Japan. Miniature pagodas, which had their origin in the Ashoka legend, became devotional artifacts in many parts of Asia and were sold and presented as gifts and devotional offerings. They often contained a written message or *mantra* of peace and dharma. Shōtoku Taishi had begun in Japan a regular mass production of such miniature gift pagodas.[130] However, more comprehensive historical research on the significance of Ashoka for, and his reception in, Japan is required to obtain a clearer picture.[131]

With the building, commissioned by Shōtoku Taishi, of the great pagoda in Nara that contains a relic of the Buddha that was brought via Korea,[132] Buddhism in Japan became the official religion of the court and of the state. Prince Shōtoku drafted in 604 the first "constitution" of Japan, in which he laid down a set of "principles of legal and social justice."[133] Named in article 2 of Prince Shōtoku's code, the "three jewels"—the Buddha (the principle or the Teacher), the Dharma (the good Doctrine) and the Sangha (the Buddhist Society)[134]—are meant to provide the basis for an ideal social order, or, in K. N. Jayatilleke's words, "the final ideal of all living beings and the ultimate foundation of all nations."[135] Shōtoku Taishi's work, at the time the Meiji Constiution was drafted, was considered one of the early forerunners of modern Japanese constitutional government. Article 1 of Prince Shōtoku's "constitution" reads:

> Harmony (*wa*) is to be valued, and an avoidance of wanton oppositon (*tōtoshi*) to be honored. All men are influenced by partisanship, and there are few who are intelligent. Hence there are some who disobey their lords and fathers, or who maintain feuds with the neighboring villages. But when those above are harmonious and those below are friendly, and there is concord in the discussion of business, right views of things spontaneously gain acceptance. Then what is there which cannot be accomplished?[136]

In 710 the Japanese imperial capital city of Nara (at that time officially known as Heijōkyō, which literally means "capital of peace") was established, and in 794 a newer and larger capital city known as Heiankyō (meaning "capital of peace and tranquility"), later called Kyōto, was founded some twenty-five miles to the north.[137] Both cities were built after the model of Chang'an,[138] the capital of the Chinese Tang Dynasty (618–906). Tang culture in particular impacted Buddhism in Japan, which was then directly linked with the international trade network extending over the Silk Roads all across Asia and by sea through the Strait of Malacca to India and further. This period of blooming Buddhist culture in Japan is called the Nara Period, after the eighth-century capital at Nara (710–794). Emperor Shōmu, who reigned from 724 to 756, followed the example of Ashoka and other Buddhist kings and joined the Buddhist order.[139] Under his rule the large bronze image of Maha-Vairocana (*Dainichi Nyorai*) or "Birushana Buddha" (popularly called the Nara Daibutsu)[140] was erected. It was meant to be "all-encompassing," as the "symbol of the spiritual unity of the universe."[141] In the popular perception of the time, the Nara Daibutsu at the same time "stood as a symbol of Japan's rise from a backward country to a highly developed one."[142]

Soon after, Saichō (Dengyō Daishi, 767–822) and Kūkai (Kōbō Daishi, 774–835), two of the most influential cultural icons in Japanese history, further shaped Buddhist development in Japan.[143] From their teachings two "mountain-top" schools emerged, the Tendai and Shingon sects. Kūkai studied in China between 804 and 806,[144] where he traveled together with Saichō in 804 on a mission sent by Emperor Kanmu, and became successor to the seventh patriarch of the school of the "True Word" (j. *shingon*, ch. *zhenyan*). He is considered to be the founder of the Japanese *kana* writing system, which was phonetically adapted from the Sanskrit *devanagari* script. He compiled a critique (known as the *Sango shiichi*) of the "three doctrines" of Confucianism, Buddhism, and Taoism, and continues to be popular with the Japanese people today. A great educator, he founded the first Japanese private school for Buddhist and Confucian studies.[145]

Saichō, founder of the Japanese Tendai (ch. *tiantai*) school of Buddhism,[146] from which numerous other Japanese Buddhist schools originated, emphasized the importance of the community. He taught that individuals should always work for the good of all, as parts of a network of the greater community, like the individual meshes of a net. Only if in our thought and activities we have the whole world in mind can we ourselves be happy.[147]

Interestingly, the Japanese monks who traveled to China since the end of the sixth century to acquire Buddhist writings from the monasteries there had chosen from among a large number of teachings (*sutras*) "those that gave evidence of a 'lay' and world-oriented tendency," putting—like in no other Buddhist country—emphasis on "economically meaningful work . . . thus preparing the ground for the rapid economic development of Japan today."[148] In this way the practice of Japanese Buddhism seems to match what Max Weber has called an "inner-worldly asceticism" in the context of a modern Christian "Protestant ethic."[149] Arcadio Schwade sees it as an auspicious "conjuncture of history that Japan came to know Buddhism in its northern form, or *Mahayana* Buddhism, which differs from southern Buddhism, the *Hinayana*, through its social orientation." Thus "compassion, patience and tolerance . . . [are] the characteristics which still today mold the life of the Japanese and also inspire pacifist movements."[150]

Although between ca. 900 and 1400 contacts with the Asian mainland had become sparse, the Shingon monks Chōgen (1121–1206) and Myōan Eisai

(1141–1215, founder of the Japanese Zen school) traveled to China to pursue their studies, proceeding on pilgrimages to Mount Tiantai and Mount Ayuwang (named after King Ashoka).[151] The thousand-meter-high Mount Ayuwang (j. Aikuōzan) in Zhejiang Province, with which Japan had since ancient times maintained trade relations, was during the Southern Song Dynasty (420–479) one of the five mountains in the Buddhist Chinese administrative system which Japan imitated in the twelfth century[152]—a system representing a peaceful sociopolitical order based on law (*dharma*) and Asian spiritual pragmatism. Thus, during the eighth and ninth centuries, an "international form of Mahayana Buddhism"—the above-mentioned *ecumene*—whose main characteristic was "its individualistic character," spread across Asia.[153] Art objects like the so-called Pala Bronzes, and Buddhist philosophy and practice emanating from the Indian universities of Nalanda and Vikramashila, profoundly influenced the arts and thoughts including political institutions, in Burma, Siam, Java, and Tang dynasty (618–906 AD) China, and consequently Japan.[154]

At the same time, in the late Heian Period (794–1185) a court literature, romantic poetry and the world's oldest extant novel, and art and architecture continued to develop. The superb accomplishments in architectural and garden design had a strong popular appeal. At the end of the twelfth century, following the two invasion attempts of Mongolian naval flotillas (manned partly by Koreans) in 1274 and 1281, which were successfully repelled with the help of two great storms (the so-called divine winds, *kamikaze*),[155] effective political power shifted from the bureaucratic court nobility (*kuge*) to the "armed nobility" (*buke*). In 1192, Minamoto Yoritomo gained the title of "supreme military commander" (*shōgun*).

It seems, however, this shift to a more firmly established military regime did Japan not much good. Around the middle of the fifteenth century a civil war began that lasted nearly a hundred years. Nonetheless, at the same time cultural contacts and trade relations with the continent grew remarkably and even led to a regular boom in Japanese overseas settlements, as, for example, in the Buddhist kingdom of Ayuthaya in Thailand. Overseas trade seemed at times to be controlled by semi-pirates under the patronage of local chieftains, but officially organized, coordinated, and financed largely by the Zen monasteries. Finally, between 1573 and 1603, Japan was unified, in successive stages, by Oda Nobunaga (1534–1582), Hideyoshi Toyotomi (1536–1598), and Tokugawa Ieyasu (1542–1616). Oda Nobunaga succeeded, with the help of Christian converts (in this regard he promoted Christianity) in breaking the secessionist tendencies of the feudal lords and Buddhist monasteries that were equipped with their own standing armies.[156]

The appearance of the so-called warrior monks around the year 1000 is problematic for the question of a Buddhist foundation of Japanese pacifism.[157] An "indifference to death"—not of others, but one's own—and the perception of the transitoriness of worldly life in the Japanese tradition may lie at the root of this: "The life of the warrior is compared with the cherry blossom which, scarcely having reached full bloom, now passes away."[158] Is it possible this was due also to some untimely panic[159] about *mappō* (the "latter or final days of the law," or *pascimadharma*),[160] when the faithful would have to prepare for the last battle to reestablish the rule of the "good law" in the world?[161] We have no conclusive judgment in this matter.

The competing temple mountains as centers of administration had frequently been subject to threats.[162] In the autumn of 963, the Emperor Murakami summoned an assembly in which twenty priests from Nara and Mount Hiei took part, to discuss important issues. The dispute could not be settled and the temples armed themselves to protect their interests. The monasteries of Kyoto and Nara were soon able to muster thousands of armed men, who in the following two centuries terrified the "superstitious courtiers" and common citizens of Kyoto.[163] The weakness of an incompetent administration as well as the priests' greed and hunger for power, the proclivity to mix worldly and spiritual affairs, and self-righteous reserve may have been the reason for this unhappy situation. As a result of the association between religion (Buddhism) and the administration, the transition from pure Buddhist brotherhoods to Confucianist *bushi* communities with their cultivation of both *bun* (letters) and *bu* (military affairs) was unproblematic; the samurais' transformation from warriors to bureaucrats at the end of the Tokugawa Period was similarly easy.[164]

After the destruction and overthrowing of the Buddhist temples by Oda Nobunaga and Hideyoshi Toyotomi, the Tokugawa Shōgunate brought Confucianism politically into the foreground. Shintoism and Buddhism came to be excluded from worldly affairs. Between these two religions since the eighth century, and effectively until the Meiji Restoration, a broad and profound syncretism prevailed. On the other hand, Confucian ethical and social doctrine emphasized the ideal and smooth functioning of societal relationships, and in this way promoted peace.

Marius Jansen has pointed out that old traditions at the beginning of the Meiji era (1868–1912) had become something of an empty vessel "into which modernity could be inserted." As Japan modernized, Buddhism also faced persecution, though only for a short period.[165] Oddly, the government attempted "to restore Japanese antiquity"[166] and championed the slogan "Abolish Buddhism, and discard Buddhist images" (*haibutsu kishaku*).[167] However, this was met with substantial resistance and, following the "rediscovery" of Buddhism (which was greatly facilitated by Europeans), and with the advent of the pan-Asian independence movements and, notably, the large-scale assembly known as the World Parliament of Religions in Chicago in 1893, a number of Japanese Buddhist priests traveled through the United States and Europe.[168] In 1889 the Ceylonese Dharmapala, who was considered a "leading representative of the early Buddhist revival," journeyed to Japan, together with the Englishman Henry Steel Olcott,[169] "the white Buddhist," and in 1903 the first International Buddhist Society (Buddhasasana Samagama) was founded in Rangoon. One of its main objectives was to bring together students from the various Buddhist countries.[170] Following the foundation of a "World Buddhist League" in Tokyo in 1925, the first "Pan-Pacific Buddhist Conference" was held in Honolulu, which was followed by a large-scale second conference, as a follow-up to the first, which took place in Tokyo and Kyoto in 1934.[171] Peter Alles has commented: "Connecting up with . . . the best tradition of the Nara Period, Buddhism displayed quite notable activities in the field of education and social welfare."[172]

During the war a number of Buddhists were imprisoned in Japan because of their pacifist convictions. Fujii Nichitatsu, the founder of one of the important Buddhist schools deriving from the Nichiren sect, during the war had declared himself in favor of pacifism. He later recollected: "The Pacific War raged ever more brutally. I could not any longer . . . keep silence about the war, in which people were killing one another. Thus I traveled through the whole of Japan and preached resistance against the war and [advocated] the prayer for peace. It was a time in which any person who only spoke about resistance to the war, would go to prison because of that alone."[173] Also the Risshō Kōseikai founded in 1938 and the Sōka Gakkai should be mentioned. Sōka Gakkai's founder Makiguchi Tsunesaburō died in prison in 1944.[174]

The Japanologist Peter Fischer, far from disavowing the consistently constructive role of Buddhism, writes: "Japanese Buddhists and researchers on Buddhism in the period between 1868 and 1945 looked into the past for ideas and forms of organization which, remolded in concrete ways to meet the [expansionist aims and] circumstances of the times, they could offer."[175] The Japanese government in the 1930s and during the Second World War promoted "quite consciously 'pan-Buddhist' endeavors . . . [merely] out of political motives."[176] Thus, Buddhism was ultimately unable to hold back Japanese militarism between 1932 and 1945 and in some instances seems to have supported it.

It should have become clear that Buddhism, like other great religions, does not lack a political dimension. In the contest over the relation between ends and means, Buddhists seem to believe and feel that for all practical purposes it is more advantageous to look for faults and shortcomings in oneself than in others. Thus, with regard to the subject in question (i.e., of the use of force and violence), the Buddhist teaching of "not causing harm to others (Sanskrit *ahimsa*) . . . prohibits *unambiguously* the killing or injury of living creatures in any way."[177]

The adoption of the concept of "freedom from fear" in the Atlantic Charter of 1941, first signed by U.S. President Franklin D. Roosevelt and British Prime Minister Winston Churchill, may have been inspired by Buddhist teachings and certainly had a precedent there, and it is this concept that was later taken up in the Japanese constitution.[178] This fact is less surprising than one might assume, because of the intensive cultural exchange between the West and the old Asian civilizations that had taken place in the past five hundred years.

CHRISTIAN PACIFIST THOUGHT IN JAPAN

For the early Christians peace was to be realized in the coming Kingdom of God. This was the highest good.[179] In the early modern period this promise, as a postulate of faith and pragmatic aim in the wake of the "discovery" of the world, was relevant also with respect to the newly encountered, non-European peoples. Christianity assumed the task of pacifying various indigenous, more or less "civilized" peoples. Francis Xavier (1506–1552), the "Apostle of Asia," a Jesuit, who had undertaken missionary activities in India, arrived in Japan in 1549 and wrote with effusive enthusiasm about his meeting with the Japanese: "The people whom we have met so far, are the best who have as yet been discovered, and it seems to me that we shall never find among heathens another race to equal the Japanese. They are a people of very good manners . . . and prize honour above all else in the world."[180] Around the year 1606 there were some seven hundred fifty thousand Christians in Japan, and every year the number was increasing by five or six thousand: "Nagasaki could vie with Manila and Macao for the title of the 'Rome of the East.'"[181]

The German physician Engelbert Kaempfer describes (writing around 1690, while in Dutch service at Nagasaki) the situation before the "exclusion" (*sakoku*) laws of the early seventeenth century: "The worldly undertakings of the Portuguese took place just as successfully as their spiritual undertakings. They married the daughters of the richest citizens, acquired houses and riches, and their trade continued according to their hopes. . . . Annually over 300 tons of gold were exported from Japan, as the Portuguese had the unlimited liberty of import and export."[182] Oda Nobunaga, one of the "three unifiers" of Japan, had made a pact with the Christians in order to break the power of the overbearing Buddhist monasteries and it was perhaps as a result of this that he had been able to push forward the unification of the country. In any case the Christians had increasingly become politically accountable and influential.

Although Christianity in Europe during the first three centuries had no claim to political power, the church would in the following centuries increasingly engage itself in worldly affairs, and by the fourth century AD "cultural developments had completely overridden the fundamental tenets of the teaching of Jesus," with the result that even "large-scale homicide was once again acceptable, so long as one was fighting on the side of God."[183] The claim of the clergy to worldly rule, however, met an energetic opposition on the part of the Japanese.[184] H. G. Wells, who was at once an ardent peace activist, researcher, and historian, writes about this process:

For a time Japan welcomed European intercourse, and the Christian missionaries made a great number of converts. A certain William Adams,[185] of Gillingham in Kent, became the most trusted European adviser of the Japanese, and showed them how to build big ships. There were voyages in Japanese-built ships to India and Peru. There arose complicated quarrels between the Spanish Dominicans, the Portuguese Jesuits,[186] and the English and Dutch Protestants, each warning the Japanese against the evil political designs of the others. The Jesuits, in a phase of ascendancy, persecuted and insulted the Buddhists with great acrimony. These troubles interwove with the feudal conflicts of the time. In the end the Japanese came to the conclusion that the Europeans and their Christianity were an intolerable nuisance, and that Catholic Christianity in particular was a mere cloak for the political dreams of the Pope and the Spanish monarchy—already in possession of the Philippine Islands; there was a great and conclusive persecution of the Christians; and in 1638 Japan, with the exception of one wretched Dutch factory on the minute island of Deshima [Dejima] in the harbour of Nagasaki, was absolutely closed to Europeans, and remained closed for over 200 years.[187]

During the "exclusion" period, Japanese Christians continued to practice their faith in secret. Such "hidden Christian communities" existed especially in Kyushu, where the missionaries had first landed.[188] In the 1850s and 1860s the question of a rehabilitation of Christianity received prominence, and many Japanese saw a causal relationship between modern knowledge and the Western religion.

The Confucian scholar and educator Nakamura Masanao (1832–1891) had observed in 1872 that without Christianity the Western arts and technology were a "hollow shell without a soul."[189] Between 1873 and 1880, according to John Hall, approximately thirty thousand Japanese, many of samurai background, converted to Christianity. In the space of the next ten years this number tripled. Schools established by Protestant Christians early on appeared in Sapporo, Kyoto, Kumamoto (on the island of Kyushu), and Yokohama. In November 1889 Christians in Tokyo, who were inspired by British Quakers, founded the first Japanese peace association, the Nihon Heiwakai.[190] The founders, Katō Kazuharu (1861–1932) and Kitamura Tōkoku (1868–1894), published a journal called *Heiwa* (Peace), of which twelve issues appeared between March 1892 and May 1893. Kitamura had, as a nineteen-year-old, written to his wife Mina that he wanted "to become like Victor Hugo, who propounded his political ideals through the power of the pen."[191]

There were many enthusiastic Christian pacifists in Japan, some of the same generation as Shidehara. The most famous is Uchimura Kanzō (1861–1930), who was during 1897–1904 the chief editor of what was then Japan's largest daily newspaper, the *Yorozu Chōhō*.[192] With him a remarkable and unique Christian pacifism that was at the same time typically Japanese exerted great influence. Karl F. Zahl describes Uchimura Kanzō as the

> most impressive person confessing the Christian faith and founder of Japanese pacifism in the second half of the Meiji Period . . . whose way of living merits special attention since from him sprang the strongest impulses for the political generation-building of Christian socialism. . . . In his writings he protested against the idea that wars had always been central to Man's history. . . . In the longer view war was no suitable means to protect peoples or to keep them from going to ruin. History showed that all world empires had gone to ruin due to their wars.[193]

Uchimura concluded that "the world will be gradually entrusted to those peoples who detest war,"[194] and he appealed directly to the conscience and patriotism of the Japanese:[195] "As a self-centered man is the least and meanest of mankind, so a self-seeking and self-satisfied nation is the weakest and most backward of all nations. Japan cannot be an exception to this eternal law."[196] He also expressed himself about Japan's role as mediator between the worlds of East and West:

> There she stands as an "arbiter," a "middle man" (*nakahodo*) between the Democratic West and the Imperial East, between the Christian America and the Buddhist Asia. . . . Quick to perceive and receive, Japan can readily assimilate to herself anything she comes in contact with. *The Japanese alone of all Oriental people can comprehend the Occidental ideas, and they alone of all civilized peoples have a true conception of the Oriental ideas.* In intellectual spheres, no less than in commercial, Japan is a stepping stone between the East and the West. . . . *To reconcile the East with the West; to be the advocate of the East and the harbinger of the West;* this we believe to be the mission which Japan is called upon to fulfill. . . . Here we shall adopt Laws, Religion, and Politics, as they come from Europe and America, and nursing them in our familiar Oriental atmosphere, we shall give them in marriage as fit brides to our less flexible brothers. We shall, if must be, lead humble Asia to curb the march of proud Europe; but we desire peace.[197]

Uchimura preached an original Christianity, wholly rejecting church organization. His "no-churchism" (*mukyōkai*) movement, as he called it, found numerous adherents. After the Second World War Uchimura's books were republished, inspiring numerous Japanese. Jan Swyngedouw has rightly observed that "the encounter between Japan and the West drove forward not only the modernization process but also exercised an influence in the sense of Christian thought, Christian ethics, and Christian practice."[198]

In Japan, as in other parts of the world, Quakers had a significant bearing on the understanding of Christianity and pacifism. The most famous Japanese Quaker was Nitobe Inazō (1862–1933; his portrait had been depicted on a five-thousand yen note still used today). Nitobe was an educator, civil servant, and intermediary between East and West, who served as Under-Secretary General of the League of Nations until 1926, and thereafter headed the renowned Institute of Pacific Relations. While he was in the United States, he wrote his famous book *Bushido: The Soul of Japan* (1899), which impressed writers like H. G. Wells and Rabindranath Tagore (1861–1941), and continues to be published and widely read.[199]

The name of the Christian socialist Kagawa Toyohiko (1888–1960) should also be mentioned. His English-language book *Love, the Law of Life*, contains chapters on "the ethics of love," "love and law," and "love and violence."[200] Kagawa, however, especially disappointed his numerous American followers and admirers,[201] and did not remain invulnerable to Japanese nationalism and its "Greater East Asia liberation ideology." Kagawa is known also for his practical engagement in the spheres of social welfare and agriculture. At the end of the 1920s and the beginning of the 1930s he led the so-called Kingdom of God (*tenmikuni*) movement, a Christian socialist version for alleviating the sufferings of the poor and aspiring to a prosperous and holy life for all. In this way, Japanese socialism was in many ways wedded to Christian ideas.

Christianity is an important element for assessing the pacifist background in which Shidehara's foreign policy flourished for a time. Also, Shidehara's wife was a practicing Japanese Christian. It was above all Protestant Christians (and some communists) who went to prison during the Second World War because of their pacifist convictions.

In the postwar years, the German-speaking Catholic (Jesuit) Bishop of Hiroshima, Ogihara Akira, argued persuasively for world peace and for the elimination of atomic weapons. A "defender of the Peace Constitution"[202] after the war, the jurist Tabata Shinobu (1902–1994), a Christian and democratic socialist, made a name in scholarly publications. The former Japanese Socialist Party Chairman Doi Takako had studied under Professor Tabata as a university student. In connection with article 9 of the Japanese postwar constitution, Tabata referred to Uchimura Kanzō, who in his later years propounded, as Ueda Katsumi pointed out, the "legal renunciation of war and total disarmament as the command of divine providence." And as far as this is concerned, "Uchimura had been convinced that to strive for this task was the true mission of a patriot."[203] Another great socialist leader and politician, as well as Protestant Christian minister and a pacifist, was Abe Isoo (1865–1949), with whom we will deal in the next chapter.

JAPANESE LIBERAL AND SOCIALIST TRADITIONS

Liberalism[204] provided valuable answers to the question of peaceful coexistence. In this respect, Shidehara's economic policy also wanted

> to take powers away from the State in favor of the individual and his economic gain; at the same time it promised the elimination of war [which had acted] as the power instrument *par excellence*, and the bringing about of peace. Because: the "essence of trade" disagrees with the "spirit of conquest." Economy binds nations together, while domination divides them. For classical liberalism therefore, political economy came to be the peace science *par excellence* and economy a strategy for peace.[205]

The project of a new era at the end of the nineteenth century inspired intellectuals to attempt to combine their traditions with the vision of an ideal future, to create a world order that could better serve the general welfare. For the modern thinkers of the nineteenth and twentieth centuries, whether Asian, European, or American, there was not only a desire to fathom the common origins of civilization—mutual interests also had to be defined and coordinated. The imminent task was to participate effectively in the organization of the world, to rationally understand the conditions of mutually beneficial interaction in the framework of the emergent global interdependence, and to fervently explore the desired options for peace and prosperity. In the new world, war was more and more coming to be regarded as obsolete.

However, it was not enough to trust in the self-regulating mechanisms of the market to ensure a durable peace. John Stuart Mill (1806–1873), who in the Meiji Period had also been widely read in Japan, like Jeremy Bentham, had come to understand that generally binding norms had to be based on an ethical foundation, deduced from what had been found to be morally correct and empirically valid. The concept of an ethic of peace should be seen in this context.

For the modern period, Wolfgang J. Mommsen identifies the German sociologist Max Weber as the "spiritual vanguard of modernization" in Japan.[206] The assertion may be accurate,[207] although Japan's unique phase of internal seclusion was indispensable as a precondition to prepare for this modernization process.[208] As we have seen, soon after opening the country in the 1850s, Japan attempted a synthesis of Eastern and Western ways of dealing with the world. This permitted a certain tolerance and created a rational basis, following world trends, to realize a pragmatic, practice-oriented political culture and foreign policy. Both Confucianism and Buddhism had been necessary prerequisites to produce an intellectual environment that was politically relevant if not always effective, as can be seen for example in the work of Ogyū Sorai. In fact, Tokugawa Ieyasu earlier on had "relied more on the counsel of Zen priests Sūden and Tenkai" than on the aforementioned Hayashi Razan.[209] The late eighteenth century had also brought to Japan elements and features of an indigenous "Enlightenment" that already reflected and anticipated European developments.

Toward the end of the *bakumatsu* years (1853–1868)—the final days of the Tokugawa Shōgunate (*bakufu*) that led to the Meiji Restoration—laws and guidelines were issued "along the lines of modern constitutions" that included "ideological and political moments" that clearly stood in a liberal tradition, and compare well to Europe's constitutional history: the decree of 10 November 1867 on "general consultation" (*shūgi*) over matters of government and foreign relations, the "great command for the restoration of monarchical rule" (*Ōsei fukko no daigōrei*) of 3 January 1868 that similarly stipulated "making every effort toward appropriate public discussions" (*shitō no kōgi o tsukusu*) and the "wide and thorough use of consultative meetings and the deciding of all [state] affairs taking account of public opinion" (*hiroku kaigi o tsukushi banki kōron ni kessubeshi*), the "Five Article Oath" (*Gokajō no goseimon*) of 6 April 1968, and the *Seitaisho* of 17 June 1868.[210]

Meiji liberals and human rights activists had in the 1880s drafted so-called *shigi kenpō*, "privately proposed constitutions" for the new Japanese state that were, however unfortunately, hardly replicated in the Meiji constitution of 1889,[211] but that after the Second World War were again called to mind and played a role in the process of the making of the Japanese postwar constitution.[212] The most significant of these constitutional proposals came from Ueki Emori (1857–1892).[213] Not commonly known in Japan today, Ueki was a Meiji intellectual of the "freedom and people's rights movement" (*jiyū minken undō*), a "Tom Paine of the democratic movement," as Andrew Roth described him in a much-read book after the war. In fact he was the "theoretician and tactician"[214] (i.e., the "brain") behind the famous leader Itagaki Taisuke (1837–1919), who, though originally of a patriotic-conservative disposition, founded the Jiyūtō (Freedom Party), the first large political party, and the first to have a genuine political program, together with Ueki Emori, Nakae Chōmin, and Baba Tatsui. Itagaki was from the Tosa clan on the southern side of the island of Shikoku, and his civil courage is well remembered in

Japan, even among high school students. When a fanatic nationalist attacked him with a dagger in April 1882, he is said to have exclaimed, "Itagaki may die, but freedom will never die."[215] Quite ahead of his time, Ueki underscored in his writings the need to establish an international government (*bankoku kyōgi seifu* or *bankoku kōhō*) that would guarantee all countries' and peoples' democratic rights and secure world peace.[216]

> Ueki, like Paine, defended the principles of the French revolution, though he was careful not to claim baldly that republicanism was necessarily suitable to Japan. He favoured a thorough democratic renovation, including the introduction of representative institutions based on universal suffrage and a bill of civic rights. . . . The intoxicating ideas of a liberal democracy propagated by the followers of Ueki created a ferment among the poorer classes.[217]

Between 1873 and 1875 the left chamber of the *Dajōkan* (the new central organ of government of the early Meiji Period) was occupied with elaborating constitutional drafts, and after 1876 the *Genrōin* or Council of Elders was made responsible for gathering materials relating to the new constitution to be enacted. In 1878 it laid forth its draft, titled "Nihon kokken'an."[218] After 1879 there were public debates on the issue, in which the liberal movement, newspapers, and private persons could voice their opinion.[219] The result was that the government largely neglected these proposals and instead adopted the authoritarian Prussian constitution as a model.[220]

Following the promulgation of the Meiji constitution (1889) and the first Diet elections of 1890,[221] eventually a party-based cabinet headed by Ōkuma Shigenobu (1838–1922) was sworn in (1898).[222] Although the makers of the Japanese constitution had, in their putting together of this basic law, been abundantly well informed and had allowed themselves to be counseled by foreign jurists, what emerged was a traditional format; it featured a somewhat "antiquated" concept of *kokutai* (literally "body of the state"),[223] with the Tennō as "head" of the government body.

Ōkuma Shigenobu, probably the most remarkable liberal politician at the turn of the century, described (a few years later) the situation of his country in these words:

> For twenty centuries the nation has drunk freely of the civilizations of Korea, China, and India, being always open to the different influences impressed on her in succession. Yet we remain today practically unaltered under one Imperial House and Sovereign, that has descended in an unbroken line for a length of time absolutely unexampled in the world. This fact furnishes at least an incontestable proof that the Japanese are not a race of people who, inconstant and capricious, are given to loving all that is new and curious, always running after passing fashions.[224]

At times self-complacent and presumptuous when it came to following ethical norms, a certain eclecticism constitutes perhaps one of the character-istics of early Japanese liberalism (*jiyūshugi*). In political reality, however, in keeping with Japanese tradition, the concept of a "middle way" as guideline to avoid extremes also seems to have been adhered to.

> [The Japanese] have ever made a point of choosing the middle course in every-thing, and have aimed at being always well balanced. To keep exclusively in one direction, or to run to extremes, or to look forward only without looking back-ward, or to remember one side of a thing, forgetting the other, is not a character-istic of our people. We are conservative simultaneously with being progressive; we are aristocratic and at the same time democratic; we are individualistic while being also socialistic. In these aspects we may be said to somewhat resemble the Anglo-Saxon race.[225]

It was perhaps understandable that Japan, after its entry into the comity of the nations, was at first oriented toward Great Britain, another island nation. England's industrial revolution, its "free trade imperialism," liberalism, and not least its navy incited the admiration of the Japanese and contributed to defining an identity. The earlier mentioned Nakamura Masanao translated and published in 1872 John Stuart Mill's *On Liberty*. In 1883 the politician Mutsu Munemitsu (1844–1897) translated Jeremy Bentham's *Introduction to the Principles of Morals and Legislation*. British pragmatism, capitalism, and utilitarianism, and especially also parliamentarism and the state form of the constitutional monarchy, tallied with the Japanese national character in many ways.

The concept of the state as an "organic entity" was certainly not alien to the West, as the concept of the "body of the state" with the king as its "head" was known also in France. This concept, however, appeared antiquated with the advent of liberalism and socialism, which had evolved in the wake of the French Revolution. Also in Japan there had been a "period of gradually increasing civil ascendancy."[226] The British model was then perhaps the most appealing, and Ōkuma Shigenobu, the successful politician, diplomat, and economist who possessed a predilection for British parliamentary ways, was its most ardent advocate.

Ōkuma had developed a concept, which came to be known as the Ōkuma Doctrine,[227] that reflected Japan's growing commercial and ideological inter-est in China. In his youth he had studied Dutch and English from foreign-ers residing in Nagasaki as well as methods of modern finance, trade, and industry, and had traveled in Europe and America. To improve and develop positive relationships with China had definite priority. Since Japan had al-ready joined the ranks of the progressive nations on near-equal terms with the

West, it was reasonable that "having modernized first, [it] should repay her ancient cultural debt to China by now guaranteeing her freedom and aiding her modernization."[228]

The nineteenth-century liberalism that had shaped the political mentality of the intellectual elite in Japan suited the Confucian mindset and tolerance of Buddhism. Itagaki Taisuke had fought with Saigō Takamori against the shōgunate. Having founded the Liberal Party (Jiyūtō) in 1881, in 1898 Itagaki and his Jiyūtō, together with Ōkuma and his Shimpotō (Progressive Party), formed an alliance that became the Kenseitō (Constitutional Rule Party). Immediately afterward it formed a new government, and the first "party cabinet," which, however, did not last long.[229] Shortly afterward Itagaki left active politics to dedicate himself to writing. By the end of the century, socialism had also become a factor to be reckoned with in Japan.

Abe Isoo (1865–1949) is known as the "father of Japanese socialism."[230] The son of a lower-ranking samurai, he became a Protestant Christian minister and a pacifist, and one of the leaders of the workers' movement. Social concerns, philanthropy (*hakuai katsudō*),[231] and Christian love for one's neighbor were central to Abe's outlook. Like most Japanese who had converted to Christianity, Abe was an internationalist. The following, published in 1903, was penned by two of his coworkers, Kōtoku Shūsui and Sakai Toshihiko: "Freedom, equality, brotherhood—these are the great principles which make human life in the world worth living. . . . We stand up for pacifism as an expression of the practical exercise of the way of brotherhood (*hakuai no michi*) for all humankind."[232]

Leo Tolstoy's pacifism also had a strong influence on Abe, as did the monumental work of the Polish banker and pacifist Ivan (Jean) de Bloch.[233] Between 1899 and 1911 Abe, as publisher of the Unitarian magazine *Rikugō Zasshi*, wrote numerous articles on the topics of pacifism and socialism.

> Democracy is stubbornly opposed by militarism. It is opposed on three counts: because arms actually protect capitalist class interests at the expense of the common people; because war aids the exploitation of weak countries by strong powers, as arms are used to open up markets by force; and because militarism always grows into despotism, a retrogression from civilization to barbarism.[234]

Soon after the first Hague peace conference,[235] two editorials appeared in *Rikugō Zasshi* with the titles "Sensō ka heiwa ka?" (War or peace?, October 1900) and "Shusenron no byūmō" (The falsity of the war argument, April 1901). In an article which appeared in the same magazine in 1904, during the Russo-Japanese War, Abe concludes:

We cannot envision a double morality. . . . We socialists are absolutely opposed to both brigandage and war. As there cannot be "good bandits" so there can never be a just war. We can sympathize with those who have been forced into banditry by the imperfections of the social order. By the same token those who argue that protective tariffs force nations into a struggle for survival demand a hearing. If free trade were allowed throughout the world, wars would be fewer. But none of these reasons can justify either banditry or war.[236]

The anti-militaristic manifesto of the first socialist party, the Shakai Minshutō (Social Democratic Party), came largely from Abe's pen.[237] It proclaimed the "total abolition of armaments as a first step toward the establishment of peace among nations."[238] The manifesto was published in its entirety in the 20 May 1901 issue of the journal *Rōdō Sekai* (Labor World). Because of its anti-militarism, however, the government banned the Shakai Minshutō almost immediately after its foundation. Despite the ban socialist activities continued, though they now focused on educating the masses while secretly propagating socialist ideas.[239] In 1926, when Shidehara was foreign minister in the liberal Wakatsuki cabinet, the party, under the same name, and with Abe Isoo as chairman, reemerged.

Having become in 1918 one of the cofounders of the Japanese Fabian Society, Abe in 1928, as chairman of the new Shakai Minshutō, was for the first time elected to the Diet. Later, as chairman of the larger "Socialist Mass Party" (Shakai Taishūtō), a union of various democratic-socialist groupings founded in 1932, Abe continued to oppose Japan's militarization. In 1938 he barely escaped an assassination attempt by right-wing extremists.[240]

Cyril H. Powles emphasizes Abe's view that the reason for wars is to be found in the "individualism" and national egotism of states, "expressed concretely through protective trade policies, combined with the aggressive use of armies in the search for markets."[241] Free trade was for Abe a landmark of mutual trust among nations and the quickest way to peace.[242] In this he at once supported Shidehara's free-trade-oriented peace diplomacy.

Abe not only made a name for himself as a publisher of magazines,[243] but also as the translator of Norman Angell's book *The Great Illusion*, published in Japan under the title *Gendai sensōron* (On modern warfare; Tokyo: Hakubunkan, 1912).[244] He boldly declared: "If peace is to be a law of humanity (*jindō*), it should be proclaimed in the world, even if this should mean the dissolution of the nation."[245] In the 1930s still, Abe could win a considerable portion of the electorate for himself and his anti-militarist program.[246] He stepped down as chairman of his party in 1940, after it had become impossible for him, in view of the superior numbers and force of his opponents, to continue and give unhindered expression to his convictions.

The success of socialism (and liberalism) in Japan in the interwar period was relative and frequently foiled. The attempt of radical socialists and anarchists in 1910, under the banner of "world revolution," to assassinate the imperial family not only miscarried,[247] but this attempt stymied all hope of winning broad popular support for socialist ideals for a long time. The man accused of leading the assassination plot, Kōtoku Shūsui (1871–1911),[248] had been one of the founding members of the Social Democratic Party in 1901 and a coworker under Uchimura Kanzō on the staff of the *Yorozu Chōhō* daily newspaper. In 1903 he left this newspaper and, with friends and sympathizers, founded the *Heimin Shimbun* (People's Newspaper), in which much of what he wrote was in opposition to war and Japanese militarism.[249] Its first issue, which came out just before the outbreak of the Russo-Japanese War, declared: "Regardless of racial distinctions or differences in government structures, we demand the abolition of military armaments and the *prohibition of war on a world scale*."[250] After the Russo-Japanese War social democrats split into Christian socialists (Abe Isoo), state socialists, revolutionaries, and anarchists. Kōtoku became increasingly radical in his outlook and was consequently arrested as the instigator of the 1910 attempt on the life of the imperial family and hanged together with ten alleged accomplices.[251]

Kōtoku had studied under Nakae Chōmin (1847–1901), who published many books on political theory, and had translated Rousseau's *Contrat social*. In the mid-1860s Nakae Chōmin had worked as an interpreter for Léon Roches, the French envoy to Japan. He had studied *Shushigaku* (the teachings of the neo-Confucianist Zhu Xi school), *Yōmeigaku* (the teachings of Wang Yangming), and *Rangaku* (Dutch studies) prior to traveling to France in 1871, where he made the friendship of Saionji Kinmochi (1849–1940), the early twentieth-century prime minister and later *genrō*. Nakae, the "Rousseau of the Orient" (as he was often called), and prominent cofounder of the Jiyūtō, was very much a "born idealist." His translations of Jean-Jacques Rousseau's works were even read in China. "His translation of *Le contrat social* [The Social Contract] was called the 'Bible' of the radicals within the Liberal Party."[252] After his return from France in 1880, he founded with Saionji Kinmochi (who later became Shidehara's guardian benefactor) the weekly *Tōyō Jiyū Shimbun* (Oriental Free Press), a publication that promoted parliamentarian democracy and the freedom and human rights movement. Government officials, however, soon closed down the publication. In 1882, Nakae published the Japanese translation of Rousseau's *Le contrat social* in his own periodical *Seiri Sōdan* (Discourses on Statecraft). Banned from Tokyo, together with Ozaki Yukio (1858–1954) and over five hundred other liberals, under the provisions of the so-called "Law on the Maintenance of Public Peace and Order" (1887), Nakae founded in Osaka the *Shinonome Shimbun* (Dawn News) and

won an elective seat in Japan's first Diet election in 1890. At this time Kōtoku was still a schoolboy. In this intellectual climate the young Shidehara, while studying in Osaka, grew up.

In 1901, the year in which Nakae died, Kōtoku published his work *Nijūseiki no kaibutsu: Teikokushugi* (Imperialism: The monster of the twentieth century), which he wrote in part as a way of expressing opposition to the sending of Japanese troops during the Boxer Rebellion in China. Also at this time he published articles in the *Yorozu Chōhō*, the popular daily newspaper of which the chief editor was, as we have seen, Uchimura Kanzō. In 1903 this newspaper attained a daily circulation of one hundred fifty thousand copies. In the spring of 1903 the Japanese government decided to intensify its preparations for war, since the conflict with Russia seemed no longer avoidable, which provoked opposition from the pacifists. When it became impossible for him to publish his articles in the *Yorozu Chōhō*, Kōtoku, together with Sakai Toshihiko (who had also written for the *Yorozu Chōhō*), founded the aforementioned *Heimin Shinbun*. Afterward—becoming ever more isolated and radical in his views, as we have seen, and also due to the falling circulation of the *Heimin Shinbun* during the Russo-Japanese War—Kōtoku disappeared from public view.[253] His name was practically forgotten until after the end of the Second World War.

Japan in the first two decades of the twentieth century was not a homogenous political and social entity. While until the beginning of the 1920s, controversial points of view were widely discussed, secret societies also gained popularity among nationalists in the interwar period, advocating a nationalist missionary zeal, in clear contrast to the parties and labor unions. Outwardly, within this field of tension among conservative nationalists, progressive liberals, radical socialists, and Communists, liberal forces could nonetheless flourish in the 1920s.[254] For some time "the ideas of liberalism and equality, which were evolving under the banner of democracy and economic advance as well as universal suffrage . . . were advancing in all areas."[255]

Another great liberal to be remembered and mentioned here was Ozaki Yukio, a noted parliamentarian and early follower of Ōkuma Shigenobu, whose Progressive Party he supported as a journalist. Visiting Europe to witness the devastation of the First World War, he became convinced of the necessity for disarmament and international cooperation. At the entrance to the Ozaki Yukio Memorial Foundation in Tokyo, just behind the Parliament building, the following sentence in English is engraved on a memorial stone slab:

YUKIO OZAKI (1858–1954) Member of the House of Representatives for 63 years from the establishment of the Diet until his death, being elected 25 times consecutively, thus setting a world record for all times, he is revered as

the father of Japanese parliamentarianism. Champion, all his long life, for the democratic order of society, he was a consistent and courageous opponent of all aggressive militarism and in his later years, a zealous proponent of world federation. This Hall, dedicated to the memory of Yukio Ozaki and the advancement of Japanese democracy, was erected by the people and presented to the Diet, February 25, 1960.[256]

NOTES

1. Quoted in Wolfgang Bauer, *China and the Search for Happiness: Recurring Themes in Four Thousand Years of Chinese Cultural History* (New York: Seabury Press, 1976), 287. The full quote reads: "He who respects the dignity of man, and practices what love and courtesy require—for him all men within the four seas are brothers."

2. "It would seem that this axis of history is to be found in the period around 500 B.C., in the spiritual process that occurred between 800 and 200 B.C. . . . The most extraordinary events are concentrated in this period . . . simultaneously in China, India, and the West, without any of these regions knowing of the others. . . . The fact of the threefold manifestation of the Axial Period is in the nature of a miracle." Karl Jaspers, *The Origin and Goal of History* (London: Routledge & Kegan Paul, 1953), 1, 2, and 18. See also Heiner Roetz, *Confucian Ethics of the Axial Age* (New York: State University of New York, 1993) (orig. Frankfurt, 1992) and S. N. Eisenstadt, *Japanese Civilization. A Comparative View* (Chicago and London: University of Chicago Press 1996), 13, and (in German) S. N. Eisenstadt (ed.), *Kulturen der Achsenzeit* (Cultures of the Axial Age), two vols. (Frankfurt: M. Suhrkamp, 1987).

3. Jaspers, *The Origin and Goal of History*, 20: "Confucius and Lao-tse [Laozi] were living in China, all the schools of Chinese philosophy came into being, including those of Mo-ti [Mozi], Chuang-tse [Chuangzi], Lieh-tsu [Liezi] and a host of others." A fourth school, the Legalists, should also be mentioned, though they, unlike the other three schools, apparently "favoured the joint promotion of militarism and agriculture." L. Tomkinson, "Chinese Historical Attitudes to Peace and War," *Journal of the North China Branch of the Royal Asiatic Society* LXXI (1940): 60, also 58.

4. Jacques Gernet, *A History of Chinese Civilization*, second ed., trans. J. R. Foster and Charles Hartmann (New York and Melbourne: Cambridge University Press, 1996) (orig. Paris, 1972), 118.

5. *Ibid.*, 131–33. See 132: "Probably no other country in the world has ever made such an effort to supply its neighbours with presents, thus elevating the gift into a political tool."

6. Gernet, *A History of Chinese Civilization*, 117.

7. "The identity perspective of the Chinese ancestor cult. . . . War, i.e., the death of the warrior meant . . . not only the breaking of the ancestral chain, but also to rot unaccounted for in the moonlight far from one's home: 'to be nobody's ancestor,' that is to say, not to have been." Gudula Linck, "'Gezwungen nur greift er zur Waffe'—Chinesische Gedichte für und wider den Krieg: Methodische Überlegungen

zum Epochenvergleich" ("Only when forced he takes up arms"—Chinese poems for and against war), *Historische Anthropologie*, 3.Jg., H.2 (1995): 287. I owe thanks to Prof. Gudula Linck (chair for Sinology at Kiel University) for this reference.

8. It should be pointed out that—also with respect to Japan—it was the school of Mozi whose political rhetoric and social teachings influenced in a significant way the peace discourse for over two thousand years. On the political significance of Taoism in China, see the work of Anna Seidel, *Taoismus, die inoffizielle Hochreligion Chinas* (Taoism, the unofficial religion in China) (Tokyo: Deutsche Gesellschaft für Natur- und Völkerkunde Ostasiens, 1990) (*OAG Aktuell*, no. 41).

9. An official "School of Mozi" ceased to exist following the persecution of fol- lowers of Confucius and Mozi during the Qin Dynasty (221–206 BC) and the great burning of books in 213 BC. Yet the teachings somehow continued to be remembered and relevant. See Hu Shih, *The Development of the Logical Method in Ancient China* (New York: Paragon Book Reprint, 1963) (orig. Shanghai, 1922), 62.

10. See Y. P. Mei, *Motse, the neglected Rival of Confucius* (London: Arthur Prob- sthain, 1934) (repr. Westport, Conn.: Greenwood Press, 1973).

11. According to A. Forke, *Geschichte der alten chinesischen Philosophie* (His- tory of ancient Chinese philosophy) (Hamburg: Kommissionsverlag L. Friederichsen, 1927), 371, Mozi also was an inventor "who had constructed a flying bird, a defender of cities." Bauer writes: "At the same time they [the Chinese] were surprised to find in the Mohist writings the rudiments of those very sciences which had led the West to power and success: logic and technology" (*China and the Search for Happiness*, 27).

12. Forke, *op. cit.*, points out that according to the "histories of the Daoists . . . Mozi is one of their genies who were said to have achieved immortality through the taking of the elixir of life" (371).

13. *The Texts of Taoism*, trans. James Legge, *The Sacred Books of China*, in two parts, Part I—The Tao Te Ching of Lao Tzŭ (New York: Dover Publications, 1962) (The Sacred Books of the East, ed. F. Max Müller, Vol. XXXIX), 73–74 (orig. Oxford University Press, 1891). A somewhat different rendering is given by Professor Lok Sang Ho, "The Living Dao: The Art and Way of Living a Rich and Truthful Life," ac- cessible at www.ln.edu.hk/econ/staff/daodejing(22%20August%202002).pdf. I thank Mrs. Samantha Xu for this reference.

14. Thus the *Book of Mencius*, which is one of the "four books" of the neo- Confucian canon, contains numerous passages in which its author, Mengzi, carries on argumentation with Mozi.

15. See Forke, *Geschichte der alten chinesischen Philosophie*, 405: "I. Dialectics. Mê-tse [Mozi] set much store on correct thinking and correct manner of expression, but he established no rules for this. That was reserved for his disciples. . . . Their goal was thus less to research the law of thinking than to establish practical rules for the art of argumentation, for overcoming their opponents in debate. Therefore the name *dialectics* would seem more suitable for this than *logic*, since it is not logic in our sense." Richard Wilhelm, *Gesellschaft und Staat in China. Zur Geschichte eines Weltreiches* (Society and state in China. On the history of a world power) (Hamburg: Rowohlt, 1960), 27, says: "We thank him [Mozi] and his School for a textbook of logic which allows us to leave that of Aristotle on the side." A similar view is given by

Gernet when he writes about the "dialectic of the school of Mo-tzu," in contrast to the Nominalists, Legalists, and to "philosophical Taoism" (*Chinese Civilization*, 166).

16. Gernet, *A History of Chinese Civilization*, 88. In any event, Jacques Gernet in his work gives to Mozi hardly more than a page, and little credit. He goes on to say: "This strange sect, which seems to have made numerous converts in the two centuries preceding the imperial unification, was to leave little impression on the history of Chinese thought. Its most noteworthy contribution was to the art of oratory. Mo-tzu and his disciples cultivated rhetoric preaching purposes, thus contributing to progress in the articulation of ideas and to greater suppleness in sentence construction" (89). The School of Mozi was concerned with, among other things, logical problems of definition, inference, and so on. The following three criteria were used to prove a hypothesis (the "triple test of a proposition"): (1) the foundation/reason/cause of the proposition; (2) the probability of the proposition; and (3) its practical applicability.

17. Forke refers also to an "edition within the Daoist canon, the *Tao-tsang pêng* edited [and published] by *Ku Tch'ien-li* in 1445 . . . the best of the early editions with the fewest errors, but without commentary" (*op. cit.*, 372). In Japan, Mozi's name appears, for example, in Ogyū Sorai's *Bendō* (1717).

18. The doctrine of "universal love and mutual profit." See Yi-Pao Mei, Mo ti, *Encyclopedia Britannica*, vol. 15 (Chicago, London, Toronto: Genf, 1962): "Universal love is the cornerstone of Mo-tzu's system." The following is from Mozi:

> The robber loves his own house and does not love the house of the other, therefore he steals from another house, in order to benefit his own house. . . . When, however, in the whole world borderless love were dominant, then states would not mutually attack one another, then families would not mutually become entangled, and there would be no more thieves and robbers. . . . When therefore borderless love were dominant in the world, the world will be in order; when however people mutually hate each other, then it is in disorder. . . . Now however the people of the world will come and say: "Good, borderless love is something quite beautiful, but it is a hard-to-reach ideal." To this I reply: To besiege a town and to fight on the battlefield in order to make a name at the sacrifice of one's life, it is that which is difficult in this world. If one however encourages the masses with appropriate words, then they will do what is suggested. And how much more so with unlimited love and mutual help? He who loves the people will be loved by them; who helps people will be helped by them. . . . What should then be so difficult about unlimited love? (Hellmut Wilhelm, *Gesellschaft und Staat in China*, 29–30).

19. L. Tomkinson, "The Social Teachings of Meh Tse," *Transactions of the Asiatic Society of Japan*, second series, vol. IV (December 1927), 5. Compare Daisetz[u] T. Suzuki, *A Brief History of Chinese Philosophy* (London: Probsthain, 1914), 93f, who emphatically praises Mozi for having "a clear and logical head, something quite unusual in Chinese philosophy." Cited in Forke, *op. cit.*, 393.

20. Tomkinson, *op. cit.*, 18.

21. Forke, *op. cit.*, 381–90.

22. Wilhelm, *Gesellschaft und Staat in China*, 29.

23. Bauer, *China and the Search for Happiness*, 290.

24. Bauer, *op. cit.*, 55: "Confucius could still 'preach,' Mencius had to engage in disputes."

25. See Goat Koei Lang-Tan, *Konfuzianische Auffassungen von Mitleid und Mitgefühl in der Neuen Literatur Chinas (1917–1942): Literaturtheorien, Erzählungen und Kunstmärchen der Republikzeit in Relation zur konfuzianischen Geistestradition* (Confucian conceptions of compassion and kindness in the new literature in China [1917–1942]: Literary theory, narratives and literary tales of the Republican era and its relation to the Confucian intellectual tradition) (Bonn: Engelhard-Ng Verlag, 1995). The author names as "representatives of the Chinese tradition" Mengzi, Lu Jiuyan (Lu Xiangshan, 1139–1193) and his "Idealist" School, the "School of the Heart" (*Xinxue*), Wang Yangming, Kang Youwei, and Hu Shi. I am grateful to Prof. Gudula Linck in Kiel for this reference.

26. Gernet, *op. cit.*, 96.

27. Gudula Linck, book review (5 March 1996) of Goat Koei Lang-Tan, *op. cit.*, Bonn 1995; personally received manuscript. Mengzi preached the "four heart virtues": compassion, diffidence, distinguishing between good and bad, and humility.

28. Tomkinson, *op. cit.*, 8.

29. The term "Ruism" (as an alternative for "Confucianism") is used by Robert Eno, *The Confucian Creation of Heaven: Philosophy and the Defense of Ritual Mastery* (Albany: State University of New York, 1990), 6–16.

30. Eno, *The Confucian Creation of Heaven*, 109 and 112. Compare also the comparative analysis of "Mohists" and "Legalists" in Cheng Chung-Ying, *New Dimensions of Confucian and Neo-Confucian Philosophy* (Albany: State University of New York Press, 1991), 219: "[T]he Mohists and the Legalists stress importance of wealth and/or power of state and society for different reasons. . . . The Mohists would primarily stress the importance of the wealth of society whereas the Legalists would primarily stress the importance of the power of the state."

31. Burton Watson, *Mo Tzu, Basic Writings* (New York and London: Columbia University Press, 1970 [1963]), 14.

32. Forke, *op. cit.*, 392.

33. The author possesses a copy of this bibliography. Mozi is mentioned also in the diary of the Japanese monk Ennin (ninth century) as well as in the sixteenth-century book *Saiyūki* (Journey to the West), about a Chinese Buddhist pilgrimage to India, which was (and still is) also very popular in Japan. See Edwin O. Reischauer (trans.), *Ennin's Diary: The Record of a Pilgrimage to China in Search of the Law* (New York: Ronald Press, 1955), 332.

34. Two books of Confucius, namely a possibly lost version of the "Thousand Character Script" (*Qianziwen*) and the "Dialogues" (*Lunyu*), in ten volumes, are said to have come to Japan at that time. See Gregor Paul, *Philosophie in Japan: Von den Anfängen bis zur Heian-Zeit—Eine kritische Untersuchung* (Philosophy in Japan: From the beginnings to the Heian period—a critical investigation) (München: Iudicium, 1993), 31. Most authors, however, place the arrival of Wani at the beginning of

the fifth century. See, for example, John Whitney Hall, *Japan—From Prehistory to Modern Times* (Rutland, Vt., and Tokyo: Tuttle, 1971/New York, Dell 1970), 38–39, originally published in German in 1968 under the title *Das japanische Kaiserreich* (The Japanese empire). George Sansom takes as a hypothetical date the period between 270 and 310—*A History of Japan, To 1334*, vol. I (Tokyo: Charles E. Tuttle, 1990) (orig. Stanford University Press, 1963), 41f. Gregor Paul ("Die Anfänge der Philosophie in Japan: Die Rezeption chinesischer Kultur in vorbuddhistischer Zeit" [The beginnings of philosophy in Japan: The reception of Chinese culture in pre-Buddhist times], *OAG Aktuell*, no. 47–54, Jg. 1991 [Tokyo: Deutsche Gesellschaft für Natur- und Völkerkunde Ostasiens, 1992], 400) writes: "At the latest since 240 concepts of state and social philosophy of Han Period Confucianism were known at the Japanese courts." Thus the introduction of the Confucian School in Japan would have been at approximately the same time as the introduction of Christianity in Germany (for example, in ca. 325 in Cologne).

35. *The Kojiki, Records of Ancient Matters*, trans. Basil Hall Chamberlain (Rutland, Vt., and Tokyo: Charles E. Tuttle, 1990) (1981, orig. 1882, reprinted 1919), 313f.; Roger Bersihand, *Geschichte Japans—von den Anfängen bis zur Gegenwart* (History of Japan—from the beginnings to the present) (Stuttgart: Alfred Kröner, 1963), 47. According to the translator's preface to the *Nihongi—Chronicles of Japan from the Earliest Times to A.D. 697*, trans. W. G. Aston (Rutland, Vt., and Tokyo: Charles E. Tuttle, 1993) (orig. 1896), xi, "the Corean national genius seems to have left no impression of its own on the civilization which it received from China and handed on to Japan. Medicine, Buddhism, painting, and the mechanic arts were transmitted, as far as we can see, without modification, and there is little trace of any special Corean character in the knowledge of Chinese literature and science which Coreans communicated to Japan. They had themselves taken up this study only thirty years before Wani's departure."

36. See also Eisenstadt, *Japanese Civilisation*, 259–60 and 14: "In China, except for a short period under the Tang, Buddhism did not become a major component of the center and, even more importantly, the Buddhist establishment did not become part of the hegemonic ruling groups. . . . In Japan the situation was, in a sense, the opposite. There Buddhism became a key component of the general culture and of the center" (259). This "gave rise to a highly sophisticated and reflexive philosophical, religious and aesthetic discourse" (260), which included "a tendency to continuous internal institutional change" (14).

37. The Five Classics or "canonical books" (*Wujing*) are (1) the Book of Changes (*Yijing*); (2) the Book of Sources (*Shujing*); (3) the Spring and Autumn Annals (*Chunqiu*), also called the "Local Chronicle of Lu"; (4) the Book of Rites (*Liji*); and (5) the Book of Songs (*Shijing*). According to Gregor Paul, *Philosophie in Japan*, 40, the Five Classics probably reached Japan in the early sixth century.

38. Wilhelm, *Gesellschaft und Staat in China*, 42.

39. The quote is from Chapter Five, "Who can best enjoy Life?" of Lin Yutang's widely read book, *The Importance of Living*, available online at www.grassy.org/Book/BKContent.asp?BookID=6378. The author continues: "After all allowances are made for the necessity of having a few supermen in our midst, explorers, con-

querors, great inventors, great presidents, heroes who change the course of history, the happiest man is still the man of the middle-class who has earned a slight means of economic independence, who has done a little, but just a little, for mankind, and who is slightly distinguished in his community, but not too distinguished. It is only in this milieu of well-known obscurity and financial competence with a pinch, when life is fairly carefree and yet not altogether carefree, that the human spirit is happiest and succeeds best. After all, we have to get on in this life, and so we must bring philosophy down from heaven to earth." I owe thanks to Mrs. Samantha Xu, Shanghai, for this reference and her precious opinion on the matter.

40. Personal correspondence with Mrs. Samantha Xu.

41. Bauer, *China and the Search for Happiness*, 208. In addition there was the "Idealist" school of Wang Yangming, which was also quite influential and would appear to stand nearer to the Mozi school.

42. Shimada Kenji defines these *shengren* as "the wise rulers of ancient times, who created culture, who created . . . the forms for governing human communal living . . . and who [became] the educational ideal of Neo-Confucianism" (*Die neo-konfuzianische Philosophie—Die Schulrichtungen Chu Hsis und Wang Yang-mings* [The neo-Confucian philosophy—the schools of Chu Hsi and Wang Yang-ming] [Berlin: Dietrich Reimer, 1987], 247).

43. According to Shimada, *op. cit.*, 195, this utterance is "included in the sum total of Neo-Confucianism, [i.e.] the *Chin ssu lu* [*Jin si lu*] compiled by Chu Hsi." Sources given in Shimada, *loc. cit.*

44. See Daniel K. Gardner, *Chu Hsi and the "Ta Hsüeh": Neo-Confucian Reflection on the Confucian Canon* (Cambridge, Mass., and London: Council on East Asian Studies [Harvard University Press], 1986), with comprehensive bibliography and commentaries. Zhu Xi (Chu Hsi) cites Cheng Hao (1032–1085), who said the *Daxue* was "the gate through which the beginning students achieve virtue." *Ibid.*, 4.

45. The "Daxue" and the "Doctrine of the Mean" (*Zhongyong*) are two chapters taken from the Book of Rites (*Liji*). The other two texts are the "Book of Mencius" and the "Book of Analects" (*Lunyu*). The latter contains the sayings of Confucius.

46. Cited in Bauer, *op. cit.*, 210. Bauer comments: "Everyone is thus individually responsible for 'peace' and, consequently, for happiness in the world" (*ibid.*). This text derives, in Zhu Xi's view, from Confucius himself. See Gardner, *op. cit.*, 87 and 94.

47. "[E]ven the least educated Chinese became thoroughly conversant with this text, and most of them adopted these ideas as maxims guiding all thought." Bauer, *op. cit.*, 210.

48. The "five mountains" in Japan originally included only the three great Buddhist establishments in Kyoto and the two large Zen monasteries in Kamakura.

49. From the Japanese *bōzu*, or Buddhist priest.

50. George Sansom, *Japan—A Short Cultural History* (revised ed., Charles E. Tuttle, 1991) (orig. 1931), 383. The so-called *jusō* were Buddhist monks who also concerned themselves with the study of Confucian texts.

51. *A Biographical Guide*, 236.

52. Bauer, *op. cit.*, 208.

53. Herbert Scurla, *Einführung, Reisen in Nippon—Berichte deutscher Forscher des 17. und 19. Jahrhunderts aus Japan* (Introduction, Travels in Nippon—reports from German explorers of seventeenth- and nineteenth-century Japan) (Berlin: Verlag der Nation, 1982), 20. See also Richard H. Minear, *Japanese Tradition and Western Law—Emperor, State and Law in the Thought of Hozumi Yatsuka* (Cambridge, Mass.: Harvard University Press, 1970), 148 ff.

54. Sansom, *A Short Cultural History*, 504.

55. Tokugawa Ieyasu "tried to secure peace both inside and outside [the country]." Scurla, Introduction to *Reisen in Nippon*, 20.

56. Sansom, *op. cit.*, 505.

57. Hermann Ooms speaks of a "Tokugawa ideology" as represented and disseminated in numerous writings and oral discourses by Fujiwara Seika and Hayashi Razan, whom he calls the "founding fathers" of this ideology ("Neo-Confucianism and the Formation of Early Tokugawa Ideology, Contours of a Problem," in Peter Nosco [ed.], *Confucianism and Tokugawa Culture* [Princeton, N.J.: Princeton University Press, 1975], ix). There is evidence that Fujiwara had also studied the Mohist teachings.

58. Hall, *op. cit.*, 214.

59. These were "housemen" of the shōgun, to use Hall's term (*op. cit.*, 92), or, in other words, vassals who originally derived from two thousand warrior families who existed at the beginning of the Kamakura Period, comparable perhaps to the Prussian *Junker*. From among the *Gokenin* were recruited the military land administrators (*jitō*) and the military governors (*shugo*).

60. Also followers (*jikisan*) of the shōgun, "banner carriers." Between 1600 and 1651, approximately seventeen *gokenin* and five thousand *hatamoto* were settled, according to a new reapportionment of land holdings, on lands directly administered by the shōgun's family. Hall, *op. cit.*, 166.

61. This sort of concept of a "cosmic dynamic" is typical for China; it may be comparable to the Western concepts of "might" and "right" (*Recht* and *Macht* in German.)

62. James McMullen, "Confucianism," *Encyclopedia of Japan*, vol. 2, 356. Wolfgang J. Mommsen notes in *Max Weber, Gesellschaft, Politik und Geschichte* (Max Weber, society, politics and history) (Frankfurt: Suhrkamp, 1974), 118: "The ethic of Confucianism, which insists on the adaptation to the Dao, the impersonal and eternal, universal law and the political ordering which flows from it, can be considered quite the opposite from Max Weber's personal *Weltanschauung*." A different view is expressed, however, by Gregor Paul, *Die Aktualität der klassischen chinesischen Philosophie* (The contemporary relevance of classical Chinese philosophy) (München: Iudicium, 1987), 63n5: "Among the accomplishments of Max Weber is his interpretation of Confucianism as a *rational* program. His view, however, that the Confucianists saw the world as something 'given' and that 'Confucian rationality' meant a 'rational adaptation to the world' (while Protestant-Puritan rationalism is taken to mean a rational dominion over the world) is surely erroneous."

63. See Edwin O. Reischauer, who says of the Tokugawa regime: "Adopting the social theories of Confucianism . . . created a hierarchy of four social classes—the warrior administrator, the peasant, the artisan, and the merchant" (*Japan—Past and Present* [London: Duckworth, 1947], 85–86).

64. Robert Neelly Bellah, *Tokugawa Religion: The Values of Pre-industrial Japan* (New York: Free Press, 1985) (orig. 1957), 94.

65. Najita Tetsuo, *Japan—The Intellectual Foundations of Modern Japanese Politics* (Chicago and London, Phoenix edition 1980) (orig. 1974, University of Chicago Press), 34–35: "Ogyū was by far the most outstanding political thinker who provided the most thoroughgoing theory of bureaucracy based on social utility . . . [he] stressed the importance of bureaucratic codes, or 'law,' in human society." In this respect he was similar perhaps to Jeremy Bentham. Richard M. Minear compares Ogyū Sorai with Erasmus of Rotterdam (*Kôdansha Encyclopedia of Japan*, vol. 6, 73).

66. Najita, *op. cit.*, 34–35.

67. *Ibid.*

68. "Indeed, Carl Steenstrup has pointed out a preference for rationalistic as against metaphysical (Buddhist and Confucian) orientations, manifest in the examples of Ogyū Sorai and other thinkers of the Tokugawa era" (Eisenstadt, *Japanese Civilization*, 308). A pragmatic rationalist, it seems, Sorai was "indeed informed by a strong moral vision" (*ibid.*, 247), though Maruyama Masao apparently thought of him "as the Japanese Machiavelli" (*ibid.*).

69. Oga Shigeru, "International Law in a Multi-Cultural World—Japan's Encounter with the Law of Nations in the Nineteenth Century," in Atle Grahl-Madsen and Jiri Toman (eds.), *The Spirit of Uppsala—Proceedings of the Joint UNITAR-Uppsala University Seminar on International Law and Organizations for a New World Order (JUS 81)*, Uppsala 9–18 June 1981 (Berlin, New York, 1984), 252. See also Donald Keene, *The Japanese Discovery of Europe: Honda Toshiaki and Other Discoverers, 1720–1798* (London: Routledge & Kegan Paul, 1952).

70. See Fukuzawa Yukichi, *The Japanese Parliament*, in Ōkuma Shigenobu (ed.), *Fifty Years of New Japan* (Kaikoku gojūnen shi), vol. III (New York: Kraus Reprint Co., 1970/London: Smith, Elder, & Co., 1910), an English translation of *Kaikoku gojūnen shi*, 578: "[T]he law strictly forbade more than three persons to meet together and talk about politics."

71. The term first appears in the seventeenth century. An older expression was "not . . . Bushido . . . (but) 'the way of the horse and bow,' a term analogous to our word 'chivalry'" (Sansom, *A Short Cultural History*, 292). See also Hall, *op. cit.*, 217; Marius B. Jansen, *The Making of Modern Japan* (Cambridge, Mass., and London: The Belknap Press of the Harvard University Press, 2002 [2000]), 103, and, of course, the famous Nitobe Inazō, *Bushido, The Soul of Japan*, revised and enlarged, with an introduction by William Elliot Griffith (Rutland, Vt., and Tokyo: Charles E. Tuttle, 1969) (orig. 1900).

72. Central to this was the idea of "loyalty" and a fair understanding of the duties "of those above" and "those below," which were, however, complementary or based on the principle of reciprocity. They were "obligations on both sides." Jansen, *ibid.*, 191.

73. Tsunoda Ryusaku, William Theodore de Bary, and Donald Keene, *Sources of Japanese Tradition*, vol. II (New York: Columbia University Press, 1964), 113 (translated from Yoshida Shōin, *Zenshū*, Bd. II, 145).

74. On Yoshida Shōin, see Bersihand, *op. cit.*, 275: "When Commodore Perry came back to Shimoda in 1854, [Yoshida and his friend] . . . tried to arrange employment on one of his ships so as to travel to America, but they were arrested and put

in prison." Yoshida at the time used the slogan "Honor the Emperor, drive away the foreigners!"

75. Bersihand, *op. cit.*, 372–73: "The first wanted a peaceable state, the second wanted a military empire without regard to a parliament. Itō was in an inferior position."

76. Bauer, *op. cit.*, 306: "Here, he did not need the example of Western pacifist movements, but could simply go back to the teachings of the ancient philosopher Mo Ti."

77. Gernet, *A History of Chinese Civilization*, 595–96.

78. Bauer, *op. cit.*, 302. See also Iriye Keishirō, "The Principles of International Law in the Light of Confucian Doctrine," *Recueil des Courts* (Leiden: Teil I, 1967), 54 ff. Kang Youwei had successors and predecessors. Hong Xiuquan (Hung Hsiu-ch'üan, 1813–1864), the leader of the Taiping Rebellion (1851–1864), was probably the most well-known of his predecessors; one of his most prominent successors might have been Sun Yat-sen, if only the two had been able to be on more understanding terms with one another. See also John K. Fairbank, Edwin O. Reischauer, and Albert M. Craig, *East Asia—The Modern Transformation* (London: George Allen & Unwin, 1965), 633ff.

79. "The classical ideal of 'Ta T'ung' . . . was enunciated by Confucius, who taught: 'Where the "right course" (*ta tao*) reigns, there everything in the world is common property (*res publica*). . . . This is called universality'" (Iriye Keishirō, *op. cit.*, 54).

80. Gernet, *op. cit.*, 596.

81. Bauer, *op. cit.*, 306.

82. A. Forke, *Geschichte der alten chinesischen Philosophie*, S. 376.

83. Forke, *op. cit.*, 373. Mei Yi-pao, *Motse, the Neglected Rival of Confucius* (1934), 51, wrote: "Pi Yuan published the first modern edition of *The works of Motse*, with his commentaries in 1783 A.D. It is still existent and widely used." According to another source, *The Book of Mozi* was first printed in Japan in 1757 (it had earlier existed only as hand-copied manuscripts). This translation was based on a Chinese edition put out by the popular and radically inclined Li Chuo-wu and his publisher Mao Hsien (1512–1601).

84. L. Tomkinson, "The Social Teachings of Meh Tse," 14.

85. Gernet, *op. cit.*, 548. The work appeared first in 1894 and then in 1907 in a revised edition under the title *Mê-tse hsien-ku* (Mozi xiangu).

86. Forke, *op. cit.*, 373.

87. Ibid., 373.

88. See Tsunashima Ryōsen, *Tōzai rinri shisōshi* (History of East-West thinking on ethics) (Tokyo: Shunjūsha, 1921). Then in 1928–1929 there appeared from the pen of the famous poet, novelist, and essayist Kōda Rohan (1867–1947) in the series of "textbooks on world history" published by Iwanami Shoten (*Iwanami kōza sekaishicho*), vol. 5, 239–58, a text with the title *Bokushi*.

89. Kobayashi Ichirō published in 1938–1939 two volumes of the Mozi texts, with commentary, under the title *Bokushi* (Keisho Daikō Series, vols. 16–17), and during the Japanese occupation of China there appeared in 1943 a work by Ōtsuka Banroku with the title *Bokushi no kenkyū* (Research on Mozi).

90. Bauer, *op. cit.*, 302.

91. Gernet, *op. cit.*, 505 and 541–42.

92. See Joyce C. Lebra, *Ōkuma Shigenobu, Statesman of Meiji Japan* (Canberra: Australian National University Press, 1973), 122: "As early as 1898 Ōkuma's Pan-Asianism had become known as the 'Ōkuma Doctrine,' a kind of analogue of the Monroe Doctrine. Ōkuma was convinced that Japan could perform a dual service for China, guiding her on the path toward modernization and enlightenment and at the same time preventing further incursion by Western nations."

93. K'ang Yu-wei, *Ta T'ung Shu: The One-World Philosophy of K'ang Yu-wei*, trans., with introduction and notes, Laurence G. Thompson (London: George Allen & Unwin, 1958).

94. Bauer, *China and the Search for Happiness*, 331. See also "International Education and Communication (Round Table Discussions)," in *Problems of the Pacific 1927*, 185: "The number of Chinese students in Japanese universities . . . was estimated as between four and six thousand. Japanese-trained students are becoming more and more prominent in political and judicial life in China."

95. See Marius B. Jansen, *The Japanese and Sun Yat-sen* (Cambridge, Mass.: Harvard University Press, 1954), 76ff.

96. Already in 1918 Japan had indicated its intention to return the Boxer indemnities, following the example of the Americans, who had started using the funds to finance exchange programs for Chinese students to study in the United States. Later, at the Washington Conference, Shidehara was encouraged by the Americans to do something about "waiving of Boxer indemnity payments," which eventually he did as foreign minister. See Ian I. Nish, *Japanese Foreign Policy in the Interwar Period* (Westport, Conn.: Praeger/Greenwood, 2002), 27.

97. See *Problems of the Pacific 1927*, 185: "Chinese spokesmen reported a general feeling that students returned from Japanese universities without the good will that most returned students feel for the countries in which they were trained, and attributed this largely to the different social reception they received. It was stated on the other hand that this relationship was improving."

98. See Fairbank, Reischauer, and Craig, *East Asia—The Modern Transformation*, 654.

99. I here express my thanks especially to Professor Heinrich Dumoulin, who gave me many valuable suggestions for this discussion of the East Asian Buddhist heritage. Unfortunately Father Dumoulin passed away in 1995.

100. In the literature, one finds both dates for the "official introduction" of Buddhism into Japan. W. G. Aston, who translated the *Nihongi* into English, notes, in *Nihongi—Chronicles of Japan from the Earliest Times to A.D. 697* (Rutland, Vt., and Tokyo: Charles E. Tuttle, 1993) (orig. 1896), 262n5: "There are clear indications that the Chinese language and character were not wholly unknown in Japan from a time which may be roughly put as coinciding with the Christian epoch. But this knowledge was probably confined to a few interpreters."

101. It may be asserted that, overall, the Indian *Weltanschauung* is "universalistic." In pre-Buddhist times already, extensive cosmological conceptions testified to a detailed knowledge of the universe: "Indians conceive of the idea of the unity of all things." Nakamura Hajime, *The Ways of Thinking of Eastern Peoples* (Tokyo: Yūshōdō, 1960), 39 (Classics on Japanese Thought and Culture, vol. I).

102. In his first sermon, Gautama Buddha analyzed the human situation. The result of this analysis is the Four Truths: (1) the truth of suffering; (2) the truth that suffering has a beginning or cause; (3) the truth that suffering has an end; and (4) the truth that there is a way to end suffering.

103. "Ethics seems to have played a more important role in Buddhism than in many other world religions." Cheng Hsueh-li (Zheng Xueli) in *Encyclopedia of Ethics*, ed. Lawrence C. Becker and Charlotte B. Becker (New York and London: Garland, 1992), 103.

104. *Ibid.*, with the further observation: "Buddhist morality seems to have treasured the value of life much more than Christian and Hindu ethics . . . loving kindness is not limited to human beings, but is extended to all sentient beings."

105. This line is attributed to Sariputra, a disciple of the Buddha, according to *Milindapanha*, verse 394, cited in Nakamura Hajime, *op. cit.*, 32.

106. Nakamura Hajime, "Die Grundlehren des Buddhismus: Ihre Wurzeln in Geschichte und Tradition" (The basic teachings of Buddhism, and their roots in history and tradition), in Heinrich Dumoulin (ed.), *Buddhismus der Gegenwart* (Buddhism in our time) (Freiburg: Herder, 1970), 33, in reference to the *Digha-Nikaya* II, 186f.

107. See also the *Dictionary of Chinese Buddhist Terms*, compiled by William Edward Soothill and Lewis Hodous (Delhi: Motilal Banarasidass, 2000) (orig. London, 1937), 178. Étienne Lamotte, *History of Indian Buddhism: from the origins to the Saka era*, trans. Sara Webb-Boin (Louvain-La-Neuve: Université Catholique de Louvain, Institut Orientaliste, 1988), 631 (paragraphs 698/699); Heinrich Dumoulin, *Geschichte des Zen-Buddhismus* (History of Zen Buddhism), Bd. I, "Indien und China" (Bern and München: Francke Verlag, 1985), 286n22: "W. L. King (Buddhism and Christianity, Some Bridges of Understanding [London, 1963], 175ff) and H. de Lubac (Aspects du Bouddhisme, Paris 1951, chapter 1) positively appraise this Buddhist meditation practice comparing it with the Christian love for one's fellow man."

108. Karen Armstrong, *Buddha* (London, Phoenix: Orion Books, 2002/Weidenfeld & Nicolson, 2000), xxiv–xxv.

109. See Annemarie von Gabain, "Maitreya und Mithra," in Walter Heissig and Hans-Joachim Klimkeit (eds.), *Synkretismus in den Religionen Zentralasiens* (Syncretism of the religions of central Asia) (Wiesbaden: Otto Harassowitz, 1987), 24.

110. The traditional dating of the lifetime of Gautama Buddha (556–486) has recently been questioned by Heinz Bechert, who would place it approximately one hundred years later. Heinz Bechert (ed.), *The Dating of the Historical Buddha: Die Datierung des historischen Buddha* (Symposiums on Buddhist Research, IV, 1) (Göttingen: Vandenhoeck & Ruprecht, 1991).

111. Edmund Hardy, *Der Buddhismus nach älteren Pali-Werken* (Buddhism according to the older Pali works) (Münster: Aschendorffsche Buchhandlung, 1926 [1890]), 52. See also Étienne Lamotte, *History of Indian Buddhism*, 17 (paragraph 18) and 297 (paragraph 325). In Lamotte's view, Buddhism was from the beginning "a religion of propaganda" (*ibid.*, 297).

112. See Hermann Kulke and Dietmar Rothermund, *A History of India* (Calcutta, Allahabad, Bombay, and Delhi: Rupa, 1991), 58.

113. See *ibid.*, 56: "Magadha's warfare against the strong tribal confederation of the Vrijis [north of the Ganges] is supposed to have continued for 14 years, and it is said that Buddha himself advised Ajatashatru against starting this war."

114. Max Weber, *The Religion of India. The Sociology of Hinduism and Buddhism*, trans. and ed. Hans H. Gerth and Don Martindale (New Delhi: Munshiram Manohar-lal, 1992) (orig. The Free Press, 1958), 238. See also K. N. Jayatilleke, "The Prin-ciples of International Law in Buddhist Doctrine," *Recueil des Courts*, Part I (Leyden, 1967), 554: Ashoka "gives up war as an instrument of policy." Lamotte, *History of Indian Buddhism*, 227–34 (paragraphs 249–56), describes the *dharma* of Ashoka.

115. "Through him [Ashoka] Buddhism received its first great push toward be-coming an international world religion" (Max Weber, *op. cit.*, 241). See also Lamotte, *History of Indian Buddhism*, 292–310 (paragraphs 320–39).

116. See Edward Conze, *Buddhist Wisdom Books, Containing the Diamond Sutra and the Heart Sutra* (London: George Allen & Unwin, 1966 [1958]), preface, 10: "In spite of many differences caused by the social and cultural background, the wisdom tradition at that time achieved a fair degree of universality and its Indian form was distinguished more by its uncompromising sublimity, than by the peculiarity of its tenets. The works of Proclus and Dionysius Areopagita, and even the *Academica* of Cicero, show that some of the specific teachings of the Prajnaparamita were once quite familiar to the West."

117. The discovery was made in 1837 by James Prinsep, Calcutta Mint Master and Secretary of the Asiatic Society of Bengal. The first comprehensive translation of the inscriptions was made by Sir Alexander Cunningham and published in 1888 (London: Routledge). A standard work is Eugen Hultzsch (ed.), *Inscriptions of Asoka*, new edition (Oxford: Printed for the government of India at the Clarendon Press, 1925) (reprinted in Tokyo, 1977).

118. Hermann Kulke, "Ausgrenzung, Rezeption und kulturelles Sendungsbewußt-sein" (Segregation, reception and the mentality of cultural mission), in S. N. Eisen-stadt (ed.), *Kulturen der Achsenzeit* (Cultures of the Axial Period), vol. II (Frankfurt: Suhrkamp, 1992), 28. See *The Edicts of Asoka*, ed. and trans. N. A. Nikam and Richard McKeon (Chicago and London: University of Chicago Press, 1965); Ulrich Schneider, *Die großen Felsen-Edikte Asokas* (Ashoka's great rock edicts), critical edi-tion, translation, and analysis of the texts (Wiesbaden: Otto Harassowitz, 1978).

119. A. L. Basham, "Ashoka, in Mircea," in Eliade (ed.), *The Encyclopedia of Religion* (New York: Macmillan [London, Collier Macmillan], 1987), vol. 1, 468–69. See also Romila Thapar, *Ashoka and the Decline of the Mauryas* (Bombay: Oxford University Press, 1961).

120. It is possible that Ashoka's successors, some of whom were known as *charkravartins*, continued Buddhist missionary activities abroad.

121. On a visit to the Ashoka mountain in December 2005 the author found a thriving Buddhist community and vast temple complex and monastery at the site (Erik Zürcher, *The Buddhist Conquest of China—The Spread and Adaptation of Buddhism in Early Medieval China* [Leyden: E. J. Brill, 1959], 277f). A later tradition should also be mentioned (*loc. cit.*): "There had been an 'Ashoka-monastery' at P'eng-ch'eng, the capital of the kingdom of Ch'u and one of the earliest Buddhist centres

in China in the middle of the first century AD." Here, on the coast of the Yellow Sea, in northern Jiangsu in the trade center of Pengcheng (today's Xuzhou), one finds the "earliest reliable evidence of the presence of Buddhism in China" from the year 65 AD (Gernet, *A History of Chinese Civilization*, 211).

122. Zürcher, *The Buddhist Conquest of China*, 152: "[T]he fame of emperor Hsiao-wu as a dharmaraja [dharma king, K.S.] had already reached what was to the Chinese the very limits of the known world. In or shortly after 395 the king of Ceylon . . . dispatched the sramana T'an-mo-I . . . to the Chinese court with a valuable Buddha-statue of jade, four feet and two inches high. . . . For unknown reasons the journey lasted more than ten years. . . . This mission marks . . . the beginning of Sino-Singhalese relations." See also the "Notes," *ibid.*, III, 378.

123. See Arnold Toynbee, *A Study of History*, vol. VIII (London, New York, and Toronto: Oxford University Press, 1955), 451: "The Mahayana [Buddhism] was transmitted to the Sinic from the Indic world without the two societies ever falling into war with one another and the peacefulness of the intercourse that produced this historic effect was advertised in the traffic of Buddhist missionaries *en route* from India to China, and Buddhist pilgrims *en route* from China to India, which found its way to and fro by both the sea-route via the Straits of Malacca and the land-route via the Tarim Basin from the fourth to the seventh century of the Christian Era."

124. "[It] . . . was destined to play a very peculiar role in early Chinese Buddhism." Zürcher, *op. cit.*, 70–71. See also *ibid.*, 277ff., as well as the "Notes," *ibid.*, 423–24. The significance of this fact for the Chinese and also the Japanese empire and its state ideology still remains largely unexplored.

125. *Das Asokarajavadan* (j. *Aikuô-den*, ch. *Yuan Wang chuan*), which contains the Ashoka legend, was handed down in two translations. Fa Qin made the first in the year 306, and the second is from the year 512. Both Chinese versions have also been known in Japan early on. Zürcher, "Notes," *op. cit.*, 423.

126. See, for example, K. N. Jayatilleke, who points out the difference between the Brahmanical and Buddhist *Dharma-vijaya*: "It has been said that the concept of *Dharma-vijaya* is found in the *Arthasastra* but as Barua has shown the Brahmanical *Dharma-vijaya* was undoubtedly a conquest by the sword. The Buddhist *Dhamma-vijaya* [in the Pali pronunciation] was to be achieved . . . without the employment of the sword or armed force (*adandena asatthena*)" ("The Principles of International Law in Buddhist Doctrine," 555).

127. Wilhelm Emil Mühlmann, "Pacifism and Nonviolent Movements," *Encyclopedia Britannica*, vol. 13, fifteenth edition, 1980, 846.

128. This concept found its expression in the *panca-sila* concept, a customary law based on Buddhist ethical norms. A familiar concept in Buddhist Asia, this concept derives from the five basic Buddhist precepts. See also Ulrich Schneider, "Asketenethik und Politik in Indien" (Recluse ethics and policy in India), in *Vom Frieden* (Hannover, 1967), 252.

129. Jambudvipa is often equated with the "whole world," having the mythical Mount Meru in the middle. Thus the Buddhist stupas can be found in many parts of Asia. Reischauer (trans.), *Ennin's Diary: The Record of a Pilgrimage to China in*

Christian missionaries') liberal attitude was not characteristic of the contemporary Roman Church as a whole, and was not even consistently maintained by the Jesuits themselves. . . . Opposition on the part of the Franciscans and Dominicans finally ruined the Jesuits' work, and, with it, Christianity's prospects, first in Japan and then in China."

187. Herbert George Wells, *The Outline of History, Being a Plain History of Life and Mankind by H. G. Wells*, Revised and Brought up to the End of the Second World War by Raymond Postgate (Garden City, N.Y.: Garden City Books, 1949 [1920]), 1030. The Jesuits were, however, also known for their tolerant attitude, open to the world, toward foreign cultures and civilizations.

188. See Tsurumi Shunsuke, *An Intellectual History of Wartime Japan 1931–1945* (London, Sidney, and Henley: KPI, 1986), 43.

189. Hall, *op. cit.*, 291.

190. Bamba Nobuya, "Kitamura Tōkoku: His Pursuit of Freedom and World Peace," in Bamba Nobuya and John F. Howes, *Pacifism in Japan: The Christian and the Socialist Tradition* (Kyoto: Minerva Press, 1978), 35. See also Francis Mathy, "Kitamura Tōkoku: Essays on the Inner Life," *Monumenta Nipponica* 19, no. 1/2 (1964): 66–110.

191. Bamba, "Kitamura Tōkoku," 42, citing a letter to Mina of 18 August 1887, found in *Kitamura Tōkoku zenshū*, 3:168 (Bamba's translation.)

192. John E. Howes, "Pacifism," in *Kōdansha Encyclopedia of Japan*, vol. 6, 144: "[T]he *Yorozu Chōhō*, under Uchimura's editorial direction, had developed into a highly readable yet strongly principled newspaper." See also John E. Howes, *Japan's Modern Prophet: Uchimura Kanzō, 1861–1930* (Vancouver and Toronto: University of British Columbia Press, 2005).

193. Karl F. Zahl, *Die politische Elite Japans nach dem 2. Weltkrieg (1945–1965)* (The political elite in Japan after the Second World War) (Wiesbaden: Otto Harassowitz, 1973), 196. In 1891, Uchimura, while an instructor at the First Higher School in Tokyo, refused to bow to the imperial portrait because of his Christian beliefs. See John F. Howes, "Uchimura Kanzō: The Bible and War," in Bamba and Howes (eds.), *Pacifism in Japan*, 93.

194. Uchimura Kanzō, "Hisenron no genri" (Basic principles of pacifism), in *Seisho no Kenkyū* (Studies on the Bible), August 1908. Cited in Zahl, *op. cit.*, 196.

195. Uchimura Kanzō, *How I Became a Christian* (Tokyo: Kyobunkan, 1895).

196. Uchimura Kanzō, "Japan: Its Mission," *The Japan Daily Mail*, 5 February 1892, in Yamamoto Taijirō (ed.), *Uchimura Kanzō Zenshū* (Complete works of Uchimura Kanzō), vol. V, "Essays and Editorials I, 1886–June 1897" (Tokyo: Kyōbunkan, 1972), 55.

197. Uchimura, "Japan: Its Mission," *op. cit.*, 59–60, 63–64.

198. Jan Swyngedouw, "Christliche Einflüsse auf die japanische Kultur" (Christian influences on Japanese culture), in Constantin von Barloewen and Kai Werhahn-Mees (eds.), *Japan und der Westen* (Japan and the West), vol. 3: Politik, Kultur, Gesellschaft (Frankfurt: Fischer TB, 1986), 202.

199. See, for example, John F. Howes (ed.), *Nitobe Inazō, Japan's Bridge Across the Pacific* (Boulder, San Francisco, and Oxford: Westview Press, 1995).

200. Kagawa Toyohiko, *Love, the Law of Life* (Chicago, Philadelphia, and London: The John C. Winston Co., 1929).

201. See Ōta Yūzō, "Kagawa Toyohiko: A Pacifist?," in Bamba and Howes, *op. cit.*, 189.

202. Ueda Katsumi, "Tabata Shinobu: Defender of the Peace Constitution," in Bamba and Howes, *Pacifism in Japan*, 221–46.

203. Ueda, *op. cit.*, 231, quoting Tabata Shinobu, "Kenpō kyūjō no hatsuansha, Shidehara Kijūrō" (Shidehara Kijūrō, the originator of article 9 in the Japanese constitution), in Kenpō Kenkyūsho (ed.), *Teiōken* (The right of resistance) (Kyoto: Kenpō Kenkyūsho, 1965), 352–56. Thomas W. Burkman, "Japanese Christians and the Wilsonian World Order," *The Japan Christian Quarterly* XLIX, no. 1 (Winter 1983): 43, gives another view of Uchimura's role, pointing out Uchimura's depiction of the League of Nations as a "Tower of Babel" and quoting these words from 1919: "It is even more impossible to establish permanent peace among mankind without first eliminating sin." Of course, as H. G. Wells noted in his 1933 *The Shape of things to Come* about the League of Nations: "It was a League not to end sovereignties but preserve them" (Book the First, Chapter 10; Versailles: Seedbed of Disasters).

204. This refers especially to Anglo-Saxon liberalism. In Germany, "liberalism" as such no longer existed after the failure of liberal forces to achieve a breakthrough at the "Hambach Festival" of 1832 or, at the latest, after the failure of the Paulskirche movement to establish a German parliament in 1849.

205. Ernst-Otto Czempiel, *Friedensstrategien—Systemwandel durch internationale Organisationen, Demokratisierung und Wirtschaft* (Strategies for peace—system change through international organizations, democratization and economy) (Paderborn, München, Wien, and Zürich: Ferdinand Schöningh, 1986), 15ff.

206. Cited in Gregor Schöllgen, "Max Weber," in *Das Parlament*, no. 11 (10. März 1989), 13. See also Helwig Schmidt-Glintzer, "Intellektueller Imperialismus? Außereuropäische Religionen und Gesellschaften im Werk Max Webers" (Intellectual imperialism? Extra-European religions and societies in Max Weber's work), in Christian Gneuss and Jürgen Kocka (eds.), *Max Weber, Ein Symposium* (München: dtv, 1988), 84: "This intensive occupation with Max Weber in Japan . . . stemmed also from the fact that in Japan the aim was modernization without internal upheavals."

207. However, one might ask, with respect to Max Weber, if perhaps in Germany the sort of national liberalism Weber represented, and the possibility, derived from his political philosophy, of a rationalization of Machiavellianism based on an ethic of responsibility might in some way have led to fascism. Compare also Friedrich Meineke, who in his book on *Staatsraison* (reason of state), puts forth the thesis that Hegel may have incorporated Machiavellianism "into the context of an idealistic Weltanschauung that simultaneously took in and supported all moral values, while he later directed his own existence always solely in keeping with the moral cosmos which he himself posited. What took place was almost like the process of legitimizing a bastard" (435). Cited in Willibald Apelt, *Hegelscher Machtstaat oder Kantsches Weltbürgertum* (Hegelian power of the state or Kantian world-citizenship?) (München: Leibnitz Verlag, 1948), 13.

208. Although Max Weber was not sufficiently informed about Japan and his attempts at explanation in this regard are generally not very productive and often incorrect, much of what he has to say about Buddhism and Confucianism can be related to Japan. Thus he writes at the end of volume 2 of *The Sociology of Hinduism and Buddhism* (trans. and ed. Hans H. Gerth and Don Martindale, 332–23), that through the "experientially-conditioned inner-attitude to the world . . . the world of real life won a relatively rational meaning. According to the most highly developed rational representations, the world was dominated by the laws of determinism. Especially in the Japanese form of Mahayanistic teaching, causality in our sense appears in external nature." Weber names as one of the possibilities of dealing rationally with this philosophical outlook, which is based on an outer-worldly doctrine of salvation that yet displays an orientation toward the "beyond," the ways of the higher educated strata like the "literarily cultivated, secular knighthood . . . such as the old Kshatriya in India and the court knighthood of Japan." See also Karl-Heinz Golzio, "Max Weber on Japan: The Role of the Government and the Buddhist Sects," in Buss, *Max Weber in Asian Studies*, 90–101; Reinhard Bendix and Guenther Roth, *Scholarship and Partisanship: Essays on Max Weber* (Berkeley, Los Angeles, and London: University of California Press, 1971), chapter X, "Japan and the Protestant Ethic," 188–206.

209. Jansen, *The Making of Modern Japan*, 201.

210. Wilhelm Röhl, "Das japanische Verfassungsrecht" (Japanese constitutional law), *Oriens Extremus*, 33.Jg., no. 1 (1990): 19–20. The *Seitaisho* served after the opening of the country as the first written draft of a true constitution.

211. See Reinhard Zöllner, "Lorenz von Stein und kokutai," *Oriens Extremus*, 33.Jg., no. 1 (1990): 67, who sees a link between some of these *shigi kenpō* and the Meiji constitution. See also Irokawa Daikichi, *Jiyū minken* (Freedom and people's fights) (Tokyo: Iwanami Shinsho, 1981). He states that at the time there were more than forty such constitutional drafts.

212. Irokawa Daikichi, *Jiyū minken*, 105.

213. His draft, called "Tōyō Dai Nihonkoku kokken'an," which was based on the principle of people's sovereignty, basic rights, and a right to resistance, was published in the press and publicly discussed.

214. Andrew Roth, *Dilemma in Japan* (London: Victor Gollancz, 1946), 100.

215. Tsunoda, de Bary, and Keene, *Sources of Japanese Tradition*, vol. II, 178. See also *ibid.*: "It is noteworthy, therefore, that in his address to members of the Liberal Party in 1882, Itagaki should stress liberty as a means of achieving greater national unity, requiring a strong sense of personal responsibility and discipline in the promotion of public interest." Ōkuma liked to call Itagaki the "spiritual successor of Rousseau" (*ibid.*, 187). On the movement for civil rights, see also E. H. Norman, *Japan's Emergence as a Modern State: Political and Economic Problems of the Meiji Period* (New York: Institute of Pacific Relations, 1946), and Ike Nobutaka, *The Beginnings of Political Democracy in Japan* (Baltimore: The John Hopkins Press, 1959).

216. See, for example, Ienaga Saburō, *Ueki Emori kenkyū* (Studies on Ueki Emori) (Tokyo: Iwanami Shoten, 1960); also see Bamba Nobuya, in *Kindai Nihon heiwa shisō* (Peace thinking in modern Japan), i. I am indebted to Professor Kurino Ohtori for these references.

217. Roth, *Dilemma in Japan*, 100.

218. Röhl, *op. cit.*, 20–21. "The press overwhelmingly favored the idea that an assembly elected by the people should first be called together" (*ibid.*, 21).

219. The government, however, rejected it because it would have severely limited the powers of the tennō (emperor).

220. Of equal significance for Japan as the Prussian constitution of 1850, especially for the critical area of "internal security," seems to have been the *Preußische Allgemeine Landrecht* (Prussian General Civil Code) of 1794, which placed "in the foreground . . . the protection against [as opposed to just reacting to] dangers as an essential element of the policing concept" (Horst Herold, "Innere Sicherheit: Organe, Zuständigkeiten, Aufbau" [Internal security: bodies, competencies, organization], in *Deutschland, Portrait einer Nation* [Germany, portrait of a nation] [Gütersloh: Bertelsmann Lexikothek, 1985], vol. 2, "Gesellschaft, Staat, Recht" [Society, nation, law], 298). The relevant paragraph 10, part II, title 17, of the Prussian General Civil Code read: "The duty of the police is [to take] the necessary precautions for the maintenance of public peace, security and order, and for the prevention of [possible] approaching dangers to which the public or individual members thereof are subject" (*ibid.*, 298).

221. In the Diet elections, at first only a little more than 1 percent of the (male) population—on the basis of annual tax payments—could take part.

222. Röhl, *op. cit.*, 23.

223. See Röhl, who discusses "the formula of the 'state as a family'" (*op. cit.*, 23). See also Klaus Antoni, "Kokutai—Das 'Nationalwesen' als japanische Utopie," *Saeculum* 38, nos. 2–3 (1987): 267ff.

224. Ōkuma Shigenobu, "Conclusion," in Ōkuma (ed.), *Fifty Years of New Japan*, vol. III, 571. See also *ibid.*, 571–72: "They have welcomed Occidental civilization while preserving their old Oriental civilization. They have attached great importance to *Bushidō*, and at the same time held in the highest respect the spirit of charity and humanity."

225. Ōkuma, "Conclusion," *op. cit.*, 572.

226. See, for example, Yale Candee Maxon, *Control of Japanese Foreign Policy: A Study of Civil-Military Rivalry, 1930–1945* (Berkeley: University of California Press, 1957) (repr. 1973), 72.

227. See Lebra, *Ōkuma Shigenobu*, 1973.

228. Fairbank, Reischauer, and Craig, *East Asia—The Modern Transformation*, 633. A similar explication is given in Jansen, *The Japanese and Sun Yat-sen*, 53.

229. See Edwin O. Reischauer and Albert M. Craig, *Japan: Tradition and Transformation* (Tokyo: Charles E. Tuttle, 1978), 181: "But the parties were not ready for such heavy responsibilities. The army and navy ministers, who were always military men, held themselves disdainfully aloof from the rest from the rest of the cabinet, and the bureaucracy as a whole proved uncooperative. Moreover the old factional divisions remained strong."

230. Cyril H. Powles, "Abe Isoo: The Utility Man," in Bamba and Howes, *Pacifism in Japan*, 143.

231. The concept obviously derives from Confucianism. In the words of Han Yu (768–824), the forerunner of Neo-Confucianism: "Universal love is called humanity (*hakuai no aware wa jin nari*)" (*ibid.*, 153).

232. Kōtoku Shūsui and Sakai Toshihiko (1870–1933), in their manifesto published on behalf of the Heiminsha (Society of Common People) in the *Heimin Shimbun*, 15 November 1903; reprinted in *Meiji shakaishugi shiryō-shū* (Collection of materials on Meiji period socialism), ed. Ōkoshi Kazuo et al., twenty vols. (Tokyo: Meiji Bunken Shiryō Kankōkai, 1960–1963), supplement 3.

233. "Bloch's work is a veritable *Das Kapital* of pacifism" (Powles, *op. cit.*, 156). Abe dedicated five issues of the journal *Rikugō Zasshi*, between May and October 1902, to the contents of this monumental six-volume work.

234. Cited in Powles, *op. cit.*, 151. See also *ibid.*, 152: "If we recognize the murder of one individual by another to be a crime, is it not also criminal for one country to invade another, or for one class of people to slaughter the members of another class? These are the reasons why Tolstoi opposes war. It is said that war is necessary to uphold social order. Yet many calamities and evils follow from war. It is said that war is necessary to uphold the independence of a nation. Yet he would say that the real purpose in maintaining thousands of soldiers has shifted away from the necessity of guarding against foreign foes to the necessity for protection against an internal enemy . . . for the oppression of the lower classes by the upper" (from *Rikugō Zasshi*, July 1885, 13).

235. On the First Hague Peace Conference, see chapter II (section 2) and chapter III (section 2).

236. Abe Isoo, "Shakaishugisha wa nani yue ni hisenronsha naru ka?" (Why do socialists become pacifists?), *Rikugō Zasshi* (August 1904), 4. This article was written during the Russo-Japanese War and published before the signing of the Treaty of Portsmouth by which the war came to an end. Cited in Powles, *op. cit.*, 155.

237. The Shakai Minshutō was supported by Abe Isoo, Kōtoku Shūsui, Sen Katayama, and other intellectuals as well as the labor union. According to George O. Totten, the founding of the party marks the beginning of socialism in Japan (*The Social Democratic Movement in Prewar Japan* [New Haven, Conn.: Yale University Press, 1966], 23).

238. Cited in Powles, *op. cit.*, 151.

239. See Totten, *op. cit.*, 27: "The Peace Police Law crushed the incipient labor union movement and the order to disband the Social Democratic Party left no room for even moderate political reformist activities. The socialist movement after 1901, therefore, was confined to educational and propaganda activities."

240. Powles, "Abe Isoo," 150.

241. *Ibid.*, 156.

242. Abe Isoo, "Hogo seisaku to heiwashugi" (Protectionism and pacifism), *Shin kigen*, 10 January 1906, reprinted in *Meiji shakaishugi shiryō-shū*, vol. 3, 34.

243. One of these magazines was the monthly magazine *Shin Kigen* (New Era), which he put out together with Kinoshita Naoe (1869–1937) and Ishikawa Sanshirō (1876–1956), and that even criticized the Imperial Rescript on Education.

244. For the prominent "left-liberal" German politician, publicist, and pacifist Hellmut von Gerlach (1866–1935), Angell's book was right on the mark. He wrote: "The conservative Englishman . . . demonstrated, with the most audacious fact-finding logic of the Anglo-Saxons, that under today's conditions every war is equally destructive for the winners as for the losers. *War is in all cases a bad busi-*

ness." Hellmut von Gerlach, "Der Weg zum Pazifismus," cited in Wolfgang Benz (ed.), *Pazifismus in Deutschland. Dokumente der Friedensbewegung 1890–1939* (Frankfurt: Fischer, 1988), 210–11 (from Hellmut von Gerlach's memoirs, *Von Rechts nach Links 1937*, new printing 1987; emphasis added). Norman Angell's work appeared in German under the title *Die große Täuschung. Eine Studie über das Verhältnis zwischen Militärmacht und Wohlstand der Völker* (Leipzig: Dieterich, 1910).

245. Cited in Tabata Shinobu, "Abe Isoo (1865–1949): No mugunbi, muteikō no shisō" (Abe Isoo [1865–1949]: his ideas on a society without arms and nonresistance), chapter 7 of *Nihon no heiwa shisō* (Pacifist thinking in Japan) (Kyoto: Minerva Shoten, 1972), 64.

246. Powles, "Abe Isoo," 163. Abe received strong public support in the second most important electoral district in Tokyo. Altogether from his party there were elected to the Diet four representatives in 1928, twenty-two in 1936, and thirty-eight in 1938. In 1929 his photograph was a "bestseller" in Tokyo. However, the all too rigid dogmatism of many leftist forces hindered the realization of a united front against militarism—much like in Germany.

247. This is known as the "High Treason Incident" (*Taigyaku jiken*). The alleged leaders of the assassination attempt were subsequently executed. See Peter Duus, *op. cit.*, 169.

248. See Asukai Masamichi, "Kōtoku Shūsui: His Socialism and Pacifism," in Bamba and Howes, *op. cit.*, 123–41.

249. See John F. Howes, "Pacifism," in *Kōdansha Encyclopedia of Japan*, vol. 6, 144: "As relations with Russia worsened, both Kōtoku and Uchimura proclaimed the cause of peace, Uchimura on the basis of biblical teachings and Kōtoku under the influence of the Russian thinker Leo Tolstoy. When the owner of the *Yorozu Chōhō* ordered that his paper side with the Japanese Government against Russia [in the Russo-Japanese War], Uchimura and Kōtoku resigned."

250. Cited in Maruyama, "Some Reflections on Article IX," 307 (emphasis added). This refers to the aforementioned first issue of the *Heimin Shimbun* (15 November 1903).

251. Asukai Masamichi writes: "Since 1945, some materials about the 1910 conspiracy have become accessible to scholars, but not until 1963 were all the records of the trial published. They show that this 'assassination plot' resulted for the most part from an official conspiracy, as the young left-wingers had suspected. It has been proved that Kōtoku was not the chief conspirator and that he himself doubted the value of the assassination" ("Kōtoku Shūsui," *op. cit.*, 123).

252. Asukai, "Kōtoku Shūsui," in Bamba and Howes, *op. cit.*, 126.

253. Asukai, "Kōtoku Shūsui," 139–41. See also F. G. Notehelfer, *Kōtoku Shūsui: A Portrait of a Japanese Radical* (Cambridge, Mass.: Cambridge University Press, 1971). Kōtoku had earlier predicted war with the United States in the case that Japan pursued an aggressive, imperialistic policy (*ibid.*, 1).

254. J. Salwyn Schapiro points out that, in a global context, the forces opposed to liberalism became more active after 1914: "[A]fter 1914 communism and fascism declared war against liberalism. Openly and insistently did these movements proclaim

their intention to destroy every vestige of liberalism throughout the world" (*Liberalism and the Challenge of Fascism* [New York: Octagon Books, 1964], vii).

255. Abe Teruya, "Betrachtungen zum Zusammenbruch der japanischen Meiji-Verfassung" (Views on the collapse of the Meiji constitution), in *Epirrhosis—Festgabe für Carl Schmitt* (Berlin: Duncker & Humblot, 1968), 6.

256. See also *The Autobiography of Ozaki Yukio*, trans. Fujiko Hara, with a foreword by Marius B. Jansen (Princeton, N.J., and Oxford: Princeton University Press, 2001).

Shidehara at the Antwerp Mission

Shidehara in London, early 1914, with Katō Takaaki

At The Hague, 1914–1915

Shidehara with his wife and two sons

Ambassador in Washington

Ambassador in Washington

II

The International Environment and the Emergence of Modern Japan

Historical and geographical conditions define a country's development and politics. They determine how people see themselves in relation to their environment, and how others see them. James Bryce stated that "geography is the key to history."[1] Foreign policy is the sum total of a country's geography, history, and ambitions.[2] Optimal conditions exist for progress and cooperation when a country thrives both in terms of its interaction with its neighbors as well as its undisturbed development and growth, to be able enjoy the fruits of its labor and freely share them with others.

THE "OPENING" (*KAIKOKU*)
AND MEIJI RESTORATION (*ISHIN*)

To assess and understand the phenomenon of the "opening of Japan" (*kaikoku*) in 1853, and its subsequent diplomacy, we should discuss briefly the circumstances of Japan's nearly two-hundred-year "seclusion" (*sakoku*) prior to the opening.[3] Some Christian influences from the sixteenth century survived the Edo Period (1603–1868) into the "modern period" that followed the Meiji Restoration of 1868. C. R. Boxer has in fascinating detail described the issue of the impact of early Christianity in his seminal work on *The Christian Century in Japan 1549–1650* (that is, the years that ended with the Seclusion Laws). The events during the second half of the sixteenth and the first three decades of the seventeenth century first shaped Japan's relations with the West.[4] After 1800 the "West" appeared once more on the horizon, threatening Japan as it was accosted from three sides by "imperialist" powers: the tsarist empire in the north,[5] Great Britain in the south, and the United States in the east.[6] Russian and Japanese explorers and traders had encountered one another from time to time to the north of Hokkaido, on the Kurile Islands and on Sakhalin at the end of the eighteenth century.[7] Attempts by Russia, however, to initiate trade relations in Hokkaido in 1792 and in Nagasaki in 1804 failed.[8] Only Chinese and Dutch ships traded in Nagasaki, and Japanese ships during the seclusion were not allowed to venture abroad.

What measures might best be adopted to avert the perceived dangers from outside was something the Tokugawa government (*bakufu*) officials, *daimyō* feudal lords, scholars, and others who were familiar with the situation often disagreed over. One school of thought, the *jōi*, wanted to "drive out the barbarians" while the other, the *kaikoku* faction, meant to "open the country."[9] These two factions had an impact in shaping the period between 1853 and 1868, known as the *bakumatsu* ("end of the Tokugawa *bakufu*") era,[10] which prepared Japan, both psychologically and materially, for the drastic changes that were to come.[11]

Maruyama Masao points out that arguments over seclusion philosophy—one side wanting to drive away the barbarians, the other to open the country—were not wholly irreconcilable. Both *jōi* and *kaikoku* advocates "acted from the same motives and toward the same objective. They differed, in fact, not about the end but about the means of attaining it."[12] Some of the most eloquent representatives of the opening idea (*kaikokuron*) were at the same time the most zealous advocates of noninterference by foreign powers in Japanese affairs, as seen in the cases of publicists Sakuma Shōzan (1811–1864), Yoshida Shōin (1830–1859), and Ōkuni Takamasa (1792–1871).[13] At any rate, as when the first Christians landed in the sixteenth century, Japanese were prepared to accept Western techniques and knowledge, under the condition of keeping their Japaneseness, and maintaining "Eastern morality, Western techniques" (*tōyō no dōtoku, seiyō no gijutsu*).[14]

The motive to improve Japan's living conditions, and at the same time guard against foreign influences, was always present. Strong utopian and idealist elements were present in the writings of Satō Nobuhiro (1769–1850), for example, who proposed ways of improving the harsh living conditions in Tokugawa Japan while also raising awareness of the perceived threats to Japan from foreign powers.[15] In the seventeenth century the nearly complete closing of the country to the West had seemed the only way to safeguard Japan's national and cultural identity. The German physician Engelbert Kaempfer (1651–1716), who in the eighteenth century had lived for a period at the Dutch trading station on the artificial Dejima Island in Nagasaki Harbor, added his voice to those defending the seclusion philosophy.[16] The Japanese seem to have driven the foreign Catholics away and persecuted them not so much on religious grounds but for political reasons.

The fact that Japan, with the elimination of the Catholic missionaries,[17] had for over two centuries deliberately shut itself off from Occidental influence and dominance[18] meant that it could not only protect its cultural distinctiveness and assets but also develop them undisturbed. The Seclusion Laws did not apply to Chinese merchants (and presumably other Asians who could pass as Chinese), or the Dutch, who were allowed from 1641 to operate a trading post on Dejima.[19] Dejima was thereafter "Japan's ear to the outside world, by which over the next two centuries, despite or maybe *precisely because of*, its extreme seclusion Japan could observe the advances of the Europeans, perhaps more consistently and more reflectively than was the case in other countries of Asia."[20] Thus a decisive amount of information on the development and details of European intellectual and political progress and natural sciences were received.

Historians have pointed out that Japan had not fallen into a "250-year sleep of the Sleeping Beauty" during the seclusion era or stopped being an accountable partner in Asian international relations, as Wilhelm Solf, Germany's ambassador in Japan from 1920–1928, had assumed.[21] Japan did not only trade with China, but also had diplomatic relations with Thailand,[22] Korea, and the kingdom of the Ryūkyū Islands, all of which periodically sent diplomatic missions to the shōgunate court in Edo. The traditional concept for the system of international relations in the Far East was what the Chinese called *hua-yi zhixu* (j. *ka-i chitsujo*),[23] which distinguished between civilized states like India, China, and Japan, on the one hand, and "barbarian," uncivilized, peoples on the other.

Around the middle of the seventeenth century Dutch studies by the Japanese had begun, "and by 1670 there were interpreters at Nagasaki who could read as well as speak the language."[24] Well-educated Japanese, who cultivated contacts with the Dutch, came to see an advantage in becoming versed in "Dutch learning" (*rangaku*).

Among the first Japanese who cultivated "Western learning" (*yōgaku*) and did pioneering work for its development in Japan were the astronomer and geographer Nishikawa Joken (1648–1724) and the Confucian scholar Arai Hakuseki (1657–1725).[25] The eighth shōgun, Tokugawa Yoshimune (1684–1751; in office 1716–1745), became known for his enthusiastic promotion of Western sciences. He not only wanted to reform the Japanese calendar and to improve agriculture; in 1720, he ended—on the advice of Arai Hakuseki—the prohibition against the import of foreign books (with the exception of books on Christianity) and commissioned the Confucian scholars Aoki Kon'yō (1698–1769)[26] and Noro Genjō (1693–1761), a physician and authority on herbology, to become fluent in the Dutch language. Between 1750 and 1790, Maeno Ryōtaku (1723–1803), Sugita Genpaku (1733–1817), and Ōtsuki

Gentaku (1757–1828)[27] published books on Western subjects. Noteworthy is the *Kaitai shinsho* (New book of anatomy), which Maeno and Sugita translated into scholarly Chinese.[28] Allowing books of European knowledge, Western or "Dutch" learning to be imported, the so-called *rangaku* that had previously been cultivated in secret "ventured into the light of day" and advanced rapidly.[29] The domestic peace that the shogunal government maintained within Japan facilitated European studies, and allowed Japanese scholars to supplement the study of the Chinese classics with new insights into the essence of Western intellectual and natural sciences, to the extent that books on these subjects became available.[30]

Under the influence of Tanuma Okitsugu (1719–1788), an upstart *daimyō*, and one of the top officials responsible for the handling of state affairs for Shōguns Ieshige (in office 1745–1760) and Ieharu (in office 1760–1786), active exchange of information with the Dutch in Dejima accelerated.[31] From 1769 until 1786, the Swedish physician Karl Peter von Thunberg and the Dutch scholar Isaak Titsingh were able to personally instruct many Japanese in Western knowledge. In 1789, the first school for studying Dutch language was opened in Edo (today's Tokyo), and at the beginning of the nineteenth century the shōgunate created a special bureau to translate Dutch books.[32] Up until 1869 several thousand Japanese studied Western sciences, mostly through the Dutch language, and some 670 works were translated into Japanese from Dutch, in addition to the number of books translated from English, French, German, and Chinese.[33] Shiba Kōkan (1738–1818) explained to other Japanese the Copernican world principles of the planetary system.[34] The result of the Dutch-studies movement was that educated Japanese since the eighteenth century were, as Donald Keene has noted, more at home with European culture than any other non-Western peoples,[35] except the Bengalis—to be sure.

World political events like Britain's 1757 victory in Plassey, Bengal, were of great interest to the Japanese leadership. By this victory, England was able to dislodge the French, establish its colonial dominion in India, and build and consolidate its empire over the following hundred years.[36] Britain's world empire depended above all on its Navy. In 1808 a British Navy frigate brought some Dutch merchants to Dejima in Nagasaki port, and in 1813–1814 the British governor of Java, Thomas Stanford Raffles, tried unsuccessfully to bring the Dutch trade in Nagasaki under British control.[37] Then, in 1824, on a small island south of Kyushu, an armed clash between some British seamen and the Japanese occurred. Such incidents did not escape the attention of the Japanese authorities. In 1825, Aizawa Seishisai (1782–1863) in a book titled "New Proposals" (*Shinron*) argued against foreign trade and contact with foreigners, which he felt would undermine traditional morals. He plied for defensive measures to be taken, strengthening national unity, and beating back the barbarians with their own weapons.[38]

Despite the official isolation, there were increasing contacts between Japanese and Europeans, whose ships now appeared more frequently in Japanese waters. A Russian expedition under Ivan Fyodorovich von Krusenstern, who was accompanied by the German physician Georg Heinrich von Langsdorff, paid a visit to Japan during its voyage around the world in 1804, and for several months, until the middle of April 1805, its ships lay at anchor in Nagasaki Harbor. Langsdorff made this diary entry of 12 October 1804 about the Japanese he had met: "The noble class of Japanese evidenced a refined and very well-behaved attitude in all their dealings. With the exception of the language and clothing, we believed ourselves to be among the most cultured Europeans."[39]

Increasingly, foreign whalers, sealers, and others were sailing off the Japanese coasts, interested in anchoring at Japanese ports to stock up on provisions or on occasion deliver shipwrecked Japanese fishermen. The foreigners aggressively demanded the right to free access and free trade, so the *bakufu* in 1825 decreed that all non-Dutch European ships in Japanese waters should be indiscriminately fired upon.[40] Intelligence about foreign movements was obtained through Dutch and Chinese merchants in Nagasaki who had the duty of communicating regularly to *bakufu* officials about developments outside Japan.

India having been subjugated by Great Britain, China alone among the old empires remained as yet unconquered. For the purchase of tea and other products from China, since it was in the British interest to hold back the export of gold and silver ingots that otherwise would have to be paid, opium trade was introduced, and opium was imported in great quantities into China. The Chinese resisted this violation of their interests. In 1839 British and Chinese warships clashed near the island of Hong Kong,[41] spurring Japanese fears, although there was no indication yet that the colonialists of India meant to physically attack Japan. However, the Opium War somewhat changed the perception, as more British ships began to be seen around Japan,[42] and the appearance of British warships at the mouth of the Yangzi River put the threat to the Japanese islands in a new and glaring light.[43]

In this first British-Chinese war (the Opium War, 1839–1842), China was for the first time defeated by a European power.[44] By the Treaty of Nanjing, China had to open five ports as of 29 August 1842, pay an indemnity—among other things, for the British products that had been destroyed by the Chinese government—and lease Hong Kong to England. As a direct consequence, China also had to conclude treaties with France and with the United States. Some Japanese feared a similar fate. Consequently Tokugawa Nariaki

(1800–1860), the *daimyō* of Mito, fortified parts of the coast, and made preparations for the repulsion of the foreigners.[45] Englishmen on their part had begun in 1843 to survey and explore the southern Ryūkyū Islands.

In 1845 the British government decided to send a mission to initiate trade relations with Japan, following a warning by the Dutch king in 1844 that Japan should take steps to end its artificially maintained seclusion before it would be forced to do so by circumstances.[46] The decision was supposed to be implemented as soon as enough large naval units were ready for service in nearby waters.[47] In 1844 the French had also surveyed the Ryūkyū Islands and tried to initiate trade relations there. Two years later, in June 1846, the frigate *Cléopâtre* with two corvettes under Admiral Cécille arrived, and then sailed from the Ryūkyūs to Nagasaki, where it arrived on 29 July 1846. Just a few days earlier, on 20 July 1846, two American ships, the *Columbus* and the *Vincennes* under Commodore James Biddle, appeared off the coast of Uraga at the entrance to Edo Bay, hoping to deliver a letter from President James Polk. In 1849 the American survey ship *Mariner* under Commodore Matheson anchored in Edo Bay and tried without success to establish contact with the local governor. In the same year, another American, Commodore Glyn, sailed from Guangzhou (Canton) to Nagasaki in order to take on board fifteen shipwrecked American sailors who were being held there in captivity. Voyages by newly developed coal-burning, steam-powered vessels to distant places were increasing, and in 1851 Commodore John H. Aulick was commissioned to conclude a treaty with Japan to secure supplies of coal. However, the plan for the Aulick expedition was never carried out.[48] Until the arrival of Commodore Perry at Uraga on 8 July 1853, all attempts by foreign powers to make direct contact with *bakufu* authorities were repelled in one way or another.[49]

The *bakufu* upheld its seclusion policy, while at the same time preparing for any eventuality. Intellectuals like the aforementioned Satō Nobuhiro,[50] Takano Chōei (1804–1850), and Watanabe Kazan (1793–1841) advocated the building of fortifications for coastal defense, though at the same time they advocated the opening of Japanese ports. Due to their criticism of the *bakufu*'s seclusion policy, Takano and Watanabe along with others were arrested in 1839,[51] and later made to commit suicide. Other intellectuals who supported and promoted political reforms and the opening of the country included Egawa Tarōzaemon (1801–1855),[52] Sakuma Shōzan,[53] Yokoi Shōnan (1809–1869), and Katsu Kaishū (1823–1899). Katsu was the first said to have mastered Western military technology and to cross the Pacific as captain in his Japanese-made steamer that accompanied the American vessels that took the *bakufu*'s first visitors to the United States in 1860 to San Francisco, and the coast of Panama.

Within the Japanese political and intellectual leadership there was a consensus regarding the need to introduce Western military science and technology.[54] Clearly the foreigners were most advanced in military technology, and their effective weaponry compelled the Japanese to forge and develop bilateral relations with their countries. This led to a surge of armaments "and other war material, information on techniques of warfare, and instructors to teach their use" being brought to Japan.[55]

Optimistic *rangaku* scholars recognized the advantages of Western science and research and their "positive results"[56] and were eloquently advocating the introduction of Western techniques and sciences, though under condition that Oriental ethics and ways of living would be upheld.[57]

With the widening horizon of knowledge and growing threats from outside, it was not surprising that the progressive forces increasingly challenged the supremacy of the shōgunate government (the Edo *bakufu*). Late Edo intellectuals such as Honda Toshiaki (1744–1821) were "deeply concerned over the foreign military threat and wanted Japan to become an imperial power like England."[58] Honda—a mathematician, astronomer, ship captain, and economist—hoped that Japan could profit from the achievements of the West and assert itself as the "England of the East."[59]

All pressed now for opening the country, the European powers from the outside, and the leading Japanese intellectuals from inside.[60] Commissioned by the American government, U.S. Commodore Matthew Calbraith Perry arrived in July 1853 at the mouth of Edo Bay (today's Tokyo Bay) with the two steam frigates *Susquehanna* and *Mississippi* and the sloops *Plymouth* and *Saratoga*, and took anchor off the port of Uraga.

The *bakufu* judged that, with its outdated weapons, it was not in a position to effectively engage in an armed opposition and resolved to negotiate—above all, in order to win time. Shimazu Nariakira (1809–1858), an important *tozama daimyō* ("outside feudal lord")[61] from Satsuma in the southern part of Kyushu, and a loyal vassal of the shōgun, argued as follows: "If the barbarians know that we give in to their threats, this will bring us continual difficulties"[62] He advocated a holding tactic, to gain time for arming the country.[63] Tokugawa Nariaki, who was much more influential than Shimazu Nariakira in *bakufu* councils and until he died in 1868 the outspoken leader of the *jōi* movement (to which the majority of the *daimyōs* adhered), held the view that a war could not in any case be avoided:

> It is my conviction that the first and most important task of the *bakufu* is to make a choice between war and peace and then to follow the chosen policy without wavering . . . I will give ten reasons why we should in no case choose a peace policy.[64]

Commodore Perry finally succeeded in going ashore, officially delivering a letter from the American President Millard Fillmore that was addressed to the Japanese emperor—he did not know that the shōgun, and not the emperor, was in fact responsible for diplomatic and government affairs.[65] With the promise, which seemed more like a threat, that he would return the next spring to receive an answer, on 19 July 1853 Perry set sail for Shanghai, where the Taiping Rebellion demanded his presence.[66] The letter from President Fillmore had been received by Abe Masahiro, a *fudai daimyō*[67] and since 1845 head of the Rōjū,[68] and then copied and shared with all the other *daimyōs*, of both the *tozama* and *fudai* categories, with the request that they give their opinions on how the matter should best be dealt with. The replies reflected the differing stances of the *kaikoku* and *jōi* advocates,[69] as well as the views of a third group, which took a middle position. With the distribution of the letters by Abe Masahiro, however, the door was also thrown open to criticism of Tokugawa policy.[70]

In February 1854 Commodore Perry returned, this time with eight ships—one-fourth of the U.S. navy at the time—and in March of the same year a treaty was signed with the *bakufu* that opened to the Americans the ports of Shimoda and Hakodate, granted the setting up of consulates in both ports, and provided for the repatriation of shipwrecked Japanese who had been rescued by American ships and the taking on of food and other supplies by American vessels.[71] Soon Great Britain (1854) and Russia (1855) concluded similar treaties with the Japanese. These treaties were not yet the "trade treaties" the Western powers hoped for, but they were soon widened in scope through the supplementary "Ansei Conventions."

The first American who took up his post as resident consul in Japan, Townsend Harris, settled in the small port of Shimoda, near the southern end of the Izu Peninsula, considerably to the south of the entrance to Edo Bay. A new agreement with Russia signed on 24 October 1857, which recognized the same conditions, allowed a Russian consul to also reside in Shimoda. This same year, 1857, Hotta Masayoshi (1810–1864), who had become Rōjū chairman (under Shōgun Iesada) two years earlier, stated in a memorandum on Japanese foreign policy:

> Our policy should be to stake everything on the present opportunity, to conclude friendly alliances, to send ships to foreign countries everywhere and conduct trade, to copy the foreigners where they are at their best and so to repair our own shortcomings.[72]

Curiously, Tokugawa Yoshinobu, who became shōgun in 1866, continued by stating that the purpose of this policy was "to foster our national strength and complete our armaments, and so gradually subject the foreigners to our influence until in the end all the countries of the world know the blessings of perfect tranquility and our hegemony is acknowledged throughout the globe."[73]

Through Harris's tenacious efforts Japan at last opened itself fully to trade, which led to the conclusion of the so-called Ansei Trade Treaties, or, in Japanese, the *Ansei gokakoku jōyaku* ("Ansei Five-Country Treaties"), the first of which was signed for the United States by Townsend Harris on 29 July 1858.[74] Apparently the emperor in Kyoto, who "looked down upon" the foreigners, gave "his agreement against his will."[75] Treaties with the Netherlands (18 August 1858), the Russian Empire (19 August 1858), Great Britain (26 August 1858), France (9 October 1858), Portugal (3 August 1860), and Prussia (24 January 1861) followed. Through these treaties the ports of Kanagawa (today's Yokohama) and Nagasaki (in 1860 and 1863, respectively), as well as Niigata on the west coast and Hyōgo (today's Kobe), were opened to trade. Subsequently, foreigners were allowed to settle in Edo and Osaka.[76] These trade treaties also stipulated that criminal proceedings against foreigners were to be conducted under consular jurisdiction ("extraterritoriality"), and not by the Japanese authorities. In accordance with colonial practice, the Western contracting powers had devised the treaties in such a way that they were "seemingly eternal since they had no termination dates or machinery for revision."[77] To neglect such provisions reflected "colonial" practices. Wilhelm Grewe notes: "The principal, practical effect of the linkage of international law to the standards of civilisation was the system of 'capitulations' or, in other words, the 'unequal' treaties by which the civilised nations reserved a special jurisdiction ('consular jurisdiction') over their own nationals, whom they did not wish to have subjected to the legal order and justice system of a half-civilised or uncivilised land."[78]

Writing in 1900 about the years he spent in Japan in the early Meiji Period, Alexander von Siebold (1864–1911) recounted that the "unequal treaties" had given rise to "unbearable and, as it turned out, untenable" conditions. A convention of 25 June 1866 additionally reduced what were at first still favorable import and export duties to an *ad valorum* basis of only 5 percent. Thus the possibility of capital accumulation, that is to say, "bringing about increased government revenues from this source, was excluded."[79]

In any event the treaties also met with sharp protests from many *daimyōs*, particularly from Satsuma and Chōshū. In the "Ansei purge" the protests were forcefully suppressed, and in the spring of 1860 the top advisor of the *bakufu*, Ii Naosuke (1815–1860), who had been seen as responsible for the approval of the treaties, was assassinated in the so-called Sakuradamongai Incident.

As the struggle within Japan against the *bakufu* by those who felt it yielded too much to the foreign powers intensified, the *bakufu* saw itself increasingly incapable of coping with the situation. A major reason for this was economic difficulty,[80] since the new international trade developed to Japan's disadvantage. One of such negative aspects was that while gold reserves dwindled,[81] the import of weapons of war flourished.

With the slogan "revere the Emperor and drive away the barbarians (*sonnō jōi*),"[82] those opposing the *bakufu* as well as the foreigners, led by the *daimyōs* of Satsuma and Choshu, gained prominence. In this way, national unity against the common enemy was invoked in a way that was extremely effective from the point of view of domestic policies. Now the emperor became the rallying point in the struggle for self-assertiveness and against the danger of being overtaken by the foreign powers. Toward the end of 1862, it seemed the leadership in Edo would be forced to accept both the policy of expulsion of foreigners (*jōi*) as well as a gradual shift of power to the emperor.[83]

To bind the two "courts," the emperor's court in Kyoto and the court of the shōgun in Edo, more closely together and reinforce national integrity, on 11 March 1862 Shōgun Iemochi married the younger sister of Emperor Kōmei. At the same time the clans of Satsuma and Chōshū were ordered by the emperor to protect Kyoto. In this way the political standing of the emperor improved. One year after his marriage, in April 1863 Iemochi came to Kyoto to become the first shōgun in 230 years to pay formal respects at the emperor's court. At the beginning of June 1863, the emperor designated 25 June 1863 as the date for beginning to expel the foreigners.[84] The *daimyōs* were to bring together troops in each of their feudal domains, while Iemochi waited in Kyoto to see how things would develop.

There had been instances of violence and incidents showing Japanese hostility to the foreigners before. In January 1861, Henry Heusken (1832–1861), Townsend Harris's secretary and translator during the negotiations over the Ansei treaties, had been killed in an attack by the Japanese,[85] and in September 1862 the Englishman Richardson was killed in the so-called Namamugi Incident. Between 1863 and 1865 there were further clashes between the "emperor-supporting" *daimyōs* and their adherents, on the one hand, and the Westerners on the other.

Activists working for the overthrow of the *bakufu*, the *shishi*, attempted to provoke a war with the Western powers. In 1863 they burned down the British Legation in Edo. On 25 June 1863, the *daimyō* of Chōshū, whose domain along the Straits of Shimonoseki controlled the passage to the Inland Sea, opened fire on an American ship and then on three other foreign ships over the next several days. However, on 20 July 1863 two French warships temporarily put an end to the attacks by the Chōshū coastal batteries. The British then fired on and took Kagoshima in the Satsuma domain. Soon Emperor Kōmei had to concede that Japan could not openly carry on war against the great powers. He officially dismissed the Chōshū troops in Kyoto and issued a decree suspending the campaign to drive away the barbarians.

Chōshū, though it had lost the emperor's favor, continued to attack foreign ships, while the already weakened shōgun at the beginning of 1864 again made a call at the imperial court in Kyoto. Eventually, on 4 September 1863 an allied squadron, composed of nineteen ships (nine British, four Dutch, three French, and one American) assembled off the coast of Hiroshima, and, moving westward managed to clear the Straits of Shimonoseki with heavy fire. Mōri Motonori (1839–1896), the leader of the revolting Chōshū troops, surrendered, and prepared to open the port of Shimonoseki to trade. Still wanting to stand up and fight for the emperor, toward the end of 1864 the large clans of Japan's southwest began to form an alliance—centered around the domains of Hizen, Tosa, and Chōshū—to carry on their struggle against the Tokugawa bakufu, prompting the bakufu, which had recently come to have at its disposal well-trained soldiers outfitted with the most modern weapons, to prepare a large-scale expeditionary force against Chōshū.[86] Finally, in the following year a British-French squadron sailing up from the southern coast of China to carry out a naval demonstration in Osaka Bay succeeded in obtaining the ratification of the treaties.[87]

While the bakufu was still trying to impose punishments to bring the shishi agitators to reason, those who had survived the Ansei "purge" proclaimed new goals, which found expression in the slogan fukoku kyōhei, meaning "a wealthy country and a strong military." In spite of the miscarriage of the expulsion policy, the transfer of government power to the emperor was achieved in the end.[88]

After the Europeans had obtained due ratification of the treaties from the emperor on 22 November 1865 and a revision of the tariff settlement,[89] troops of the bakufu and the emperor's supporters clashed once more, on 19 July 1866. By 16 September 1866 the Edo troops loyal to the government were encircled within Hiroshima and defeated. On 19 September 1866 Shōgun Tokugawa Iemochi died at the age of twenty-one in Osaka, and on 10 January 1867 the new shōgun, Tokugawa Keiki (Yoshinobu), was installed in office in the Nijō Palace in Kyoto. On 3 February 1867 Emperor Kōmei died and was succeeded by his fifteen-year-old son Mutsuhito, who would become the "Meiji emperor."

The opening to international trade of the ports of Hyōgo (Kobe) and Osaka, which Keiki had recommended to the emperor in April 1867, became effective as of 1 January 1868. Yoshinobu resigned on 19 November 1867, to hand over power to the emperor. On 3 January 1868, however, in a coup d'état, the Satsuma and Chōshū troops seized the palace in Kyoto and announced another imperial restoration.[90] The next day, the emperor was installed at the

apex of a newly established government, which consisted of a prime minister (*sōsai*), ten ministers (*gijō*), and twenty advisors (*san'yo*), among them
Saigō Takamori and Ōkubo Toshimichi (1830–1878). It was a victory of the
western and southern over the eastern clans. Keiki, who was not made part of
the new government (though the emperor had previously designated him to
handle foreign affairs), departed for Kyoto on 27 January in order to officially
submit to the emperor his declaration to step down. The loyal *bakufu* officials
who accompanied the shōgun, however, remained opposed to his abdication
and to the new political order. Meanwhile, the Satsuma and Chōshū troops
continued to struggle against the *bakufu* troops, in the course of which Keiki's
supporters were defeated, and he too had to flee.[91] Following further tussles in
Osaka, in the course of which Osaka Castle as well as the French and Dutch
consulates were torched, the imperial army marched to Edo, which was occupied without struggle on 3 May 1868. Armed clashes continued in other
areas. Finally, with the capitulation of the last *bakufu*-loyal troops on 27 June
1869, the civil war ended. Thus the revolutionaries' political goal of "revering
the emperor" (*sonnō*) was accomplished.

The new leaders got to work assimilating the new order. The modernization process had positive effects:

> Japan was . . . thrust into new worlds of thought and action—into the political
> world of Rousseau and the French Revolution, of British liberalism and the stat-
> ism of Prussia; into the economic world of Malthus, Smith, Mill, and List; into
> the intellectual world of Kant, Hegel, Darwin, Huxley, and Spencer. It would
> not be long before each new current in Western thought would have its native
> spokesman in Japan, its great works made available in translation.[92]

Due to the long interaction with the Dutch, schoolbooks and modern scientific texts in the second half of the nineteenth century could be published
in Japanese, so people "became acquainted with the scientific conceptual
world in their mother tongue."[93] The assimilation of European knowledge
was, as Najita Tetsuo has pointed out, supported by the fact that "a great part
of the language [the Japanese] reverted to in the process of these translations
derived from the eighteenth century discourse on knowledge and perception, i.e., from an intellectual environment in which Western scientific and
political predominance did not yet play an essential role."[94] For this reason
the Japanese were able to assimilate Western technology earlier than other
Asian countries. As a result, control and management as well as financing of
large projects during the country's industrialization and modernization period
remained in Japanese hands. Most hired foreign specialists were soon replaced by trained Japanese, many of whom had studied abroad.[95] The "quick

knowledge-transfer in the early phase of modern Japan" was carefully guided and facilitated through such an "independent translation policy."[96]

Great Britain especially inspired Japan's intellectual avant-garde.[97] The above-mentioned Fukuzawa Yukichi, the founder of Keiō University and probably most prominent representative of the Japanese "Cultural Enlightenment" (*bunmei kaikaku*), played a major role. His books, in which he reported on Western ways of thinking and observations he made during his trips in Europe and America, were sold in editions of over a million copies.[98]

> Fukuzawa's influence was the greater because of the practical and popular character of his writings. . . . If there is any single influence from the West which Fukuzawa most clearly exemplified and fostered it is British utilitarianism and liberalism. . . . Linked closely to this was the prevailing belief in human progress through the wider application of the methods of the natural sciences.[99]

The politically liberal social theories that went along with the utilitarianism of a Jeremy Bentham, the positivism of a John Stuart Mill (1806–1873), and the evolutionism and evolutionary individualism of a Herbert Spencer (1820–1903) were quickly popularized in Japan thanks to Fukuzawa Yukichi.[100] In liberalism, as it developed from the French Revolution and in the Anglo-Saxon political culture, the Japanese found similarities with their own political culture and tradition. This facilitated the gradual taking over of political responsibility from the hands of the sword-nobility (*buke*) to the newly self-confident land-nobility (*shizoku*),[101] which were recruited from among the former samurai.[102]

Between 1854 und 1868, new official posts were established, especially concerning foreign affairs and defense, including, for example, the *gaikoku-gakari*, responsible for foreign relations, and the *gaikoku-bugyō* (Magistrate of Foreign Affairs) established in 1858. New posts were established, of plenipotentiary commissioners known as *ōsetsu-gakari*, experts who were called in negotiations involving the treaties concluded with the Western powers. Clearly, as Beasley notes, "in this brief period . . . something resembling a [modern] diplomatic service [was] taking shape."[103]

With the opening of the country between 1853 and 1868, new information about Japan reached the West. Japanese and Oriental thoughts and ways were studied in America and Europe in much the same way as were European and American lifestyles and ideas in Japan. As previously mentioned, on the occasion of the World Parliament of Religions held in Chicago in 1893[104] several Japanese Buddhist priests traveled to the United States and Europe in order to publicize Buddhist teachings in the West. Conversely, it was Western influences that in Japan stimulated radical social and political change through modernization and industrialization. Nonetheless, like Germany, Japan has been called a latecomer (*verspätete Nation*)[105] in the concert of nations.[106]

In any event, with the "opening of the country" (*kaikoku*), the attempt was made to achieve a synthesis of East and West, to gain new perspectives on the world, and catch up with the industrial revolution, which was beginning to show its effects also in Asia.

> The Orientals, struck by the material superiority of the Occident, dreamed of having their countries participate in the advantages of modern science. They were persuaded that an exclusive spiritual culture was the cause of the political and economic subjection of the Orient. . . . And they preached a sort of synthesis of spiritualism and material science. Japan was the first to apply these principles.[107]

Having come into contact with the Western powers, the question of "world peace" also posed itself for Japan for the first time.

Japan now had to prove and assert itself in the international context. Whether the events surrounding the opening of the country and the subsequent new political orientation were a revolution[108] or a "restoration" (i.e., merely a new edition following traditional patterns) is a question that is still discussed in Japan today.[109]

From 1869 until the promulgation of the Meiji constitution in 1889, numerous reforms were carried out. Following the defeat of the shōgunate loyalists, all the *daimyōs*, in response to this new situation, had declared their allegiance to the young emperor, Mutsuhito, and turned over to the new government their feudal registers.[110] The domains of all the *daimyōs* were formally dissolved in 1871 and replaced by "prefectures" (*ken*). In 1872 universal military conscription[111] was introduced as well as compulsory schooling; in the same year the official prohibition of Christianity, which had existed for over two centuries, was revoked.

Among the samurai, however, the loss of their former privileges had also brought discontent, protests, and uprisings.[112] In 1877 the so-called Southwest War (*Seinan Sensō*) broke out, in the course of which rebelling samurai, led by Saigō Takamori (1827–1877),[113] fought government troops for eight months before they were finally defeated. With this victory the government's power was firmly and unshakably established. Japan could now speak with one voice to the outside world and take on new responsibilities in Asia and in the emerging universal "concert of the nations."

Though rising from a feudal past into a modern era, Japan after 1890 took also a "romantic" look back to more traditional, imperial concepts.[114] An edict of 1871 by the young Meiji emperor invoked the ancient principles of *hakkō ichiu* (the "eight directions under one roof") and *kōdō* (the "imperial way").[115]

This eventually opened the gates wide for misuse by the military for their expansionist policies.[116] Yet, in general, the Meiji Period distinguished itself for its enlightened and progressive reforms. In China, too, the Meiji government could be seen as the embodiment of modern reform movements in East Asia.[117]

> Not since the seventh century, when a band of Sinophiles around the throne tried to remake Japan on the Chinese model, had all aspects of Japanese life been so much altered by political action or Japanese thinking so much directed along lines laid down by a few master planners.[118]

Such "masterful planning," which had evolved out of the disputes among the various factions concerning the "correct way," ultimately brought a consensus—a remarkable characteristic of Japanese political culture.[119] The opening of the country, while in some degree imposed upon Japan by the Western powers, was thus at the same time guided and carefully planned and prepared by the various political forces in Japan itself. External circumstances, domestic needs, and a flexible and—based on historical experience—creative and adaptable regime produced the Japanese entrance into the existing dominant world political system.

JAPANESE FOREIGN RELATIONS AND THE RECEPTION OF INTERNATIONAL LAW AFTER THE MEIJI RESTORATION

> "May the hopes which were attached to this new epoch be fulfilled and may above all the Japanese people not forget that the entry into European international law brings with it not only rights but also duties, and that only a continuation of the enlightened progress shown so far and of the earnest work on the still to be completed cultural tasks will secure for Japan the place which it has achieved for itself with so much effort and patience."
>
> Alexander von Siebold[120]

To understand Japanese foreign policy and international relations in the twentieth century we have to look into the question of Japanese foreign policy during the period of the Tokugawa shōgunate (*bakufu*).[121] As has been shown the exclusion policy did not mean the eschewing of all diplomatic and other foreign relations. Intensive, though strictly channeled, relations with other countries were cultivated; the older picture of Japan in this respect had to be revised[122]—it could not explain the country's quick and dramatic development after the "opening" to the outside world.

Doubtless the channels through which Japan associated with the outside world were constrained and narrow,[123] and the number of foreign contacts limited. However, during the early decades of the exclusion period, up until the end of the seventeenth century, Japanese trading ships from the Tsushima and Satsuma domains sailed regularly to Korea and Okinawa in order to exchange goods with China and Southeast Asia. To continue observance of the outside world, the *bakufu* renewed diplomatic relations with the kingdoms of Chōsen (i.e., Korea) and Ryūkyū around 1640.[124] Between 1607 and 1850 altogether twenty-one diplomatic missions from the Ryūkyū Kingdom and twelve from Korea visited Japan.[125] In 1674, at the urging of the Siamese king, Japan took up diplomatic relations with the Buddhist kingdom.[126] Japan's strategic role in the area and for the economy of the East Asian region was substantial and politically significant. The multiple official cords of these connections extended out from Edo (today's Tokyo), and stretched via the Tsushima Islands to Pusan and Seoul in Korea and via Nagasaki to the Chinese coast as far as Fujian, the province south of Zhejiang, and as far as Southeast Asia. They constituted a far-reaching information network. Ronald Toby has pointed out these foreign relations, which also helped legitimize *bakufu* rule, were part of the early Tokugawa shōguns' "foreign policy strategy," which "served in later decades and centuries to define the Japanese conception of the structure of international order and of Japan's relationship to that order."[127]

Evidently it had not been the intention of the Japanese government to pursue a self-complacent isolationism but only to keep out the *namban* or "southern foreigners" (i.e., the Catholics), and put a stop to the "subversive ideology" of the Roman Catholic Church. When, for example, Britain tried to initiate relations with Japan in 1673, it was refused mainly because the English King, Charles II, had married a Portuguese princess: "Japan now regarded England as a Catholic collaborator and an enemy."[128]

Japan's traditional view of international relations was shaped by the Confucian (Chinese) concept of national identity, the *ka-i* concept of the "inner" in relation to the "other" or "outside." The traditional *ka-i chitsujo* was the model of interstate relations,[129] which made a distinction between civilized states (*ka*) like India, China, and Japan,[130] and less civilized "barbarians" (*i*),[131] who were conceived as posing a permanent, potential threat. Maruyama Masao, in an article published in 1949, referred to the relationship between the *ka-i chitsujo* and the astounding phenomenon of the rapid and rationally carried out modernization of Japan after the "opening." Without this "prehistory," the transformation of the Tokugawa *bakufu* into a modern state could not have taken place as it did.[132]

This overall perception is vital for assessing Japan's place in the world; it is a precondition for Japan's appearance during the Edo Period as an equal and active partner in the East Asian political and strategic environment, successfully projecting its interests in the region. The arrival of the first Europeans in Asia during the sixteenth century put this Asian order in question. Within this order, from Japan's point of view, Korea and the "Indianized" portions of Southeast Asia functioned as a "bridge," while Japan oriented itself mainly, at least outwardly, toward nearby China.[133] Being the farthest outpost of the Silk Road, Japan, the easterly island kingdom, became a gathering post, and treasure store for the culmination of various cultural traits accumulated on the sea-trade routes from the West.

Between 1690 and 1693 the Dutch had defeated the chief South Indian kingdoms of Madura, Ramnad, and Tanjur, which had controlled important trade routes in the Bay of Bengal and along the Indian Eastern ghats (Coromandel coast). With the victory of the English at Plassey, Bengal, in 1757 India was finally subjugated and dropped out as an independent political actor within the Asian "security community," which was held together by traditional codes of conduct based on Buddhist-Brahmanistic and Confucian principles. Thus only Japan and China remained as "guarantors" for upholding the balance vis-à-vis the West. Since the formerly ruling Ming dynasty had been replaced in 1636 by "barbarian" Manchu (Tartar) tribes (who adopted the Chinese name Qing),[134] in the face of the growing impact of the Western powers on Asia, Japan began to perceive itself as a natural "hegemon" and protector of Asian values, a role that was reflected upon eloquently within Japan.

This designation is important to understand subsequent developments in the region. Japan was perhaps less aggressively inclined and more interested in being a responsible actor in the overall security environment in East Asia. Insofar as Japan wanted to assert its own centrality and its equality with the Western powers (as well as its hoped-for, mutually benefiting ties with China),[135] Japan set the course for its future development and position in its international relations. For this Japan had consciously pursued a policy of *sakoku* that was, in fact, no strict closure, but a self-restrained and contained assertion, a way of taking stock, by way of "remote control."

With the "opening" of the country, Japan was again confronted with the same problems it had faced three hundred years earlier, only this time the problems came from another side and were considerably more threatening and incalculable than during the "Christian Century" between 1549 and 1650. The effects of the industrial revolution, the growing political impact of the United States and Russia in international relations and especially in the Pacific region and in Northeast Asia, but above all the expansive European colonialism and imperialism posed a challenge that Japan could no longer counter by relying solely on its own tradition and means.

Following Hugo Grotius's (1583–1645) groundbreaking work on the freedom of the seas, European international law had developed, and subsequently, in the course of the Enlightenment a secular, novel universal law of nations gained prominence. Together with the rights of man and modern constitutional law, a legal system evolved that could claim worldwide adherence, corresponding with and complementing the univeralism of Confucianism, which had similarly put harmony and ethical principles at the center, and fostered the "benevolence" of government.[136] Fukuzawa had been able to welcome and accept the law of nations since it was based on some kind of "natural law" that was akin to the *ri* of neo-Confucian teachings.[137] With the rise of the modern, independent nation-states, diplomacy began to tread a new course. To find a common denominator in international relations that was universally valid, in the first two decades after Japan's "opening," the role of international law was widely discussed.[138]

Thus in 1860, having concluded the first treaties opening ports to trade, an eighty-one-member Japanese delegation—the *Man'en kembei shisetsu*—journeyed for the first time to the United States to negotiate terms favorable to Japan with the government in Washington.[139] In 1862 a second delegation went to England, France, the Netherlands, Prussia, Russia, and Portugal.[140] The objective of these missions was initially to delay the opening of ports and cities.[141] A third embassy went to the West in 1864, and the *bakufu* sent additional delegations to France in 1865, to Russia in 1866, and again to Europe in 1867.[142] From 1862 onward, students were sent to Europe, where they enrolled in universities in the Netherlands, England, and France, and by 1885 more than three hundred Japanese had gone to study in the United States. The most well-known mission, decisive for the further development of Japanese foreign policy, was the Iwakura Mission (*Iwakura kengai shisetsu*) under the leadership of Iwakura Tomomi (1825–1883), which traveled abroad for eighteen months between 1871 and 1873, visiting the United States and fourteen European countries with which Japan had concluded treaties. Its dual purpose was the revision of the "unequal treaties" and the study of Western societies.[143] The Iwakura Mission's lack of success in revising the "unequal treaties" led to an elemental change in Japan's attitude with respect to the possibility of obtaining international law guarantees for its national security and independence, which was evident in Fukuzawa Yukichi's changing outlook and disillusionment.[144]

With the abdication of the last Tokugawa ruler (1867) and the restoration of emperor rule (the Meiji Restoration), Japan's rise to a modern industrial nation and a leading military power in the region began.[145] Emperor Mutsuhito (the "Meiji tennō") moved the capital from Miyako (Kyoto) to Edo, now renamed Tokyo. The new slogan of the young samurai who constituted the Meiji government proclaimed "a wealthy country and a strong military" (*fukoku kyōhei*). Kido Takayoshi (Kōin, 1833–1877), one of the great statesmen of the Meiji Period, accordingly advocated a powerful Japan. At the end of 1868 Kido recorded in his diary:

There is an urgent need for Japan to become strong enough militarily to take a stand against the Western powers. As long as our country is lacking in military power, the law of nations is not to be trusted. When dealing with those who are weak, the strong nations often invoke public law but really calculate their own gain. Thus it seems to me that the law of nations is merely a tool for the conquest of the weak.[146]

In any event, on the fifteenth day of the first month of the first year of Meiji[147] (that is, 8 February 1868, by the Gregorian calendar) the young Meiji emperor officially received for the first time the foreign emissaries, declaring on this occasion that Japan would from now on conduct its foreign affairs in keeping with international law.[148] On the seventeenth day of the second month (17 March 1868), an official public notice affirmed Japan's commitment to cultivating foreign relations in accordance with public international law (*bankoku kōhō*).[149]   Interestingly, at the same time, progressive political thinkers in Japan also advocated an international administration—in line with progressive thinking in the West—as evidenced in the writings of the afore-mentioned Ueki Emori (1857–1892), the constitutional scholar and intellectual of the *jiyū minken undō* (Freedom and Human Rights Movement).

However, to assert also in the military dimension its sovereignty as a state in international relations, Japan needed the help and recognition of the Western powers, which had already made considerable "progress" along these lines. While the Japanese government looked to France and Germany for guidance in the domestic sphere (i.e., when it came to criminal and civil law), and for this purpose invited German and French experts on public law to Japan,[150] the navy adopted the English model.[151] The army was built first on the French and then on the German example. The perceived need for defense and a military establishment corresponded to the generally accepted responsibilities and prerogatives of sovereign states (*Staatsräson*). An official announcement on the emperor's edict of 29 November 1872 introducing conscription[152] stated:

> So long as there is a state, there is military defence; and if there is military defense, there must also be a military service. Therefrom it follows that the [setting forth of a law] which makes military provisions is a natural right and no accidental man-made right.[153]

"Militarization" and "democratization," according to the European model, were two sides of a coin.[154]

After the Japanese government had at first turned to France for the provision of military training officers, the later preference for the German military system took the upper hand to such a degree that gradually the French instructors were

replaced by Germans and individual Japanese officers were dispatched to the
German Army [for training].[155]

As Japan approached the end of the nineteenth century, its military power
increased. Alexander von Siebold's (1846–1911) figures, compiled from
newspaper reports, speak for themselves.

> At the end of the year 1899 there will be at the disposal of the three Army com-
> mands (of the East, the Center, and the West, each of which consists of four
> divisions, while the guard division is directly responsible to the Emperor) the
> following: 15 divisions with 26 infantry brigades, 52 regiments, 156 battalions,
> 13 cavalry regiments with 65 squadrons, 13 field artillery regiments for the
> present with 79 field and mountain batteries, reaching however in 1900 the full
> strength of 117 batteries in 39 divisions each with 3 batteries, 13 pioneer bat-
> talions until the end of 1900 with 28, then 39 companies, 13 training battalions
> with 26 companies, 1 railroad and telegraph battalion with 3 companies. In
> stocks of weapons absolutely nothing is lacking.[156]

With these forebodings—one of which was a cautious reserve toward the
West—and with the intention of ending the unequal treaties and achieving a
full and equitable partnership with the West, Japan entered the twentieth century.[157] For many Asians Japan was a bringer of hope, as Peter Duus points
out: "All these young Asians saw Japan as a potential liberator of Asia, a notion shared by a great many Japanese as well."[158] One of these was Mohandas
K. Gandhi.

In the reception of international law the Western "model" had played a
pivotal role. The laws of war (as part of international law) were regarded
as a function of "natural law." If Japan's vital national interests were to be
recognized and fittingly protected, this included the concession of certain prerogatives on the Asian mainland on the grounds of cultural and geographical
proximity and perhaps also its assumed civilizational lead. For some nationalists and the military, warfare appeared as a legitimate tool to assert national
interests. The empire had to be on guard against the European colonial powers. In this constellation, peace as an ultimate goal helped legitimize the military establishment; threats from outside Japan were perceived as very real.

Did Japan really have grounds to distrust Western international law? Distrust has been a cause of war time and again.[159] Alexander von Siebold, eldest
son of the famous Japanologist Philip Franz von Siebold[160] and from 1870
to 1911 advisor to Japan's Ministry of Foreign Affairs, writes that after the
Japanese government had at first

> committed itself in the same way as Turkey and had given up for an undefined
> period the independent exercise of important governmental activities . . . it now

became the first non-European state which succeeded after efforts of many years, in the recent treaty agreements, which entered into force on 17 July and 4 August [1899] respectively . . . to achieve the recognition by the Western powers of its full rights under international law. . . . Formerly European international law, in keeping with its historical development, had full validity only among the Christian countries inside and outside of Europe.[161]

In 1865 Japan had become a founding member of the International Telegraph Union (established in Paris that year), an event that the German international law scholar and parliamentarian Walther Schücking identified as "the first of all international administrative bodies operating under international law."[162] Having acceded to the General Postal Union (Treaty of Berne, 1874; renamed Universal Postal Union in 1878), the administration of Japan's postal services after 1877 was wholly in Japanese hands. At the 1878 Paris Convention of the Universal Postal Union Japan already took part "as an equal treaty-signing power and in July 1879 we see it . . . take its seat at the conference in London as a member of the International Telegraphic Union."[163]

In 1875 Japan acceded to the Metric Convention (signed in Paris in that year), and became a member of the International Bureau of Weights and Measures, which was established for the diffusion and standardization of the metric system. In 1884 Japan joined the international treaty for the protection of undersea telegraph cables, and in 1886 the Bern Convention on the Protection of Works of Literature and Art. In the same year it also joined the International Red Cross Society. From 1888 onward, both Japan and China were among those states that "had come together to ensure unhindered shipping through the Suez Canal."[164] In 1890 Japan, China, Siam, and other countries acceded to the International Convention for the Publication of Customs Tariffs formed in Brussels.[165] In 1905 Japan became a member of the International Institute for Agriculture in Rome, and in 1908 the International Union of Scientific Radio Telegraphy.

The Japanese reception of the law of nations, despite pragmatic reservations, and despite the change in attitude since the end of the 1870s and beginning of the 1880s, nevertheless got the country positively involved. Abiding by the "law of nations" (*ius gentium*), Japan's aim as a subject in international law was to be acknowledged and acquire for itself, in the modern Western sense, a stake in the assets—in the sense of "legal entitlements" to the world's available resources—which on principle were supposed to be accessible to all.

Wheaton's Elements of International Law, a comprehensive textbook on the law of nations, had been translated into Chinese and made accessible to Japanese scholars in 1864.[166] The author, Henry Wheaton (1785–1848), a diplomat, "rediscovered" the law of nations doctrine of the Dutch scholar Hugo de Groot (Grotius, 1583–1645), who had insisted that the interest of the international community must be placed above that of the nation-state.[167] Also, already in 1887 (presumably) a Japanese-language edition had appeared of Immanuel Kant's *On Perpetual Peace*, a work that the German scholar Klaus Dicke has called "probably the most influential proposal . . . in which is put forward the institution of a civil society that administers law—domestic public law, international law, law of world citizens/cosmopolitan law—as an imperative of practical reason."[168]

By the early 1880s, at the Imperial University in Tokyo[169] there existed, according to Alexander von Siebold, a well-staffed and well-equipped law faculty.

> In 1882–83, the law department included the following courses: an overall survey or encyclopedia of law, traditional Japanese law, modern Japanese law, English law, French law, Roman law, international law and general jurisprudence and legal philosophy. . . . The literature on which these studies were based [consisted of] the best European and American works in the respective disciplines.[170] . . . In the international law division the following works were assigned reading: Wheaton, *International Law*; Wharton, *Conflict of Laws*; Bluntschli, *Droit International Codifié*;[171] de Martens, *Précis du Droit des Gens Moderne de l'Europe*; Foelix, *Traité du Droit Internationale Privé*; Vattel, *Droit des Gens*, etc.[172]

The first modern constitution that Japan adopted in 1889, after a meticulous study of Western models, was fashioned after the Prussian model of a constitutional monarchy. Since it was strongly marked by Prussian concepts of public law and order, it centered on the stability and continuity of the "national identity" (*kokutai*). The political philosophy of the Prussian monarch greatly influenced the thinking of Japanese statesmen in the 1880s.[173] In contrast, Ueki Emori had in 1881 presented the draft of a liberal, enlightened constitution that was, however, rejected by the political leadership at the time in favor of the authoritarian Prussian model.[174] All in all, the promulgation of the Meiji constitution had a positive effect on constitutional development in general—not merely in Japan.

There were few impulses from the German side for the reception of "international law."[175] Instead, social Darwinist ideas abounded on the "right of the mightier" (*Recht des Stärkeren*) that gave physical (including military) might precedence over legal right.[176] Katō Hiroyuki, who had been president of the Imperial University of Tokyo from 1877–1886 and again from 1890–1893, an eminent jurist and constitutional scholar who also concerned himself with the issue of "world law," was one of the "leading Japanese advocate[s] of Social Darwinism" in Japan.[177] Considered at first a "liberal," who had translated Bluntschli's *Allgemeines Staatsrecht* into Japanese (under the title *Kokuhō hanron*, 1872), and propagated democratic human rights, he later turned into an advocate of the doctrine of "the struggle for survival."[178] "It was ironical," writes Maruyama Masao in *Nihon no shisō*, that here an "*ultra-progressive sort of thinking*" should join with "the most extreme political reaction."[179] Katō's influence on the development of Japanese militarism and chauvinism was significant, laying some of the theoretical foundations and legal grounds for Japan's aggressive politics in later years.

An ambiguity in modern public and international law, which became apparent in the course of the nineteenth century, was that while on the one side the maintenance of a standing army was considered essential for ascertaining national sovereign power, the "law of nations" increasingly tended to aim at outlawing war—a development that did not go unnoticed by the Japanese,[180] and that eventually after 1945 led to significant constitutional revisions in many countries. In line with this trend in international law, which became stronger in the interwar period, Japan showed itself an active and trusted partner within the League of Nations order—at least until the eclipse of "Shidehara Diplomacy," at the end of 1931.

Kido Kōin, the nineteenth-century samurai political leader, considered that historical imperatives determine the rise and fall of nations and peoples: only "loyalty to the constitutional order" could, as a criterion of cultural and political development, secure progress and constancy. This was, according to Kido, a universal law.[181]

Like the Europeans, the Japanese now diligently used "the law of nations" to obtain territorial and political advantages. The Sino-Japanese War (1894–1895) was both power politics carried out in the national interest and, from the point of view of international law, a legitimate action in response to a particular situation that had arisen in Japan's relations with its neighbors.[182] Japan's national interest required a liberated, pacified Asia as a precondition for assuring her prosperity and progress.

When the Sino-Japanese War was in the making Shidehara, who was born in 1872, was a secondary school and university student. A thoughtful student and motivated by patriotism, these events most likely provided Shidehara with the motivation for his decision to follow a diplomatic career. A first-hand eyewitness account of the events before and during the Sino-Japanese War is to be found in Mutsu Munemitsu's diplomatic memoirs, *Kenkenroku*.[183]

Japan, having maintained diplomatic relations with Korea during the Edo Period, twice sought to reestablish its ties with the "hermit kingdom," eager to explain the new circumstances and changes after its opening, but was repulsed on both occasions. In the meantime China had come to regard Korea, the "sick man" of the Far East, as a vassal state.[184] Finally Japan forced the opening of Korea in 1876, an act that in some ways replicated the opening of Japan in 1853/1854. In the Treaty of Kanghwa Korea was recognized as an independent sovereign state, and "her tributary relationship to China was abolished."[185]

Causes of the war, in the broadest sense, were the opposing interests of the "Western powers" in China. The emerging rivalry among the Western powers and Japan on the continent complicated and held up reforms needed for Korea's modern advance. Since China itself was in need of reforms, Japan sought a leading role to carry out reforms in Korea. In this Japan ran up against the opposition of the seclusionist prince regent or *taewŏngun* (literally, "prince of the great court"), who carried out affairs of state in the place of his young son, King Kojong, while facing at the same time opposition from the reactionary Min faction, the family clan of the queen, who was supported by China and strove above all to monopolize power and secure government offices for family members. Striving for modernization, the pro-Japanese faction of the Independence Party became increasingly powerful.

In the Treaty of Tianjin (18 April 1885), Japan (Itō Hirobumi) and China (Li Hongzhang) agreed that both countries would withdraw their troops stationed in Korea, and stop making officers available to train the Korean armed forces. In case serious unrest or boycotts in Korea should necessitate the engagement of Japanese or Chinese troops in the future, the Chinese and Japanese governments were to inform one another beforehand of their activities, and immediately withdraw troops after completion of the engagement.[186]

Although China had in effect with the Treaty of Tianjin given up its suzerainty over Korea, the Korean queen and her party continued to recognize the Chinese overlordship. The rigid leadership of the Min faction, however, soon led to a revolt of the farmers who were demanding a new apportionment of agricultural lands. In 1893 some of the farmers occupied the royal palace.[187] At the beginning of June 1894 the whole southern portion of Korea had risen up against the government, and Chinese ships and army units were sent to support the Korean forces in an attempt to put down this so-called Tonghak ("Eastern Learning") Rebellion.[188]

The suppression of the Tonghak Rebellion turned out to provide the cause for Japan's war with China. The Chinese, called in for assistance by the Min queen, occupied a region south of Seoul. Thereupon the Japanese also sent ships and troops, and soon Chinese and Japanese soldiers were facing each other in the vicinity of Seoul. The Chinese dismissed a Japanese proposal to work together to put down the rebellion and initiate reforms.[189]

The war, in the opinion of a contemporary American observer, could have been prevented if Great Britain had made effective use of its considerable influence in Beijing and demanded compromises by the Chinese.[190] On 26 June 1894, Japan unilaterally called upon the Korean king to carry out the needed reforms, demanding two days later, in a sort of ultimatum, that Korea declare its independence from China. One month later, on 23 July 1894, Japanese units occupied the royal palace and took King Kojong prisoner. A new government was installed and the king was forced, on July 25, to abrogate all existing agreements with China. Chinese troops were to leave Korea, with the Japanese overseeing their withdrawal.

On the morning of 25 July 1894, a battle at sea south of Seoul finally set off the war when Japanese cruisers under Captain Tōgō Heihachirō and two Chinese warships that were accompanied by the *Kow-shing* sailing under the command of a British captain named Galsworthy clashed. The *Kow-shing* had twelve thousand people, Chinese officers and crew, on board. Also on board was a German army captain named von Hanneken, who managed to flee; the Japanese captured Galsworthy and several other Europeans.[191] Field Marshall Yamagata Aritomo expressed his strong support for Togo's engagement, even if Itō Hirobumi and Admiral Saigō Tsugumichi (brother of Restoration activist Saigō Takamori) felt the incident would be detrimental to Japan's reputation.

Later that same week, on 29 July 1894, the chief of the Japanese army's general staff, Ōshima Ken'ichi (1858–1947), put a Chinese corps near Asan out of action. Three days later, on 1 August 1894, Japan formally declared war. The Japanese troops were better equipped and more numerous than the Chinese. At sea, although the Chinese had at their disposal a greater number of ships, they were poorly equipped. By September, the Chinese had been driven out of Korea. When Admiral Itō Sukeyuki had defeated the Chinese ships, the "Manchurian Expedition" began. From early October until early December, the Japanese army advanced onto the Liaodong Peninsula and took control of Dalian and Port Arthur (Ryojun in Japanese). On 12 February 1895, China's Admiral Ding Yuan capitulated in the Gulf of Liaodong, after the forts at Weihaiwei on the northern coast of the Shandong Peninsula had been destroyed by Japanese troops. By March 1895 the Japanese had defeated all the Chinese troops and occupied large areas. When the way to Beijing was open, Count Itō Hirobumi, as head of government, called off the operation.

On 17 April 1895, Japan and China signed the Treaty of Shimonoseki, in which China (1) recognized the independence of Korea; (2) ceded to Japan its control over Taiwan and the nearby Pescadores Islands as well as (3) the Liaodong Peninsula; (4) agreed to pay Japan a war indemnity of 364 million yen; and (5) gave Japan "most favored nation" status equal to the European powers in all respects. Although the Europeans tried to intervene to prevent its conclusion, the treaty favoring Japan was ratified on 8 May 1895.[192]

Shortly afterward, however, the Russians, together with the Germans and French, protested in Tokyo—in what came to be known as the "Triple

Intervention"—against the presence of Japanese troops in the Liaodong Peninsula, which Russia needed as final station of its Trans-Siberian Railroad; as a consequence Japan had to give up some of its new treaty rights. While the intervention had been spearheaded by Germany,[193] the Japanese victory was badly timed for the Russians, who were just penetrating northeastern China, "in order to take firm hold on the Manchurian market"[194] and develop and exploit its resources. Thus—according to the *Frankfurter Zeitung*—Russia had shown itself to be the "true friend" of the Chinese, and "with the sympathetic backing of Germany and France happily managed to almost completely maneuver the Japanese out of the Asian mainland." It offered "not only consoling words, but also a handsome sum of money," to obtain a position in the region that it increasingly cemented both militarily and through the building of the Trans-Siberian Railway.[195]

In July 1896, Russia concluded an accord with China in order to consolidate its position in East Asia and especially vis-à-vis Japan. The secret agreement, in essence a military pact, branded Japan as an aggressor. Though Japan eventually concluded a trade agreement with China, as had been provided for in the Shimonoseki Peace Treaty, and in which on 21 July 1896 Japan was formally recognized as a "most favored nation," still the Japanese felt they were treated unfairly, having been denied the fruits of what had been, from their point of view, a just and fairly fought war.

The interference of the powers had deeply humiliated the Japanese—statesmen and the common people alike—hurting their national pride. The trade treaty [with China], on the other hand, placed them on a level of equality with other foreigners. Both aroused nationalistic feelings; *they developed the understanding that they could only achieve the rank of a great power if they elevated their country's military power.*[196]

Two years later, those same powers, which "had claimed to have noble intentions and deprived Japan of the fruits of its victory,"[197] occupied those same regions they had denied the Japanese.[198]

The Triple Intervention was, in the words of historian Hatada Takashi, "the spark that set off the so-called 'second partition' of the Far East by the powers."[199] Russia received in 1898 not only Port Arthur and Dalian (Ta-lien, renamed "Dalny" by the Russians), but also (already in 1896) had obtained rights for mining, railway construction, and police administration in the Three Eastern Provinces of China (which non-Chinese often collectively referred to as "Manchuria"). France obtained special rights and privileges in southern China (especially in Yunnan Province, which would soon be connected by rail to Hanoi in French Indo-China), and Germany annexed the region around the port of Qingdao on the Shandong Peninsula—the Chinese "heartland"—and subsequently occupied also the Bay of Jiaozhou (Chiao-chou, Kiaochow). In response, Great Britain in 1898 obtained a twenty-five-year lease of Wei-haiwei and a ninety-nine-year lease of the Jiulong (Kowloon) Peninsula opposite the island of Hong Kong, which was already in British possession. In 1898, too, the United States annexed Hawaii and, as a result of the Spanish-American War, also the Philippines. The next year, 1899, the United States formally announced the "open-door policy" toward China, which was meant to hold in check any aggressive intentions the various powers might cherish. In an unofficial capacity, Japanese reacted to these Western démarches with the founding (in 1903) of the Tōa Dōbunkai, to promote Japanese-Chinese cultural cooperation.

Russia seemed to be achieving a position of predominance not only in "Manchuria" but also in the Korean Peninsula:

What the unbiased friends of Japan warned her would happen when she attacked China in order to secure the independence of Corea, has come to pass, and Russia has now established her protectorate over the Corean Court and the Government . . . [and] she has turned China out only, as she was forewarned, to let Russia in.[200]

Nonetheless, "as a result of the treaties concluded between 1894[201] and 1896 and the abolition of consular jurisdiction, Japan was accepted into the comity of civilized nations, and this was thanks also to its unique [economic and social] development and its strict observation of the law of nations in the war of 1894 with China."[202] Subsequently, in 1899, Japan took part as a fully accredited participant among some two dozen states, in the First Hague Peace Conference, to which the Russian Tsar Nicholas II, on the counsel of his Chancellor Muraviev, had invited them.[203] Even if these were not altogether peaceful times for Japan, the two Hague peace conferences were significant as the first "truly international assemblies meeting in time of peace for the purpose of preserving peace, not of concluding a war then in progress."[204] With the coming together at the first Hague Peace Conference in 1899 a pinnacle was reached, advancing international relations and the development of international law. Although this was also the peak of imperialism, when national interests were paramount, a lasting peace, too, at the time seemed to be in most of the great powers' interest.[205]

The bringing together of diverse cultural and legal traditions may have seemed "utopian" at the time. Certainly, the compilation, at the Hague peace conferences in 1899 and 1907, of legal codes aimed at making wars more "human" was a futile undertaking, albeit shortsighted, and later proved elusive. In its two wars—with China in 1894–1895 and with Russia in 1904–1905—Japan had meticulously followed the law of nations "in a manner that could even have set an example for old Europe." However, Japan could "hardly be enthusiastic over a law of nations that to all appearances was merely written down in order to be taught and [then] transgressed."[206] As for the binding jurisdiction of an international court to settle disputes between states, and with regard to disarmament, the two main objectives at The Hague, a lot remained to be done, to assure a peaceful and profitable future for all of mankind.

THE ORGANIZATION OF THE WORLD—
SCIENTIFIC PACIFISM AND THE ABOLITION
OF WAR BEFORE AND AFTER THE FIRST WORLD WAR

"Utopians [said Mr. Bloch], and they call us Utopians, idealists, visionaries, because we believe that the end of war is in sight? But who are the Utopians, I should like to know? What is a Utopian, using the term as an epithet of opprobrium? He is a man who lives in a dream of the impossible; but what I know and am prepared to prove is, that the real Utopians who are living in a veritable realm of phantasy are those people who believe in war. War has been possible, no doubt, but it has at last become impossible, and those who are preparing for war, and basing all their schemes of life on the expectation of war, are visionaries of the worst kind, for war is no longer possible." (1899)[207]

Ivan S. Bloch

The idea of world peace and an international league has its European origin in the cosmopolitanism of ancient Greece and Italy.[208] Similarly, the Indian book of statecraft, the *Arthashastra*, whose origins go back to the third century BC, includes, with its *mandala* system, federalist elements which transcend the notion of a "single state."[209] Comparable state models can be found in ancient China.[210] In modern history, in the context of the European Enlightenment, the idea was advocated by Immanuel Kant in Germany. In the United States, William Ladd (1778–1841) gained prominence with his *Essay on a Congress of Nations*.[211] At the beginning of the twentieth century, the neo-Kantian Walther Schücking, a parliamentarian and professor of international law at the universities in Marburg and Kiel, also championed a world-encompassing league of nations.[212]

The modern history of the organization of the world essentially started with the First Hague Peace Conference,[213] focusing on disarmament and the peaceful settlement of disputes through compulsory international jurisdiction. The so-called humanitarian international law (*ius in bello*)[214] aimed at regulating the conduct of belligerents in times of war, which was also discussed and codified at The Hague, could not prevent the atrocities and ever-increasing fatalities among civilian populations in the wars of the twentieth century and after.[215] The real issue at The Hague was the "right to war" (*ius ad bellum*). Those who questioned that right looked toward the limitation of the traditional sovereign right of belligerency of the state and sought the ultimate total and general abolition of warfare. The failure of the Hague conferences in their two main objectives, disarmament and binding jurisdiction, made the failure of its minor objective, the *ius in bello*, inevitable. Nevertheless, as a positive outcome of the peace efforts an international court was actually created,[216] albeit its decisions were to be nonbinding. That the binding character of international jurisdiction, the "main task" of the conferences, could not be achieved was—according to Philipp Zorn, the German delegate to both the peace conferences, and an international jurist of some renown who voiced what was the overall judgment among the participants, as well as among the public—"Germany's fault."[217]

The aforementioned Schücking[218] represented the evolving "scientific" pacifism of his time, which was also known as "organizational" pacifism, that is to say, a pacifism aiming at the organization of the world in a legally binding, mutually beneficial system, subject to the rule of law.[219] Such "organizational" or scientific pacifism contrasted with the "utopian" pacifism, which, like anarchism, tended to reject state institutions, laws, and sanctions.[220] The difference between these two orientations was also recognized in Japan: "Just as the scientific socialism of Marx followed utopian socialism, one should expect that, in the same way, scientific pacifism (*kagakuteki heiwashugi*) . . . would follow the utopian pacifism of [Woodrow] Wilson."[221]

Pacifism had, in the course of the nineteenth century, become a movement transcending national borders.[222] When it claimed its rightful position to become an academic discipline, its authority and international bearing were effectively strengthened. Political scientists, sociologists, historians, and philosophers, as well as jurists and international law experts, took up the issue to declare peace the object of academic research.[223] The basic idea behind the new rational-pacifist trend was the understanding that peace and an *organized* world society must be permanently secured by creating effective institutions founded on principles of justice and equality, and that war must be abolished. A peaceable *disposition* was a necessary, though not a *sufficient*, condition for the possibility of a world without war. The goal was to be the creation of a binding, supranational legal order for all states, in which ultimately individuals, too, would be subjects under international law who could be brought to justice. Enforceable *world law* should apply to individuals and not only to states. The decisive step forward was to be that "war ceases to be a legal institution. For the militarists . . . admittedly a hard blow."[224] Standing armies should be completely abolished.

This was the objective pursued at the Hague peace conferences (1899 and 1907), which came together largely as a result of growing public awareness. Public opinion had already been mobilized in the nineteenth century by an international peace movement that had begun to articulate and pursue its ideals vociferously.[225] Liberal governments of the democratic countries were prepared to seriously discuss the objectives of the peace movement and to contribute to their realization. For the "undoubtedly existing community of interests" it was now necessary to establish "the corresponding international organization."[226] In Schücking's view, with the Hague conferences "a process had begun which, in brief, one could describe as international law being on the point of becoming transformed into world law (*Weltstaatsrecht*)."[227]

It is not surprising that around the turn of the century the idea of a world-encompassing league found adherents in Japan too.[228] As mentioned above, enlightened liberals of the *Jiyū Minken Undō* had already endorsed Ueki Emori's idea of an "international government" that would be equipped to guarantee justice and peace to all nations. The Japanese knew well how to organize responsibilities and interests in a common administration at the national level. On 6 April 1868, at an assembly of the representatives of the feudal domains, over two hundred *daimyōs*—out of some 260 in all—acknowledged the newly established central government brought about by the Meiji Restoration, giving up voluntarily not only their inherited prerogatives but also their castles and other assets in favor of the national enterprise and the public interest.[229] Similarities exist between the Swiss Confederacy and the Swiss League established in 1848[230] (i.e., the famous oath of the Japanese feudal lords and that of the Swiss confederates).[231]

The Inter-Parliamentary Union (IPU) founded by the Englishman Sir Randell Cremer (1838–1908) and the Frenchman Frédéric Passy (1822–1912) in 1889—the same year the Meiji constitution was promulgated—also aroused much interest in Japan at the beginning of the twentieth century, in line with the general ideas of scientific, political pacifism. At the founding session "a large number of participants," among them parliamentarians from Italy, Austria, Germany, Switzerland, Belgium, Denmark, Great Britain, France, the United States, Sweden, the Netherlands, Spain, Portugal, and some Central and South American states, had advocated the "establishment of a world parliament, or global federation," and announced their willingness to cooperate in this regard.[232] Japanese Diet members participated for the first time in the 1906 IPU session, held in London, and from then on "contacts between the Union leadership and interested Japanese parliamentarians gradually increased."[233] In 1910, Japan became a "full member" of the IPU and Diet members regularly participated in the IPU sessions.

The First Hague Peace Conference pursued similar objectives. Albert Gobat, the general secretary of the IPU, in an address on 24 September 1904 at a White House reception by President Roosevelt for IPU participants who had that year (during the Russo-Japanese War) met together in St. Louis, reiterated: "We look at this institution [i.e., 'the work of The Hague'] as the starting point of the most important evolution ever entered upon by mankind."[234] An IPU Resolution produced in St. Louis requested the American president to call a second Hague Peace Conference. In 1905 an IPU "Committee on the Establishment of an International Parliament" recommended that "the Hague Conference should become the world tribunal and . . . the Inter-Parliamentary Union should itself be converted into a universal legislature."[235] The IPU's contribution in the twentieth century to the development of international law and order and the idea of an organized peace has been substantial.

At the Second Hague Peace Conference (15 June–18 October 1907) fifty-one so-called civilized nations participated.[236] The cardinal question was the arbitration for the peaceful settlement of international disputes through an international court of law.[237] At the first conference in 1899, a general but nonbinding obligation of states to resolve their disputes peacefully had been established, and there was a desire to further institutionalize procedures for the resolution of international disputes and make arbitration obligatory: "The great majority of states . . . declared themselves in favor of the principle of obligatory arbitration; [however] it was rejected by Germany and Austria-Hungary, together with the following states: Romania, Greece, Bulgaria, Turkey. Japan abstained from voting."[238]

After the First World War, the international lawyer Professor Philipp Zorn from Königsberg, and the only German who took part in both Hague peace conferences, addressed this question in these words:

The . . . great task was the successful institution of the *Obligatorium* [i.e., the principle of submission to obligatory arbitration]. With impatient longing, the world awaited its realization. And that Germany did not recognize this world expectation, and even believed it had to repudiate it, was its prime and fatal mistake.[239] . . . What could very well have been Germany's title to fame for the shaping of international relations [was] from the start belittled and then fully shattered through an immense political miscalculation . . . which must have provoked, and in fact brought about, the most serious consequences, which . . . today, in the horrible light of the universal conflagration of 1914–18 appears *precisely to have been a cause of the world war.*[240]

At the third peace conference that was being prepared for 1914 at The Hague, it was anticipated that the principle of unanimity would be discarded in favor of a majority vote. When Germany marched into Belgium to attack

France—war was declared on 3 August 1914[241]—the principle agreed upon at The Hague, that international disputes should be settled peacefully, was thrown into the dustbin,[242] and the generally accepted principles of international law were breached by violating Belgium's neutrality.[243]

After the failure of the Second Hague Conference in the question of obligatory arbitration, a worldwide arbitration "boom" began, with multiple bilateral and multilateral arbitration treaties concluded among the states that had taken part in the conferences. Most of these proceedings, including the deposition of documents, took place under the auspices of The Hague.

By the year 1911 the peace movement had reached another peak, with chances for the implementation of the concepts of organizational pacifism greater than at any time before, although the danger of war had also increased proportionally. Already on 20 and 24 June 1910 the American Congress had moved:

> *Resolved*, by the Senate and House of Representatives of the United States of America in Congress assembled, that a commission of five members be appointed by the President of the United States to consider the expediency of utilizing existing agencies for the purpose of limiting the armaments of the nations of the world by international agreement, and of *constituting the combined navies of the world as an international force for the preservation of universal peace*, and to consider and report upon any other means to diminish the expenditures of government for military purposes and to lessen the probabilities of war.[244]

The efforts of the British Foreign Secretary Sir Edward Grey to prevent the outbreak of war are also well known. Shidehara closely observed all these efforts in his official capacity. Since the Second Hague Peace Conference had determined that preparations for the third conference were to commence two years before the projected event in 1914—the event was, however, later postponed to 1915—it was important that Shidehara would be at The Hague at an appropriate time.

On 13 March 1911, in a speech before the House of Commons, Sir Edward Grey called to mind the general benefits of arms reductions and stated the conditions to bring it about: "I can conceive but one thing which will really affect the military and naval expenditure of the world on the wholesale scale on which it must be affected if there is to be real and sure relief. You will not get it until nations do what individuals have done—come to regard an appeal to the law as the natural course for nations instead of an appeal to force." The British foreign minister then went on to name a further condition: "Some armies and navies would remain, no doubt, but they would remain then not in rivalry with each other, but as the police of the world."[245] Grey then quoted from a recent speech by American President William H. Taft:

I do not see any reason why matters of national honor should not be referred to Courts of Arbitration as matters of private or national property are. I know that is going further than most men are willing to go, but I do not see why questions of honor should not be submitted to tribunals composed of men of honor who understand questions of national honor, to abide by their decision as well as in other questions of difference arising between nations.[246]

This was certainly relevant to Japan, and to Shidehara, as it addressed some key concerns for maintaining relations among the powers[247] that could ensure their progress and peace. In July 1911, Foreign Minister Komura Jutarō renewed the British-Japanese Alliance of 1902. It had been intended that Germany, too, should participate in the renewed alliance, but Germany declined. A new cabinet headed by the liberal Saionji Kinmochi was installed in August, with Uchida Yasuya (Kōsai, 1865–1936) replacing Komura as foreign minister. Komura died three months later.

It was only natural that the question of an international executive would also be on the agenda for the third Hague conference. The international law professor at Leyden University, Cornelis van Vollenhoven in the Netherlands, a pacifist, considered the establishment of naval units as being most practicable for an international police force, better than land-based troop contingents,[248] a view shared by the German Walther Schücking. At the end of February 1915, after the war had already begun, a further resolution was introduced in the American Congress, which aimed at "providing a special committee to prepare plans looking to the neutral government and control of the seas." It was planned to get for this purpose the support "of all neutral states" and "possibly of the belligerents" and in this way to provide an impulse toward "arbitration or some other settlement of the present war."[249]

In October 1914, through the initiative of the Dutch organization *Vrede door Recht* (Peace through Law, founded in 1909), the Nederlandse Anti-Oorlog Raad (Netherlands Anti-War Council) was formed, and in April 1915—the same year the Third Hague Peace Conference was to have taken place, the Anti-Oorlog Raad organized an international conference of "neutral countries," which resulted in an international movement of nonbelligerents, in which pacifist circles in the United States, the Netherlands, and Scandinavia were prominent, and which also supported the semiofficial plan for an international police of the seas.[250] It was during this time that Shidehara resided in The Hague—from June 1914 until August 1915—as chief of the Japanese diplomatic representation to the Netherlands and Denmark. Naturally he became acquainted with some of the proponents and their ideas, which were relevant for Japan's future foreign and security policy as well.

During the war various plans for a future worldwide association of nations that would guard the peace of the world were prepared.[251] After the armistice of 11 November 1918, "[a]ll thinking people in Europe and America earnestly sought to establish some kind of international organization in order to prevent a future catastrophe."[252] The universal League of Nations became the rightful successor to the "Hague Confederation," which had already aimed at abolishing war.[253]

For the Allies, obviously, the Peace of Versailles was, though "born of the world war . . . a peace of justice."[254] As the British ambassador in Washington, James Bryce, however, warned in his lectures in August 1921, which Shidehara obviously also had attended or taken notice of, the postwar settlements at Versailles had also created problems, which were so many and so great, and the "list . . . of the dangers which now threaten the peace of the world . . . [being such] a long one," that although no country may be "in a position to resume fighting this year or next year or the year after," if the "fires" are "allowed to smolder long," they "are likely ultimately to break out" once more—that is, if the nations and the League did not proceed to "rake out the embers and quench them with all the water that can be found." And this, in Bryce's opinion, could not be accomplished "without the help of the New World,"[255] a new world that now also included Japan.

On the Japanese side Shidehara had been involved as chairman of the Preparatory Committee between 1916 and 1918 to coordinate plans for the proposed League and postwar settlements. The arrangements of 1919 were shaped by idealist conceptions for a durable peace and, with respect to establishing the principle of sovereign equality, self-determination, and collective security, quite revolutionary. Indeed, the new order created after the First World War brought greater freedom to the peoples of Europe. Wilson had announced on 4 July 1918 in his address at Mount Vernon: "What we seek is the reign of law, based upon the consent of the governed and sustained by the organized opinion of mankind."[256] The Japanese in 1918 also called for a "genuine system of sanctions" to operate after the war.

In Paris, Woodrow Wilson presented his Fourteen Points. An embryonic system of collective security was to guarantee peace among nations. Since the Hague Confederation had not been able to prevent the First World War, the goal was now, after the proclaimed "war to end all wars," to prevent, at all costs, another such catastrophe. A "new type of thinking" marked the years after Versailles. How could the abolition of the institution of war and the related establishment of an institution of law, a "World Court" with an appropriate "code of law," be pushed forward?[257] The Permanent International Court remained an institution outside the League, but it was closely related, and Americans were participating in it.

Like Japan, the United States also had a strong interest in not getting drawn again into a European war.[258] Nevertheless, in March of 1921, after the inauguration of the new president, Warren G. Harding, the American Senate, contrary to expectations, chose not to ratify the League covenant[259] because, among other things, too many senators disapproved of the decision taken by the League Council regarding Japan's occupation of Shandong Province.[260] Also, and perhaps more importantly, for a significant number of senators and representatives, the Versailles agreements had not gone "far enough."[261]

> A few individuals dissented *because the League did not go far enough toward supranational government or even a federation of nations.* Considering the fact that the League to Enforce Peace could not unite internationalists behind a comprehensive plan . . . [so] it is no wonder that the League of Nations divided the peace movement when it came before the United States Senate. *The general idea had been given a stronger base of public support than its specific terms could carry.*[262]

In February 1923, a year after the successful conclusion of the Washington Conference, where Shidehara acted as main speaker on the Japanese side, a resolution was introduced in the American Senate by Senator William Edgar Borah (1865–1940),[263] chairman of the Senate Foreign Relations Committee from 1925–1933. This resolution, which continued to be the object of congressional debates for many years,[264] advocated the abolition of war and aimed at a comprehensive organization that would go beyond the inadequate League of Nations system. Instead of the institution of war, institutions of public law would in future guarantee the peaceful resolution of international disputes and a balance of interests based on the principle that they should be adjudicated in a court of law. The "Borah Resolution" highlighted three points:

> (1.) war between nations should be outlawed as an institution . . . making it a public crime under the law of nations . . . (2.) a code of international law of peace based upon the outlawing of war and on the principle of equality and justice between all nations . . . should be created and adopted . . . (3.) a judicial substitute for war should be created (or, if existing in part, adapted and adjusted) in the form of an international court, modelled on our federal supreme court in its jurisdiction over controversies between our sovereign states; such court shall possess affirmative jurisdiction to hear and decide all purely international controversies, as defined by the code.[265]

A world federation was, according to American progressive thinking, not only desirable but also imperative to secure the economic, political, and social progress of mankind.[266] A precedent to such a solution was seen in the historic coming together of the thirteen original states of the American confederation to create a unified federal state. American democracy had successfully passed its probation in the eyes of history. The unifying of the world under the rule of law was the declared goal for the future. A major problem in these deliberations was the question of "sanctions."

Not only American Christians like Charles Clayton Morrison, publisher of the *Christian Century*, but also broad sectors of the public saw the United States as a champion for the abolition of war.[267] U.S. President Calvin Coolidge frequently advocated in his speeches in the mid-1920s the "outlawry" of war,[268] which became the catchword, notably in the Anglo-Saxon world. These ideas were not new. Their foundations had been laid by William Ladd in the United States, Immanuel Kant in Germany, Jeremy Bentham in England, Victor Hugo in France, and the Enlightenment, which had, it should not be forgotten, received inspiration from the writings and spirit of the Orient.[269] In the course of the economic, political, and cultural "discovery" and opening up of the world, Jeremy Bentham had advocated a global federation that would eventually encompass the entire globe. Victor Hugo (1802–1885), one of the spiritual fathers of the peace movement, at the great Paris Peace Congress in 1849, had outlined a "United States of Europe" and called for the political unification of the diverse peoples of the world, which would make general disarmament possible.[270] A later advocate was British pacifist writer H. G. Wells (1866–1946).[271] All these concepts had a common objective: the abolition of the institution of war, and, as a result, the attainment of the common progress and welfare of mankind.

It was the "spirit of Geneva" of the 1920s that motivated the friends of peace. In 1924 the League of Nations Assembly unanimously approved the "Geneva Protocol." This almost impeccably crafted document with its provisions intended to do away with war worldwide was not, however, ratified the following year due to a change of government in Britain.[272] What little remained of its spirit, however, led to the conclusion of the Locarno Treaties of 1925, which in turn in the early 1930s inspired Japanese proposals for a "Far Eastern Locarno," i.e., a security system for the Pacific region and East Asia in cooperation with the United States, China, France, Great Britain, and the Soviet Union.[273] However, as some Asians have seen it, the European Locarno Pact was the first step leading to the failure of the League of Nations.[274]

The Kellogg-Briand Pact of 1928, outlawing war, was an important milestone in the history of organizational pacifism. The Resolution prepared by Senator Borah which outlawed "war as an instrument of national policy" was first endorsed by the National Grange, a farmers' association with some eight hundred thousand members. Soon "the press and the public were expressing such support for the proposal that the State Department could no longer remain impassive."[275] On 27 January 1927, Secretary of State Frank B. Kellogg presented a "Declaration of American Policy" in which he declared the initiative for outlawing war—the draft had been completed with French collaboration—

to be a prime goal of American foreign policy. Presently Britain supported the initiative, though with some reservations.[276] After further deliberations with French Foreign Minister Aristide Briand, the Kellogg-Briand Treaty, or Pact of Paris, as it came to be known, was signed on 27 August 1928, first by nine countries, including Germany (represented by Gustav Stresemann) and Japan (represented by Uchida Kōsai). The Soviet Union and China both joined in 1931. When the Second World War broke out in 1939, a total of sixty-four nations—practically all the world's sovereign states—had signed on.

Why did the League of Nations' system of collective security fail, in spite of the fact that the peace of 1919 had been, not only in the view of a good number of Americans, "a peace of justice and of freedom"?[277] Although the United States had not joined the League, it had followed a foreign policy in consonance with the "principles of international justice"[278] to effectively contribute to the maintenance of a lasting peace. The League machinery, however, meaning to secure the progress of mankind, possessed no enforcement powers; there was no mechanism to equip the organization with real competencies to adequately guarantee member states' peace and security. The people involved in trying to create a "world without war," men like Aristide Briand, Shidehara Kijūrō, William Edgar Borah, and Frank B. Kellogg, in time came to see their enlightened policies fail. The British historian R. B. McCallum writes:

> But those who refused to believe that a sufficient number of the nations of the world would ever combine in positive action to prevent war passed very quickly into supposing that the League did not even imply an attempt at realizing such a policy. They chose to consider that the creators and advocates of the League were all pacifists, people who thought that aggression could be conjured away without force.[279]

This was quite to the point, since obviously collective security could not function effectively, if nation-states did not agree to limitations of their national sovereignty in favor of the world organization, and pool their resources to form a world executive that would also enable nations to disarm to a required minimum—a subject that had been debated since the Hague peace conferences. There was a lesson to be learned; a new legal paradigm was to emerge meant to compel national lawmakers to take action.

When the Second World War started in Europe in September 1939, Professor James T. Shotwell (1874–1965), a historian of Canadian-American origin who taught at Columbia University, founded the "Commission to Study the Organization of Peace." Numerous antiwar groups came into being in the United States, many of them backed by the Federal Council of Churches, the Church Peace Union, the Carnegie Endowment for International Peace, the League of

Nations Society, and the Council on Foreign Relations. A committee to study questions of peace was established in the State Department.[280] In the spring of 1940, at the annual conference of the American Academy of Political and Social Science in Philadelphia, American and European academics, historians, and scholars met to discuss "The United States and Durable Peace." At issue were not only the possible entry into the war of the United States and its foreseeable consequences,[281] but also, and most importantly, the question of the constitution of the envisaged postwar global association of nations. Which institutions in the League of Nations system should be modified, and which principles ought to be retained? With the Japanese *de facto* capture of northeastern China, the Italian "adventure" in Abyssinia (Ethiopia), the *Anschluss* (annexation) of Austria, the German *Einverleibung* (incorporation) of Czechoslovakia, and finally the German attack on Poland and the beginning of the Second World War, the international order had collapsed. Academics and pacifists wanted to find answers.

The Philadelphia conference participants unanimously agreed that those institutions of the League of Nations system that had proven their worth should continue to operate after the war: the International Labour Organization (ILO), the humanitarian, social, and cultural institutions, the council, the assembly, and the secretariat, as well as an international court.[282] The task was to ensure the effectiveness of the future world organization without imposing a preordained order.

In contrast, the fascist powers had organized themselves in the 1930s to order international relations according to ideological and racial concepts. The principle of self-determination was considered redundant and replaced by the "leader principle" (*Führerprinzip*).[283] As the forces of fascism turned *against* law and order to take recourse to violence, they placed themselves in an *a priori* unjustifiable position. Fascism did not seek to eliminate injustices but posit itself as the measure of all things, to arbitrarily rule over others. The Axis Powers rejected the ideas of organizational pacifism that had essentially shaped Allied policy. In Japan Shidehara's foreign policy was bypassed. Wilhelm Grewe's assessment of this situation is questionable (in the chapter "League of Nations and the Kellogg-Briand Pact as Instruments of the Anglo-American Condominium"). Grewe writes:

> At the same time that the new Great Power formation of Germany indicated the existence of a counter-system directed against the Anglo-American world order, it turned out that this counter-system, too, had a similar structure. It centered around two focal points: Berlin-Rome and Tokyo.[284]

Liberal statesmen and intellectuals like Walther Schücking, Wilhelm Solf, Matthias Erzberger (1975–1921), and others in Germany had also advocated a binding international arbitration system and wished to abolish war as a legal institution.[285] Grewe does not recognize that by equating the two systems, he denounces not only the strong pacifist elements of the Anglo-Saxon, the French, Scandinavian, East Asian, and also Indian and Latin American political cultures, but those in Germany, too. These were expressions of a truly humanistic and universalistic tradition aimed at putting a stop to war and the use of force as an instrument of policy. The "counter-system" might have been similarly *structured*, but the "structural violence" that now spread all over the world destroyed, in its blind zeal, those structures which organizational pacifism, in the course of its laborious and carefully crafted work, had been erecting.

JAPAN IN THE LEAGUE OF NATIONS

"Justice, not force, governs international relations."

Yomiuri Shimbun, 19 February 1919

Edwin O. Reischauer (1910–1990), the great American scholar born in Japan, and one-time ambassador there, wrote in 1974 about the period before the Second World War:

The Japanese, claiming equality with China and in contact with all of the other units of East Asia . . . came closest to the Western concept of international relations, but could hardly develop a family of nations without reciprocity from the others.[286]

The entry of Japan onto the world diplomatic stage had brought radical and revolutionary changes not only for Japan. Many Japanese had entertained the idea that to withstand the impact of the West, their country would have to become a match economically and militarily, and perhaps with China and Korea by its side. If in its foreign policy Japan sought to achieve a prosperous and peaceful order in Asia, in concert with the Western powers, it upheld the institution of war endorsed by international law to counter the challenges inherent in the Western-dominated international setting and in order to consolidate its position in Asia—to be better able, if necessary, to defend its interests. It is understandable that Japan wished to have a part in collective security, and to cooperate in the various Western plans and endeavors aimed at building up a comprehensive economic, political, and social order at the European and global levels,[287] an international order from which it hoped to profit in material ways.[288] Japan felt itself called upon to make a contribution in ways that would fit its particular identity, on the grounds of its historical experience and geographical position. A policy of isolation was not an option.[289]

It had been a long and arduous path toward fully equal membership in the society of nations. The Japanese victory in the war with China and in the Russo-Japanese War had established for Japan a position of predominance in Asia and satisfied the Japanese need for security by removing ambiguities in its foreign relations and reducing the Russian-European threat potential. For the first time a European great power had been put in its place.[290] Though the annexation of Korea in 1910 had somehow detracted from Japan's high standing, Japan later in significant ways, as a partner of the Western allies in the First World War, consolidated its position in the international arena.

With the Republican Revolution in China in 1911, and the fall of the Manchu (Qing) Dynasty, it had seemed for a time as if the progressive political forces in Japan and China might work in tandem:

> Japan was alike the model of the Ch'ing government reformers and (until about 1907) the home base for anti-Ch'ing revolutionaries. Republican China went to school in Tōkyō. . . . *In fact, the revolution of 1911 was largely made in Japan* . . . Japan's influence in this brief period was more direct, profound, and far-reaching than that of Britain in the nineteenth century or of the United States from 1915 to 1949, or even one may suspect of the Soviet Union after 1949. One reason for this was Japan's much closer cultural as well as geographical propinquity. Another reason was the historical circumstance that, in this dawn of their modern age, China was most eager to learn and Japan most eager to teach, as yet without serious conflicts of national interest.[291]

There were other noteworthy events around the year 1911, apart from the foundation of the Chinese Republic: the First Universal Races Congress in London (1911), the general broadening of the international organization that now included the independent sovereign states of Asia and South America,[292] the efforts of the United States,[293] Great Britain, and France[294] to establish an international legal order, and the preparation for the Third Hague Peace Conference scheduled for 1914/1915.[295]

The First Universal Races Congress convened at the University of London (26–29 July) also discussed some of the questions that Japan later brought forward at the Versailles Peace Conference. Although it was not a peace congress "in the sense of aiming specifically at the prevention of war,"[296] the object was "to discuss, in the light of science and the modern conscience, the general relations subsisting between the peoples of the West and those of the East, between so-called white and so-called coloured peoples, with a view to encouraging between them a fuller understanding, the most friendly feelings, and a heartier co-operation."[297] Around twenty civilizations were present on that occasion,[298] statesmen,[299] religious figures, and other personages from fifty countries, some of "the most brilliant representatives of the intellectual culture of the Hindus, the [American] Indians, the negroes of America and South Africa, the Turks, Persians, Japanese, Chinese, Egyptians, etc." [300] The congress was followed with special attention also in Japan. The spokesmen for the Japanese attendees were Takebe Tongo (1871–1945), professor of sociology at the Imperial University of Tokyo, his colleague Kobayashi Teruaki, and Katō Genchi (1873–1965), lecturer on the science of religion at the Imperial University of Tokyo, who led a session on Shintoism. In Walther Schücking's opinion, "the entire event was permeated with the spirit of modern organizational pacifism,"[301] and naturally the Japanese too had high hopes that their interests would be recognized.

Shidehara's official duties as chief of the Information Bureau of the Ministry of Foreign Affairs between 1904 and 1911 included the preparation and following of the proceedings of the Second Hague Peace Conference. He studied Western legal philosophy and treaty law under Henry Willard Denison (1846–1914), the American who served as legal advisor (*hōritsu komon*) in Japan's Ministry of Foreign Affairs.[302] An assignment in Washington between September 1912 and December 1913 led Shidehara to discuss the California legislation that discriminated against Japanese immigrants.[303] Returning via London,[304] where he again met James Bryce (1838–1922), the one-time teacher of his law professor at Tokyo Imperial University,[305] whom he first got to know around the year 1900, he proceeded to The Hague. In June 1914 he took up his post as minister for the Netherlands and Denmark, which lasted until September 1915. His diplomatic missions abroad between 1912 and 1915 found him in diplomatic circles where the ideas of organizational pacifism were being debated as a rational option for a permanent world peace. A keen observer, who spoke impeccable English, and besides had a wide circle of friends among diplomats, Shidehara comported himself skillfully on the diplomatic stage. From October 1918 until his appointment as Minister of Foreign Affairs in June 1924, his name was on the list of judges for the Permanent Court of Arbitration in The Hague.

Shidehara was well acquainted with the plans and ideas that revolved around the founding of a "League of Nations." Back in Tokyo, in early 1916, as vice foreign minister he secured the chairmanship of the preparatory committee for what would become the Versailles Peace Conference. Some of the most important materials he had at hand were the British parliamentary group's reports and those by League of Nations advocates grouped around James Bryce (the "Bryce Group"), who had begun their work in 1914,[306] as well as the documents prepared by Theodore Marburg, who had together with journalist Hamilton Holt founded the American League to Enforce Peace.[307] The "Preparatory Committee for the Making of Peace following the Japanese-German War" (*Nichi-Doku sen'eki kōwa junbi iinkai*) eventually, however, did not put forward any proposal for a League of Nations of its own,[308] while the continental Europeans and the Americans developed different concepts. The Americans, having entered the war on a pledge to put an end to wars once and for all, sought to take the initiative. Not only in the United States, but also in Japan, many saw the questions under discussion as a European problem, which the Europeans had not been able to appropriately deal with. And besides, the Japanese had their own problems closer to home. All the same, the Japanese contribution to the Versailles Peace Conference, which Shidehara took a part in preparing and later on did his best to uphold, was significant, as Japan was a founding member of the League.

Japan had asserted its position in East Asia—in an imperialist context, no doubt—and, having come out of the First World War as a victor, was set to help create stable conditions in the region. Shidehara evaluated the League of Nations in a more realistic way, like many of his American friends. The question of racial equality was, for the Japanese, closely linked to the question of freedom of trade—including Japanese trade in the European colonies. Despite the failure of the Japanese proposal to include a provision on racial equality in the League covenant, Shidehara was determined to uphold and defend the idealism of the League, like his older colleague Nitobe Inazō.

When the armistice of 11 November 1918 at last brought to the world the peace it had been yearning for, the responsible forces "in Europe and America earnestly sought to establish some kind of international organization in order to prevent a future catastrophe."[309] In Japan, on the very day of the European armistice, the "Political Affairs Bureau" (*seimukyoku*) in the foreign ministry presented a six-page report in which "three conditions" for the success of an international organization after the war were named: (1) its general endorsement by the world's political leaders; (2) the readiness of states "to accept restrictions on their behavior"; and (3) "a viable system of sanctions." The report further identified five "issues of concern to Japan": (a) arms limitations/disarmament; (b) "economic opportunity: . . . opening of the closed economic systems created by the colonial powers"; (c) compatibility of the League of Nations principles with bilateral agreements such as, for example, the Anglo-Japanese Alliance; (d) the limitation of national sovereignty; and (e) the question of Germany's membership. The report at the same time prophesied that the League of Nations would probably have difficulties in reaching its high-placed goals.[310]

On 19 November 1918, Foreign Minister Uchida Kōsai (Yasuya, 1865–1936) gave his agreement to the report, but added further thoughts: "The persistence of narrow racial attitudes among nations casts doubt upon the feasibility of the League's goals and creates the possibility that its establishment will be disadvantageous to the Empire."[311] On 30 November, the chief of the European Section of the Bureau for Political Affairs, Komura Ken'ichi, presented a memorandum in which he urged: (1) Japan must strive for acceptance of the principle of equal treatment; (2) Japan must promote an active world peace policy and a conciliatory foreign policy; and (3) Japan must fundamentally revise its arrogant China policy. Regarding point 3, the memorandum went on to say that Japan should grasp the initiative in the abolishment of extraterritoriality and spheres of special interests in continental China, should cancel the indemnity payments accruing to Japan for its part in militarily suppressing the "Boxer Rebellion" of 1899–1900, should pull out all its troops from China, and should support the four-power financial consortium proposed by the United States.[312] A few days later, Makino Nobuaki, who had been appointed plenipotentiary at the Versailles Peace Conference, took up Komura's proposals at a meeting of the *Gaikō Chōsakai*. Foreign Minister Uchida agreed in all points. At a further meeting of the *Gaikō Chōsakai* on 8 December, the idea of a League of Nations was formally approved,[313] although during the preparations for the Japanese participation in the peace conference, domestic political tensions between the conservative *Gaikō Chōsakai* (Committee on Foreign Relations), founded in 1917, and the "internationalist" camp had surfaced. The latter had disapproved of the Siberian Expedition during the war and stood for a policy of nonintervention.[314]

On 18 January 1919, the French prime minister, Georges Clemenceau, who had been minister of war under President Raymond Poincaré, opened the Peace Conference in the Paris Ministry of Foreign Affairs with seventy delegates from the twenty-seven countries on the winning side of the 1914–1918 war. On 25 January the conference approved the establishing of a League of Nations "to promote international cooperation, to insure the fulfillment of accepted international obligations and to provide safeguards against war."[315]

The Covenant of the League of Nations formed the first part of the peace treaties of the Entente with the German empire, Austria, Bulgaria, Hungary, and Turkey, who had lost the war.[316] The League of Nations Committee thus was set to "work out the details of the constitution and functions of the League," under the chairmanship of the American president, Woodrow Wilson.[317] On 3 February 1919 it met for the first time. The Japanese delegation, officially led by *genrō* Saionji Kinmochi, consisted of eighty members; however, due to ill health Saionji was unable to take part in the early sessions of the conference.

The top representatives besides Saionji were Baron Makino Nobuaki (1861–1949), who (like Saionji) also arrived late in the French capital and became the main speaker, the ambassador in London Chinda Sutemi (1856–1929), and the ambassador in France Matsui Keishirō (1868–1946). Though outwardly reserved in negotiations, Saionji "was an active and significant participant in the internal workings of the Japanese delegation."[318] A committed advocate of the League idea, he believed that the spread of culture would secure world peace, and thus disarmament and "cooperative diplomacy" were the realistic options.[319]

Three drafts, one Anglo-American, one French, and one Italian, were laid before the committee for consideration.[320] Baron Makino apologized that Japan had prepared no draft of its own to put forward, although already in October 1914, Foreign Minister Katō Takaaki (Kōmei, 1860–1926) had entrusted the head of the Bureau for Political Affairs in the Ministry of Foreign Affairs, Nagaoka Shun'ichi, with the tasks of compiling materials relating to the future peace and studying historical precedents.[321] Shidehara, in the beginning phase of the Versailles negotiations, and until he became ambassador in Washington in early 1919, remained in close contact with the Japanese delegation and acted as an intermediary between Tokyo and Paris.

On 14 February, the Anglo-American draft, representing "the concepts and movements concerning peace that had developed in various countries as a result of self-examination regarding World War I,"[322] was adopted by the committee for its deliberations at Versailles. By 11 April the committee's work was completed, and the final text was laid before the conference on 28 April, which was subsequently unanimously approved. The league's headquarters were to be in Geneva. In spite of its unanimous approval, the League of Nations was a compromise.[323]

In the debates the Japanese had been committed to three areas: disarmament, arbitration, and racial equality. On the other hand there were the "demands": (1) an extension of the Japanese occupation of Jiaozhou, and (2) the taking over of the former German Pacific islands, which Japan had occupied in 1914.

The Japanese were frequently seen as "silent partners of the Conference," yet they "never lost sight of a single angle in the discussion."[324] David G. Egler describes the Japanese commitment to the League: "Some optimistic intellectuals of the 'Taishō democracy' school openly heralded the coming league as the touchstone of human progress . . . Western influenced diplomats in the foreign ministry . . . promoted Japanese participation as a means to assure cooperative relations with the Anglo-American powers."[325] Among early strong supporters immediately after the war were eminent intellectuals like Yoshino Sakuzō and Anesaki Masaharu, and labor leader Suzuki Bunji.[326] In spite of that an attitude of skepticism prevailed,[327] since the League of Nations was seen by many as a European affair (with Europe being at the heart of the problem), and a possible instrument for maintaining the status quo in Asia.[328]

Japan had previously, in its declaration of war against Germany (23 August 1914), emphasized that its interest was above all the continuation of free trade, which Germany appeared to jeopardize, as well as the general peace in East Asia. Naturally, the alliance with Great Britain being key to Japanese foreign policy and security, this provided another "reason why Japan participated in this war."[329]

Japan took part in the Versailles Peace Conference as a new military industrial power (i.e., one of the "Big Five")—together with the United States, Great Britain, France, and Italy. In September 1918 Uchida Kōsai became foreign minister in the civilian cabinet of Hara Kei (Takashi). The Japanese delegates at the peace conference were thus all civilian, liberal statesmen of the "Anglo-Saxon faction."[330] Moreover, the Japanese delegates comported themselves not as debutants, but as experienced diplomats.[331]

Although Baron Makino, the delegation spokesman, spoke little English, the Japanese effected a change in the wording of article 8 of the League Covenant, approved on 3 February 1919: "The Members of the League recognize that the maintenance of peace requires the reduction of national armaments to the lowest point consistent with *national safety* and the enforcement by common action of international obligations." The Japanese had proposed the words "national safety" instead of the earlier "domestic safety" and thus added clarity when it came to questions of disarmament.[332]

On the question of arbitration for the peaceful settlement of disputes and the moratorium, which was of special interest to the conference, Japan proposed to supplement certain wording to article 12—that is, the arbitration clause submitted by Woodrow Wilson to the League of Nations Committee at its first meeting on 3 February 1919, which read:

1. The High Contracting Parties agree that should disputes arise between them which cannot be adjusted by the ordinary processes of diplomacy, they will in no case resort to war without previously submitting the questions and matters involved either to arbitration or inquiry by the Executive Council three months after the award by the arbitrators or a recommendation by the Executive Council; and that they will not even then resort to war as against a member of the League which complies with the award of the arbitrators or the recommendation of the Executive Council.

2. In any case under this Article, the award of the arbitrators shall be made within a reasonable time, and the recommendation of the Executive Council shall be made within six months after the submission of the dispute.[333]

Baron Makino proposed adding the following words at the end of the second paragraph:

From the time a dispute is submitted to arbitration or to inquiry by the Executive Council, and until the lapse of the aforesaid term of three months, the parties to the dispute shall refrain from making any military preparations.[334]

This amendment, however, was not approved, when on 11 April 1919, at the fifteenth and last session of the committee, the Japanese initiative was discussed, at which time the British delegate Lord Robert Cecil pointed out difficulties which might arise if the Japanese amendment were adopted, saying:

> Such a provision would give an important advantage to such States as maintained their military establishment in a highly developed state. Should a crisis arise, the small and peaceful nations with a low military establishment would find themselves at a serious disadvantage if they could not make use of the period of three months in order to prepare a better defence against a nation with superior armaments and effectives.

Baron Makino said in reply:

> The whole spirit of the Covenant was opposed to the principle that nations might make military preparations in a crisis. If they should undertake warlike measures, a tense and anxious atmosphere would be created which would hardly conduce to a peaceful settlement. Moreover, if the nation whose military preparations were inadequate should augment them, the better armed nation would do the same and the discrepancy between the two military forces would remain the same.

Lord Cecil, to defend his argument, put forth a hypothetical case as follows:

> Suppose that an unscrupulous nation should be considering an attack against a neighboring State. She mobilizes all her troops, amasses them on the frontier, and thereupon starts a dispute of a nature calculated to lead to a rupture. The dispute would then be submitted to arbitration,[335] and while the case was being examined the aggressor State would have all its forces ready for action. On the other hand, the State which was threatened would not be able to take any preparatory measures. As far as Naval Power was concerned, a State might quite easily without violating Article 8 mobilize its fleet with a view to aggression.

The British delegate thus concluded: "The Japanese amendment would therefore seem to impose obligations too great for human nature and to put tremendous advantages into the hands of unscrupulous States."[336] Instructions from Tokyo must have shaped Makino's proposal, and to that extent Shidehara and possibly Denison's hand in formulating the contents would have been decisive.

Lord Cecil's view was shared by the French delegates Ferdinand Larnaude and Léon Bourgeois, the Serbian delegate Milenko Vesnić, the Portuguese delegate Jayme Batalha Reis, and the Chinese delegate Wellington Koo (Gu Weijun). The Italian delegate Vittorio Emanuele Orlando backed the Japanese initiative, saying it was "unquestionably in harmony with the spirit of the Covenant." Woodrow Wilson himself seemed to back Lord Cecil's view in that he felt the majority of the member states would not welcome the "inconveniences which would arise if it were incorporated," although he admitted he had "a sentimental interest in the Japanese amendment." Thereupon Japan retracted its proposal.

However, it was the much disputed Japanese motion to adopt an article in the League covenant to stipulate racial equality that presented a dramatic climax, which "was said to be one of the most impressive proposals taken up during the whole peace conference."[337] The chief motivation for the Japan's initiative was its aspiration, as a trading nation, to be recognized as an equal partner in African and Asian regions that were under European colonial rule, so as to freely pursue its commercial activities in these areas. In contrast, as the Japanese were well aware, Germans could trade freely in the colonies and even had positions in directorates of banking and business conglomerates, especially in the British Commonwealth.[338]

We have seen, when Shidehara was residing as Japan's chief diplomatic representative to the Netherlands and Denmark in The Hague, in October 1914, the Nederlandse "Anti-Oorlog Raad" (Anti-War Council) was founded at the initiative of the Dutch organization "Vrede door Recht" (Peace through Law). Subsequently, from 7–12 April 1915, an international peace conference, sponsored by the Anti-Oorlog Raad, took place in The Hague. Shidehara must have witnessed the event; most likely he took part in some of the proceedings and discussed the pertinent issues with the participants. He was well acquainted with the Netherlands foreign minister, Dr. John Loudon, who had been ambassador in Tokyo in 1907 (i.e., the year of the Second Hague Peace Conference), and whom he had no doubt met again in 1913 in Washington.[339] Loudon, like his colleague, the Dutch jurist and diplomat Cornelis van Vollenhoven, emphasized Grotius's ideas on international security, which aimed "to organize for peace the whole society of mankind."[340] Hugo Grotius had warned against going to war, even for a just cause.[341] At the April 1915 peace conference in The Hague, a "Minimum Program" was adopted, which stated in point 2:

The states are to agree to enforce, in their colonies, protectorates and spheres of interest, freedom of trade or at least the equality of all nations.[342]

Soon after Shidehara had left The Hague in September 1915, he returned to Japan, where he took over the chairmanship of the Commission for the Making of the Peace following the Japanese-German War (*Nichi-Doku sen'eki kōwa junbi iinkai*).[343] The Japanese proposal on racial equality of 7 February

1919, based on the foreign ministry's instructions dated 9 December 1918,[344] therefore came as no surprise, and was well premeditated. Without the Hague precedent it is unlikely that Japan would have exposed itself as it did at Versailles. The Japanese proposal read:

> The equality of nations being a basic principle of the League of Nations, the High Contracting Parties agree to accord, as soon as possible, to all alien nationals of States members to the League equal and just treatment in every respect, making no distinction, either in law or in fact, on account of their race or nationality.

At first the Americans appeared to react positively and even proposed to present the article themselves, with a few minor emendations. However, the British delegation was not of one mind since Britain had to take account of its dominions, which followed their own policies on racial questions and matters of immigration. The Australian prime minister, William Hughes, voted against the Japanese proposal.[345] The two spokesmen of the Japanese delegation, Makino and Chinda,[346] therefore made assurances that the adoption of the racial equality clause was not meant to entail unrestricted immigration allowances for the Japanese. An ardent campaign on the part of the Japanese to soften William Hughes's determined opposition began.[347]

David Hunter Miller, Woodrow Wilson's legal advisor, reports on a conversation that took place on 9 February 1919 between Wilson's personal advisor "Colonel" House and Balfour:[348]

> Colonel House called me in and talked to me about the Japanese proposal. While I was discussing it Mr. Balfour came in. There was a general discussion of the matter between Colonel House and Mr. Balfour. Colonel House handed me a pencil memorandum which he showed to Mr. Balfour, commencing with the proposition taken from the Declaration of Independence, that all men are created equal.[349]

Balfour is said to have replied that the American Declaration of Independence was a document of the eighteenth century, and though it was true "in a certain sense that *all men of a particular nation were created equal*," he disputed that "*a man in Central Africa was created equal to a European*." Colonel House countered "that he did not see how the policy toward the Japanese could be continued. The world said that they could not go to Africa; they could not go to any white country; they could not go to China, and they could not go to Siberia; and yet they were a growing nation, having a country where all the land was tilled; they had to go somewhere."[350]

The Japanese proposal on the racial question was again discussed on 13 February, at the tenth session, in connection with a proposal on religious freedom. Baron Makino pointed out that *"racial and religious animosities have constituted a fruitful source of trouble and warfare among different peoples throughout history, often leading to deplorable excesses,"*[351] and he now proposed that the article on religious freedom be supplemented with exactly the same clause as previously suggested, i.e.:

> The equality of nations being a basic principle of the League of Nations, the High Contracting Parties agree to accord, as soon as possible, to all alien nationals of States members to the League equal and just treatment in every respect, making no distinction, either in law or in fact, on account of their race or nationality.[352]

Makino pointed out that in the war just ended the various races had struggled against a common enemy to achieve a common objective, and that according to the League Covenant nations were obligated to stand by one another against a possible aggressor: "[E]ach national would like to feel and in fact demand that he should be placed on an equal footing with people he undertakes to defend even with his life." Wellington Koo openly sympathized with the Japanese proposal. Eventually, however, the committee accepted Lord Cecil's motion to adjourn.

The Japanese government meanwhile made every effort to come to an understanding with the Western powers. Japan's ambassador to the United States, Viscount Ishii Kikujirō, sent the State Department a note, as President Wilson prepared for Europe on 4 March 1919, stating *inter alia*:

> The Japanese Government are much gratified to perceive the just and disinterested spirit in which the President is using his best endeavors to secure an enduring peace of the world. They also are sincerely grateful for the sympathy and support which the President and the American peace delegation were friendly enough to give to the proposition of the Japanese delegation on the question of doing away with race discriminations. In view of the fundamental spirit of the League of Nations the Japanese Government regards as of first importance the establishment of the principle that the difference of race should in no case constitute a basis for discriminatory treatment under the law of any country. Should this great principle fail of general recognition, the Japanese Government do not see how a perpetual friction and discontent among nations and races could possibly be eliminated.[353]

On 14 March 1919, Ambassador Ishii spoke on the subject in New York. To placate Prime Minister Hughes, the Japanese, following Colonel House's advice, proposed a somewhat shortened text for the covenant's preamble. Although the South African General Smuts and Sir R. Borden now declared themselves in favor, they could not move the Australian prime minister. On

11 April, the last session held by the commission, Baron Makino merely suggested adding to the words "relations between nations" in the preamble the phrase "by the endorsement of the principle of equality of nations and just treatment of their nationals." The Chinese delegate Wellington Koo backed the Japanese initiative, declaring:

> I should be very glad to see the principle itself given recognition in the Covenant, and I hope that the Commission will not find serious difficulties in the way of its acceptance. I should like to have my statement appear in the Minutes.[354]

Delegates from Italy (Orlando), France (Bourgeois and Larnaude), Greece (Venizelos), Czechoslovakia (Kramar), and Poland (Dmowski), some of whom had previously voted against the clause on 13 February, now also backed the Japanese initiative. Lord Cecil regretted that he could not vote for the proposal though "the British Government realized the importance of the racial question," arguing that "its solution could not be attempted by the Commission without encroaching upon the sovereignty" of member States.[355] In his reply, Viscount Chinda referred to the negative effects that a rejection of the Japanese proposal would have on public opinion in Japan.[356]

Indeed, the agitation in Japan, nourished by press reports about the dispute, had reached a high point. At that moment President Wilson ruled that the principle of unanimity be adopted for the vote, and the amendment was finally rejected by a vote of seventeen to eleven. Naturally this was a "bitter blow to the Japanese psyche,"[357] which may well have cleared the stage for future discrimination and genocide in the twentieth century. However, Japan was now able to gain concessions with regard to the administration of the territories formerly leased by China to Germany around Jiaozhou Bay and elsewhere in Shandong Province.[358] In his written report to the Japanese emperor, Saionji stated:

> I am sad that we could not accomplish our wishes in total. . . . Over racial equality, we had ten private discussions with British and American delegates. . . . Although we put up a good fight in the Committee on the League covenant there was persistent opposition from the British colonies and Anglo-American delegates finally went back on their earlier acceptance. What more could we do? The Japanese delegate announced that Japan would raise this problem again at the 5th plenary Assembly, made clear our standpoint and left the decision to a later date . . . Japan stands among the five great Powers in the world and has passed the threshold which allows her to take part in the affairs of Europe. Again, we have been granted an important place in the League of Nations and acquired the right to take part in future more and more in every aspect of the affairs of east and west. This . . . can be said that we can identify a new turning-point in Japan's history.[359]

Among the critics and opponents of the League of Nations was "a young bureaucrat of the Interior Ministry with the name Konoe Fumimaro" (1891–1945),[360] who had been "Saionji's choice of personal secretary"[361] at the Versailles conference, and who published an article with the title "*Ei-Bei hon'i no heiwashugi o haisu*" (Rejecting the pacifism represented by England and America) in the 15 December 1918 issue of the nationalistic periodical *Nippon oyobi Nipponjin* (Japan and the Japanese), in which he wrote of Versailles and the League of Nations:

> The peace that the Anglo-American leaders are urging upon us amounts to no more that maintaining a status quo that suits their interests. . . . The true nature of the present conflict is a struggle between the established powers and powers not yet established. . . . The former call for peace, and the latter cry for war. In this case pacifism does not necessarily coincide with justice and humanity.[362]

Young Konoe warned:

> In the coming peace conference, should we decide to join the League of Nations, we must demand as the minimum *sine qua non* the eradication of economic imperialism and discriminatory treatment of Asian peoples by Caucasians. Militarism is not the only force that violates justice and humanity. . . . Should the peace conference fail to suppress this rampant economic imperialism . . . Japan, which is small, resource-poor and unable to consume all its own industrial products, would have no resort but to destroy the status quo for the sake of self-preservation, just like Germany . . . we must reject economic imperialism. . . . We must require all the powers to open the doors of their colonies to others, so that all nations will have equal access to the markets and resources of the colonial areas. It is also imperative that Japan insist on the eradication of racial discrimination. At the coming peace conference we must demand this in the name of justice and humanity. Indeed the peace conference will provide the opportunity to determine whether or not the human race is capable of reforming the world on those principles.[363]

Not only Konoe, but also most politically awake Japanese believed that a world order founded on justice[364] would end racial discrimination between nations and respect Japan's special interests in Manchuria. Thus Konoe's critique gained momentum as a result of Japan's failure to get the "race equality" clause accepted.[365] Military men like Ugaki Kazushige (1868–1956), an influential general who became army minister and was for a short time in 1938 foreign minister, also saw the League of Nations as a pretext for the Anglo-American policy of maintaining a status quo among the world powers.

It was only natural, since Japan's wish for equal treatment remained unfulfilled, that the focus of interest necessarily shifted to nearby areas, to enhance Japan's economy, trade, and industry. The decision taken at Versailles not to make concessions on the Shandong question thus was understandable. The Japanese no doubt felt the Europeans were presumptuous in claiming privileges for themselves that they did not wish to afford to others. What purpose did it serve Japan to take part in an organization that was unable or unwilling to grant the people of Asia equal standing in their own region?

Shidehara may have shared the views of many Americans that the League of Nations did not go far enough in providing for an effective administration of justice, and organization of peace, which could guarantee equal treatment and opportunities, and would oftentimes have preferred bilateral, rather than multilateral, agreements with China. An official report from the European and American division of the Japanese Ministry of Foreign Affairs stated:

> It will be very much to our disadvantage to have our fate decided at this sort of a large round table discussion rather than in direct negotiations with a party whose interests are involved. I would prefer [the League proposal] go unrealized. But since it is likely to come about, there is no alternative but to align with world trends and give it serious consideration.[366]

Indeed, Japan threatened to leave the Versailles Conference if its demands for concessions on the mainland were not fulfilled. Shidehara on this point had to follow the line of his government. The majority of the conference's council of the "Big Ten,"[367] and especially the Americans, were negative toward the Japanese wish to take over the former German concessions in Shandong. Around the end of April instructions arrived from Tokyo that the Japanese delegation should not sign the League covenant if the unconditional transfer of Qingdao to Japan was not granted. This proved effective. Even President Wilson was convinced and took the threat seriously: "They are no bluffers, and they will go home unless we give them what they should not have."[368]

The Japanese demands in regard to Shandong were, however, only partly fulfilled, and only after Saionji made a call on French President Georges Clemenceau (1841–1929), an old friend from his student days in Paris,[369] and persuaded him that Japan harbored no unfair intentions on the mainland. Clemenceau was then able, at the next foreign ministers' meeting, to win Wilson over to the Japanese position on the basis of the assurance that Saionji had given that Japan would return Shandong to China at an agreed-upon time.[370] This, however (i.e., the conference's decision to transfer to Japan the German rights in Shandong), in turn led to China's refusal to sign the treaty.[371]

Japan, together with the other powers, signed the Versailles Treaty on 28 June 1919 as one of the five permanent members of the League Council.[372]

With the transfer to Japan of former German rights in Shandong and the Pacific islands north of the equator, Japan became (with respect to the latter) a "mandatory power" in the League of Nations system for the protection and development of these territories. Nitobe Inazō accepted the influential post of the League's under-secretary general.[373] Although Japan was geographically far from Europe, it had a paramount interest in the peace of Europe, sensitive to the fact that a European conflict, as Adachi Mineichirō pointed out, "might, according to the circumstances, entail consequences dangerous to world peace."[374] Adachi (1869–1934) was an international jurist who had played an important role in the discussions that had taken place in the legal division of the Ministry of Foreign Affairs in connection with the League. Later, in 1930, as successor to Oda Yorozu (1868–1945), he became a judge on the Permanent International Court of Justice at The Hague where he also served for three years, until his death, as its president.

Japan would also play a leading role in the Washington Conference on Naval Limitation (1921–1922) and in the Kellogg-Briand Pact on the outlawry of war (1928), as well as in the London Naval Disarmament Conference of 1930. The Kellogg-Briand Pact of 1928, which Japan was one of the first nations to sign, represented a milestone in the development of the international law of peace. U.S. Secretary of State Henry Lewis Stimson (1867–1950) assessed the importance of the Washington treaties and the Kellogg-Briand Pact in a letter to his longtime friend, U.S. Senator William Edgar Borah (1865–1940):

> These two treaties represent independent but harmonious steps taken for the purpose of aligning the conscience and public opinion of the world in favor of a system of orderly development by the law of nations including the settlement of all controversies by methods of justice and peace instead of arbitrary force.[375]

The Kellogg-Briand Pact notwithstanding, Japan's military under Tanaka Giichi as prime minister in 1928 got involved in the Liaodong Leased Territory trying to forcefully regulate political affairs in the region. It was too tempting, as the conspiracy of Japanese military officers in the so-called Manchurian Incident in September 1931 would show, to resort to the use of force to ensure the Japanese interests on the Asian mainland, since "a vast semi-colonial territory as large as France and Germany combined" only waited to be exploited; the "creation of puppet states and buffer states has been a well-recognized tactic of nineteenth century imperialism." The editors of the Proceedings of the Fifth Conference of the Institute of Pacific Relations (IPR), held in Banff, Canada, in 1933, referring to China's Three Eastern Provinces plus those parts of "Inner Mongolia" that were included in the new state of "Manchukuo" (proclaimed 1932), observed that there had "never been a puppet of such gigantic dimensions and of such potential wealth and economic importance as the newly formed state in Manchuria."[376]

To resolve the dilemma that the "independence" of Manchukuo had created for Japan's international relations, in August 1933 Professors Takagi Yasaka and Yokota Kisaburō (both of the Imperial University of Tokyo) at the fifth IPR conference in Banff proposed to conclude a "regional security pact" modeled after the Locarno Pact that would include China and the other powers that had interests in China, and thereby relieve Japan of its responsibility. Nitobe Inazō had already emphasized the regional element[377] at the third conference of the IPR in Kyoto in 1929:

> As the League grows in membership and geographical dimensions, it will presumably be compelled to conduct some of its business in regional congresses. For, though theoretically and ideologically the concern of one nation is the concern of the whole world, there are, in practice, international questions that affect only restricted areas. Questions of this character can be best discussed by the parties interested in a regional gathering, under the general direction or oversight of the central body.[378]

Shidehara, too, after the successful conclusion of the Locarno Pact in 1925, had welcomed the principle of regional arrangements to support the League of Nations system. A regional order in the Far East did not come about, however, and on 27 March 1933 Matsuoka Yōsuke (1880–1946), then the head of the Japanese delegation to the League of Nations, announced Japan's departure from the world body, following Japan's condemnation by the League for the seizure of Manchukuo.

Since the law of nations and its new world order had already begun to fail, the proposal for a regional order seemed only reasonable. After Japan had left the League of Nations, in the summer of 1933, Dr. Nitobe, who headed the Japanese delegation at the IPR conference in Banff, remarked:

> [The] fundamental causes of international conflict . . . have their roots in divergent national economic policies. . . . Some nations are endowed with the material blessings of nature out of proportion to the size of their populations, while the reverse is the case with others. How to adjust those obvious inequalities with the principle of "live and let live" is the supreme test of enlightened statesmanship. The trend of economic self-sufficiency when carried to excess will inevitably create a psychology in the less fortunately situated countries that the only way to guarantee their own material economic security is to establish economic blocs of their own by bringing outside territories into their own political orbit. If this policy is carried to its logical conclusion it may finally divide the world into many isolated camps, and the rivalry resulting from it may end sooner or later in a great disaster for humanity.[379]

THE NEW DIPLOMACY—
SHIDEHARA AS FOREIGN MINISTER

According to historian Ian Nish, the 1920s were "the age of Shidehara in Japanese diplomacy."[380] This epoch in the history of Japanese diplomacy was unique with respect to its adaptability to the international environment, and the attempts to carry out policies conducive to world peace. Its roots lay a quarter-century earlier, when Mutsu Munemitsu (1844–1897), in the last decade of the nineteenth century, had pushed through significant reforms in the Ministry of Foreign Affairs.[381] Not long after, Shidehara had been on an assignment in Korea just when the Korean reformer So Chaep'il, alias Philip Jaisohn, was having his greatest successes following his return from his American exile,[382] and Kang Youwei in China was preparing his "hundred days reform." There can be no doubt that the "spirit" displayed in these efforts also related to the worldwide peace movement that culminated in the Hague peace conferences. Even if these reform movements in China and Korea failed due to their suppression by the reactionary regimes in power at the time, and perhaps also due to the failure of related peace activities in Europe,[383] clearly most Japanese encouraged and supported these efforts.

The parameters for determining Japan's position in international relations had been set during the "Iwakura Period" (1868–1883).[384] Mutsu Munemitsu,[385] foreign minister in the cabinet of Itō Hirobumi, had reorganized the ministry in 1893 to meet Western standards, introducing a new, rigorous, and very selective examination system for the diplomatic corps, which Shidehara underwent to make his career in the foreign service. Representatives serving abroad received new designations: ambassador, minister, and *chargé d'affaires*; the foreign minister, formerly called *gaimukyō*, was renamed *gaimu daijin*.[386] By 1894 there were fourteen overseas embassies with full diplomatic staff. The army and navy attachés held important posts.[387] The cabinet system, too, continued to develop along modern lines. Diplomatic and military affairs at first, however, were not yet subject to parliamentary control. The ministers were responsible to the emperor only.[388] Mutsu himself was a new type of political personality who had come to prominence, and turned out to be one of the greatest statesmen of the Meiji era.[389] His reforms had paved the way for "Shidehara diplomacy." Mutsu was, one might say, the "spiritual father" of Shidehara diplomacy. A brief description of Mutsu Munemitsu's life and work may here be in order.[390]

After a short stay in London in 1870, Mutsu—returning in May 1871—took part in the rebellion led by Saigō Takamori against the emperor and went to prison for five years in 1878, where he translated Jeremy Bentham's *Introduction to the Principles of Morals and Legislation*. The book was published in Japanese in 1883, the year he was released from prison. He was rehabilitated, and took an active part in the preparations for the new Japanese constitution that was promulgated in 1889. Between 1884 and 1886 Mutsu traveled widely in Europe and, while in Vienna, visited Lorenz von Stein (1815–1890), an authority on international law, with whom he later corresponded. Back in Japan in 1887, he rejoined the government and for two years became Japan's minister in Washington, achieving a breakthrough with the revision of the "unequal treaties" between the United States and Japan, and Japan and Mexico in 1888, making the new treaties more equal. The Anglo-Japanese commercial treaty[391] signed by Mutsu in July 1894 was a further decisive step on the way to Japan's being treated on an equal basis with the Western powers.[392] His time in office as foreign minister saw the war with China and the subsequent deep disappointment of Japan because of the "Triple Intervention" of Russia, Germany, and France within a few months of the Treaty of Shimonoseki with China. Mutsu represented the Japanese side at the signing of the Shimonoseki peace treaty on 17 April 1895.[393]

Nonetheless, Japan was now more than ever diplomatically and internationally recognized. In the war with China, it had "behaved" in accordance with "modern" Western concepts befitting a civilized nation.[394] The times, when international politics were determined in the European chancelleries alone,[395] were changing. Japan's rise on the international stage was a precedent and it altered the provisions and constellations for international cooperation and competition. Accordingly, a new situation had emerged.

Japan's development at the end of the nineteenth century in fact replicated the "transition between the old diplomacy and the new"[396] described by Harold Nicholson that took place in Europe and in the United States of America.[397] In Europe the transition had started with the Congress of Vienna, and continued after the Franco-Prussian War of 1870–1871.[398] Japan, too, was not inexperienced in diplomatic affairs—it had carried out diplomatic relations with other Asian countries even during the "seclusion" period—and quickly adopted the international usages. Mutsu Munemitsu was a "man of the new age," an intellectual, jurist, and internationalist, and the most likely model for Shidehara.[399] Under Mutsu the course was set for eventually bringing the Ministry of Foreign Affairs to the pinnacle of its power—to become, in the 1920s, the high point of a policy aimed at peace, international understanding, and economic cooperation, and a distinctive body that throughout Shidehara's tenure was accountable both to the Diet and the electorate, where its public appeal increased considerably.

The dramatic events surrounding the "rising of Japan," the introduction of parliamentary democracy and the promulgation of the Meiji constitution, as well as the perceived injustice of the Triple Intervention, which had compromised the Treaty of Shimonoseki, had enticed Shidehara to enter a diplomatic career and serve his country. After graduation from the Imperial University in Tokyo in 1895 (with a bachelor of law degree), Shidehara in 1896, at age twenty-three and one year after the conclusion of the Sino-Japanese War, passed the examination to enter the diplomatic service.[400]

He passed his examinations with exceptional marks, "the most successful of the early entrants" and remaining unrivaled for decades after.[401] Following the Anglo-Japanese Commercial Treaty of 1894, promising the abolishment of extraterritoriality within five years,[402] three years later similar treaties were concluded with other Western powers. Eventually, Foreign Minister Komura announced the termination of all unequal treaties in February 1909. At the same time the government confirmed new treaties with the powers would be concluded in keeping with the principle of equality and mutuality.[403] The promulgation of full tariff autonomy in 1911 finally recognized Japan's unrestricted national sovereignty.

The political ups and downs of the Meiji Period paved the way toward a diplomacy that, in Harrison Holland's portrayal of the "Shidehara era," was exemplary, following a distinctive and creative policy the prestige and influence of which hardly finds its equivalent either before or after that period.[404] Earlier foreign ministers like Inoue Kaoru (1836–1915), who was foreign minister between 1879 and 1887, Ōkuma Shigenobu (who served as foreign minister in 1888–1889 and 1898), Aoki Shūzō (1889–1891 and 1898),[405] and later foreign ministers like Komura Jutarō (1901–1906 and 1908–1911), Uchida Kōsai (1911–1912, 1918–1923, and 1932), and Katō Takaaki (1900–1901, 1906, 1913, and 1914–1915) were important liberal statesmen, but they still belonged to the "old school." Shidehara stands out as "a new type of diplomat in a new age for Japan,"[406] very much in contrast to diplomats like Gotō Shimpei (1857–1929, foreign minister 1918), Ijūin Hikokichi (1864–1923, foreign minister 1923), and Hayashi Gonsuke (1860–1939), who were more beholden to chauvinistic traditions.

Influential military-bureaucratic cliques, whose traditionalism was rooted in a chauvinistic understanding of Japan's role in the world, tried also to gain control over Japan's foreign policy and carry out their policies to define and expand Japanese spheres of interest according to their own ways of thinking.[407] These men, for whom the end justified the means, wished to realize the dream of "empire" on the Asiatic mainland. To this group had belonged early Meiji leaders like Saigō Takamori, Soejima Taneomi (1828–1905), and Itagaki Taisuke.[408] The rivalry between traditionalists and militarists on the one hand and the democratic-liberal forces on the other resurfaced toward the end of the First World War, when a decision was taken in 1918 to send troops to Siberia. Those opposed to this "Siberian Expedition" were *genrō* Saionji Kinmochi, Hara Kei (1856–1921), Inukai Tsuyoshi (1855–1932), Count Makino Nobuaki, and Shidehara Kijūrō.[409]

Shidehara was one of the chief architects of the system of agreements that came out of the Versailles and Washington treaties.[410] Aspects of "Shidehara diplomacy" already became apparent from around 1911, when Japan achieved full sovereignty and equal diplomatic status with respect to the Western powers. In various important "key positions" he began to influence foreign policies in keeping with the progressive spirit of the time.[411] Shidehara was, according to Lesley Connors, "a favourite of Saionji" and he soon "came to personify the Saionji group's approach to foreign policy."[412] Saionji represented the strong democratic currents in Japan during the Taishō Period (1912–1925) having its roots in the enlightened conceptions of Japan's early democratic movements.

Following the fall of the Manchu (Qing) dynasty in China in 1911, a new time of peace and prosperity, it was hoped, would manifest itself in East Asia. Japan wanted to make a generous contribution toward this end since it had progressed economically and held an advantageous position in the international community. Geographical proximity and traditionally close cultural ties to the Asian mainland seemed to make Japan destined to assume such a role. Idealists and political adventurers like Miyazaki Tōten had dedicated their lives to the task.[413] It was not unreasonable to suppose that, similar to the way in which Western Europe had "discovered" and "opened up" new lands in America, Africa, and the East, or Russia had done in Siberia, large areas in East Asia, especially in the eastern provinces, might also be opened up, developed, and guided toward a greater and beneficial role in the context of the wider world. Or was it?

In a positive sense, like those European undertakings inspired by a pioneering spirit, the realization of this concept was seen as the task of the (new) century, which, in the context of the emerging new world order that had begun to take shape with the Hague peace conferences, would benefit the whole of mankind. Seen in this way, Japan, now on an equal footing with the Western powers, claiming legitimate rights in Asia and setting an example, should take the initiative to carry through the much-needed reforms. Obviously, though, there was a disparity between such "objective" motivations, and the more "subjective" national parochial interests. The goal of protecting and consolidating national security and sovereignty had, in its essential points, been achieved through the revision of the unequal treaties. Now the boundaries had to be staked out within which Japan could address its national concerns and define and create a sphere of interests that was appropriate to its growing economy and industry, and political clout.[414] To work toward this end was the task for diplomats who could effectively represent Japan's positions and interests. Shidehara's aim, however, was not only to further Japanese interests. He advocated reconciliation and international cooperation on a wide scale to accommodate China's interests and the interests of the other powers who had invested in East Asia.[415]

On the question of the means for realizing Japan's objectives, opinions were divided. For Shidehara the choice of means was decisive. He knew Japan could succeed only if it would adjust to the current policies of effective interdependence and peaceful cooperation. This was not pacifism in the guise of a peaceful imperialism.[416] Peaceful coexistence, a recognized community of interests, and the progressive rule of law in international relations, to safeguard the future, should bring the efforts on all sides to a successful conclusion. Shidehara's attitude reflected public opinion at the beginning of the 1920s. Japanese soldiers in uniform—militarism in general—were not looked on favorably by the public,[417] which also favored a policy of international cooperation and understanding.

Already as vice foreign minister between 1914 and 1919 Shidehara had acquired the reputation of being an outspoken antimilitarist,[418] who persistently countered the plans of the military to exploit the lawlessness in international relations for war and expand their influence on the Asian mainland. The Versailles Peace Conference, to which Shidehara had contributed by preparing Japan's part in it, and the League, had raised expectations worldwide for a new era of peace. Bamba Nobuya describes the international environment after the First World War:

> [T]he dominant note in the international situation after the Great War was the general world aspiration for peace and order. Anti-imperialism, a democratic order, and international co-operation were common goals among nations. The *Wilsonian and Leninist attacks on imperialism* continued strong, and China, which had been a major victim of imperialism enthusiastically supported both American and Russian assertions. Wilson emphasized self-determination and the sovereign rights of all people. In Great Britain Lloyd George advocated "diplomacy by conference," by which he hoped to bring about "open diplomacy" and the "mobilization of world opinion." All denounced the "old diplomacy" and agreed on the need for establishing a "new diplomacy." *The main elements of the "new diplomacy" were peaceful settlements, open negotiations, multinational conferences and agreements, the mobilization of world opinion, renunciation of economic and military exploitation of weaker nations, respect for national sovereignty, and the self-determination of all peoples.*[419]

A significant step toward securing international peace and strengthening the international order was the Washington Naval Disarmament Conference.

This "Versailles-Washington system" was not a military alliance against a common, external enemy but a universal treaty system oriented toward peace, security, and disarmament. It was meant to produce stability and provide for a just settlement of interests through improved networking and interdependent efforts toward these goals. Shidehara's new diplomacy was based on negotiations and compromise. For the resolution of international disputes this meant, as his friend the British diplomat James Bryce stated in a speech in August 1921, the readiness to submit to procedures of arbitration, mediation, conciliation, and negotiation.[420]

As foreign minister in the 1920s, Shidehara continued the policies established by Mutsu Munemitsu and Komura Jutarō (1855–1911),[421] known as Kasumigaseki[422] diplomacy, under a new paradigm. The policies of the militarists and nationalists lost momentum and were driven back, and the military was subjected to parliamentary control. The Ministry of Foreign Affairs, not the military, had the decisive voice in important foreign policy questions related to armament or disarmament.

The peculiar structure of the military organization in contrast to that of the civil administration, however, posed a danger that made the challenge of the military perilous for the Ministry of Foreign Affairs. The fact was that the army was "a complete social system, a kind of military microcosm,"[423] which allowed sectors of the military to conspire to undermine Shidehara's policy. This included parliamentarians belonging to the "military faction" who sought to promote their own autonomous foreign policy. Thus, in 1925 Army Minister Ugaki Kazushige tried to organize a conspiracy between certain Japanese and Chinese military factions "behind foreign minister Shidehara Kijūrō's back, to take advantage of the civil war in China."[424]

These problems had to be taken care of with pragmatism, determination, and patience. Shidehara was not prone to dogmatism, and not even an outspoken anti-Communist. A pragmatist and an idealist, pacifist, and a politician of *realpolitik*, he wanted to make Japan, as a modern industrial and trading nation and producer of civilian industrial goods, accountable and competitive in the international market. His internationalism had a patriotic component. Again and again Shidehara stressed that if Japan was to exercise "leadership" in Asia, it would be only with the objective of furthering peace, progress, and prosperity in the region. He had learned from James Bryce's lectures, delivered in August 1921:[425] "So soon as the peoples of each country have become convinced that they have more to gain by one another's prosperity than they have by raising obstacles to free intercourse, so soon will the facilities of trade throughout the world have their proper chance of being extended."[426] Disarmament, economic cooperation aiming at common prosperity, and the international rule of law would work to stabilize peace.

Shidehara was also—quite in contrast, for example, to Foreign Minister Aoki Shūzō—not interested in "power." His pragmatism and unsentimental commitment of purpose were reminiscent of Max Weber's ethics of rationalism. Prince Saionji Kinmochi, the last *genrō* and one of the great Japanese liberals, greatly valued Shidehara's integrity—an impression that foreign newspaper reporters frequently took satisfaction in confirming.[427] He did not give great import to conventions of hierarchy, rituals, and sentiments of social obligation or showing off,[428] which in Japan could traditionally be very meaningful. He represented a "nonpartisan diplomacy" (*chōtō gaikō*), as he called it. Discreet and persevering, in an exemplary fashion Shidehara seemed to fulfill the prerequisites for successful diplomacy described by diplomat Harold Nicolson—that is, "those principles of courtesy, confidence and discretion which must for ever remain the only principles conducive to the peaceful settlement of disputes."[429] Not belonging to any political party until after the Second World War, he remained unaffected by the squabbles of party politics.

Prewar Seiyūkai politician Nagai Ryūtarō in 1927 described Shidehara's political philosophy as that of a principled anti-imperialist statesman:

> There have been two types of thoughts in our diplomacy. One is imperialism and the other, liberalism. . . . Most of our Foreign Ministers without strong determination and definite principles vacillated between the two types of policies. . . . However, a characteristic of Shidehara's policy is its consistent liberalism.[430]

If measured against world standards, Shidehara's foreign policy in the 1920s would have stood at the apex of progressive, liberal politics. In the Japanese context, marred by certain bias and misconceptions, Shidehara diplomacy is, however, perhaps not easy to "explain." For this reason, and also because of his links to "capital" (especially the Mitsubishi *zaibatsu* represented by his father-in-law) he was after the Second World War subjected to "left-wing" and Marxist criticism.[431] The Marxist critique overlooked some important aspects.[432] Since it did not want to acknowledge Shidehara's accomplishments, some critics invented the idea of "dual diplomacy,"[433] which will be discussed in some detail later.[434]

Shidehara was partial to Anglo-Saxon liberalism and American pragmatism, with their aim to achieve a worldwide peaceful regulation of interests in the era after 1919.[435] He put much stock in the sorts of ideas which American humanists were putting forward, as one political philosopher of the time remarked: "Politics has to do with ideals which are bringers of action," in other words ideals are "signposts" for politicians' orientation.[436] This "pacifism of philosophical reason" is typical for the American approach.[437] Shidehara's unadulterated pragmatism[438] and essential liberalism seemed most appropriate in the East Asian context. However, at the beginning of the 1930s Shidehara had to face the same dilemma as some American political figures, who became "prisoners of the contradiction between a national ideology (that war is a crime and that the rule of law must prevail in the relations between nations) and . . . the distinctive nature of international or interstate relations [that] . . . lay in the legitimacy or legality of the use of military force."[439]

NOTES

1. James Bryce, "The Importance of Geography in Education," *The Geographical Journal* (Great Britain), 1902, 308, quoted in Alan R. H. Baker, *Geography and History, Bridging the Divide* (Cambridge: Cambridge University Press, 2003), 16.

2. There may be some similarities here with Germany. See Karl Kaiser, Hans Maull, et al. (eds.), *Deutschlands neue Außenpolitik, Grundlagen* (Germany's new foreign policy, fundamentals) (München: R. Oldenbourg, 1994), especially the article by Michael Stürmer, "Deutsche Interessen" (German interests), 39–61, in the same book.

3. According to Hall, the efforts of Tokugawa Ieyasu "to obtain full control of the destinies of the country and to assure complete loyalty to his regime led step by step in the direction of closure. The history of the adoption of the seclusion policy therefore shows an intermingling of three strands of concern: 1) the Tokugawa effort to secure internal political stability, 2) the Tokugawa desire to secure a monopoly of foreign trade, and 3) fear of Christianity" (*Japan—From Prehistory to Modern Times*, 187).

4. Boxer, *The Christian Century*, gives in his introduction this view: "The period of Japanese history known as the Christian century was decisive for the development of Japan's relations with the West. But for the introduction, growth, and forcible suppression of militant Christianity in the sixteenth and seventeenth centuries, it seems probable that Tokugawa Japan would not have retired into its isolationist shell. This in turn implies that Japan's overseas expansion in that period would not have proved abortive. The Japanese, whether peacefully or otherwise, would have established themselves in the Philippines, Indo-China, and in parts of Indonesia by the turn of the seventeenth century; and they would, in all probability, have been able to share in the fruits of Europe's industrial revolution, for several decades before they actually did" (vii).

5. "The Russians were the first to exert pressure on Japan" (Fairbank, Reischauer, and Craig, *East Asia—The Modern Transformation*, 116).

6. See, for example, William G. Beasley, *The Meiji Restoration* (Stanford, Calif.: Stanford University Press, 1972), 76.

7. In 1809 a Japanese explorer, Mamiya Rinzō (1780–1845), carried out an expedition that took him beyond the northern end of Sakhalin and then up the Amur River (Fairbank, Reischauer, and Craig, *East Asia—The Modern Transformation*, 116).

8. Then Japanese outposts to the north of Hokkaido were attacked by Russians in 1806 and 1807, and later, in 1811, the Japanese captured several Russians and kept them in captivity on Hokkaido for two years (*ibid.*, 116–17).

9. For a detailed account of the decisive period of the formulation and application of this policy and of its further development, see Conrad Totman, *The Collapse of the Tokugawa Bakufu, 1862–1868* (Honolulu, University of Hawaii Press, 1980). *Jōi* means "drive out the barbarians" while *kaikoku* meant to "open the country."

10. Fairbank, Reischauer, and Craig, *East Asia—The Modern Transformation*, 119. See also William G. Beasley, *Select Documents on Japanese Foreign Policy, 1853–1868* (London, New York, and Toronto: Oxford University Press, 1955), 5. Beasley in this work was the first scholar to access, document, and discuss this theme in considerable detail in a Western language. In his introduction (15ff), he compares and analyzes these two political tendencies.

11. "The need for strengthening defences to meet the threat of foreign attack was the one subject on which unanimity could be achieved. On other questions of foreign policy Japan's leaders were sharply divided" (Beasley, *op. cit.*, 5).

12. This argument can be found in Beasley, *Select Documents*, 15.

13. Maruyama Masao, *Studies in the Intellectual History of Tokugawa Japan* (Tokyo: University of Tokyo Press, 1974), 351.

14. This was a well-known slogan of the time, which expressed a widely shared standpoint and was conspicuously publicized by Sakuma Shōzan (Maruyama, *Studies in the Intellectual History of Tokugawa Japan*, 307). See also Beasley, *The Meiji Restoration*, 74–87, and Conrad Totman, *The Collapse of the Tokugawa Bakufu* (1980).

15. See Maruyama, *Studies in the Intellectual History of Tokugawa Japan*, 289ff.

16. Engelbert Kaempfer (*The History of Japan* [New York: AMS, 1971] [reprinted from the edition of 1906, Glasgow, originally published in 1727], 301–40) makes the case that "the Japanese . . . confined within the limits of their Empire enjoy the blessings of peace and contendedness" (304) and "that it is not only advisable, but very much to its advantage, that its inhabitants . . . should be kept . . . from . . . vices, from covetousness, deceits, wars, treachery, and the like" (305)."

17. See the account of the Shimabara Uprising by Japanese Christians in northern Kyushu that led to the "seclusion laws" of the *bakufu* (shōgunate) in Fujii Masato, *Die Wahrheit über Japan* (The truth about Japan) (Tokyo: Japanisch-Deutsche Gesellschaft, 1982), 10–11: "On the Shimabara Peninsula there broke out in 1637 a large organized uprising of the Christians, who had been persecuted with brutal cruelty. They carried out a stubborn and dogged resistance. Only with the employment of 124,000 warriors could the *bakufu*, after a long and hard fight, put down the 34,000 rebels (1638)."

18. The term *sakoku* first appeared among Japanese historians and publicists only around the beginning of the nineteenth century: Ronald Toby, *State and Diplomacy in Early Modern Japan, Asia in the Development of the Tokugawa Bakufu* (Princeton, N.J.: Princeton University Press, 1984), 12–13. In point of fact, Japan after 1638 did not disappear from the political stage of East Asia and continued to have diplomatic exchanges in this part of the world. See chapter I, section 1. In any case, for some

time "Hideyoshi's seven-year war with Korea and China had left Japan isolated from Asia" (Toby, *op. cit.*, 23).

19. See the account in Fairbank, Reischauer, and Craig, *East Asia—The Modern Transformation*, 34–35.

20. Hermann Kulke, "Überlegungen zur Begegnung Europas und Asiens bis ins 19. Jahrhundert" (Considerations on the meeting of Europe and Asia up to the nineteenth century), *Oriens Extremus* 33, no. 1 (1990): 11.

21. Wilhelm Solf, *Wie kam es zum Konflikt im Fernen Osten?* (How did the conflict in the Far East come about?), a special supplement (Sonderabdruck) to the *Berliner Börsen-Zeitung* (Berlin Financial Paper), no. 143, 25 March 1932, 5.

22. See Ishii Yoneo, "Ayutthayam-Japanese Relations in the Pre-Modern Period: A Bibliographic Reflection," *The Transactions of the Asiatic Society of Japan*, fourth series, vol. 10 (1995): 1–9.

23. This refers to a world order based on a division between barbarian and civilized peoples. See section 2 of this chapter.

24. Paul A. Cohen, "Europe goes East: The first impact of the West on China and Japan," in Toynbee (ed.), *Half the World*, 292.

25. Arai published two books on the West: *Seiyō kibun* (Curious writings on the West, 1715) and *Sairan igen* (Various views on world geography, 1713, revised 1725). The latter comprised five volumes and was commissioned by Tokugawa Ienobu. It is based on the work of the Jesuit priest Matteo Ricci, who had been an advisor to the Chinese court (Fujii Masato, *Die Wahrheit über Japan*, 11). See also Arai's autobiography, *Told Round a Brushwood Fire—The Autobiography of Arai Hakuseki*, translated and with introduction by Joyce Ackroyd (Tokyo: University of Tokyo Press, 1980).

26. In 1745 Aoki compiled a Dutch-Japanese dictionary (Hall, *Japan—From Prehistory to Modern Times*, 224).

27. Ōtsuki Gentaku translated, among other things, the *Lehrbuch der Chirurgie* (Textbook on surgery) of the German surgeon Laurenz Heister, from a Dutch-language edition, giving it the Japanese title *Yōi shinsho* (New book of Western medicine), two vols. (1793). In 1788 Ōtsuki Gentaku published his *Rangaku kaitei* (Explanation of Dutch studies). See Hall, *op. cit.*, 224.

28. The Dutch-language edition, *Ontleedkundige Tafelen*, from which the Japanese was translated, was in turn a translation of the work *Tafel Anatomia* of the German scholar Johan Adam Kulmus. See the detailed account given in Fujii Masato, *Die Wahrheit über Japan*, 13–19. Sugita Genpaku also published an important small book with the title *Rangaku kotohajime* (First steps in Dutch studies). This book was newly published in 1890 by Fukuzawa Yukichi, and appeared in a still newer edition (under the supervision of Ogata Tomio) in 1959.

29. Fujii Masato, *Die Wahrheit über Japan*, 13.

30. See Tsunoda, DeBary and Keene, *Sources of Japanese Tradition*, vol. II, 49: "Indeed many of the best minds of the late eighteenth century were turning to the West for new information and guidance as the isolation of the country grew increasingly oppressive. . . . [I]t was towards the [Dutch] trading station at Nagasaki that many young Japanese looked for knowledge."

31. Hall, *op. cit.*, 224: "[T]he importation of Western curiosa took on the proportions of a fad. Daimyos collected clocks and field glasses, drank out of glass goblets and watched experiments in electricity."

32. Cohen, "Europe goes East," 292. In 1811 the "Bansho Yawarage Goyō" (Institute for the Translation of Foreign Books) was founded in Edo. There developed from this in 1857 the newly established "Institute for the Study of Foreign Books," which became a center for the study of Western scholarship and languages. Similar schools were established in the feudal domains of Chōshū, Satsuma, Mito, Tosa (in Shikoku), Hizen (in Kyushu), and elsewhere.

33. Fujii Masato provides a categorized list of these publications. One hundred thirty of the six hundred seventy texts were books on medicine, seventy had to do with military affairs, fifty were on chemistry and physics, forty were on astronomy, thirty were on politics, and so on (*Die Wahrheit über Japan*, 19).

34. Cohen, "Europe goes East," 292.

35. Donald Keene, cited in Cohen, "Europe goes East," 292.

36. From the British-French colonial wars of 1754–1763 England emerged victorious. The victory of Admiral Nelson (1758–1805) at Trafalgar secured British domination of the seas and maritime route to India. See also Klaus Schlichtmann, "The West, Bengal Renaissance and Japanese Enlightenment: A Critical Inquiry into the History of the Organisation of the World around 1800," in Stephen Conermann and Jan Kusber (eds.), *Asien und Afrika* (Schenefeld: EB-Verlag, 2003), 411–40.

37. William G. Beasley, *The Meiji Restoration*, 77.

38. Fujita Tōko (1806–1855) developed this idea further. Both individuals here mentioned belonged to the Mito school (Fairbank, Reischauer, and Craig, *East Asia— The Modern Transformation*, 118). Najita writes that Aizawa Seishisai believed that the maintenance of the seclusion policy toward the West could not be carried out and that "as a matter of practical strategy, Japan must break out of its present seclusion and confront that threat" (*Japan—The Intellectual Foundations*, 47–48). Cited in Conrad Totman, "From *Sakoku* to *Kaikoku*: The Transformation of Foreign Policy Attitudes, 1853–1868," *Monumenta Nipponica* 35, no. 1 (Spring 1980): 6n7.

39. Cited in Bersihand, *op. cit.*, 294.

40. In 1806 the *bakufu* had given instructions to local authorities in coastal regions to drive away foreign ships. However, to avoid confrontations, in 1842 this rigorous policy was somewhat revised and permission granted to provide foreign ships with provisions (Fairbank, Reischauer, and Craig, *East Asia—The Modern Transformation*, 117).

41. Kenneth Scott Latourette, *The Chinese, their History and Culture* (New York: Macmillan, 1959), 345–46.

42. Beasley, *The Meiji Restoration*, 77–78.

43. See also Beasley, *Select Documents on Japanese Foreign Policy, 1853–1868*, 4: "[T]he warning voices were comparatively few until after 1840. It was the Opium War in China, presented as evidence both of British strength and British aggression, that finally persuaded the Japanese that an attack on their own country was not only possible but even imminent."

44. Sakuma Shōzan believed that China had lost the war "because foreign learning is rational and Chinese learning is not." Cited in W. G. Beasley, *The Meiji Restoration*, 81. On the Opium War, see Arthur Waley, *The Opium War Through Chinese Eyes* (London: Allen & Unwin, 1958). The "Second Opium War," also known as the "Arrow War," took place between 1856 and 1860.

45. *Ibid.*, 312. According to this work (276) the emperor secretly gave Tokugawa Nariaki the order to "place himself at the head of the disaffected and to drive away the barbarians." However, in 1844 Nariaki had to appear in Edo where he was taken prisoner: "Ostensibly, then, Nariaki was an advocate of the so-called 'war' policy of the *jōi* party" (Beasley, *Select Documents on Japanese Foreign Policy, 1853–1868*, 12).

46. Beasley, *The Meiji Restoration*, 78. Slightly later, an article published in the *Edinburgh Review* of October 1852, 383, stated: "The compulsory seclusion of the Japanese is a wrong not only to themselves, but to the civilized world. . . . The Japanese undoubtedly have an exclusive right to the possession of their territory; but it must not abuse that right to the extent of debarring all other nations from a participation in its riches and virtues." Cited in Beasley, *The Meiji Restoration*, 76.

47. *Ibid.*, 78. All in all, many unsettling rumors about foreign plans for conquest were making the rounds. After about 1790, books and pamphlets in which foreign affairs and international relations increasingly played a role appeared quite regularly.

48. Bersihand, *op. cit.*, 277–79.

49. "In July 1853, when Perry's squadron entered Uraga Bay, the *bakufu* did not have a foreign policy of any description" (Beasley, *Select Documents on Japanese Foreign Policy, 1853–1868*, 21).

50. Satō Nobuhiro was well versed in Dutch studies as well as in history, geography, astronomy, and botany. He traveled widely in Japan offering his advice to feudal lords (Hall, *op. cit.*, 220).

51. This affair is known as the *Bansha no goku*—"the imprisonment of the companions in foreign studies." Altogether twenty-six intellectuals were arrested, among them Koseki San'ei (1787–1839), who had been a student of the German physician Philip Franz von Siebold, who served on Dejima. The Shōshikai study group headed by Watanabe and Takano was not allowed to carry out further activities (Maruyama, *Studies in the Intellectual History of Tokugawa Japan*, 335).

52. Egawa Tarōzaemon was a pioneer in Western military science and industrial technology. Between 1842 and 1857 he built a reverbatory furnace and carried out experiments that laid the groundwork for a large-scale installation producing heavy artillery canons. On the history of ironworks and production in Japan, see, for example, *Tatara Nihon korai no seitzetsu* (Tokyo: JFE21 Seiki Zaidan, 2004).

53. Sakuma Shōzan had studied under Egawa Tarōzaemon and later became Yoshida Shōin's teacher. He was assassinated in 1864. He once said: "When I was twenty I knew that people were linked together in one province; when I was thirty I knew that they were linked together in one nation; when I was forty I knew that they were linked together in one world of five continents." Translation by Henricus van Straelen, in *Yoshida Shōin, Forerunner of the Meiji Restoration, A Biographical Study* (Leiden: E. J. Brill, 1952), 14n1. The author (*loc. cit.*) goes on to point out: "However, he did not acquire a pacific, global philosophy. On the contrary, just as Shōin he

remained the fiery patriot." See also Maruyama, *Studies in the Intellectual History of Tokugawa Japan*, 306–7.

54. "[I]t was essential that Japan's entry into world affairs be preceded by creation of the unity and consciousness of danger which would enable her people to adopt such Western ideas as could be made to serve them, while firmly rejecting all those that threatened the national ethos. This could not be achieved by mere exhortation. The *bakufu* would have to make its sincerity plain by effecting thorough reform of the economy and administration. It must also announce publicly a policy of expulsion, affirming all foreign demands would be refused even at the risk of war. Indeed, war itself would play a part in achieving the desired end. Only the sound of cannon could arouse Japan from her lethargy" (Beasley, *Select Documents*, 10).

55. Conrad Totman, "From *Sakoku* to *Kaikoku*," 18.

56. *Ibid.*, 84. Among the "leading spirits" who prepared the way for the "downfall of the tottering shōgunate" were Sakuma Shōzan, adherents of the so-called Mito school like Lord Tokugawa Nariaki, Fujita Tōko, and Aizawa Seishisai, and, in a third group, Sugita Genpaku, Takano Chōei, and Fukuzawa Yukichi.

57. Some, like Ōtsuki Gentaku and Ogino Kyūkoku, who were proficient in Dutch studies, categorically declared that Chinese scholarly studies were now at an end and that genuine wisdom and knowledge came from the Dutch. (They also adopted the view that the wellsprings of civilization lay in Egypt and Asia Minor.) Dutch science was seen to rest upon provable facts and not empty theory: "In these . . . the method of attack is already shifting from the imputation that Chinese are not better than other people to the more positive statement that they are not as good as the Japanese or Dutch. . . . *The emergence of this attitude is of the greatest significance in the history of Japanese thought.*" Donald Keene, *The Japanese Discovery of Europe, Honda Toshiaki and other Discoverers 1720–1798* (London: Routledge & Kegan Paul, 1952), 35 (emphasis added).

58. Cohen, "Europe goes East," 292. Compare also Maruyama, *Studies in the Intellectual History of Tokugawa Japan*, 286–88 and 346–50.

59. See translated passages of writings by Honda Toshiaki in Tsunoda, De Bary, and Keene, *Sources of Japanese Tradition*, vol. II, 50.

60. See Cohen, "Europe goes East," 292: "Japan was opening herself, and by the time the Perry Expedition arrived in 1853, her intellectual preparation for entry into the modern world was already well under way." On the "opening" process, see also Schwebell (ed.), *Die Geburt des modernen Japan*, 78–147.

61. Those *daimyōs* who submitted to the victorious general Tokugawa Ieyasu only after the Battle of Sekigahara (1600) are known as the sixty-four *tozama daimyōs*, all of whom had maintained a certain degree of independence.

62. Cited in Gertrude C. Schwebell, *op. cit.*, 123–24. See also Bersihand, *op. cit.*, 312–13.

63. Schwebell, *op. cit.*, 123–24.

64. *Ibid.*, 121. There was a range of reasons, from trying to uphold the traditional seclusion policy and the prohibition against Christianity to concerns about moral decay and loss of authority by the regime. The shōgun carried, after all, the hereditary

title of *Sei-i Tai-Shōgun* ("great general who controls the barbarians") bestowed by the imperial house, and so would seem to have a clear mission in this regard. See also Maruyama, *Studies in the Intellectual History of Tokugawa Japan*, 336.

65. See the chapter on "The Perry Expedition" in Beasley, *The Meiji Restoration*, 87ff.

66. Bersihand, *op. cit.*, 280. A few days later, on 27 July, Shōgun Ieyoshi died.

67. The *fudai daimyō* controlled hereditary domains under the overlordship of the Tokugawa.

68. This was a sort of council of elder statesmen that was entrusted with the highest-level decisionmaking.

69. Beasley, *Select Documents*, 23. The Confucian scholars, who were also consulted, came to the conclusion that no compromises should be made and that the foreigners must be driven away.

70. "[A]dvocacy of expulsion . . . proved an invaluable weapon against the Tokugawa *bakufu*" (Beasley, *Select Documents*, 15).

71. The Treaty of Peace and Amity between the United States and Japan (*Nichibei washin jōyaku*) of 31 March 1854 was also known as the "Kanagawa Treaty" after the place of the negotiations (in what is today a part of Yokohama) (Fairbank, Reischauer, and Craig, *East Asia—The Modern Transformation*, 200ff.; see also Duus, *op. cit.*, 60ff.)

72. Cited in Miyoshi Masao, *As We Saw Them, The First Japanese Embassy to the United States (1860)* (Berkeley, Los Angeles, and London: University of California Press, 1979), 5.

73. *Ibid.*

74. See also Townsend Harris, *The Complete Journal of Townsend Harris, First American Consul General and Minister to Japan*, ed. M. E. Cosenza (Rutland, Vt., and Tokyo: Tuttle, 1969) (orig. New York, 1930).

75. Bersihand, *op. cit.*, 310.

76. "The most serious consequence of the treaties was the presence in Japan of considerable numbers of Westerners, whom most Japanese regarded with great distrust and hostility . . . foreign traders began to settle in large numbers at the harbor of Yokohama" (Fairbank, Reischauer, and Craig, *East Asia—The Modern Transformation*, 121).

77. Louis G. Perez, "Mutsu Munemitsu and the Diet Crisis of 1893," *Journal of Asian History* 25, no. 1 (1991): 35.

78. Wilhelm Grewe, *The Epochs of International Law*, trans. and rev. Michael Byers (Berlin and New York: Walter de Gruyter, 2000), 457. See also table 3, "Concessions and Concessionaires in Korea, 1896–1900," in Hatada Takashi, *A History of Korea*, trans. and ed. Warren W. Smith Jr. and Benjamin H. Hazard (Santa Barbara, Calif.: ABC-Clio, 1969), 105.

79. Alexander Georg Gustav von Siebold, *Der Eintritt Japans in das europäische Völkerrecht* (The entry of Japan into the European Law of Nations) (Berlin: Kisak Tamai, 1900), 4–5. (A French translation appeared in Paris in 1900, and an English translation appeared in London in 1901.) On the history of the "unequal treaties," see

Francis C. Jones, *Extraterritoriality in Japan and the Diplomatic Relations Resulting in its Abolition, 1853–1899* (New Haven, Conn.: Yale University Press/London: H. Milford, Oxford University Press, 1931).

80. "[T]he injection of foreign currency thoroughly disrupted the Japanese monetary system. This together with the heavy foreign demand for certain export commodities, particularly silk and tea, the inflow of cheaper foreign manufactures, particularly cotton textiles, frantic efforts to increase armaments, and growing political disruption resulting from the foreign threat, set off a severe inflationary spiral" (Fairbank, Reischauer, and Craig, *East Asia—The Modern Transformation*, 121).

81. The Japanese had not been in a position to easily adjust their gold currency. The ratio of the exchange rate between gold and silver stood at 1:5 in Japan, while outside Japan it was 1:15. Thus foreign traders could for a period earn enormous profits, while Japan lost almost all its gold. Sir Rutherford Alcock, the first British diplomatic envoy in Japan, writes:

> Japanese and foreigners seemed equally to have had a fit of insanity; the first from fear and rage combined, and the second from the "*auri sacra fames*," the unquenched and unquenchable thirst for gold, more gold, and still [more] gold! . . . There can be no doubt it tended much to excite feelings of hostility, and to array all their prejudices against the foreigner, his trade, and all that belonged to him or was connected with his presence in the country. It equally certainly and seriously warped their better judgment in regard to the possible benefits of foreign commerce. It was about this time that they first began to exhibit a desire, which soon ripened into a distinct proposition, to defer the opening of any more ports for a term of years, and even . . . limit the exports from those already opened (Sir Rutherford Alcock, *The Capital of the Tycoon: A Narrative of a Three Years' Residence in Japan* [London: Harper & Brothers, 1863], 254).

82. The Western equivalent to such utterances is a remark by U.S. Senator William Mangum about the Japanese in connection with the Perry Mission, cited in Miyoshi, *As We Saw Them*, 5: "You have to deal with barbarians as barbarians."

83. Totman, *The Collapse of the Tokugawa Bakufu*, 33.

84. On 5 November 1862 the imperial court decided to order the ejection of the foreigners. On 8 November, Matsudaira Katamori (Aizu) underscored in a memorandum the need to take back the concessions allowed in the treaties of 1858 and to punish those *bakufu* officials who been responsible for concluding the treaties (Totman, *The Collapse of the Tokugawa Bakufu*, 34). An English translation of the text of the memorandum is found in Beasley, *Select Documents*, 225–27.

85. Totman, "From *Sakoku* to *Kaikoku*," 11. See also Reinier Hesselingk, "The Assassination of Henry Heusken," *Monumenta Nipponica* 49, no. 3 (Autumn 1994): 350, describing the background of Heusken's assassination, for details.

86. At the same time ever more well-armed foreign troops were stationed in the vicinity of the foreign diplomatic legations: "More and more foreign activities were taking place on Japanese soil: trade, tourism, religious proselytizing, and arms selling" (Totman, "From *Sakoku* to *Kaikoku*," 12).

87. See Wells on the subsequent response in Japan: "The humiliation of the Japanese by these events was intense . . . [but with] astonishing energy and intelligence they set themselves to bring their culture and organization up to the level of the European powers. Never in the history of mankind did a nation make such a stride as Japan did then" (*Outline of History*, 1031–32).

88. Beasley, *The Meiji Restoration*, 197–240.

89. However, the opening of the ports of Hyōgo (today's Kobe) and Osaka was postponed.

90. Reischauer and Craig, *Tradition and Transformation*, 132.

91. *Ibid.*, 131–33, for a fair description of the events. See also the documents reproduced in Henricus van Straelen, *Yoshida Shōin, Forerunner of the Meiji Restoration*, 143ff.

92. Tsunoda, De Bary, and Keene, *Sources of Japanese Tradition*, vol. II, 131. See also Bamba Nobuya, *Japanese Diplomacy in a Dilemma—New Light on Japan's China Policy, 1924–29* (Kyoto: Minerva Press, 1972), 44–45: "Western political theory—such as Rousseau's theory of social contract, Locke's idea of inalienable natural rights of the individual, and Bantham's utilitarian concept of the government—had become extremely influential, and was greatly damaging to the traditional concept of the state and Imperial authority based upon the Shintō mythology."

93. Najita Tetsuo, "Die historische Entwicklung der kulturellen Identität im modernen Japan und die humanistische Herausforderung der Gegenwart" (The historical development of the cultural identity in modern Japan and the humanistic challenge of the present), in Constantin von Barloewen and Kai Werhahn-Mees (eds.), *Japan und der Westen* (Japan and the West), vol. 3 on "Politics, Culture and Society" (Frankfurt: Fischer, 1986), 177–78.

94. *Ibid.*

95. Hazel J. Jones, *Live Machines—Hired Foreigners and Meiji Japan* (Vancouver: University of British Columbia Press, 1980), xiii. Jones (*ibid.*, 145) gives for the period from 1868 to 1900 the following figures for the numbers of foreign government- or military-related advisors and consultants (compiled from foreign ministry records, navy records, prefectural government records, the cabinet, and the Ōkuma and Griffis collections): Great Britain = 1034; France = 401; United States = 351; Germany = 279, and so on. The term "live machines" comes from Sufu Masanosuke, an official from Chōshū, who once so designated European teachers and instructors. See also Murakami Yōichirō, "Japan and die moderne Wissenschaft, " in Barloewen and Werhahn-Mees, *op. cit.*, 173–74.

96. Najita Tetsuo, *op. cit.*, in Barloewen and Werhahn-Mees, 177.

97. Compare also Tsurumi Yūsuke, in *Problems of the Pacific 1927* (Chicago: University of Chicago Press, for the Institute of Pacific Relations, 1927), 502: "The Japanese people entertain a kind of historical affection for the British people. English gentlemen were often compared to Japanese samurai. We felt that there were some common traits, owing to the insular nature of the two countries, and some similarities in their system of government."

98. Tsunoda, De Bary, and Keene, *Sources of Japanese Tradition*, vol. II, 116. Najita similarly states: "Fukuzawa's 'Conditions in the West' (*Seiyō jiyō*) of 1866 and

'An Encouragement to Learning' (*Gakumon no susume*) of 1872 . . . were enormously popular classics all through the Meiji era, their total sales soaring into several million copies" (*Japan—The Intellectual Foundations*, 88).

99. Tsunoda, De Bary, and Keene, *op. cit.*, vol. II, 117. See also 116: "No other Japanese in those turbulent pre-Restoration days had such wide vision as Fukuzawa Yukichi . . . nor in the reconstruction period which followed did any Japanese of his renown and ability live the life of an independent commoner with such native dignity." See also Carmen Blacker, *The Japanese Enlightenment: A Study of the Writings of Fukuzawa Yukichi* (Cambridge: Cambridge University Press, 1964).

100. Bersihand, *op. cit.*, 358.

101. Fukuzawa Yukichi, "History of the Japanese Parliament," *Japan Weekly Mail*, 6 April 1889, printed in McLaren, *Japanese Government Documents*, 585: "The political power of the state fell into the hands of the *shizoku*."

102. See Lebra, *Ōkuma Shigenobu*, 55: "It has been estimated that while only 5 percent of the population at the time of the Restoration were of Samurai or *shizoku* class, in 1882 61.2 percent of the bureaucracy were still *shizoku*. For this reason the *shizoku* have been termed the 'political class' of the Meiji period."

103. Beasley, *Select Documents*, 20.

104. The centenary of this event was commemorated in 1993.

105. According to Helmut Plessner, *Die verspätete Nation* (Latecomer Nation) (Frankfurt: Suhrkamp, 1974).

106. See, for example, Maruyama, *Thought and Behavior in Modern Japanese Politics* (expanded edition); Bamba Nobuya, *Japanese Diplomacy*; and Bernd Martin (ed.), *Japans Weg in die Moderne, Ein Sonderweg nach deutschem Vorbild?* (Japan's way to modernity, a special way following a German model?) (Frankfurt and New York: Campus, 1987).

107. Fan-Fô-ngai, "Das Lebensproblem in China und Europa" (The problem of life in China and Europe), in *Archiv für Geschichte der Philosophie*, vol. 34, new series (Berlin, 1922), 142–43.

108. Tsurumi Yūsuke answers the question positively in "The Meiji Revolution and Its Consequences," in Arnold Toynbee (ed.), *Half the World* (London: Thames & Hudson, 1973), 308–10.

109. For a discussion of the *rōnō-ha* and the *kōza-ha*, see Harry D. Harootunian, *Toward Restoration: The Growth of Political Consciousness in Tokugawa Japan* (Berkeley, Los Angeles, and Oxford: University of California Press, 1970), "Preface," xxvi–xxxii. Before the Second World War there were two groups that addressed in quite different ways the question of whether the Meiji Restoration was a "revolution." The *rōnō-ha* (worker-farmer faction) took a positive stance, while the *kōza-ha* (seminar group) took a negative stance.

110. Article 5 of the "Five-Article Oath" (*Gokajō no goseimon*) of 6 April 1868 reads: "Knowledge should be sought throughout the whole world, in order to strengthen the foundations of the imperial power."

111. The Confucian class differences were abolished in the Army and overall equality was proclaimed for the lower classes of society in general, including the so-called *eta*, who had formerly been considered an inferior outcaste.

112. For details on the samurai unrest, see Beasley, *The Meiji Restoration*, 338ff.

113. Saigō Takamori had ten years earlier brought together the troops from Satsuma and Chōshū and had in 1867–1868 led to victory the military forces arrayed against the shōgunate. He was subsequently involved to a considerable extent in the negotiations over the conditions for the transfer of political power to the emperor.

114. Some of the ideological elements of the so-called tennō system were *kokutai*, *kōdō*, and *hakkō ichiu*. See also Maruyama Masao, *Thought and Behavior in Modern Japanese Politics*, and chapter IV.

115. "Hakko Ichiu" meant "the bringing of the corners of the world under one roof, or the making of the world one family. This was the alleged ideal of the foundation of the Empire; and its traditional context meant no more than a universal principle of humanity which was destined ultimately to pervade the whole universe. The second principle of conduct was the principle of 'Kodo,' a contraction of an ancient phrase which meant literally 'The oneness of the Imperial Way.' The way to the realization of Hakkō Ichiu was through the benign rule of the Emperor; and therefore the 'way of the Emperor'—the 'Imperial' or the 'Kingly way'—was a concept of virtue, and a maxim of conduct. Hakkō Ichiu was the moral goal; and loyalty to the Emperor was the road which led to it. These two ideas were again associated with the Imperial Dynasty after the Meiji Restoration. The Emperor proclaimed them in an Imperial Rescript issued in 1871. They then represented a constitutional rallying point, and an appeal to the patriotism of the Japanese people . . . In the decade before 1930, those Japanese who urged territorial expansion did so in the name of these two ideas." B. V. A. Röling and C. F. Rüter (eds.), *The Tokyo Judgment: The International Military Tribunal for the Far East (IMTFE), 29 April 1946–12 November 1948*, part I: "The Majority Judgment" (Amsterdam: University Press Amsterdam, 1972), 53–54.

116. In Bamba's view, "traditionalism" was characteristic of Japanese "national politics," which represented the concept of *kokutai* (i.e., the national, specifically Japanese state body with the Tennō at the top as the divinely legitimized ruler and with the Japanese people as the incarnation of the imperial will) (Bamba, *op. cit.* 25ff). According to Maruyama, the term *kokutai* appeared "as a legal concept for the first time in the first paragraph of the Law for the Upholding of Peace and Order (*chian iji hō*)" (*op. cit.*, 47). See also Klaus Antoni, "Kokutai—Das 'Nationalwesen' als japanische Utopie," *Saeculum* 38, nos. 2–3 (1987): 267ff; and Reinhard Zöllner, "Lorenz von Stein und *kokutai*," *Oriens Extremus* 33, no. 1 (1990): 65–76.

117. "Meiji" means "bright rule" or "enlightened government": "No one questioned the appropriateness of this name for the ruler, who became known, even to reformers in nineteenth-century China, as a symbol of the modern East" (Tsunoda, De Bary, and Keene, *op. cit.*, vol. II., 136). These authors then (*ibid.*) state: "If subsequently the imperial institution has been able to withstand the shocks of the twentieth century, and survive in the esteem of the people, it is due largely to the prestige won for it by Meiji, in demonstrating that the Throne could be a constructive and steadying force in the new era. . . . [W]e must not neglect the central fact of Meiji's rule—that it brought Japan out of the feudal past and into the modern world."

118. Tsunoda, De Bary, and Keene, *op. cit.*, vol. II, 132. The great "master planners" were above all the "Big Three" (*ibid.*, 193): "Of the so-called Big Three of the Meiji Era, Itō was usually identified in the popular mind with the Constitution, Ōkuma with 'public opinion,' and Yamagata Aritomo (1838–1922) with the Army. Among them Yamagata also most conspicuously represented the forces of traditionalism."

119. One should not, however, overlook the fact that the "outer daimyō" (*tozama daimyō*) had during the entire Edo period intrigued against the *bakufu* (shōgunate) and that often bitter, although generally nonviolent, struggles for power took place between certain feudal domains.

120. Alexander Georg Gustav von Siebold, *Der Eintritt Japans in das europäische Völkerrecht* (The entry of Japan into the Law of Nations), 49.

121. For a detailed account, see Ronald Toby, *State and Diplomacy in Early Modern Japan, Asia in the Development of the Tokugawa Bakufu* (Princeton, N.J.: Princeton University Press, 1984). This book brings together discussions among historians that began in the mid-1970s.

122. Nakamura Hajime could still in 1967 represent the view that Japanese feudalism had wholly "crushed" foreign trade and "obstructed the development of a civil society in the European sense of the word." See Nakamura Hajime, "Suzuki Shōzan 1579–1655, and the Spirit of Capitalism in Japanese Buddhism," *Monumenta Nipponica* XXII (1967): 1.

123. Toby, *op. cit.*, xiv.

124. Toby, *op. cit.*, xv. For the history of the Ryūkyū Islands, see George H. Kerr, *Okinawa, The History of an Island People* (Rutland, Vt., and Tokyo: Charles E. Tuttle, 1958).

125. Toby (*op. cit.*, 36–37) gives a list of the Korean embassies, also giving a list of the embassies from the Ryūkyū Kingdom (48–49).

126. See Iwao Seiichi, "Reopening of the Diplomatic Relations between Japan and Siam during Tokugawa Days," *Acta Asiatica*, no. 4 (1963): 1–31.

127. Toby, *op. cit.*, xvi–xvii. Toby names Asao Naohiro as one of the first authors who, in contrast to the then dominant view in Japan, recognized "foreign relations as one of the central elements in the development of the Tokugawa state."

128. Toby, *op. cit.*, 14. "The analogy with England is perhaps useful for comparison, for England, too, was confronted with what she perceived as a Catholic menace" (Toby, *ibid.*, 21).

129. Ronald Toby, *op. cit.*, 217. Compare also Nishikawa Joken, *Ka-i tsūshō kō* (Commercial considerations relating to the *ka'i* [model of interstate relations]), 1695, on Japan's trade with "barbarian" lands. I thank Prof. Nakai Akio of Sophia University for recommending this title. Compare also the Mediterranean/Roman concept of the civilized world under the rule of law confronted and threatened by lawless barbarians.

130. In the consciousness of the Japanese there had been until the arrival of the first Europeans in the East Asian region in the sixteenth century only three approximately equal-ranking (in Japanese eyes) cultures, each in itself central: the Chinese, the Japanese, and the Indian. See Mori Katsumi, "International Relations between the 10th and the 16th Century and the Development of the Japanese International

Consciousness," *Acta Asiatica*, no. 2 (1961): 69—"The world consisted of Honchō (Japan), Kara (China) and Tenjiku (India)."

131. *Ka* literally signifies a "flowering" (in this case of culture) and in our context could be translated as "civilization." For the Japanese the Manchus, which ruled all of China from 1644 until 1911, and also the Mongols, which conquered China's Song Dynasty between 1268 and 1279 and founded the Yuan Dynasty (lasting until 1368), were considered "uncivilized" (*i*).

132. Maruyama Masao, "Kindai Nihon shisōshi ni okeru kokka risei no mondai (1)" (The problem of the rationality of the national state in modern Japanese history), *Tenbō* (January 1949): 4–15. In Toby's paraphrase: "For it was, in Maruyama's view, only through the catalysis of a Japan-centered vision of *ka* and *i* that the Japanese were able to transform late-Tokugawa isolationism and xenophobia . . . into the thesis that Japan's survival depended on the autonomous opening of the country to full foreign intercourse (*kaikoku*)" (Toby, *op. cit.*, 218).

133. This way of seeing things was expressed in the already mentioned late seventeenth-century work by Nishikawa Joken, *Ka-i tsūshō kō*, on trade with Korea, Siam, and Holland, in which China is represented as central and India has largely disappeared from view. Thus China, as the "Middle Kingdom" between India and Japan, was a center of civilization in East Asia.

134. See Toby, *op. cit.*, 223ff., especially 225: "Japanese intellectuals, government officials, and popular writers all [had] identified the Manchus as the 'Tatars,' and considered them to be the same people who had tried to invade Japan in the thirteenth century." See also John King Fairbank and Merle Goldman, *China, a New History* (enlarged edition) (Cambridge and London: The Belknap Press of Harvard University Press, 1998), 1: "2 million or so Manchus took power over 120 million or so Chinese."

135. The Confucian scholar Hayashi Razan, in the early Edo Period, in the letters he was commissioned by the *bakufu* to send to the Chinese government representative in Fujian Province included the phrase "to restore the old relations between the two countries will surely bind together the joyous hearts of the *two heavens*" (emphasis added). See *Hayashi Razan bunshū*, 132, cited in Toby, *op. cit.*, 172. See also Toby, 219n125, and 221 (quote from Fujiwara Seika, who was Hayashi Razan's mentor). Already earlier, Japanese written communications to the Chinese court were meant to establish equal status by using phrases like "from the son of heaven from the land of the rising sun to the son of heaven from the land of the setting sun."

136. Harootunian, *Toward Restoration*, 18.

137. Miyoshi, *As We Saw Them*, 171, referring to Albert Craig, Fukuzawa Yukichi, "The Philosophical Foundations of Meiji Nationalism," in Robert E. Ward, *Political Development in Modern Japan* (Princeton, N.J.: Princeton University Press, 1968) (e.g., 114 and 145).

138. For a detailed account, see John Peter Stern, *The Japanese Interpretation of the "Law of Nations," 1854–1874* (Princeton, N.J.: Princeton University Press, 1979).

139. The delegation, of which the young Fukuzawa Yukichi was a member, was led by Shinmi Masaoki, Muragaki Norimasa, and Oguri Tadamasa. It left Yoko-

hama in January on the American warship *Powhatan* and was accompanied by the *Kanrin Maru* with a Japanese crew under Captain Katsu Kaishū. On 17 May 1860 the Japanese exchanged credentials in Washington with President James Buchanan. What impressed the *bakufu* representatives most of all was the American election system, whose functioning they could observe first-hand as presidential elections were soon in progress, which would lead to the selection of Abraham Lincoln in November.

140. Townsend Harris, the American representative in Edo, sponsored the first mission. The second mission was sponsored by the British Minister Rutherford Alcock and French Minister Duchesne de Bellecourt. See also Miyoshi Masao, *As We Saw Them, The First Japanese Embassy to the United States (1860)*.

141. For a complete list of the members of all the missions to the West prior to the Meiji Restoration see Osatake Takeshi, *Iteki no kuni e* (To the lands of the aliens) (Tokyo: Banrikaku Shobō, 1929) (with the full membership of the second mission given on 222–24).

142. This mission took part in the Universal Exposition in Paris. It was the last of the missions sent to the West by the Tokugawa Shōgunate (*bakufu*). Led by the young Tokugawa Mimbudayū Akitake, the shōgun's brother, "this delegation was clearly a strategic one, and the Tokugawas emphasized its importance by sending, for the first time, a real prince. . . . By this time, however, all was too late. While the young boy was beginning to behave like a Japanese version of the Prince of Wales at the courts of Napoleon III, Queen Victoria, and other European monarchs, the foundation of the Tokugawa House was rapidly caving in. . . . And by the time he hurried home, his brother no longer ruled over Japan" (Miyoshi, *As We Saw Them*, 175).

143. The attempt by the Japanese mission to the United States to revise the treaty that had been concluded in 1858 with the American envoy Townsend Harris was unsuccessful. On the other hand the Japanese delegation successfully acquired useful knowledge about modern economic life, methods of industrial production, and modern techniques utilized in agriculture, transportation, and communications. The delegation's findings and impressions were published in 1878 in a five-volume report on their travels. On the history of the "unequal treaties," see Francis C. Jones, *op. cit.*.

144. Miyoshi, *As We Saw Them*, 171. Fukuzawa was soon disillusioned: "As he gradually realized that the Western nations did not live up to the so-called 'law of nations,' Fukuzawa began to adjust to the changed understanding of the West all his socio-political ideas from civil rights to international justice. The West was wealthy and powerful; Japan too should be wealthy and powerful. How? Militarily and economically. During his entire career as the head of the *Jiji Shinpō* after 1882, he supported every single administration program for military expansion, strengthening of capitalism, and territorial invasion of Korea and China." See also *ibid.*, 16. Compare some of the discussions which took place in Japan between 1854 and 1874 on the law of nations as either a "shield of the weak" or as an "instrument of the mighty" and on the state as a "moral entity," as presented by John Peter Stern, *op. cit.*, 63–100. See also Miwa Kimitada, "Fukuzawa Yukichi's 'Departure from Asia,'" *Monumenta Nipponica*, Special Issue: Centennial of the Meiji Restoration, ed. Edmund Skrzypczak (Tokyo: Sophia University and Charles E. Tuttle, 1968): 1–26.

145. Japan's rapid technological and material progress in the second half of the nineteenth century is lauded by Wells in his *The Outline of History* (1032 of the 1949 Garden City Books edition): "In 1866 she was a medieval people, a fantastic caricature of the extremist romantic feudalism: in 1899 hers was a completely Westernized people, on a level with the most advanced European powers, and well in advance of Russia. She completely dispelled the persuasion that Asia was in some irrevocable way hopelessly behind Europe. She made all European progress seem sluggish and tentative by comparison."

146. Quoted in Miyoshi Masao, *As We Saw Them*, 143. Kido Kōin five years later took part in the already mentioned Iwakura Mission to Europe, together with Itō Hirobumi, Ōkubo Toshimichi, and others. During a dinner in the residence of Prince Bismarck in Berlin, the German chancellor warned the Japanese not to put too much faith in the law of nations. Bersihand refers to this occasion in these words: "Bismarck explained that Japan should make itself so strong that it could rely on its own strength alone: nations observed their international obligations only insofar as this was in their own interests. This lecture was not without effect [sic!]" (*op. cit.*, 339). The text of Bismarck's remarks at this dinner is reproduced in Alfred Milatz (ed.), *Otto von Bismarck: Werke in Auswahl*, vol. 5 (Darmstadt: Wissenschaftliche Buchgesellschaft, 1973), 311–12. See also Yanaga Chitoshi, *Japan since Perry* (New York: McGraw-Hill, 1949), 179.

147. The first-named date is according to the Japanese lunar calendar, which was officially replaced by the Gregorian calendar two years later.

148. This was surely in part thanks to the efforts of the American envoy Townsend Harris, who between 1856 and 1858 negotiated the Treaty of Amity and Trade (the "Harris Treaty") between Japan and the United States of America. In the words of Miyoshi Masao, *op. cit.*, 16: "To bring the heathen country under the 'laws of nations' was his personal mission, reflecting the Manifest Destiny of the United States." Also of the greatest importance here was the influence of Fukuzawa Yukichi, who in the 1860s and early 1870s "assumed that the civilized countries of the world should, and in fact *did* abide by the 'law of nations' (*bankoku no kōhō*)" (Miyoshi, *As We Saw Them*, 171).

149. *Nihon gaikō nenpyō narabi ni shuyō monjo* (Chronology and major documents of Japanese diplomacy), Gaimushō 1969, vol. 1, 33–34.

150. See Najita, *Japan—The Intellectual Foundations*, 82–83.

151. Hall, *Japan—From Prehistory to Modern Times*, 287.

152. "Thus the moral power of the state reached its greatest possible extent: in exchange for guaranteeing the natural rights of man, the state could demand the willingness to accept discipline, danger and ultimately death in its defence. What transformed warfare was therefore a revolution in the power of the state, acting in the name of the general will. Military service, from having been the lot of a small section of society, could now in theory be truly universal." Hew Strachan, "Nation in Arms," in Geoffrey Best (ed.), *The Permanent Revolution, The French Revolution and its Legacy, 1789–1989* (London: Fontana Press, 1988), 49–50. This passage also can apply to Japan, which had in this respect learned a good deal from France.

153. Cited and translated in Tsunoda, De Bary, and Keene, *Sources of Japanese Tradition*, vol. II, 197–98. See also Miyoshi, *As We Saw Them*, 171, referring to

Albert Craig, "Fukuzawa Yukichi: The Philosophical Foundations of Meiji Nationalism," in Robert E. Ward, *Political Development in Modern Japan* (Princeton, N.J.:
Princeton University Press, 1968) (e.g., 114 and 145), who asserts that Fukuzawa had
been able to welcome and accept the law of nations because it was based on a sort of
"natural law" which was akin to the *ri* of neo-Confucian teachings.

154. In Europe the French King Charles VII established the first standing, regularly
salaried army in 1445. Until then there had been neither a duty of military service nor a
right of the king to exact taxes. Within two centuries the number of soldiers increased
from twelve thousand under Charles VII to one hundred eighty thousand under Louis
XIV. There were soon similar developments in other parts of the world. However, wars
until the end of the Middle Ages were still to an extent ritual. War was a legitimate
means for deciding a dispute over rights between states. Interestingly, an international
"arms race" began around the same time as the "discovery of the world" by the Europeans. On the "democratizing" of the institution of war, see the tendentious argument in
Karl Dietrich Erdmann, in "Toynbee—eine Zwischenbilanz" (Toynbee—an intermedi-
ate assessment), *Archiv für Kulturgeschichte* 33 (1951): 218–19.

> The French Revolution . . . brought forth a new age of fanaticism. The institu-
> tion of war was democratized. From a sport of kings it became an affair of
> [whole] peoples. In the place of costly, small, cautiously employed mercenary
> armies (*Söldnerheere*) there appeared cheap, ruthlessly exploitable mass armies.
> Industrial development put new frightful weapons into the hands of fanatical
> peoples' armies [*Volksheere*]. The manufacture and operation of these weapons
> became ever more complex, engaged ever wider sectors of a country's total
> life activities, until we in our days have experienced the monstrosity of "total
> war." But how was it possible that democracy, in which its admirers like to see
> a political manifestation of the Christian faith, could at the same time fall into
> contradiction with itself, insofar as it influenced the development of warmaking
> in such an unhealthy way?
>
> *The answer is to be found in the circumstance that democracy and industrial-
> ism, instead of other natural tendency to overcome the sovereignty of individual
> states, on the contrary allied themselves with these individual states. The mod-
> ern nationalism that springs from such an idea, the driving force behind the
> terror of conducting a total war, is thus a historical abnormality, an anachro-
> nism through which it has come to pass that the old institution of single-state
> sovereignty had lost, in a process of sclerosis, the capacity to adapt itself to the
> essentially 'universal' impulse of industry and democracy* [emphasis added].
>
> The conviction that the world will ultimately regulate itself through a free
> economy rested, however, on still another misconception. It did not take account
> of the evidence from the past that man does not live by bread alone.

Nonetheless the French Revolution brought with it, for the first time, the *constitutional outlawing of war*. See Boris Mirkine-Guetzévitch, "La Renonçiation à la
Guerre dans le Droit Constitutionnel moderne," *Révue Héllénique de Droit Internationale* 4 (1951): 1–16.

155. Siebold, *op. cit.*, 20.

156. Siebold, *op. cit.*, 20.

157. One should not make comparisons only with the European powers (and the United States), but should also take account of Asian neighbors and their identity. The Bengali poet-philosopher Rabindranath Tagore (1861–1941) wrote at the start of the twentieth century: "Japan's example has given heart to the rest of Asia. . . . We have seen the life and strength are there in us, only the dead crust has to be removed." Cited in Peter Duus, *The Rise of Modern Japan* (Boston, Atlanta, and London: Houghton Mifflin Co., 1976), 189. See also Rabindranath Tagore, *Der Geist Japans* (The spirit of Japan) (Leipzig: Der Neue Geist Verlag, n.d.).

158. Duus, *op. cit.*, 189–90. However, many Asians looked on Japan's development with an increasingly critical eye: "[E]vents were soon to prove these hopes false. Although many Japanese continued to be Pan-Asianist in word, the Japanese government was emphatically imperialist in deed, working hand in glove with the very Western colonialist powers against whom the other Asian nationalist movements struggled" (*loc. cit.*). See also Klaus Schlichtmann, "Gandhi and the Quest for an Effective United Nations: The Stakes, 1917 to 1947," *Gandhi Marg* 26, no. 1 (April–June 2004): 55–79.

159. See the famous passage in Friedrich Nietzsche, *Human, All too Human II*, The Wanderer and his Shadow, 1880, Nr. 284:

The means to real peace.—No government nowadays admits that it maintains an army so as to satisfy occasional thirsts for conquest; the army is supposed to be for defence. That morality which sanctions self-protection is called upon to be its advocate. But that means to reserve morality to oneself and to accuse one's neighbour of immorality, since he has to be thought of as ready for aggression and conquest if our own state is obliged to take thought of means of self-defence; moreover, when our neighbour denies any thirst for aggression just as heatedly as our State does, and protests that he too maintains an army only for reasons of legitimate self-defence, our declaration of why we require an army declares our neighbour a hypocrite and cunning criminal who would be only too happy to *pounce upon* a harmless and unprepared victim and subdue him without a struggle. This is how all states now confront one another: they presuppose an evil disposition in their neighbour and a benevolent disposition in themselves. This presupposition, however, is a piece of *inhumanity* as bad as, if not worse than, a war would be; indeed, fundamentally it already constitutes an invitation to and cause of wars, because, as aforesaid, it imputes immorality to one's neighbour and thereby seems to provoke hostility and hostile acts on his part. The doctrine of the army as a means of self-defence must be renounced just as completely as the thirst for conquest. And perhaps there will come a great day on which a nation distinguished for wars and victories and for the highest development of military discipline and thinking, and accustomed to making the heaviest sacrifices on behalf of these things, will cry of its own free will: *"we shall shatter the sword"*—and demolish its entire military machine down to its last foundations. *To disarm while being the best armed,* out of an *elevation* of sensibility—that is the means to *real* peace, which must always rest on a disposition for peace: whereas the so-called armed peace such as now parades about in every country is a disposition to fractiousness which trusts neither itself nor its neighbour and fails to lay down its arms half out of hatred, half out of fear. Better to perish than to hate and fear, and *twofold better to perish than to make oneself hated and feared*—this must one day become the supreme maxim of every individual state!—As is well known, our liberal representatives of the people lack the time to reflect on the nature of man: otherwise they would know that they labour in vain when they work for a "gradual reduction of the military burden." On the contrary, it is only when this kind of distress is at its greatest that the only kind of god that can help here will be closest at hand. The tree of the glory of war can be destroyed only at a single stroke, by a lightning-bolt: lightning, however, as you well know, comes out of a cloud and from on high (trans. R. J. Hollingdale, in *Human, All Too Human. A Book for Free Spirits* [Cambridge: Cambridge Texts in the History of Philosophy, 1996], 380–81).

160. Alexander von Siebold, after attending a gymnasium in Germany through the fourth class, came to Japan with his father in 1859, was an employee of the English legation in Tokyo, served in 1867 as interpreter during the Tokugawa Akitake Mission to Europe, in 1869 served as English consul in Tokyo and as interpreter for the Austro-Hungarian Japan Mission and in 1879 as honorary secretary of the Japanese Legation in Berlin. See Hans Körner, *Die Würzburger Siebolds, eine Gelehrtenfamilie des 18. und 19. Jahrhunderts* (The Siebolds of Würzburg, a scholar family of the eighteenth and nineteenth centuries) (Leipzig: J.A. Barth, 1967).

161. Alexander von Siebold, *op. cit.,* 1–2. This is not quite correct, since there had already been treaties based on the law of nations with Muslim states, for example, with the Ottoman Turks, and international law had thus already been applied beyond the borders of Europe.

162. Walther Schücking, *Der Bund der Völker, Studien und Vorträge zum organisatorischen Pazifismus* (Leipzig: Der Neue Geist Verlag, 1918), 64.

163. *Ibid.*

164. *Ibid.*

165. 5 July 1890, *ibid.*

166. *Wheaton's Elements of International Law,* first edition, Philadelphia, 1836.

167. "It was perhaps Grotius's combination of realism and idealism which struck Wheaton." C. van Vollenhoven, "Grotius and Geneva," lectures delivered in Columbia University, July 1925, *Bibliotheca Visseriana Dissertationum Ius Internationale Illustratium,* Bd.6 (Leyden: E. J. Brill 1926), 35.

168. Klaus Dicke, "Gerechtigkeit schafft Frieden" (Justice creates peace), in Max Müller (ed.), *Senfkorn, Handbuch für den katholischen Religionsunterricht* (The Mustard Seed, Handbook for Catholic religious instruction) vol. III/1, Stuttgart 1987, 363. Relevant also to the modern age is Dicke's comment (*ibid.*): "In particular the idea expressed therein of a peace-securing federation of states as a 'surrogate' for the lack of a centralized administration of order in international politics . . . was the

godfather for the creation of the peace-securing world organizations after both world wars, the League of Nations and the United Nations."

169. There were six imperial universities in Japan.

170. Siebold, *op. cit.*, 27.

171. The Swiss-born international law professor at Heidelberg University Johann Caspar Bluntschli in 1878 also published a peace plan, for an international (European) federation.

172. *Ibid.*, footnote.

173. On the origin of the Meiji constitution, see Johannes Siemes, *Die Gründung des modernen japanischen Staates und das deutsche Staatsrecht* (The founding of the modern Japanese state and German civil law) (Berlin: Duncker & Humblot, 1975). See also Rolf-Harald Wippich, "The Beginnings of German Cultural Activities in Meiji Japan," *Sophia International Review* 15 (1993): 61. "The year 1881 was a turning point, because it practically paved the way for the adoption of Prusso-German models . . . [showing that there was] a clear preference for German patterns in establishing an authoritarian structure of the state" (*ibid.*, 60–61.)

174. Ueki's draft came to play a vital part in the making of the 1946 "Peace Constitution" (*heiwa kempō*).

175. But see Otfried Nippold, *Die Wahrheit über die Ursachen des Europäischen Krieges* (The Truth About the Causes of the European War), ed. Harald Kleinschmidt with an introduction by Akio Nakai (München: Iudicium, 2005) (backcover of book), where Nippold is said to have "developed his political ideas from the experience during his visit as law professor [teaching] in Japan from 1885–1889."

176. Quite the opposite concept is proclaimed by Mathias Erzberger, *The League of Nations. The Way to the World's Peace*, trans. Bernard Miall (New York: Henry Holt, 1919), 176: "It is part of the conception of justice which is to be established in the collective life of the nations that it must replace the 'right' of might by the right of right, which will be available for all, without exception."

177. Wippich, "The Beginnings of German Cultural Activities in Meiji Japan," 61.

178. See Katō Hiroyuki, *Der Kampf ums Recht des Stärkeren und seine Entwicklung* (The struggle for the right of the mightier and its development) (Berlin: R. Friedländer & Sohn, 1894). In this book, published in German and strongly influenced by Rudolf von Jhering, Katō makes a distinction between, for example, "active and passive (feminine) human races." According to his thesis, the Asiatic peoples were still "at a low level of civilization" (63). The "German race—certainly the strongest of all races" must in this situation take the leadership in "the struggle for the right of the more mighty." (66). On Katō, see also Maruyama Masao, *Denken in Japan* (Japanese thought), ed. and trans. Wolfgang Schamoni and Wolfgang Seifert, (Frankfurt: Suhrkamp, 1988), 39. (The original Japanese edition is *Nihon no shisō*, Iwanami Shoten, 1961).

179. Maruyama, *Denken in Japan*, 39. In reference to Katō Hiroyuki, the author states that the international community of states "found itself in the second half of the nineteenth century at a turning point both with regard to political-economic trends and with respect to the intellectual and cultural situation" (*ibid.*, 42).

180. Kido Kōin's diary (see following note) undoubtedly permits such an interpretation, as do expressions of opinion by other Meiji Period statesmen. International law since the nineteenth century was concerned with creating a legally binding framework for the peaceful settlement of disputes and mutually beneficial intercourse of nations with one another, eventually—in the twentieth century—favoring disarmament in the interests of economic and social progress.

181. Kido Kōin, *Shōgiku Kido-kō den*, 1563–68. Cited in Tsunoda, De Bary, and Keene, *Sources of Japanese Tradition*, vol. II, 143; McLaren, *Government Documents*, 571–75.

182. Evidently, the Chinese broke the Treaty of Tianjin (1885). See Bersihand, *op. cit.*, 356–57. According to the treaty, both Japan and China had been required to remove their troops from Korea. Perhaps the Japanese had had more sympathy from the Korean *people*, but China in 1894 sent troops to Korea, in violation of the treaty agreement, in order to support the government against the populace: "Japan's victory in its support for the Korean popular uprising in 1894 was for China a huge psychological shock. In a battle near the mouth of the Yalu River four out of twelve Chinese ships sank—the Japanese had no losses. China could at first not admit this defeat and published woodcut-print posters on which its navy was shown destroying the Japanese navy and winning back Korea." See also Tsurumi, "The Meiji Revolution and Its Consequences," in Arnold Toynbee (ed.), *Half the World*, 313.

183. See also Marius B. Jansen, *Japan and China, from War to Peace 1894–1972* (Chicago: Rand McNally College Edition, 1975).

184. On the history of Korea and its relations with Japan and China see Ku Dae-Yeol, *Korea under Colonialism: The March First Movement and Anglo-Japanese Relations* (Seoul: The Royal Asiatic Society, Korea Branch, 1985); Melvin Frederick Nelson, *Korea and the Old Orders in East Asia* (New York: Russell & Russell, 1967); Benjamin Weems, *Reform, Rebellion, and the Heavenly Way* (Tucson: University of Arizona Press, 1964); Lee Ki-baik (Yi Ki-baek), *A New History of Korea* (trans. Edward W. Wagner and Edward J. Shultz) (Cambridge, Mass., and London: Harvard University Press, 1984, for the Harvard-Yenching Institute); and Homer B. Hulbert, *History of Korea* (London: Routledge & Kegan Paul, 1962).

185. Hatada, *A History of Korea*, 92.

186. On the background to the Japanese-Chinese disputes and Japan's relationship to Korea, see also Duus, who gives a fitting description of the events (*op. cit.*, 127ff.). A less Japan-friendly description is given in Beasley, *op. cit.*, 48 ff.

187. Duus, *op. cit.*, 128. For additional details, compare also the following accounts, which variously emphasize certain elements: C. I. Eugene Kim and Kim Han-kyo, *Korea and the Politics of Imperialism 1876–1910* (Berkeley and Los Angeles: University of California Press, 1967); *The Observations of Ernest Satow, British Minister Plenipotentiary to Japan (1895–1900) and China (1900–1906)*, selected and edited with a historical introduction by George Alexander Lensen (Tokyo: Sophia University/Tallahassee, Fla.: The Diplomatic Press, 1968) (1966); George Alexander Lensen, *Balance of Intrigue—International Rivalry in Korea and Manchuria, 1884–1899*, vol. II (Tallahassee: University Press of Florida, 1982).

188. On the "Tonghak" rebellion, see Mutsu Munemitsu, *Kenkenroku—A Diplomatic Record of the Sino-Japanese War, 1894–95*, ed. and trans. Gordon Mark Berger, chapter I, "The Tonghak Rebellion," 19–33 (Tokyo: University of Tokyo Press, 1982), 5–10; Lee Chong-sik, *The Politics of Korean Nationalism* (Berkeley and Los Angeles: University of California Press, 1965). The ideological background of this revolutionary movement, which had similarities with the Christian-inspired Taiping Rebellion in China (1850–1864) and with the later Boxer Rebellion of 1900, included a mixture of religious elements, nationalism, the declared struggle against the government, and a cleverly contrived organizational structure for the attainment of its revolutionary goals. The movement was generally ill-disposed toward all foreign powers including the Japanese. See Lee, *op. cit.*, 26; C. I. Eugene Kim and Kim Han-kyo, *op. cit.*, 75–77; Lensen, *op. cit.*, vol. 1, 121–35.

189. See Mutsu, *Kenkenroku*, chapter IV, "The Proposal for a Joint Sino-Japanese Commission on Korean Domestic Reform," 21–26; Duus, *op. cit.*, 129. Lee Chong-sik, *op. cit.*, 288n25, states: "As the Japanese government had expected, the Chinese government rejected the offer of joint efforts."

190. "So marked was the predominance of British influence in Peking that the Tsungli Yamen could have been easily induced to make such timely and generous concessions in the matter of Corea as would have stopped the outbreak of hostilities" (*The North-China Herald*, 3 October 1898; the name of the American is unknown). Lord Rosebery, the British prime minister at the time, pursued a policy of peace throughout. This course apparently made him overlook other, substantial aspects of the situation.

191. Bersihand, *op. cit.*, 365. See also Fairbank, Reischauer, and Craig, *East Asia—The Modern Transformation*, 382–83.

192. On the Treaty of Shimonoseki, see the detailed discussion in *Kenkenroku*, chapters 16–18. According to Fairbank, Reischauer, and Craig, the following dialogue occurred during the first meeting at Shimonoseki between Itō Hirobumi and Li Hung-chang representing the Chinese High Command: "Itō said to him, 'Ten years ago at Tientsin I talked with you about reform. Why is it that up to now not a single thing has been changed or reformed?' Li replied, 'Affairs in my country have been so confined by tradition'" (*East Asia—The Modern Transformation*, 383).

193. See Otfried Nippold, *Die Wahrheit über die Ursachen des Europäischen Krieges*, "introduction," xlii: "[T]he French envoy Harmand and even the Russian, Hitrovo, had made a definite endeavour to use a conciliatory language, while Baron Gutschmid added a lengthy written statement to his actual explanation, in which he—and he alone—bluntly threatened [the Japanese] with war."

194. Baron S. A. Korff, *Russia's Foreign Relations During the Last Half Century* (New York: Macmillan, 1922), 75. On the other hand the Russian plans for the Pacific coastal region were still unclear.

195. *Frankfurter Zeitung*, 23 March 1896.

196. Bersihand, *op. cit.*, 371 (emphasis added). Wilhelm Grewe, in discussing the 1894–1895 war, curiously omits any mention of Japan's acquisition of Taiwan (*The Epochs of International Law*, 441).

197. Bersihand, *op. cit.*, 376. See also Grewe, *op. cit.*, 441.

198. Compare Korff, *op. cit.*, 76–77: "What could Japan think of European diplomatic methods after that? And this was the start of her intimate dealings with Russia . . . [T]hese relations from the beginning took the shape of mutual distrust and dislike . . . Japan found nothing but double play and trickery and when later during the suppression of the Boxer uprising she witnessed the looting and robbing of Chinese homes by Europeans, she must necessarily have felt grave doubts about the lofty ideals of European civilization. The Chinese riots on the Russian frontier . . . when the riots occurred along the Amur River the Russian generals there behaved most cruelly, for not only did they shoot promiscuously all Chinese in sight, but ordered some of them to be placed on barges in the river and the barges sunk."

199. Hatada Takashi, *A History of Korea*, 104.

200. *The North-China Herald*, 21 February 1896.

201. The treaty concluded with Great Britain in 1894 would not enter into force until 1899. The revision of the "unequal treaties" was, after the promulgation of the Meiji constitution of 1889, the main theme of political discussion.

202. Walther Schücking, "Die Annäherung der Menschenrassen durch das Völkerrecht, address given before the First Universal Races Congress (London, 26–29 July 1911)," in Schücking, *Der Bund der Völker* (1918), 60. See also Siebold, *op. cit.*, 1f. According to Siebold, Japan's membership in the comity of nations was decisively established as a result of the treaties of 17 July and 4 August 1899. See also the letter of 18 July 1899 from Minister Aoki to Lord Kimberly, cited in Siebold, 47–48: "The new treaty opened for Japan a new era in its foreign relations, because it for the first time pronounced the full and legitimate acceptance of Japan into the family of civilized powers." Siebold also reflected: "Thus finally . . . on 17 July and 4 August of that year, the reestablishment of Japan's sovereign rights, which it had long hoped for and struggled for, entered into force and the whole empire was opened to trade and intercourse under the generally accepted conditions of international law" (*op. cit.*, 48). However, as Maruyama points out, the "struggle for the revision of these treaties [found] its successful conclusion only in 1911" (*Denken in Japan*, 85).

203. On the tsar's rescript, see Arthur Eyffinger, *The Peace Palace. Residence for Justice—Domicile of Learning* (The Hague: Carnegie Foundation, 1992 [1988]), 9–19. The letter from Muraviev was addressed to the foreign legations accredited in St. Petersburg; Calvin DeArmond Davis, *The United States and the First Hague Peace Conference* (Ithaca, N.Y.: Cornell University Press [for the American Historical Association], 1962), 37ff. See also Jost Dülffer, *Regeln gegen den Krieg? Die Haager Friedenskonferenzen 1899 und 1907 in der internationalen Politik* (Rules against War? The Hague Peace Conferences of 1899 and 1907 in international politics) (Berlin, Frankfurt, and Wien: Ullstein, 1981), 39–53, and Klaus Schlichtmann, "Japan, Germany and the Idea of the two Hague Peace Conferences," *Journal of Peace Research* 40, no. 4 (2003): 377–94; Ralph Uhlig, *Die Interparlamentarische Union 1889–1914* (Stuttgart: Franz Steiner, 1988 [*Studien zur modernen Geschichte*, vol. 39]), 226, 249.

204. Francis Harry Hinsley, *Power and the Pursuit of Peace: Theory and Practice in the History of Relations between States* (Cambridge: Cambridge University Press, 1963), 139.

205. The opening words of the Uno Resolution A/RES/51/159 of the general assembly marking the centenary of the First Hague Peace Conference are: "Recognizing the invaluable contribution of the first International Peace Conference to the settling or resolving of international disputes or situations which can cause the infringement of peace, by its adoption of the Convention for the Pacific Settlement of International Disputes and the establishment of the Permanent Court of Arbitration."

206. C. van Vollenhoven, *Die drei Stufen des Völkerrechts* (The three stages of international law) (The Hague: Martinus Nijhoff, 1919), 98. Vollenhoven was later, like Shidehara, placed on the list of judges for the Permanent Court of Arbitration in The Hague.

207. I. S. Bloch, "Conversations with . . . W. T. Stead," in Bloch, *Is War now Impossible? Being an Abridgement of "The War of the Future in its Technical, Economic and Political Relations"* (London: Grant Richards, 1899), ix.

208. See Wolfgang Preiser, "Völkerrechtsgeschichte—Altertum, Mittelalter, Neuzeit bis zum Westfälischen Frieden" (History of International Law—ancient, medieval, modern until the Peace of Westphalia), in *Wörterbuch des Völkerrechts* (Dictionary of International Law), vol. 3, 680–703. A fairly comprehensive list of all published writings on European and international peace plans is found in Jakob Ter Meulen, *Der Gedanke der internationalen Organisation in seiner Entwicklung* (The Idea of International Organization and Its Development), three vols. (The Hague: Nijhoff, 1917), and in Hans-Jürgen Schlochauer, *Die Idee des Ewigen Friedens—Ein Überblick über Entwicklung und Gestaltung des Friedenssicherungsgedankens auf der Grundlage einer Quellenauswahl* (The Idea of Perpetual Peace—A review of the development and shaping of the idea of peace based on a selection of sources) (Bonn: Ludwig Röhrscheid, 1953); Kurt von Raumer, *Ewiger Friede: Friedensrufe und Friedenspläne seit der Renaissance* (Perpetual Peace: Appeals and Plans for Peace since the Renaissance) (Freiburg and München: Karl Alber, 1953). See also Peter Brock, *Studies in Peace History* (New York: Syracuse University Press, 1991); David Barash (ed.), *Approaches to Peace: A Reader in Peace Studies* (New York and Oxford: Oxford University Press, 2000); *Uniting the Peoples and Nations: Readings in World Federalism*, compiled by Barbara Walker, with an introduction by John Logue (New York: World Federalist Movement & World Federalist Association, 1993).

209. M. V. Krishna Rao speaks of "federal units centering around a dominant ruler" (*Studies in Kautilya* [Delhi: Munshi Ram Manohar Lal, 1958], 135). See Hartmut Scharfe, *Untersuchungen zur Staatsrechtslehre des Kautilya* (Investigations into Kautilya's Doctrines of Statecraft) (Wiesbaden: Otto Harrassowitz, 1968). Compare also Gerald Fussman, who also disagrees with the view that the Mauryan Empire, based on the doctrines of the *Arthashastra*, was a centralist state ("Central and Provincial Administration in Ancient India: The Problem of the Mauryan Empire," *The Indian Historical Review* XIV, nos. 1–2 [July 1987 and January 1988]: 43–72).

210. Compare, for example, the state concepts of Confucius. One might compare the passage in the "Sayings of Confucius," the *Lun-yü* (Japanese reading: *Rongo*), 2. I: "The Master said: 'To exercise government through virtue is, figuratively speaking, analogous to the North Star: it stays fast in its place and all the other stars gather around it.'" Cited in Bauer, *China and the Search for Happiness*, 47. Compare also Mozi's "ideal state" and the "idea of equity" (*ibid.*, 56).

211. William Ladd, *An Essay on a Congress of Nations, for the Adjustment of International Disputes without Resort to Arms* (New York: Oxford University Press, 1916) (reprint of the original edition of 1840).

212. Walther Schücking, *Die Organisation der Welt* (Leipzig: Alfred Kröner, 1909). According to this work, the modern concept of a pacifist, universal league of nations, which Kant favored, had its origins in the work of Pierre Dubois (ca. 1250–1325), a Norman lawyer serving Philip the Fair. In Schücking's opinion, this was "the most interesting, and at the same time the oldest document . . . relating to the history of the modern peace movement" (*ibid.*, 28). Dubois described in his work *De recuperatione terre sancte* the means and conditions for establishing a comprehensive, just, and durable peaceful international order. An "international league" consisting of a parliament of princes and a court of arbitration, and universal school education for young men and women were all part of this plan. Otto Gerhard Oexle saw Pierre Dubois had "since the time of the Hague Peace Conferences [been] a precursor of modern pacifism and of the idea of international arbitration . . . a pioneer of the league-of-nations idea . . . [and] since the end of the Second World War a leading representative of the idea of the Europe [-an union]" ("Utopisches Denken im Mittelalter: Pierre Dubois" (Utopian Thought in Medieval History: Pierre Dubois) *Historische Zeitschrift* 224 [1977]: 332–33).

213. On the 1899 peace conference, see Eyffinger, *The Peace Palace: Residence for Justice—Domicile of Learning*, 21–35; DeArmond Davis, *The United States and the First Hague Peace Conference*, especially 81ff.

214. See Albrecht Randelzhofer, "Entwicklungstendenzen im humanitären Völkerrecht für bewaffnete Konflikte," *Die Friedens-Warte* 59, nos. 1–2 (1975): 30: "The prohibition of violence, the *ius ad bellum*, threatens to take precedence over the *ius in bello*. . . . Between *ius ad bellum* and *ius in bello* there exists today a conflict."

215. In a sobering article published in 1994, Chris af Jochnick and Roger Normand have shown that, in regard to the legal standing and applicability of the *ius in bello*, "the entire work was in vain." Chris af Jochnick and Roger Normand, "The Legitimation of Violence: A Critical History of the Laws of War," *Harvard International Law Journal* 35, no. 1 (Winter 1994): 49–95.

216. See the article by Hans-Jürgen Schlochauer, "Internationale Gerichtsbarkeit" (International jurisdiction), *Wörterbuch des Völkerrechts* 2, 56–64, and his definition: "International jurisdiction is the institution of a permanent court of law which engages independent international judges who are not subject to influence from the disputants, and which decides international legal disputes between states in accordance with valid international law."

217. Philipp Zorn, *Deutschland und die beiden Haager Friedenskonferenzen* (Germany and the Two Hague Peace Conferences) (Stuttgart and Berlin: Deutsche Verlags-Anstalt, 1920), 64.

218. Hans Wehberg described Schücking at the time as "perhaps the greatest among the living international law scholars of the German Empire. . . . [N]obody has portrayed himself so openly as a pacifist" ("Walther Schücking, Ein deutscher Völkerrechtslehrer," *Die Friedens-Warte* 29 [March 1929]: 65).

219. Fritz Münch, "Walther Schücking (1875–1935)/Völkerrechtler und Poli-titker," in Ingeborg Schnack (ed.), *Marburger Gelehrte in der ersten Hälfte des 20. Jahrhunderts* (Marburg scholars in the first half of the twentieth century) (Marburg, 1977) (Lebensbilder aus Hessen, vol. 1. Veröffentlichungen der Hist. Kommission für Hessen 35, 1) (special publication), 474. See also Walther Schücking, *Der Bund der Völker: Studien und Vorträge zum organisatorischen Pazifismus* (Leipzig: Der Neue Geist Verlag, 1918), and Detlev Acker, *Walther Schücking (1875–1935)* (Münster: Aschendorffsche Verlagsanstalt, 1970) (XXIV), 37: "The term '*Internationale Organisation*' (international organization) was first used in Germany by Walther Schücking."

220. Politicians in the past hundred years have taken advantage of this internal discord between these two pacifist trends, ever since the nineteenth century, under the pretext of carrying forward a so-called *realpolitik* based on a presumed ethic of responsibility.

221. Murobuse Takanobu, "Kōwa kaigi ni okeru kakkoku no shuchō to sono hihan" (Claims of the various countries at the Peace Conference and a critique), *Chūō Kōron* 34, no. 6 (June 1919): 63. Translated by Miwa Kimitada, in "Japanese Opinion on Woodrow Wilson in War and Peace," *Monumenta Nipponica* 22, nos. 3–4, 388.

222. "Indeed, its expansion marks a major social phenomenon of the period" (Eyffinger, *The Peace Palace: Residence for Justice—Domicile of Learning*, 14).

223. This movement received a decisive impulse toward the establishment of modern peace research through the work of the Russian-Polish banker Ivan (Jean) de Bloch on the causes and consequences of war. De Bloch's *Der zukünftige Krieg in seiner technischen, volkswirtschaftlichen und politischen Bedeutung*, six vols., was first published in Russian in 1898, followed by a French translation in 1898 and a German translation in 1899: "Bloch . . . said first and foremost that the image of war in the future would be the mutual attrition of the opponents in a vicious circle; the end result would be the total decimation of all who take part, hunger catastrophes, social and political upheavals" (Karl Holl, *Pazifismus in Deutschland* [Frankfurt: Suhrkamp, 1988], 73). Bloch's work also appeared in English in an abridged version, as I. S. Bloch, *Is War Now Impossible? Being an Abridgement* (London: Grant Richards, 1899); and *The Future of War* (Toronto: W. Briggs, 1900). "Bloch's work is a veritable *Das Kapital* of pacifism" (Powles, *op. cit.*, 156).

224. Schücking, *Die Organisation der Welt*, 83.

225. Among them the Quakers, the Baha'I, and in Japan Ueki Emori.

226. Schücking, *Der Bund der Völker*, 63.

227. *Ibid.*, 73. See also Walther Schücking, *The International Union of the Hague Peace Conferences*, trans. Charles G. Fenwick (Oxford: Clarendon Press; London, Edinburgh, New York, Toronto, Melbourne, and Bombay: Humphrey Milford, 1918) (Carnegie Endowment for International Peace, Division of International Law, James Brown Scott, Director).

228. "It may cease to be a mere dream to look for the day when the nations of the world will federate under one code of international law and form one organic system, creating a new era of fellowship and good will" (Ōkuma, "Conclusion," in Ōkuma

(ed.), *Fifty Years of New Japan*, 575). See also the following commentary by Lebra, *Ōkuma Shigenobu*, 143–44: "Such was the visionary . . . goal to which Ōkuma aspired . . . it was incumbent on Japan in turn to transmit her knowledge to the rest of Asia. Japan had the unique capacity to graft the scientific civilisation of the West, having its origin in Greek knowledge and analysis, onto the substratum of the ancient civilisations of China and India."

229. Alexander Freiherr von Siebold, *Der Eintritt Japans in das europäische Völkerrecht*, (The entry of Japan into the European Law of Nations) (Berlin: Kisak Tamai, 1900), 15.

230. MacArthur sometimes spoke of Japan as the "Switzerland of the East." See, for example, General Douglas MacArthur in an interview with G. Ward Price, correspondent of the London *Daily Mail*, 2 March 1949, cited in Martin E. Weinstein, *Japan's Postwar Defense Policy, 1947–1968* (New York and London: Columbia University Press, 1971), 16n14. See also *The Mainichi*, 3 March 1949.

231. Von Siebold, *op. cit.*, 16, notes: "The famous session of the [French] National Assembly of 4 August 1789, where the French nobility, carried away by the general trend, voluntarily sacrificed their prerogatives, had a certain similarity with the behavior of the western and eastern daimyōs."

232. Ralph Uhlig, *Die Interparlamentarische Union 1889–1914—Friedenssicherungsbemühungen im Zeitalter des Imperialismus* (The IPU 1889–1914—Efforts at maintaining peace in the era of imperialism) (Stuttgart: Franz Steiner, 1988) (Studien zur modernen Geschichte, vol. 39), 65–66.

233. *Ibid.*, 480–81.

234. Calvin DeArmond Davis, *The United States and the Second Hague Peace Conference*, American Diplomacy and International Organization 1899–1914 (Durham, N.C.: Duke University Press, 1975), 110; Uhlig, *op. cit.*, 335.

235. Hinsley, *Power and the Pursuit of Peace*, 143.

236. On the Second Hague Peace Conference, see Eyffinger, *The Peace Palace. Residence for Justice—Domicile of Learning*, 77–91.

237. On the concept of arbitration and its history, see Kurt Rabl, *Die Völkerrechtsgrundlagen der modernen Friedensordnung* (The foundations of the contemporary order of peace in international law), part I, Geschichtliche Entwicklung (Hannover: Schriftenreihe der Niedersächsischen Landeszentrale für Politische Bildung, 1967) (Friedensprobleme, no. 2).

238. Philipp Zorn, *op. cit.*, 72.

239. Philipp Zorn, *op. cit.* (1920), 75.

240. *Ibid.*, 57 (emphasis added). Zorn (*ibid.*, 73), addressing the various reactions in the German and international press, notes that in Germany "no single one of the larger German press organs, and neither the 'Frankfurter Zeitung' nor the 'Berliner Tageblatt,' came forward decisively in favor of the Russian proposals. If directives from the foreign ministry had an effect here or perhaps were even of determining importance, I am unable to say; [however], I suspect it [to be the case]" (*ibid.*, 15–16). At the end of the conference "the mood . . . over the lamentable outcome in the main question of the conference's work . . . was extremely uneasy. . . . In the press of the whole world these laments and accusations echoed and re-echoed."

241. The wording of the relevant passages in the Hague conventions may suggest that this sort of aggression was already contrary to the law of nations as considered valid at the time.

242. There exists a wide-ranging literature on the question of the German responsibility for the First World War. See, for example, John Horne and Alan Kramer, *German Atrocities 1914: A History of Denial* (New Haven, Conn., and London: Yale University Press, 2001); see also Walter Fabian, *Die Kriegsschuldfrage* (The question of war guilt) (Bremen: Donat Verlag, 1988 (reprint of the 1925 edition), for Germany's "sole responsibility" for the First World War. Wilhelm Muehlon, *Ein Fremder im eigenen Land: Erinnerungen und Tagebuchaufzeichnungen eines Krupp-Direktors 1908–1914* (A foreigner in his own land: Memoirs and diary entries of a Krupp Director 1908–1914) (Bremen: Donat Verlag, 1989), 98 and 101–3. The German negotiator at the Versailles Conference, Count Brockdorff-Rantzau, who refused to sign the Versailles Treaty, in an interview of 17 February 1919 for the League of Nations, advocated the development of the "assembly of delegates into a world parliament," but this idea was subsequently completely forgotten; Count Brockdorff-Rantzau, *Dokumente und Gedanken um Versailles* (Documents and thoughts around Versailles) (Berlin: Verlag für Kulturpolitik, 1923), 152.

243. Friedrich Wilhelm Foerster has the following episode concerning Belgium: "In November 1913, King Albert visited the Kaiser at Potsdam. Moltke was invited to attend their meeting and heard the Kaiser inform the royal guest that war with France was inevitable, would shortly break out, and would certainly end in the defeat of France. If the small states wished to secure their national existence they would do well to join Germany in good time. King Albert ordered the Belgian ambassador in Berlin to acquaint the French ambassador Jules Cambon with this conversation, which so closely concerned the guarantees of Belgium's neutrality. Some ten years earlier the Kaiser had made the same proposition to King Albert's father and promised him several French provinces if he would permit the German army to march through Belgium" (*Europe and the German Question* [New York: Sheed & Ward, 1940], 215).

244. House Joint Resolution (H.J.Res.) 223, "Universal Peace Commission," 24 June 1910. *Congressional Record*, 20 and 24 June 1910, 8545–48, 9028.

245. Grey continued: "Public opinion has been moving; the number of arbitrations has been increasing; but you must take a large step further before the increase of arbitration will really affect this increase of expenditure on armaments." *Sir Edward Grey on Union for World Peace*, from his speech in the House of Commons, 13 March 1911, World Peace Foundation Pamphlet Series, Boston, April 1911, no. I, part II, 10.

246. U.S. President Taft on 22 March 1910, in *Sir Edward Grey on Union for World Peace*, 17. And in a speech in Washington on 17 December 1910 the American president explained: "If we can negotiate . . . agreements with some other nation to abide by the adjudication of International Arbitration Courts in every issue which cannot be settled by negotiations, no matter what it involves, whether honor, territory, or money, we shall have made a long step forward by demonstrating that it is possible for two nations at least to establish between them the same system which, through the process of law, has existed between individuals under government" (*ibid.*, 18).

247. Among the mix of realities that channeled the great powers' actions was also the promulgation of the upgrading of the German navy (*Flottennovelle*) in 1908, which was reciprocated in turn by increased British "Naval Estimates" in 1909.

248. See C. van Vollenhoven, *The Enforcement of Sanctions in International Law By Means Of an International Police System*, a paper sent to the International Peace Bureau for transmission to the Hague Peace Congress, Publications of the International Peace Bureau, August 1913, 7: "[O]ne could begin with an international navy, as the sum of all . . . individual navies."

249. House Joint Resolution 432, 27 February 1915, *Congressional Record*. This resolution more or less foundered amid the confusions of the war. Henry Ford declared that he favored the concepts it expressed.

250. The proposal of a certain Carroll Livingston Riker, published as *International Police of the Seas*, New York (April 1915), also found a substantial readership. In the U.S. House of Representatives, a further resolution was introduced, "looking to the neutral government and patrol of the seas, by an international Commission who shall control all armed vessels."

251. Also during the war, on 4 January 1916, a resolution was introduced in the House of Representatives that sought the creation of a world federation. H.J.Res.75, 64th Congress, "Joint resolution proposing the establishment of an International Federation of the World" (16, article VII). A copy is found in the Netherlands foreign ministry Archives, *Ministerie van Buitenlandse Zaken, Inventaris van de A-dossiers, 1871–1918*, 5 February 2003, DOOS 177.

252. Matsushita Masatoshi, *Japan in the League of Nations* (New York: Ames Press, 1968 [1929], Columbia University Studies in the Social Sciences), 15.

253. The founder of "anthroposophy," Rudolf Steiner, in his *Kernpunkte der sozialen Frage* (Central points of the social question) (Dornach: Steiner Verlag, 1919), 114, welcomed the establishment of the League of Nations "from realistic impulses," and discarded the view to "regard such things as 'utopian.' . . . *[I]n truth* the reality of life strives toward such institutions . . . *the damage to this reality comes precisely from the fact that these institutions are not in place*" (emphasis added).

254. William Rappard, *op. cit.*, 3–4.

255. James Bryce, *International Relations, Eight Lectures Delivered in the United States in August 1921* (New York: Macmillan, 1923), lecture II, "The Great War and Its Results," 72–73. Bryce's list is indeed long and worth studying.

256. Cited in Kurt Rabl, *Die Völkerrechtsgrundlagen der modernen Friedensordnung*, part I, "Geschichtliche Entwicklung" (Hannover: Schriftenreihe der niederländischen Landeszentrale für politische Bildung, 1967) (Friedensprobleme, 2), 3.

257. On the history of the Permanent Court of International Justice, see Hans-Jürgen Schlochauer, "Ständiger Internationaler Gerichtshof" (Permanent International Court), in *Wörterbuch des Völkerrechts*, vol. 3, 342: "During the first World War, the idea of an international court to be created after the war's end was put forward partly in connection with plans for a world organization, but it was advocated mainly apart from academic associations—[i.e.] for the most part by the Interparliamentary Union, the Central Organisation for a Durable Peace, the British Fabian Society, the American Society for the Judicial Settlement of Disputes, and the World Court's League (with its journal *The*

World Court, 1915–1919)—as well as through Commission Drafts by neutral states like Denmark, Norway, Sweden and Switzerland." On 27 October 1920, the statute for the new court was approved by the League Assembly. Adachi Mineichirō (1869–1934), councilor at the Japanese Embassy in Paris and later (from 1928) Japan's ambassador there, was a member of this commission, representing ten nations.

258. Two years before the founding of the League of Nations, the American lawyer S. O. Levinson had published a proposal for the "outlawry of war" that he and associates continued to pursue and which contributed to the realization of the Kellogg-Briand antiwar pact of 1928. See also Charles Clayton Morrison, *The Outlawry of War—A Constructive Policy for World Peace* (Chicago: Willett, Clark & Colby, 1927), 22. The proposal also found support among British politicians, diplomats, and publicists. J. L. Garvin, publisher of the *London Observer*, wrote in 1925: "The absolute outlawry of war is the attainable ideal of the world" (cited in Morrison, *op. cit.*, 29).

259. U.S. Senator William Borah had opposed the entry of the United States to the League of Nations largely because in his opinion the league's proposals did not go far enough. *Encyclopedia Britannica*, vol. 13, 1962, 893.

260. At the Washington Conference on Naval Limitations, with support from Shidehara, the "return" of Shandong Province to China was achieved.

261. Another reason was that the treaty appeared to conflict with the American Monroe Doctrine.

262. Charles Chatfield (ed.), *Peace Movements in America* (New York: Schocken, 1973), xvi–xvii (emphasis added).

263. For additional material on W. E. Borah and the war outlawry movement, see Claudius Osborne Johnson, *Borah of Idaho* (New York and Toronto: Longmans, Green & Co., 1936); John Chalmers Vinson, *William E. Borah and the Outlawry of War* (Athens: University of Georgia Press, 1957); James Maddox, *William E. Borah and American Foreign Policy* (Baton Rouge: Louisiana State University Press, 1970); and John E. Stoner, *S. O. Levinson and the Pact of Paris: A Study in the Techniques of Influence* (Chicago: University of Chicago Press, 1942).

264. See also Hans Wehberg, "The Outlawry of War," Washington, Carnegie Endowment for International Peace (Pamphlet Series, Division of International Law No. 52), 1931, 17ff., on "The American movement to outlaw war." (In German: *Die Ächtung des Krieges*, Berlin, Verlag von Franz Vahlen, 1930, 22ff.)

265. Cited in Charles Clayton Morrison, *op. cit.*, 51. See also the discussion of the "American War Outlawry League" in Ishii, *op. cit.*, 226–30. On efforts within the League of Nations, see also (for a critical assessment) E. H. Carr, *International Relations between the Two World Wars (1919–1939)* (London: Macmillan, 1950), chapter 6, "The Campaign against War," 113–30. See also Frances Kellor and Antonia Hatvany, *Security Against War* (New York: MacMillan, 1924), vol. II, 789ff.

266. This initiative reflected the perspective outlined decades before by William Ladd in his *An Essay on a Congress of Nations*, published in 1840. William Ladd wrote that the United States, as an enlightened and in many respects the most progressive nation, should take a leadership role, since the Europeans were obviously incapable, on their own, of bringing about a greater world unity.

267. See Morrison, *op. cit.*, 45–46: "Here is the only nation that came out of the great war with no ends to serve except the single moral end for which her sons were told they were fighting, namely to end war . . . *America would seem to be in a peculiar position to take the initiative in a world-embracing crusade to abolish war as an institution for the settlement of international disputes*" (emphasis added).

268. *Ibid.*, 28. Coolidge had been vice president under the Republican President Harding, but became president when Harding was assassinated in 1923 and was then elected for a four-year term beginning in 1925.

269. See Klaus Schlichtmann, "The West, Bengal Renaissance and Japanese Enlightenment: A Critical Inquiry into the History of the Organization of the World Around 1800," in Conermann and Kusber (eds.), *Asien und Afrika* (Festschrift: Hermann Kulke for his 65th birthday), 411–40.

270. From Victor Hugo come the words: "A day will come when the only fields of battle will be markets opening up to trade and minds opening up to ideas. A day will come when the bullets and the bombs will be replaced by votes. . . . A day will come when we will display cannon in museums just as we display instruments of torture today, and are amazed that such things could ever have been possible." The last sentence is cited in Schücking, *Die Organisation der Welt*, 1, and had been printed in a German-language "Führer durch Paris" (Guidebook through Paris) published at the time of the Paris Universal Exposition of 1867.

271. On the history of socialist and pacifist internationalism, compare H. G. Wells, *Experiment in Autobiography*, 643ff. Wells was in the twentieth century one of the most significant pioneers of social-liberal and pacifist internationalist thinking in Great Britain and, as a friend of Churchill already during the First World War, had an important influence on the thinking of the later British governing elite. He was himself an engaged pacifist and federalist: "I was already trying to get the world state recognized as a war objective in 1916" (*ibid.*, 681). Already at that time Wells had met personally with Churchill and had been able to interest him in his ideas. A somewhat earlier representative of this mode of thinking was the "Queen's poet," Alfred Tennyson (1809–1892).

272. R. B. McCallum, *Public Opinion and the Last Peace* (London: Oxford University Press, 1944) (German trans.: *Der Weltfrieden und die öffentliche Meinung nach 1919* [Berlin: Suhrkamp, formerly S. Fischer, 1948]), 134), citing Harold Butler, who in his book *The Lost Peace* (33–35) held the Geneva Protocol to be the "the best and last" attempt "to put teeth into the League," in McCallum's words, "to make it a practical instrument of security." See also Thomas W. Burkman, "The Geneva Spirit," in Howes (ed.), *Nitobe Inazō*, 177–214.

273. See Klaus Schlichtmann, "Ein fernöstliches Locarno? Japanische Vorschlage für ein regionales Sicherheitsbündnis in den dreißiger Jahren" (A Far-Eastern Locarno? Japanese proposals for a regional security pact in the nineteen-thirties), *Japans Kultur der Reformen, Referate des 6. Japanologentages der OAG in Tokyo*, ed. Werner Schaumann (München: Iudicium, 1999), 103–15.

274. "Any international collaboration must presuppose a limitation on the sovereignty of individual states. . . . The civilized nations have failed in the case of the League of Nations, and I may not be quite wrong if I say the Locarno Pact was the

first step leading to that failure." A. C. Guha, at the IPU's 1952 conference in Berne, *Compte Rendu de la XLIe Conference tenue a Berne du 28 aout au 2 septembre 1952*, published by the Bureau Interparlementaire, Geneva, 1952, 651–55.

275. Lawrence H. Battistini, *Japan and America, From the Earliest Times to the Present* (New York: John Day Co., 1954) (Tokyo 1953), 81–82.

276. Compare Viscount Cecil of Chelwood, "Peace Through International Cooperation," in a special edition of *The Annals of the American Academy of Political and Social Science* titled When War Ends (Addresses at the forty-fourth annual Meeting of the American Academy, 12–13 April 1940), Philadelphia 1940 (hereafter *The Annals*), 62: "Some years ago a group of able young men—for they were young then—with the countenance of Lord Milner set about constructing a Federal Constitution for the British Empire. They called themselves the Round Table, and they had considerable financial and literary backing. With great industry and imagination they drew up a sketch of the proposed constitution."

277. William E. Rappard, "Why Peace Failed," *The Annals*, 1: "The peace of 1919 had failed precisely because it was a peace of justice and of freedom."

278. *Ibid.*, 4.

279. R. B. McCallum, *Public Opinion and the last Peace*, 131.

280. Charles Chatfield, *op. cit.*, xviii. For a detailed discussion, see also Robert A. Divine, *Second Chance: The Triumph of Internationalism in America during World War II* (New York: Atheneum, 1967).

281. William E. Rappard, "Why Peace Failed," in *The Annals*, 2.

282. See Viscount Cecil of Chelwood, "Peace Through International Cooperation," *The Annals*, 63.

283. Rappard, *The Annals*, 1: "[T]he guiding principle of self-determination has been discarded in favor of considerations of strategy and economics, summed up in the synthetic formula of 'Lebensraum' . . . democracy and political freedom have . . . given way to dictatorship and totalitarianism. The philosophy of the Rights of Man has been abrogated, and the conquests of the French Revolution derided."

284. Grewe, *The Epochs of International Law*, 585. This kind of thinking continued to be a serious flaw in German legal culture even after the Second World War.

285. S. Matthias Erzberger, *Der Völkerbund—Der Weg zum Weltfrieden* (The League of Nations—The way to world peace) (Berlin: R. Hobbing, 1918). See also Klaus Epstein, *Matthias Erzberger and the Dilemma of German Democracy* (Princeton, N.J.: Princeton University Press, 1959), 281: "Erzberger placed special importance on the obligatory element in arbitration."

286. Edwin O. Reischauer, "The Sinic World in Perspective," *Foreign Affairs* 52, no. 2 (January 1974): 344.

287. Rolf Hellmut Foerster, *Europa, Geschichte einer politischen Idee* (Europe, history of a political idea) (München: Nymphenburger Verlagshandlung, 1967), enumerates 182 such plans between 1306 and 1945.

288. Compare the statement made by Foreign Minister Komura Jutarō (1855–1911) before the Diet on 2 February 1909: "The foreign policy of this empire should have for its objects the maintenance of peace and the development of national resources. . . . [T]he maintenance of peace . . . has now been practically assured. It is believed

that in the face of such a situation we can permit ourselves to devote our endeavours to the development of the natural resources." Cited in Ōkuma, *Fifty Years of New Japan*, vol. II, 592–93 (appendix C). This of course meant the economic development of Japan in the East Asian region, where after the two wars of 1894–1895 and 1904–1905 it could now proceed in a secure environment favorable to Japan.

289. Compare also Baron Tsuzuki Keiroku, "Social Intercourse between Japanese and Occidentals," in Ōkuma, *Fifty Years of New Japan*, vol. II, 492: "For us a 'splendid social isolation' is an impossibility if we want to play a part in the future development of the world's history."

290. Compare H. G. Wells, *A Short History of the World* (New York: Penguin Books, 1970), 295: "The European invasion of Asia was coming to an end and the retraction of Europe's tentacles was beginning."

291. Fairbank, Reischauer, and Craig, *East Asia—The Modern Transformation*, 631–32 (emphasis added).

292. The 1907 Hague Peace Conference had newly incorporated the South American states; 1910 saw the founding of the Pan-American Union, with headquarters in Washington.

293. See the aforementioned resolution of the U.S. Congress of 20 and 24 June 1910 on international disarmament and "the combined navies of the world as an international force for the preservation of universal peace." Also see chapter II, section 3.

294. The coming into a closer alignment of the naval policies of several of the great powers—the French-British naval agreement of 1912 and the Russian-French naval convention of the same year—must be seen in the light of the aforementioned proposals for an international naval force for the maintenance of peace. See Vollenhoven, *The Enforcement of Sanctions in International Law By Means Of an International Police System*.

295. Vollenhoven, *ibid.*, 4.

296. Quoting from the Congress Program text.

297. Congress Program ("Advance Copy" in the author's possession).

298. According to the program, among the "supporters" of the Universal Races Congress were "the majority of the Members of the Permanent Court of Arbitration and of the Delegates to the Second Hague conference, twelve British Governors and eight British Premiers, over forty Colonial Bishops, some hundred and thirty Professors of International Law, the leading Anthropologists and Sociologists, the officers and the majority of the Council of the Inter-Parliamentary Union, and other distinguished personages. The list of the writers of papers includes eminent representatives of over twenty civilizations."

299. The congress supporters included "over thirty Presidents of Parliament."

300. Schücking, "Der erste Weltrassenkongreß" (The First Universal Races Congress), *Die Friedens-Warte* (August–September 1911), 231.

301. Schücking, "Der erste Weltrassenkongreß," 232.

302. See chapter III, section 3.

303. Already during his stay in Washington, he had nurtured contacts with the British ambassador, James Bryce.

304. Shidehara in fact stayed in London for half a year between December 1913 and June 1914. During this period he also had several conversations with British Foreign Secretary Sir Edward Grey.

305. Hozumi Nobushige (1856–1926) had received a Ministry of Education scholarship in 1876 to study in both England and Germany; Shidehara studied under him in the law faculty of the Imperial University of Tokyo in the mid-1890s.

306. Parts of it were published in 1917 as "Proposals for the Prevention of Future Wars," reprinted in Henry R. Winkler, *The League of Nations Movement in Great Britain, 1914–1919* (New Brunswick, N.J.: Rutgers University Press, 1952), 16–20.

307. This is known also from the post–Second World War reminiscences of two of Shidehara's colleagues in the Gaimushō's Division of European and American Affairs (*Ōbeikyoku*), Mushanokōji Kimitomo and Tamura Kōsaku, submitted to the compilers of the *Shidehara Kijūrō* official biography, published by the Shidehara Heiwa Zaidan in 1955 (see *op. cit.*, 136–37). "The League to Enforce Peace and the Bryce group provided the Japanese government with valuable reports on the League movement prior to the Armistice"; Thomas W. Burkman, "The Geneva Spirit," in Howes (ed.), *Nitobe Inazō*, 180. See also Burkman, "Japan, the League of Nations, and the New World Order, 1918–1920," 97. On Theodore Marburg, see John H. Latané (ed.), *Development of the League of Nations Idea: Documents and Correspondence of Theodore Marburg* (New York: Macmillan, 1932).

308. See chapter III, section 4. In Japan at the time, the First World War was usually called the "Japanese-German War" (*Nichi-Doku sensō*).

309. Masatoshi, *Japan in the League of Nations*, 15.

310. Thomas Wesley Burkman, *Japan, the League of Nations, and the New World Order, 1918–1920* (The University of Michigan, Ph.D. diss., 1975), 98–99.

311. *Suisō nikki* (Itō Miyoji's notes and personal commentary on the Gaikō Chōsakai meetings), ed. Kobayashi Tatsuo (Tokyo: Hara Shobō, 1966), 286, cited in Burkman, *op. cit.*, 99.

312. Burkman, *Japan, the League of Nations, and the New World Order, 1918–1920*, 102.

313. How deeply the war and the hope for a lasting peace molded people's minds is clearly shown in the following quote from Ernst Bloch, *Geist der Utopie* (Spirit of Utopia) (München and Leipzig: Duncker & Humblot, 1918) (Faksimile Suhrkamp Gesamtausgabe, vol. 16), 432: "It will come pass, no longer to be delayed, the federative rapprochement of nations . . . by which the extravagances of closed cultures will cease and the holy fellow of man, the universal Christ, will be born." Another passage from this book by Ernst Bloch (who is not a relative of Ivan de Bloch) reads: "For it is so . . . that the Messiah can only come when all the guests have been accomodated at the table; this, however, is first of all the Table of Work and only then the Table of the Lord—the organization of the World, in the mystery of the [divine] kingdom (*He Basileia thou uranon*), possesses its immediately effective, and at once deductive, metaphysic" (411). In Versailles, however, it was decided not to give Japan a place, as "racially equal," at the common table.

314. This internationalist camp included Makino Nobuaki, *genrō* Matsukata Masayoshi, the "Shidehara clique" in the Ministry of Foreign Affairs, Admirao Katō

Tomosaburō, Prime Minister Hara Kei, and Saionji Kinmochi; Lesley Connors, *The Emperor's Advisor, Saionji Kinmochi, and pre-war Japanese politics* (London: Croom Helm, 1987), 66–67.

315. David Hunter Miller, *The Drafting of the Covenant* (New York: G. P. Putnam's Sons, 1928), vol. I, 76, cited in Matsushita, *Japan in the League of Nations*, 15.

316. "The word Völkerbund [the German name for the League of Nations], which stands in a great German tradition, going back to, among other things, Kant's famous essay 'On Perpetual Peace,' became a customary designation in Germany." Carl Schmitt, *Der Völkerbund und das politische Problem der Friedenssicherung* (The League of Nations and the political problem of securing peace) (Leipzig and Berlin: B. G. Teubner, 1930), 7.

317. Miller, *The Drafting of the Covenant*, 76, *ibid.*

318. Connors, *The Emperor's Advisor*, 64.

319. *Ibid.*, 68. See also in Matsushita the statement made by Count Makino en route from San Francisco to Paris in 1919: "We are on our way from East to West seeking to assist our friends to conclude a just and honorable peace. . . . We are going to Paris first to take counsel and cooperate with our Allies and our friends" (*Japan in the League of Nations*, 17).

320. Woodrow Wilson presented the Anglo-American draft, Léon Bourgeois presented the French draft, and Orlando presented the Italian draft.

321. Burkman, *Japan, the League of Nations, and the New World Order, 1918–1920*, 82.

322. Unno Yoshirō, "League of Nations and Japan," *Kōdansha Encyclopedia of Japan*, vol. IV, 373.

323. See, for example, the report of 4 August 1919 by a delegation from the Swiss Bundesrat to the Swiss Federal Assembly on the question of the possible accession of Switzerland to the League of Nations, cited in Schmitt, *op. cit.*, 24–25: "The Paris League of Nations treaty is unmistakably a compromise [of basic principles]. . . . Measured against a true League of Nations the Paris treaty is something very imperfect," and (28) "A main objection that will be made to the the the draft, from an organizational point of view, is that it is no League of Nations but a mere league *of governments*. . . . The League of Nations should be more democratic."

324. Ray Stannard Baker, *Woodrow Wilson and World Settlement* (New York: Doubleday, 1922), vol. I, 145, cited in Matsushita, *Japan in the League of Nations*, 17.

325. David G. Egler, "Pan-Asianism in Action and Reaction," in Harry Wray and Hilary Conroy (eds.), *Japan Examined: Perspectives on Modern Japanese History* (Honolulu: University of Hawaii Press, 1983), 302.

326. Burkman, "The Geneva Spirit," 184.

327. Burkman quotes a statement from the period by *genrō* Yamagata Aritomo, saying that "the hope of some Japanese for permanent peace is a utopian dream" (*Japan, the League of Nations, and the New World Order, 1918–1920*, 77).

328. Egler, "Pan-Asianism," 304: "Reference to the league as a European club was common in the Japanese press." See also Thomas W. Burkman, "The Geneva Spirit," 194.

329. Address by the Japanese foreign minister, Viscount Motono Ichirō (1862–1928), before both houses of the Japanese Diet, 22 January 1918, published in *World Peace Foundation Pamphlets*, Boston 1917–1918, 445, and cited in Matsushita, *Japan in the League of Nations*, 17.

330. The United States ambassador in Tokyo, Roland Morris, informed the U.S. Secretary of State on 2 December 1918 that "none of the peace conference delegates on the part of Japan are classed as belonging to the German school." *Foreign Relations of the United States*, 1918, I, 492, cited in Burkman, *Japan, the League of Nations, and the New World Order, 1918–1920*, 104.

331. Mermeix, *Le Combat des Trois, Notes et Documents sur la Conférence de la Paix*, 11.édition, Paris 1922, 104: "Ils se comportèrent non comme des débutants, mais comme des vétérans de la diplomatie" (They behaved not like amateurs, but like veterans of diplomacy). Cited in Ludwig Waldecker, *Die Stellung der menschlichen Gesellschaft zum Völkerbund—Versuch einer Darstellung des Kampfes um die Weltorganisation* (The public attitude toward the League of Nations—An attempt to portray the struggle for the organization of the world) (Berlin: Carl Heymanns, 1931), 144.

332. See Carl Schmitt for the text of the article and a discussion of its genesis (*Der Völkerbund*, 12).

333. Matsushita, *Japan in the League of Nations*, 20–21.

334. Miller, *op. cit.*, vol. II, 392, cited in Matsushita, *Japan in the League of Nations*, 21.

335. On "Obligatory Arbitration" see, for example, chapter VII in Matthias Erzberger, *The League of Nations: The Way to the World's Peace*, 167–88.

336. All quotations from Miller, *op. cit.*, vol. II, 376, cited in Matsushita, *Japan in the League of Nations*, 22–23. David Hunter Miller was legal advisor to President Woodrow Wilson at Versailles.

337. Matsushita, *Japan in the League of Nations*, 25. See also Shimazu Naoko, "The Japanese Attempt to Secure Racial Equality in 1919," *Japan Forum* 1, no. 1 (April 1989): 97: "Throughout the Peace Conference, the racial equality proposal was the most highly debated issue. Perhaps the Japanese public took it more seriously than their delegates." See also Harold Nicholson, *Peacemaking 1919* (New York: Grosset & Dunlop, 1965) (The Universal Library), 145; F. P. Walters, *A History of the League of Nations* (London, New York, and Toronto: Oxford University Press, 1960), 63–64.

338. Friedrich Wilhelm Foerster, *Mein Kampf gegen das militaristische und nationalistische Deutschland* (My battle against militaristic and nationalistic Germany) (Stuttgart: Verlag Friede durch Recht, 1920), 195f. And *ibid.*, 83: "Until August 1914, a German business man in Nigeria, Bombay, Calcutta, Singapore and Hong Kong could do business under the same conditions as English companies."

339. In April, Loudon received a letter from Lord Bryce, who had returned from Washington to England, in which he recalled with a certain amount of nostalgia "the peaceful days of Washington . . . I receive many communications from a body in Holland called the Anti Oorlogs Raad, working for peace, but do not know how much influence it may have. One would like to be more sanguine about the possibilities for averting future wars than one can be after seeing how the Hague

Convention has been trampled under foot" (Omslag 20, *Rijksarchiv Den Haag, A-Dossiers*, 2.21.205.37).

340. C. van Vollenhoven, "Grotius and Geneva," *Bibliotheca Visseriana Dissertationum Ius Internationale Illustrantium*, vol. VI (Leiden: E. J. Brill, 1926), 44. Grotius's work was also given much attention in Japan, especially after the mid-1920s.

341. Hugo Grotius, *De jure belli ac pacis* (On the Law of War and Peace), chapter XXIV (1625); see the English translation by A. C. Campbell, London, 1814, online URL www.constitution.org/gro/djbp.htm.

342. Below the printed text, and preceded by a star-shaped mark, appears the handwritten note: "This is the principle of the 'open door'" (Federal Archives, Koblenz, Papers of Georg Gothein, folio 170).

343. Thomas Burkman, *Japan, the League of Nations, and the New World Order, 1918–1920*, 82. The committee was set up on 10 September 1915 and met altogether approximately thirty times. A comprehensive report of 25 December 1916 was published in *Gaimushō no hyakunen*, vol. 1, 697–700.

344. The instructions from the foreign ministry to Count Makino had read: "If concrete plans were to be submitted for the establishment of the League of Nations, the plenipotentiaries should make efforts as far as situations would allow them, to prevent the Japanese government from having to accept a disadvantaged position arising out of racial discrimination." In Shimazu, "The Japanese Attempt to Secure Racial Equality in 1919," 94. See also Gaimushō, *Kokusai Renmei: Jinshu sabetsu tekkai* (League of Nations: Eliminating racial discrimination), vol. 3, "Jinshu sabetsu taigū tekkai mondai sōkatsu hōkoku" (Summary report on the question of eliminating racially discriminating treatment), 1.

345. Neville Bennett, "Bitter Fruit: Japanese Migration and Anglo-Saxon Obstacles, 1890–1924," *TASJ*, fourth series, no. 8 (1993): 80. "Australia led the opposition" (Shimazu, "The Japanese Attempt to Secure Racial Equality in 1919," 95).

346. Chinda Sutemi supported the Zionist movement for a Jewish state: "When the peace conference convened, Dr. Chaim Weizmann, chairman of the English Zionist federation, approached the Japanese ambassador in London, Chinda Sutemi, with a request that the Japanese government endorse the Balfour Declaration. On January 6, 1919, Chinda, who was about to join the Japanese delegation at the conference, sent . . . (a positive reply) to Weizmann." Ben-Ami Shillony, *The Jews and the Japanese: The Successful Outsiders* (Rutland, Vt., and Tokyo: Charles E. Tuttle, 1991), 152–53.

347. During this period, when Matsuoka Yōsuke was chief of the Japanese Press and Information Section in Paris, a veritable "paper warfare" began (Nish, *Japanese Foreign Policy, 1869–1942*, 120).

348. See Matsushita, *Japan in the League of Nations*, 26.

349. Miller, *op. cit.*, vol. I, 183–84.

350. *Ibid.*

351. *Ibid.*

352. See also the account in Marilyn Lake and Henry Reynolds, *Drawing the Global Colour Line: White Men's Countries and the International Challenge of Racial Equality* (Cambridge: Cambridge University Press, 2008), 284ff.

353. Baker, *op. cit.*, vol. II, 236, cited in *Japan in the League*, 30.

354. Miller, *op. cit.*, 391.

355. Miller, *op. cit.*, vol. II, 389. Instead of this, Lord Cecil suggested: "Japan would be permanently represented on the Executive Council and this fact would place her in a situation of complete equality with the other Great Powers. This being so, it would always be possible for her to raise the question of equality of races and of nations before the Council itself" (*ibid.*).

356. "The Japanese newspapers took delight in attacking the Australian Prime Minister, Billy Hughes" (Shimazu, *op. cit.*, 97).

357. Bennett, "Bitter Fruit," 81.

358. Ian Nish, *Japanese Foreign Policy 1869–1942, Kasumigaseki to Miyakezaka* (London and Boston: Routledge and Kegan Paul, 1977), 122: "Japan's failure here may have worked to her advantage over her other demands."

359. *Report to the Emperor by Prince Saionji, 27 August 1919*, cited in Nish, "Document 20," *op. cit.*, 287–88.

360. Egler, *op. cit.*, 302. I cannot agree with Tsuzuki Chushichi, where the author claims that Japan's "attitude to the League of Nations was negative on the whole," and that its "proposal for racial equality was in fact [merely] an afterthought" (*The Pursuit of Power in Modern Japan, 1825–1995* (Oxford: Oxford University Press, 2000), 208).

361. Barbara J. Brooks, *Japan's Imperial Diplomacy: Consuls, Treaty Ports, and War in China, 1895–1938* (Honolulu: University of Hawaii Press, 2000), 31.

362. Oka Yoshitake, *Konoe Fumimaro, A Political Biography* (Tokyo: University of Tokyo Press, 1983), 11.

363. *Ibid.*, 13. See also David G. Egler, *op. cit.*, 302. Later, in the 1920s, this view was reinforced: "Anti-Japanese discrimination in California, capped by the exclusion of Orientals by the 1924 U.S. Immigration Act, confirmed the Japanese suspicion that universal morality was a myth" (Egler, *loc. cit.*).

364. Many, like Baron Sakatani, also hoped for an actual "world federal union." Sakatani Yoshio, "Sengo keiei to sekai tōitsu" (Postwar reconstruction and world unification), in *Heiwa jihō* 6, nos. 9–10 (October 1918): 2, 11, and 12, quoted in Burkman, *op. cit.*, 205–6.

365. "[C]omplaints were reinforced when the principle of racial equality which Japan sought to inject into the League Covenant was rejected by the powers at the peace conference" (David G. Egler, *op. cit.*, 302).

366. *Shidehara Kijūrō*, 136–37, cited in Burkman, *Japan, the League of Nations, and the New World Order, 1918–1920*, 98.

367. These were for the United States, Wilson and Lansing; for Great Britain, Lloyd George and Balfour; for France, Clemenceau and Pichon; for Italy, Orlando and Sonnino; and for Japan, Saionji and Makino.

368. Connors, *op. cit.*, 73.

369. Nish, *Japanese Foreign Policy 1869–1942*, 119: Saionji "had been educated in France and claimed to have a long-standing friendship with Georges Clemenceau."

370. Connors, *op. cit.*, 74.

371. In 1922, toward the end of the Washington Conference, Shidehara, "a favourite of Saionji . . . [who] came to personify the Saionji group's approach to foreign

policy," was instrumental in the decision to return former German concessions in Shandong Province to China (Connors, *op. cit.*, 68).

372. See Edwin O. Reischauer, *Japan, Past and Present* (Rutland, Vt., and Tokyo: Tuttle, 1991 (London 1947), 141: "Japan went to the Peace Conference at Versailles in 1919 as one of the great military and industrial powers of the world and received official recognition as one of the 'Big Five' of the new international order."

373. On Nitobe Inazō, see Howes (ed.), *Nitobe Inazō*, 1995.

374. Adachi Mineichirō in *9th Year Official Journal*, 894–95, cited in Matsushita, *Japan in the League of Nations*, 113.

375. Henry Lewis Stimson, *The Far Eastern Crisis, Reflections and Observations* (New York and London: Harper & Brothers, 1936) (for the Council on Foreign Relations), 172.

376. Bruno Lasker and William L. Holland, "Introduction," *Problems of the Pacific 1933—Economic Conflict and Control* (Proceedings of the Fifth Conference of the Institute of Pacific Relations, Banff, Canada, 14–26 August, 1933) (London: Oxford University Press/Chicago: University of Chicago Press, 1934), 11 (hereafter cited as *Problems of the Pacific 1933*).

377. Nitobe had also been a cofounder of the International Committee for Intellectual Cooperation (ICIC), which was founded under the auspices of the League of Nations in 1922 and became the forerunner of UNESCO.

378. Cited in Burkman, "The Geneva Spirit," 202.

379. *Problems of the Pacific 1933*, vii–ix.

380. Ian Nish, *Japanese Foreign Policy 1869–1942, Kasumigaseki to Miyakezaka* (London, Henley, and Boston: Routledge and Kegan Paul, 1977), 126.

381. Nish, *op. cit.*, categorizes the new era in Japanese foreign policy during the half-century between the Meiji Restoration and the end of the First World War into six periods: the Iwakura Period (1869–1883), the Mutsu Period (1884–1896), the Aoki Period (1896–1901), the Komura Period (1901–1911), the Katō Period (1911–1915), and the Ishii Period (1913–1919), which is followed by the Shidehara Period in the years from 1920 to 1932.

382. See chapter III.

383. It must not be forgotten that German policies and political philosophy exerted a considerable influence in China and other parts of Asia, which may also have been a contributing factor, apart from the impact of the failure of the Hague peace conferences caused by Germany.

384. See the description in chapter II, 2.

385. See Ian Nish, who calls him "the founder of Japanese diplomacy" (*op. cit.*, 42). See also Bamba, *op. cit.*, 145.

386. Nish, *op. cit.*, 28. *Kyō* is an old title meaning "master" or "excellency." *Gaimu* means "foreign affairs" and *daijin* means "minister."

387. Nish, *op. cit.*, 61.

388. "The foreign minister might make statements to the Diet but these were made by grace rather than by duty; nor was he required to reply to interpellations" (Nish, *op. cit.*, 28). "The system here described held good in the main until the new constitution was introduced in 1947" (*ibid.*, note 3, 312).

389. *Ibid.*, 26: "He was an exceptional character in his own right—a man of spirit and intellect with wide international interests."

390. Mutsu Munemitsu's diplomatic memoirs, which appeared in Japanese in 1896, were translated into English by Gordon Mark Berger under the title *Kenkenroku: A Diplomatic Record of the Sino-Japanese War, 1894–95* (Princeton, N.J., and Tokyo: Princeton University Press and University of Tokyo Press, 1982). The *Kenkenroku* ("Record of tribulations") was at the time confiscated and banned (until 1929). The book was newly issued by Iwanami Publishers in 1939 and is today considered one of the world's great masterpieces of diplomatic literature. See also Marius B. Jansen, "Mutsu Munemitsu," in Albert M. Craig and Donald H. Shively (eds.), *Personality in Japanese History* (Berkeley: University of California Press, 1970), 309–34.

391. For interesting background information see Ian Nish, *The Anglo-Japanese Alliance: The Diplomacy of Two Island Empires 1894–1907* (London and Dover, N.H.: The Athlone Press, 1985 [1966]), 10.

392. "The Anglo-Japanese commercial treaty was the vital step in resolving the problem of treaty revision" (Ian Nish, *Japanese Foreign Policy 1869–1942*, 33).

393. Protests by a dissatisfied Japanese public following the "Triple Intervention" of Germany, France, and Russia, by which Japan was forced to give up its claim on the lease of the Liaodong Peninsula that China had agreed to in the treaty, obliged Mutsu to step down from his post as foreign minister one year later. He died not long afterward.

394. This fact is generally well known. See *Kenkenroku*, 5: "[T]he two empires signed the Treaty of Shimonoseki, bringing about profound changes in our traditional diplomatic relationship and evoking world recognition of Japan as the preeminent power of the Far East." It seems almost certain that Shidehara would have in the late 1890s obtained and read a copy of Mutsu's *Kenkenroku* since several copies of the book are known to have made the rounds within the Ministry of Foreign Affairs. Berger's introduction (xvii) to the translated text states that "one version or another of *Kenkenroku* became privately available from early in 1896." Although the book was officially banned, it was customary that such confidential papers and books make the rounds within "insider circles" without this being officially objected to.

395. See Harold Nicholson, *The Evolution of Diplomatic Method* (Westport, Conn.: Greenwood Press, 1977) (orig. 1954), 73: "It was in the chancelleries of Europe alone that the final issue of general peace or war would be decided. . . . Japan, when she arose, appeared an exceptional phenomenon."

396. *Ibid.*, 72.

397. Nicholson points out that "America, until 1897, remained isolated behind her oceans and her Doctrine. . . . Europe was regarded the most important of all continents" (*op. cit.*, 73).

398. Nicholson refers, in the context of the European "concert of powers," to the pace-setting French diplomacy as "the theory and practice of international negotiation originated by Richelieu, analysed by Callières, and adopted by all European countries during the three centuries that preceded the change of 1919" (*op. cit.*, 72).

399. Shidehara was during Mutsu's years as foreign minister a junior aspirant to a high post in Japan's diplomatic corps and found Mutsu's idealism and sense of justice,

expressed through a diplomatic talent and an engaged standing up for Japanese interests, something he could easily relate to. Possibly, however, he was somewhat dissatisfied with the older diplomat's *datsua nyūō* attitudes (rejection of backward, "Oriental" manners and ways and adoption of Western manners and ways). See Bamba, *op. cit.*, 364: "Mutsu, Komura, and Katō all were extremely oppressive to other Asian nations. In fact, *datsua nyūō* implies an attitude of subservience to the West and arrogance toward Asia." Such an attitude was not one that Shidehara shared.

400. "He was from a young age picked out for his special capacity" (Nish, *op. cit.*, 127).

401. Nish, *loc. cit.*, makes the point that Shidehara was "the most successful of the early entrants . . . [being] the first product of the examination system to become foreign minister."

402. Signed on 16 July (Nish, *op. cit.*, 32–33). The treaty provided for ending consular jurisdiction in criminal cases involving nationals of one's own country arrested abroad, five years after its signing.

403. "With regard to the question of treaty revision, the government has decided to give notice next year to the various Powers of the termination of the existing commercial treaties. In accordance with the provision, one year after such notice is given the operation of the treaties is to be arrested. It is the intention of the Government to approach the different Powers severally on the subject of the negotiation of the new treaties, unhampered by any unequal engagement, and to conclude suitable compacts based entirely on the principle of reciprocity with a view to the free development of international commerce." "Précis of a Speech Delivered by Baron Komura, Minister of Foreign Affairs, in the Imperial Diet, February 2, 1909, on Japan's Foreign Policy," in Ōkuma Shigenobu, *Fifty Years of New Japan*, vol. II, 593.

404. Harrison M. Holland, in assessing the quality of the Ministry of Foreign Affairs following the Second World War, notes that "[one] could be more imaginative and innovative in attempting to persuade the media to give the ministry a 'better press'—*solid successes on the diplomatic front could be pointed to in creating the image of power and prestige that existed, for example, when Baron Shidehara Kijūrō was foreign minister*" (*Managing Diplomacy: The United States and Japan* [Stanford, Calif.: Hoover Institution Press, Stanford University, 1984], 191–92) (emphasis added). See also Bamba, *op. cit.*, 360ff. One might offer the thesis that the "economic pacifism" of the post–World War II period, on which Japan's prosperity has been based, rests—even if this is rarely acknowledged as such—on the preliminary work accomplished by Shidehara.

405. Aoki's wife Elisabeth was a member of the Austrian nobility. Before and during the time Aoki was foreign minister, Japan was "much influenced by happenings in the German empire and especially by the personality of Bismarck. Japanese politicians like Itō Hirobumi, his disciples like Itō Miyoji and diplomats like Aoki Shūzō had fallen under his spell" (Nish, *Japanese Foreign Policy 1869–1942*, 67).

406. Cited in Bamba, *op. cit.*, 148, from Itō Jusshi, "Nihon no shingaikō to Shidehara-san" (Japan's new diplomacy and Shidehara-san), *Shoka no Shidehara-kan*, 279. Itō Jusshi was chairman of the foreign ministry's Information Bureau.

407. This refers to the group that had traditionally formed around *genrō* Yamagata Aritomo (Kyōsuke, 1838–1921). See Bamba, *op. cit.*, 158n33: "From 1916 to 1923,

except during the period of the Hara Cabinet [autumn 1918–1921] . . . the 'old' politics controlled by the military bureaucratic clique prevailed in Japan. Consequently, Foreign Ministers were also somewhat of the old type."

408. Itagaki Taisuke later changed his attitude and became a leader of the Movement for Freedom and People's Rights (*jiyū minken undō*), under the influence and working with Ueki Emori. According to Bamba, he opposed the government because it gave advantages to his political rivals (*op. cit.*, 35n19). The aggressive continental policy of the militarists was taken to task by Iwakura Tomomi, Ōkubo Toshimichi, and Kido Kōin.

409. "[Shidehara was] opposed to the idea of military intervention, because it was anti-democratic in principle, too costly, and impractical" (Bamba, *op. cit.*, 38). A political extremist murdered Hara Kei in 1921 and another political extremist murdered Inukai Tsuyoshi in 1932. Advocates of the "Siberian Expedition" included Tanaka Giichi, *genrō* Yamagata Aritomo, Foreign Minister Gotō Shinpei, Prime Minister and General Terauchi Masatake (1852–1919), Army Minister Ōshima Ken'ichi, and General Ugaki Kazushige.

410. See chapter III, section 5.

411. When he had been chief of the foreign ministry's telegraphic division, Shidehara had played a significant role in the formulation and distribution of relevant information.

412. Lesley Connors, *The Emperor's Adviser, Saionji Kinmochi, and pre-war Japanese politics* (London: Croom Helm, 1987), 68.

413. See the detailed autobiography of Miyazaki Tōten, *My Thirty-three Years Dream*, translated with introduction by Etō Shinkichi and Marius B. Jansen (Princeton, N.J.: Princeton University Press, 1982).

414. See Roger F. Hackett, "The Meiji Leaders and Modernization: The Case of Yamagata Aritomo," in Marius B. Jansen (ed.), *Changing Japanese Attitudes Toward Modernization* (Princeton, N.J.: Princeton University Press, 1965), 248ff, especially with respect to the two concepts of *shukensen* (line of sovereignty) and *riekisen* (line of interest), as set forth, for example, in Yamagata Aritomo, *Yamagata den*, III, 4–5: "The independence and security of the nation depend first upon the protection of the line of sovereignty (*shukensen*) and then the line of advantage (*riekisen*). . . . [I]f we wish to maintain the nation's independence among the powers of the world at the present time, it is not enough to guard only the line of sovereignty; we must also defend the line of advantage . . . and within the limits of the nation's resources gradually strive for that position. For this reason it is necessary to make comparatively large appropriations for our army and navy" (cited by Hackett [his translation], 248).

415. See Ishii Kikujirō, *Diplomatic Commentaries*, 125–26: "Thus the special interests of Japan and Great Britain in China are (1) the maintenance of China's independence and territorial integrity, and (2) the maintenance of equality of opportunity for the commerce and industry of all nations."

416. See Shidehara's inaugural speech as foreign minister in 1924, and his assertion that "Imperialistic and nationalistic ways and means which the Western powers have pursued are already out-of-date" (cited in Bamba, *op. cit.*, 361).

417. "Wherever soldiers went, passers-by bore a scornful air on their faces. Even when soldiers rode streetcars, they could not but feel small when they were wearing their uniforms. For example, in the streetcar people whispered aloud—so that the soldiers could also hear them—'Are spurs necessary in the streetcar?' Passengers treated soldiers' long swords as a nuisance." Shigemitsu Mamoru, *Shōwa no dōran* (The Shōwa Upheaval), two vols. (Tokyo: Chūō Kōronsha, 1952), cited in Bamba, *op. cit.*, 197. See also Kawaya Tsuguo, *Tanaka Giichi-den* (Biography of Tanaka Giichi) (Tokyo, 1929), 160–61: "These days [1922] young officers tend to take off their uniforms and wear civilian suits while travelling. This is only a familiar example. In streetcars and trains, when we are wearing uniforms, we feel a certain scorn from the public . . . In this way, the soldiers' spirit is gradually eroded" (cited in Bamba, *op. cit.*, 198n20).

418. "[He was] regarded as anti-militarist." John M. Maki, *Japanese Militarism, Its Cause and Cure* (New York: Alfred A. Knopf, 1945), 213.

419. Bamba, *op. cit.*, 186 (emphasis added).

420. James Bryce, *International Relations*, lecture VII, "Methods Proposed for the Settlement of International Questions and Disputes," 226ff. Bryce names sixteen wars between 1849 and 1914 (224–25), of which he says only two or three might possibly have been prevented or resolved through law-based arbitration.

421. Komura Jutarō had studied in the United States at Harvard University in the 1870s, and was foreign minister 1901–1906 and 1908–1911. "The people in the next generation who furthered 'Kasumigaseki Diplomacy' were Katō Takaaki [Kōmei] and Hara Kei [Takashi]" (Bamba, *op. cit.*, 363).

422. In the Edo Period, many *daimyō* families had maintained residences in the Kasumigaseki (the name of which literally means "haze barrier") section of the city. This geographical name became a sort of synonym for the Ministry of Foreign Affairs, which was located there.

423. James B. Crowley, "Japanese Army Factionalism in the Early 1930's," *Journal of Asian Studies* 21, no. 3 (May 1962): 116.

424. Ikei Masaru, "Ugaki Kazushige's View of China and his China Policy, 1915–1930," in Iriye Akira (ed.), *The Chinese and the Japanese, Essays in Political and Cultural Interactions* (Princeton, N.J.: Princeton University Press, 1980), 199.

425. "During his stay in Washington, Shidehara established a close association with the British ambassador, James Bryce, from whom he learned pragmatic and rational ways of thinking in diplomacy" (Bamba, *op. cit.*, 151); in *Gaikō gojūnen* Shidehara describes his friendship with Bryce (28–44). James Bryce also had been professor of history at Oxford. According to historian Karl Lamprecht, Bryce, the historian, deserved to be placed in the same class as Leopold von Ranke and Heinrich Treitschke (*Shidehara Kijūrō*, 70).

426. James Bryce, *International Relations*, lecture VII, "Methods Proposed for the Settlement of International Questions and Disputes," 209–10.

427. Bamba, *op. cit.*, 166, and footnote 44.

428. Including conventions of hierarchy like *oyabun-kobun* (conscious distinctions between "leaders" and "followers") and ritualized affectations of the sorts expressed by terms like *onshi* (a former teacher for whom one has a feeling of special respect),

giri-gimu (sentiments of social obligation), or *ninjô* (professions of "humanity" even though these might be largely for show), and so on. See Bamba, *op. cit.*, 144–45, for an example.

429. Nicholson, *The Evolution of Diplomatic Method*, 91.

430. Nagai Ryūtarō, "Shidehara gaikō no honshitsu" (The essence of Shidehara Diplomacy), *Chūō Kōron* XLII (March 1927): 91–95, cited in Bamba, *op. cit.*, 221n51.

431. As in Europe and elsewhere, after the Second World War, historians and political scientists were under strong Marxist "methodological" influence.

432. Certain aspects of Japan's modern political development and culture should be continually reassessed, also to put "Shidehara diplomacy" in proper perspective. Compare Maruyama Masao, "Nationalismus in Japan—Theoretischer Hintergrund und Perspektiven" (Nationalism in Japan—Theoretical background and perspectives), in Ulrich Menzel (ed.), *Im Schatten des Siegers: Japan* (In the shadow of the victors: Japan) (Frankfurt: Suhrkamp, 1989), 33–56. This was originally an essay from the year 1951 in which Maruyama addresses the "difficulty of incorporating Japan into world history" (a phrase which appears on 33 of the above). In many respects things have changed little up until today.

433. See Bamba, who under the heading "The Meaning of Double Diplomacy" writes: "Japan in the 1920's and the 1930's was frequently criticized abroad for carrying out 'double diplomacy.' This criticism meant two things. First, it sometimes referred to the competition between civilians and military leaders for control of diplomacy, the former being thought of as peaceful and the latter as aggressive. Second, it sometimes suggested that Japan is 'two-faced' and therefore untrustworthy" (*op. cit.*, 359).

434. Compare also the Marxist critique of the historian Imai Seiichi, in "Seitō seiji to Shidehara gaikō" (Party politics and Shidehara Diplomacy), *Rekishigaku Kenkyū*, no. 219 (May 1958): 20–26. See also Bamba, *op. cit.*, 8n1: "Imai Seiichi for example, asserts that both policies were 'imperialistic.' Shidehara's was economic, while Tanaka's [as foreign minister 1927–1929] was military imperialism."

435. It was the pacifism of the 1920s that some apologists of the "Third Reich" later asserted was responsible for Hitler's grasping of power and for the Second World War.

436. I share this view, for example, with the American political philosopher Thomas Vernor Smith, cited in Ludwig Marcuse, *Amerikanisches Philosophieren* (Hamburg: Rowohlt, 1959), 23. This view is also reminiscent of the well-known statement attributed to the German-born newspaperman and U.S. Senator Karl Schurz (1829–1906), made in the mid-1800s: "Ideals are like stars; one can never reach them, but one can orient oneself by them." For this reference I am grateful to the Japanologist Reinhard Zöllner.

437. Marcuse, *op. cit.*, 25. But this is not *appeasement*.

438. Compare also John C. Farrell, "Editor's Foreword," *International Affairs* XXV, no. 2 (1967): ix: "The pragmatic bent of Americans, their bias against the theoretical and abstract and in favor of the practical and concrete, is a commonplace."

439. Raymond Aron, "What is a Theory of International Relations?" *International Affairs* XXI, no. 2 (1967): 205.

III

Shidehara Kijūrō, 1872–1922

Canadian historian E. H. Norman described Field Marshall Yamagata Aritomo as the "evil genius" of Japanese militarism. As minister of war, Yamagata had in 1873 introduced "universal" three-year military conscription for Japan's male population, and in 1883 promoted a revision and extension of these military obligations. Substantial increases in the arms expenditures of the army and navy were considered necessary to prepare for the possibility of war on the Asian continent and defend Japanese interests against hostile and aggressive powers.[1] In this Japan merely followed the example of Europe. However, between 1871 (the end of the Franco-Prussian War) and 1914 Europe had been quite peaceful, and there was a trend to find new nonviolent and more civilized ways of governing international affairs that went beyond previously held balance-of-power concepts and alliances. Transcending the confines of the individual nation-state, these were to include methods for the fair and impartial adjudication of international disputes. The Hague conferences of 1899 and 1907 were the most prominent attempt in this direction at the turn of the century. Though this was at the height of European imperialism, governments made a sincere effort to alter and adapt state practice with regard to the use of force in international relations and the supposed "right" to wage war. These chances were deliberately lost during the century's second decade. It was not until the 1920s, when Shidehara became Japan's minister of foreign affairs, that a universal and comprehensive plan for peace once more appeared within reach.

During the interwar years after 1920, Shidehara was probably the most consequential representative of the tradition of a specifically Japanese type of liberalism and internationalism developed within the Ministry of Foreign Affairs. This capable statesman for a time played a determining role in Japan's foreign relations, defining Japan's place in world politics. Though often called a "career diplomat," it is doubtful if this description does him justice. The American diplomat William Franklin Sands, who served as ambassador in both Japan and Korea around the turn of the century, fittingly described a new type of government servant, the "professional executive," who could form his own judgment and maintain autonomy in decisionmaking, handling affairs, and formulating and applying political concepts. Sands contrasted this new type with the traditional "obedient" office-beholden bureaucrat who was little more than a receiver of orders.[2] Shidehara represented this new type.

Japanese historians like Bamba Nobuya and Takemoto Tōru, but also Western authors, have pointed to the nonauthoritarian, humanist-pacifist, or antimilitaristic character of "Shidehara diplomacy,"[3] which after the Second World War was often referred to as "peace diplomacy" (*heiwa gaikō*).[4] Shidehara diplomacy augmented the chances for a durable and peaceful order in the interwar period, within the framework of the Versailles-Washington treaty system.[5] These chances were affected by four key settings that determined the international environment: (1) the degree of observed stability in European-American relations, especially among England, France, and the United States;[6] (2) the relationship of the powers to China; (3) the relationship of Japan to the United States; and (4) the political trends in Germany, including relations with Russia.

Shidehara stood for a progressive and economy-oriented foreign policy, urging political cooperation to create and maintain a workable order in Asia and the world. Evaluating Shidehara's work during this period, American scholar and pacifist Lawrence Battistini notes:

> Shidehara hoped to win the confidence and trust of both China and the United States in the motives and intentions of Japan in the Far East. However, his policy was from the beginning opposed by the militants and nationalists.[7]

Adding to that, if it was not the immediate cause, European politics and European conflicts determined much of what was happening in Asia, and eventually nullified all attempts at a permanent peace, including the Japanese efforts in the Far East. This was the background, and the stage, where Shidehara's life and work took shape.

THE EARLY YEARS: CHILDHOOD, EDUCATION, AND THE "APPRENTICE YEARS" IN KOREA, TO SPRING 1899

> "He was a spirited child who occasionally needed disciplining from adults."
>
> Takemoto Tōru

Shidehara Kijūrō was born on 11 August 1872, as the second son of a wealthy and influential landholding family in Kadoma, near Osaka, which was a major center of commerce.[8] It was a world of rapid change. The year 1872 saw the introduction of the Gregorian calendar (from November 9) and compulsory education for children, as well as the opening of Japan's first rail line, between Tokyo and Yokohama, and the introduction of Arabic numerals in the import-export trade. The previous year, a new postal service had been opened between Tokyo and Osaka, and the first undersea telegraph cable was laid between Nagasaki and Shanghai. In 1872 the Russian empire occupied the Chinese region of Ili on its advance eastward along the ancient Silk Roads, and American naval vessels occupied the fortified island of Kanghwa in the estuary of the Han River below Seoul. In 1873, Japan would see the creation of a new financial system, the start of universal military service, and the lifting of the old prohibition of Christianity. In 1874, in Brussels, a second conference on "the humanization of wartime international law" would convene at the initiative of the Russian tsar, Alexander II.[9]

Unlike most who took up prominent posts in government or politics at the time, Shidehara did not come from a samurai family. In the late 1870s the general trend in Japan favored Western models and methods in education and science. In all parts of the country new educational programs were getting underway;[10] *bunmei kaika* (civilization and enlightenment) was the watchword of the times. In his memoirs, Shidehara describes his parents' home in Kadoma, which was surrounded by a white wall and, like the clothing and demeanor of the Shidehara family, appeared to have an aristocratic air. During the Tokugawa period (1600–1868), members of the Shidehara family had been respected as village heads, and some held religious offices.[11] Despite its refinement and forward-looking stance on education, the Shidehara family appeared conservative in the eyes of the world. Its male members cut their hair in what was called a *chasen* ("tea-brush") style.[12] Since its youngest members were not supposed to play with the village's farm children, Kijūrō often found himself alone, expected to look after himself and not to stray from the courtyard of the family home.[13]

Buddhist doctrine and ethics formed the literary and religious backdrop to Kijūrō's education. Buddhism was made part of his everyday awareness by a priest from a nearby temple who was also director and head teacher at Kijūrō's elementary school.[14] Shidehara began his school education at the age of six in the new Kadoma Elementary School in his home village. From the first grade onward, the young scholars were presented with a fairly comprehensive picture of the wider world.[15] One of Kijūrō's elementary school teachers achieved fame as a writer (using the pen name Takeda Ten). In 1883, at age eleven, Kijūrō was sent to the Osaka Middle School, where special pains were taken to teaching the English language with the help of instructors from England and America.[16] A certain incident Shidehara mentions in his memoirs speaks to his pluck, innate wit, and readiness for repartee. When their American teacher asked the pupils if they could say something in English, all remained silent until Kijūrō drew attention and brought merriment when he exclaimed "See the moon!" At the end of the class, the teacher called him forward to praise his courage and humor. Shidehara's biographer Takemoto Tōru notes that he was unusually resourceful, lively, and quick to show enthusiasm, even if adults on occasion felt they had to apply disciplinary measures.[17]

Shidehara was still a pupil when the Osaka Middle School was integrated into the Third National Middle School in Kyoto. Kijūrō thus had to spend most of his school years in one or another boarding school separated from his parents, and found himself in large cities: Osaka, Kyoto, and finally—for his higher education—Tokyo. He seems to have had few close friends among his schoolmates and showed little interest in social occasions. He was gifted and appeared eager for learning, accustomed from an early age to fend for himself, and generally was of a thoughtful disposition. In Osaka, he developed a close friendship with one of his schoolmates, Hamaguchi Osachi ("Lion Hamaguchi," 1870–1931),[18] who came from Kōchi Prefecture on the island of Shikoku. He later served as prime minister (1929–1931) and died from a bullet wound inflicted by an ultranationalist assassin at Tokyo Station.

Shidehara's father, Shinjirō, had determined that he would invest the family assets in the education of his children. The family's progressive inclinations and openness to the larger world[19] were reflected in the fact that Shidehara's elder sister, Setsu, was the first woman in Osaka to pass the state examination to enter the medical faculty and earn a degree in medicine. Another sister, Masako, took over the administration of the family property and took public office as village chief. Shidehara's elder brother, Hiroshi (Taira), started on an academic career, became a well-known historian,[20] and served as president of the Hiroshima Higher Teachers College. From 1928–1937 he was the first president of the Imperial University in Taipei. For a short period after 1946, he was also a member of the emperor's privy council, a group of special advisors created in 1887 that was abolished when the new constitution entered into force in 1947.

In 1892, Shidehara passed the entrance examination for the law faculty of Tokyo Imperial University. Trained according to the new international standards of jurisprudence, he would be counted in the first rank to become influential in Japanese government and politics. Immediately upon his graduation with a baccalaureate in "English law" in 1895, Shidehara wanted to take the examination for the Foreign Service, but ill health kept him from doing so.

His head professor, Hozumi Nobushige (1856–1926),[21] tried to accommodate him elsewhere, but was fervidly opposed by the prospective young diplomat, who refused his mentor's well-intentioned offer. One year later he passed the state examination to enter the foreign ministry, with the highest distinction.

Shidehara's university years saw the outbreak of the first Sino-Japanese War (1894–1895), a conflict that contributed significantly to Japan's political standing and security. If peaceful means, treaty law, and international agreements appeared inadequate, the young Shidehara pondered intensively the formulations of international law and the rights and duties of states, which might offer alternative possibilities for the handling of international affairs. Experience taught that it was realistic on occasion to consider and take into account the possibility of having to relinquish certain (national) rights to achieve a peaceful settlement between contesting parties. Paul H. Clyde points to an internal debate that was taking place in Japan during the peace negotiations:

> During the Shimonoseki negotiations Prime Minister Itō and Foreign Minister Mutsu [Munemitsu] knew that an unfriendly European intervention was in the making. Accordingly, Mutsu, in an effort to forestall action by the powers, had insisted that Japan make no territorial demands on the mainland, but he was overruled by pressure of the military and naval staffs. The generals were determined to have a strategic foothold on the continent.[22]

Germany's rigorous pressing ahead (acting as a sort of proxy for Russia) with the occupation of Jiaozhou (Kiaochow) on 14 November 1897, barely two years after the Triple Intervention that had obliged Japan to give up the Liaodong Peninsula as one of the spoils of war, was in Japan unanimously judged as a "robbery" and a "breach of international law without parallel."[23] It led, however, merely to further occupations of pieces of Chinese territory by interventionist foreign powers. Foreign Minister Mutsu Munemitsu's preventive diplomacy,[24] which meant to avoid needlessly provoking the other powers in Asia—even if this policy should not be entirely accepted at home and prove unsuccessful—only strengthened and confirmed in young Shidehara's mind the conviction that diplomacy should always take precedence over military means and motivations; if war was to be ruled out, Japan would need competent and motivated diplomats who could successfully deal with these challenges.

Japan's willing commitment to play a key role in the modernization and reforms in China and Korea, as well as its asserted national interests in East Asia, including economic interests and its legitimate security needs, were important components in this conviction. Like many young internationalists, Shidehara wanted to see justice done for Japan and Asia. However, to this end only legitimate means could and should be employed. He had little doubt as to his mission. If Japan had had more educated and informed diplomats, even the war with China might have been prevented.

Toward the end of 1896 Shidehara was dispatched as consular assistant (*ryōji-kanpo*) to Inch'ŏn (previously called Chemulp'o), the trading port nearest to the Korean capital Seoul. He arrived at Inch'ŏn on December 26.

The status in international law of parts of East Asia that had not been directly colonized was ambiguous. With the Hague peace conferences, however, a new chapter in the history of international relations was to begin that would challenge the balance of power. Until this time, a quasi-colonial, exploitative system of "concessions" existed that had come out of the so-called capitulations in diplomacy. The diplomat William Franklin Sands gave this assessment: "The concession system as practiced in Korea (and China) was as pernicious a form of diplomacy as any yet invented, for it hampered true business and created an artificial jealousy and hostility in the relations of all concerned."[25] Japan was the first East Asian country that managed to assert its sovereignty and interests, claiming privileges under international law, and demanding a place in a hitherto Eurocentric concert of nations. Under the existing conditions, in the opinion of many, Japan too was bound to aspire to a colonial empire.[26] In any case it was in Japanese eyes important for the country's security to gain the sympathy of Korea (and also China) and generally encourage a positive attitude toward Japanese policies.

After Japan had been forced to retreat from its posture in Korea and with respect to "concessions" on the Chinese mainland as a result of the Triple Alliance, negotiations—and confrontation—with the Russian empire intensified. The Yamagata-Lobanov Protocol,[27] signed on 9 June 1896, in Moscow, specified the "independence" of Korea as well as Japan's and Russia's shared responsibilities there, but was hardly suited to guarantee peace or adequately safeguard their mutual interests. The same is true of the agreement that was signed on 25 April 1898 in Tokyo by Nishi Tokujirō and Baron Roman Romanovich Rosen (1847–1921), which acknowledged Korean independence and sovereignty and the obligation to undertake mutual Japanese-Russian consultations on, and to prevent obstructions to, the development of Japanese-Korean commercial relations.[28]

These matters taken up in the Nishi-Rosen agreement had already been essentially agreed upon in the Moscow Protocol as well as in the "Seoul Memorandum" of 14 May 1896, in which Russia, among other things, had committed itself to maintain in Korea only the same number of troops Japan kept there.[29] A consequence of the new Russian assertiveness was that McLeavy Brown, the very able British financial advisor to the Korean government, and "with his international staff" "the only solid and really efficient body of officials the Korean government possessed,"[30] was nearly replaced, toward the end of 1897, by a Russian, Kuril Alekseyev (usually spelled "Alexieff" in non-Russian communications).[31] "Japan is fully aware how rapidly Korea is becoming a Russian province," wrote the English-language *Kobe Chronicle* (weekly edition, uncensored) in a lead article on 6 November 1897. McLeavy Brown did manage, however, partly through the intervention of the British consul-general, John Newell Jordan, but mainly by the show of force "of a strong Anglo-Japanese squadron [appearing] in the harbor of Chemulpo,"[32] to retain his post as customs commissioner. However, the increasingly aggressive policy of Russia on the peninsula compromised Japan's security and other interests,[33] and future armed conflict with Russia seemed already preordained.[34]

It was in such an environment that Shidehara began his diplomatic career in 1896 in Inch'ŏn, Korea, under Ambassador Ishii Kikujirō (1866–1945), an experienced diplomat with whom he developed a lifelong friendship.[35] Ishii was a patriotic liberal who, like Shidehara, was ideologically and temperamentally opposed to militarism. In 1936 he published a book in which he condemned militarism, identifying it as "the root of aggressive politics, [which] must be checked in time."[36] According to Ishii, the first step in the establishment of international peace must be to introduce a "system of settling disputes between nations by pacific means. . . . The times require that Japan should give support to arbitration treaties and to the movement of disarmament."[37]

Great Britain, which had agreed to forming the Anglo-Japanese Alliance, had approved of the Japanese reform policy on the peninsula,[38] at least until Japan annexed Korea in 1910. The Americans, on the other hand, seemed to regard the Japanese as rivals and disparage their efforts to aid the reforms.[39] Nevertheless, progressive political forces in Seoul had begun propagating reform ideas even before 1895; many of them were pro-Japanese and considered Japanese backing as something to be welcomed. But it was the "Independence Club" (*Tongnip Hyŏphoe*),[40] founded by Dr. Sŏ Chaep'il, that first succeeded gaining a significant following and becoming politically effective.[41] As an "assistant consul," Shidehara held no key position, yet he frequently took part in talks and negotiations and seems to have enjoyed the trust of his superiors. Apart from strategic considerations, Great Britain had placed confidence in Japan, and wished to entrust China to a more globally oriented future order in which Japan would play an important role.[42] Shidehara probably participated and assisted in facilitating these discussions. The young consular officer also developed a close friendship with Anna Sophia Jordan, the young sister of Britain's consul-general, John Newell Jordan.[43]

Although Japan had managed, through victory in war, to restrain China's role in Korea, Russia had now replaced China as a major contestant.[44] In the years to follow Japan saw itself having to protect its interests in a contest with the "Russian bear." In 1897, Japanese diplomats played a key role in negotiating the opening of two more Korean ports—namely Chinnamp'o (today's Namp'o in North Korea) and Mokp'o—to be added to the three ports already open to trade, namely Pusan (Busan, since 1876), Wŏnsan (since 1880), and Inch'ŏn (since 1882). The opening of these two ports went into effect on 1 October 1898.[45] In October of 1897, the Korean king, who at the time had resided, of his own volition, in the compound of the Russian legation, had himself crowned "emperor of Korea." Despite efforts by Koreans to modernize and improve their conditions—involving above all Dr. Sŏ Chaep'il's "Independence Movement," which was generally more friendly toward Japan—European observers at the time were apt to make the sort of assessment seen in this editorial (16 October 1897) published by the British-owned *Kobe Weekly Chronicle*:

> So far as the independence of Korea is concerned, many observers of Far Eastern politics would be pleased to see the country have the opportunity of governing itself for a few years without outside interference; but, so far as we can see, there is not the slightest possibility of this. . . . Korea is bound to come under the domination of one of three contiguous Powers—either China, Japan or Russia will have the controlling voice. It would seem, however, that China's opportunity of controlling the destiny of Korea has passed away forever; and unless the attention of Russia is diverted either by European or by Indian frontier complications, Japan's opportunity seems also to have passed. There remains Russia, which slowly and steadily, without ostentation, is securing paramount control over the peninsular kingdom.[46]

A half-year later, however, an article in the British-owned Shanghai paper *The North-China Herald* speculated as to whether Japan might not be able after all, with British backing, to secure such a paramount position for itself. Nevertheless, in the opinion of the article's author, terms like "leasehold" or "concession" to designate rights achieved by the European powers in China and elsewhere were merely euphemisms for theft. How could one expect that Japan would keep aloof? "A free hand in Corea, backed up, if necessary, by the active co-operation of England? It does not seem likely, yet who knows? Time alone will show."[47]

In St. Petersburg, Japan's ambassador, Count Hayashi Tadasu (1850–1913),[48] pursued talks with the Russian foreign minister, Vladimir N. Muraviev,[49] to sound out respective spheres of interest in East Asia and especially in Korea.[50] Hayashi cabled (7 January 1898) to his superior in Tokyo, Saionji Kinmochi, that the Russian foreign minister had said the Russian tsar, Nicholas II, had confided in him that "the continual friction between Japan and

Russia in Corea is not conducive to the interests of both countries. Keeping in view the fact that Japan has the greater interest than Russia, may not an arrangement [be] arrived at to avoid complications for the future?"[51] Japan could not be expected to undertake any further steps, however, so long as this approach was not officially endorsed, namely, "to conciliate Japan, by leaving her more freedom of action in Corea, in order to carry out her scheme in Chōsen (Korea) free from opposition."[52] On 18 January 1898, Nishi Tokujirō in Tokyo informed Hayashi in St. Petersburg that the Russian minister had visited him and put forth the opinion that Russia was ready "to assist Japan as far as possible in regard to our commercial and industrial interests in Korea. I replied immediately that unless Russia was ready to abandon her position on the subject of the drilling of the army and the engagement of the Financial Adviser a satisfactory understanding seemed difficult of realization."[53] Nishi the next day cabled this information (requesting a prompt response) also to the head of the legation Katō Masuo in Seoul. Katō doubted, however, in his reply (21 January 1898) that Nishi's demands would be acted upon, and asked if the Russian attitude was not ultimately to be attributed to the fact that Russia wanted, in whichever case, to avoid seeing Japan make a common case with England.[54]

Shidehara, as junior diplomat in Korea's southeastern port city of Pusan, followed the grand stage of world politics *en miniature*, as if through a shop window, keeping up to date with regard to all relevant events. In the ongoing diplomatic efforts relating to Korea Japan proceeded circumspectly. Its current aim was to come to an agreement whereby it would be allowed to appoint *either* the military trainers for the Korean army *or* the principal financial advisor. France meanwhile, its foreign minister intimated at the end of January 1898, was agreeable to have Japan join in a "likely European concert in the East."[55] For a short time it appeared that the powers would settle their affairs in mutual agreement, and that the new century would start under a more favorable star, with forebodings of a lasting peace and a reconciliation of interests. Other events, however, appeared to be detrimental to such purposes, like the French and British military interventions during the African Fashoda Crisis of September–October, 1898, which laid bare some of the sharp conflicts of interest among the powers.

The Koreans meanwhile announced that they wished to do away completely with the foreign advisors and instructors. Perhaps due to the unstable domestic and international political relations and entanglements in which the Korean king found himself, he had, as stated earlier, since early 1896 taken refuge in the Russian legation and been crowned "emperor" in October 1897.[56] In a note of March 1898, the Korean sovereign having spent two years as a guest of the Russians, the Korean regime communicated that "they will be able hereafter to manage by themselves, and that they will not require service of foreigners."[57] Even while it acknowledged Russia's friendly support during the king's refuge in the Russian Legation, the note gave it to be understood that "the military officers and financial adviser may be withdrawn."[58] The Russian government then announced that, having withdrawn its personnel, Korea would not be allowed to employ other foreign advisors or military trainers.

On 12 March 1898, the Russian minister of war, Alexei Nikolaevich Kuropatkin, proposed to the tsar a cutback in weapons expenditures. Foreign Affairs Minister Muraviev backed the proposals, which contrary to expectations met with the tsar's wholehearted approval. Muraviev explained: "Precisely now, when we are taking appropriate steps in the Far East, it would be very important . . . to give Europe factual evidences of our love of peace."[59] In relating the reason for his letter to Muraviev, Kuropatkin had denounced the existing "armed peace" and vividly warned of a future war where "within a month Europe could present the drama, never before seen since the creation of the world, of a bloody struggle of armies in the millions."[60]

In a realistic vein, Nishi, in St. Petersburg, suggested in a cable (22 March 1898) to Ambassador Katō Takaaki in London that Japan "propose to Russia a division of spheres of influence," with the objective "to remove all cause of irritation and to strengthen our position by throwing Russia back to a safe distance from our frontiers and to conserve our actual interests."[61] The "strictly confidential" letter reflects the apprehensions over the Russian expansion in Manchuria, which was continuing unabated, even if Russia's retreat from Korea was supposedly to become a matter of record. The next day, Katō sent his opinion to Tokyo: "Once England and Japan are united, Russia will recede [from Manchuria] even without armed opposition."[62] Noteworthy is the judiciousness with which the Japanese conducted their affairs, adjusting their tactics to each new situation in an ostensibly positive spirit. In spite of this, during the following month the progress made in the discussions was brought to naught by a sudden political about-turn of the Russians in regard to Korea.

In St. Petersburg, meanwhile, the Russian minister for foreign affairs, Vladimir N. Muraviev, at a "regular weekly reception for the diplomatic corps"[63] on 24 August 1898, delivered to the accredited envoys—including those from Japan and Korea—a circular in which Tsar Nicholas II officially extended an invitation for a peace conference.[64] The goal of the conference was to be a general diminution of armaments and the establishment of a court of justice for the arbitration of international disputes.

In Korea, the Independence Club, the party founded by Sŏ Chaep'il, had in the meantime gained in popularity. Though Sŏ Chaep'il declined the post of

Korean minister for foreign affairs, it seemed for a time as if the democratic reform movement might bring about a constitutional monarchy. At the end of October 1898, when a breakthrough seemed imminent, intrigues and internal struggles within the government apparatus and among the established power-holders prevented the democrats from pushing through the desired reforms, and occupying the government posts necessary to assure the continuation and success of their movement. Despite strong public opinion opposing them, the ultraconservative forces prevailed. In early 1899 all political activities of the Tongnip Hyŏphoe were forbidden, the Independence Club was dissolved, and the publication of its newspaper *The Independent* was banned.

By the time Shidehara left Korea in the spring of 1899, the Independence Club reform party had already ceased to exist. Only in 1919 would there again be a Korean independence movement, this time aimed against Japanese suzerainty over the peninsula. The failure in 1899 was especially regrettable because "the dispersed and outlawed Independents' Party . . . might have been a valuable instrument of administration"[65] and progress, independent of foreign domination. In August 1899 notices began appearing in the press about the drastic increase in political refugees leaving Korea. One such notice in *The Kobe Weekly Chronicle* spoke of "Korean political offenders now taking refuge in Japan" and went on to state that "the presence of so many Korean refugees is regarded as a hindrance to the policy of Japan in Korea."[66] The same issue of *The Kobe Weekly Chronicle* also mentioned the Hague peace conference that was then in session, telling readers: "It is stated that the Conference has only adopted a resolution to prohibit the Dum Dum bullets."[67]

In May 1899, Great Britain and Russia agreed (to the surprise of many) to restore China's integrity and to allow no new special rights and privileges other than those that had already been granted. The two imperial powers, through this agreement, wished to guarantee the Russian railway rights in Manchuria and the British railway rights in the Yangzi region. One British journalist put it this way: "Nobody, Russia and Germany being satisfied, is to have any more slices of China."[68] A course was set that, taking Japanese interests into account, and with an eye to the forthcoming peace conference in The Hague, could lead toward a peaceful governance of international affairs.

There seemed to be scarcely any limitations on what might be achieved by developing resources and industries for the benefit and advancement of the people—or at least so it appeared to well-meaning statesmen and other perceptive contemporaries at the time. Shidehara was actively participating in these advances, directing his hopes and aspirations toward realizing these objectives. The young diplomat committed himself—as he would soon have opportunity to show—to further the peaceful progress of his native country.

After he returned to Japan from Korea, Shidehara prepared for a new assignment, which now took him to London.

THE FIRST HAGUE PEACE CONFERENCE AND THE
ESTABLISHMENT OF THE PERMANENT COURT OF
ARBITRATION, 1899–1903; SHIDEHARA IN LONDON

Motono Ichirō (1862–1918),[69] the Japanese envoy in Russia, on 25 August
1898 received a note from the Russian minister of foreign affairs, Count
Vladimir Muraviev, proposing that an international peace conference be convened "in view of investigating most effective means to secure to all nations
benefits of real and durable peace, and to put an end to progressive development of actual armaments in all countries." The arms competition in particular, the Russian circular emphasized, had during the last two decades led to
an untenable situation. Indeed, since the Franco-Prussian War of 1870–1871
the dangers had intensified.

> Main reasons laid down in the note are as follows: During the last twenty years,
> the maintenance of peace has been considered as the object of international
> policy; and under the pretext of the maintenance of peace, Great Powers have
> formed alliances, increased and still are increasing their armaments without suc-
> cess: Financial burdens, resulting from it increase day by day, and injure public
> prosperity from its root. If this situation continues, it will finally lead to catas-
> trophe, which they intend to avoid. Russian Minister for Foreign Affairs added
> that, he does not think that such a conference may produce immediate result, but
> he hopes that it may serve to prepare solutions for the future.[70]

What had happened? It was actually 24 August, when the ambassadors
and ministers accredited to the Court at St. Petersburg had come to attend the
weekly reception there. On this occasion, Count Michael Muraviev, the Russian foreign minister, presented a rescript that the tsar, Nicholas II, had commissioned him to deliver to the diplomats. The tsar's rescript read in parts:

> This conference should be, by the help of God, a happy presage for the century
> which is about to open. It would converge in one powerful focus the efforts of
> all states which are sincerely seeking to make the great idea of universal peace
> triumph over the elements of trouble and discord.[71]

That Japan was not principally opposed to the rule of international law
had been shown early on by Fukuzawa, Ueki Emori, and others. Even if in
the national interest the country pursued a more "realistic" policy of security,
defense, and armaments, this did not mean that international law and order

had been generally discarded. During the 1880s and 1890s much emphasis was laid on defining "legal concessions" and positions that Japan could effectively claim in the global context.[72] Binding agreements under international law continued to remain the goal for the future.

Japan, in the words of the German jurist Schücking, had become "implicitly accepted into the community of civilized nations" after the victory in the 1894–1895 war with China,[73] and participated in the peace conference convened at The Hague between 18 May and 29 July 1899, together with some two dozen other sovereign states. Shidehara was still in Korea, between the end of August 1898 and spring of the following year, when the preparations for the peace conference drew considerable attention. This was not the usual congress, concluding a "peace treaty" after fighting a war, but a conference aimed at a new universal order, something that had been brewing for some time. Apart from trying to put an end to the armaments race among the European colonizing powers, which were fighting over colonial concessions and resources and disputing their spheres of influence, global solutions were required. It had not been, at first, Japan's intention to participate in the scramble for foreign possessions. As historian Miwa Kimitada has pointed out, "[f]rom the beginning, Japanese colonial thought had emphasized national defense," and in this way was different from the Europeans' colonialism of aggressive exploration and exploitation.[74]

The calling of the first peace conference by the Russian tsar thus heralded the beginning of the end to the age of "discoveries" and resultant colonial exploitation. Europe's press and statesmen reacted at first quite favorably to the tsar's initiative. Hayashi cabled from St. Petersburg to Prime Minister Ōkuma in Tokyo (1 September 1898) that he had met with the German secretary of state in the foreign ministry, Bernhard von Bülow, who had confidentially told him the German leadership would be taking a positive look at the tsar's proposals. The Japanese might have hoped that perhaps the Russian leadership had consulted the Germans before releasing their circular in St. Petersburg.[75] The same day Motono in St. Petersburg reported, almost euphorically: "It appears that European press welcome Russian proposal with almost unanimity, and considers it as one of the most important acts of international policy of this century, and expresses hopes that their respective Governments will adhere to Russian proposal."[76] Even cautious German newspapers like the *Norddeutsche Allegemeine Zeitung*, which carried an article titled "Weltfrieden" (World Peace) on 31 August, welcomed the Russian initiative. As the message "went around" to Berlin, Paris, London, and Washington, it "prompted a mixture of disbelief, skepticism and joy." However, eventually skepticism "prevailed" and gave rise to questions as to the motives. What had really driven Nicolas II, "this absolute despot and monarch of the world's

largest military power . . . to call for peace? *Realpolitiker* all over the world
were quick in detecting . . . the reasons."[77] In spite of von Bülow's positive
outlook, the first protests against the Russian circular were to come from
Berlin, arguing that "no armament could be called excessive which would
guarantee peace and that no German felt its burden."[78]

Nevertheless, all the nations who had received the tsar's rescript of 24
August 1898 had positively replied to the invitation. A second circular letter
dispatched on 11 January 1999, specified the issues that were to be debated
at The Hague, the place that had been chosen for the convention, after the
young Queen Wilhelmina of the Netherlands had, on Muraviev's suggestion,
accepted to hold the conference there.[79] The circular letter recommended the
following issues to be included in the conference program:

1. The freezing of the present military effectiveness and budgets for a
   fixed period and the examination as to the future reduction of both;
2. The immediate prohibition of any new firearms and explosives more
   powerful than the ones actually in use;
3. The restriction in wartime of the existing explosives and the prohibition
   of projectiles dropped from balloons or other aircraft;
4. The prohibition of submarine torpedo-boats and ram-equipped vessels;
5. The extension of the stipulations of the 1864 Geneva Convention to the
   area of naval warfare;
6. The neutral status of ships employed in rescue operations during or after
   an engagement;
7. The revision of the still unratified Declaration of the 1874 Brussels
   Conference on the laws and customs of war;
8. The acceptance of the principles of mediation and facultative arbitration as a means of preventing or settling international disputes, and the
   establishment of a mode and uniform practice in these respects.[80]

On January 18, Minister Hayashi cabled from Berlin to Foreign Minister
Aoki Shūzō in Tokyo: "I saw German Minister for Foreign Affairs to-day,
who told me that while the Emperor of Germany and his Government cordially sympathize [with the] humanitarian undertaking of the Emperor of
Russia, he thought there would be great difficulty in arriving at [a] practical
solution of the propositions formulated in recent circular of [the] Russian
Minister for Foreign Affairs." Hayashi's first impression was that the German leadership wanted to avoid taking a positive attitude or initiative in the
matter, preferring to observe how the other powers would respond. In the
meantime, the German government apparently had given instructions to the
German press to report little or nothing about the planned conference, so

as not to unnecessarily arouse hopes among the population or in any way to prejudice German interests overseas: *"Newspapers in this country are generally silent."*[81]

The Japanese meticulously recorded the other powers' reactions. There was no reaction from Britain yet, which did not want to commit itself prior to receiving an official invitation, which may have contributed to the Japanese restraint.[82] Japan's engagement at the peace conference would indeed depend, to a decisive degree, on the stance taken by the Western powers. The various views of the governments that were invited were already being sounded out early on. Since Shidehara was a frequent guest in the home of the British minister in Seoul, John Jordan, he must on occasion have participated in some of the discussions about the Russian initiative.

Although the growing global interdependence may have been the true cause, the heavy burden of weapons expenditures on the national budget was named as the chief motive behind the Russian initiative.[83] When Minister of War Kuropatkin demanded sixty million rubles to modernize the Russian artillery (*The Times* even spoke of 120 million that would be needed),[84] this helped breathe life into the peace initiative. While Japanese concerns may have been of little consequence in the European capitals, the question of Russian intentions was relevant to Japanese policies in the Far East. Indeed, currency had been given in early September to an idealized version of the circumstances that had led to the Russian initiative:

> I know there are two versions about the probable cause of the Russian proposal: (1) The emperor of Russia, deeply animated by sincere desire for peace, spontaneously has ordered Russian Minister for Foreign Affairs to make the said proposal, and to give publicity to the document by seizing opportunity of the unveiling [in 1898] of [the statue of] Alexander II [reigned 1855–1881] at Moscow. It is said that the Empress of Russia has exercised great influence on the Emperor of Russia on the subject. (2) Russian Government being much sensible to the violent attack made by English newspapers against her ambition, and being anxious to keep friendly relations with England, have decided to manifest to the world their peaceful intention by proposing the said conference in view of appeasing bad feeling on the part of the English people. Foreign representatives do not attach great importance to the results of the conference.[85]

Apart from the dedication of the statue of Tsar Alexander II,[86] the initiative of the British prime minister, Lord Rosebery, who called Tsar Alexander III (reigned 1881–1894) "the greatest guarantor of peace in Europe," and had urged him to take up the matter of a worldwide diminution of armaments, should be remembered.[87] Now the time was ripe and the ground well prepared.

A forerunner for the tsar's proposal, according to the London *Times* of 12 December 1898, was a conference of the Inter-Parliamentary Union (IPU, founded 1889) which had taken place 23–25 September 1896, in Budapest.[88] Russia's consul general in the Hungarian capital, Alexander von Basily (later head of the Division for Asian Affairs in Russia's Ministry of Foreign Affairs under Count Muraviev), had prepared what was probably the most eloquent and detailed report on this forward-looking conference of the IPU delegates. The introduction by the French artillery of a new machine gun and the ensuing desire of Germans, Russians, and others to invest in the development and production of the new weapon also contributed to the fact that Basily's report was again dug up, and the Russian will for peace strengthened.[89] In Budapest it had been proposed to establish a permanent international court of arbitration. This too was not a new idea, but its achievement would be a novelty. Japan had for the first time included an "arbitration clause" in its commercial treaty with Siam of 25 February 1898 ("Treaty of Friendship, Commerce, and Navigation between Japan and Siam").[90]

Other currents included the international Quakers' peace movement. The Swiss pacifist Henri Dunant's (1828–1910) initiative in creating the International Red Cross Society had similarly added to the trend of regarding war as barbaric and outmoded.[91] And, in the spring of 1898 the banker and author Jean (Ivan) de Bloch, who was then serving as honorary member on Russian Finance Minister Count Sergei Witte's "finance council," arranged to have an audience with the tsar during which he illustrated, with numerous diagrams, his views on the catastrophic consequences, and the unfeasibility of future wars.[92] And in November of that year, Tsar Nicholas II read to his wife Alexandra Fyodorovna from Tolstoy's *War and Peace*.[93]

Ōkuma on 13 September cabled Hayashi a draft for an official letter of reply to the Russian government, an optimistically nuanced directive in which the "humane motives and high aspirations" of the Russian government were praised and Japan's own tradition was cited to underline "the priceless benefits of a lasting peace." Ōkuma stressed that "the Imperial Government hasten to announce their intention to accept the proposition of the Imperial Government of Russia and to participate."[94] On 16 September Hayashi delivered to the Russian minister of foreign affairs, Count Lamsdorff, the official letter of reply (transmitted in French) by the Japanese government. Indeed, Japan welcomed the plan, but as Sir Ernest Satow, the British councilor in Tokyo, related to Lord Salisbury on 1 November 1898, Prime Minister Ōkuma also sounded a warning. Failure of the conference, he said, could lead to war—a war Japan, however, was not afraid of.[95]

It was typical for the transitional character of these international efforts that while the preparations for the peace conference were in progress and even during the conference itself, ambitions for more weaponry by the participating states continued almost unabated. Japan was no exception.[96] There seemed to be considerable support, however, for an obligation for open declarations of weapons inventories. On 7 December Hayashi cabled from St. Petersburg to the Japanese minister of foreign affairs, Aoki Shūzō (1844–1914),[97] Shidehara's superior, about Japanese military developments that were apparently still in the planning stage: "It seems advisable to publish now . . . our naval and military projects." And on 12 January of the following year Hayashi informed Aoki of the details of various points of the Russian arms limitation proposals, which had been outlined in the second circular letter of January 11.

The documents in the archives of the foreign ministry in Tokyo contain among items entered in early 1899 the handwritten copy of Leo Tolstoy's famous "Letter to the Swedes" of 23 January 1890. Like most all dispatches and other documents in English, it has an attached Japanese translation.

Armies will disappear when public opinion brands with contempt those who, whether for advantage or from fear, sell their dignity as men and enter the ranks of those murderers dressed in fools' clothes—called the army, when men will be ashamed to wear, as they now do, implements of murder, and when the word "military" will be, what indeed it is—a term [of] foul abuse. Only then will armies first diminish and then quite disappear, and a new era in the life of humanity will commence.[98]

This was of interest, relevant to Japanese thinking on peace and security, and may have inspired some of the more thoughtfully inclined statesmen, all the more so as it had to do with Russia. The Ministry of Foreign Affairs was a reservoir of information and ideas that reflected the atmosphere and environment of Japan's international relations at the time.

While Shidehara was still in Korea in early 1899 (Meiji 32), the Ministry of Foreign Affairs on 12 April sent a cable to Hayashi Tadasu[99] (who later headed the ministry) in St. Petersburg, naming him chief delegate to the forthcoming conference:

Sir: His Majesty the Emperor has been graciously pleased to appoint you as the Delegate of Japan to attend the international Conference which is to meet at The Hague on the 18th of next month for the purpose of discussing the most effective means of arresting the progressive development of armaments and of securing real and enduring peace . . . *Europe is the center of military and naval activity and it is chiefly to deal with the situation there that the Conference is convoked.* It will therefore be your first duty to watch carefully to see that the rights and interests of Japan are not sacrificed.[100]

On May 25 Foreign Minister Aoki inquired of Nishi in The Hague if the conference reports were to be published—an important query in light of the originally agreed-upon significance of involving the public.[101] On the same day Hayashi replied: "The proceedings of the Conference are to be kept secret."[102] As it turned out, even prominent pacifists like Bertha von Suttner and most especially members of the press were not allowed to attend the conference.

On 28 May, Sugimura sent Aoki a "strictly confidential" telegram, which acknowledged the draft submitted by the Russian delegation in Arbitration Committee III, introducing the plan for a convention on mediation and arbitration.[103] Wisely, it only provided that initially vital state interests and important matters of honor were to be excluded. This jurisdiction would later be expanded.[104] Recourse to the proposed court was to be obligatory in the following cases:

> First, question of pecuniary indemnity so far as not to touch vital interest nor honour of the state; Second, interpretation of the Treaties, convention on the following subjects: Post, telegraphs, railways, prevention of collision on high seas, navigation on international river and canals, patent, copyright, monetary and metric system, sanitary questions, cattle and plant disease, successions, extradition, mutual judiciary assistance, demarcation, so far as purely technical.[105]

"[A]rbitration as a substitute for war" had been vociferously advocated at the "closing decades of the nineteenth century"[106] by international lawyers, pacifists, and politicians, and numerous attempts had been made, notably in the United States, "to establish a system of peaceable adjustment of differences arising between nations."[107] In fact, as the American delegate Frederick Holls recalled, in general, "[n]o proposition before the Conference was received with more sympathy and favor than the plan for the establishment of a Permanent Court of Arbitration."[108]

A few days earlier, on 24 May, the American delegate Andrew D. White and the head of the German delegation Count Münster had met when Münster had spoken vigorously against obligatory arbitration: "I found him entirely opposed to it, or, at least, entirely opposed to any well-developed plan. He did not say that he would oppose a moderate plan for voluntary arbitration, but he insisted that arbitration must be injurious to Germany; that Germany is prepared for war as no other country is or can be; that she can mobilize her army in ten days; and that neither France, Russia, nor any other power can do this."[109]

The Arbitration Commission III had, at its first session on May 23, 1899, established an examination committee that came to be politically significant because of its expertise, and bringing together members of the other committees. Among the participants an "atmosphere of trust" developed that culminated in honest endeavors to participate in erecting the great edifice of peace. The German historian Jost Dülffer describes how, as a result of the arbitration proposals, by the end of May the "formerly pessimistic disposition among the Hague delegates and—emanating from that disposition—a similar sentiment in most capitals" had changed. This was, however, thwarted by the Germans. Nevertheless a consensus emerged, at least by some noticeable appearances, to formally "make a beginning to reform international relations," even if the "sting [had been] taken out" of the arbitration regulations by introducing exceptional clauses concerning vital state practice.[110]

On 4 June Sugimura Yōtarō[111] informed Aoki about the proposed composition of the court of arbitration, and on 7 June he sent him from St. Petersburg this cable telegram:

> SPECIAL—Russian proposal of Permanent Court is as follows:—This Conference shall, until the period when a new Conference will take place, designate five powers who shall each nominate a judge either of their nationality or a foreigner; these judges will constitute [the] Permanent Tribunal; if the litigants are other than these five powers, they shall also each choose a judge, having the same rights as other judges; central office of administration will be established in La Haye.[112]

This was changed later to a maximum of four persons from each of the signatory powers, which the governments of the membership nations would select (article 23 of the Arbitration Treaty). Thus the Permanent Court of Arbitration (*kokusai chūsai saibansho*) was first composed merely of a list from which countries could select the judges of their choice following the outbreak of a dispute. In September 1900 an administrative council was formed as a sort of "oversight council of the arbitration court which watches over the court's activities and consists of the [foreign] envoys in The Hague and the Dutch minister of foreign affairs." As adjuncts there were the International Bureau and the court's "Secretariat."[113] This examination committee met on 3 and 7 June to discuss questions of obligatory arbitration. Aoki informs Sugimura on the same day (7 June, i.e., 8 June in Europe) that the Japanese government had no objection to the "project of a convention on mediation and arbitration." Sugimura was advised, "[Y]ou are hereby authorized to agree to the whole project—*provided however that all the continental Powers do likewise.*"[114] However, by 4 July, compulsory arbitration was finally and irrevocably defeated, mainly due to German objections,[115] and nonbinding arbitration became the price the conference had to pay to avoid the otherwise certain dismissal of the whole plan for an arbitration convention and the international court idea. Similarly disappointing were the results in the area of disarmament, when the Russian proposal to freeze all armaments for a period of five years also came to naught.[116]

An undated newspaper article (most likely published in January 1900) in the Japanese archive gives the speech before the German Reichstag by the state secretary in the foreign ministry, Count von Bülow, explaining the German attitude toward the concept of obligatory arbitration:

> In the question of arbitration and mediation, we have not agreed to the proposal of an obligatory arbitration. It is our conviction that an independent state is an end in itself and can in the political field recognize no higher goals than those of protecting its own interests and of its self-assertion through the fulfillment of its own purpose of existence. *In serious political questions we will never recognize any guiding principle other than the general welfare* (Salus publica) *of the German people. . . . Obligatory arbitration has [therefore] been abandoned [by the conference].*[117]

Arbitration required but a minor curtailing of sovereignty, which in return would be expected to have a definite, positive effect on state behavior, with regards to questions of war and peace. Shidehara was likely to welcome, like his mentor Henry Willard Denison, the idea of the peaceful settlement of international disputes through the appeal to arbitration. In spite of the setbacks, the institution for the peaceful settlement of disputes continued to be, with the ratification of the Arbitration Treaty—however limited in scope—on the agenda. The idea had evolved to the status of a realistic political option for the future.

After the relative failure of the Hague peace conference in August 1899, over the most important questions (i.e., disarmament and arbitration), the Japanese government retracted its intention of publishing the results of the Hague conference, and any "reports from the Japanese representatives at the Peace Conference . . . reaching the General Army Staff Department,"[118] as had originally been planned.[119] Although the government and Ministry of Foreign Affairs seem to have refrained from instructing the press (as had been the case in Germany) to limit its reporting or report negatively, there was more disappointment than enthusiasm in Japan over the results of the conference. Discussions about the peace of the world were widely seen as a European affair, and Japan's voice in this carried little weight. Nonetheless, the general idea of international, obligatory arbitration for the peaceful settlement of disputes had been given certain substance, and the powers seemed resolved to pursue this goal further and to bring it to fruition in a not too distant future. The same was true for disarmament, which would become possible within the strong legal framework of an international order. That the Hague peace conference had public appeal was demonstrated by the initiative of Princess

Mōri, who had in June of that year (1899) personally delivered the signatures of the members of the Japanese branch of the Ladies International Peace Association to the promoters of the association's branch in Germany.[120]

All the powers that had taken part in the conference had signed the final communiqué by 31 December 1899.[121] On 6 October 1900, Japan deposited in The Hague its signatures to the three "conventions" and three "declarations" that the conference had produced, and on 10 February 1901, ratification documents were exchanged. Signing the conventions and declarations was Chinda Sutemi, "Envoy Extraordinary and Minister Plenipotentiary of his Majesty, the Emperor of Japan." The official Japanese document, composed in French with an accompanying letter by Foreign Minister Katō Takaaki, was duly delivered to the Dutch envoy in Tokyo, Jonkheer Cesta.[122] The list of judges (*liste des arbitres*) was ordered to be drawn up, with "the object of facilitating an immediate recourse to arbitration for international differences which could not be settled by diplomatic methods."[123] Those nominated for the list of judges—a list that would later include Shidehara—should possess recognized expertise in matters of international law and enjoy the highest moral integrity. The nominees carried the title "Member of the Permanent Court of Arbitration." The Japanese government nominated Motono Ichirō and Henry Willard Denison.[124] For Great Britain Sir Julian Pauncefote, for Russia Vladimir Muraviev and the jurist Feodor de Martens, for France Baron Estournelles de Constant, for Austria Lammasch, and for Italy Count Nigra made themselves available for service. After Motono's death, Shidehara followed in the footsteps of his mentor Denison from 1918–1924 who had died in 1914.

In spite of the considerable disillusionment over the meager results of the conference, especially amongst the ranks of the international peace movement, with the First Hague Peace Conference the community of nations had, according to Schücking, "undergone a thorough change in its legal structure. A new era of a world league of nations had dawned."[125] The First Hague Peace Conference had laid the foundations for a prospective new "concert" of nations, whose distinguishing features were a new internationalism (in which all states were to be treated equally) and pacifism, aiming at disarmament and the peaceful resolution of disputes through due process of law instead of going to war.

This formula appealed to the legally minded and patriotic Shidehara and likeminded Japanese who were disposed toward such a regulation of affairs, if only the Western powers were determined and united in their purpose. The peace conference gained true significance and universal value with the participation of Japan and other non-European countries. Chance was that the new scientific pacifism and the young, universally aspiring family of nations would mutually reinforce one another. Shidehara would later, as minister of foreign affairs, bring into play, in his diplomacy, the practical instruments of negotiation and compromise, mediation, conciliation, and "good offices."[126] The formula negotiated at the conference—disarmament and "arbitration"—held for the young Shidehara not only a moral promise and a political appeal to practical wisdom, but also commended itself, first and foremost, to a sound international diplomacy, which would aim at democratic institutions and a universal "legislature" in the widest sense. Disagreement among the Western powers kept Japan at first—and subsequently to a great extent—from articulating itself more clearly. The young nation wanted to avoid exposing itself unnecessarily. The chance for a clearer articulation of policy would come in the 1920s.

At the turn of the century there was a general awareness and an alertness, in Japan and the West, as a new age in international relations was about to dawn, that the next century should bring about general progress and peace. At the same time, the political climate fostered, however, not only hope but also deep fears about what could happen—possibly in the near future—if some sort of a settlement was not reached to halt certain developments, especially in the field of armaments.

During most of the duration of the Hague conference, Shidehara had been on board the ocean liner on his way from Kobe to Marseilles, making stops in Shanghai, Hong Kong, Saigon, Singapore, Colombo, Djibouti, and Port Saïd. He had left Kobe on a steamer of the Messageries Maritimes Line around 9 June, three weeks after the commencement of the conference, and reached London on 19 August—via Marseille and Paris—some three weeks after its conclusion. Although intelligence about the progress of the conference was also received on board, there remained ample room for speculation. At the ports en route—Shanghai, Hong Kong, Bombay, and so on—newspapers and other information came aboard. And no doubt reports reached Shidehara by telegraph about the conference proceedings.

After a short stay in Marseilles—in this large commercial port a number of Japanese as well as a diplomatic representative resided—Shidehara traveled onward, by train, to Paris, where just then a trade fair in which Japan participated had been opened.[127]

It appears that Shidehara was not officially received immediately upon his arrival in London by train following the short sea voyage from Calais to Dover. After a trip alone through London on the Underground, he looked for a hotel room and then got in contact with Japan's embassy. He wanted to get a feel of the great city. If he had not yet read Charles Dickens's *A Tale of Two Cities*, on the train from Paris he might have taken the opportunity to do so.

Great Britain held first place in Japan's international relations, being model, friend, and—as the premier imperial power—a practical challenge at the same time. Shortly before or during the outbreak of the Sino-Japanese

War, Great Britain had shifted its overseas priority from China to Japan, and concluded a commercial treaty with Japan in 1894. Shidehara was concerned with reconnoitering British attitudes with respect to issues of international peace and security, commerce, and British-Japanese relations in general. The British stance and political concepts in the wake of the Hague conference would have enlightened Shidehara, to see how future relationships among states—as between Japan and Great Britain—were likely to take shape. The results of the Hague peace conference were relevant, and Japan, having taken part in the conference and signed its conventions, did not intend to remain inactive and in a fog of uncertainty.

Shidehara's superior in London was Katō Takaaki,[128] a genuine liberal and practical politician who later served as foreign and prime minister and led the progressive Dōshikai and Kenseikai Parties.[129] Among Shidehara's duties— alongside the routine carrying out of liaison functions related to trade and other matters—was to regularly follow the debates in the British parliament and pre- pare reports on them. These unassuming jobs included gathering information from newspapers and keeping files of newspaper clippings on important issues. Shidehara regularly exercised his memory by learning by heart long passages from the English classics.[130] He clearly possessed the main characteristics of an outstanding diplomat: an excellent memory, integrity, and patience.

In London, Shidehara still seems to have pursued marrying the daughter of John Newell Jordan, the British minister in Korea, but he appears to have decided against it on the advice of Katō Takaaki, and sacrificed his personal wishes to his career. But what he did not give up was his faith in the pos- sibility of an international order based on law and morality. His professional interest would naturally have extended toward concepts akin to what came to be known as the school of "organizational" (i.e., scientific) pacifism.[131] It is nice to picture that such issues also played a part in his talks with his English female friend, who we can easily imagine shared Shidehara's idealism.

Little is known to date of the young diplomat's meetings with James Bryce, who had been mentor of Hozumi Nobushige, Shidehara's teacher at Tokyo Imperial University, and who at this time was a member of Parliament for Aber- deen South, Scotland. Anyway, it was then and there that the fundamental out- lines of what came to be known as "Shidehara diplomacy" were conceived and gradually consolidated. Shidehara stayed in London until December 1900.

Among the events of 1900 the Boxer Rebellion stands out, which in Oc- tober gave Russia the opportunity to militarily occupy China's Three Eastern Provinces. At the end of December Shidehara served for a short period as consul in Antwerp,[132] where obviously he must have had occasion to confer, among others, with old Auguste Beernaert (1829–1912), an international jurist and member of the Permanent Court of Arbitration who had been one of the principal organizers of the First Hague Peace Conference.[133] At the same time this was an opportunity to become acquainted with the particulars of Belgian federalism, and with Belgium's 1831 liberal "model constitution." The following year (1901) Shidehara returned to Japan to report back to his government, after which he took the post of consul at Pusan in Korea, the country he had left two years earlier. In Korea prominent configurations in international relations became visible as in a nutshell. Until shortly after the beginning of the Russo-Japanese War in February 1904, Shidehara remained in Pusan.

Shidehara's work in London had contributed to preparing the naval alliance with Japan, which Great Britain concluded on 30 January 1902. Philipp Zorn, professor of international law at Königsberg University (who also participated as German delegate in both Hague peace conferences), has pointed out that "there was the intention of bringing Germany also into this alliance," but unfortunately "this intention did not find approval in Germany,"[134] which had other plans. Until the beginning of the 1920s, this alliance remained, as Komura Jutarō (who had signed the treaty) called it, "the cornerstone of Japanese diplomacy." The alliance greatly contributed to Japan's victory not only in its war with Russia (1904–1905), but later also committed Japan to declare war on Germany in 1914.

In 1903 Shidehara married Iwasaki Masako, the youngest daughter of Iwasaki Yōtarō from the famous Satsuma family of samurai origins who founded the Mitsubishi business conglomerate (*zaibatsu*). Shidehara's former superior in London, Katō Takaaki, had married Masako's elder sister. Having followed Katō's counsel not to marry Sir John Jordan's younger sister, the marriage tie with Masako, however, was mediated not by Katō but Shidehara's superior in Korea, Ishii Kikujirō. Through this marriage, Shidehara became closely associated with Ishii, Katō, the Dōshikai (and later Kenseikai) Party, and—to a lesser extent—the Mitsubishi business concern. It is true though that a close link existed between the Dōshikai/Kenseikai Party of Ōkuma Shigenobu and the Mitsubishi concern, which promoted and financially supported the party. These forces represented Japan's liberal economic interests. The "Kenseikai cabinets" of the 1920s stood for parliamentary democracy, pacifism,[135] and "free trade."

Masako was a Christian, and the Christian pacifism of Uchimura Kanzō around the turn of the century must have appealed to her. Uchimura's articles appeared in the *Yorozu Chōhō*, of which Uchimura was copublisher.[136] In an article on Tabata Shinobu, the great constitutional scholar and pacifist who died in 1993, Ueda Katsumi wrote that "Tabata could not discover a link which connected Shidehara to Japan's past [Christian] pacifist thinkers . . . [and that] although Shidehara was not a Christian, his wife was. Tabata presumes that God's will may have been working upon Shidehara through his wife's Christian influence."[137]

Toward the end of 1903, the armed conflict with Russia was already clearly on the horizon. *The New York Times* of 20 December reported that "the Russian railway [through Manchuria] is worked to its utmost capacity for the conveyance of Russian troops eastward. . . . Russia is dispatching all her available naval forces to the Asiatic coast of the North Pacific. . . . She has left herself without naval representation in the Mediterranean in order to reinforce her Asiatic fleet." A day later (21 December) the *Frankfurter Zeitung* (evening edition) similarly came to Japan's defense: "One cannot say that the Japanese have up to now been quick-tempered; they have given the Russians time to carry out their promises on the demilitarization of Manchuria. Only after the demilitarization deadline had passed without the Russians showing signs of fulfilling their promises, did the Japanese come forth with the claim for compensation." The *North-China Herald* made quite a different point on 8 January of the following year: "The view of the crisis taken by the German Press, under direction, of course, from St. Petersburg, is that the Russian Goliath has compassionately told the Japanese David to put away his toy ships and his little wooden sword, and run and play about in Southern Corea where nobody will interfere with him." The same article continues: "For Russia, a war with Japan is an episode in her history; but Japan will be fighting for her existence; and if Russia does not withdraw from the attitude of aggression she has maintained ever since the war between China and Japan, Japan must fight."

The conflict with Russia could have been prevented if the tsar's earlier initiative had produced tangible results.[138] No doubt Russian imperialism and expansionism, backed by Germany, were to blame for the outbreak of the war. All over the world there were expressions of sympathy for the Japanese. The *Frankfurter Zeitung,* however, on 20 February changed course, placing Japan and Russia morally on the same ground: "It is good that Russian policy of conquest in Asia has come up against a hard-to-surmount impediment . . . but one can also, if the development of things is seen without bias, look upon the behavior of Japan as nothing other than the expression of a policy of conquest. To put it briefly: neither is in the right—both are in the wrong."

IN THE TELEGRAPHIC DIVISION OF THE FOREIGN MINISTRY—THE RUSSO-JAPANESE WAR, THE INTERNATIONAL PEACE MOVEMENT, AND THE SECOND HAGUE PEACE CONFERENCE, 1904–1911

Shidehara was consul in Pusan in the years from 1901 to 1904 that led up to the Russo-Japanese War. In his memoirs he describes an event that took place in February 1904, two days prior to the opening of hostilities. The consular residence was on a hill that afforded an excellent view over the city and harbor. On the morning of 8 February, when war between the two countries had become all but inevitable, Shidehara observed Japanese naval units starting to capture some Russian freighters. The Russian consul in Pusan naturally wanted to notify his superior in Seoul by telegraph, so the Russian governor general in Port Arthur would be forewarned. Suspecting as much, Shidehara promptly gave the Japanese police stationed in Pusan orders to occupy the telegraph office, and prevent the sending of the Russian cable. This coup succeeded, and two days later the Japanese were able to carry out their surprise attack on Port Arthur.[139] The Russians later complained bitterly to Japan over the incident.[140]

From 1904 to 1911, Shidehara served in the telegraphic division of the Ministry of Foreign Affairs in Tokyo, first in a subordinate position and then as head of the division (*denshin kachō*). All important intelligence went over his desk. He composed telegraphic dispatches and documents and took part in important cabinet sessions—as, for example, during the war with Russia.[141] Shidehara's colleagues regarded his extraordinary knowledge of the English language as a "national treasure" (*kokuhō*)—since English had become the international *lingua franca* and was highly valued for diplomatic correspondence.[142] Shidehara was so apt in English that he customarily wrote his drafts of diplomatic documents in English and then translated them into Japanese.[143] English had in any event become a key language ever since telegraphic communication had first been introduced toward the middle of the nineteenth century.

The expansion of telegraphic services opened a new chapter in foreign relations and marked the beginnings of a modern "communications society." In the second half of the nineteenth century, an increasingly vast, wide-ranging network of embassies and missions that were entrusted with looking after political, economic, and military matters abroad was maintained by countries worldwide. Governments might communicate with other foreign governments directly through these countries' foreign ministries, which were in close contact with their embassies or other diplomatic representations abroad, which in turn maintained contacts with relevant government offices in their host countries. Or a government could present its views through an embassy or other diplomatic representation accredited to its national capital by another state with which it wished to have dealings, and this diplomatic mission on foreign soil would then forward the matter, most often by telegraph, to the relevant departments back home.[144] This sort of communication would foster international understanding, trade, and cultural exchange, creating a network that could potentially form the basis for a peaceful order among nations.

The Denmark-based Great Northern Telegraph Company realized the first telegraphic link between Japan and Europe in 1872. An undersea cable ran from Copenhagen through Denmark's Bornholm Island to Liepāja (Libau) on the Baltic coast of Latvia. Messages could then be forwarded from there through Moscow, Omsk, and Irkutsk, along the Siberian route, to Vladivostok. Another undersea cable linked Vladivostok with Nagasaki, and yet another linked Nagasaki and Shanghai, which was extended in 1873 to Hong Kong by way of Amoy (Xiamen).

Besides this northern route, there were cables managed by British telegraphic enterprises, among them the Eastern Telegraph Company. In the 1850s, undersea cables linking London and Paris, and also Marseilles and Malta, had already been laid. By the end of the 1870s the Malta-Bombay line, which passed through Alexandria and Aden, had been completed. British domination in India had facilitated the completion in 1858 of telegraphic links between Bombay, Madras, and Karachi. In 1871, two different British enterprises, the Eastern Extension Australia and the China Telegraph Company of Britain, completed undersea cable links between Madras and Hong Kong, via Penang, Singapore, and Saigon. Eventually, the International Telegraphic Union was founded in 1875 in St. Petersburg. Its accords covered, first and foremost, telegraphic traffic and legal matters. Japan joined the organization in 1879.[145]

The telegrams that arrived in Nagasaki at the beginning of the 1870s still had to be carried personally to Tokyo by special messengers (*hikizaku*). From around 1870, a telegraphic link between Tokyo and the commercial port of Yokohama was in use.[146] Finally, in 1873, Tokyo became linked through Nagasaki with the Great Northern line. Although the government was interested in linking Japan with the Chinese mainland through a Japanese cable, it concluded a cable-linkage agreement with Great Eastern in 1882 in which Japan agreed not to interfere with the company's monopoly over a period of thirty years.

This Danish monopoly posed restrictions on Japanese plans and security efforts in Korea. However, in 1884 a cable was laid from the seaside village of Yobuko in Saga Prefecture to Pusan via the islands of Iki and Tsushima. Then, in 1891, Japan attained the rights to the cable sector between Yobuko and Tsushima. Until the outbreak of the Russo-Japanese War efforts by Japan to bring under its control the sector between Tsushima and Pusan remained unproductive. Following Japan's colonization of the island of Formosa (Taiwan) after the 1894–1895 war with China, Japan in 1897 laid a cable from Ōshima in Kagoshima Prefecture via the islands of Amami Ōshima, Okinawa, and Ishigaki, to Jilong on Formosa (Taiwan), "for both civilian and military use." Then in 1898 Japan attained the right to use the undersea cable from Fuzhou (Foochow) to Danshui (Tamsui) on Formosa, which China had laid already in 1887. The British Eastern Extension operated a relay station in Fuzhou, which was on the Shanghai–Hong Kong line, with the result that Japan could now be in telegraphic communication with Europe via the British China Telegraph Company.

Improvements in conveyance technology stemming from Thomas A. Edison's invention of the dual duplex telegraph system made it possible, by around 1905, for a telegram between Europe and Japan to require no more than eight to twelve hours. Although there was by this time also a Berlin-based route via Warsaw, Odessa, Teheran, and India, Japan for the most part used the British route. Although the trans-Pacific undersea cable, which finally linked Japan directly with the United States, was completed only in 1906, telegraphic communications played a key role during the peace negotiations held in Portsmouth, New Hampshire, at the end of the Russo-Japanese war, when instructions from St. Petersburg and Tokyo, as well as information and official dispatches from Washington, needed to be delivered daily.

The instructions and other dispatches which the Japanese foreign ministry sent to its various legations and consulates on the European continent had to be first assembled in London and from there forwarded to their destinations. During his 1899–1901 stay in London, Shidehara had thus been able to extend the knowledge he had already begun to develop, during his first posting in Pusan, about telegraphic communications techniques. Since it was necessary, for the most part, to use English-language code books in dealing with technical and other matters, almost all Japanese cablegrams were composed in English.

Telegraphically conveying political information could meet with various bureaucratic and technical difficulties. In a telegram to a certain Mimashi, Aoki asks on February 14, 1899, for information on what to do about a notice put out by the Eastern Extension Telegraph Co. that said "No telegrams containing political news or information can be accepted without first being approved by the Censor: Col. R. E. Thompson of the U.S. Signal Corps. No private telegrams from abroad containing political information can be delivered without first being submitted to the Censor."[147] The reason was the unsettled conditions in the Philippines following their annexation by the United States in 1898. Not long afterward, as if to balance the territorial scoreboard, Japan occupied the tiny Marcus Island, one thousand miles southeast of Yokohama.[148]

The Japanese experimented with sending telegrams written phonetically in Japanese using the Latin script (*rōmaji*), which was hardly understood by the Russians. In one telegram (21 December 1901) from Komura to consul Tanabe in Niuchuang (Newchwang), he complains about "discrimination against Japanese words."[149] Then four days later Komura dispatched the following inquiry: "Telegraph at once if it is true that Russian telegraph office at Yinkow and

Newchwang do not accept telegrams in Japanese."[150] For a time it appeared that Japanese texts without any "secret meaning" would be accepted. But difficulties again arose, and on 30 December 1901, Tanabe notified Komura in Tokyo from Port Arthur: "Russian Telegraph Office . . . does not accept not only those in Japanese but all kind of international telegrams."[151]

A few days earlier in a correspondence between the Japanese consulate and the head of the customs administration in Niuchuang, consul [K.] Tanabe ("H.I.J.M's consul and senior consul") had on December 14 sounded out Captain A. Eberhardt ("H.I.R.M. civil administrator") as follows: "Sir, With reference to the notice circulated yesterday that the Chinese Eastern Railway Telegraph Station at Newchwang would be closed from 1st December of Russian calendar I have the honour to enquire on behalf of the Consular Body if it is the purpose of the Civil Administration to take any steps with the view of securing to us and our nationals the telegraphic communication with China and the world which we have hitherto enjoyed, and if so, what steps are contemplated. I have the honour to be, Sir, Your obedient servant."[152] On the same day Eberhardt replied: "Sir, I have the honour to acknowledge . . . and in reply to inform you, that the contents . . . will be directly brought by me to the consideration of His Excellency, Vice-Admiral [Mikhail] Alexeieff, General-aide-de-Camp to his Imperial Majesty."[153] After some hemming and hawing, Eberhardt informed the Japanese consul on 31 December that "the Russian Imperial Military Telegraph will accept international telegrams as an exception," upon which Tanabe in a four-page letter to Tokyo denounced the overbearing tone of the Russian communication. On 2 January, Tanabe cabled Alexeieff about the matter and received a telegram in reply, composed in French, in which Alexeieff offered an apology.[154] All this must, of course, be seen against the background of Russia's expanding influence in the Far East and also perhaps the British-Russian rivalry in Asia and Japan's increasing disposition to side with Great Britain.

Back in Tokyo in 1904, working in the foreign ministry's telegraphic division (*denshinka*),[155] Shidehara kept in close contact with Henry Willard Denison, the special advisor (*hōritsu komon*) in Japan's Ministry of Foreign Affairs from 1880 until his death in 1914. Shidehara had already become acquainted with Denison during his stay in Korea.[156] Denison, born on 11 May 1846 in the small agricultural and logging village of Guildhall, Vermont, studied law at Columbia College in Washington, D.C., and first came to Japan in 1869 as an office employee in the American consulate in Kanagawa (soon to be renamed Yokohama). Saitō Hiroshi (1886–1939), who served under Shidehara in 1930 as chief of the information division of the foreign ministry in Tokyo,[157] honored Denison by including a whole chapter about him in his book *Japan's Policies and Purposes* (1935).[158]

It had presumably been Denison's idea to use the constitution of the empire of Japan (Meiji constitution) as a "weapon" to remove the practice of extra-territoriality. Given constitutional prerogatives and the constitutionally stipulated independence and unassailability of judicial authority, extraterritoriality could scarcely be in consonance with the stipulated integrity and sovereignty of the imperial government.[159] With the backing of Hugh Fraser, the British minister to Japan, successful negotiations on this issue had commenced back in the 1890s.[160] Denison is given credit for having further suggested that negotiations be carried out individually with each the various powers rather than *en bloc*, a method that proved effective.

Denison is a central figure in the following anecdote relating to the outbreak of the Russo-Japanese War: Denison had been entrusted by Foreign Minister Komura with composing a diplomatic note to address the escalating crisis, in a last effort to turn things around. He was asked to deliver the text by the following day. However, the next morning he had to report to Komura that while he had spent the whole night thinking about the matter, he had not yet put a single sentence on paper. The foreign minister wished to know what the problem was. "I must first know," the American was said to have replied, "which decision you have made—will you fight against Russia or not? I will use strong words if you do *not* wish to wage war. But in the case that Japan is ready to fight, I will compose a note expressed in the most cordial and accommodating tones." Komura is said to have answered laconically, with a thin laugh, "Go softly!"[161]

The document, which was later made public, was indeed a masterful rendering of diplomatic prose. Shidehara greatly admired Denison and "stuck with him from morning till night."[162] Denison was "one of the closest advisors working for Foreign Minister Komura Jutarō throughout the time of the Russo-Japanese War."[163] Up until his death on 3 July 1914, not long before the outbreak of the First World War,[164] Denison remained a decisive presence in the foreign ministry. In 1911, for example, he was assigned to work on the renewal of the Treaty of Trade and Navigation between Japan and the United States, which had been established in 1894. Article 1 of the renewed treaty stated, in Denison's words, "The subjects or citizens of each of the High Contracting Parties shall have full liberty, with their families, to enter and sojourn in all parts of the territories of the other."[165] Having been on the list of judges at the Permanent Court of Arbitration in The Hague,[166] between 1900 and 1912, Denison also was a member of the Japanese delegation to the Second Hague Peace Conference in 1907.

The modest American, who had already mentored such important diplomats as Kurino Shin'ichirō (1851–1937), Chinda Sutemi, Hayashi Gonsuke, and Makino Nobuaki, became a person of central importance for Shidehara's diplomatic career. Denison's living quarters were located next to Shidehara's on the foreign ministry grounds. Through his daily professional and personal contact with Denison, Shidehara's proficiency in both law and diplomacy was further developed and refined. From Denison he learned the special nuances of English diplomatic and juridical language, practiced compiling treaty texts, and studied the intricacies of international relations and international treaty law.

Denison was, on his part, so impressed by Shidehara that shortly before his death he bequeathed to Shidehara his diaries and the diplomatic papers and notebooks that he had accumulated over the years of his service with the Japanese government. These materials were no doubt useful to Shidehara for reference.[167] They were an irreplaceable source of information on Japanese foreign relations during the Meiji era, though unfortunately they appear to have been lost.

Together with routine work on technical matters like determining tele-graph costs, the correct encoding of telegrams, and everyday political and diplomatic correspondence,[168] Shidehara's work in the telegraphic division included matters concerning the Permanent Court of Arbitration, through which four cases were submitted to judgment between 1901 and 1907, as well as the war and subsequent peace treaty with Russia, and finally the Second Hague Peace Conference of 1907. In such ways Shidehara was practically and principally involved in the efforts of the international peace movement.

Shidehara's handling of telegraphic communications for the Ministry of Foreign Affairs after 1904 involved delicate matters affecting the war with Russia and the peace negotiations of the summer of 1905. By the time the peace talks began in Portsmouth, New Hampshire, Japan's army was nearly exhausted.[169] But since Japan had won the war, it claimed a stately sum of money in reparations, as well as the cession of the entire island of Sakhalin. Because of the alleged refusal of the tsar to accept those Japanese conditions which a British diplomat (who had been informed by an American diplomat) had made public prematurely, hostilities seemed about to recommence, even though the emperor and also Prime Minister Katsura Tarō (1847–1913)[170] had meanwhile resigned themselves to be flexible and not insist on the original Japanese demands. On learning this, Shidehara immediately sent a cable with this information to Japanese negotiator Komura in Portsmouth.[171] However, shortly thereafter he got wind that the Russian tsar would be quite ready to cede the southern half of Sakhalin, so he then immediately (and without hav-ing explicitly requested to be granted the authority to do so) cabled Komura to ignore the earlier communicated decision of the imperial government and to await further instructions.[172]

Japan as a whole was enthralled. They had defeated a European, white Christian power—their gunnery and naval tactics were superior; the siege of Port Arthur, costly as it had been, had succeeded. But the aftertaste of jubilation was slightly bitter. Japan's victory had been won at an enormous sacrifice—apart from the monetary expenditures, some two hundred thousand men, most of them young, had lost their lives. To better understand the overall dimensions of the threat from Russia that Japan's leaders perceived, the following factors that had a bearing on the course history would take, especially the genesis of the First World War, should be considered. For Shidehara these considerations were of fundamental consequence. On the positive side, Japan's victory in the war had brought it the admiration of many Asians, among them also of Mohandas Karamchand Gandhi.

Russian-German relations, up until the First World War, during which Germany provided safe passage for the Russian revolutionaries from Switzerland to Moscow in order to distract and put the tsar's military on the Eastern front out of action, had been of special significance. It was true, as Kurt Bloch pointed out in a publication for the Institute of Pacific Relations (IPR) in 1940 that "Germany's rapidly expanding share in the exploitation of China did not accord well with Japanese ambitions, more especially since Germany backed Russia in her Far Eastern expansion."[173] The German emperor, Wilhelm II, had, for example, written to the tsar on 3 January 1904 (he wrote in English) that it was obvious for anyone who was unprejudiced that Korea should be Russian—it was only a question of "when and how." In any case Russian annexation of Korea was said to be a foregone conclusion, which, as in the case of the unavoidable occupation of Manchuria, did not admit of foreign (i.e., Japanese) meddling, since it concerned only the tsar and his country.[174]

Bloch's description provides further insight into how the German Reich acted in consonance with the overall ambitions of Russian Far East policies, with German ships supplying the Russians' Baltic Fleet with coal—"mostly Cardiff coal"—at the beginning of the war in 1904, something that provoked strong protests from the Japanese. The kaiser had in fact wanted a formalized German-Russian alliance.[175] Then in 1907 and 1908 the kaiser tried to bring about a German-Chinese-American entente, which he hoped would also be attractive for Russia.[176]

Some of the victories by the Japanese in the Russo-Japanese war had come rather unexpectedly. "[O]n the last day" of 1904 Port Arthur fell; the Russians "were treated gallantly by their enemies, and there were many scenes of fraternization between Japanese and Russian officers."[177] Then, between 23 February and 16 March 1905, there were further clashes between the Japanese and Russian armies.[178] According to Bersihand, "Prime Minister Katsura and the Japanese army leadership would have liked to continue the struggle in order to utterly defeat the Russian army and march to Harbin," but this would have demanded another huge material expenditure and cost in human lives that Tokyo wanted to avoid.[179] Japan finally attained the decisive victory in the sea battle of Tsushima, in which the Russian Baltic Fleet was totally annihilated on 27 May. The peace negotiations began on 10 August, and the peace treaty was signed in Portsmouth on 5 September.

Already during the war, the Japanese had declared that they were willing to respond positively to an invitation by President Roosevelt to take part in a second international peace conference at The Hague, as proposed by the American president on 24 September 1904. As a precondition for such a conference, the Japanese indicated that they were, after over seven months of war with Russia, prepared to accept an armistice. This was a step, however, that the Russians, whose Baltic Fleet was already heading toward Japan, were not ready to take, being sure of victory.

A second Hague peace conference, which was expected to continue the work begun in 1899, had been envisaged by the first conference. As part of the plan put forward by the American president, Theodore Roosevelt, it was hoped that after the Russo-Japanese War had been terminated the Russian tsar would again, as in 1899, take over the initiative to call the conference, together with Queen Wilhelmina, at The Hague. A point of departure for the American president's demarche was a resolution adopted by the Inter-Parliamentary Union (IPU) at its twelfth conference in St. Louis, Missouri, in September 1904.[180]

On 24 September 1904, President Roosevelt[181] explained during a White House reception for the IPU participants that the peace conference would be called "with a view to pushing toward completion the work already begun at The Hague, by considering the questions which the first conference had left unsettled."[182] Clearly one of these unsettled questions was the question of arms reductions. In a 4 October article in the *Washington Post*,[183] Secretary of State John Hay took up the cause, in words that resonated with Leo Tolstoy's ideals and religious pacifism.[184] On 20 October, Hay dispatched a circular to all foreign governments in which he urged them to conclude bilateral arbitration treaties with other states.[185] The next day he sent a further note to the American diplomatic representatives of the countries that had signed the final act of the 1899 Hague Peace Conference. Among other things Hay stated:[186]

> Enlightened public opinion and modern civilization alike demand that differences between nations should be adjudicated and settled in the same manner as disputes between individuals are adjudicated, namely, by arbitrament of courts in accordance with recognized principles of law.[187]

At the beginning of December 1904, Japanese Ambassador Hioki Eki (1861–1926)[188] reported to Foreign Minister Komura from Washington about a talk he had with Hay, in which Hay had indicated that an early reply by the Japanese to Roosevelt's suggestion would be most welcome. Hioki intimated that, in his opinion, the Russian attitude was that the moment, at least for the time being, was still not "opportune."[189] The following day Komura cabled back: "[The] decision of Japanese Cabinet . . . will be communicated . . . at the earliest opportunity possible."[190] On 8 December, Komura sent the Japanese ambassador a memorandum with an accompanying note in which it was communicated that "the Imperial Government gladly accept the invitation."[191] In his subsequent reply, Hioki reported Hay's "greatest gratification at the manner in which [the] invitation was received." However, the secretary of state "regrets that the Russian government does not see the matter in the same light." In a subsequent U.S. State Department circular, in tune with other recent Japanese dispatches, the American government officially lamented the negative attitude of the Russians: "This reply, tending as it does to cause some postponement of the proposed Second Conference, is deeply regretted."[192]

On 31 December the Bureau International de la Cour Permanente d'Arbitrage in The Hague began mailing out a printed brochure which contained the two American circulars as well as (in copies numbered 875 and up) the letters of reply[193] of those states that had indicated their willingness to accept the invitation, among them Luxembourg (23 November 1904), Siam (28 December 1904), China (31 December 1904), Mexico (2 January 1905), Great Britain (11 January 1905, "no objection"), Switzerland (20 January 1905), Turkey, Italy, and Montenegro (each 31 January 1905) and Germany (28 February 1905).[194] In the case of Germany, however, the foreign ministry (often referred to as "Wilhelmstraße," its location in Berlin) in a separate note of 28 February 1905, protested against the promotional activities of the Hague bureau, which it claimed the bureau was not officially authorized to pursue.[195]

On 5 September, the Portsmouth peace treaty was signed and a week later, on 13 September, the Russian ambassador in Washington, Baron Rosen, delivered to the American president a memorandum in which the tsar now actively called for the convocation of a second international peace conference. On 19 September a cablegram from Inoue Katsunosuke (1860–1929)[196] in Berlin informed Katsura Tarō in Tokyo of the Russian government's willingness to invite the powers to a second peace conference in The Hague.[197] From this point onward, Shidehara occupied himself frequently with preparations for the second Hague peace conference. Almost all related documents passed through his hands, receiving his cinnabar seal and also his special, undivided attention.

On 27 September, the Japanese envoy in The Hague, Mitsuhashi Nobutaka, in a cable to Tokyo confirmed the Russian government's invitation, stating that the Netherlands had agreed to host the conference. On the same day Inoue Katsunosuke, from Berlin, informed the Japanese foreign minister: "Russian

Representatives in foreign countries . . . are instructed to declare . . . that the proposal of Russian Government is for a conference whose work is intended to have strictly practical character," adding somewhat cryptically that the conference was "principally or even exclusively to treat serious questions which have arisen during the recent war and whose immediate solution is necessary."[198]

A cabled message of similar content, written by Baron Rosen, reached the American president at "Oyster Bay."[199] The Russians initially failed to make clear, however, what exactly the second conference would concern itself with. The American memorandum of 12 October 1905 emphasized "the [American] President's keen desire that upon a favorable occasion the labors of the first international peace conference might be supplemented and completed by an accord reached by a second conference of the Powers." Roosevelt stressed how important it should be to complete the work of the first conference, through no less than "full concord upon the broad questions specifically relegated by the final act of The Hague to the consideration of a further conference."[200] An article in *The Japan Times* on 14 November covers the invitation extended by the tsar.[201] Eventually, on 6 April 1906, the Russian "program" for the conference was delivered to American Secretary of State Elihu Root (1845–1937) together with a letter from Ambassador Rosen. It did not, however, include an agenda item on "disarmament" or "arms reduction," and ended by stating that "All political questions will be excluded."[202] Russian reticence in this regard most likely had been due to intense pressure from the German side, which had also been indignant due to Russia having been defeated by Japan.

On 9 May 1906—dated 16 April according to the old Russian calendar (observed until 1917)—Russian Ambassador Boris Bakhmeteff reported in a cable in French from the Russian legation in Tokyo:

> The first conference was divided on the proposition that its task could be ultimately fulfilled in proportion to an increased level of understanding thereof among [different] peoples or could be supported by the experiences gained in this process. In this connection, the most important creation, THE INTERNATIONAL COURT OF ARBITRATION, is an institution whose first experiences are already behind it. It is, in the best interest of the general welfare, an Areopag [*sic*] of legal experts who enjoy international respect.[203]

Japan proposed not to convene the conference before April or May of 1907.[204]

In negotiating with the Russians the problem of Korea's participation in the conference proved difficult, since Japan had in a treaty imposed on Korea (17 November 1905) assumed the direction of diplomatic matters for the Korean kingdom. In a diplomatic note of 13 June 1906, on the question of Korean participation, Hayashi Tadasu gave his opinion that "participation by Corea in the work of that Assembly would give rise to serious misconceptions . . . [since] she is unable at this point to claim for herself any of the rights or to fulfill any of the obligations which would be implied by representation at the proposed Conference."[205] On 15 June, Hayashi informed Motono in St. Petersburg of the content of this note. Although the Russian government had sent an invitation to the Korean government in late summer, Bakhmeteff wrote the Japanese foreign minister a note in early October pressing for a speedy reply on the question of Japanese participation, since "the majority of interested powers have adopted entirely the programme proposed by Russia." Bakhmeteff now maintained that "the refusal of the [the] Japanese Government to sign [the] proposed Protocol would only have influence on [the] adhesion of South American Republics, and that Korea, Panama and Abyssinia were out of the question for other reasons."[206] On 16 October Hayashi communicated this new Russian stance to Aoki in Washington. But on 24 October Ambassador Kusakabe in Rome informed the Japanese foreign ministry that the circulating Russian list of invitees he had seen still included the names of the three above-named countries. Abyssinia was said to have accepted the invitation, Panama had rejected it, and Korea was said not yet to have replied. Kusakabe complained, "*Having invited these three countries, Russia now says they are out of question.*"[207] How was this possible? Ambassador Aoki in Washington cabled to Tokyo: "On hearing my statement 25th October, Mr. Root said he thoroughly understood [the] significance of Japan's objection [regarding Korea's participation in the conference] which he thought natural, but that the proper course for Japan would be to communicate explicitly [the] reasons of her objection to Russia. He gave me an impression without saying so directly that he thought [the] second peace conference would not lead to important results even if it should meet at all, which was doubtful."[208] On 9 November Japan retracted its reservations.[209]

As the ambiguities about inviting Korea to the peace conference seemed to have been put to rest, considerable attention was now given to the question of arms reduction, which was missing in the Russian invitation protocol,[210] in spite of the fact that one of the primary goals of the American initiative had clearly been to include this question. Minister Aoki in London reported: "British Government desire that the question of reduction of armaments should be included in the deliberation of [the] conference."[211] This view was reported to be in keeping with that of the Americans: "United States Government . . . in addition ([to] questions contained in the Russian proposal) propose to consider the question of reduction or limitation of armaments."[212]

According to Aoki's report to Tokyo, Secretary of State Elihu Root regretted the Russian disposition, more so since it had been Russia that had so loudly demanded arms reduction at the first Hague Conference. The Japanese ambassador did not fail to assure the Americans that Japan would welcome a British-American initiative on this matter.[213] In a note penned on 7 April (25 March by the Russian Orthodox calendar) 1907, Ambassador Bakhmeteff in Tokyo informed Foreign Minister Hayashi of the wish of Great Britain, the United States, and Spain to discuss the question of reduction of armaments at the conference.[214] Japan had apparently neglected to formulate more clearly for the Russian government its own wishes about arms reduction and to bring these to the fore.[215] On 10 April the Netherlands ambassador in Tokyo announced that 15 June had been set as the date for the beginning of the conference.[216] The proposal to discuss arms reduction put forward by the Italian foreign ministry seems to have revived Japanese attention to this matter. On 27 April, Hayashi cabled Komura in London: "The Japanese Government are disposed to give their eventual adhesion to the Italian proposition."[217] However, according to Japanese dispatches, the Italian government soon thereafter withdrew its arms reduction proposal due to objections from Germany and Austria.[218]

In world public opinion, sympathy for Japan by the beginning of 1907 was declining. Armaments were increasing everywhere, and the specter of the "Yellow Peril," which the German kaiser had done his best to resuscitate at the beginning of the Russo-Japanese war, was spreading farther afield. Also in 1907 the American navy devised its secret "Plan Orange," in which Japan was identified as the most likely future "enemy," giving impetus to a far-reaching naval arms build-up program.[219]

On 19 February 1907, Alexander von Siebold wrote to Foreign Minister Hayashi from Switzerland, offering his services for the upcoming peace conference.[220] Hayashi replied apologetically to Siebold on 2 April that preparations had already been made and that longtime foreign ministry advisor Henry W. Denison had been selected to accompany a Japanese delegation to be led by Tsuzuki Keiroku.[221] In the document of appointment signed by the Meiji emperor (Mutsuhito), Tsuzuki and Satō Aimaro were jointly named as "plenipotentiaries" of the Japanese delegation to The Hague.[222]

On 1 May, Ambassador Inoue Katsunosuke in Berlin cabled Hayashi a report on a debate in the German Reichstag that had taken place the day before. The German Chancellor von Bülow was said to have expressed himself negatively as to whether it would be useful to discuss arms reduction at the conference. The only decision that had been reached at the first conference was, according to the chancellor, that the powers were obliged to carefully investigate this question. The German government had indeed done so, but had found no means that seemed appropriate, given the geographic, economic, military, and political differences among states, to eliminate these differences that might serve as grounds for an agreement. The chancellor had no knowledge as to whether other governments had considered the question with different results.[223] In fact, the kaiser, who was against the whole idea of the Hague peace conference, had commented in 1899 already: "Just so that [the tsar] does not become the laughingstock of Europe, I agree to the foolishness! But later in practice I will, as before, rely on and entrust myself only to God and my sharp sword! I sh.. on all the declarations! [*Ich scheiße auf die ganzen Beschlüße!*]"[224]

A few weeks before the opening of the Second Hague Conference, Inoue Katsunosuke cabled (30 May 1907) to Tokyo: "I went with Ambassador Tsuzuki to see Prince von Buelow May 29th. In the course of [the] conversation the latter expressed a hope that Tsuzuki would have cordial relations with the German delegates at the Peace Conference and work together hand in hand for the cause of peace. [The] Prince, on his part, would instruct the Principal German Delegate to be always in close touch with Tsuzuki."[225] Three days later Inoue informed Tokyo that the German kaiser had received him and Tsuzuki together with the other members of the Japanese peace delegation. The kaiser had emphasized that Japan and Germany, as two great military powers, must work together at the forthcoming conference, "to which end the Emperor would command German delegate[s] to co-operate with Tsuzuki and to be in intimate relationship with him."[226] During the whole conference the Germans kept a close watch on their Japanese colleagues.

The Second Hague Peace Conference, in which now over fifty nations took part, first met on 15 June and did not conclude until 18 October. "By far the most important question" debated at the conference was that of "*universal obligation*" in matters of arbitration.[227] On 27 June Tsuzuki cabled to Tokyo: "Russian delegation has proposed, under a skillfully veiled form, a quasi obligatory *enquête internationale* [i.e., international opinion poll]. German[y] will of course oppose it."[228] Clearly the Russians remained interested in further building a legal framework for the work already begun earlier in The Hague. It is not necessary to go into any details about the discussions and provisions of the "laws of war"—the third subject besides disarmament and arbitration—in which the German delegation excelled, only to be the first, later in the First World War, to break them.

Though obviously Japan was not the driving force at The Hague, it in fact—granted the Western powers were united in their quest—favored a solution in accordance with the conference aims, i.e., arbitration and disarmament.[229] Without such unanimity, however, the Japanese delegation was instructed to show restraint.

The main speaker of the Japanese delegation at the 1907 Hague peace conference, Tsuzuki Keiroku (1861–1923),[230] "represented his country and its special interests with admirable tact and dignity using, as occasion required, French or English with equal facility and positive effect."[231] However, the

Japanese delegation at the second Hague conference refrained from participating in the discussions on obligatory arbitration. Since unanimity among
the Western powers was required and it was clear the Germans could not be
swayed, the Japanese participated only as observers. The positions being represented were too much at odds with one another for Japan to wish to voice
her opinion or take sides. Also, it should be remembered that, ever since the
defeat of France in the Franco-Prussian War of 1870–1871, Japan had been
under strong German influence. This was still true to a certain extent in 1907.
At the conference, the "tactics of the German representatives consisted . . .
in constantly coming up with new legal complications and at the same time
trying to gather around themselves so many allies that one would not have
to submit to the principle of 'quasi-unanimity.'"[232] Perhaps for this reason,
and because there was a considerable pro-German faction (*Doitsu-ha*) in
the foreign ministry, the Japanese delegates at The Hague had apparently
received instructions from Tokyo to vote against obligatory arbitration.[233]
According to historian Adolf Wild it was thanks to the personal commitment
and persuasive skills of the French delegate Baron d'Estournelles de Constant
(1852–1924) that Tsuzuki decided to abstain from casting a vote—evidence
of the power of independent judgment of Japanese diplomats abroad even in
making important decisions.[234]

Though supporting a consensus, Japan chose not to commit itself to either
side, "in order that [the] country might have further time for reflection."[235]
Finally Tsuzuki gave the following statement:

Not having received the erudite and comprehensive report of [the Belgian del-
egate] Baron Guillaume until yesterday evening at around ten o'clock, I have
not had the time even to read it, let alone study it.[236] In addition, not having been
a member of the Examining Committee, it was with great difficulty that we have
been able to discover which parts of the texts that were discussed today in such
a lively way contained the disputed passages or one might perhaps say, where
they were hidden. But that did not keep me from listening very attentively and
with the greatest interest to all the arguments pro and con. And I find myself in
a very embarrassing situation because I sense that there are reasons on the two
sides. In any case, since *we have always supported the principle of arbitration*,
since we represent a country which belongs to the small minority of states which
have actually made an appeal to the mechanism which is found at The Hague for
cutting across international differences, and also, since we profoundly appreciate the elevated, pacific and humanitarian ideals which animate the institution
of arbitration, *one must confess that the psychological balance of our delegation
is rather inclined toward those who have supported this principle, more than
toward those who have combated it.* In spite of all that, one should nevertheless admit that the consecration of the principle of arbitration to a universal
obligation, along the general lines traced by the Convention of 1899, represents

nothing less than a new approach. This consecration is of a nature that entails serious consequences and responsibilities as well as rather serious *limitation of the sovereignty of each contracting state*. Because of this, I do not believe it is unreasonable to ask that one give the Governments the necessary time to submit the material to a detailed study before they should be obliged to pronounce themselves definitively on the proposition which has been presented to us; and that we be given the time to make a preliminary and minute examination of the question in all its aspects, and in all of its repercussions on the political, economic and juridical activities of the national and international life of my country, before adopting a stance. In these circumstances, I reserve my opinion on the proposition and I shall abstain from the vote.[237]

As already mentioned, one reason for the Japanese restraint in the question of obligatory arbitration was the German delegation which had clearly stated "fundamental aversion . . . to obligatory arbitration"; the German Empire was under no circumstances ready to submit to binding international jurisdiction, which the majority of the conference participants advocated, or "to make even the most miniscule concessions in this matter."[238]

Another reason for the Japanese to abstain from voting may have been that the American delegation did likewise, having unsuccessfully pushed for a majority vote. According to the U.S. delegation's report:

The Conference was unable to agree upon a general treaty of arbitration, although a large majority expressed itself in favor. . . . The majority felt that it was desirable to conclude at The Hague a general arbitration treaty binding those who were willing to be bound, without seeking, directly or indirectly, to coerce the minority, which was unwilling to bind itself. The minority, however, refused to permit the majority to conclude such a treaty, invoking the principle of unanimity or substantial unanimity for all conventions concluded at The Hague. . . . The friends of arbitration were bitterly disappointed and the American delegation abstained from voting on the declaration; first, because it seemed to be an inadmissible retreat from the advanced position secured by an vote of four to one in favor of the arbitration convention [obtained previously], and, second, lest an affirmative vote be construed to indicate both an approval of the arguments or methods of the minority as well as of the withdrawal of the proposed treaty.[239]

Shidehara followed carefully through all these events and the reports on specialized technical, theoretical, or legal questions about war and peace, all of which came to carry Shidehara's stamp. It was Shidehara's task, as the main connection between Tsuzuki in The Hague and Hayashi in Tokyo, to communicate to Hayashi the contents of the dispatches from The Hague and draft the Japanese government instructions. Shidehara's expertise and counsel in this area was highly valued.

An event that had engaged Shidehara's attention in the beginning of the conference was the dispatch of a small contingent of Koreans to The Hague that was meant to draw the attention of the other delegations to the Korean question and to put Japan on the defensive. The affair, which finally ended with the abdication of the Korean emperor, began when at the end of June three Koreans entreated the Russian delegate Nelidof to admit them to the conference as an official delegation. Nelidof answered, even before he had seen the Koreans, that he could receive no delegates who had not been invited by the Netherlands government.[240] An irritated Tsuzuki telegraphed on 30 June: "William Stead, who is here, told me that they are professing that they intend to take full advantage of the present relations between Japan and America, which they believe to be strained on account of [the] San Francisco [school segregation] affair."[241]

The Koreans, one of whom had been a former secretary of the Korean legation in St. Petersburg, carried a letter of accreditation with the emperor's seal and were said to be on their way to the United States to deliver a letter from the Korean emperor. In keeping with the required red tape, the Netherlands minister of foreign affairs also declined them an interview.[242] Soon thereafter, a certain American named Hulbert, who was working on behalf of the Koreans, arrived in Paris and warned of a Japanese monopoly in Korea from which the Western powers would be excluded.[243] The press speculated whether, and to what extent, the Korean emperor was in fact personally behind the campaign.[244]

On 7 July Itō Hirobumi, who as "resident-general" had since 1905 been Japan's head administrator in Korea, received a telegram in Japanese, in which he was asked to explain to the Korean emperor that if the matter was found to have his backing, this could provoke military intervention on the part of Japan; the Korean actions could constitute a *casus belli* and cause Japan to declare war.[245] In order to calm his government, Tsuzuki cabled to Tokyo on the same day: "Complaint and philippics of [the] Coreans are not making much impression here as there are Georgians, Poles, and others who are trying the same sort of experiment."[246] On the evening of the same day, however, he sent a further cablegram, revealing a less complacent mood: "I think it is advisable that I should, acting under [the] authority of Article I of the Agreement of November 17th, 1905, send for [the] Coreans now here and demand to see [the] authority under which they profess to act. It is probable that they will refuse to come to [the] Legation or to show their credentials. In either case shall I not call [the] attention of [the] Dutch Government to the fact that is impossible for the Coreans to have any valid credentials and ask [the] Dutch Government, if it is possible in some way, to put a stop to the agitation of Coreans[?]."[247]

The aforementioned Hulbert reached The Hague on 10 July,[248] and nine days later, Tsuzuki reported the arrival of another Korean. On 20 July, Foreign Minister Hayashi informed Ambassador Motono in St. Petersburg that the Korean emperor had two days earlier abdicated in favor of the crown prince. He averred that "the abdication was in no way result of any insinuation or suggestion made by the Japanese Government."[249] At the same time Hayashi cabled to Aoki in Washington instructions to forward this communication to the embassies in Paris, Berlin, Vienna, Rome, Brussels, and The Hague. A short article praising Japanese policies in Korea appeared in the *New York Tribune* of the same day:

> Saved by Japanese arms from Russian conquest, Corea three years ago agreed to be guided by Japanese advice in fiscal and other administrative matters and to conduct its foreign affairs through [the] Japanese Government. In return Japan was to guarantee her territorial integrity and safety of her dynasty. This arrangement was recognized by all the world. The gravity of the offence of the Emperor of Corea sending [a] delegation to La Haye unknown to Japan may be estimated if we imagine [the] Emir [of] Bokhara sending one to ask intervention between him and Czar [Tsar] or Annamese King against France or some Indian Maharaja asking La Haye to expel British rule from Hindustan. Title of Japan to deal with Corea, as she has, is at least as good as that of Russia, France, England or any other power. . . . Peace and progress of the world are of more importance than nominal independence of a country as a bone of international contention. We may now bid farewell of Corea as a protectorate of Japan. We may welcome it to a large measure of prosperity and progress Japan herself enjoys.[250]

Despite efforts to give the impression that the abdication of the Korean emperor had come about without Japanese complicity, and although the press was on the whole favorable to Japan, most of the delegates meeting in The Hague seem to have shared the view that pressure from Japan had been the deciding factor.[251] Although at this time the German press was in general friendly toward Japan, the *Lokalanzeiger* represented the view that, since the Korean emperor had to abdicate due to his violation of treaty agreements, Japan was now going to bring Korea completely under its control.[252]

Indeed, to strengthen the Japanese position in Korea, four days after the Korean emperor's abdication, Japan concluded a new treaty (24 July 1907), signed by Itō and Yi Wanyong, which further trimmed Korea's independence. Its text was immediately forwarded to Japan's diplomatic representatives in Washington (Aoki), London, Paris (Kurino), Berlin, Vienna (Uchida), Rome (Takahira), Brussels (Akizuki), The Hague, St. Petersburg (Motono), and Beijing (Abe).[253] *The New York Tribune* of 26 July wrote: "The law of the survival of the fittest prevails among states as well as among plants and animals. Corea has been conspicuously unfit. Therefore she fails to survive. . . . It is idle to rail at Japan. It would be a perversion of facts to pretend that Japan was inferior to Corea and was degrading and corrupting the latter."[254] London's *Times* carried an article (29 July) saying: "Japan's reputation as a colonizing power is at stake. . . . If by a judicious mixture of firmness, of tact and of patience she can persuade the mass of the Corean people to acquiesce her rule, she will have achieved what we have achieved in Egypt."[255] Then, too, *The Scotsman* commented on 30 July: "In all this Japan has acted correctly according to Western examples."[256] Indeed, what else could have been expected?

This episode is significant insofar as it helps understand the international relations of the time, in which colonialism and infatuation with imperial grandeur were the order of the day. Under the circumstances, no doubt, Japan was acting responsibly and wisely and in the interest of the security and general progress of the region. Japan on the whole was convinced that it was. Considerations of national security played a key role, as did the economy. If Shidehara was concerned about the proper means to achieve the desired ends, Japan had little or no time to put too much thought into whether its actions in Korea were justified by some higher moral code.

On 20 September, Tsuzuki cabled Hayashi that the peace conference in The Hague had set its eye on a possible third conclave:[257] "This conference recommends to the powers . . . that if Her Majesty Queen [of] Netherlands approve, the following scheme shall be adopted: 1. The Conference will be invited by Her Majesty to meet in May 1914 at la Haye."[258] There was to be established an advisory committee of nine members, to which Japan would belong. Obligatory arbitration was to be recognized as a leading principle for the future,[259] and play an important role in the preparations for the third conference, as did the question of a world executive.

After the proceedings at The Hague Tsuzuki traveled via Germany to England, where he met with British Foreign Minister Sir Edward Grey.[260] In June of the following year Japan's foreign ministry made public a diplomatic note explaining that "the Imperial Government are prepared to give their consent to twelve of the thirteen conventions [approved by the Second Hague Peace Conference]. They do not, for the present, intend to sign the Convention relative to the Establishment of an International Prize Court and they have decided to withhold their agreement to the Declaration Prohibiting the Discharge of Projectiles and Explosives from Balloons. As to this latter Act it may be mentioned that complete unanimity, among the Great Powers, is lacking."[261] It was, in fact, Germany among the principal powers that had failed to sign the latter agreement.

Meanwhile, Japan's relations with the United States, which had in the past been characterized by a warm feeling of friendship, had after 1905 experienced a marked downturn. The Root-Takahira Agreement of 1908 appeared for a time to neutralize Japanese-American differences; but these differences again flared up with the suggestion by Secretary of State Philander C. Knox (6 November 1909) to transfer the Russian and Japanese railroads in Manchuria to Chinese hands through an international scheme of financial credit. The result of the "Knox initiative" was that Japan and Russia now came together bilaterally to protect the status quo.[262]

In October 1909 Itō Hirobumi, Japan's resident-general in Korea, was assassinated in Harbin, Manchuria, by a Korean patriot. In the opinion of American diplomat W. F. Sands this was "the worst thing Koreans ever did for themselves."[263] The next year Japan signed a new agreement (July 1910) on Manchuria with Russia, and the following month it finalized the "annexation" of Korea. War Minister Terauchi Masatake signed the annexation treaty on 22 August and was named "governor-general" of the new colony. Around the same time anti-Japanese agitation against Japanese immigrants in parts of the United States and the dominions of the British Empire took on a threatening posture. According to one chronicler writing in 1924, already in 1907 and 1908 "all of the settler societies on the Pacific Rim castigated the 'yellow peril' and demonstrated against Japanese migration. Australia and New Zealand [among others] . . . excitedly welcomed Roosevelt's 'Great White Fleet.'"[264]

In 1910, Foreign Minister Komura Jutarō marked as off-limits for Japanese emigrants and overseas settlers all regions controlled by the Anglo-Saxon powers. Two years later the "all-rounder" Shidehara was chosen—following the end of his work in the telegraphic division in 1911—to go to Washington as counselor to the embassy. His mission was related, among other things, to the conclusion of a revised treaty on commerce and navigation between Japan and the United States. Article 1 of the original treaty of 1894 had specified "free entry and residence" for the citizens of both countries in their respective areas of sovereignty.[265] This now had run into problems of interpretation as the legislatures in California and other states of the American West Coast voted for various measures that were prejudicial to the Japanese.

SHIDEHARA AS EMBASSY COUNSELOR IN WASHINGTON AND VICE FOREIGN MINISTER DURING THE FIRST WORLD WAR

1912–1915

After his arrival in Washington, Shidehara became Ambassador Chinda Sutemi's "right hand,"[266] having been appointed embassy counselor (*sanjikan*) at the end of April 1912. Chinda had known Shidehara since the time of the Russo-Japanese war, when he was vice foreign minister. Now in Washington he made a personal request to the foreign ministry for Shidehara's assistance.

Shidehara did not reach the American capital until 8 September 1912.[267] Though ultimately not successful, over the next few months he exerted his best efforts to prevent the passage of legislation by the state of California that was meant to prevent Japanese settlers from owning agricultural land. The debate in California over immigration-related legislation had intensified, with many Californians demanding a law on land ownership by non-American citizens. In January 1913 a bill was submitted to the California state legislature which would ban the sale of land to persons born in Asia—with the exception of Russian Siberia—whose inhabitants, according to American legal precedent, were considered "ineligible for naturalization," and thus unable to become United States citizens. The discriminatory state legislation, known as the Alien Land Law, which in practice affected mainly persons born in Japan, was passed in May and went into effect in August 1913. The efforts of the U.S. federal government to prevent this bill from becoming law failed, although Secretary of State William Jennings Bryan make a special trip to California to try to dissuade state legislators. The federal government then suggested that the Japanese government should lodge an official complaint stating the law violated the Japanese-American treaty agreements that had been concluded in 1894 and renewed in 1911, which were binding. Only then could the U.S. federal government bring about the annulment of the state law through the federal Supreme Court.

The Japanese government in fact lodged a complaint but the California state legislature now expanded the law through a supplementary clause[268] that brought the Japanese side all the more under duress since it specified that only the Japanese government (but not the American government in Washington) could appeal the matter to the U.S. Supreme Court. Shidehara, who was entrusted with the whole matter, consulted numerous jurists and composed all sorts of notes and memos. It transpired, however, that it was impossible for the Japanese side to gain access to the Supreme Court since by precedent foreign proxies were disallowed as parties to cases submitted before the Supreme Court.

In the wake of this legal subterfuge, the U.S. government found itself deprived of the possibility of appealing the case. In these circumstances, Shidehara wanted to encourage the American side to accept a supplementary clause in the bilateral American-Japanese agreements that would effect a most-favored-nation provision along the lines of treaties between the United States and Spain or between the United States and Italy. However, the U.S.

government was unable to make any commitment at this point, and ultimately was obliged to respect the decision of the state of California. It was widely held that any further intervention in the internal affairs of California would not be in keeping with federal principles.

One possibility seemed still to remain, namely an appeal to the Permanent Court of Arbitration in The Hague. To be sure, Shidehara did not fail to consider this possibility. He discussed it with his old friend and well-wisher, Britain's ambassador in Washington, James Bryce. Japan had on 5 May 1908 concluded an arbitration treaty with the United States, which was later extended by two subsequent agreements (28 June 1913 and 28 June 1918). Bryce, however, dissuaded Shidehara from pursuing this path.[269] Shidehara no doubt also recalled Japan's onetime dispute with France, Great Britain, and Germany over the real estate taxes on houses in Yokohama owned by these countries' citizens, which was decided by the Permanent Court of Arbitration (22 May 1905) unfavorably for Japan. Shidehara finally gave up his efforts of fifteen months to sway the state of affairs in California.[270] At the end of 1913, to Chinda's surprise, Shidehara was reassigned to London.

Whatever one may say about the immigration dispute, Shidehara's stay in Washington had positive results in another regard—namely, the friendship and conversations with British Ambassador James Bryce.[271] In January 1913, not long after Shidehara's arrival in Washington, Bryce was placed on the list of judges for the Permanent Court of Arbitration—a special honor for the seventy-four-year-old diplomat.[272] Shidehara had discussed with Bryce the unfortunate West Coast legislation affecting Japanese settlers, and Bryce finally counseled him to concede defeat after months of hard struggle. Diplomats, Bryce told him, should not fail to see things in long-term perspective.

Japan's Meiji emperor had died in December 1912. The beginning of the new reign, named Taishō (meaning "great rectitude," 1912–1926), was characterized by a general economic upswing and by the gradual emancipation of the individual into a "political personality." Relative prosperity, a significant measure of fundamental democratic values, a high level of education, with an expanding educational system were impressive features of the early Taishō period, in spite of some conservative or at times reactionary political currents.[273] Mass movements were seeking popular rights and organized demonstrations in the streets proclaiming their views, with great ingenuity and perseverance.[274] But in proportion to the progress attained, dangers for the social fabric of democracy were also growing.

On 21 December 1912, Katsura Tarō, an army general, was appointed prime minister for the third time, replacing the liberal Prince Saionji Kinmochi (1849–1940), who had twice served as prime minister (1906–1908 and 1911–1912). Progressive parties, workers, intellectuals, and many business entrepreneurs feared the military could squeeze the powers of the civil government; they demanded radical changes and a strengthening of constitutional government.[275] Revelations of corrupt dealings by the navy ministry in early 1913 (Siemens Affair) sparked mass demonstrations before the Diet building, and as a result of what came to be known as the "Taishō Crisis" the reactionary Katsura cabinet was replaced.[276] In the assessment of Ian Nish it was the Seiyūkai party that, through its opposition to army and navy plans in 1912–1913, brought the crisis to fruition.[277] Katsura's successors also, all of them from military circles, soon had to resign.[278]

In December 1913 Ambassador Inoue Katsunosuke in London asked Foreign Minister Makino Nobuaki for Shidehara's assistance as counselor in the London embassy.[279] Shidehara's mission in London quite possibly related to British endeavors, at the London Ambassadors' Conferences of 1912–1913, and subsequently Foreign Secretary Grey's efforts on 25 July 1914 to "reactivate the traditional system of the powers for resolving disputes" to deflect what was seen as the growing danger of war. The Russian tsar likewise tried to intervene:

> The possibility of bringing matters to The Hague was emphasized in an appeal to the Kaiser by the Russian Tsar [on 29 July], to move the Austro-Hungarian monarchy to [make use of] this [possibility]. Chancellor Bethmann Hollweg "naturally," as he himself expressed it, rejected [this idea].[280]

Shidehara certainly by now was among some of the best-informed and foremost diplomats—not only in Japan but anywhere in the world. His sincere, unassuming, friendly demeanor and his conscientious diplomacy gained him respect and sympathy. He always took care to present himself as a "gentleman"—on occasion with bowler hat and walking stick.[281] His suits were ordered from the best London tailors.[282] Foreign Secretary Sir Edward Grey's political philosophy appeared to appeal to him, and he followed every diplomatic gesture of the Britons with keen interest. Naturally the British efforts of the years 1912–1914 to maintain peace in Europe and the world were relevant for Japan also. Staying in London until June 1914, Shidehara observed those efforts at close hand.

Following his departure from London, Shidehara became Japan's chief envoy at The Hague, for the Netherlands and Denmark, among other things to represent Japan in the preparations for the third Hague peace conference. He now held the highest rank among representatives abroad, with "plenipotentiary powers," even if technically speaking the top envoy to The Hague and Copenhagen did not bear the title "ambassador." Peace was what the Japanese diplomat, who was soon to celebrate his forty-second birthday, regarded as part of his professional calling. Shidehara was now in the center of the "official" international peace establishment. The Hague was the cockpit of this international movement, with the seat of the Permanent International Court of Arbitration, which only a year earlier, in 1913, had been given a home through the donation of the Peace Palace by the American philanthropist and pacifist Andrew Carnegie.[283] Building had started in 1907.[284] A letter by the board of the Carnegie Foundation directors requested the participant nations to the Hague conferences to contribute something that would be typical of its national culture to the Peace Palace building interior.[285] Preparations for the third Hague peace conference that had by then been planned for 1915 intensified between 1912 and 1914—a noble effort that was, however, eventually foiled by Germany's war of aggression.[286]

Shidehara arrived at his posting in the Netherlands on 26 June 1914, just two days before a Serbian nationalist murdered the Austrian crown prince, Franz Ferdinand (b. 1863), in Sarajevo. Following the declaration of war on Serbia by the Austro-Hungarian Empire on 28 July (instead of going to appeal to the Hague Court; Austria-Hungary had followed Germany's lead and opposed obligatory arbitration), Germany declared war on Russia and France (1 and 3 August, respectively), and marched into neutral Belgium on 3 and 4 August, following an attack plan that had been prepared by the army chief of staff, Alfred von Schlieffen, in 1905. After a disregarded British ultimatum urging Germany to immediately withdraw its troops from Belgium, Britain on 4 August, and Japan on 23 August, declared war on Germany. The German ambassador in Tokyo, Count von Rex, who had previously headed the German legation in Beijing, however, refused to accept the Japanese declaration of war and forward it to Berlin. Foreign Minister Katō Takaaki (Kōmei) therefore immediately dispatched several cables, among others to Ambassador Funakoshi Mitsunojō in Berlin and to Shidehara in The Hague, to make sure the declaration of war was duly communicated to the German authorities.[287]

Having been unsuccessful in conveying the Japanese declaration of war to Berlin, Shidehara's main task was to inform Tokyo about the unfolding and developments in the European war. With the assistance of the Dutch foreign ministry he carried out this duty until August of the following year. As chief representative of Japan in The Hague, Shidehara automatically belonged to the Permanent Court of Arbitration's administrative Council, which had been established in September 1900. Apart from the court's International Bureau and the Court Secretariat, this body, which consisted of the foreign envoys accredited to The Hague and the Dutch foreign minister, served as "a sort of board of directors."[288] The Dutch foreign minister, Dr. John Loudon (1866–1955), who was slightly senior to Shidehara, held a doctorate in political science, and had been minister in Tokyo between 1905 and 1908. Then, until he became foreign minister in 1913, he had served as ambassador in Washington, where he met his future American wife. Shidehara was known to him from his earlier days in Tokyo.

Although the third Hague peace conference never assembled, the aforementioned representatives from a group of neutral states meeting together at The Hague formed an international executive body for "the enforcement of international law."[289] The earlier cited resolution, which had been passed by the two houses of the U.S. Congress on 20 and 24 June 1910, should be remembered in this context. This joint resolution of the American Senate and House of Representatives had suggested setting up a commission to consider the creation of an international police force made up of the "combined navies of the world . . . for the preservation of universal peace" and "to consider and report upon any other means to diminish the expenditures of government for military purposes and to lessen the probabilities of war."[290] The third Hague peace conference, while this time would have had to decide the issue of obligatory arbitration not by consensus but by majority vote, would most certainly also have debated the issue of enforcement by an international police (collective security), which Germany wanted to avoid at any cost, by manipulating the entry into war just as Bismarck had done in 1870. Germany had to avert by all means any such development. Having built up a powerful navy to challenge Britain it already planned to establish German hegemony in Europe and, if possible, the world.

Instead, the Nederlandse Anti-Oorlog Raad (Netherlands Anti-War Council) was established, to which "not only 1500 organizations, but also the country's most prominent personalities, venerable prime ministers of many years' service, retired generals, leading parliamentarians, etc., lent their cooperation, and out of which an international 'Central Organization for a Durable Peace' developed, consisting of ten countries." This international central organization (i.e., "a circle of representatives of parliamentary, political, scientific and pacifist organizations . . . from ten countries") established "a . . . Minimum Program"[291] during the first winter of the war, one of whose principal demands was: "The work of the Hague Peace Conferences concerning the peaceful organization of the society of states should be expanded. . . . The [Hague] Peace Conference should be furnished with a permanent organization and hold periodic sessions. . . . States should agree to submit all their disputes to a peaceful procedure."[292]

There can be no doubt that in the spring of 1915 Shidehara was witness to the 7–12 April proceedings of the Central Organization for a Durable Peace sponsored by the Nederlandse Anti-Oorlog Raad, and welcomed the peace movement's plans. Since Japan was one of the belligerent parties, official participation in the peace efforts of the neutral countries was not possible, and therefore Shidehara could only have attended as an observer. His attention then must have been especially drawn to point 2 of the earlier cited chapter 2 of the Minimum Program, according to which the colonial powers were to grant "freedom of trade" and "equality" to all states. This directly concerned Japanese interests and Shidehara, in his role as observer, must have taken notice and reported the event to his superiors in Tokyo.

The Minimum Program's stipulation was a necessary precedent to the "racial equality clause" that Japan later introduced at the Versailles Peace Conference. During his residence in The Hague, Shidehara had been successfully negotiating on behalf of Japanese residents in the Dutch East Indies who were working there as businessmen or wished to settle as medical doctors. He managed to see to it that these professional groups, especially the doctors, would not be disadvantaged and could enjoy rights equal to those of Europeans. Freedom of trade for Japanese in the Dutch East Indies was also substantially extended.

Naturally, in the first year of the European war, Shidehara maintained cordial, professional, and also personal relations with the foreign ambassadors and diplomats in The Hague and took part in the city's social and cultural life. Among the diplomatic corps he seems to have been popular and well-liked.[293] Foreign Minister Loudon did not fail to introduce Shidehara to the Dutch Queen Wilhelmina. But the shadow of the war weighed heavily upon everybody.

On 15 August 1915, a cablegram reached Shidehara from Paris in which his old friend and superior Ishii Kikujirō, then serving as Japan's ambassador to France, intimated he intended to recommend Shidehara for the post of vice foreign minister (*gaimu jikan*) in Tokyo. Ishii himself was suggested for the post of foreign minister following the decision that Katō Takaaki (Kōmei) would leave the ministry, and Ishii wished to confirm that Shidehara would agree to be his right-hand man. Shidehara accepted Ishii's proposal. On 6 September, Queen Wilhelmina hosted a festive farewell banquet in the Noordeinde Palace at The Hague in Shidehara's honor and conferred upon him a high decoration. Newspapers reported that Queen Wilhelmina asked Shidehara if he had any hobbies. Shidehara, who had been living in a seaside farmhouse not far from the city, replied that he had inherited a motorboat from his predecessor Satō Aimaro, and that often on Sunday mornings, after having shared a few cups and played billiards the night before with some of the young men of the village, he took the boat out to fish. "Interesting," the queen allowed, and wanted to know if he ever caught anything. The reply was "Unfortunately not," though the fish were abundantly provided with bait, Shidehara said, for which they were no doubt thankful.[294] Not long after, Shidehara left the Netherlands for Tokyo.

From 1915 to the Entry Into the War
of the United States and China in 1917

In the meantime, a confrontation in Japan-China relations had developed
and continued to brew. Still, toward the end of 1914 it seemed that friendly
cooperation—a term often used by the Japanese at the time was *teikei*—with
China should in general outline be possible. The Japanese declaration of war
against Germany (23 August 1914) opened the possibility of joint Chinese-
Japanese political action in East Asia.[295] However, China remained neutral,
and on 18 January 1915, the Ōkuma cabinet directed its so-called Twenty-
One Demands (*nijūikkajō yōkyū*)[296] to neutral China. Although they were
largely revised and eventually acceded to by the Chinese government on 5
May, they remained divisive and controversial.[297]

Shidehara had criticized Ōkuma's policy toward China, which he felt
would complicate Japanese-Chinese relations in the future.[298] The Twenty-
One Demands, as historian Takemoto Tōru has noted, proclaimed policies
"completely opposite to Shidehara's concept of liberalism . . . Shidehara
clearly envisioned the coming troubles produced by that policy, not only between Japan and China, but also between Japan and world powers that had an
interest in China."[299] They seemed to infringe upon certain principles of international law by compromising Chinese integrity and national sovereignty.
But Shidehara could not bring his views decisively to bear. Besides, Ōkuma
may have had his reasons, of which Shidehara was not aware.

It is in any way doubtful whether Shidehara, as Peter Duus has suggested,
felt himself duty-bound to the concept of a wider "Japanese empire."[300] Indeed, it is highly unlikely that this was so. Takemoto Tōru refers to a letter
from Shidehara to Foreign Minister Katō in which he laid out his reasons for
disapproving of the demands and the way in which they were presented.[301]
The decisive factor, in any event, was the choice of means: "He emphatically
rejected needless saber-rattling and bellicose gestures in China, maintaining
a policy of strict nonintervention in China's domestic troubles."[302] Shidehara
saw the demands as overly one-sided and an impermissible interfering with
China's domestic concerns.[303]

Foreign Minister Katō Kōmei, on the other hand, believed that he could
serve Japanese interests best by using the war situation to confront China with
a list of demands. He wished to bind China more closely to Japan and at the
same time prevent Chinese participation in the war on the German side. It is
probable that, at the time, this policy had the backing of the majority of Japanese politicians, who felt it would help safeguard peace in East Asia. However, in presenting the Chinese government with the Twenty-One Demands,
Katō had neglected to consult the *genrō* and other oligarchs beforehand, a

mistake that was not to be redeemed.[304] Thus the *genrō*—Saionji perhaps excepted—were rather less upset over the demands than over Katō's diffident behavior. As a consequence, in August 1915 Katō would be asked to vacate his post.[305]

In the aforementioned letter to Katō, Shidehara had aired his views after news of the demands first reached him in the Netherlands. He did not shy away from discussing with the other members of the Japanese legation what he considered to be Katō's error. One young colleague, Tani Masayuki (1889–1962), who would later play a significant role in Japan's China policy, had initially felt, unlike Shidehara, that it should be proper for Japan to demand anything from China that might serve Japanese interests. Shidehara invited him for lunch hoping to bring him around to the point of view that in practical politics one cannot do everything that might theoretically be possible. The lecture by his superior noticeably curbed Tani's appetite, and he had to accede that Shidehara had the better arguments. Tani came to the conclusion that Shidehara possessed an extraordinary knowledge of legal matters and exceptional political understanding.[306]

Shidehara was not alone in taking a position against the Twenty-One Demands. After the general election of March 1915, Ōkuma, who had been prime minister since the previous year, continued in power while Katō remained for the time being in the post of foreign minister. In June, Hara Takashi (Kei), who was the leader of the opposition Seiyūkai Party in the Diet and later served as prime minister, brought to vote a Resolution with these words:

> Resolved that the negotiations carried on with China by the present Government have been inappropriate in every respect; that they are detrimental to the amicable relationship between the two countries, and provocative of suspicions on the part of the Powers; that they have the effect of lowering the prestige of the Japanese Empire; and that, while far from capable of establishing the foundation of peace in the Far East, they will form the source of future trouble.[307]

The resolution received 130 "yea" votes, even if these were not enough to allow its passage by the House of Representatives. Thus, Shidehara saw clearly that China was not to be controlled through forceful measures and that power politics of that sort, without a consensus among the other world powers, had no chance of success.[308] Even with Germany Japan would have to get along amicably in the future, and German interests, too, had to be taken into account.

Perhaps this was also the reason why Japan declined, in November 1915, the prodding request of Great Britain, France, and Russia, to push the Chinese toward entering the war against Germany. The Australian journalist George Ernest Morrison, an attentive observer and onetime consultant to Yuan Shikai, wrote in a letter to a British friend: "On the 23rd November [1915] the three Powers, England, France and Russia formally requested the Japanese government (Baron Ishii now Viscount Ishii being minister of foreign affairs), to join with them in inviting China to join the Alliance, to place her arsenals at the service of the Allies and to expel the Germans who were carrying on serious intrigues in China especially prejudicial to British rule in India."[309]

Foreign Minister Ishii based his refusal on the fact that China was said to have already definitively arranged the matter of weapons arsenals in the context of the Twenty-One Demands. As to what approach should be taken toward the Germans in China, this should be decided on a case-by-case basis: "As regards China joining the Alliance the Japanese Government could not accept the responsibility of awakening the activities of 400 million people."[310] Possibly this holding back by the Japanese, despite the dictatorial regime of Yuan Shikai and China's lack of unity, worked for the time being to stabilize international relations in East Asia.

In fact, the Twenty-One Demands were a reaction to the threat posed by imperial Germany, which on its part had been striving to gain a position of advantage in China. In Ōkuma's words, "The Kaiser's plan was to prepare China to fight Japan, and the Japanese Government knew this."[311] Indeed before 1914 large numbers of German military trainers were active in China. And it is known that the kaiser had at one time tried to convince Russian foreign minister Sergei D. Sazanov that Russia should ally itself with China against Japan.[312] When this did not succeed, China's President Yuan Shikai was urged to make common cause with Germany. The Twenty-One Demands were thus directed, in the first instance, against Yuan Shikai and any "alliance" with the German empire. First and foremost, Ōkuma believed there was grave danger that China, without the treaty tying it to Japan as laid forth in the Twenty-One Demands, would fight in the war on the German side.[313]

The Australian publicist George E. Morrison similarly describes the situation in China. His letters describe German activities in China; the author complains that the Germans, even after the beginning of the war in 1914 and the surrender to Japan in Qingdao, generally maintained a free hand in China and carried on trade undisturbed. Germans in China received six thousand pounds every day, through the Deutsch-Asiatische Bank, as war indemnity for the German participation in crushing the Boxer Rebellion. The money was "used in China largely for carrying on propaganda against Great Britain, especially among Mohammedans, and particularly among the Mohammedans of Far Western China who are in constant intercourse with the Mohammedans of India."[314]

K. K. Kawakami, a brilliant and unprejudiced publicist and freelance mediator between Japan and the West residing in the United States, similarly

argued that Japan's declaration of war and the Japanese military action in
Jiaozhou (Kiaochow) Bay helped deflect the possible danger of German
dominance in China, which might have resulted in Beijing declaring war on
the Entente powers (also called the "Triple Alliance" of Russia, France, and
Great Britain, and then, with Japan's entering the war, the "Allied Powers").

> Had Japan delayed her action against Kiao-chow, it was more than probable that
> the Germans would have raised a large army of Chinese in Shantung, captured
> the arsenal at Techow on the Tientsin-Nanking line, virtually seized the whole
> of that province, and thus compelled the Government at Peking to declare war
> upon the Entente Powers. In the state of disorganization in which China found
> herself at that time, it was obvious that such a German plan would have easily
> been put into practice. China would have had to accept the German yoke and
> been compelled to drive all British and French interests from the country. Only
> by Japan's prompt declaration of war upon Germany was such an eventuality
> prevented.[315]

Akizuki Satsuo, a veteran diplomat who later in the 1940s (together with
Shidehara and Yoshida Shigeru) extended "peace feelers" to China, similarly
testifies to these motivations of Japan's leadership:

> When one but imagines oneself being put into the context which had been cre-
> ated out of the totality of events before and after the 1914 declaration of war, it
> is . . . without doubt that the forced undertaking of Germany against Kiaochow
> in the autumn of 1897 and the complete cession of this region as the result of
> a Chinese-German agreement signed March 6, 1898, were the factors from
> which the German danger in the Far East arose and which brought in their train
> the largest part of the difficulties for which East Asia [subsequently] provided
> the scenario (the Boxer Rebellion of 1899–1900, the Russo-Japanese War of
> 1904–1905, the World War of 1914).[316]

Fears had long circulated that Berlin might arbitrarily try to partition
China, like it did Africa during the time of Bismarck and the *Kolonialbörse*,
flouting Japan's interests in the process. In an article published in 1912 to the
German peace journal *Die Friedens-Warte*, Ōkuma Shigenobu had warned:
"During the years from 1884 to 1892 the European powers divided up Africa.
. . . Should the powers try something similar in China, they would have to
deal with far more difficult conditions. . . . *To seek a division of this Empire
in the same way as in Africa would be an undertaking fraught with great dangers. Such an attempt would call forth a general collision of opposed interests
on the part of the powers.*"[317]

Then came the war, and it is not to be denied that this war was pursued
on the German side with the goal of producing "a definitive decision as to

who should play the leading role in the world market,"[318] and to acquire new colonies.[319] In any event, in the eyes of Japan the German saber-rattling in China brought "the barrel to overflowing" and it was recognized as necessary to take countermeasures so as to stay in a position of equilibrium, compete with the European powers, and at the same time to prevent the cutting up of China.[320] Thus in the eyes of most Japanese the Twenty-One Demands were presented to Yuan Shikai "entirely for defensive purposes."[321] According to historian Ian Nish the demands were an "attempt at an 'across the board' settlement of outstanding problems in exchange for Japan's promise to return Shantung."[322] Still, Shidehara thought it would be better to stick to the principle of noninterference.

On the other hand Japan had already been branded, in the secret Moscow treaty of 22 May 1896 between the Russian empire and China, as a potential aggressor in Asia. Its first article stated unambiguously: "Any incursion by Japan, be it against the Russian area of East Asia or be it against the region of China or Korea, shall bring about the direct application of the present treaty. In this case the two high contracting parties have the obligation to mutually support one another with all military forces, on land and water, which are available to them at such a time, and to help one another insofar as possible in the servicing of their respective military forces." The treaty, whose contents were made known only in 1922,[323] served as a regular military alliance against Japan and laid the groundwork to guarantee the safety for building the Russian rail line through the Chinese provinces of Heilongjiang and Jilin to Vladivostok.[324] The Russo-Chinese Bank, which also enjoyed French support, was founded especially for the purpose of completing this "Trans-Siberian Railroad."[325]

As vice foreign minister, Shidehara was concerned, above all, with the legal foundations of peace and how these could be further strengthened in regard to Japan's position and policy vis-à-vis China, so that no dangerous misunderstandings should arise. If the Western powers should misconstrue the Japanese intentions, or if they merely wanted to conceal their own plottings, as, for example, Russia had done by raising false accusations (which the Moscow treaty had demonstrated), then all the more so Japan would have to pursue an unambiguous policy to eliminate these misunderstandings and prove through deeds the falsity of the allegations. For this, wisdom and patience were needed. The 1921–1922 Washington Conference on Naval Limitations would offer the chance to make good on such considerations.

Studied more closely, the much-criticized Twenty-One Demands were probably not as malignant as they were made out to be.[326] In his book *Japan's Pacific Policy* published in 1922, K. K. Kawakami not improperly explored the question of why the so-called wishes that made up group V of the demands should in fact be all so objectionable as their critics claimed. For example, by "wish" 1 Japan had in no way intended to keep China from employing any foreign consultants other than Japanese; the wish was only to see Japanese employed alongside other foreign consultants under the same terms. "Certainly this was no infringement upon the sovereignty of China." In 1915 there were officially employed in Chinese governmental services 1,105 British, 1,003 French, 530 Germans, and 463 Russians, while there were only 207 Japanese and 174 Americans.[327]

"Wishes" 2 and 7 were nothing more than a claim for treatment and privileges equal to those which American or European commercial and industrial firms already enjoyed. By presenting wish 3, Japan hoped to work more closely with Chinese police forces in areas with a relatively large Japanese population, while "wish" 4 proposed that Japan "supply China with a certain percentage of arms required by the latter or to establish an arsenal in China as a joint enterprise between the two countries. . . . Certainly this was no novel proposal." By "wish" 5 Japan offered to build certain rail lines, and "wish" 6 had to do with a Japanese sphere of influence in Fujian Province, which had long been a Japanese trading base, even during and before the Tokugawa era. The idea that states competed for spheres of influence in certain economic regions was, at least at that point in time, no abnormality. Nonetheless, Kawakami concedes that "[t]he essence of the 'twenty-one' proposals was the Japanese desire to secure the Japanese position in Manchuria and Shantung."[328]

The most important parts of the Japanese-Chinese agreement of 1915 had to do with Shandong Province as a Japanese sphere of interest; extensions of the treaty leases for Port Arthur, Dalian (with the Japanese pronunciation "Dairen"), and the South Manchurian Railway together with the treaty-specified rights and privileges related to these leases; and having China take it upon itself to consult with Japan about foreign investments in Fujian Province, especially in railways and harbors.

After Japan, already at the beginning of the war, had taken over the German possessions and interests in Shandong—Qingdao (Tsingtao) had surrendered after five weeks—the Japanese government hoped, with the Twenty-One Demands, to guarantee, through a treaty process, Japanese rights and so-called vital interests on the Chinese mainland. In doing so, however, Japan had to cope with faultfinding from the Western powers, especially the United States.[329] The American Secretary of State William Jennings Bryan had urged caution in a memorandum delivered to the Japanese ambassador on 13 March 1915.

A comparison of the originally presented demands of 18 January 1915 with the conditions finally agreed to on 25 May gives the impression that Japan's standpoint was neither unfounded nor inflexible. There were now not twenty-one, but only nineteen points. Group V, which comprised seven of the nineteen points, were moreover no longer classed as "demands," but as "proposals" or, to use the term used in English at the time, "wishes."[330] Group I originally comprised four points: (1) the transferal of German rights to Japan; (2) the principle that no part of Shandong should be ceded to a third party;[331] (3) the Japanese preferential right to build a rail line from Zhefu (Chefoo) or Longkou (Lungkow) to most probably Weixian (Weihsien); and (4) the opening to foreign trade of several cities in Shandong Province. Group II had to do with Manchuria and comprised five points: (1) extension of the lease treaty concerning Port Arthur and the South Manchuria Railway; (2) permission for Japanese in southern Manchuria and eastern Inner Mongolia to travel and reside, as well as settle and rent or acquire land, in order to carry out trade or agricultural pursuits;[332] (3) permission to acquire mining privileges in southern Manchuria and eastern Inner Mongolia;[333] (4) refusal to grant, without Japanese agreement, railway concessions in southern Manchuria and eastern Inner Mongolia to any third country or to use local taxes as security for the building of such railways;[334] and (5) the transferal to Japan, for ninety-nine years, of management rights for the Jilin-Changchun rail line.[335] Group III had only two points, both having to do with the Hanyehping Company, which was engaged in iron mining and steelmaking in and around the Wuhan region of the Yangzi Valley: (1) China should not give up any of the company's rights (i.e., ground and property assets) without Japan's agreement, and should agree to a joint management by China and Japanese capital investors;[336] and (2) the Chinese government, without agreement by the Hanyehping Company, should not grant to third parties permission to exploit mines in the vicinity of the company's property.[337] Group IV had only one clause, which stipulated that China should not cede to any third country harbors, islands, or bays along the Chinese coast. This was, however, ultimately neither included in the treaty as signed, nor in a separate note.

Of the seven points in group V, which were merely considered to be "wishes" or "proposals," five were neither included in the treaty text or in separate notes.[338] The two remaining points of group V had to do with a request for preferential treatment for Japanese as political, military, and financial advisors, and the wish to have China consult Japan before accepting foreign loans for the building of railways or harbors in Fujian Province. In connection with the hiring of consultants, the original Japanese proposal to have Japanese given preference (most of all in southern Manchuria) was subsequently altered, with the result that this point was also not included in the treaty text, although it was contained in a separate diplomatic note. The obligation to consult with one another about possible construction projects of various kinds in Fujian Province was likewise referred to in a separate note only.[339]

For all practical purposes the Chinese government had already on 12 February 1915 (that is, twenty-four days after the presentation of the Japanese proposals) granted in a counterproposal practically all the Japanese demands with
respect to Shandong and Manchuria, agreeing to a ninety-nine-year extension
of the lease of Dalian, Port Arthur, and the South Manchuria Railway, and accepting that Japan would take over the former German rights in Shandong.[340]
However, the United States saw itself obliged to cautiously lodge a protest
against the Japanese demands. President Wilson, who had been the first head
of state to grant diplomatic recognition to the Chinese Republic in 1913, let
the Japanese government know, through a detailed memorandum of 13 March,
that certain of the demands went against the "Open Door" policy, while others
clearly compromised China's political independence. But of still greater significance—and especially for Japan—was this paragraph of the memorandum:

> While on principle and under the treaties of 1844, 1858, 1868 and 1903 with
> China the United States has ground upon which to base objections to the
> Japanese "demands" relative to Shantung, South Manchuria and East Mongolia,
> nevertheless, *the United States frankly recognizes that territorial contiguity cre-
> ates special relations between Japan and these districts.*[341]

This was something Japan could live with and which it welcomed. Despite—or perhaps because of—the American protests, during the period up to
17 April, agreement was reached on practically all the substantive points, the
"proposals" in group V were for the most part retracted, and further Japanese
concessions were made. However, according to Kawakami, "for some incom-
prehensible reasons" China then suddenly "sought to prolong the negotiations
indefinitely,"[342] so that Japan was finally forced to send an ultimatum on 7/8
May. The negotiations with Yuan Shikai had already taken several months,
and according to Ōkuma, Yuan Shikai "himself suggested that this ultimatum
be sent because he saw in this method a way of saving his face for giving in to
Japan."[343] Somewhat indignantly, Kawakami asks: "[If on 12 February 1915]
China had in black and white agreed to extend Japan's leaseholds to 99 years
. . . how can China [later at Versailles and Washington] say that the extension
was wrested from her under duress, and upon that ground seek its annulment
at an international conference?"[344]

Kawakami gives further grounds for the supposition that China had accepted
the agreements of 1915 both *de facto* and *de jure*. Namely, when China in
1918 wanted from Japan the loan of "a handsome sum" for railway projects in
Shandong Province, "the Japanese Government persuaded Tokyo bankers to
advance $10,000,000 in gold to China in September, 1918. By this deal China
not only confirmed the validity of the treaties of 1915, but derived material
benefit from them."[345] This argument would be brought forward also at the

Versailles Peace Conference by the Japanese delegation as justification for the Japanese policy in China during the war and the formulation of the original Twenty-One Demands.[346]

Nevertheless it was Foreign Minister Katō (who was Shidehara's superior) who had acted prematurely when he accepted, without further consultations, the text of the Twenty-One Demands that had been jointly drafted by the foreign ministry and the Japanese military attaché in Beijing, and then straightaway made Prime Minister Ōkuma and the rest of his cabinet concur.[347] In point of fact there had perhaps not been any real need to take action at all. Had all the trouble really been worth Japan's while? Shidehara seems to have thought otherwise!

Though the demands were supposed initially to have been kept secret,[348] after some time a list of eleven of the demands were communicated to friendly foreign governments. In many respects the demands amounted to a revision of the rights concerning Port Arthur, Dalian, and southern Manchuria that had been compromised as a result of the Triple Intervention by France, Russia, and Germany in 1895. At the 1921–1922 Washington Conference Shidehara would bring about a total revision of the Twenty-One Demands, and for the first time show the workings of his independent "Shidehara diplomacy" before the world.

Another circumstance, also involving finance, should be mentioned—the "Nishihara Loans." In February 1917, Nishihara Kamezō (1872–1954) was dispatched to China on a secret mission by Prime Minister General Terauchi Masatake (1852–1919), who had formed his cabinet in October 1916[349] after Yuan Shikai had died in June, in order to negotiate Japanese credits[350] with the Chinese head of state Duan Qirui (Tuan Ch'i-jui, 1865–1936). This was another attempt to get China to enter the war. Neither Deputy Foreign Minister Shidehara nor Foreign Minister Motono Ichirō had been informed.[351] No doubt those involved also hoped thereby to secure a monopoly position for Japan on the Chinese mainland. The project failed, however. Terauchi had sought to brace up the so-called Anfu clique with these credits, but in the end was faced with the opposite result, namely the downfall of this powerful group. In July 1920 the Anfu clique, which had exercised power in central China, lost out to the Fengtian military clique under Zhang Zuolin (Chang Tso-lin) and the Zhili Clique supported by Great Britain.[352] The Japanese demarches associated with the Terauchi government also needlessly upset the Americans, who had their own interests in China to watch over.

1917–1919—The War Ends

Following Germany's declaration of unrestricted submarine warfare, U.S. President Woodrow Wilson, "having announced the severance of American relations with Germany,"[353] urged the neutral states to join the Allies. This won over the Chinese, who on 14 March severed ties with Germany, and declared war on 14 August.[354] In June 1918 the United States took the initiative in organizing, together with France, Great Britain, and Japan, a financial consortium that, however, initially found scant appreciation on the part of the Chinese.[355] At the same time, while the United States and Japan were competing in Beijing for financial control over China, those who succeeded Yuan Shikai between 1916 and 1928 could "only keep themselves in power by borrowing from consortiums of foreign banks" money which the mutually competing foreign powers offered them.[356] As French historian Jacques Gernet describes it, eventually

> [t]he end of the First World War was to resuscitate the rivalry between the nations which had divided up the old empire into spheres of influence and to favour the political breakup; hence the ascendancy of the men christened "warlords" by the Anglo-Saxon press—independent military governors with their own resources and their own armies.[357]

Japan was toward the end of the war able to negotiate an agreement with the United States by which its special interests on the Chinese mainland were acknowledged. In the diplomatic notes that were exchanged on 2 November 1917 between American Secretary of State Robert Lansing (1864–1928) and Ishii Kikujirō, words similar to those of the earlier Bryan memorandum were used:

> Territorial propinquity creates special relations between countries, and consequently, the Government of the United States recognizes that Japan has special interests in China, particularly in the part to which her possessions are contiguous.[358]

The binding force of this diplomatic note was later contested by Lansing and still later, in a joint Japanese-American note of 1923, at the Washington Naval Disarmament Conference, declared void and no longer relevant.[359]

Shortly after Shidehara had returned to Tokyo from The Hague, Ishii Kikujirō became foreign minister, in October 1915, subsequent to Ōkuma having for a short time exercised the duties of the office following Katō's dismissal. Shidehara now served as vice foreign minister in the cabinet of the aging Count Ōkuma and in fact remained in this post for five years, under three prime ministers (Ōkuma Shigenobu, Terauchi Masatake, and Hara Kei) and seven different foreign ministers. Already during the war political parties had increasingly exercised control over the cabinet, and determined who would fill important political posts.[360] The frequent changes of government during the war were in part the result of this trend but had nonetheless confused Japanese voters and contributed to destabilizing the situation. The political crisis reached its high point with the large-scale "rice riots" of 1918. The protests were directed primarily against a small group of industrialists who had gained large profits while serving the war effort.[361] There were noticeable inequalities in people's living standards, too. At the same time, an enlightened, politically concerned middle class that enjoyed rising if modest incomes was becoming increasingly outspoken and articulate.[362]

Writing after the Second World War, Shidehara remembered those earlier economic developments:

> Before the first World War, Japan had usually been a debtor nation, with the balance of trade against her. The war suddenly turned the scale, and she emerged as a creditor nation. She was called upon to supply ships and munitions to her then Allies and Associates, and in return a considerable amount of money flowed into the country. A large number of nouveaux riches grew up. Luxuries and amenities of life were all the rage.[363]

Facilitated by its participation in the First World War, Japan had built up something like a "military-industrial complex," and arms exports during the war had brought exceptional monetary returns. Not only the naval operations, but also the material support of the Allies with armaments and destroyers built in Japanese shipyards for use against the submarine peril in the Mediterranean, as well as other provisions and services, brought Japan into a supplier's role and "a very remarkable flourishing of the economy." The positive balance of trade made it possible to pay back foreign loans and build up gold reserves: "Industry developed with giant strides, and the number of workers grew. . . . The merchant marine, which was in the hands of large companies, increased its volume both in total tonnage as well as in the capacity of individual ships. Textile, machine, chemical and other factories shot up from nowhere."[364] With the ending of the war this lucrative business had to be given up, and one had to turn again primarily to production of civilian goods.

Japan had in the course of the war some losses to register as well, since the new Soviet republic announced the annulment of the treaties with tsarist Russia that had recognized for Japan certain special rights in Manchuria and Korea; and then too the United States, in the wake of President Wilson's "New Diplomacy," ultimately announced the ending of American assurances regarding Japanese special interests in China (arising from the "territorial propinquity" of the two countries), which had rested upon the Taft-Katsura Agreement of 1905 and the Lansing-Ishii Agreement of 1917.[365] Evidently, the Japanese were denied their own "Monroe Doctrine." However, at the Versailles Peace Conference and the Washington Conference, Japan was able, after intensive negotiations with the Western powers and China, to define its interests and, without resorting to a "Japanese Monroe Doctrine," to consolidate its security[366] as well as its general position as a global power and its standing in Asia.

Japanese "imperialism" for that matter had run into criticism even at home as a result of growing public awareness, toward the end of the First World War (influenced by Wilson's Fourteen Points), that eschewed colonial excesses or imperialistic behavior. It was Shidehara's conviction "that traditional imperialism was no longer the most productive means for Japan to achieve her objectives."[367] The Chinese, on the other hand, saw Wilson's proposals as a useful tool to push through their nationalist ambitions. Japan had, through the annexation of Korea, and as a result of the Twenty-One Demands, lost sympathies abroad, in spite of the fact that it had during the 1914–1918 war fulfilled its obligations, and supplied the Allies and Russia with munitions, foodstuffs, and other provisions, and provided a sustained and often crucial support to the war effort.[368]

Undeniably, some of the Japanese military actions on the Asian mainland had reinforced this image. The army and navy had tried, in 1916, to take advantage of the war situation, attempting to establish in Manchuria an independent buffer state under the authority of a military clique. Shidehara had gotten wind of this and foiled the plot by immediately alerting Foreign Minister Motono (until then wholly in the dark about the clandestine affair),[369] who thereupon managed to call the military to account. In this way Shidehara quickly made himself unloved by the military.

Another event that involved Shidehara was the revolutionary unrest in Russia, which led to the decision of England and France, taken at an inter-Allied conference in Paris in December 1917, to intervene in the Russian struggle in order to apply pressure on the Bolsheviks. The two European powers approached their ally Japan with the request that Japan intervene in Siberia, "take over the Trans-Siberian Railway,"[370] and—if it should prove necessary—even "to advance as far as [European] Russia."[371] Although the United States at first protested and denied its consent, it finally agreed, though only under condition that Japan would "not make incursions into Russia."[372] In January 1918 the Japanese government and the emperor approved the sending of two shiploads of troops to Vladivostok, where the Allies managed a large warehouse of war supplies.

In March 1918 Japan concluded with China an agreement to promote a common plan in Siberia. At first, nominally, the Siberian intervention had only to do with the security of the consular corps in Vladivostok and the matter of protecting freed Czech war prisoners from Bolshevik attacks, and accompanying them as they made their way eastward to Vladivostok to return home from there by ship. The anti-Communist Japanese military were eager, however, to take part directly in opposing the Bolshevik Revolution in Russia. After China's cooperation with the Japanese military expedition in Siberia had been assured in March,[373] U.S. Secretary of State Robert Lansing officially urged Japan, in July, to support the Czechs. In August eleven Japanese divisions landed in Vladivostok and soon advanced into much of the rest of the Russian Maritime Province, into the Lake Baikal region and, in between, along the upper Amur basin, where it was felt they could remain in place for a considerable period. Shidehara, who was no friend of imperialistic power politics, perceived the grave dangers such a situation could entail for Japan.

Meanwhile, the so-called Shidehara party in the Ministry of Foreign Affairs had been built up around men from the moderate political camp including Saionji Kinmochi, Hara Kei (president of the Seiyūkai), Inukai Tsuyoshi, and Makino Nobuaki, who worked together with, and supported, Shidehara in bringing their influence to bear against the expansionist plans of the military.[374] In contrast to military figures like General Tanaka Giichi, former Prime Minister Yamagata Aritomo, and War Minister Ōshima Ken'ichi, who wanted to halt, by force of arms, the expansion of Bolshevik influence to the east and south into China,[375] statesmen of the Shidehara party felt a Japanese intervention was uncalled for and could be allowed only under extraordinary circumstances. Yamagata himself feared that a Japanese intervention in Siberia could unnecessarily provoke and upset the United States.[376] The Shidehara party's argument that sending in military forces could damage Japanese-Russian trade in the area also carried weight.[377]

It seems that Shidehara and the Japanese government at first tried to defuse the situation in Siberia by recognizing the provisional government under Admiral Kolchak in Omsk,[378] and in this way to effect the withdrawal of the Japanese troops. On 24 May 1919 Shidehara, who had in the meantime become ambassador to the United States, delivered to the American government in Washington an *aide mémoire* from the Japanese government that stated:

Having regard to the known desire of all the Allies and associated powers, [Japan] wishes the early reestablishment in Russia of an orderly and efficient government with reasonable promise of stability, and believing it proves official acknowledgement by foreign powers of the international standing of the Omsk government will materially be much to the maintenance of peace, the Japanese government feel the moment is opportune to consider the question of provisional recognition to be extended to the Omsk Government.[379]

After the end of the war, Shidehara tried, through diplomatic maneuvering, to secure Japan's "retreat with honor from its Siberian adventure."[380] But although as ambassador in Washington he had done almost everything he could to prepare for such a withdrawal of Japanese troops, he was overruled by the "autonomous command" of the military leadership.[381] The military, always professing loyalty to the emperor, saw the Communist revolution in Russia as a threat and was eager to engage in battle, all the more so because in 1919 a revolutionary democratic-socialist wave hit Japan that could potentially endanger the home country.[382] For many Japanese intellectuals, Russia's October Revolution was not only a noteworthy event in world history but something well worth emulating. President Woodrow Wilson's answer, on the other hand, although he "saw Lenin as a fellow visionary,"[383] was a "democratic world revolution," which found its expression in the proposals for a league of nations.

Japanese troop contingents still remained in the Maritime Province until October 1922 and in northern Sakhalin until 1925.[384] The U.S. government had already in April 1920 withdrawn U.S. military personnel from Siberia without apparently informing its ally Japan beforehand. Ambassador Shidehara frankly and bitterly complained to Secretary of State Lansing over this breach of trust:

> What kind of a terrible thing have you done to us? If the troops were despatched after a consultation between our two countries, they should have also been evacuated after a consultation. Now that you have done this, not having given us a word of notice beforehand, it may be understood from now on that the United States will have no right to object no matter what Japan may do as to the continuation or termination of Japanese occupation, or the increase or decrease of troops, without consulting your country.[385]

Because of the fact that Washington withdrew its troops without consulting Japan during the stage of planning and decision and not even informing the Japanese Ministry of Foreign Affairs at an appropriate time, Shidehara was all the more deprived of the possibility of exercising effective leadership to bring about an early withdrawal of Japanese troops. Apparently, the Americans were poorly informed about Japan's domestic politics and also about its constitutional provisions on the "autonomy of command" by the military when engaged outside Japan, and the dangers that might ensue from this situation.[386]

On 26 October 1918, Shidehara had been appointed to become one of the judges on the list for the Permanent Court of Arbitration in The Hague,[387] filling a vacancy that had earlier been occupied by Motono and still earlier (until 1912) by Shidehara's mentor Denison. More important, however, was Shidehara's assignment, from 1916 until the beginning of 1919, as chairman of the Japanese preparatory committee for the Versailles conference.[388] This "preparatory committee for peace negotiations after the Japanese-German war" (*Nichidoku sen'eki kōwa junbi iinkai*) had been established in September 1915 after Shidehara's return from The Hague.[389] The committee's members were recruited from the foreign ministry, the army and navy ministries, and the cabinet's legal bureau (*hōseikyoku*).[390]

Shidehara did not uncritically accept the Allied plans for a league of nations. Should the new league be built on the earlier Hague coalition or would it be better to create something entirely new? As the German jurist Walther Schücking, whom Shidehara my well have met at The Hague in 1915, explained: "In Holland as well as in Switzerland,[391] expectations were that this league for peace (*Friedensbund*) will, needless to say, be founded upon the work of The Hague, and that this will be enlarged upon accordingly."[392] Schücking observed: "Now strange as this might seem, this 'league to enforce peace,' if I am correctly informed, will completely break with the [earlier] work of The Hague (*Haager Werk*). The work of The Hague is to lie as a ruin along the way, and coming from America something absolutely new is to be created."[393] Shidehara may have been susceptible also to James Bryce's criticism, who thought the league was "already" in "need" of "amendments" and to a great extent "condemned by [the negative] results already visible . . . leading straight to future wars."[394]

The Japanese were "sitting between chairs," since the Europeans and the Americans were advancing different concepts. How should Japan conduct itself under these circumstances? Also, unlike the Hague organization, the League of Nations was to come about not "out of free will," but was forced into being by the war. Insofar as such criticism was justified, one was dealing here with an "imperialistically created legal order.[395] . . . An adroit organization of the world might also have come about without the war. . . . It would have come about upon a democratic foundation, with the contributions of all participating states. The two Hague Peace Conferences would have provided its points of departure."[396] Shidehara was sensitive to Bryce's argument that the Hague peace conferences, like the Washington Naval Disarmament Conference that was to "resume the effort, defeated at The Hague, to secure an all-round reduction of military and naval armaments," "belong[ed] to a different category."[397]

It is difficult to guess how close Shidehara's contacts after 1915 were either with the American or with the British and—via The Hague, Denmark, or Switzerland—other intellectual progressive diplomats developing the idea of a league of nations, but most importantly, the proposals of the "Bryce group" in England and the American proposals communicated by Theodore Marburg reached the peace preparatory committee in Japan, which Shidehara chaired from 1916 onward.[398] Since Japan was not elaborating any "league

of nations" plan of its own, until December 1916 the work of the committee focused in great part on a report concerning the taking over of the former German concessions in Shandong Province of China and the formerly
German-administered islands in the Pacific.[399]

Japanese Christian pacifists also played an important part in promoting
ideas for the new international organization, with plans extant during the
war that "an organization to promote the League of Nations be planted in
Japan."[400] In June 1916 Theodore Marburg, in his capacity as chairman of
the LEP's (League to Enforce Peace) Committee on Foreign Correspondence,
sent a letter to Prime Minister Ōkuma in which he explained the American "league of nations" idea. This might have prompted Shidehara, Ishii
Kikujirō's trusted deputy in the foreign ministry, to now intensively engage
himself with this issue. Marburg himself had lent his moral support to a "Japanese Monroe Doctrine" and was of the view that "a backward country which
is unable to maintain law and order at home" should not be a member of the
proposed league and that "a Japanese hegemony in China" would bring great
benefits to the Chinese; that was something Shidehara, being more farsighted
and perhaps better informed, would have disagreed with. In November 1916,
Motono, who replaced Ishii as foreign minister, now also busied himself
with the "league of nations" idea and, assisted by Ambassador Satō Aimaro
in Washington, sent to Marburg in January of the following year a message
signaling Japan's basic agreement with the American plans.[401]

The connection to London was, however, according to historian Thomas
Burkman, better than that to the American League of Nations advocates,
which might have been due to Shidehara's personal connections. In general,
"public foreign policy statements by Allied statesmen, replete with reference
to a postwar League . . . [were] dutifully transmitted by Japanese embassies
and translated by foreign ministry functionaries during the war."[402] In these
preparatory stages it was Shidehara—aided by his close associate Saburi
Sadao—who evaluated the input, and then prepared the policy options.
Almost certainly one of those inputs was the already mentioned "Minimal
Program" presented in 1915 by the Netherlands Anti-War Council at The
Hague, which had counseled the powers to allow "liberty of commerce" and
"equal treatment for all nations" in their "colonies, protectorates and spheres
of influence."

At some point after 11 April of the following year (1917), the official "Tentative Draft of a Treaty for a League of Nations" put forward by the League
to Enforce Peace reached the foreign ministry in Tokyo. This proposal advocated (in section 17) the setting up of an "executive body of the League"; and
the decisions and stipulations of the League of Nations were "to be enforced
. . . using their whole economic and military power" (section 2). In a letter

to Marburg dated 17 November, Harvard-educated senior statesman Kaneko Kentarō (1853–1942) wrote he had studied the draft that "was translated and published in *The Hōchi Shimbun*, one of our influential newspapers. Ever since, the subject of the League of Nations has been discussed everywhere. . . . However, can you tell me and explain more fully in regard to the 'Economic and Military Measures' which you speak of, in the case of any nation which disregards the decision of the Court or violates the international law?"[403] The reference to enforcement measures was of interest to the Japanese concerned about national security, and binding and enforceable regulations.[404]

The Japanese side was aware of the implications of these proposals for Japan and for the future framing of international relations. A six-page report by the foreign ministry's Political Affairs Bureau was presented on 11 November 1918 (the day of the European armistice) and included a historical outline of the international efforts to organize peace from the "Holy Alliance" up to Woodrow Wilson's famous speech of 27 October 1918. It also incorporated the proposal for limitation of armaments and of national sovereignty as well as the application of the principle of the "open door," including the colonies. This report, together with a memorandum of 30 November 1918 in which Japan's conciliatory policy favoring global peace was outlined, reflected the general tendency after the war, as it prevailed also in Japan.[405]

Despite the various misgivings in Japan and some doubts about the efficacy of the Western peace plans, Shidehara wholeheartedly welcomed the establishment of the League of Nations. Speaking at Keiō University nearly a decade later, he gave this assessment:

The horrible experiences of the World War have made the realization of a League of Nations necessary. Today, there are such organizations as the League of Nations Assembly, the League of Nations Council, the [Permanent] Court of International Justice [since 1922], and also outside the League of Nations the [Permanent] Court of Arbitration [since 1899] and the Deliberative Council on International Disputes. All have been established, at multiple levels, to regulate the relations among countries with the help of world public opinion (*sekai no kōron o motte*).[406]

Given, however, the lack of institutions and organs of international law enforcement that would be more genuinely representative on the global level, Shidehara also placed his hope above all on the effective power of public opinion. As he himself put it, "Just as most bacteria cannot survive in strong sunlight, so the international crimes that are carried out in a dark age must melt away by themselves with the increasing light of the world's public opinion."[407] The *power of public opinion* had been decisive for the advancement of the international peace movement in the nineteenth century and contributed to the convening of the First Hague Peace Conference of 1899. This movement, Shidehara was well aware, originated with the Age of Enlightenment, with thinkers such as Rousseau, Kant, Bentham, and Victor Hugo. Shidehara staked his faith in global communication and the interdependence of social, economic, political, and cultural interests, and the triumph of the power of public opinion in eventually bringing about the reduction of armaments and rejection of the institutions of war and indeed an end to war, which increasingly visited horrible suffering not only on combatants but on civilian populations.[408]

It was in a similar vein that Sun Yat-sen once expressed some of the hope he had come to have for postwar Japan.

> At the Versailles Peace Conference, Japan sat as one of the Five Great Powers. She was spokesman for the affairs of Asia, and the other Powers listened to her proposals, looking upon her as the "leading horse." We may infer, therefore, that what the white races can do, Japan can evidently also do; although the races show variation of colour, there are no marked differences in intelligence and ability. Because Asia possesses a strong Japan the white races now dare not disparage the Japanese or any Asiatic race. So Japan's rise has brought prestige not only to the Yamato race, but it has raised the standing of all Asiatic peoples. We once thought we could not do what the Europeans do; we see now that Japan has learned from Europe and that, if we follow Japan, we, too, will be learning from the West as Japan did.[409]

With the ascendancy of Shidehara diplomacy, this hope seemed to be not wholly unfounded. The Shidehara party in the foreign ministry was influential and the League of Nations idea seemed likely to be an effective means to further erode the unwholesome influence of the military.

Shidehara was well prepared. After the delegates began arriving at Versailles for the Peace Conference he was first and foremost responsible for communications and coordination between Tokyo and Paris. At a banquet on 10 August 1920, his efforts were officially commended when the emperor bestowed the rank of baron on him. To recommend this entitlement, Foreign Minister Uchida Yasuya presented a statement assessing the services of the "Envoy Extraordinary and Ambassador Plenipotentiary, Shidehara Kijūrō" in these words:

> During the years of war after 1915, [he] assumed the difficult tasks of Deputy [i.e., Vice] Foreign Minister. In assistance of the Minister, he presided over the duties and works generated and expanded as a result of that war, and his execution of his duties was prompt, very detailed, and very appropriate. Particularly, *when difficult issues were raised in the course of the peace conference, he always participated and contributed greatly in crucial phases.* His preparation and

policy formulation has never been irrelevant. When the committee for the peace treaty preparation was formed in the Ministry, he presided over it as Chairman and properly executed his duties.[410]

Having attained the rank of "Baron," Shidehara became a member of Japan's emperor-appointed "peerage" (*kazoku*) established in 1884, whose princes, marquises, counts, viscounts, and barons were subject to the imperial household ministry and enjoyed significant financial subsidies. Together with the unofficial institution of "elder statesmen" (*genrō*), the official court bureaucracy, the cabinet, the privy council, the imperial Diet (consisting of the House of Peers and the House of Representatives), and the various organs of the military leadership, this *kazoku* institution was an important factor in the "tennō system" until it was abolished, as a part of the post–Second World War reforms, in 1947.

AMBASSADOR IN WASHINGTON (1919–1922) AND CHIEF NEGOTIATOR AT THE WASHINGTON NAVAL DISARMAMENT CONFERENCE (12 NOVEMBER 1921–6 FEBRUARY 1922)

"We are now, it seems, standing in the centre of the world's history. After five years of the terrible war, a new era of international relationship has dawned."

Shidehara Kijūrō, 4 March 1920

Shidehara had already during the war made himself unloved by the military because of his conciliatory and cooperative diplomacy (*kyōchō gaikō*) with respect both to the Western powers and China. This policy was based, among other things, on the conviction that a bellicose advance onto the Asian mainland would not only provoke the censure and intervention of the Western powers but above all stifle any possibility for constructive cooperation and development in Sino-Japanese relations. When Shidehara at the beginning of 1919 was assigned the post of ambassador to the United States, he made sure that his policies in this regard would not be misunderstood. In a speech before the Fifth Avenue Association of New York in March the following year, he stressed that with the end of the war and the founding of the League of Nations "a new age in international relations had dawned."[411] With regards to China, he confirmed Japan's intentions to return Shandong saying that "Japan knows her responsibilities to China and to civilization. She will go forward unswervingly along the pathway which she believes leads to international peace and stability."[412]

As I ponder on the future of our mutual relations, I see every hopeful sign of a firm and enduring friendship. We are neighbors, and yet divided by a substantial barrier which effectually prevents frontier incidents. You were our sponsors when we entered the Family of Nations. You have evinced a sympathetic appreciation of our qualities. We entertain an immense appreciation for your practical achievements, for your constructive genius and for your resourceful energy. We are both in spirit young nations, quick to ride on the crest of the wave of progress. Is it possible to imagine any question on which our interests seriously clash? On the Shantung question, or on any other Chinese questions?[413]

At the Washington Conference of 1921–1922 on naval limitations and the position of Japan and the European powers in China, Shidehara as chief negotiator on the Japanese side, and one of the architects of the "Versailles and Washington treaties system," would fulfill this promise. But there were other problems also Shidehara had to tackle.

Not long after the Versailles conference's rejection of the Japanese proposal to include in the League of Nations Covenant a stipulation on racial equality, Shidehara became once again occupied with this sort of question in Washington. Already in 1913 agricultural land ownership had been denied to the Japanese in the state of California; now in 1920 they were also deprived of the right to rent agricultural land. Negotiations in Washington between Shidehara and former U.S. ambassador to Tokyo Roland S. Morris (1872–1945) took place between mid-September 1920 and the end of January 1921, but led to no concrete results in reversing the legal measures passed by the California legislature.

While Japan had apparently no intention to make the United States into a destination for new emigrants to relieve its overpopulation problem,[414] its concern was rather over the principle of enjoying equal rights vis-à-vis the United States and the other races and peoples living in America and elsewhere. Shidehara underlined this in a May 1921 address before the Cleveland, Ohio, Chamber of Commerce:

One of the charges constantly brought against the Japanese is that he is not assimilable. . . . The entire question is one of delicacy because it seldom defines its premises. No Japanese claims that he is identical in blood with the white man. . . . He has his own pride of race and offers no apology for the fact that his hair is black and his skin of a darker tint than that of the Caucasian. . . . What he does claim is that, when given the opportunity and the privilege, he is capable of those intellectual and spiritual assimilations which are compatible with good citizenship, dignified manhood and loyal service to the community in which he resides. . . . No race has a monopoly of all the virtues and none possesses all the unworthy characteristics. . . . There is such a thing as the blending of civilizations and aspirations and common interests which ignore the lesser ties of blood. . . . The Japanese race is itself a mixture of immigrant races which have been molded into homogeneity during historic time.[415]

In regard to China and especially to its Three Eastern Provinces in Manchuria, Shidehara nevertheless held the view that Japan might properly have certain special interests there taking into consideration such matters as cultural affinities, geographical proximity, and the fact that parts of China were still economically undeveloped.[416] In an address before the Japan Society in New York in March 1920, Shidehara referred to this as follows:

> It should be borne in mind that Japan has in China a special position which is not shared by the United States or by any of the European powers. *Her future destiny is closely interwoven with that of China, and her own national safety and vital interests are in many cases directly involved in Chinese problems*, which America and Europe can afford to approach from purely sentimental or economic points of view. I feel sure, however, that this special position of Japan is fully realized by her American and European friends, and that she will not be called upon to renounce *her undoubted right of self-protection and self-preservation.*[417]

What this meant was that Japan wanted to be given equal opportunity to what the other powers already possessed, and which Japan had fought hard to assert. At the Washington Conference, which took place from 12 November 1921 to 6 February 1922, Japan demonstrated it was open to compromise and claimed only equal rights to those of the other powers in China. Asada Sadao has shown that "Shidehara believed that Japan, because of her geographical position, needed *no preferential or exclusive economic rights in China*; on the contrary, it was Japan that really benefited from fair competition. But the Japanese plenipotentiary went too far in the eyes of his superiors in Tokyo when he declared that Japan demanded no special privileges in the purchase of raw materials and foodstuffs from China."[418] In his reply to the foreign ministry Shidehara pointed out that "it is not the purpose of our policy to establish a definite exception to the principle of the Open Door and equality of opportunity." To pursue such an aim at the conference "would occasion many controversies, give the Chinese a most effective tool for anti-Japanese agitations" and so on, and he, "therefore, refrained from bringing up this problem" during the deliberations.[419] Keeping to his principles, Shidehara would work tirelessly, to the point of utter physical exhaustion, to help bring the Washington Conference to a successful conclusion.

The idea for a disarmament conference had been conceived, and brought to fruition when in December 1920, U.S. Senator William E. Borah introduced in the Senate a resolution encouraging the American president to call a conference with the aim of moving the powers to drastically reduce their naval armaments, initially over a period of five years.[420] An overwhelming majority (Senate 74:0; House of Representatives 330:4) in both houses of Congress voted for the proposal, and the American government proceeded to invite at first Great Britain, France, Italy, and Japan, and later also Belgium, China, the Netherlands, and Portugal, to take part in the conference.

Germany's ambassador in Tokyo, Wilhelm Solf, reported to his government the Japanese reaction (as of late February 1921) to the Borah initiative:

> Spurred forward by Borah, this question has here awakened in public opinion an undoubtedly great and—apart from a very few imperialistic voices in the press—favorable echo . . . Japan's largest newspapers [have] . . . without reserve adopted Borah's point of view. Ozaki [Yukio] took the matter up in Parliament, where he introduced a Resolution in favor of reducing the Japanese Navy. . . . His arguments are simple and convincing.[421]

It seems quite plausible that Shidehara was involved in the initial preparations for the planned conference program.[422] The American ambassador in Tokyo, Edward Bell, in an official note to Foreign Minister Count Uchida, on 12 September 1921 communicated the proposed "Agenda for the Conference on the Limitation of Armament."[423] It had two parts: "Limitation of Armament" and "Pacific and Far Eastern Questions." The first part had three subsections: first of all, the limitation of naval armaments, with the following points: (1) principles of limitation; (2) scope of limitation; and (3) execution of limitation. The second subsection listed "rules for control of new agencies of warfare," and the third had to do with limitation of land armaments.

The agenda's second part was likewise subdivided into three subsections. The first had to do with questions concerning China. Which principles should be applied in which areas, and how? The topics to be explored were: (1) matters of territorial integrity; (2) integrity of administration; (3) the "open door"—commercial and industrial equality of opportunity; (4) "concessions"—monopolies or economic privileges; (5) development of railways, including the Russian-owned Chinese Eastern Railway across north-central Manchuria; (6) preferences in railway charges; and (7) the status of already existing obligations.[424] The second subsection had to do with Siberia—again subdivided into subpoints 1–7; and the third subsection with mandated administrative areas in the various Pacific islands.

The United States naturally had an interest both in applying a brake to any projected or actually existing expansionist ambitions on the part of Japan in the East (especially in China), and in consolidating its own position of power in the Pacific. The Lansing-Ishii Agreement had already served a purpose in this regard. At the same time, the United States wished to see the dissolution of the Anglo-Japanese Alliance, through which it saw itself—in spite of the 1911 amendments to the Alliance treaty—indirectly threatened. The view of one foreign newspaper correspondent that Japan was initially not enthusiastic about the conference proposal since it had "never been closer than in 1921 to realizing Yoshida Shōin's dream of a hegemony over Asia"[425] was no doubt one-sided. Anyway, the Japanese government, no less than the Japanese public, had a genuine interest in reducing armaments, and the invitation was duly accepted.

The Washington Conference, in President Warren Harding's view, was meant to be the groundwork of "a larger association of nations" that would go beyond the goals and capabilities of the League of Nations (in which the United States was not a part), and in fact complement the latter.[426] Germany, too, in Harding's conception, should be invited to the final phase of the arms limitation conference in the hope that it would also sign and ratify the treaties.[427] Great Britain generally welcomed the American proposals as a meaningful complement to the League system.[428] The Japanese view of President Harding's campaign for an "Association of Nations" was expressed by a Japanese correspondent for *The New York World*, Adachi Kinnosuke: "Nothing would please Japan more. She would naturally join the Association wholeheartedly."[429] The conference was overshadowed throughout, however, by British-French antagonisms.[430]

Nevertheless, with Harding's campaign a new beginning seemed to have been made, giving added encouragement to many during the Washington Conference.[431] One of the declared goals of this idealistic concept was to declare war illegal.[432] It must not be forgotten that the American secretary of state at the time, Charles Evans Hughes (1862–1948), belonged to what one might call the "hard core" of the American "outlawry of war" movement. Hughes was convinced that "[w]ar should be made a crime, and those who instigate it should be punished as criminals."[433] He was no advocate of alliances, "so far as the maintenance of peace is concerned."[434] The limitation or giving up of the sovereign right of nations to go to war should be of their own free will—a hope that was frustrated, as the future would reveal.

The outlawry of war necessarily implies a self-imposed restraint. . . . The outlawry of war, by appropriate rule of law making war a crime, requires the common accord needed to establish and maintain a rule of international law, the common consent to abandon war; and the suggested remedy thus implies a state of mind in which no cure is needed. As the restraint is self-imposed, it will prove to be of avail only while there is a will to peace.[435]

The British proposals went even farther than a mere "common accord" or facultative agreement. The great hope was that, similarly to what had been aspired to in the Hague peace conferences, world peace could permanently be secured through adequate institutions. This was linked, in addition, to the need to achieve, in concert with Japan, a durable peace in the Far East.[436] In this respect, the Chinese delegate, Dr. Wellington Koo (Gu Weijun), had announced early on that he wanted to bring the Shandong question and the Twenty-One Demands to the conference table for deliberation. This did not mean that China was opposed to the idea of an effective association of nations.

Shidehara could dispense with the usual media-centered public relations activities which diplomacy made use of in the preparatory stage of the negotiations as well as during the conference itself. Harvard-educated Frederick Moore, who at the time worked closely with Shidehara as an advisor, testifies to Shidehara's tactics of dealing with others on a personal, one-to-one basis. According to Moore, he declined an offer by an American publicity agent to be of service to him on the grounds that he had already found someone who adequately represented the Japanese standpoint. "Who?" the American wished to know. Shidehara's reply was: "The Secretary of State!"[437] Between Shidehara and Secretary of State Hughes, from the start, a relationship of trust had developed that in due course enabled Shidehara to have a positive influence, during the negotiations, on differences of opinion between the Britons and the Americans. Shidehara, however, did perhaps not quite share the above-cited standpoint of Hughes, who was wary of balance-of-power alliances. He perhaps preferred a more comprehensive (collective) security alliance of the sort the British delegate Arthur James Balfour proposed.

As a point of departure for the naval negotiations among the United States, Great Britain, and Japan, a capital-ship ratio of 5:5:3 was adopted. Japan was not satisfied, however, and the cabinet instructed the Japanese delegation to strive for a 10:10:7 ratio. With sportive ease, or so it seemed, throughout the conference Japan showed itself in its negotiations both diligently tough, while at the same time ready to make concessions. Although Prince Tokugawa Iesato, a nondiplomat, had been formally designated by the emperor to head the Japanese delegation, it was the other two plenipotentiaries, Admiral Katō Tomosaburō and in particular Baron Shidehara (with his special language and diplomatic skills), who effectively held the reins and led the Japanese negotiating team.

An alleged "dispute" between Prince Tokugawa Iesato and the "chief Japanese negotiator" Admiral Katō Tomosaburō caused what H. G. Wells in an article published on 30 November in *The Baltimore Sun* referred to as "Conference Spirit at Ebb." Admiral Katō had announced that Japan would hold fast to the "70 percent ratio" under any circumstance. To this Prince Tokugawa had remarked that it was only "the expression of the [admiral's] personal view," which enraged the latter.[438] In any event, Japan still tried to hold fast to the 10:10:7 position.

The negotiations over Shandong began in early December. Because of the controversial nature of the issue, on which views diverged sharply, the Chinese and the Japanese at first confronted each other fervently.[439] However, in return for compromises by the other powers on Far Eastern matters, Japan was now disposed to accept the 5:5:3 ratio.[440] France was brought into the negotiations for the purpose of resolving certain Pacific problems, also in regard to China. The powers, including Japan, were generally willing to compensate China, and made conciliatory offers to own up to past injustices. France was willing to give up its leaseholds in the "treaty ports," but only if the other colonial powers did likewise.[441] On 4 December, accords were reached when the United States, France, and Great Britain announced their principle willingness to give up their leaseholds on Chinese territory—in fact, the first positive result, and one that could partly be accredited to the Japanese.[442] China, which had refused to sign the Versailles Treaty, now enjoyed a favorable negotiating position.

It was Japan, however, that now was not yet quite ready to give up its hard-won concessions on the Chinese mainland for nothing. Chung Chu Kwei (Zhong Zhugui) addressed this in *The New York Times*, in an article titled "Conference Doings Disappoint Chinese."[443] Because of this, the conference for a time seemed to drag on, and lose some of its momentum.

While the Japanese delegation waited for new instructions from Tokyo,[444] the conference was receiving horrific news reports of adversities, hunger, and terror in Russia.[445] This and the fact that Japan continued to maintain troops in eastern Siberia and found itself generally in a fire of criticism because of its perceived dawdling over the negotiations also weighed on the negative side.[446] *The Christian Science Monitor*, generally critical of Japan, maintained that in Tokyo it was the militarists who held the greatest power,[447] and on 7 December *The Baltimore Sun* made the case that Japan was the only country that still had not made any concessions.[448] Responsibility was attributed, among other things, to Japan's "secret diplomacy."[449] A pessimistic mood prevailed.[450]

One reason for Japan's perceived delays was apparently that Shidehara—assisted throughout by his trusted colleague Saburi Sadao—was concerned with the treaty draft of the British delegate Lord Balfour that had to be modified to be made acceptable to the Americans. Balfour had proposed a sort of security alliance of the three "sea powers"—Great Britain, Japan, and the United States—that would replace the Anglo-Japanese Alliance. Instructions from Tokyo had called for a "Japanese-British-American entente for the maintenance of a durable peace in the Pacific and the Far East." France should also, in the Japanese view, be part of the alliance. Shidehara believed that the Americans would only agree if the proposed treaty were modified into a consultative pact without too far-reaching commitments. The Shidehara draft, elaborated from these premises, was in the end compared with the draft prepared by U.S. Secretary of State Charles Evans Hughes. Out of all this was born the Four Power Treaty.[451] The naval agreement—also known as the "Pacific Treaty"—in essence stipulated a freezing of the current status of fortifications and naval supply points in the Pacific, as spelled out in article 19. The "final draft, which formed the basis for the treaty" in many important points reflected the input of Shidehara,[452] and the wording of article 19 in particular appears to have come from Shidehara's pen.[453] One delegate referred to "dry" America under the Prohibition Law (and accompanying U.S. constitutional amendment of 1919), which was not meant to suggest any watering down of the new peaceably-arrived-at and peace-promoting accord, but rather, quite the contrary, was meant to emphasize its universal applicability and recognition.[454] Journalist K. K. Kawakami was convinced it was Shidehara's sober and realistic policy approach that had taken the rough edges off the original British treaty draft and made it acceptable to the skeptical Americans.[455] On 13 December the treaty, by which the four states secured mutual respect for their stipulated rights in the Pacific, was signed.[456]

The New York Times had a few days earlier published the main points of the treaty. The new pact was said to include the commitment to mutual consultations, mediation, and adjudication: "*First*—It fixes territorial integrity in the region of the Pacific, each of the Powers being bound not to attack the territory of any other. *Second*—It provides that if the vital interests of any of the Powers in the Pacific are menaced, it will be morally required to consult the other Powers before taking action. *Third*—It provides that in case of disagreements between any two of the contracting parties the other two Powers will be asked to mediate and arbitrate. *Fourth*—It provides for the abolition of the Anglo-Japanese Alliance, which ends with the exchange of ratifications of this new treaty."[457] It was a big and important step for Japan to take.

The fact had been that so long as Japan was allied bilaterally with England, the United States could be distrustful toward Japan. The new arrangements, however, gave no impetus to any further fears, although some opponents of the agreements in the United States saw the Monroe Doctrine compromised.[458] In truth, the treaty was a sort of moral codex for civilized behavior in regard to China. In Kawakami's words: "The value of this four-power agreement is moral. Its importance lies not so much in what it says as in what it implies."[459]

With the mere signing of this treaty, however, China's concerns had barely come under discussion, to say nothing of reaching specific negotiated outcomes in regard to Chinese objectives and claims.[460] Nevertheless—according to Lady Astor commenting in *The Washington Times*—it is likely that some further substantial steps forward with respect to Chinese wishes were being made through the secret consultations that were simultaneously taking place.[461] One reason for this lack of progress had most likely been Shidehara's illness that had kept him in bed for some time.

On 15 December the Japanese delegation announced that it was ready to accept the ratio for naval strengths proposed by the Americans for the "Five Power Naval Treaty" (United States, Great Britain, Japan, France, and Italy). This agreement would stipulate a stop to the construction of battleships and cruisers over a period of ten years (until 31 December 1931), the scrapping of certain ships that were already built and ready to be commissioned or in the process of being built—845,000 tons for the United States and 583,000 tons for both Japan and Great Britain—as well as limiting the tonnage of capital ships and aircraft carriers (for all three countries) to thirty-five thousand and twenty-seven respectively, and limiting their gun calibers to sixteen and eight inches respectively.[462] The newspapers emphatically welcomed the compromises made by the Japanese. Thanks to them, a future "arms competition at sea will be avoided for ten years," declared *The Washington Post*. A "new epoch in international relations" had dawned.[463] The goal of the treaty, to guarantee Japan security in its own waters and to guarantee the other treaty powers—especially the United States and Great Britain—security vis-à-vis Japan, seemed to have been met.[464] Somewhat disheartening in the midst of the general enthusiasm was the piece of news that Japan would continue, in spite of the planned treaty agreements, the construction of its super-battleship *Mutsu*, which would be the world's largest.[465] However, *The Baltimore Sun*, in a Tokyo dispatch of 19 December 1921, assured readers that this would be the last battleship that Japan would build over the coming ten years.

Much more negative were the reports which American newspapers carried on 17 December about French plans to built super-battleships, over the next decade, with a total 350,000 gross tonnage: "This proposal, if carried out, means the naval holiday . . . would be totally wrecked . . . [and] expanded to such an extent [that] . . . naval disarmament would become a joke."[466] Meanwhile, significant progress had been achieved in Sino-Japanese negotiations over Shandong. Generally, the success of the Japanese negotiators in Washington was underscored, with *The New York Times* of 17 December noting:

> It must be admitted that so far Japan has had amazing success in this conference . . . Japan came to Washington with many misgivings. Her chief fear was of isolation, in other words, loss of the English alliance with nothing of much value as a substitute. What she now receives is much wider in scope—a mutual pledge by Big Pacific Powers that makes the ocean in which the Island Empire is situated absolutely safe. The agreement not to fortify islands puts the final seal on Japan's security.[467]

Negotiations over submarines were carried forward over the Christmas holidays. After agreement was reached between France and Great Britain, a further accord between France and Japan seemed forthcoming.[468] France continued to pose difficulties but announced that it would now abstain completely from submarines "if the British Government will guarantee to protect the French coast in the event of another unprovoked German attack."[469] The matter was taken up in the context of the British-French bilateral discussions.

Following the negotiations between the Japanese and Chinese delegates, Shidehara spoke before the Far Eastern Committee on 18 January, at which time he referred to a remark made before the full committee by Chinese delegate Dr. Alfred Sze on 16 November of the previous year: "China wishes to make her vast natural resources available to all people who need them!" Developing this theme, Shidehara went on to assert:

That statement evidently represents the wisdom and foresight of China, and the Japanese delegation is confident that the principle which it enunciated will be carried out to its full extent. It is to be hoped that, in the application of that principle, China may be disposed to extend to foreigners, as far as possible, the opportunity of cooperation in the development and utilization of China's natural resources. Any spontaneous declaration by China of her policy in that direction will be received with much gratification by Japan and also, no doubt, by all other nations interested in China. Resolutions which have hitherto been adopted by this committee have been uniformly guided by the spirit of self-denial and self-sacrifice on the part of foreign powers in favor of China. The Japanese delegation trusts that China, on her part, will not be unwilling to formulate a policy which will prove of considerable benefit, no less to China herself than to all nations.[470]

However, concrete matters vis-à-vis China were at this point not taken up. Rather, on 23 January, Shidehara first "took the Siberian bull by the horns," placing the Siberian question on the agenda of the Far Eastern Committee. "It was good strategy," writes Kawakami. "For the first time the Japanese have taken the offensive."[471] In the course of his detailed presentation of 23 January before the Far Eastern Committee, Shidehara explained:

The military expedition of Japan to Siberia was originally undertaken in common accord and in cooperation with the United States in 1918. It was primarily intended to render assistance to the Czecho-Slovak troops who, in their homeward journey across Siberia from European Russia, found themselves in grave and pressing danger at the hands of hostile forces under German command. The Japanese and American expeditionary forces, together with other allied troops, fought their way from Vladivostok far into the region of the Amur and the Trans-Baikal Provinces to protect the railway lines which afforded the sole means of transportation of the Czecho-Slovak troops from the interior of Siberia to the port of Vladivostok.[472]

The last group of Czech troops had left Vladivostok by ship in September 1920. While indeed Japanese troops were still stationed in the southern part of the Maritime Province around Vladivostok and Nikolsk "defending themselves" against Bolshevik attacks and rebellious Koreans, the province was by no means "under Japan's military occupation." It was not a matter of "occupation" by a foreign power, since no civil or military administration by the Japanese existed, and Russian officials were generally not hindered in carrying out their functions. Until the conclusion of Japanese-Russian negotiations in Dalian (Dairen), Japanese troops would, however, remain stationed in the region.

> The Japanese Government are anxious to see an orderly and stable authority speedily re-established in the Far Eastern possessions of Russia. It was in this spirit that they manifested a keen interest in the patriotic but ill-fated struggle of Admiral Kolchak. They have shown readiness to lend their good offices for promoting the reconciliation of various political groups in Eastern Siberia. But they have carefully refrained from supporting one faction against another. It will be recalled, for instance, that they withheld all assistance from General Rozanov against the revolutionary movements which led to his overthrow in January, 1920. They maintained an attitude of strict neutrality and refused to interfere in these movements which it would have been quite easy for them to suppress if they had so desired.[473]

Shidehara admitted, however, that Japan had, with other allied nations, supported the Cossack leader Ataman Semenoff, who had organized a movement to block Bolshevik activities and, supposedly, to maintain a certain amount of order: "It will be remembered that the growing rapprochement between the Germans and the Bolshevist government in Russia in the early part of 1918 naturally gave rise to apprehensions in the allied countries that a considerable quantity of munitions supplied by those countries, and stored in Vladivostok, might be removed by the Bolsheviki to European Russia for the use of the Germans."[474] The Japanese had continued to support Ataman Semenoff for a while even after assistance from the other allied countries had ended, but when it became clear that this was unwanted interference in Russia's domestic affairs and could no longer help pacify the internal situation, the Japanese government had, as Shidehara emphasized, stopped its assistance. The Japanese policy could be considered as both balanced and predictable.

The negotiations in Dalian were supposed to facilitate, as soon as possible, the withdrawal of Japanese troops from the Maritime Province. They were meant, in Shidehara's words, to remove "the present threat to the security of Japan as well as to the life and property of Japanese residing in eastern Siberia." They also had to do with giving the Japanese guarantees that they would be free to carry on commercial occupations in the region and there would be prohibition against Bolshevik propaganda activities going on beyond Russia's borders: "Should adequate provisions be arranged on the lines indicated the Japanese Government will at once proceed to the complete withdrawal of Japanese troops from Maritime Province."[475]

Things stood differently with the question of Sakhalin. Japan would keep troops in the Russian-administered northern half of the island until in Russia "a responsible administration has been firmly established, which can negotiate with Japan over a compensation" for the massacre by Russians in Nikolaievsk (near the mouth of the Amur River) of seven hundred resident Japanese, including many women and children as well as the Japanese consul, in the spring of 1920. This wanton massacre understandably engendered anger and protests among the Japanese public.[476]

In Japan itself public opinion was clearly on Shidehara's side, and conciliatory. It even went so far as to almost unanimously condemn much of the government's policy in Siberia. Ever since August 1921 the foreign ministry had been trying to deal with the government in Chita to bring about something like a security guarantee for Japanese life and property in the region. However, the Japanese press emphasized that any demonstration of force would be misguided and urgently demanded the withdrawal of troops even without a declaration of security guarantees, although no responsible policy on the part of the Chita government could be expected.[477] Interestingly, Kawakami comments that if Japan's objective in Siberia were the blocking of Bolshevism, one had to take into account that Bolshevism was only an idea, "an intangible thing, whose spread cannot be prevented by a 'sanitary cordon' formed by the guns of soldiers."[478]

Finally, negotiations with the Chinese delegation got well under way. Shidehara did not neglect to refer to the fact—which he took as an essential point of departure for considering any possible revision of the Twenty-One Demands—that these accords, concluded between Japan and China in 1915, continued to have validity in international law. The fact that the Chinese themselves were asking for a "revision" of the accords meant that they were acknowledging their legality. These earlier negotiations, Shidehara pointed out, had resulted in the exchange of ratification documents and thus were in keeping with international norms. In his "statement" of 2 February before the Washington Conference's Far Eastern Committee, Shidehara warned against questioning the legality of international treaties lightly: "If it should once be recognized that rights solemnly granted by treaty may be revoked at any time on the ground that they were conceded against the spontaneous will of the grantor, an exceedingly dangerous precedent will be established, with far-reaching consequences upon the stability of the existing international relations in Asia, in Europe and everywhere."[479]

Shidehara met the argument of the Chinese side—namely, that the treaty violated the principles of sovereignty and independence that had been adopted as a basis for the Conference proceedings—with the reminder that, as the Conference had acknowledged at various junctures, territorial or other "concessions" which China had granted *ex contractu*, in the course of exercising its sovereign rights, could not be seen as "inconsistent with her sovereignty and independence." To the surprise of the conference participants Shidehara ended his "more or less academic discussion" of the Twenty-One Demands by announcing that Japan would withdraw from Shandong. It was not the work of the conference, Shidehara maintained, to allow old disputes to take on new life. The official announcement of 2 February comprised three sections. The first section was aimed at regulating the "right of option" for investors in Chinese enterprises through the newly formed International Financial Consortium. Japan was willing to renounce certain loans affecting southern Manchuria as well as "priority purchase rights" for Japanese capital investors in favor of opening things up, through a consortium of this type, to more multilaterally oriented financial projects. The second section addressed Japan's decision not to insist on former requests for giving priority employment to Japanese financial and military advisors, or to police and political advisors. And thirdly the complete abandonment of group V of the Twenty-One Demands was announced.[480] In addition, although Japan had at Versailles been given the right to take over the former German lease of Qingdao (Tsingtao) on the coast of Shandong Province, the administration of this port city and the surrounding region was now to be fully restored to China.[481]

In his detailed statement of response made the next day,[482] Chinese delegate Wang Zhengting (C. T. Wang) expressed himself positively in regard to each of the three sections that Shidehara had outlined, but nevertheless indicated his regret that the Japanese government had not likewise renounced the remaining "demands" presented in 1915. He took up Shidehara's formulation that a total abrogation of the treaty accords would create a dangerous precedent with wide-ranging consequences for the stability of currently existing international relations, and countered this claim by saying that an even more dangerous precedent would be created if a nation were given the right to extract concessions from a friendly but militarily weaker nation without respect for the principle of *quid pro quo*.

According to Wang Zhengting, the American government was said to have made clear—and he cited the exact wording—in a diplomatic note (13 May

1915) sent to *both* Asian governments that it would not countenance a diminution of the treaty rights of the United States and its residents in China, or any diminution of the territorial integrity of the Republic of China or of the "Open Door policy."

From the fact that this note was addressed to both treaty partners, it could at least be concluded that the American government was not sure if China had concluded the accords in concert with Japan or had been coerced by Japan to accept them. According to Wang, "in cognizance of its obligations vis-à-vis the other powers," the Chinese government had immediately after the signing of the Twenty-One Demands given out a formal statement in which it "protested [the 1915 accord with Japan] . . . and declined to take responsibility for the eventual impairment of existing treaties with other powers."[483] The Chinese delegate was still at this juncture eloquently advocating the "abrogation" of the Sino-Japanese treaties and of the exchange of notes of 25 May 1915.[484] Perhaps he had not quite grasped the subtle implications and true significance of Shidehara's arguments.

Then on the same day (3 February), U.S. Secretary of State Hughes produced a statement in which he repeated once again the wording of the American note of 13 May 1915, making no reference, however, to his predecessor's deliberation. He formally repeated once more the rights no longer to be retained by Japan and then, with regard to those rights which remained, he confirmed that the American government did not see these as "exclusive rights" that would possibly contradict the American point of view:

> The Chinese Government granted the Japanese subjects the right to lease land for building purposes in South Manchuria and to engage in any kind of business and manufacture there, and to enter into joint undertakings with Chinese citizens in agricultural and similar industries in Eastern Inner Mongolia. With respect to this grant, the Government of the United States will, of course, regard it as not intended to be exclusive, and, as in the past, will claim from the Chinese Government for American citizens the benefits accruing to them by virtue of the most favored nation clauses in the treaties between the United States and China.[485]

Following Hughes's presentation, the Chinese showed themselves willing to give up previous objections, and on 4 February 1922 the first Sino-Japanese agreement was signed. The Nine Power Treaty, which was also signed on the same day and has been called "the culmination of nearly a century of American policy in the Far East," would guarantee China's security as Japan, Great Britain, the United States, France, Italy, Belgium, the Netherlands, and Portugal committed themselves to respect Chinese independence and sovereignty as well as the principle of "equality of business opportunity, in all regions of China, for all states pursuing trade with China" (applying the treaty's "most favored nation clause").[486] In the Nine Power Treaty the national unity of China as a sovereign state and, "in contradistinction to the vague enunciations of the prewar accords among the great powers, the principle of the 'Open Door' in China was *for the first time*, in an agreement with the Chinese, *clearly* put into writing [for future reference]."[487] Thus "finally, at Washington China received the satisfaction she had failed to obtain at Versailles."[488] In 1925 Germany was urged by the United States to join its name to this treaty. Although it appears that the German government was at first favorably disposed, for various reasons, among them vehement protests by the Chinese,[489] the German participation was never brought to fruition.[490]

In the Nine Power Treaty and in the Sino-Japanese Agreement of 4 February 1922, Shidehara had approved a broad retraction of what remained of the Twenty-One Demands. In this context American Secretary of State Henry L. Stimson would later (in 1936) identify Shidehara as a man "well known for his enlightened and liberal policies in foreign affairs and particularly towards China."[491] On 6 February the Five Power Naval Treaty was signed among the four principal powers and Italy.

Shidehara's influence was evident during each phase of the Washington negotiations. In the negotiating process he in no way slighted Japanese interests and neglected no opportunity to assure the Western powers of Japan's peaceful intentions and to discuss and agree upon compromises that were not inconsistent with his country's long-term interests. The earlier cited American scholar and writer Raymond Leslie Buell also saw the Japanese negotiating policy in a positive light: "The policy of the Japanese Delegation was consistently successful. That policy was first, to make impossible the military intervention of any western power in the Orient. Secondly, it was to prevent the diplomatic intervention of the Western World in the suzerainty Japan has attempted to set up on the Asiatic mainland."[492]

H. G. Wells, who had left his native England to report at first hand on the historic proceedings in the American capital, assessed the Japanese negotiating strategy and the Washington Conference as follows:

If there is one thing to be noted more than another about the work that has led up to this settlement it is the adaptability, the intelligent and sympathetic understanding shown by Japan in these transactions. The Japanese seem to be the most flexible minded of peoples. They win my respect more and more. In the days of imperialistic competition they stiffened to a conscientious selfishness and a splendid fighting energy. Now that a new spirit of discussion, compromise and the desire for brotherhood spreads about the world, they catch the new note and they sound it with obvious sincerity and good will. . . The idea of them as of a people insanely patriotic, patriotically subtle and treacherous, mysterious and mentally inaccessible has been largely dispelled. I myself have tried that view over in my mind and dismissed it, and multitudes of the commonplace men have gone through the same experience here. Our Western world, I am convinced, can work with the Japanese and understand and trust them.[493]

This assessment was no doubt an appraisal and acknowledgment of Shidehara and his superb negotiating style, moral purpose, and sense of direction. For Peter Duus, the Washington system and its agreements reflected acknowledgement by the Japanese—and no doubt the other participants as well—that peacefully oriented policies in international affairs were possible and worth striving for, more so since the alternative would be an extremely "costly and purposeless arms race. Further territorial expansion on the continent was no longer a realistic option, and it made more sense to defend Japan's national security . . . through a peaceful collective security arrangement."[494] Wilhelm Solf's assessment that the Washington Conference meant for Japan "in relation to the other great powers . . . a back-slide in terms of power politics" seems, from this point of view, shortsighted and ill informed.[495] Not only had the Versailles peace arrangements with the founding of the League of Nations for the first time brought into play some of the basic tenets for a functioning system of collective security, in Washington genuine disarmament measures were agreed upon according to which warships were scrapped and weapons limitations adhered to—if only for a time.

Thoughtful observers at the time, like K. K. Kawakami, nonetheless urged sober circumspection:

Japan has gone home from the Washington Conference on probation. Although she made a fairly good impression at the Conference, that impression is, as I see it, neither profound nor durable. What America and Europe will really think of her will depend upon what she does in China and Siberia in the coming few years.[496]

Kawakami's hopes showed some promise of fulfillment. And the main bearer of this hope for a solid and realistic peace policy in the Far East was undoubtedly Shidehara. He embodied what Kawakami was asking of Japan, if its political morality was meant to persist in concert with the other powers. The young nation's liberal credo hung in the balance. Yet a comparison like the following by Kawakami may put an interesting light on the situation: "Would it not have been embarrassing to the United States, had Japan proposed, for instance, that an international conference be convened at Tokyo to discuss Near Western and Caribbean Problems, the agenda of which might include such matters as foreign troops in Haiti and Puerto Rico, the territorial and administrative integrity of the West Indies, and the open door and equal opportunity in Mexico?"[497] One thing, however, seemed clear:

[T]he old framework of imperialist diplomacy was no longer adequate for reconciling Japanese interests and those of other countries . . . they were willing to work together with other countries to develop new rules of the game.[498]

One of these new rules was collective security, a new concept that had been developed following the failure of the Hague Peace Conferences and during the First World War. Together with the objectives discussed at The Hague (i.e., disarmament and binding international jurisdiction), this concept was to gain in importance in the interwar period.

The conclusion of the Washington treaties and the League covenant, however, did not yet bring about the ultimate renunciation of the culture of militarism. Some of the leading military figures in Japan harbored the feeling that peace would not last and that the time at hand should be utilized "to prepare the country, internally and externally, for a global conflict that was sure to come in the long run."[499]

Nevertheless, under the cabinet of Katō Tomosaburō (1861–1923), a navy admiral of the old school who—having been the formal head of the negotiating team in Washington—became prime minister, began a series of cuts in the Japanese military budget, from 39 percent of the government budget in 1919 to an average 16 percent between 1923 and 1931. In 1924–1925 the Kenseikai cabinet of Prime Minister Katō Kōmei reduced the army by four divisions or about thirty-five thousand men including several thousand officers.[500] The economic effects of the Japanese arms reduction policy were positive, removing from the population the burden of the extraordinarily high taxes to support the military budget, such as had existed during the war and even for some time after the war had already ended: "Between 1917 and 1921, Japan's average military expenditure in relation to its total budget was 43.5 percent, and this amounted to 7.72 percent of the total national income. The respective figures were 23 percent and 2.26 percent for the United States and 22.6 percent and 3.3 percent for Britain."[501]

The figures make clear that the armaments expenditures weighed much more heavily on the Japanese population than on that of the United States or Great Britain: "In this situation, Shidehara's successful conclusion of the Washington Treaty was more than welcome to Japan."[502] Japan's expectations were above all else economic. With these treaties a new era in international relations was to be initiated and the relationship to the United States of America could be placed on a new foundation of mutual respect, trust, and cooperation.[503]

Successive cabinets, irrespective of their party affiliations, adhered to the agreements resulting from the Washington Conference.[504] In Takemoto's view, the positive results of the Washington Conference—and later the 1930

London Naval Conference—were due to the successful Shidehara diplo-macy.[505] With regard to the question of Chinese customs and trade autonomy, the nine powers had agreed in Washington to convene, in the near future, a conference to consider a further revision of the still extant customs accords and the revision of the so-called unequal treaties affecting China.[506]

Shidehara, the cosmopolitan, had by now spent nearly ten years abroad when he returned to Japan in 1922.[507] His untiring advocacy of the Washing-ton Conference's objectives had found at last recognition. Many diplomats "remembered his heroic efforts."[508] Due to the physical exertion during the conference, Shidehara's health had visibly suffered and President Harding, as a token of his concern, had sent him a bouquet of flowers at the beginning of December while he was bedridden and recovering.[509] His colleagues at the em-bassy advised him to return to Japan to take a respite. Shidehara acknowledged the need for a change of pace and asked the foreign ministry for a furlough, which was granted him on 12 March. On 27 March he left Washington and after a land journey across the American continent sailed on 8 April for Kobe from San Francisco on the *Korea Maru*. The voyage lasted two weeks.

NOTES

1. E. H. Norman, *Soldier and Peasant in Japan: The Origins of Conscription* (Westport, Conn.: Greenwood Press, 1973) (orig. 1943], 47: "The evil genius behind Japan's militarism and black reaction, Field Marshal Yamagata, openly stated that the purpose for the revision and extension of conscription in 1883, with the accompany-ing enormous increase in military and naval expenditure, was a preparation for war on the continent."

2. William Franklin Sands, *Undiplomatic Memories (The Far East 1896–1904)* (New York: McGraw-Hill [Whittlesey House], 1930), 7–8.

3. Takemoto, *Failure of Liberalism in Japan*, 7, 166, 202–4, 361; Fukase Ta-dakazu, "Shidehara Kijūrō no gunshuku heiwa shisō to jikkō" (Shidehara Kijūrō's thought and actions regarding disarmament and peace), in Ashibe Nobuyoshi (ed.), *Nihon kokukempō no riron—Satō Isao sensei koki kinen* (Foundations of the Japa-nese Constitution—Memorial Edition for Satō Isao on his 70th Birthday) (Tokyo: Yūhikaku, 1986), 74–114.

4. Bamba, *op. cit.,* 7; Fairbank, Reischauer, and Craig, *East Asia—The Modern Transformation*, 371, 584.

5. This term refers to the total corpus of new rules, resulting from the Versailles and Washington conferences, which defined the framework for international rela-tions in both East and West in the interwar period, with the aim of securing a durable peace.

6. See, for example, Ian Nish, "Japan's Policies Toward Britain," in James Wil-liam Morley (ed.), *Japan's Foreign Policy, 1868–1941—A Research Guide* (New York

and London: Columbia University Press, 1974), 214, where he says, "Japan and Britain were united in emphasizing the need for peace and disarmament in the world at large." Nevertheless, writes Nish: "[T]hey were often at cross-purposes in China" (*ibid.*)

7. Lawrence Battistini, *Japan and America—An Objective and Constructive Account of Japanese-American Relations from Earliest Times to the Present* (Tokyo: Kenkyūsha, 1953), 89.

8. For Shidehara's biography, see Bamba, *op. cit.*, 137–81, and also Takemoto, *op. cit.*, 7–12.

9. On the initiative of Alexander II delegates of fifteen European states came together in Brussels on 27 July 1874 "to examine the draft of an international agreement concerning the laws and customs of war submitted to them by the Russian Government. The Conference adopted the draft with minor alterations. However, since not all the governments were willing to accept it as a binding convention it was not ratified." International Humanitarian Law—Treaties and Documents, www.icrc .org/ihl.nsf/INTRO/135?OpenDocument

10. Peter Enderlein, in his presentation on "Moralkunde-Schulbüchern" (ethics textbooks used in schools) before the German East Asia Society Tokyo (Ostasiatische Gesellschaft—OAG) in December 1994, very observantly detailed the process by which new textbooks were systematically introduced from Western school systems and how their contents were at first—and indeed just as thoroughly and systematically as in the traditional method of instruction—simply memorized.

11. According to Takemoto, papers documenting the family tree were unfortunately destroyed by a flood (*Failure of Liberalism in Japan*, 7).

12. This refers to a specially trimmed plait of hair the shape of which reminded one of the bamboo whisks used to prepare tea during a tea ceremony.

13. Shidehara Kijūrō, "Watakushi no yōshō jidai" (The era of my childhood), *Yomiuri shimbun gakkōban* (Yomiuri Newspaper School Edition), 27 November 1950.

14. *Ibid.*

15. Bamba, *op. cit.*, 142. Among other things, schoolchildren learned that in the world there were five "races": the Asiatic, the Malay, the European, the American, and the African.

16. *Ibid.*, 143.

17. Takemoto, *op. cit.*, 7–8.

18. Shidehara Heiwa Zaidan (ed.), *Shidehara Kijūrō* (Tokyo: Dainippon Hōrei Insatsu, 1955), 18.

19. Shidehara Kijūrō, "Watakushi no yōshō jidai."

20. "Taira Shidehara (1870–1953) . . . was a historian specialized in Japan, Ryūkyū, Formosa and Korea. As to Korea, he was one of the Japanese pioneers of the study of its history." Quoted from Enoki Kazuo, "Dr. G.E. Morrison and the Tōyō Bunko—In Celebration of the Fiftieth Anniversary of the Transfer of Dr. G.E. Morrison Library to Baron Hisaya Iwasaki (1917–1967)," *East Asian Cultural Studies* VII, nos. 1–4 (March 1968): 41.

21. Hozumi Nobushige had studied in England, under Prof. James Bryce and other jurists, and in Berlin, and became an "English barrister of the Middle Temple." See Arthur Taylor von Mehren, *Law in Japan* (Cambridge, Mass.: Harvard Univer-

sity Press, 1963), 30. According to Guntram Rahn, Hozumi represented *bürgerlich-bürokratische* (urban-bureaucratic) points of view (*Rechtsdenken und Rechtsauffassung in Japan* [Legal Thought and Legal Interpretation in Japan] [München: C. H. Beck, 1990], 106).

22. Paul Hibbert Clyde, *The Far East—A History of the Impact of the West on Eastern Asia* (Englewood Cliffs, N.J.: Prentice-Hall, 1958), 306.

23. Rolf-Harald Wippich gives various examples and documentary sources ("Deutschland und Japan am Scheideweg—Eine Skizze des deutsch-japanischen Verhältnisses in den 1890er Jahren" [Germany and Japan at Crossroads—A Sketch of German-Japanese Relations in the 1890s], in Josef Kreiner [ed.], *Japan und die Mittelmächte im Ersten Weltkrieg und in den zwanziger Jahren* [Japan and the Middle Powers in the First World War and in the 1920s] [Bonn: Bouvier Verlag Herbert Grundmann, 1986], 47). He shows that it was above all the "Progressive Party" (Shimpotō) that was especially conspicuous with its "sharp attacks against the German Reich."

24. Mutsu Munemitsu, in his memoirs, *Kenkenroku*, presents in detail and with the greatest possible objectivity the prehistory and the main events and significance of the first Sino-Japanese War.

25. Sands, *Undiplomatic Memories*, 197.

26. It was above all the German colonial policy of the 1880s that, in addition to England's status as a world power, strengthened Japan's ambition to assert what it thought were legitimate interests in East Asia.

27. The text of the protocol, which consisted of four publicly announced and two secret articles, is reproduced in George Alexander Lensen, *Balance of Intrigue—International Rivalry in Korea and Manchuria, 1884–1899*, vol. II (Tallahassee: University Press of Florida, 1982), 633–34.

28. *Ibid.*, 811, gives the full text of the protocol.

29. This memorandum (14 May 1896) was signed by Komura Jutarō and the Russian diplomat Veber (usually spelled "Waeber" in non-Russian documents). Apparently the Russian side was not interested in publishing the agreement and did not take the Japanese side seriously. See, for example, the telegram (5 June 1896) from the Japanese Foreign Minister Saionji Kinmochi to the Japanese ambassador in Moscow Nishi Tokujirō: "Ask Russian Government whether they intend to publish or keep secret memorandum signed by Komura and Waeber on 5/14. Reply at once." On 10 June Nishi cabled back: "Russian Government intend to keep memorandum in secret."

30. William Franklin Sands, *At the Court of Korea: Undiplomatic memories*, introduction by Christopher Hitchens (London: Century, 1987), 52.

31. See the lead article in *The Kobe Weekly Chronicle*, 6 November 1897, 373–74: "There is no suggestion of any charge of incapacity against Mr. McLeavy Brown, who by universal consent has managed the financial affairs of Korea more satisfactorily, succeeding in the course of his brief tenure of office in paying off two-thirds of the Japanese loan of three million yen, in checking misappropriation of funds, and in putting the finances of the kingdom in such order as has never previously been known in Korea in modern times . . . Japan is fully aware how rapidly Korea is becoming a Russian province. . . . The Korean question is rapidly approaching a crisis—more rapidly . . . than Count Okuma believed when a few weeks ago he took up a determined attitude

respecting the threatened annexation of Hawaii." See also the lead article in *The Kobe Weekly Chronicle* of 15 January 1898, 21: "Mr. McLeavy Brown has had thirty-five years' experience of the Far East, and is besides an accomplished Chinese scholar, reading Chinese characters as well as understanding the spoken language. The chief members of foreign staff under him are also Chinese scholars, and have been resident for many years in the East. On the other hand, neither M. Kuril Alexieff nor his foreign assistant knew a single Chinese character, and their experience in the Far East has been *nil*. They are consequently entirely in the hands of Russian-speaking Koreans."

32. Clyde, *The Far East*, 315. See also Sands, who, however, only mentions "nine British cruisers [which] gathered quietly in Chemulpo harbour," adding that "McLeavy Brown shipped all the customs funds to Shanghai on deposit, to be held there until the question should be decided" (*At the Court of Korea*, 52).

33. Interestingly, Ian Nish relates that in 1900, when "the Koreans through their British adviser, [Sir] John McLeavy Brown, asked for a substantial loan, either 1,000,000 or 500,000, [Foreign Minister] Aoki [Shūzō] went out of his way to assist them through financial circles in Japan. . . . Eventually the amount was granted" (*Japanese Foreign Policy*, 55).

34. In this context the following assessment of *The New York Times* (24 April 1898) in regard to the "partition of China" may be noted: "In the event of a final and definite partition of China, Japan had always intended to take over the Korean Peninsula as her share of the spoils. This fact is well known in St. Petersburg."

35. *Shidehara Kijūrō*, 29–30. According to Takemoto, Ishii Kikujirō was also of the view that it was more advantageous for Japan to expand international trade and cooperation with other countries than to build a great Japanese overseas empire (*op. cit.,* 8).

36. Ishii Kikujirō, *Diplomatic Commentaries* (Baltimore and London, 1936), 34. See also 61, 68f, 81, 85f, 129, 169–72, 268f, and 315; and the review of Ishii's work by George H. Blakeslee, in *Political Science Quarterly* LII, no. 4 (December 1937): 599–602: "Japanese militarism is frequently condemned throughout the book . . . including the expedition to Siberia . . . (viii), the Nishihara loans (vii), and Tanaka's Tsinan expedition in 1927 (viii)."

37. Ishii, *op. cit.,* 269–70.

38. Ku Dae-Yeol, *Korea under Colonialism: The March First Movement and Anglo-Japanese Relations* (Seoul: Royal Asiatic Society, Korea Branch, 1985), 18ff. Although voices of criticism against Japan increased after 1905, the British minister in Seoul, John Newell Jordan, in the first half of 1905 "rejected such reproaches as 'exaggeration,' in part because her [Japan's] soldiers were regarded as 'a model of restraint' and the Japanese were undertaking 'the stupendous task' of reforms" (*ibid.,* 19).

39. Sands, *At the Court of Korea*, gives this impression.

40. Sŏ Chaep'il had, after his participation, together with Kim Ok-kyun, in a *coup d'état* in 1884 against the Min clan of Korea's queen, spent twelve years in American exile. He returned to Korea in 1896 as an American citizen with the name Philip Jaisohn and established the "Independence Club" in the spring of 1896, and the first number of its journal *Tongnip* (The Independent, which always had at least one English-language page) came out on 7 April. The organization held a formal founding ceremony on 2 July. See Ku Dae-Yeol, *op. cit.,* 1; also see Se Eung Oh, *Dr. Philip*

Jaisohn's Reform Movement 1896–1898—A Critical Appraisal of the Independence Club (Lanham, Md.: University Press of America, 1995), 20.

41. The Independence Club was composed, in large part, of groupings of a sort which make it possible, in one scholar's view, to characterize the Independence Club as "a Confucianist reform party, a persuasion that evolved out of the 'Eastern ways, Western machines' school of thought" (Ki-Baik Lee, *A New History of Korea*, trans. Edward W. Wagner with Edward J. Shultz [Seoul: Ilchokak Publishers, 1984], 302). An outward manifestation of the movement was the building of a so-called Independence Gate, begun in November 1896. In May of the following year, the "Independence Hall" was completed.

42. Sands recounts a conversation with Itō Hirobumi in which the count, who was at the time governor in Korea, told him about his proposal, "sanctioned by the emperor of Japan, to form a close alliance between Japan, China, and Korea. It seemed to mean a union of the Far East, possibly a federation in which Japan having been more successful than the others in assimilating Western knowledge, should guide them both in general policy and in practical Western training" (*At the Court of Korea*, 207–8).

43. I am grateful to Linda Kwan of Canada, a distant relative of Jordan, for providing me, in a letter of 28 January 2005, with the name of Sir John Jordan's sister Anna Sophia.

44. See "The Independent" of 20 July 1899, stating that the "Koreans may be said to be divided into two sections—pro-Russian and pro-Japanese. Those living close to the Russian quarter imitate the Russian in every possible way; while those living near the Japanese quarter prefer Japanese models. Sometimes the youngsters of the two sections engage in sham fights, not infrequently leading to serious disturbances."

45. News article in *The Kobe Weekly Chronicle*, 31 July 1897, 90. See also Takashi Hatada, *A History of Korea*, trans. and ed. Warren W. Smith Jr. and Benjamin H. Hazard (Santa Barbara, Calif.: ABC-Clio, 1969), 93.

46. Lead editorial in *Kobe Weekly Chronicle*, 16 October 1897, 310.

47. *North-China Herald*, 25 April 1898.

48. Hayashi Tadasu was Japan's foreign minister between 1891 and 1895, and then served as minister to China (1895–1896) and Russia (1897–1899). As head of legation in St. Petersburg he was given the task of taking part in the Hague peace conference of 1899. Afterward he served as head of legation in London until 1906.

49. After the death of Prince A. B. Lobanov-Rostovsky, who was Russia's foreign minister in 1895–1896, Count Muraviev (usually at the time spelled "Muravieff" in non-Russian communications) took over the foreign ministry. Both of these men distinguished themselves, according to one writer, by their "limited intellects and their crass ignorance of some matters (especially the Far East)" (Baron S. A. Korff, *Russia's Foreign Relations During the Last Half Century* (New York: MacMillan, 1922], 3). (Muraviev was foreign minister from the end of 1896 to 1900.)

50. After 1899 Japan saw itself obliged to try to negotiate simultaneously with Russia and Great Britain: "Japan set out to find a friend and an ally. . . . Very carefully did she begin to study the complex situation in Europe, testing the relative strength of the powers, learning their history, studying their mutual relations and trying to find

out future possibilities. . . . In 1901 she began negotiations with England and Russia simultaneously; Hayashi had talks with Landsdowne and Ito came to St. Petersburg to consult with Witte and Lamsdorff" (Korff, *op. cit.*, 78–79).

51. Gaikō Shiryōkan, MT 2.1.1.2, vol. III, 957.

52. *Ibid.*, 955–56.

53. *Ibid.*, 966.

54. Korff, *op. cit.*, 63f, writes: "The fatal years of 1897–1899 saw . . . Germany . . . land a force [late in 1897] on the Kwantung Peninsula, without any intention of leaving it there, but simply for the purpose of egging Russia on . . . Count Muraviev . . . caught at the bait . . . to the great satisfaction of Berlin . . . Germany had thus scored a brilliant victory. The policy of territorial aggression was well started, but the initiative and moral responsibility fell entirely upon Russia."

55. Cable from Hayashi to Nishi in Tokyo, 28 January 1898. (Gaikō Shiryōkan, MT 2.1.1.2, vol. III, 990.)

56. After fleeing to the Russian legation in February 1896, the Korean king ordered the execution of several ministers, reported in a letter of 15 February from Saionji to Nishi: "The Corean King took refuge in the Russian Legation . . . [and] he caused the execution of several of his ministers of state." (Gaikō Shiryōkan, MT 2.1.1.2, 15.) The Japanese dispatched numerous inquiries to the Russian government, always requesting it to exert a moderating influence on the Korean government. In one such message, for example, it was stated: "It is the custom in Corea for those in power to inflict most cruel punishment on their political opponents, thereby keeping alive a revengeful spirit which is detrimental to national tranquility. Japanese Government therefore propose to Russian Government in the interest of all that Japan and Russia should instruct their respective representatives at Seoul to counsel Corean Government not to inflict such inhuman penalties" (Saionji to Hayashi Tadasu in St. Petersburg and Komura Jutarô in Seoul, telegram no. 31 of 25 February 1896, Gaikō Shiryōkan, MT 2.1.1.2, 72–74). Mikhail [K]hitrovo replied on 2 March: "The Representatives of Russia and Japan shall aim at recommending to the King moderate Ministers and at inducing him to show clemency towards his subjects" (Gaikō Shiryōkan, MT 2.1.1.2, 104–5).

57. Communication (14 March 1898 from Nishi to Hayashi. Gaikō Shiryōkan, MT 2.1.1.2, vol. III, 1063–64. The reason was said to be that "both the Military system and financial affairs . . . through the efforts of the military officers and financial adviser specially dispatched for the purpose, [have] been brought to a condition approaching perfection . . . King of Korea intends to express his thanks personally to Emperor of Russia by dispatching special envoy for the purpose" (*ibid*).

58. *Ibid.*

59. Dülffer, *Regeln gegen den Krieg?*, 22–23.

60. *Ibid.*, 23. It would be interesting to investigate whether such announcements could have been the reason for the Korean refusal of foreign military assistance, even though this seems unlikely.

61. Gaikō Shiryōkan, MT 2.1.1.2, vol. III, 1144–47.

62. *Ibid.*, 1149.

63. Dülffer, *op. cit.*, 19.

64. See DeArmond Davis, *The United States and the First Hague Peace Conference*, 43–45, and, by the same author, *The United States and the Second Hague Peace Conference*, 4–5. For some of the dates and other sources, see also Dülffer, *Regeln gegen den Krieg?*, 22–23.

65. Sands, *Undiplomatic Memories* (1930), 154.

66. *Kobe Weekly Chronicle*, 2 August 1899.

67. On 5 July the *Kobe Weekly Chronicle* (549) carried this Reuter dispatch of 27 June from London: "The German delegates to The Hague have definitely opposed the Russian proposal for suspension of armaments."

68. The Anglo-Russian Agreement, *The North-China Herald*, 8 May 1899.

69. Motono had studied in France and served as Japan's envoy in Belgium (1898–1901), France (1901–1906), and Russia (1906–1916) before serving as foreign minister in the Terauchi cabinet between May 1916 and July 1918.

70. Motono to Ōkuma, Gaikō Shiryōkan, MT 2.4.1.2, vol. I. A segment of the original document of Count Muraviev (12 August 1898) and of the official note are also found in the Ministry of Foreign Affairs archives in Tokyo (Gaikō Shiryōkan, MT 2.4.1.2, vol. II).

71. Quote in DeArmond Davis, *The United States and the First Hague Peace Conference*, 37 and 36ff; see also Eyffinger, *The Peace Palace: Residence for Justice—Domicile of Learning*, 9ff.

72. Since a "shortcut" to an international order based on ethical and legal norms did not seem feasible at the time, Fukuzawa Yukichi's "departure from Asia" (*datsua ron*) seemed to be the sole possible objective attainable and in keeping with *realpolitik*. See Miwa Kimitada, "Fukuzawa Yukichi's 'Departure from Asia'" (*Monumenta Nipponica* Special Issue, Centennial of the Meiji Restoration), ed. Edmund Skrzypczak (Tokyo: Sophia University and Charles E. Tuttle, 1968), 1–26.

73. Walther Schücking, "Die Annäherung der Menschenrassen durch das Völkerrecht" (The mutual approach of the human races through international law), lecture given at the First Universal Races Congress, London, 26–29 July 1911, in Walther Schücking, *Der Bund der Völker—Studien und Vorträge zum organisatorischen Pazifismus* (The League of Nations—studies and lectures on organizational pacifism) (Leipzig: Der Neue Geist Verlag, 1918), 60. Japan's membership in the comity of nations (*Völkerrechtsgemeinschaft*) was finally sealed and formalized through the treaties of 17 July and 4 August 1899. "The new treaty [of 17 August 1899 with England] opened for Japan a new era in its foreign relations because it articulated for the first time Japan's full and legitimate accession to the family of civilized powers (*Kulturmächte*)." Letter of envoy Aoki Shūzō (18 July 1898) to Lord Kimberley, quoted in Alexander von Siebold, *op. cit.*, 47–48. See also Gabriele Schirbel, *Strukturen des Internationalismus—First Universal Races Congress, London 1911*, Teil I, Studien zur Friedensforschung, Band 3 (Münster and Hamburg: Lit Verlag, 1991).

74. Miwa Kimitada, "Colonial Theories and Practices in Prewar Japan," in Howes (ed.), *Nitobe Inazō*, 159.

75. "German Government was disposed to take into favourable consideration the proposal of the Emperor of Russia. . . . Report which appeared in some newspapers that Russian Government consulted German Government before sending out circular,

seems pretty well borne out by evidence" (Hayashi to Ōkuma, 1 September 1898, Gaikō Shiryōkan, MT 2.4.1.2, vol. I).

76. Motono to Ōkuma, Gaikō Shiryōkan, MT 2.4.1.2, vol. I.

77. Eyffinger, *The Peace Palace. Residence for Justice—Domicile of Learning*, 9.

78. *Ibid.*, 10.

79. Quoted in Eyffinger, *The Peace Palace: Residence for Justice—Domicile of Learning*, 17.

80. Quoted in Eyffinger, *The Peace Palace: Residence for Justice—Domicile of Learning*, 17.

81. Motono to Ōkuma, Gaikō Shiryōkan, MT 2.4.1.2, vol. I (emphasis added).

82. Hayashi to Aoki, 31 March 1899, *Gaikō shiryōkan*, MT 2.4.1.2, vol. II.

83. "It was largely because Russia was the first of the Great Powers to find that she was being crippled by the growing armaments burden" (cited in Hinsley, *op. cit.* [1963], 276).

84. *The Times*, 12 December 1898. Copy in the Gaikō Shiryōkan, MT 2.4.1.2, vol. I.

85. Motono to Ōkuma, 1 September 1899, Gaikō Shiryōkan, MT 2.4.1.2, vol. I.

86. At the Brussels Conference on 27 July 1874 an international agreement concerning the laws and customs of war had been organized at his initiative. The predecessor of Alexander II already, Alexander I "in the midst of the Napoleonic turmoil had made the suggestion that after the general war and Napoleon's downfall the nations of Europe should unite in a treaty which would determine 'the positive rights of nations . . . [and] assert the obligation of never beginning war until all resources which the mediation of a third party could offer have been exhausted.' On such principles, he maintained, one could proceed to a general pacification, and give birth to a league of which the stipulation would form 'a new code of the law of nations'" (Eyffinger, *The Peace Palace. Residence for Justice—Domicile of Learning*, 10–11).

87. William L. Langer, *The Diplomacy of Imperialism, 1890–1902* (New York: Alfred A. Knopf, 1972), 582.

88. Uhlig, *Die Interparlamentarische Union*, 243; see also 233ff on the Budapest conference.

89. *The Times*, 12 December 1898, documents, Gaikō Shiryōkan, MT 2.4.1.2, vol. I. The article continues: "[A]bout this new gun . . . it is even said that the French military authorities refused to let their Russian allies have it unless they consented to be supplied from French Government factories only at the end of three years."

90. The treaty was concluded on the Japanese side by Inagaki Manjirō and stipulated that "arbitration shall be binding."

91. The International Red Cross was established in 1864; in 1901 Dunant shared the first Nobel Peace Prize with Frédéric Passy.

92. On Bloch, see Peter van den Dungen, *The Making of Peace: Jean de Bloch and the First Hague Peace Conference* (Los Angeles: Center for the Study of Armament and Disarmament, California State University, 1983) (Occasional Papers Series, no. 12), which points to the strong influence Bloch had on the tsar.

93. Dülffer, *op. cit.*, 362n31.

94. "You are hereby authorized . . . to reply . . . in the following sense: The Government of His Majesty the Emperor of Japan do not fail to appreciate the humane motives and elevated sentiments which have inspired the proposal of the Imperial Russian Government, and, true to their own traditions and history, they cordially sympathize with the endeavor to secure the inestimable blessings of enduring peace. Wishing as far as possible, to contribute to the full realization of the high ideal which the Imperial Cabinet at St. Petersburg has placed before the world" (Gaikō Shiryōkan, MT 2.4.1.2, vol. I).

95. DeArmond Davis, *The United States and the First Hague Peace Conference*, 41.

96. Later, the Japanese proposed at the Versailles Peace Conference that a provision should be put into the League of Nations Covenant, for a three-months' moratorium before the imposition of court jurisdiction to arbitrate conflicts.

97. Aoki (1844–1914) became a viscount and served as deputy foreign minister (1886–1889), foreign minister (1889–1891 and 1898–1900), and minister in Berlin (1892–1897) and London (1894–1895). Ian Nish speaks in his work on the history of foreign policy (1869–1942) of the years from 1896 to 1901 as the "Aoki Period" (*Japanese Foreign Policy 1869–1942* [London, Henley, and Boston: Routledge & Kegan Paul, 1977], 44–58). Assisted by his Austrian wife, "Aoki was probably the most Europeanized among the prominent Meiji diplomats . . . a bold, independent thinker" (*ibid.*, 45).

98. Gaikō Shiryōkan, MT 2.4.1.2, vol. II. Of course, Tolstoy was in any case a widely read author and enjoyed a great following among Japanese intellectuals and students.

99. Together with Hayashi, the other Japanese delegates who took part in the first conference were Motono Ichirō, Uyehara M., and Sakamoto M. Later Ariga Nagao, a jurist and professor of international law at the Army and Navy Academy in Tokyo, also joined as an advisor. The chief delegate at the Second Hague Peace Conference, Tsuzuki Keiroku, a member of the cabinet of Yamagata Aritomo, resigned on 9 April 1899 as vice foreign minister and after that date no longer took part in the conference (*Kobe Weekly Chronicle*, 12 April 1899, 283). On 6 April, Hayashi inquired with Aoki whether Siebold could not participate for the Japanese as a delegate at The Hague and asked: "Would it not be of advantage to order me to join Japanese Delegates in peace conference to take advantage of the opportunity for promoting objects of your letter of January. Siebold" (MT 2.4.1.2, vol. II).

100. Gaikō Shiryōkan, MT 2.4.1.2, vol. II.

101. *Ibid.*

102. Telegram no. 34, Gaikō Shiryōkan, MT 2.4.1.2, vol. II.

103. Compare Schücking, *League of Nations*, 70: "The significance of the first Hague Conference lies not in the codification of the laws of land warfare [*ius in bello*], which was taken up there [as a matter for discussion], but in the establishment of the Permanent Court of Arbitration (Cour permanente d'arbitrage.)"

104. Frederick W. Holls, *The Peace Conference at The Hague*, 227–31; DeArmond Davis, *op. cit.*, 146–47; Dülffer, *op. cit.*, 90.

105. 28 May, Special Telegram no. 35, Gaikō Shiryōkan, MT 2.4.1.2, vol. II.

106. DeArmond Davis, *The United States and the First Hague Peace Conference*, 1.

107. See the historical account in Frederick W. Holls, *The Peace Conference at The Hague and Its Bearings on International Law and Policy* (New York: Macmillan, 1900), 231–36.

108. Holls, *op. cit.*, 231: "It formed from the first the keystone of the proposals formulated and presented on behalf of the United States."

109. *Autobiography of Andrew Dickson White* (New York: The Century, 1904), vol. II, 265.

110. Dülffer, *op. cit.*, 89.

111. Sugimura (1856–1938) was around 1894 chargé d'affaires in Seoul.

112. Gaikō Shiryōkan, MT 2.4.1.2, vol. II.

113. Hans Wehberg, *Die internationale Friedensbewegung* (The international peace movement), M. Gladbach, Volksvereinsverlag 1911 (Staatsbürger-Bibliothek H.22), 21. The Permanent Court of Arbitration in fact had no permanent abode until Andrew Carnegie donated the Hague Peace Palace, completed in 1913.

114. Gaikō Shiryōkan, MT 2.4.1.2, vol. II. The entire delegation was again on 9 June informed that there was "no particular objection on the part of the Japanese Government either to the Projects for mediation and arbitration, *provided all the principal Powers give their adhesion thereto*" (emphasis added).

115. DeArmond Davis, *op. cit.*, 165–67. As one critic later remarked, the "substantive provisions contained in the Arbitration Convention amount really to nothing, since everything in them which savoured of an obligatory character was omitted, in deference to the arguments of which the German delegation was the mouthpiece" (*ibid.*, 188). Already on 23 June, the German minister for foreign affairs had instructed the German delegation, if the conference was to continue with German participation and the arbitration treaty project be upheld in some moderate form, among other things, "omission of all references to obligatory arbitration" was a must. DeArmond Davis, *The United States and the Second Hague Peace Conference*, 31–32.

116. Brigitte Hamann, *Bertha von Suttner, a Life for Peace*, trans. Ann Dubsky, foreword by Irwin Abrams (Syracuse, N.Y.: Syracuse University Press, 1996), 151.

117. Gaikō Shiryōkan, MT 2.4.1.2, vol. II (my emphasis). An explanation for the imperial German government's self-assertiveness may be the expectation (by Germany) of a "German century" among the great powers. The archival materials of the Japanese Ministry of Foreign Affairs include reports by a certain Frederick Marshall, an informant who, similarly to Alexander von Siebold, compiled reports for the Japanese government. See, for example, his Report No. 266 of 7 January 1901 addressed to Katō (Kōmei): "[W]ithout counting the momentary successes of Holland and Portugal, or the fluctuating prosperities of Austria it may be said, in general terms, that the sixteenth century was the age of Spain and the seventeenth of France; that the eighteenth saw the commencement of the lead of England, which was developed in the nineteenth; *and now, with the twentieth, it seems to be the turn of Germany*" (Gaikō Shiryōkan, MT 1.6.3.5 [emphasis added]).

118. From the Japanese press (8 August 1899), cited in *The Kobe Weekly Chronicle*, 9 August 1899.

119. To be sure, as has already been remarked, Hayashi in St. Petersburg had already telegraphed Aoki on May 25: "The proceedings of the Conference are to be kept secret." This referred, however, not to Japanese public relations activities but to the conference itself, which was not open to the public.

120. *The Kobe Weekly Chronicle*, 28 June 1899, 521.

121. Sugimura to Aoki, 4 January 1900: "[A]ll the remaining powers signed up to 12. 31. [December 31] although some made reserves [*sic*]" (Gaikō Shiryōkan, MT 2.4.1.2, vol. VII). Of the eight volumes containing correspondence and documents from the First Hague Peace Conference, volumes III to VI were reserved primarily for printed documents.

122. Gaikō Shiryōkan, MT 2.4.1.2, vol. VII. The texts were reproduced in vol. VI.

123. Article 20 of the First Convention for the Peaceful Adjustment of International Differences of 29 July 1899. Quoted in Frederick W. Holls, *The Peace Conference at The Hague*, 393. Holls gives the texts of both conventions in English and the original French. Compare also Jürgen Schlochauer, "Ständiger Schiedshof" (Permanent Court of Arbitration), in *Wörterbuch des Völkerrechts* (Dictionary of International Law), vol. 3, 364–71.

124. On 26 November 1900 Foreign Minister Katō Takaaki inquired from Chinda Sutemi in The Hague whether government officials or diplomats were to be chosen as arbitrators. Chinda replied (27 November): "[A]mong arbitrators thus far designated are found 1 Minister of Justice, 4 Ex-Ministers of State, 3 professors, 1 [illegible], 1 Senator, 1 public prosecutor general etc." Thus both were considered possible. Three days later (30 November) Alexander von Siebold had also offered his services (Gaikō Shiryōkan, MT 2.4.1.3, vol. I). Sugimura (in St. Petersburg) to Katō (5 December). Siebold's letter containing the proposal was addressed to Inouye in Berlin. Since Siebold was already stationed in Europe, no special financial burden was to be incurred for Japan. There was, apparently, no stipulation whereby the number of arbitration judges which any given country could nominate would be restricted (Gaikō Shiryōkan, MT 2.4.1.3, vol. I).

125. Schücking, *League of Nations*, 69. Schücking argued that "a(n international) confederation under international law may be assumed wherever a majority of the states have created common organs" (of governance or adjudication). He uses the terms "Hague Confederation of Nations" (*Haager Staatenverband*) and "world league of nations" (*Weltstaatenbund*) when referring to the association of the Hague Conferences. As documented in an essay by Fritz Münch, similar ideas had been set forth also by a number of authors (for example Franz von Liszt), who had in the nineteenth century expounded the *genossenschaftlich* (cooperative-like) and thus league-like character of "international organizations" and were of the opinion that "the legal community of nations might be organized in a cooperative-like way as a *Staatenverband* (association of states) and might be strengthened as such as a result of recurring congresses" ("Walther Schücking [1875–1935], Völkerrechtler und Politiker, " in Ingeborg Schnack [ed.], *Marburger Gelehrte in der ersten Hälfte des 20. Jahrhunderts* [Marburg scholars in the first half of the twentieth century] [Marburg: Philipps-Universität Marbug, 1977], 473).

126. A good example is the Morris-Shidehara Memorandum of 1921 that he and former American ambassador in Japan Roland S. Morris worked out while Shidehara was ambassador in Washington.

127. Among them were Hamada Renjirō, Yabu Masaichi, Fujimoto Sōichi, and Zasui Sei.

128. On Katō, see Ian Nish, "Kato Takaaki, 1860–1929: Japanese Ambassador to London and Japanese Foreign Minister," in Hugh Cortazzi (ed.), *Britain and Japan. Biographical Portraits*, vol. IV (London: Japan Library, 2002), 14–27.

129. Nish characterizes Katō as being "a westernized Japanese, who spoke good English; a clear thinker with a direct manner" (*op. cit.,* 86).

130. Shidehara, *Gaikō gojūnen*, 245. Later, when he was prime minister after the Second World War, Shidehara liked to recite quotations from Shakespeare's works. His private secretary, Fukushima Shintarō, on the other hand was fond of quoting passages from Bunyan's *The Pilgrim's Progress*, and in such a way the two Anglophile diplomats took to "vying with one another" when it came to English recitation. (Fukushima entered the Ministry of Foreign Affairs in 1931.) Interview with Fukushima's widow in Tokyo, 7 May 1995.

131. This required, in the words of American publicist Raymond L. Bridgman, a kind of "world self-consciousness," since "joint action by the nations of the world would not be possible unless there were an identity in the world" greater than mere national self-consciousness. Quoted in Thomas Peyser, *Utopia and Cosmopolis: Globalization in the Era of American Literary Realism*, (Durham, N.C.: Duke University Press, 1998), viii, from Raymond L. Bridgman, *World Organization* (Boston: Ginn & Co., 1905). See also David S. Patterson, who quotes Bridgman as an early "example of an anti-imperialist whose enthusiasm for future international cooperation resulted in bold suggestions for creation of a new world order. As early as 1899 he had argued that the Hague Conference was but the first step in an inevitable trend toward a world constitution consisting of judicial, executive, and legislative branches . . . he hoped that the Hague Court would become a truly judicial body and that an executive agency would gradually evolve" (*Toward a Warless World: The Travail of the American Peace Movement 1887–1914* [Bloomington and London: Indiana University Press, 1976], 111–12).

132. According to *Gaikō gojūnen* (230), Shidehara reached Antwerp on 22 December.

133. Auguste Marie François Beernaert received the Nobel Peace Prize together with Baron d'Estournelles de Constant in 1909.

134. Philipp Zorn, *Deutschland und die beiden Haager Friedenskonferenzen* (Germany and the two Hague Peace Conferences) (Stuttgart and Berlin: Deutsche Verlags-Anstalt, 1920), 49; see also Korff, *Russia's Foreign Relations During the Last Half Century*, 79–80: "In February 1902 Komura, then minister of foreign affairs, had a talk with the German ambassador at Tokyo, and asked him if Germany would like to join, but the latter refused."

135. That is, calling for "retrenchment touching even the military establishment" (*Saionji-Harada Memoirs,* 82).

136. In the first years after the turn of the twentieth century Japan experienced a strong movement that bore the stamp of a socialist, and even more of Christian, pacifism. See John F. Howes, "Uchimura Kanzō: The Bible and War," in Bamba and Howes, *Pacifism in Japan*, 91–122.

137. Ueda Katsumi, "Tabata Shinobu: Defender of the Peace Constitution," in Bamba and Howes, *op. cit.*, 231.

138. Thus, for example, the court prevented a conflict in 1902 in the so-called California Church Property Conflict, and in 1903–1904 the conflict that had pitted Venezuela against Germany, England, and Italy was judicially settled through a decision of the Permanent Court of Arbitration. See Dülffer, *op. cit.*, 209ff.

139. Shidehara, *Gaikō gojūnen*, 5–9; *Shidehara Kijūrō*, 40–43. According to Takemoto, the incident in Pusan harbor stemmed from the misbehavior of a small naval unit that clearly acted without orders from superiors (*Failure of Liberalism in Japan*, 25). One might here give Shidehara some allowances: (1) he was still young; (2) he represented no "pacifism at any price;" (3) he was a loyal patriot; (4) in the absence of a higher legal resort the interest of the Japanese state took priority over other interests; (5) to have done nothing could be seen as being objectionable from a point of view of an "ethics of responsibility"; (6) Russia was in fact the aggressor having violated the agreement with Japan to withdraw its military from Manchuria; and (7) Russian telegraph stations in Newchwang and Yinkow had previously similarly obstructed the sending of Japanese telegraphic cables.

140. Gaimushō (ed.), *Komura gaikōshi* (A history of Komura diplomacy) (Tokyo: Hara Shobō, 1966), 384–85, cited in Takemoto, *op. cit.*, 25.

141. *Shidehara Kijūrō*, 50–53.

142. Shidehara Heiwa Bunko, *Shoka no Shidehara kan* (Various persons' views of Shidehara), unpublished, 277, cited in Bamba, *op. cit.*, 138.

143. Bamba, *op. cit.*, 139.

144. After the early development in the United States of a telegraphic cable system by Samuel F. B. Morse in the 1830s, the practical use of such a system spread at first in Europe and America. With the development of a special protective coating for the "wires," already in the 1840s some deep-sea telegraphic cables had been laid.

145. I am here largely following Inaba Chiharu, "International Telecommunications during the Russo-Japanese War—The Development of the Telegraphic Service between Europe and Japan and the Russian Interception of Japanese Telegrams," *Kenkyū kiyō* 32 (Tōyō Eiwa Jogakuin Tanki Daigaku 1993): 25–41. I thank A. M. Cohen for having brought this article to my attention.

146. Gaikō Shiryōkan, MT 3.6.11.1, vol. I. The Gaimushō archives contain also an inquiry about telegraphic matters (30 August 1873) from a Peruvian delegation in Tokyo, inquiries about telegraphic traffic regulations, and a list, dated 28 February 1872, of telegraph fees ("Tarif annexé à la convention internationale télégraphique" and "Règlement de service international"), which had been sent to the foreign diplomatic representations.

147. Correspondence, Gaikō Shiryōkan, 3.6.11.2, vol. III-1.

148. *The Times*, 24 May 1899, document, Gaikō Shiryōkan, 3.6.11.2, vol. III-1. Marcus Island is the easternmost of the Ogasawara Islands.

149. Komura to Tanabe, 21 December 1901, Gaikō Shiryōkan, 3.6.11.2, vol. III-1.

150. Komura to Tanabe in Niuchuang, 25 December 1901, Gaikō Shiryōkan, 3.6.11.2, vol. III-1.

151. Tanabe to Komura, Gaikō Shiryōkan, 3.6.11.2.-3-1.

152. Gaikō Shiryōkan, 3.6.11.2.-3-1.

153. *Ibid.*

154. *Ibid.*

155. "Communications intelligence work in the foreign ministry was the responsibility of the Cable Section (*Denshin-ka*)" (Jeffrey T. Richelson, *Foreign Intelligence Organizations* [Cambridge, Mass.: Ballinger, 1988], 253).

156. Denison was in the second half of the 1890s engaged as a facilitator for the sale to a Japanese firm of American concessions for the building of a railway line.

157. Saitō Hiros[h]i, *Japan's Policies and Purposes—Selection from Recent Addresses and Writings* (Boston: Marshall Jones Co., 1935), 179–89. Saitō had earlier won popularity as Japan's consul general in New York. "[H]e had unusual popularity for a Japanese" (*Saionji-Harada Memoirs*, 144n21), was designated by Shidehara to be the "right-hand man" to Wakatsuki Reijirō, the chief Japanese delegate at the London Naval Conference, and served as ambassador in The Hague before serving as ambassador in Washington between 1934 and 1939. He died in the United States in 1939.

158. *Ibid.,* 179. Saitō wrote of Denison: "[He] enjoyed work for the joy of working, service for the joy of serving."

159. "[I]n the Constitution, [Denison] contended, the independence of the judicial prerogative was firmly established and extraterritoriality was incompatible with the integrity of the Imperial authority" (*ibid.,* 184).

160. On Fraser see Hugh Cortazzi, "Hugh Fraser, 1837–1894: British Minister at Tokyo, 1889–1894," in Hugh Cortazzi (ed.), *Britain and Japan: Biographical Portraits*, vol. IV (London: Japan Library, 2002), 41–52.

161. This episode is related in Saitō Hiros[h]i, *ibid.,* 186–87. The story goes further: One winter evening Shidehara paid a call on Denison in his office, and noticed there some old documents, among them the drafts for the onetime correspondence with the empire of the Russian tsar which needed to be sorted out. When Shidehara asked if he could have the drafts as a souvenir, Denison is said to have thought about it a while and then thrown the papers into the fireplace where they were soon burned up, explaining with these words: "It is better that they are not preserved."

162. Ōta Tamekichi, "Shidehara-san o kataru" (Comments about Mr. Shidehara), in *Shoka no Shidehara-kan*, collection of unpublished manuscripts, 216, cited in Bamba, *op. cit.*, 150.

163. Takemoto, *Failure of Liberalism in Japan*, 15.

164. Bamba, *op. cit.*, 138, n. 3, mistakenly prints the year of Denison's death as 1924 instead of 1914.

165. Cited in Okamoto Shumpei, "Meiji Imperialism: Pacific Emigration or Continental Expansionism?" in Harry Wray and Hilary Conroy (eds.), *Japan Examined—Perspectives on Modern Japanese History* (Honolulu: University of Hawaii Press, 1983), 147. Denison's successor as foreign legal advisor to the Ministry of Foreign Affairs was the English jurist Dr. Thomas Baty (1871–1954).

166. There was during this period only one other person on the list, namely, Motono Ichirō, who from 1912 until the nomination of Shidehara stood alone on the Japanese list.

167. Shidehara, *Gaikō gojūnen*, 220–40, cited in Bamba, *op. cit.*, 147.

168. Compare for example an inquiry of 11 August 1890 from the acting envoy for Communications (and thus Shidehara's predecessor in the office) to Ambassador Kurino in London: "Referring to proposals for reducing rate via Siberia, Cabinet asks under what authority the Russian delegate acts and whether on your side you require Imperial letter of authority or Minister's authority only." On 15 August 1890 came the reply: "Agreement, if made, to be approved by Government. The Russian delegate acts under general authority (of his office) so the Minister's telegraph authority is quite sufficient."

169. This was less true of the navy.

170. Katsura Tarō, who had studied military affairs in Berlin in the 1870s, was during the first Sino-Japanese war (1894–1895) commander of the third army division; from 1898–1900 he served as minister of war, and was three times prime minister, 1901–1906, 1908–1911, and 1912–1913. In January 1882 he had, together with Katō Hiroyuki (the "leading Japanese exponent of Social Darwinism") and others, founded the Doitsugaku Kyōkai (Gesellschaft für deutsche Wissenschaft, or the German Association of Science); Rolf-Harald Wippich, "The Beginnings of German Cultural Activities in Meiji Japan," Tokyo, Sophia University, *Sophia International Review* 15 (1993): 61.

171. See "The Portsmouth Peace," in Nish, *Japanese Foreign Policy*, 72–77, for further details.

172. *Shidehara Kijūrō*, 50–53.

173. Kurt Bloch, *German Interests and Policies in the Far East* (New York: Institute of Pacific Relations, 1940), 3.

174. This was the assertion made by Roy H. Akagi, *Japan's Foreign Relations, 1542–1936* (Tokyo: Hokuseidō Press, 1936), 232, cited in Bloch, *German Interests*, 3.

175. Bloch, *ibid.*

176. "The idea, however, met defeat at the hands of Japanese diplomats through the so-called Root-Takahira Agreement" (Bloch, *ibid.*, citing Akagi, *op. cit.*, 291).

177. Storry, *A History of Modern Japan*, 140.

178. Storry presents the matter as follows: "Just after the Battle of Mukden Marshal Ōyama Iwao (1842–1916), the Japanese *generalissimo*, sent his chief of staff, Kodama, on a confidential mission to Tokyo to impress upon the government the need for an early peace with Russia. And indeed, with admirable foresight, the *Genrō* and cabinet had decided, just before the war began, to ask the United States to mediate at a suitable moment and a special envoy had been sent to Washington for this purpose. Thus President Theodore Roosevelt was not taken by surprise when, within a week of the Battle of Tsushima, he was asked by the Japanese to propose peace to the Russians" (*op. cit.*, 141).

179. Bersihand, *op. cit.*, 383–84.

180. On the history of the twelfth conference of the IPU in St. Louis see Uhlig, *op. cit.*, 326ff. See also Albert Gobat, general secretary of the Inter-Parliamentary Union, who had said, in President Roosevelt's presence, at the IPU Congress in St. Louis in 1904: "We look at this institution [The Hague Movement] as the starting point of the most important evolution ever entered upon by mankind" (cited in Uhlig, *op. cit.*, 335).

181. Although Theodore Roosevelt was, according to Wild, "anything but a paci-fist," he nevertheless "in contrast to the European statesmen was not tied in his politi-cal thinking and actions by the narrow juridical traditions and basic casuistry with respect to power" (*Baron d'Estournelles de Constant (1852–1924)*, 100). In such a context the stagnating Court of Arbitration in The Hague was saved by Roosevelt's initiative since he referred to the Court the case of the church properties dispute between the United States and Mexico: "Upon settlement of the first case there natu-rally followed other cases" (*ibid.*). See also James Brown Scott, "Der kalifornische Kirchengüterstreit zwischen den Vereinigten Staaten und Mexiko" (The California church properties dispute between the United States and Mexico), in Walther Schü-cking (ed.), Das Werk vom Haag, 2. Serie (The Work of The Hague, 2nd series): *Die gerichtlichen Entscheidungen* (The legal decisions), vol. 1, *Die Judikatur des ständi-gen Schiedshofs von 1899–1913* (The rulings of the Permanent Court of Arbitration 1899–1913), part 1 (München: Duncker & Humblot, 1917), 43–247.

182. Gaikō Shiryōkan, MT 2.4.1.7.-1.

183. The article carries a Boston dateline of 3 October 1904.

184. "Agrees with Tolstoi," Gaikō Shiryōkan, MT 2.4.1.7.-1. Another article from the *Washington Post*, which is found among the public papers in the archive of the Ministry of Foreign Affairs (see "Communication from London," 26 September 1904), reports the restrained reception given by the Europeans toward the proposed conference in St. Louis and toward Roosevelt's initiative. The headline reads "Europe Skeptical."

185. Eyffinger, *The Peace Palace: Residence for Justice—Domicile of Learning*, 77; Dülffer, *op. cit.*, 246. This had been preceded by various treaties between the states of North and South America, concluded in the framework of the Pan-American movement, which also aimed at obligatory arbitration. See Dülffer, *op. cit.*, 229ff. After 1899 these states recognized The Hague as the court of jurisdiction.

186. For the genesis of the American resolution, see DeArmond Davis, *The United States and the Second Hague Peace Conference*, 106–7.

187. Gaikō Shiryōkan, MT 2.4.1.7.-1. Indeed, article 19 of the arbitration treaty of 1899 foresaw still more extensive bilateral agreements, toward the conclusion of which the various states were given encouragement. Statesmen like Pierre Marie Waldeck-Rousseau and Jean Jaurès created together with Baron d'Estournelles de Constant a *groupe d'arbitrage*, which represented successfully the ideas behind the subjection of disputes to legal arbitration. In a compilation of documents published by the French foreign ministry shortly after the second Hague conference one finds a ré-sumé which documents, on two sides of a page giving various statistics and illustrated with maps of the world printed in color, "Les Progrès d'Arbritrage Obligatoire de 1903 à 1908." The tightly intertwined net of bilateral and multilateral arbitration trea-ties, which at the time were considered important aspects of international relations, would, it was hoped, make war impossible. On 14 October 1903 an arbitration treaty was concluded between England and France, and Japan had signed its first arbitration treaty as early as June 1873, with Peru. Thus after the first conference in The Hague the project of establishing an obligation to submit disputes to arbitration was carried forward in more than a hundred treaties (up to 1911) and in this way arbitration was

realized, albeit not as a universally recognized principle, but beyond the framework of the conferences.

188. Hioki Eki was in Japan's diplomatic service in China during 1900–1903 and became Japanese minister in Beijing in 1914; during 1920–1924 he was ambassador in Berlin. His name often appears in connection with the Twenty-One Demands that Japan presented to China in 1915.

189. "A conversation with Secretary of State December 1st gives me the impression that he is anxious to obtain early reply of Japanese Government . . . Russian Government . . . not consider the moment opportune" (Gaikō Shiryōkan, MT 2.4.1.7.-1).

190. Gaikō Shiryōkan, MT 2.4.1.7.-1.

191. *Ibid.*

192. Hioki to Komura, 9 December 1904, Gaikō Shiryōkan, MT 2.4.1.7.-1.

193. 31 December 1904, Gaikō Shiryōkan, MT 2.4.1.7.-1. The circular letters bear an attached letter in French, and the original, found among the official letters in the Japanese archives, is addressed to Ambassador Mitsuhashi Nobutaka, "Envoie Extraordinaire et Ministre Plénipotentiaire," in The Hague.

194. Gaikō Shiryōkan, MT 2.4.1.7.-1. The Bureau of the Permanent Court of Arbitration (*jōsetsu kokusai saibansho*) informed, via authenticated copies of an official notice, all the foreign ambassadors accredited in The Hague—including Mitsuhashi Nobutaka from Japan—of every occasion when another country became a party to the work of the court. In a circular distributed by the U.S. State Department on 16 December 1904 the names of Austria-Hungary, the Netherlands, Portugal, Spain, Sweden, and Norway were added as having accepted the invitation to the second peace conference (Gaikō Shiryōkan, MT 2.4.1.7.-2).

195. Note of 28 February 1905, in Dülffer, *op. cit.*, 279, with source data.

196. Inoue Katsunosuke was minister to Belgium (1898) and Germany (1898–1906), and then continued his diplomatic career in Germany until 1908 as ambassador after the post was created in 1906. During 1913–1916 he was ambassador in London.

197. "Russian Government intend to approach foreign powers for the purpose of convoking second Peace Conference in La Haye" (Gaikō Shiryōkan, MT 2.4.1.7.-1). There is also a cablegram (15 June 1905) from the U.S. ambassador in Athens, John B. Jackson, to John Hay, in which he informs the secretary of state that Romania has accepted the American president's invitation and will attend the conference ("to my surprise I have just received a note from General Lahovary, Roumanian Minister of Foreign Affairs") (*ibid.*). The telegram from Inou(y)e to Katsura bears at its top Shidehara's seal, who received such dispatches in the telegraphic division and acted as conveyor and interpreter. Until 1907 and even during the Second Hague Peace Conference almost all the telegraphed documents found in the Gaimushō archives bear Shidehara's stamp, affixed very neatly on the left upper side above the name of the addressee.

198. Gaikō Shiryōkan, MT 2.4.1.7.-1.

199. *Ibid.* (emphasis added). The Russian foreign minister Muraviev had on 27 September sent a letter to Italian foreign minister Tittoni (the same official who had already accepted Roosevelt's invitation on 30 January), attaching a diplomatic note

saying the following: "After the hostilities were ended and peace agreed upon between Japan and the Russian Empire, the Russian tsar in his capacity as initiator of the international Peace Conference of 1899 has found the time appropriate to embark upon a progressive and systematic improvement of the foundations of this international gathering. His Imperial Majesty felt himself encouraged by the expression of full sympathy for his plan, to which President Roosevelt in the course of the last year also gave renewed emphasis. . . . Supported by this sort of sympathetic manifestation, his Imperial Majesty has during the foregoing year recommended to the Italian government that it take part in the new international Peace Conference." Similar letters were sent to the governments of other states.

200. Gaikō Shiryōkan, MT 2.4.1.7.-1.

201. "The Tsar's Invitation to the Hague Peace Conference," *Japan Times*, 14 November 1905, official documents, Gaikō Shiryōkan, MT 2.4.1.7.-1.

202. Gaikō Shiryōkan, MT 2.4.1.7.-2.

203. Gaikō Shiryōkan, MT 2.4.1.7.-1 (translated from the original French).

204. This comes from the Russian-Japanese correspondence of May 1906 concerning the scheduled Hague peace conference. See "Correspondence Concerning the Second Hague Peace Conference," printed documentation, Gaikō Shiryōkan, MT 2.4.1.7.-2.

205. Gaikō Shiryōkan, MT 2.4.1.7.-1.

206. Printed documentation: "Correspondence Concerning the Second Hague Peace Conference, October 1906" (before 16 October), Gaikō Shiryōkan, MT 2.4.1.7.-2. See also the letter by Bakhmeteff of 26 September/9 October to the Japanese minister of foreign affairs: "[L]e refus du Gouvernement Japonais de signer le protocole proposé par la Russie, pourrait seulement influer sur adhésion des Républiques de l'Amérique du Sud, qui n'ayant pas été représentées à la première Conférence, seront invités à la seconde—*la Corée, le Panama et l'Abyssinie étaient déja hors de cause pour d'autres raisons*" (The refusal of the Japanese government to sign the protocol proposed by Russia could only influence the accession of South American Republics which, not having been represented at the first Conference, will be invited to the second—Korea, Panama and Abyssinia were already out of the question for other reasons) (Gaikō Shiryōkan, MT 2.4.1.7.-1).

207. Kusakabe to Hayashi, 24 October 1906, Gaikō Shiryōkan, MT 2.4.1.7.-1.

208. "He said that as United States had no question similar to that of Corea it did not occur to her to make any comments on protocol proposed by Russia" (Gaikō Shiryōkan, MT 2.4.1.7.-1).

209. On 9 November 1906, Hayashi informed Aoki of the Japanese note of reply to the Russian envoy in Tokyo: "[T]he Imperial Government infer [from the Russian note] . . . that in addition to the Powers represented at the last Conference, only the South American Republics are to be invited . . . if that inference is correct, the Imperial Government . . . will withdraw their objection" (Gaikō Shiryōkan, MT 2.4.1.7.-2).

210. Gaikō Shiryōkan, MT 2.4.1.7.-1. The foreign ministry archives contain the correspondence and in most cases a certain amount of commentary. One can gather from them a vivid portrayal, from the Japanese perspective, of the progress of the discussions and negotiations surrounding the peace conference.

211. Komura in London to Hayashi, 26 October 1906, Gaikō Shiryōkan, MT 2.4.1.7.-1.

212. Aoki to Hayashi, 17 November 1906, Gaikō Shiryōkan, MT 2.4.1.7.-2. It is also interesting to note this further content of the communication, referring to what may have been German objections: "At an interview with Secretary of State November 15th, he told me confidentially that Russian answer to these proposals of United States was that the programme communicated by Russia to the interested powers was the *result of understanding with great Powers of Europe* and could not be changed without going over the whole subject again with those Powers" (emphasis added).

213. "I deemed it prudent to say at once as my personal opinion that it seemed to me hardly likely that the Japanese Government would have any objection if an understanding has been reached between United States and Great Britain" (Aoki to Hayashi, 17 November 1906, Gaikō Shiryōkan, MT 2.4.1.7.-2). On 9 March 1907 Inou(y)e cabled Hayashi from Berlin, "The question of disarmament has not as yet been included in the programme and it was not yet certain in what manner, and if the question at all, would be treated" (*ibid.*).

214. Gaikō Shiryōkan, MT 2.4.1.7.-2.

215. There is, however, a letter from the Italian Foreign Minister Tittoni to Baron Romano Avezzana, "chargé d'affaires d'Italie à Tôkyô," which includes specific disarmament proposals. On April 17 Hayashi replies: "The Imperial Government congratulate the Italian Minister of Foreign Affairs upon his eminently conciliatory propositions respecting limitations of armament. Although the Imperial Government fear that there is no present prospect of a general accord among the Powers on that important subject, they would have no objection to Monsieur Tittoni's propositions in principle as an eventual mode of procedure" (Gaikō Shiryōkan, MT 2.4.1.7.-3).

216. Gaikō Shiryōkan, MT 2.4.1.7.-3.

217. *Ibid.*

218. Komura to Hayashi, 28 April 1907: "British Government . . . have not as yet made any definite proposal . . . Italian proposition has been withdrawn owing to objection of Austria and Germany" (Gaikō Shiryōkan, MT 2.4.1.7.-3).

219. However, see Kawakami (*Japan's Pacific Policy*, 62), who gives the following quote from Colonel [!] Theodore Roosevelt (circa 1902), which preceded the "Plan Orange" and brings to the fore the keen American sense of mission: "The Mediterranean era declined with the Roman Empire and died with the discovery of America. The Atlantic era is now at the height of its development and must soon exhaust the resources at its command. *The Pacific era, destined to be the greatest of all, and to bring the whole human race at last into one great comity of nations, is just at the dawn.* Man, in his migration westward, has at last traversed the whole round of the planet, and the sons of the newest West now stand on the Pacific Coast of America and touch hands across the greatest of oceans with those ancient races of Asia which have from time immemorial dwelt in their present seats. It is the fate of the American nation to be placed at the front of the turmoil that must accompany this new placing of peoples" (emphasis added).

220. Von Siebold reported: "The legal advisor of the Russian Foreign Office Monsieur von Martens has been visiting most of the Capitals of Europe and although a

profound secret is kept of his object, sufficiently has transpired to justify the conclusion that his object is to secure a majority for the Russian projects the program of which was communicated to the Powers. . . . There seems however the intention to introduce also those questions which were brought forward during the Japanese Russian war. Here I have reason to suspect that an opportunity will be seized to open a critical discussion on Japan's action . . . there was a tendency to question the justice of Japan's action at Port Arthur (the attack on the Russian fleet) previous to the declaration of war. . . . On the . . . question, it will be impossible for Russia to say anything, for Mr. von Martens in his work on international law maintains that a declaration of war is unnecessary for the opening of hostilities. (Russia marched in the last war with Turkey its troops into Turkey, without any previous declaration of war.)" Copy of the letter, addressed to the Japanese Embassy in Berlin, document, Gaikō Shiryōkan, MT 2.4.1.7.-2.

221.　Hayashi to Baron von Siebold, 2 April 1907: "[B]efore I knew your disposition . . . the Government, in view of several problems interesting to Japan, had set themselves to work to make the necessary preparations and had designated a number of persons to assist Mr. Tsuzuki Keiroku who is to represent Japan at the coming Conference. Among them is Mr. Denison." Von Siebold had in his letter referred to Denison and offered his help in the event that Denison's presence in Tokyo might be indispensable (Gaikō Shiryōkan, MT 2.4.1.7.-2).

222.　The other delegates are Major Akiyama Yoshifuru, Counter Admiral Shimamura Hayao, the attachés Kurachi Tetsukichi (advisor in the foreign ministry), Yoshimura Yasozō (advisor in the war ministry), and Yamakawa Tadao (advisor in the navy ministry), Frigate Captain Moriyama Keizaburō, Commander Takatsuka Kyō, Tatsuki Shitchita, and Nagaoka Harukazu (Gaikō Shiryōkan, MT 2.4.1.7.-3).

223.　"At the First Conference the only decision arrived at was that Powers should carefully examine the question. German Government had done so but had found no means which in view of the great difficulties in the geographical, economical, military and political situation of the different States would be justifiable and suitable to remove these differences and to serve as a basis for an agreement. Chancellor had no knowledge whether other Governments were more successful . . . no hopes that anything would come out of discussions" (Gaikō Shiryōkan, MT 2.4.1.7.-3). Attached to this document are several newspaper clippings from 3 March 1907 on the question of arms limitations, from *Journal des Débats*, *Le Siècle*, and *Le Temps* (the latter also from the issue of 15 March 1907).

224.　Dülffer, *op. cit.*, 93.

225.　Gaikō Shiryōkan, MT 2.4.1.7.-3.

226.　Inoue to Hayashi, 2 June 1907, Gaikō Shiryōkan, MT 2.4.1.7.-3. Attached to the report is a short description by Tsuzuki of a half-hour-long conversation with the German emperor at a gala dinner: "[T]he German Emperor had a long talk with me lasting about thirty minutes. The General trend of which made me feel that he was trying to impress upon me possibility and the desirability as well of the close friendship and the intimate understanding between the two nations which based their greatness on the strength of their self-defence as of the strong sympathy between the two heroic peoples animated so thoroughly by military spirit and so willing to fulfill their duties towards the respective bodies politic. The frankness and the erudition with which he spoke coming from a Sovereign on a Gala occasion made me feel that it was something more than an ordinary after-dinner conversation" (*ibid.*).

227. Philipp Zorn, *op. cit.*, 67.

228. Gaikō Shiryōkan, MT 2.4.1.7.-3. In fact the proposal for an obligatory international investigatory commission was dropped in early July. Tsuzuki to Hayashi, 9 July 1907, Gaikō Shiryōkan, MT 2.4.1.7.-4.

229. Walther Schücking, *Der Bund der Völker*, 73.

230. For insight into Tsuzuki's career and personality see also his article, "Social Intercourse between Japanese and Occidentals," in Ōkuma (ed.), *Fifty Years of New Japan*, 477–93, in which he quotes in German (485) from Goethe's poem "Orient und Okzident": "Ob von Buddha oder Christ/Nur das Licht verkündet ist/Es versteht sich allerwärts/Freier Geist und freies Herz" (Whether by Buddha or Christ/the Light is revealed/Everywhere it is understood/free spirit and free heart).

231. James Brown Scott, *The Hague Peace Conferences of 1899 and 1907*, two vols. (Baltimore: The John Hopkins Press, 1909), vol. I, 160.

232. Adolf Wild, *Baron d'Estournelles de Constant (1852–1924)*, 306.

233. In preparing to send the Japanese delegation to the first Hague conference in 1899, the Japanese government had left the question of "obligatory arbitration" open, giving the delegation instructions to follow the majority of the participating states on this matter.

234. See Adolf Wild, *op. cit.*, 309: "His greatest success came, however, with the Japanese delegate Tsuzuki, who at his remonstrance, withheld his vote instead of—as his instructions were intended—voting against the world arbitration treaty. D'Estournelles had both luck and the lack of it with the Bulgarians, whom he could also influence to vote for the project (against their instructions), even though they then had to quickly change their vote to a 'no' under German pressure."

235. James Brown Scott, *The Hague Peace Conferences*, vol. I, 160.

236. "Some of the strongest statements against obligatory arbitration were coming from . . . Baron Guillaume of Belgium. . . . arbitration enthusiasts had not expected to find Belgians cooperating so closely with Germany. Rumours circulated that King Leopold was hoping Germany would support his Congo policy in return for assistance in blocking the arbitration treaty . . . critics disgusted with his pro-German attitude were soon calling him Guillaume Deux." Calvin DeArmond Davis, *The United States and the Second Hague Peace Conference. American Diplomacy and International Organization 1899–1914* (Durham, N.C.: Duke University Press, 1975), 283.

237. This refers to Tsuzuki's abstention on the question of the proposed "Convention rélatif à l'arbitrage obligatoire (Annèxe 72)" on which a vote was taken on 5 October 1907 at the fifth session of commission I, toward the end of the conference. See *Actes et Documents*, Deuxième Conférence Internationale de la Paix. Le Haye 15 Juin–18 Octobre 1907. Tome II. Première Commission. Ministère des Affaires Étrangères. Le Haye 1909, 82 (translation from the original French; emphasis added).

238. Adolf Wild, *op. cit.*, 306. Ishii Kikujirō suggests a further reason: "[I]t has been characteristic of Japan to dislike arbitration. . . . Over a long period there had continued between the Japanese government and the several governments of foreign

residents owning houses in the former foreign settlement areas in Japanese ports, a controversy over the payment of the house tax on this property, and as the dispute seemed to have no end the matter was finally submitted to a court of arbitration [Hague Court. Award given 22 May, 1905]. The plaintiff was Japan and the defendants France, Great Britain, and Germany. Japan fought the case from every angle, but the decision was completely against her. Out of this experience the feeling has grown among Japanese that even though they might entrust a domestic or external issue to foreign arbitration they cannot expect a fair judgment" (*Diplomatic Commentaries*, trans. and ed. William R. Langdon [Baltimore: The John Hopkins Press/London: Humphrey Milford, Oxford University Press, 1936], 214). This case is described and analyzed in a published doctoral dissertation: Edmund Simon, *Natur und völkerrechtliche Tragweite des Urteils des Haager Permanenten Schiedsgerichtshofes vom 22. Mai 1904 betreffend die zeitlich unbegrenzte Ueberlassung von Grundstücken in Japan an Fremde* (Range of relevance for natural and international law of the judgment of 22 May 1904 by the Hague Permanent Court of Arbitration concerning the temporally unlimited transfer of plots of land in Japan to foreigners) (Greifswald 1908).

239. James Brown Scott (ed.), *Instructions to the American Delegates to the Hague Peace Conferences and their Official Reports* (New York: Oxford University Press/London, Toronto, Melbourne, and Bombay: Humphrey Milford, 1916) (Carnegie Endowment for International Peace, Division of International Law), Report of the American Delegation, 129–30.

240. Tsuzuki to Hayashi, "Den Haag," 29 June 1907: "These Coreans are said to have sent to all first Delegates, except probably English, printed protestation against our regime in Corea" (Gaikō Shiryōkan, MT 2.4.1.9.-1).

241. Tsuzuki to Hayashi, 30 June 1907, Gaikō Shiryōkan, MT 2.4.1.9.-1. The San Francisco affair refers to a decision taken by the San Francisco school board in 1906 to have children of Asian parentage study in segregated public schools, a step that lead to a formal protest from the Japanese side, and intervention by President Roosevelt.

242. Satō Aimaro to Hayashi, 3 July 1907, Gaikō Shiryōkan, MT 2.4.1.9.-1.

243. Tsuzuki to Hayashi, 2 July 1907: "[H]e instigates that European Powers will one day repent the present indifference to Corean affairs, as the Japanese are going to monopolize all the resources of the country to the exclusion of both Westerners and natives" (Gaikō Shiryōkan, MT 2.4.1.9.-1).

244. Tsuzuki to Hayashi, 5 July 1907: "New York Herald, Paris Edition, of July 5th publishes cablegram from the East and says the appearance of the Coreans in The Hague caused much sensation to Japanese authorities, who suspect of the connivance of Corean Emperor, although he repudiates the mission and denounces the credentials as forgery. It further states that the revelation will precipitate the crisis, and that Marquis Itō's Cromer policy will be in accord between the two fires, viz: Tokyo influence demanding the iron hand and even annexation on the one hand and the renewed activity of anti-Japanese Corean intrigues on the other hand" (Gaikō Shiryōkan, MT 2.4.1.9.-1).

245. Hayashi to Itō, Japanese-language dispatch of 7 July 1907, Gaikō Shiryōkan, MT 2.4.1.9.-1.

246. Tsuzuki to Hayashi, Gaikō Shiryōkan, MT 2.4.1.9.-1. In the same telegram Tsuzuki speaks also of a detailed brochure (which is also found in the archival folder together with photographs of the three Koreans) that relates in French the process of the gradual taking over of power by the Japanese in Korea, beginning with Itō Hirobumi's arrival in Korea on 10 November 1905 and going up through the successful signing of the protectorate agreement later the same year.

247. *Ibid.*

248. Tsuzuki to Hayashi, 11 July 1907, Gaikō Shiryōkan, MT 2.4.1.9.-1. The dispatch also speaks about a so-called Pagoda Affair.

249. Hayashi to Motono, 20 July 1907, Gaikō Shiryōkan, MT 2.4.1.9.-1.

250. The contents of the article were sent in telegram format, Aoki to Hayashi, 21 July 1907, Gaikō Shiryōkan, MT 2.4.1.9.-1.

251. "General impression here among the representatives is that abdication of the Corean Emperor was due to pressure from Japan" (Tsuzuki to Hayashi, 21 July 1907, Gaikō Shiryōkan, MT 2.4.1.9.-1).

252. Inoue to Hayashi, 21 July 1907, Gaikō Shiryōkan, MT 2.4.1.9.-1.

253. Gaikō Shiryōkan, MT 2.4.1.9.-2, circa 25 July 1907.

254. "The Assertion of Japanese Sovereignty of Corea," *New York Tribune*, 26 July 1907. Gaikō Shiryōkan, MT 2.4.1.9.-2.

255. Gaikō Shiryōkan, MT 2.4.1.9.-2.

256. Gaikō Shiryōkan, MT 2.4.1.9.-2.

257. "Conférence recommende aux puissance, réunion d'une troisième Conférence de Paix" (Gaikō Shiryōkan, MT 2.4.1.7.-4). See also Scott (ed.), *Instructions to the American Delegates to the Hague Peace Conferences and their Official Reports*, 137f.

258. Gaikō Shiryōkan, MT 2.4.1.7.-4.

259. Tsuzuki to Hayashi, 12 October 1907: "La Commission est unanime 1. à reconnaitre le principe de l'arbitrage obligatoire" (Gaikō Shiryōkan, MT 2.4.1.7.-4).

260. Tsuzuki from Paris to Hayashi, 14 November 1907: "Sir Edward Grey promised me that he will keep in close touch with our Embassy" (Gaikō Shiryōkan, MT 2.4.1.7.-6).

261. Note of the Ministry of Foreign Affairs, 19 June 1908, Gaikō Shiryōkan, MT 2.4.1.7.-6.

262. Latourette, *The Chinese, Their History and Culture*, 396.

263. Sands, *At the Court of Korea*, 207. Sands thought that Itō, who was able to "listen to the opinion of others . . . could have inaugurated a better system of government" that would have satisfied the Koreans.

264. Neville Bennett, "Bitter Fruit: Japanese Migration and Anglo-Saxon Obstacles, 1890–1924," *Transactions of the Asiatic Society of Japan*, fourth series, no. 8 (1993): 78. See also *ibid.*, 79: "By 1907 Japan contemplated the 'bitter fruit' of the virtual exclusion of her people from the British Empire and the United States. The only compensation was that her status was intact, on paper. Conversely the repercussions to her migration policy were very serious: the United States began to look upon Japan as an enemy. . . . Australia adopted compulsory military service in peacetime which was hitherto unheard of in British societies and Australia and New Zealand in 1909 bought dreadnought battle cruisers to be based in Singapore to counter Japan."

265. The renewed treaty was signed 21 February 1911; Shumpei Okamoto, "Meiji Imperialism: Pacific Emigration or Continental Expansionism?" in Harry Wray and Hilary Conroy (eds.), *op. cit.*, 147.

266. Chinda Sutemi had signed the Hague conventions in 1900. During the last years of the Meiji period he served as vice foreign minister (*gaimu jikan*), before taking up his post as ambassador to the United States.

267. *Shidehara Kijūrō*, 66.

268. The supplementary clause also stipulated that, in keeping with the bilateral agreements, "naturalized Japanese immigrants could own land," even though in the American interpretation of who could become a naturalized American citizen, there were not any Japan-born naturalized immigrants. However, their American-born offspring automatically had American citizenship.

269. See Shidehara's conversation with Bryce as recorded in *Shidehara Kijūrō*, 70–71.

270. *Shidehara Kijūrō*, 69. Later, when Shidehara was ambassador in Washington, Ishii Itarō, a secretary in the embassy, found Shidehara's numerous manuscripts and legal proposals in the files which he had earlier prepared for Chinda during their endeavor to resolve the "California question."

271. *Shidehara Kijūrō*, 46–66. Bamba writes: "In his memoirs Shidehara wrote that he was very much impressed by Bryce's teaching and felt as if he had been taught by his grandfather" (*op. cit.*, 152).

272. Gaikō Shiryōkan, MT 2.4.1.4, vol. 4. At the time the Japanese judges on the Permanent Court of Arbitration list were Motono, Watanabe, and Miyako. Denison (who died in 1914) after 1912 no longer appeared on the list.

273. Karl F. Zahl, *op. cit.*, 26.

274. Cf. Bamba, *op. cit.*, 42: "The Taishō era saw a remarkable social phenomenon, the rise of the masses."

275. Bamba, *op. cit.*, 50.

276. According to Bamba, *op. cit.*, 50: "This was the first case in which the masses played a decisive role in the fall of a cabinet." Hara Kei includes these words in Hara's diary entry for 10 February 1913: "If Katsura had not resigned, a revolution might have occurred" (*Hara Kei nikki*, Tokyo, Kangensha 1950/1951, nine vols., v, 191). Incidentally, Katsura had also been responsible for the execution in 1911 of socialist thinker Kōtoku Shūsui (unjustly accused of complicity in a plot to assassinate the emperor).

277. Ian Nish, *op. cit.*, 93.

278. After the Meiji Restoration a predominantly nationalistic and reactionary military clique was built up around former members of the samurai class.

279. Although Shidehara had been expected to arrive at his new post already in November, he arranged to postpone his departure from Washington by about two weeks.

280. Dülffer, *op. cit.*, 11. See also Otfried Nippold, *Die Wahrheit über die Ursachen des Europäischen Krieges* (The truth about the origin of the European war), ed. Harald Kleinschmidt, with a preface by Akio Nakai (München: Iudicium, 2005), 55: "Undoubtedly, had the German government found anything wanting in the modalities of Grey's proposition, it could have made counter-proposals."

281. Ishii Itarō, "Shidehara-dan no omoide" (Memories of Baron Shidehara), in *Shoka no Shidehara-kan*, 275–76, cited in Bamba, *op. cit.*, 139.

282. Kishi Kuramatsu, "Shidehara Kijūrō no omoide o kataru" (Relating memories of Shidehara Kijūrō), in *Shoka no Shidehara-kan*, 25–35, cited in Bamba, *op. cit.*, 139.

283. The British journal *The Independent* had on 4 December 1913 published an article titled "Call the Third Hague Conference without Delay" (vol. 77, no. 3392, 429), cited in Uhlig, *op. cit.*, 703. See also Alfred H. Fried, "Die dritte Haager Konferenz" (The Third Hague Peace Conference), *Die Friedens-Warte* 16, no. 1 (April 1914): 121–24. *Die Friedens-Warte* (The Peace Watch) was founded by academics and adherents to the peace movement in German-speaking countries in 1899, originally as a weekly publication to report on the proceedings of the First Hague Peace Conference, and is still published today in Berlin.

284. The stone-laying ceremony took place on 30 July 1907; Eyffinger, *The Peace Palace: Residence for Justice—Domicile of Learning*, 95, with details. The opening ceremony was on August 28, 1913.

285. This was based on the unanimously adopted resolution of 16 October 1907 (Gaikō Shiryōkan, MT 2.4.1.10), which also gives a copy of the letter, dated 17 January 1908, with Japanese translation, and bearing Shidehara's seal. For a photo of the Japanese Room, see Eyffinger, *The Peace Palace: Residence for Justice—Domicile of Learning*, 128.

286. "From 1912 onwards commissions were raised in several countries to arrange a proper agenda for 1915. Detailed studies were made of a fairly promising nature. However, the outbreak of *La Grande Guerre* put an end to these lofty ideals" (Eyffinger, *The Peace Palace: Residence for Justice—Domicile of Learning*, 89).

287. See Otfried Nippold for the text of the Japanese ultimatum handed to the German government on 17 August by Funakoshi in Berlin, and Germany's reply (*Die Wahrheit*, 203–4). The Japanese declaration of war, following the presentation of the ultimatum in Berlin, was transmitted to Berlin via Sweden and received on 23 August.

288. Hans Wehberg, *Die internationale Friedensbewegung* (The international peace movement) (M. Gladbach: Volksvereinsverlag, 1911) (Staatsbürger-Bibliothek Heft.22), 21.

289. See, for example, the report in English by C. van Vollenhoven, *The Enforcement of Sanctions in International Law by Means of an International Police System*, referring to the Twentieth Universal Peace Congress that coincided with the opening of the Peace Palace at The Hague in August 1913.

290. See chapter II, subchapter 3: House Joint Resolution (H.J.Res.) 223, Universal Peace Commission, 24 June 1910. *Congressional Record*, 20 and 24 June 1910, 8545–48, 9028.

291. Walther Schücking, *Der Weltfriedensbund und die Wiedergeburt des Völkerrechts* (The world peace league and the rebirth of international law) (Leipzig: Verlag Naturwissenschaften, 1917), 10–11. The author goes on to point out: "A particularly strong movement grew up . . . during the first winter of the war on Dutch soil in the form of the [Nederlandse] Anti-Oorlogs Raad." For details of the Minimum Program, see also De Jong van Beek en Donk, *History of the Peace Movement in the*

Netherlands (The Hague, 1915). According to A. C. F. Beales, the 1915 conference at The Hague of the Central Organisation for a Durable Peace "was the successor of the Inter-Parliamentarian and Universal Peace Conferences" (*The History of Peace* [London and New York, 1931], 299).

292. Walther Schücking, *ibid.*, 12 and 15.

293. *Shidehara Kijūrō*, 79.

294. Shidehara wrote in the *Yomiuri Shimbun* (evening edition of 15 November 1950) about his stay in Holland, cited in *Shidehara Kijūrō*, 85. Other details are given in a copy of a letter of 7 November 1996 to the author from Dr. B. Woelderinck, director of the royal household.

295. In a sense, one upshot of these considerations was the Twenty-One Demands, which many Chinese felt were an abomination of the worst kind.

296. In the words of Haru Matsukata Reischauer, *Samurai and Silk, A Japanese and American Heritage* (Rutland, Vt., and Tokyo: Charles E. Tuttle, 1987), 325: "[T]he Twenty-One Demands Japan had forced on China in 1915 had made the Japanese the most hated imperialists in China and the greatest threat to nascent Chinese nationalism."

297. Among the twenty-one points that were laid before Chinese President Yuan Shikai (Yüan Shih-k'ai) on 18 January 1915 were new concessions (prospecting rights, etc.) in southern Manchuria and Eastern Mongolia, the transformation of the Hanyehping coal and steel company into a joint Chinese-Japanese enterprise, as well as railway rights and the demand that China should not grant any rights to Western powers which would stand in opposition to Japanese interests. Regarding the genesis of the proposal of presenting the Twenty-One Demands, see Nish, *op. cit.*, 96–99; also see Beasley, *op. cit.*, 112.

298. See Takemoto, *Failure of Liberalism in Japan*, 10: "Shidehara had obviously been, from the very beginning, against the Twenty-One Demands of Katō Takaaki's Cabinet in 1915, but he was still too young and uninfluential." Compare also Beasley, *op. cit.*, 108ff.

299. Takemoto, *op. cit.*, 54–55.

300. Duus, *op. cit.*, 199. In this connection the relevant literature often uses the term "dual diplomacy." This problem will be discussed in more detail later on.

301. Takemoto, *op. cit.*, 55, which refers to *Shidehara Kijūrō*, 85–86.

302. *Ibid.*

303. Kita Ikki had also spoken out against Japan's interference in China's domestic affairs. See Nomura Kōichi, "Profile of Asian Minded Man II: Ikki Kita," *The Developing Economies* 4, no. 2 (June 1966): 137, cited in Wilson, *op. cit.*, 1969, 161: Kita "found that Japan's attitude represented a definite self-deception, since as *self-appointed* representative of the East in China it had to accede to Western methods."

304. Nish, *op. cit.*, 100–101; Fairbank, Reischauer, and Craig, *East Asia—The Modern Transformation*, 232–33.

305. *The Correspondence of G. E. Morrison*, vol. II (1912–1920), ed. Lo Hui-min (Cambridge: Cambridge University Press, 1978), 539n2: "Katō . . . remained however one of the most powerful political leaders in Japan. He was a supporter of Ōkuma's aggressive policy towards China under Yüan Shih-k'ai." See also *ibid.* (540n3) where

it is intimated that Ariga Nagao (1860–1921), a Japanese legal scholar (fluent in both French and German) and former participant in the 1899 Hague peace conference who reported to the *genrō* as an emissary from Yuan Shikai (for whom he had been employed as a legal advisor since 1913), had much to do with bringing about Katō's replacement in August.

306. *Shidehara Kijūrō*, 85–87.

307. Cited in Karl K[iyoshi] Kawakami, *Japan's Pacific Policy—Especially in Relation to China, The Far East, and the Washington Conference* (New York: E. P. Dutton & Co., 1922, 296. *Ibid.,* 293–96, reproduces in its entirety, as appendix B, "Mr. Wang [Zhengting]'s Statement before the Far Eastern Committee [of the Washington Conference], February 3, 1922," which details Chinese criticisms of the treaties and notes of 1915 and ends by quoting the above resolution.

308. See also Dan Kurzmann, *Japan sucht neue Wege. Die politische und wirtschaftliche Entwicklung im 20. Jahrhundert* (Japan seeks new ways—political and economic development in the twentieth century) (München: C.H. Beck, 1961), 98: "Shidehara was of the opinion that no foreign power would ever be in the position to impose a political or social structure on the Chinese people. He furthermore held it to be unethical to make even the attempt to do so."

309. Letter to the British journalist L. G. Fraser, 12 October 1916, *The Correspondence of G.E. Morrison*, vol. II (1912–1920), 562.

310. "There the case ended" (letter to the British journalist L.G. Fraser, October 1916. *Ibid.*).

311. Ōkuma Shigenobu, "Japanese Prime Minister Who Negotiated '21 Demands' Tells Inside Story," published on 9 November 1931 in *The Japan Times* (in English) and in *Hōchi Shimbun* (in Japanese). The article had been dictated by Ōkuma on 7 July 1921 from his sickbed as part of a series of signed articles in 1920 and 1921, which, translated into English by Yamakawa Yoshihiro, were submitted for publication once or twice monthly to *The Philadelphia Public Ledger* syndicate. The posthumously published 1931 article, which had until then been withheld from the public, attracted much attention. A copy is found, among other places, as an attachment to Report J.Nr. 2620 of the German embassy in Tokyo, dated 18 November 1931 (foreign ministry Archive (AA), Bonn, K625466).

312. There probably stood in connection with this also the Potsdam Agreements of November 1910 and August 1911. Sazanov in 1910 began his period in office as Russian foreign minister "with the attempt to bring about an entente with Germany, which in Paris and London caused great anxiety." B. H. Sumner, "Der russische Imperialismus in Ostasien und im Mittleren Osten 1880–1914" (Russian imperialism in East Asia and the Middle East 1880–1914), in Hans-Ulrich Wehler (ed.), *Imperialismus* (Königstein, Taunus: Athenäum/Droste, 1979), 340.

313. "China would have been ranged alongside Germany in the struggle for the mastery of the world. . . . [It] would have entered the war on the side of Germany, because the Chinese army was then largely under German influence, although not to the extent that the Turkish army was" (Ōkuma, *loc. cit.*, 9 November 1931, in *The Japan Times*).

314. Letter to the journalist L. G. Fraser, 12 October 1916, in *The Correspondence of G. E. Morrison*, 563–64.

315. Kawakami, *Japan and World Peace* (New York: Macmillan, 1919), 9.

316. Akidzuki Satsuo, *La question du Chantoung* (Paris: Librairie Plon, 1919), 9–11 (translation from the original French).

317. Ōkuma Shigenobu, "Die chinesische Revolution und der Weltfriede" (The Chinese Revolution and world peace), *Die Friedens-Warte*, August 1912, 164.

318. This phrase is taken from the *Deutsche Arbeiterzeitung* of 7 February 1915. A letter of 7 September 1914 from Walther Rathenau to Chancellor Bethmann Hollweg had stated: "The end objective should be that situation which alone can bring a future European balance: Central Europe united under German leadership, against England and America on the one side and against Russia on the other, stabilized politically and economically" (Walther Rathenau, *Politische Briefe* [Dresden, 1929], 12). Both citations are found in Dieter Groh, "Imperialismus," in *Geschichtliche Grundbegriffe, Historisches Lexikon zur politisch-sozialen Sprache in Deutschland* (Historical basic concepts, historical lexicon of socio-political language in Germany), ed. Otto Brunner, Werner Conze, and Reinhart Koselleck (Stuttgart: Klett-Cotta, 1982), 209.

319. See Wilhelm Solf, "Das deutsche und das englische koloniale Kriegsziel" (The German and English colonial war aim), an address given in Leipzig 7 June 1917 at a celebration held by the Deutsche Kolonialgesellschaft (German Colonial Society), printed by Königliche Buchdruckerei v. E. S. Mittler & Sohn (Berlin) 1917. In *Wachtfeuer* (Watchfire), "Künstlerblätter zum Krieg 1914/18," no. 179, Kolonial-Nummer, Solf writes these prefatory remarks in March 1918: "Germany's colonial war objective is the creation of a fair balance of the colonial territories (*gerechter Ausgleich der kolonialen Besitzungen*), a balance which does justice to our civilizational power (*kulturelle Kraft*) and our economic needs. Only by this can there be achieved a lasting relaxation of tensions in international relations and a durable, peaceful living together of the peoples (*Nebeneinanderleben der Völker*)" (Solf-Nachlaß Archiv Koblenz, Akte 7, 25). See also Solf's *Kolonialpolitik, Mein politisches Vermächtnis* (Colonial policy, my political legacy) (Berlin: Verlag von Reimar Hobbing, 1919).

320. Fairbank, Reischauer, and Craig name as grounds for the Japanese demands "an attempt to strengthen the position it had won in Manchuria as a result of the Russo-Japanese War and to make new advances in China" (*East Asia—The Modern Transformation*, 234).

321. Ōkuma Shigenobu, "Japanese Prime Minister Who Negotiated '21 Demands' Tells Inside Story," *The Japan Times*, 9 November 1931.

322. Nish, *Japanese Foreign Policy 1869–1942*, 98.

323. Shidehara goes into some of the particulars in his address "Gaikō kanken" (Personal views on diplomacy) delivered at Keiō University on 19 October 1928; see *Shidehara Kijūrō*, 274. Sections of the entire speech are reproduced, in somewhat rearranged order, in Shidehara Kijūrō (272–77). The full text is available as an unpublished document (36) from the former Shidehara Heiwa Bunko (no. R-7, 13), in the National Diet Library.

324. The full text of the secret agreement signed on the Russian side by Lobanov and Witte and on the Chinese side by Li Hongzhang is found in German translation from the original French in B. A. Romanov, "Rußlands 'friedliche Durchdringung' der Mandschurei," in Wehler (ed.), *Imperialismus*, 382–83. Article V specified: "It is

to be understood that Russia, in the case of a war, will have the free use of the railway according to Article I . . . for the transport and the provisioning of its troops" (*ibid.*).

325. Romanov, *op. cit.,* 356–57.

326. See also Walter LaFeber, *The Clash* (New York and London: W.W. Norton, 1997), 109ff; Jansen, *The Making of Modern Japan*, 515f.

327. Kawakami, *Japan's Pacific Policy, especially in relation to China, the Far East, and the Washington Conference* (New York: E. P. Dutton & Co., 1922), 182–83.

328. *Ibid.,* 183. "Had Japan wisely confined herself to demands relating to those territories, that desire would have been more readily recognized by China."

329. Storry, *A History of Modern Japan*, 153: "The unfortunate Twenty-One Demands were a turning point in American-Japanese relations." Criticism had come especially also from the American Minister to China Paul Reinsch, a "passionate defender of China and an outspoken critic of Japan" (LaFeber, *Clash*, 110).

330. Karl K. Kawakami, *Japan's Pacific Policy*, 175.

331. This point was not taken up in the main body of final treaties but in a separate note in which the nonalienation principle was said to be applicable to all "foreign powers" instead of to "third powers," as originally proposed by Japan (*ibid.*, 177).

332. This was ultimately adopted only in part, with the result that Japanese were to be allowed to rent, but not to own, land in southern Manchuria. In eastern Inner Mongolia only joint Japanese-Chinese agricultural and livestock-related enterprises were to be permitted. Travel was to be freely allowed in southern "Manchuria" but not in eastern Inner Mongolia. China declared itself ready, however, to open certain towns in eastern Inner Mongolia for trade in the future (Kawakami, *Japan's Pacific Policy*, 178).

333. This point was not embodied in the "Manchuria Treaty" (25 May 1915), but was accepted by China, with qualifications, in a note (29 May 1915) from the Chinese foreign minister to the Japanese minister to Beijing, which permitted Japanese to work mines in ten mining lots in Fengtian and Jilin Provinces (South Manchuria) but disallowed similar privileges in eastern Inner Mongolia (Kawakami, *Japan's Pacific Policy*, 178).

334. This point was not embodied in the treaty, but was nonetheless confirmed on the same day in a separate note (*ibid.,* 179).

335. This point was not put into the treaty as such, although in the treaty text China agreed to "revise" earlier treaty-based agreements with respect to the Jilin-Changchun Railway on the basis of railway loans made by other foreign parties (*ibid.*).

336. This point was not adopted in the treaty but was acknowledged the same day in a slightly altered wording in a note from the Chinese Ministry of Foreign Affairs to the Japanese minister in Beijing (Kawakami, *Japan's Pacific Policy*, 179–80).

337. This point was not accepted (*ibid.*, 180).

338. It is interesting to list briefly those points which were not accepted: (1) the privilege to maintain Japanese hospitals, churches, and schools in the Chinese interior; (2) the establishment, in certain large cities with a high percentage of Japanese residents, of a joint Chinese-Japanese police administration or employment of Japanese police officers; (3) an obligation by China to procure a certain percentage of weapons and munitions from Japan and to establish a joint Japanese-Chinese arsenal;

(4) allowing Japan to build the Wuzhang-Nanzhang and Nanzhang-Hangzhou rail lines; and (5) guarantees to Japanese of the same rights of religious proselytization as had been granted to other foreigners (Kawakami, *Japan's Pacific Policy*, 181–82).

339. *Ibid.*

340. Kawakami, *Japan's Pacific Policy*, 183–84. The document was delivered to the Japanese minister in Beijing on 12 February 1915.

341. Clyde, *The Far East*, 423 (emphasis added). American Secretary of State Bryan had delivered the Memorandum to the Japanese ambassador. After the Chinese government had accepted the Japanese ultimatum, the American government in identical notes to Japan and China gave them to know that "any agreement or undertaking which has been entered into or which may be entered into between the governments of Japan and China, impairing the treaty rights of the United States and its citizens in China, the political or territorial integrity of the Republic of China, or the international policy relative to China commonly known as the open door policy" would not be recognized by the United States (*ibid.*, 423–24).

342. Kawakami, *Japan's Pacific Policy*, 184.

343. Ōkuma, "Japanese Prime Minister Who Negotiated '21 Demands' Tells Inside Story," *loc. cit.*

344. Kawakami, *Japan's Pacific Policy*, 184. See also Frank C. Langdon, "Japan's Failure to Establish Friendly Relations with China on 1917–1918," *Pacific Historical Review* XXVI, no. 3 (August 1957): 256: "Even the evil motives attributed to the Japanese leaders, such as buying up valuable rights and attempting to seize control of China, seem to be an exaggeration."

345. Kawakami, *Japan's Pacific Policy*, 185.

346. *The Correspondence of G. E. Morrison*, II, 764n2.

347. Storry, *A History of Modern Japan*, 152: "But foolishly Kato, the Foreign Minister, overplayed his hand."

348. However, Paul Reinsch in Beijing had already "learned about the demands in late January 1915" (LaFeber, *Clash*, 110).

349. See also Tani Hisako, "Terauchi naikaku to Nishihara shakkan" (The Terauchi Cabinet and the Nishihara loans), *Hōgakkai zasshi* 10, no. 1 (October 1969): 57–142 ("1. The negotiations were promoted secretly by Mr. Nishihara who was given authority by Premier Terauchi and Finance Minister Katsuda without the foreign ministry being informed . . . 2. Japan attempted to monopolize concessions in China at the time when all the European countries and the U.S. were wholly involved in World War I. 3. That agreement did not bring about any advantages to Japan while it hampered the unification of China by helping the Dankizui [Duan Qirui] government" [English abstract, 2]). See also Frank D. Langdon, *The Japanese Policy of Expansion in China 1917–1928* (diss., University of California, Berkeley, 1953), and his "Japan's Failure to Establish Friendly Relations with China in 1917–1918," *Pacific Historical Review* 26, no. 3 (August 1957).

350. Clyde, *The Far East*, 451, names the sum as 120 million yen: "These were not investments in the usual meaning of the word. Rather, they were payments to officials then in power in exchange for certain agreements that would promote Japanese policy, particularly in Manchuria."

351. Tani Hisako, "Terauchi naikaku to Nishihara shakkan," 68ff. As for the Japanese military faction's repeated history of offering loans to Chinese warlords, Takemoto makes the general case that "the Japanese army had long been playing the game of balance of power in China among Chinese warlords by using its personnel and secret political funds. This manipulation was totally outside Shidehara's control and most often occurred without the foreign office's knowledge" (*Failure of Liberalism in Japan*, 62).

352. *The Correspondence of G. E. Morrison*, II, 583n4.

353. After the United States itself formally declared itself a belligerent on 6 April 1917 the peace movement and opponents of American participation in the war were now subject to various types of repression. See H. C. Peterson and Gilbert C. Fite, *Opponents of War, 1917–1918* (Seattle and London: University of Washington Press, 1957). See also the famous essay of Randolph S. Bourne, "Trans-National America," *Atlantic Monthly* cxvii (July 1916), reprinted in Bourne, *War and the Intellectuals, Collected Essays, 1915–1919*, edited and with an introduction by Carl Resek (New York, Evanston, and London: Harper & Row, 1964), 107–23.

354. Clyde, *op. cit.*, 425ff.

355. *Ibid.*, 452.

356. Gernet, *A History of Chinese Civilization*, 630.

357. Gernet, *op. cit.*, 630–31.

358. Willoughby, *op. cit.*, 625; Nish, *op. cit.*, 116.

359. See Ishii Kikujirō, *op. cit.*, 124–35, which reproduces this document.

360. Takemoto, *op. cit.*, 9.

361. See Wilhelm Solf, "Wie kam es zum Konflikt im Fernen Osten?" (How did the conflict in the Far East come about?), special edition of the *Berliner Börsenzeitung* (Berlin Financial Newspaper), no. 143, vol. 25 (March 1932): 7: "In and for Japan the World War was not the catastrophe which it was for almost all other lands and peoples that had taken part. For Japan it was a means to unheard-of progress, a spring of material wellbeing, and politically seeing its high point with Japan's inclusion among the 'Big Five' [orig. English] of Versailles."

362. See Bamba, *op. cit.*, 46: "Between 1895 and 1925 the number of students in high school had increased almost tenfold. The number of universities had increased from 2 to 34."

363. Shidehara Kijūrō, "Genesis of the Manchurian Incident of 1931, Manshū mondai," *Shidehara documents* 44 (reel 2), 20 (unpublished English manuscript, date uncertain).

364. Bersihand, *op. cit.*, 406–7.

365. Bamba, *op. cit.*, 188–89.

366. John H. Maurer stresses that "Japan derived important benefits from the Washington settlement that enhanced its security" ("Arms Control and the Washington Conference," in Erik Goldstein and John Maurer [eds.], *The Washington Conference, 1921–22: Naval Rivalry, East Asian Stability and the Road to Pearl Harbor* [Portland, Ore.: Frank Cass, 1964], 288).

367. David Armstrong, "China's Place in the New Pacific Order," in Goldstein and Maurer (eds.), *The Washington Conference*, 255. And *ibid.*: "In Shidehara's view,

Japan stood to gain more from trade and overseas investment than from territorial acquisition and this entailed a more liberal and conciliatory international posture, particularly towards the United States, with whom Japanese trade was growing faster than the trade of either country with China."

368. Even George E. Morrison shows in a long letter (*op. cit.*, 429–46) to Liang Shiyi (Shih-yi, 1869–1933), a onetime imperial bureaucrat and later Republican, sympathies for Japan, warning against too one-sided an assessment and praising the Japanese entry into the war: "Has England any reason for dissatisfaction? From the outbreak of the war Japan has acted with faithfulness to her alliance. She has given assistance of the most important kind. Immediately on the declaration of war she mobilised one third of her Navy and placed it at the service of her ally. Her ships have helped to sweep the German ships from off the seas" (*ibid.,* 430).

369. *Shidehara Kijūrō,* 94, cited in Takemoto, *Failure of Liberalism in Japan,* 37–38: "Working through Prime Minister Terauchi Masatake, General of the army, it [the army] proposed the idea of combining military and diplomatic control of Manchuria and then placing the combined responsibility in the army's hands. Being totally ignorant of the plan, Foreign Minister Motono unwittingly gave his approval. In fact, when Terauchi asked him for his approval of the plan, he gave his agreement verbally without first consulting the foreign ministry's senior officers. Shidehara was taken by surprise by such army politicking, but he counteracted immediately by briefing Motono and explaining the implications of such a plan."

370. "[A] daring move that Lansing immediately condemned as the first Anglo-Japanese giant step to dominate Russia. In Tokyo, most officials viewed the British proposal as heavensent" (LaFeber, *Clash,* 117, with more details).

371. Bersihand, *op. cit.,* 405.

372. *Ibid.* On how this developed, see also Nish, *op. cit.,* 145ff.

373. This assistance included, among other things, joint strategic planning, Japanese use of transport facilities, and the introduction of Japanese military advisers.

374. Bamba, *op. cit.,* 38: "There was a clear contest over the Siberian expedition . . . between two clusters of leaders." See also James W. Morley, *The Japanese Thrust into Siberia, 1918* (New York: Columbia University Press, 1957); and Takeuchi Tatsuji, *War and Diplomacy in the Japanese Empire* (London: George Allen & Unwin, 1935) (repr. New York, 1967), chapter 18.

375. They were backed in this by Foreign Minister Gotō Shimpei and Prime Minister (and General) Terauchi Masatake.

376. Duus, *op. cit.,* 197.

377. Bamba, *op. cit.,* 38–39.

378. However, a proposal put forward by Woodrow Wilson to mediate the calling together of a conference of all the Russian parties to the conflict was rejected during February 1918 by the "White Russians."

379. Woodrow Wilson Papers, Manuscript Division, Library of Congress, 24151–52, CF 2106, Washington-Paris, 27 May 1919. The cablegram in its entirety read:

Japanese Ambassador handed me the following aide mémoire on May 24: "More than six months have elapsed since the provisional government becoming organized at Omsk under the direction of Admiral Kolchak to undertake the restoration [of] order and security in Russia. It has so far borne with admirable tact and determination the most difficult task that has ever fallen upon the lot of any government, while its position seems now to be further strengthened by the recognition reported to have recently accorded to it as the central authority in Russia by the group at Archangel and Ekaterinburg. Having regard to the known desire of all the Allies and associated powers, [Japan] wishes the early reestablishment in Russia of an orderly and efficient government with reasonable promise if stability, and believing it proves official acknowledgement by foreign powers of the international standing of the Omsk government will materially be much to the maintenance of peace, the Japanese government feel the moment is opportune to consider the question of provisional recognition to be extended to the Omsk government. The recognition might be made subject to such conditions as may be found essential to safeguard the legitimate interest of foreign nations and the government to assume all international obligations and indebtedness undertaken by Russia before the overthrow of [the] Kerensky administration. In bringing these considerations to the notice of the government to which you are accredited the Japanese government desire to suggest that the questions might conveniently be discussed among the delegates of the principal Allied and associated foreign powers now assembled at Paris." Please advise me what reply to make. Polk, Acting.

380. Takemoto, *op. cit.*, 51.

381. Article XI of the constitution of the empire of Japan (often called the "Meiji constitution") read: "The Emperor has the supreme command of the Army and Navy." As a result of this provision the military leadership, by invoking the emperor's authority, could in an ambiguous situation that might develop outside Japan evade control by the Diet and civil government.

382. Bamba, *op. cit.*, 45.

383. LaFeber, *Clash*, 117.

384. There had apparently even been plans by the Japanese secret service to rescue the Russian tsar and his family from the Bolsheviks.

385. *Gaikō gojūnen*, 90. This English translation is by Miwa Kimitada, in "Japanese Opinions on Woodrow Wilson in War and Peace," *Monumenta Nipponica* 22, nos. 3–4 (1967): 379.

386. The *Survey of American Foreign Relations*, prepared under the direction of Charles Howland (New Haven, Conn.: Yale University Press, 1930), 62, asserts on the other hand: "[O]n January 12, 1920, the United States announced to Japan its intention to withdraw its forces from Siberia. This began on the seventeenth." On 31 May 1921 the State Department stated, in a diplomatic note to Tokyo, that it recognized no Japanese rights related to the continuing military presence in Russia.

387. Together with Shidehara, there also appeared on the list of potential Japanese judges Tomii Masaakira and Hozumi Nobushige (Gaikō Shiryōkan, MT 2.4.1.3, vol. 5, note 11). In December 1924 Adachi Mineichirō (Adatci Mineitcirô), then serving as Japanese ambassador in Brussels, was appointed to take Shidehara's place. After

25 November 1921 the neo-Kantian German jurist Walther Schücking also appeared on the list of potential judges. Oda Yorozu from Japan was also added to the list on 25 August 1921 (Gaikō Shiryōkan, MT 2.4.1.3, vol. 6).

388. *Shidehara Kijūrō*, 147. The Versailles Peace Conference began on 13 January 1919 and ended with the signing of the Treaty of Versailles on 28 June 1919.

389. One might assume that Shidehara, having served in The Hague until recently, was already well informed about plans for the future world organization.

390. Thomas Burkman, *Japan, the League of Nations, and the New World Order, 1918–1920* (Ph.D. diss., University of Michigan, 1975), 82. The committee was established on 10 September 1915 and officially met some thirty times. A comprehensive report of 25 December 1916 is found in *Gaimushō no hyakunen*, vol. 1 (1969), 697–700.

391. Interestingly, in October 1914 there had already taken place consultations sponsored by the Schweizer Vereinigung zum Studium der Grundlagen eines dauerhaften Friedensvertrages (Swiss Association to Study the Foundations of a Durable Peace Treaty), which Shidehara may also have known about.

392. Walther Schücking, *Der Weltfriedensbund und die Wiedergeburt des Völkerrechts* (A world peace league and the rebirth of international law) (Leipzig: Verlag Naturwissenschaften, 1917), 11.

393. Walther Schücking, *Der Weltfriedensbund*, 12.

394. James Bryce, *International Relations*, lecture II, "The Great War and Its Results," 39–40.

395. Géza von Magyary, *Die internationale Schiedsgerichtsbarkeit im Völkerbunde* (International arbitration in the League of Nations) (Berlin: Otto Liebmann, 1922), 12, citing F. Klein, *Der Völkerbund der Friedensverträge* (The League of Nations of the Peace Treaties) (Wien, 1919), 41: "In the democratic-parliamentary age all power derives from the people, including that of the League of Nations."

396. Géza von Magyary, *op. cit.*, 12, who then continues: "Only now, when the grand spirit of both Hague Peace Conferences has faded away, is revealed to us the true knowledge of its meaning."

397. James Bryce, *International Relations*, lecture VII, "International Questions and Disputes," 208 and 210.

398. Thomas Burkman, *op. cit.*, 97 (on Bryce group) and 83–84 (on Theodore Marburg). It is possible that information had reached Shidehara and the preparatory committee via personal contacts with the Japanese legation in the Netherlands. See also H. Latané, where Theodore Marburg on 16 May 1917 had arranged for the sending of the "Japanese text of the League literature" which had "been forwarded" to a publisher in Tokyo "with the request that he have 2,000 copies printed and placed in the hands of the intellectual leaders of Japan, including the statesmen and members of Parliament" (*Development of the League of Nations Idea—Documents and Correspondence of Theodore Marburg* [New York: Macmillan, 1932], vol. 1, 300–301).

399. Thomas Burkman, *op. cit.*, 82: The so-called comprehensive report referred "almost exclusively to the transfer of former German territories and economic rights to Japan." It was reported, for example, that "the Japanese Government sold all the

enemy property which was seized during the War, notwithstanding its promise at the beginning of the War that enemy subjects should not be disturbed in their possessions." See also Howland, *Survey of American Foreign Relations*, 513.

400. Burkman, "Japanese Christians and the Wilsonian World Order," 39. It was believed that Japan was "one of the great powers whose participation was essential to the viability of any League scheme" (*ibid., 40*).

401. See Latané, where in response to a letter from Theodore Marburg the Japanese ambassador Satō Aimaro is confirming a telegraphic message that had been sent by foreign minister Motono and that stated: "I [Motono] have noted with interest your unremitting efforts to secure the world against a repetition of the present convulsion. All proposals directed to effect so desirable an end must be welcomed and carefully studied by everyone to whom peace and good will are not empty names and who has any regard for humanity." Marburg's message had stated among other things that "the establishment of such a league (to ensure peace and justice throughout the world) [was now] almost certain" (*Development of the League of Nations*, vol. 1, 246–47).

402. Burkman, *op. cit.*, 87. In German there is an excellent dissertation by Swiss scholar Ursula Fortuna, *Der Völkerbundgedanke in Deutschland während des Ersten Weltkrieges* (The League of Nations idea in Germany during the First World War) (Zurich: Europa Verlag, 1974).

403. Latané, *Development of the League of Nations*, vol. II, 549.

404. Later, with regard to the Washington Naval Disarmament Conference, Thomas H. Buckley concludes that "[t]he experience of the Washington Conference suggests that those who believe that world peace can be secured through disarmament alone, without making political arrangements concurrently, are ignoring reality" (*The United States and the Washington Conference* [Knoxville: University of Tennessee Press, 1970], 190).

405. Burkman, *op. cit.*, 98–99 (Reports of the Political Affairs Bureau, vol. 11, November 1918) and 102 for the text of the "memorandum" (also Political Affairs Bureau, 30 November 1918), which includes point 3 on China policy, with the proposal that Japan should take the initiative in doing away with judicial extraterritoriality in its spheres of interest in continental China, should return the Boxer indemnity payments, withdraw all troops from China, and support the Four-Power Financial Consortium being put together under American leadership.

406. Shidehara Kijūrō, "Gaikō kanken" (My personal views on diplomacy), address before students of Keiō University (19 October 1928), in *Shidehara Kijūrō*, 274. A similar translation of this passage is found in Bamba, 162 (emphasis added).

407. *Ibid.*

408. Perhaps first and foremost, Thomas Hobbes, who was well known to the Japanese through translations, had identified the mobilization of public opinion as a precondition for peace.

409. Cited in Helen Mears, *Mirror for Americans—Japan* (Boston: Houghton Mifflin, 1948), 301.

410. English translation as published in Takemoto, *Failure of Liberalism in Japan*, 34, with emphasis added.

411. Shidehara Kijūrō, "Japan's Attitude Towards America," speech before the Fifth Avenue Association, New York (4 March 1920), published in *The Japan Review* IV (May 1920): 205.

412. Quoted in *The Far Eastern Republic* 1, no. 6 (March 1920): 2 (The Chinese National Welfare Society, San Francisco). This publication assigned to the Japanese "the most sinister designs" in their policies with regards to China (*ibid.*, 19).

413. Shidehara Kijūrō, "Japan's Attitude Towards America," *ibid.*

414. See Edward Price Bell, giving the following exchange: Question (Bell)— "You found, nevertheless, that Shidehara feels deeply about the discriminatory clause in our immigration act?" Reply (Bancroft)—"I knew that already. But, if I had not known it, Shidehara would have enlightened me . . . *Japan wants the quota, and nothing more*" (*World Chancelleries*, with an introduction by Calvin Coolidge, Chicago, *The Chicago Daily News*, 1926, interview with Edgar Edison Bancroft, U.S. ambassador in Tokyo, 114) (emphasis added). Harvard-educated Frederick Moore, who had been appointed by Shidehara as advisor to the Japanese Embassy in Washington in 1921 and later served as an advisor to the Japanese foreign ministry in Tokyo during Shidehara's tenure as foreign minister, notes in the second paragraph of his book *With Japan's Leaders: An Intimate Record of Fourteen Years as Counsellor to the Japanese Government, Ending in December 1941* (New York: Scribners, 1942), 1: "The refusal of Congress to permit a token quota of a little more than a hundred [Japanese farmers or blue collar workers] a year to enter this country had a profound effect upon the nation. The Government and people were severely hurt. The passage of the Act was a turning point in the Japanese attitude toward Americans."

415. Shidehara Kijūrō, "The United States and Japan," speech before the Cleveland Chamber of Commerce (3 May 1921), published in *The Japan Review* V (May 1921): 117–18.

416. After the Second World War the American government in effect proposed a sort of Monroe Doctrine for the Pacific region. See *The New York Times* of 17 February 1951: "The United States has suggested a 'Monroe Doctrine' for the Pacific, under which it would join Australia, New Zealand, the Philippines and Japan in a mutual defense pact against Communist aggression."

417. Shidehara Kijūrō, "The Future of American-Japanese Relations," speech before the Japan Society of New York (3 March 1920), published in *The Japan Review* IV (April 1920): 170–71 (emphasis added).

418. Asada Sadao, "Japan's 'Special Interests' and the Washington Conference, 1921–1922," *American Historical Review* LXVII (October 1961): 68 (emphasis added).

419. Asada, "Japan's 'Special Interests,'" 68–69.

420. Raymond Lesley Buell, *The Washington Conference* (New York and London: D. Appleton, 1922), 147.

421. Documents in the Political Archive of the German foreign ministry, Bonn, Roll 1, J.No.686. Nr.

422. Gaikō Shiryōkan, MT 2.4.3.3.-1. Shortly before, on the same day, Shidehara had already telegraphed the contents, via the Bonin Islands, to the Ministry of Foreign Affairs, with the designation "URGENT." According to Nish, Secretary of State

Hughes personally intimated to Shidehara in March 1921 the plans of the American government to host a naval disarmament conference. "[T]he ambassador responded quite favourably" (*op. cit.*, 139).

423. Edward Bell to Uchida Yasuya, 12 September 1921, Gaikō Shiryōkan, MT 2.4.3.3.-1.

424. *Ibid.*: "Under the heading 'status of existing commitments,' it is expected that an opportunity will be afforded to consider and reach an understanding with respect to unsettled questions involving the nature and scope of commitments under which claims of rights may hereafter be asserted.—I have the honor to add that these suggestions as to the Agenda will be communicated to all the Powers invited to the Conference and will be brought to the attention of his Excellency Baron Shidehara at Washington."

425. Buell, *op. cit.*, 148–49.

426. See John Chalmers Vinson, *William E. Borah and the Outlawry of War* (Athens: University of Georgia Press, 1957), 41ff, for more details.

427. See "Summary of News," in English, Gaikō Shiryōkan, MT 2.4.3.5.-4. However, almost immediately the French government expressed itself in opposition to the above-named proposal. See Boyden Sparks, "French oppose asking Berlin to Conference," *The New York Tribune*, 26 November 1921.

428. See Joseph W. Grigg, "Britain expects to back Harding's Association Plan," *New York World*, 26 November 1921. A copy is found in Gaikō Shiryōkan, MT 2.4.3.5.-4.

429. Adachi Kinnosuke, 28 November 1921, in the *New York World*.

430. The dispute was said to have been triggered by a speech of Lord Curzon, to which the French Foreign Minister Briand reacted sharply (Gaikō Shiryōkan, MT 2.4.3.5.-4).

431. See "The Association-of-Nations Plan finds Favour with Congress," *Baltimore Sun*, 27 November 1921; Charles Michelson, "Foreign Delegations agree 'in principle' to President's Plan," *New York World*, 27 November 1921; and Albert W. Fox, "Harding World Conference Idea dominates Delegates," *Washington Post*, 28 November 1921. Only Borah attacked the president's plan. See, for example, "Borah attacked Harding Plan for Family of Nations," *Philadelphia Public Ledger*, and "Harding Proposal attacked by Borah," *New York Herald*, both on 28 November 1921. See also Vinson, *William E. Borah and the Outlawry of War*, 42ff.

432. "'Outlaw' Weapons Big Issue at Parley," *New York Herald*, 28 November 1921.

433. "The Pathway to Peace," an address by the Honorable Charles E. Hughes before the Canadian Bar Association, Washington, Government Printing Office 1923, 2.

434. *Ibid.*

435. *Ibid.*, 2–3.

436. According to Frederic William Wile in the *Washington Post* of 3 December 1921: "There is to be a three-power understanding between the United States, Japan and Great Britain for preservation of peace in the Far East, if not actually in the whole world."

437. Frederick Moore, *With Japan's Leaders: An Intimate Record of Fourteen Years as Counsellor to the Japanese Government, Ending December 7, 1941* (New York: Charles Scribner's Sons, 1942), 57–58.

438. Kato's view personal, declares Tokugawa, *New York Times*, 30 November 1921. The previous day the same newspaper carried an article under the title "Shidehara Better," referring to the health problems Shidehara had encountered when he suffered from kidney stones. Surprisingly, he was able to continue to "influence things despite his illness and despite being confined to bed" (personal communication from Professor Ian Nish in a letter of 28 June 2007).

439. Cornelius Vanderbilt even went so far as to publish an article in the *New York American* (2 December 1921) with the title "Japan Shows No Peace Desire."

440. See Charles Michelson in the *New York World* (3 December 1921): "Japan Accepts 5-5-3 Ratio, but Expects Concessions in East."

441. Ralph Courtney, "France to give up China Leases only if others do," *New York Herald*, 4 December 1921.

442. See, for example, Carter Field, who speaks of "important concessions" in his article "Pacific Problem to be Solved by Agreement of Four Powers" (4 December 1921) in the *New York Tribune*; Thomas Steep, "China wins Marked Concessions," *New York Tribune* (4 December 1921) writes: "China achieved historic progress toward relief from foreign control." The correspondent of the *New York Times*, Edwin L. James, saw matters not quite so positively, saying "China will not get all she asks" ("Powers Agree to End some China Leases," 4 December 1921).

443. Chung Chu Kwei, "Conference Doings Disappoint Chinese," *New York Times*, 4 December 1921.

444. "Japanese Delegates await Word from Tokyo on Ratio," *Washington Post*, 4 December 1921.

445. See, for example, "A foreign Traveller describes Terrors of Bolshevist Russia," *New York Tribune*, 4 December 1921, and "Famine Conditions in Russia," *New York World*, 4 December 1921.

446. For example, Albert W. Fox published in the *Washington Post*, 5 December 1921, an article titled: "Japanese Diplomacy of Delay checks Arms Parley Progress."

447. "Militarist Party in Power in Japan," London dispatch of 5 December 1921 in *The Christian Science Monitor*.

448. Philip C. Tyan on 7 December 1921 in the *Baltimore Sun*: "Not a Concession yet made by Japan."

449. Frank H. Simonds, "Secret Diplomacy causing Trouble," *Washington Herald*, 7 December 1921.

450. "Pessimism's Bad Week," *New York Tribune*, 7 December 1921.

451. Akira Iriye, *After Imperialism: The Search for a New Order in the Far East, 1921–31* (Cambridge, Mass.: Harvard University Press, 1965), 16–17.

452. See Kawakami, *Japan's Pacific Policy*, 61: "It is not correct to say, as has been said by some writers, that Japan initiated this treaty, although there is reason to believe that its final draft, which formed the basis of the treaty, was Baron Shidehara's work. . . . If we are to credit any single nation with the initiative of the new treaty, that credit should go to England. But perhaps it is nearer the truth to say that the treaty was initiated spontaneously and simultaneously by Japan, Britain and America. Each felt almost intuitively what the others had in mind."

453. "Rumor has it that Article 19 [of the naval treaty], as it now stands, was drafted by Baron Shidehara. It was a happy solution of the knotty problem, and was readily accepted by Mr. Hughes and Mr. Balfour" (Kawakami, *Japan's Pacific Policy*, 40). Similarly Nish has noted: "[I]t appears that the critical clause of the four-Power naval treaty was drafted by Shidehara" (*op. cit.*, 140). He modifies this statement by a note (320n12) saying "Shidehara's [own] account of the naval issue in his 'Inside view (*rimenkan*) of the Washington Conference' [published by the Ministry of Foreign Affairs in 1939] is slight." The note refers to 220 of *Shidehara Kijūrō*, where the editors conclude from Shidehara's reminiscences in *Gaikō gojūnen* that the "rumors" at the time about Shidehara's likely authorship of article 19 of the naval treaty were well founded.

454. Hanihara Masanao, one of the Japanese delegates (who would later be ambassador to the United States), compared the expiring Anglo-Japanese Alliance with the new agreement and thought it fair to comment: "We have discarded whiskey and accepted water." Cited in Kawakami, *Japan's Pacific Policy*, 61.

455. "It was perhaps Baron Shidehara who took the 'kick' out of the original British draft, and thus converted it to wholesome 'water' acceptable to 'dry' America" (*ibid.*).

456. The official title read: *Treaty between the Four Powers Concerning Their Insular Possessions and Insular Dominions in the Region of the Pacific Ocean.*

457. "4-Power Treaty pledges Consultation, Mediation, Arbitration, ends the Anglo-Japanese Alliance," *New York Times*, 9 December 1921.

458. See, for example, Henry Woodhouse, "Pacific Pact 'Blow to Monroe Doctrine'" (*New York American*, 14 December 1921). Taken to task, too, was what to some appeared to be increasing tactics of covertness. See, for example, "Secrecy grows at Conference as Settlement draws near," *Baltimore Sun* (14 December 1921).

459. Kawakami, *Japan's Pacific Policy*, 60.

460. Paul S. Reinsch, "China losing Hope of Peace," *New York American* (10 December 1921).

461. Lady Astor, "Material Progress has been made," *Washington Times* (11 December 1921).

462. Clyde, *The Far East*, 480–81. "Japan had won tangible and specific advantages [and] her security was greatly increased" (*ibid.,* 481).

463. Albert W. Fox, in "Ten Year World Naval Holiday Assured," writes of the agreement in the *Washington Post* (16 December 1921): "It virtually assures a ten-year naval holiday . . . and the end of the race for naval armaments. It marks a new epoch in international relationships and ushers in a day which may prove the most important since the Armistice in its effect on the future of world events." The *Washington Herald* speaks of "the greatest single step ever made toward permanent and lasting peace," and the *Baltimore Sun* points out that the budgetary savings for the United States would be 170 million dollars in the following year and 100 million dollars per year thereafter.

464. Fairbank, Reischauer, and Craig, *East Asia—The Modern Transformation*, 236.

465. "Japanese to keep Mutsu in return for Agreement on Naval Ratio," *Washington Herald* (16 December 1921). See also Shiba Takao, "The Loss of Japanese

Shipbuilding Industry caused by the Conclusion of the Naval Armaments Limitation Treaty of 1922—The case of Mitsubishi Shipbuilding and Engineering Co," *Acta Humanistica et Scientifica Universitatis Sangis Kyotoiensis* 24, no. 4 (March 1994): 59–85.

466. See Charles Michelson, "French Plan of ten new Warships threatens to upset naval Accord," *New York World* (17 December 1921); "France calls for 350.000 tons of new ships by 1941," *Washington Post* (19 December 1921).

467. J. G. Hamilton, "Japanese Success is called Amazing," *New York Times* (17 December 1921).

468. Carter Field, "France and Japan are to yield on Submarines," *New York Tribune* (26 December 1921), which goes on to note that "absolute confidence that both France and Japan will accept the reasonable ratio for their submarine tonnage . . . is felt here tonight."

469. Frederic William Wile, "French reject Hughes Ratio on Submarines," *Philadelphia Public Ledger* (28 December 1921).

470. Cited in Kawakami, *Japan's Pacific Policy*, 309.

471. Kawakami, *op. cit.*, 242.

472. Shidehara Kijūrō, "Statement before the Far Eastern Committee," 23 January 1922, cited in Kawakami, *Japan's Pacific Policy*, appendix XIII, "Siberia," 354. The same statement by Shidehara also appears in full in a French translation in D. C. H. d'Avigdor et Windsor, *La Sibérie orientale et le Japon, Études politiques et économiques suivies de la déclaration du baron Shidehara* (Paris: Roger et Cie, 1922).

473. *Ibid.*, 356.

474. *Ibid.*, 357.

475. *Ibid.*, 357–58. Such provisions would include "the removal of the existing menace to the security of Japan and to the lives and property of Japanese residents in Eastern Siberia, the provision of guarantees for the freedom of lawful undertakings in that region, and the prohibition of Bolshevist propaganda over the Siberian border."

476. *Ibid.*, 358.

477. Cited in Kawakami, *Japan's Pacific Policy*, 243.

478. *Ibid.*, 244, where the author goes on to explain "[t]he best way to prevent its propagation in Japanese territories would be to recall Japanese soldiers from Siberian soil and expend the money thus saved on necessary internal reform both in Korea and in Japan."

479. "Baron Shidehara's Statement before the Far Eastern Committee," 2 February 1922, given as appendix IV-A to Kawakami, *Japan's Pacific Policy*, 290–92.

480. Kawakami, *Japan's Pacific Policy*, 174–75. See also Baron Shidehara's Statement before the Far Eastern Committee, 2 February 1922, in *ibid.*, 292; Hugh Borton, *Japan's Modern Century—from Perry to 1970* (New York: The Ronald Press, 1970), 344–45: "In January 1922, Japan's delegate [at the Washington Conference], Foreign Minister [at the time ambassador to the United States] Shidehara, made a conciliatory move. He announced that his country had no designs on either Chinese or Russian territory and would begin immediate withdrawal of its troops from Shantung. Under these circumstances, China had little choice but to agree to the Sino-Japanese Treaty of February 4, 1922, in which Japan promised to restore Shantung to China in full

sovereignty and to grant it a loan to enable it to buy the Tsinan-Tsingtau Railway";
see also Storry, *A History of Modern Japan*, 165.

481. "Baron Shidehara's Statement before the Far Eastern Committee," 2 February
1922, in Kawakami, *Japan's Pacific Policy*, 291.

482. "Mr. Wang's Statement before the Far Eastern Committee," 3 February 1922,
ibid., 293–96.

483. *Ibid.*, 294. Wang explained that in this statement the Chinese government
had declared that it had been "constrained to comply in full with the terms of the
[Japanese] ultimatum."

484. The Chinese delegation gave the following justification: "(1.) In exchange
for the concessions demanded of China, Japan offered no *quid pro quo*. Thus any
benefits derived from the agreements were wholly unilateral. (2.) The agreements, in
important respects, are in violation of treaties between China and the other Powers.
(3.) The agreements are inconsistent with the principles relating to China which have
been adopted by the Conference. (4.) The agreements have engendered constant misunderstandings between China and Japan, and, if not abrogated, will necessarily tend,
in the future, to disturb friendly relations between the two countries, and will thus
constitute an obstacle in the way of realizing the purpose for the attainment of which
this Conference was convened." Cited from "Mr. Wang's Statement before the Far
Eastern Committee," 3 February 1922, included as appendix IV-B in *ibid.*, 293–96.
Wang then cites the aforementioned resolution introduced in the Japanese Diet in June
1915 by Hara Takashi (Kei), who three years later became Japan's prime minister,
garnering "the support of some 130 of the members of the parliament."

485. "U.S. Secretary of State Charles Evans Hughes before the Far Eastern
Committee," 3 February 1922, in appendix IV-C to *ibid.*, 297.

486. Gottfried-Karl Kidnermann, *Der Ferne Osten in der Weltpolitik des industriellen
Zeitalters* (The Far East in the world politics of the industrial era) (München: dtv-
Weltgeschichte des 20. Jahrhunderts, Bd. 6, 1970), 101; Storry, *op. cit.*, 164.

487. Udo Ratenhof, *Die Chinapolitik des Deutschen Reiches 1871 bis 1945.
Wirtschaft-Rüstung-Militär* (The China policy of the German Empire 1871 to
1945—economy-armaments-military) (Boppard am Rhein: Harald Boldt, 1987), 273.
Also, *loc. cit.*: "The Four Power Treaty and the Washington naval agreement of 13
December 1921 continued the great powers' balance-of-power and security policies
in the Far East which had [already] existed since before the First World War, even if
with an obvious increase in the strength of the Americans" (emphasis added).

488. Storry, *op. cit.*, 164. China had in 1919 refused to sign the Versailles Treaty.

489. Already on 20 May 1921 Germany had signed with China the "first treaty
on the basis of equality with a foreign partner" and thereby in fact took the initiative
in the lifting of the "unequal treaties," which was eyed by the Washington Conference for some time in the future (Udo Ratenhof, *Die Chinapolitik des Deutschen
Reiches*, 290).

490. See Beverley D. Causey, "Why Germany Never Signed the Nine-Power
Treaty," *The Far Eastern Quarterly* I (1941): 364–77; Gabriele Ratenhof, *Das
Deutsche Reich und die internationale Krise um die Mandschurei, 1931–1933, Die
deutsche Fernostpolitik als Spiegel und Instrument deutscher Revisionspolitik* (diss.,

Freiburg) (Frankfurt, Bern, and New York: Peter Lang, 1984), 17–18. Peter Krüger, in *Die Außenpolitik der Republik von Weimar* (The foreign policy of the Weimar Republic) (Darmstadt: Wissenschaftliche Buchgesellschaft, 1985), 326, makes this noteworthy assertion: "Politically in the Far East most important and significant for the overall framework of German foreign policy was in any case the [proposed] accession, as of 17 December 1925, to the Washington agreement, namely the Nine Power Treaty." He goes on to discuss the advantages for Germany that would have come from this cooperation, which never materialized. He wrongly assumes, however, that Germany joined the treaty.

491. Henry L. Stimson, *op. cit.*, 9. See also Takemoto, *Failure of Liberalism in Japan*, 31: "Secretary of State and later Secretary of War, Henry L. Stimson wrote many flattering comments about Shidehara in his book, 'The Far Eastern Crisis,' although the book was written in criticism of Japan's expansion into Manchuria. In Stimson's mind, Shidehara's name was associated with 'a closer cooperation with the social and political views of the western world.'"

492. Buell, *op. cit.*, 313–14.

493. H. G. Wells, *Washington and the Riddle of Peace* (New York: Macmillan, 1922), 283–84. A German translation by Robert West under the title *Hoffnung auf Frieden* (Hope for peace) also appeared in 1922 (München, Kurt Wolff), where this passage is found on 340–41. H. G. Wells stayed in the American capital during the conference, writing articles every day or two in quasi-diary form, which were first published in the *New York World* and then compiled, together with a concluding essay, in book form.

494. Peter Duus, *The Rise of Modern Japan* (Boston: Houghton Mifflin, 1976), 199.

495. Wilhelm Solf, "Wie kam es zum Konflikt im Fernen Osten? " (How did the conflict in the Far East come about?), *Berliner Börsenzeitung*, 25 March 1932.

496. K. K. Kawakami, *Japan's Pacific Policy—Especially in Relation to China, The Far East, and the Washington Conference* (New York: E. P. Dutton & Co., 1922), v. Following this modest introduction, the author continues: "In saying this, I am advancing no opinion that Japan is the sole, or even chief, sinner among the Powers. So far from it, I am prepared to assert that her diplomatic history is bright enough when compared with the dark leaves recording the international dealings of some Western Powers."

497. *Ibid.*

498. Iriye, *After Imperialism*, 18.

499. Duus, *op. cit.*, 202.

500. *Ibid.*, 201.

501. Institute of Pacific Relations, *Problems of the Pacific* (1927), 67.

502. Takemoto, *Failure of Liberalism in Japan*, 35.

503. *Ibid.*, 34.

504. *Ibid.*, 33–34, where the author refers to the "most fundamental policy guideline."

505. *Ibid.*, 32: "Together with the London Conference of 1930, the Washington Conference can be regarded as the major accomplishment of the Shidehara diplomacy."

506. In Washington preliminary plans for made for a future conference in Beijing (held in 1925) on Chinese customs and trade autonomy.

507. In September 1923 Shidehara experienced the Great Kantō Earthquake in Tokyo. The shattering event gave rise to apocalyptic fears and was felt by many to symbolically cast a shadow over future developments.

508. "[D]espite the excruciating pain he suffered from kidney stones," which had confined him to bed during parts of the conference (Takemoto, *op. cit.*, 33).

509. Shidehara thanked the president and his wife in a letter of 5 December 1921 in which he writes: "I am happy to inform you that I am much improved" (The Harding Papers, Library of Congress, 76785).

Bibliography

I. PRIMARY SOURCES

Actes Et Documents: Deuxième Conférence Internationale de la Paix. La Haye 15 Juin–18 Octobre 1907. Tome II. Première Commission. Ministère des Affaires Étrangères. La Haye: Martinus Nijhoff, 1909.

A Chronicle of Gods and Sovereigns: Jinnō Shōtōki of Kitabatake Chikafusa, trans. H. Paul Varley. New York: Columbia University Press, 1980.

Blaustein, Albert, and Gisbert H. Flantz (eds.). *Constitutions of the Countries of the World.* Dobbs Ferry, N.Y.: Oceana Publications, Inc., n.d.

The Charter of the United Nations, With Addresses Selected from the Proceedings of the United Nations Conference, San Francisco, April–June 1945, foreword by Frederick Lewis Allen. Scranton, Penn.: The Haddon Craftsmen, 1945.

Conférence Internationale de la Paix. La Haye 18 Mai–29 Juillet 1899. Ministère des Affaires Étrangères. La Haye: Imprimerie Nationale, 1899.

Giuliano, Maurizio, Bruno Simma, Hermann Mosler, Andreas Paulus, and Eleni Chaitidou. *The Charter of the United Nations: A Commentary.* Oxford: Oxford University Press, 2002.

Hultzsch, Eugen, *Inscriptions of Asoka* (Corpus Inscriptionum Indicarum, vol. 1), new edition. Oxford: Printed for the Government of India at the Clarendon Press, 1925 (Tokyo: Meicho-Fukyû-kai, 1977).

International Court of Justice (ICJ), Reports, 1970.

The Kojiki (Records of Ancient Matters), trans. Basil Hall Chamberlain. Rutland, Vt., and Tokyo: Charles E. Tuttle, 1990 (1981, orig. 1882, repr. 1919).

McLaren, W. W. *Japanese Government Documents.* Tokyo: Transactions of the Asiatic Society of Japan, vol. XLII, part I (1914).

Nihongi—Chronicles of Japan from the Earliest Times to A.D. 697, trans. from the original Chinese and Japanese by W. G. Aston. Rutland, Vt., and Tokyo: Charles E. Tuttle, 1993 (orig. 1896).

Pal, Radha Binod. *International Military Tribunal for the Far East—Dissentient Judgment.* Calcutta: Sanyal & Co., 1953.

Der Parlamentarische Rat 1948–1949, Akten und Protokolle, ed. vom Deutschen Bundestag und vom Bundesarchiv, 2 Bde., Bd. 2—Der Verfassungskonvent auf Herrenchiemsee, Bonn: 1975 and 1981.

Prichard, R. John, and Sonia Magbana Ziade (eds.). *The Tokyo War Crimes Trials* (The Complete Transcription of the Proceedings of the International Military Tribunal for the Far East), twenty-two vols. New York: Garland, 1981–1983.

Röling, B. V. A., and C. F. Rüter (eds.). *The Tokyo Judgment: The International Military Tribunal for the Far East (IMTFE), 29 April 1946–12 November 1948, Part I: The Majority Judgment—Part II: Dissenting Opinion PAL—Part III: Other Dissenting Opinion and Charter of the IMTFE*, two vols. Amsterdam: University Press of Amsterdam, 1972.

Supreme Commander for the Allied Powers, Government Section. *Political Reorientation of Japan: September 1945 to September 1948*, two vols. Washington, D.C.: Government Printing Office, n.d.

Survey of American Foreign Relations, prepared under the direction of Charles Howland. New Haven, Conn.: Yale University Press, 1930.

Trial of Japanese War Criminals, Documents: 1. Opening Statement by Joseph B. Keenan, Chief Counsel; 2. Charter of the International Military Tribunal for the Par East; 3. Indictment. Washington, D.C.: U.S. Government Printing Office, 1946 (Department of State Far Eastern Series 12).

Union Interparlementaire. *Compte rendu de la XXIIe Conférence tenue a Berne et Genève du 22 au 28 Août 1924.* Lausanne, Genève: Librairie Payot, 1925.

U.S. Army. *Reports of General MacArthur*, vol. 1 supplement, *MacArthur in Japan, The Occupation: Military Phase*, prepared by his general staff. Washington, D.C.: U.S. Government Printing Office, 1966.

U.S. Department of State, *Activities of the Far Eastern Commission, February 26, 1946–July 10, 1947*, Report by the Secretary General, Department of State Publication 2888, Far Eastern Series 24. Washington, D.C.: U.S. Government Printing Office, 1947.

———. *Foreign Relations of the United States, Diplomatic Papers: The Conference of Berlin [Potsdam] 1945*, vol. 1. Washington, D.C.: U.S. Government Printing Office, 1960.

———. *Foreign Relations of the United States 1944*, vol. 5, *The Near East, South Asia and Africa, the Far East.* Washington, D.C.: U.S. Government Printing Office, 1965.

———. *Foreign Relations of the United States 1946*, vol. 8, *The Far East.* Washington, D.C.: U.S. Government Printing Office, 1971.

War and Peace Aims: Extracts from Statements of United Nations Leaders (Special Supplement No. 2 to the United Nations Review), 1943.

II. SHIDEHARA KIJŪRŌ SPEECHES, INTERVIEWS, STATEMENTS, ETC., IN WESTERN LANGUAGES; MEMOIRS AND OTHER WRITINGS IN JAPANESE

Ambassador Shidehara's Address (Japan Society of New York, 15 December 1920), *The Japan Review* V, no. 1, 39–41 (January 1921).

Ambassador Shidehara's Statement of the Anglo-Japanese Alliance, *The Japan Review* V, no. 7, 157–58 (July 1921).

Déclaration du baron Shidehara Kijūrō. In D. C. H. d'Avigdor, *La Sibérie orientale et le Japon*, (Études politiques et économiques). Paris: Roger et Cie, 1922.

"The Future of American-Japanese Relations." *The Japan Review* IV, no. 6, 170–71 (April 1920).

Interview with Shidehara Kijūrō. *Bungei Shunjū*, October 1933. English trans. in *Contemporary Japan* 2, no. 3, December 1933, 533–36.

"Japanese-American Relations." *The Outlook*, 317 (June 1920).

"Japan's Attitudes Towards America." *The Japan Review* IV, no. 7, 204–5 (May 1920).

"The United States and Japan" (address before the Cleveland Chamber of Commerce, 3 May 1921). *The Japan Review* V, no. 5, 115–18 (May 1921).

"Views of Japan's Foreign Minister, Interview." In Edward Price Bell, *Japan Views the Pacific*. Chicago: The Chicago Daily News, 1925, 13–18.

Shidehara Kijūrō. "Chūkoku taishi Ō Eihō to watashi (The Chinese Ambassador Wang Rongbao and I)." In Nomura Taizō (ed.), *Sekai no kokoro to sugata* (Heart and shape of the world). Tokyo: Fujitōsha, 1949.

———. *Gaikō gojūnen* (Fifty Years of Diplomacy). Tokyo: Yomiuri Shinbunsha, 1951 (new ed.: 1976; Chūō Kōronsha, 1987).

———. *Gaikō kanken* (Personal views on diplomacy), 1928 (Pamphlet in "Shidehara documents," 11).

———. *Wasureenu hitobito* (People one doesn't forget). *Bungei Shunjū*, January 1951, 54–65.

———. *Watakushi no yōshō jidai* (My childhood). *The Yomiuri Shinbun gakkō-ban*, 27. November 1950.

Shidehara Heiwa Zaidan (ed.). *Shidehara Kijūrō*. Tokyo: Dainippon Hōrei Insatsu, 1955.

III. UNPUBLISHED "SHIDEHARA DOCUMENTS" IN NATIONAL DIET LIBRARY (FROM *SHIDEHARA HEIWA BUNKO MOKUROKU*)

Shidehara Heiwa Bunko. *Nihon koku kempō seitei kankei shiryō*. Tokyo: Shidehara Kijūrō-shi (Herr Shidehara Kijūrō). Shidehara documents, reels 1–8.

———. *Shidehara jihitsu shoronbun*. Shidehara documents, reels 9–10.

———. *Shidehara sensei gaikō ronbun shū*. Shidehara documents, reel 11.

————. *Shidehara sensei eibun genkō*. Shidehara documents, reel 12.

————. *Nihachi dōsōkai kiji*. Shidehara documents, reel 13.

————. *Ōta Taiwan sōtoku-ate shokan*. Shidehara documents, reel 14.

————. *Kyokutō gunji saiban ni okeru Hirota hikoku bengo kankei shiryō*. Shidehara documents, reels 15–23.

————. *Shidehara naikaku no shokuryō taisaku to nōgyō shisaku*. Shidehara documents, reel 24.

————. *Shidehara naikaku no senkyohō kaisei to dai nijūni kaisō senkyo*. Shidehara documents, reel 25.

————. *Shidehara naikaku no fukuin taisaku*. Shidehara documents, reel 26.

————. *Shidehara naikaku ni okeru tsuihō ni kansuru kankei shorui*. Shidehara documents, reel 27.

————. *Shidehara naikaku to Sensō Chōsakai*. Shidehara documents, reel 28.

————. *Shidehara naikaku no keizai kiki kinkyū taisaku*. Shidehara documents, reel 29.

————. *Shidehara naikaku ni taisuru rengōgun shireibu no shirei oyobi oboegaki—rengōgun no tainichi seisaku*. Shidehara documents, reel 30.

————. *Shoka no Shidehara-kan*. Shidehara documents, reel 31.

————. *Kimura Takeshi, Shidehara Kijūrō hakugenkō*. Shidehara documents, reels 32–34.

————. *Shidehara Kijūrō sensei shokan shū zen-rokukan*. Shidehara documents, reel 35.

————. *Eibun shokan narabini eibun kiji*. Shidehara documents, reel 36.

————. *Rondon gunshuku kaigi*. Shidehara documents, reel 37.

————. *Washington kaigi kankei*, Shidehara documents, reel 38.

————. *Shidehara gaikō hihan*. Shidehara documents, reel 39.

————. *Shidehara keizai gaikō shiryō*. Shidehara documents, reel 40.

————. *Shidehara-Morisu kōshō kiroku*. Shidehara documents, reel 41.

————. *Chōtōha gaikō mondai*. Shidehara documents, reel 42.

————. *Shina mondai kankei*. Shidehara documents, reel 43.

————. *Manshū mondai*. Shidehara documents, reel 44.

————. *Tennōsei ni kansuru mono*. Shidehara documents, reel 45.

————. *Shinpotō yori Minshutō*. Shidehara documents, reel 46.

————. *Gichō jidai*. Shidehara documents, reel 47.

————. *Shidehara naikaku*. Shidehara documents, reel 48.

————. *Shidehara naikaku no ippan shisei*. Shidehara documents, reel 49.

IV. LITERATURE IN THE JAPANESE LANGUAGE

Agawa Hiroyuki. *Inoue Shigeyoshi*. Tokyo: Shinchōsha, 1986.

Asao Naohiro. *Sakoku*. Tokyo: Shōgakkan, 1975.

Ashibe Nobuyoshi (ed.). *Nihon koku kempō no riron (Satō Isao, sensei koki kinen)*. Tokyo: Yūhikaku, 1986.

Baba Tsunego. "Shidehara Kijūrō-ron." *Gendai Jimbutsu Hyōron*. Tokyo: Chūō Kōronsha, 1980.

Bamba Nobuya. *Manshū jihen e no michi*. Tokyo: Chūō Kōronsha, 1972.

Eguchi Keiichi. *Nihon teikokushugi no gaikō* (Die Diplomatie des japanischen Imperialismus). Tokyo: Shōmoku Shobō, 1975.

———. "Shidehara Kijûrō." *Sekai denki daijiten* (Großer biographischer Weltalmanach), vol. 3. Tokyo: Porupu Shuppan, 1978.

Fukase Tadakazu. "Heiwa shugi no oitachi to shikumi—Konnichiteki shiten kara sōgōteki ni kangaeru." *Hōgaku Kyōshitsu*, no. 128 (May 1991): 10–15.

———. "Kempō no heiwashugi: dai kyūjō no kaishaku to jieitai." *Hanrei Jihō*, no. 712 (1973).

——— (ed.). *Sensō no hōki*, three vols. Tokyo: Sanseidō, 1977.

———. "Shidehara Kijûrō no gunshuku heiwa shisō to jikkō." In Ashibe Nobuyoshi (ed.), *Nihon koku kempō no riron (Satō Isao, sensei koki kinen)*. Tokyo: Yûhikaku, 1986, 74–114.

Gaimushō hyakunen-shi hensan iinkai (ed.). *Gaimushō no hyakunen*, two vols. Tokyo: Hara Shobō, 1969.

Gendai-shi shiryō, forty-five vols. 1962–1976.

Hara Kei (Takashi). *Hara Kei nikki*, ed. by Hara Keiichirō, nine vols. Tokyo: Kangensha, 1950, 1951.

Harada Kumao. *Saionji kō to seikyoku*, eight vols. Tokyo: Iwanami Shoten, 1952.

Hata Ikuhiko. *Shōwa tennō itsutsu no ketsudan*. Tokyo: Bungei Shunjû, 1994.

Hattori Ryūji. *Shidehara Kijūrō to nijuu seiki no Nihon: Gaikō to minshu shūgi*. Tokyo, Yūhikaku, 2006.

Hirakawa Sukehiro. *Heiwa no umi to tatakai no umi*. Tokyo: Kōdansha Gakujitsu Bunka, 1993.

Honda Wataru. *Bokushi*. Tokyo: Kōdansha, 1978 (Jinrui no chiteki isan 6—"Man's Intellectual Heritage").

Ienaga Saburō. *Ueki Emori kenkyû*. Tokyo: Iwanami Shoten, 1960.

Imai Seiichi. "Seitō seiji to Shidehara gaikō." *Rekishigaku Kenkyû*, no. 219 (May 1958): 20–26.

Iriye Akira and Ariga Tadashi (eds.). *Senkango no Nihon gaikō*. Tokyo: Tokyo University Press, 1984.

Irokawa Daikichi. *Jiyû minken*. Tokyo: Iwanami Shinsho, 1981.

Ishii Itarô. *Gaikôkan no isshô*. Tokyo: Yomiuri Shinbunsha, 1950.

———. "Shidehara-dan no omoide." In *Shoka no Shidehara-kan*. Shidehara documents, reel 31.

Kishi Kuramatsu. "Shidehara Kijūrō no omoide o kataru." In *Shoka no Shidehara-kan*.

Kobayashi Ichirô. *Bokushi* (Keisho Daikô series, vols. 16–17). 1938–1939.

Kobayashi Tatsuo, et al. *Taiheiyô sensô e no michi*, eight vols. Tokyo: Asahi shinbunsha, 1962, 1963.

Kurino Ōtori. "Nihon koku kenpô no heiwa genri ni tsuite no ikkôsatsu." *Hiroshima Heiwa Kagaku*, Hiroshima Peace Science 7 (1984): 1–21.

Kuroki Yûkichi. *Akizuki Satsuo*. Tokyo: Kôdansha, 1972.

Makino Nobuaki (ed. Ito Takashi, etc.). *Makino Nobuaki nikki*. Tokyo: Chūō Kōronsha, 1990.

Maruyama Masao. *Nihon no shisō* (Japanese thought). Tokyo: Iwanami Shoten, 1961.

————. "Kindai Nihon shisôshi ni okeru kokka risei no mondai (1)." *Tenbô* (January 1949): 4–15.

Minobe Tatsukichi. *Nihon koku kempô genron*. Tokyo: Yûhikaku, 1954.

Nakae Chômin. *Sansuijin keirin mondô*. Tokyo: Iwanami Bunko, 1995 (orig. 1887).

Nihon gaikô monjo. Tokyo: Gaimushô, 1936.

Nihon gaikô nenpyô narabi ni shuyô monjo, two vols. Tokyo: Gaimushô, 1955.

Nihon Kokusai Seiji Gakkai (ed.). *Kokusai seiji: Nihon gaikô-shi kenkyû—Meiji jidai*. Tokyo: Yûhikaku, 1957.

————. *Kokusai seiji: Nihon gaikô-shi kenkyû—Taishô jidai*. Tokyo: Yûhikaku, 1958.

————. *Kokusai seiji: Nihon gaikô-shi kenkyû—Shôwa jidai*. Tokyo: Yûhikaku, 1959.

Nihon-shi jiten, expanded edition. Tokyo: Sôgensha, 1960.

Nomura Kichisaburô. *Beikoku ni tsukai shite*. Tokyo: Iwanami Shoten, 1946.

Ôtsuka Banroku. *Bokushi no kenkyû*. Tokyo: 森北書店, 1943.

Shigemitsu Mamoru. *Shōwa no dōran*. Tokyo: Chūō Kōronsha, 1952.

Shioda Ushio. *Saigo no gohôkô, saishô Shidehara Kijûrô*. Tokyo: Bungei Shunju, 1992.

Tabata Shinobu. "Abe Isoo (1865–1949) no mugunbi, muteikō no shisō." Chapter 7 of *Nihon no heiwa shisō*. Kyoto: Minerva Shoten, 1972.

————. *Gendai Nihon no heiwa shisô, heiwa kenpô no shisôteki genri to hatten*. Kyoto: Minerva Shobô, 1993.

————. "Kempô kyûjô no hatsuansha, Shidehara Kijûrô." In Tabata Shibobu, *Teikôken*, ed. Kenpô Kenkyûsho Shuppankai. Kyoto: Minerva Shobô, 1965, 352–56.

Tanaka Kotarô. *Sekai-hô no riron*, vol. 2. Tokyo: Iwanami Shoten, 1932–1934 (new edition 1954/1972, anthology of writings by the author).

Tobe Ryôichi. *Piisu Fiira*. Tokyo: Ronsôsha, 1991.

Tōgō Shigenori. *Tōgō Shigenori gaikō shūki* (Diplomatic memoirs of Tōgō Shigenori). Tokyo: Hara shobō, 1967.

Ujita Naoyoshi. *Shidehara Kijûrô*. Tokyo: Jiji Tsûshinsha, 1958 (Nihon Saishô Retsuden 17).

Uno Shigeaki. "Shidehara gaikô hossoku zengo no Nihon gaikô to Chûgoku (Die japanische Außenpolitik und China vor und nach der Einsetzung der Shidehara-Diplomatie)." In Irie Akira and Ariga Tadashi (eds.), *Senkanki no Nihon gaikô* (Japanische Außenpolitik in der Zwischenkriegszeit). Tokyo: Daigaku Shuppankai, 1984, 97–123.

Usui Katsumi. "Shidehara gaikô oboegaki." *Nihon Rekishi*, no. 126 (December 1958): 62–68.

————. "Tanaka gaikō ni tsuite no oboegaki." In Nihon Kokusai Seiji Gakkai (ed.), *Nihon gaikōshi kenkyū: Shōwa jidai*. Tokyo: Yushindo, 1959.

Watanabe Yukio. *Shigemitsu Mamoru, Shanhai jihen kara kokuren kamei made*. Tokyo: Chūō Kōronsha (Chūkō Shinsho 1318), 1996.

Yamamoto Yôichi. *Nihonsei genbaku no shinsô*. Tokyo: Yûkisha, 1976.

Yoshida Shigeru. *Kaisō jūnen* (Ten Years in Retrospect). Tokyo: Shinshōsha, 1957.

Yoshizawa Kenkichi. *Gaikô rokujû-nen* (Sechzig Jahre Diplomatie). Tokyo: Jiyû Ajiasha, 1958.

V. LITERATURE IN WESTERN LANGUAGES

1. Monographs and Anthologies

Abe, Shintarô. *Creative Diplomacy; Japan's Initiative for Peace and Prosperity*. Tokyo: Ministry of Foreign Affairs, 1985.

Acker, Detlev. *Walther Schücking (1875–1935)*. Münster: Aschendorffsche Verlagsanstalt, 1970 (XXIV).

Aduard, Baron E. J. Lewe van. *Japan—From Surrender to Peace*, with a foreword by John Foster Dulles. Den Haag: Martinus Nijhoff, 1953.

Akidzuki, Satsuo. *La Question du Chantoung*. Paris: Librairie Plon, 1919.

Allen, G. C. *A Short Economic History of Modern Japan, 1867–1937*. London: George Allen & Unwin, 1953 (1951).

Anesaki, Masaharu. *History of Japanese Religion: With Special Reference to the Social and Moral Life of the Nation*. Rutland, Vt.: Charles E. Tuttle, 1963.

Angell, Norman. *The Great Illusion: A Study of the Relation of Military Power to National Advantage*. London: Heinemann, 1910.

Apel, Karl-Otto. *Diskurs und Verantwortung—Das Problem des Übergangs zur postkonventionellen Moral*. Frankfurt: Suhrkamp, 1992.

Apelt, Willibald. *Hegelscher Machtstaat oder Kantsches Weltbürgertum*. München: Leibnitz Verlag, 1948.

Aron, Raymond. *Peace and War: A Theory of International Relations*. Garden City, N.Y.: Doubleday & Co., 1966.

Asada, Sadao. *International Studies in Japan: A Bibliographical Guide*. Kunitachi-shi, Tokyo: Japan Association of International Relations, ca. 1988.

——— (ed.). *Japan and the World, 1853–1952: A Bibliographic Guide to Japanese Scholarship in Foreign Relations*. New York: Columbia University Press, 1989 (A Study of the East Asian Institute).

d'Avigdor, D. C. H. *La Sibérie orientale et le Japon* (Études politiques et économiques) "survies de la déclaration du baron Shidehara." Paris: Roger et Cie, 1922.

Ball, W. MacMahon. *Japan, Enemy or Ally?* Melbourne: Wilkie and Co., 1948/New York: The John Day Co., 1949 (for Institute of Pacific Relations).

Bamba, Nobuya. *Japanese Diplomacy in a Dilemma—New Light on Japan's China Policy, 1924–29*. Kyoto: Minerva Press, 1972.

Bamba, Nobuya, and John F. Howes. *Pacifism in Japan: The Christian and the Socialist Tradition*. Kyoto: Minerva Press, 1978.

Baratta, Joseph Preston. *The Politics of World Federation*, vol. 1, The United Nations, U.N. Reform, Atomic Control. Westport, Conn.: Praeger, 2004.

Barloewen, Constantin von, and Kai Werhahn-Mees (eds.). *Japan und der Westen*, three vols. Frankfurt: Fischer TB, 1986.

Barnhart, Michael A. *Japan Prepares for Total War: The Search for Economic Security, 1919–1941*. Ithaca, N.Y.: Cornell University Press, 1987 (Cornell Studies in Security Affairs).

Baruch, Bernard. *Baruch: My Own Story*. New York: Henry Holt, 1957.

Battistini, Lawrence H. *Japan and America, From the Earliest Times to the Present*. New York: The John Day Co., 1954 (Japan, 1953).

Baty, Thomas. *Alone in Japan: The Reminiscences of an International Jurist in Japan, 1916 1954*. Tokyo: Maruzen, 1959.
————. *International Law in Twilight*. Tokyo: Maruzen, 1954.
Bau, Mingchieh Joshua. *China and World Peace—Studies in Chinese International Relations*. New York, Chicago, London, and Edinburgh: Fleming H. Revell Co., 1928.
Bauer, Wolfgang, *China and the Search for Happiness: Recurring Themes in Four Thousand Years of Chinese Cultural History*. New York: Seabury Press, 1976.
Beasley, William Gerald. *The Meiji Restoration*. Stanford, Calif.: Stanford University Press, 1972.
————. *The Rise of Modern Japan*. Tokyo: Charles E. Tuttle, 1991.
————. *Select Documents on Japanese Foreign Policy 1853–1868*. London, New York, and Toronto: Oxford University Press, 1955.
Bechert, Heinz, and Richard Glombrich (eds.). *Der Buddhismus, Geschichte und Gegenwart*. München: C. H. Beck, 1984 (orig. English ed.: London, 1984).
Beek en Donk, de Jong van. *History of the Peace Movement in the Netherlands*. Den Haag: Morikita Shoten, 1915.
Bell, Edward Price (ed.). *Japan views the Pacific, conversations on vital international issues with Viscount Kato, premier, and Baron Shidehara, foreign minister in the Imperial Japanese cabinet*. Chicago: The Chicago Daily News Co., 1925.
Bellah, Robert Neelly. *Tokugawa Religion: the Values of Pre-industrial Japan*. New York: Free Press/London: Collier Macmillan, 1985 (1957).
Bendix, Reinhard, and Roth, Guenther. *Scholarship and Partisanship: Essays on Max Weber*. Berkeley, Los Angeles, and London: University of California Press, 1971.
Benedict, Ruth. *The Crysanthemum and the Sword: Patterns of Japanese Culture*. Rutland, Vt., and Tokyo: Charles E. Tuttle, 1992 (orig. 1946).
Bennett, Edward M. and Burns, Richard D. (eds.). *Diplomats in Crisis*. Oxford, Santa Barbara: ABC-Clio Press, 1974.
Benz, Wolfgang (ed.). *Pazifismus in Deutschland. Dokumente der Friedensbewegung 1890–1939*. Frankfurt: Fischer, 1988.
Bersihand, Roger. *Geschichte Japans—Von den Anfängen bis zur Gegenwart*. Stuttgart: Alfred Kröner, 1963.
Bikle, George B., Jr. *The New Jerusalem—Aspects of Utopianism in the Thought of Kagawa Toyohiko*. Tucson: The University of Arizona Press, 1976 (The Association of Asian Studies: Monograph No. XXX).
Blacker, Carmen. *The Japanese Enlightenment: A Study of the Writings of Fukuzawa Yukichi*. Cambridge: Cambridge University Press, 1964.
Blacker, Richard. *The Needle-Watcher—The Will Adams Story, British Samurai*. Rutland, Vt., and Tokyo: Charles Tuttle, 1986 (orig. 1932).
Bloch, Ernst. *Geist der Utopie*. München and Leipzig: Faksimile der Ausgabe von Duncker & Humblot, 1918 (Suhrkamp Gesamtausgabe vol. 16).
Bloch, Jean de. *Is War now Impossible? Being an Abridgement of "The War of the Future in its Technical, Economic and Political Relations"*. London: Grant Richards, 1899.
Bloch, Kurt. *German Interests and Policies in the Far East*. New York: Institute of Pacific Relations, 1940.

Borg, Dorothy. *The United States and the Far Eastern Crisis of 1933–1938*. Cambridge: Harvard University Press, 1964.

Borg, Dorothy, and Okamoto Shumpei (eds.). *Pearl Harbor as History. Japanese-American Relations 1931–1941*. New York: Columbia University Press, 1973 (Studies of the East Asian Institute).

Borton, Hugh. *American Presurrender Planning for Postwar Japan*. New York: East Asian Institute, Columbia University, 1967.

———. *Japan's Modern Century: From Perry to 1970*. New York: The Ronald Press Co., 1970 (1955).

Boxer, Charles Ralph. *The Christian Century in Japan 1549–1650*. Berkeley: University of California Press, 1967 (1951).

Brockdorff-Rantzau, Graf. *Dokumente und Gedanken um Versailles*. Berlin: Verlag für Kulturpolitik, 1925.

Buckley, Thomas H. *The United States and the Washington Conference*. Knoxville, University of Tennessee Press, 1970.

Buell, Raymond Leslie. *The Washington Conference*. New York and London: D. Appleton, 1922.

Bürkner, Alexander. *Probleme der japanischen Wehrverfassung von der Meiji-Zeit bis in die Gegenwart*. Phil.Diss., Bonn: Rheinische-Friedrich-Wilhelm-Universität, 1973.

Burkman, Thomas Wesley. *Japan, the League of Nations: Empire and World Order, 1914–1938*. Honolulu: University of Hawaii Press, 2007.

———. *Japan, the League of Nations, and the New World Order, 1918–1920*. The University of Michigan, diss., 1975.

Butow, Robert J. C. *Japan's Decision to Surrender*. Stanford, Calif.: Stanford University Press, 1954 (The Hoover Library on War, Revolution and Peace, 24).

———. *Tojo and the Coming of the War*. Stanford, Calif.: Stanford University Press, 1972.

Butler, Harold. *The Lost Peace*. New York: Harcourt, Brace and Company, 1942.

Carr, Edward Hallett, E. H. *Conditions of Peace*. London: Macmillan, 1944.

———. *International Relations Between the Two World Wars (1919–1939)*. London: Macmillan, 1950.

Cary, Otis. *Eyewitness to History*. Tokyo: Kōdansha International, 1975 (reprint 1995).

Chatfield, Charles (ed.). *Peace Movements in America*. New York: Schocken, 1973.

Close, Upton. *Behind the Face of Japan*. New York and London: D. Appleton-Century Co., 1942.

——— (Josef Washington Hall). *The Revolt of Asia—The End of the White Man's World Dominance*. New York and London: G.P. Putnam's Sons, 1927.

Clyde, Paul Hibbert. *The Far East—A History of the Impact of the West on Eastern Asia*. Englewood Cliffs, N.J.: Prentice-Hall, 1958.

Cohen, Theodore, and Herbert Passin (eds.). *Remaking Japan. The American Occupation as New Deal*. New York: The Free Press, 1987.

Colcord, Samuel. *The Great Deception—Bringing into the Light the Real Meaning and Mandate of the Harding Vote as to Peace*. New York: Boni and Liveright, 1921.

Collcutt, Martin, *The Five Mountains: The Rinzai Zen Monastic Institution in Medieval Japan*. Cambridge, Mass.: Harvard University Press, 1981 (Harvard East Asian Monographs 85).

Connors, Lesley. *The Emperor's Advisor: Saionji Kinmochi and Pre-war Japanese Politics*. London, Sydney, and Wolfeboro, N.H.: Croom Helm and Nissan Institute for Japanese Studies, University of Oxford, 1987.

Conze, Edward. *Buddhist Wisdom Books, Containing the Diamond Sutra and the Heart Sutra*. London: George Allen & Unwin, 1966.

Coox, Alvin D., and Hilary Conroy (eds.). *China and Japan: Search for Balance since World War I*. Santa Barbara, Calif., and Oxford: ABC-Clio, 1978.

Cortazzi, Hugh (ed.). *Britain and Japan: Biographical Portraits*, vol. IV. London: Japan Library, 2002.

Crowley, James B. *Japan's Quest for Autonomy, National Security and Foreign Policy 1930–1938*. Princeton, N.J.: Princeton University Press, 1966.

Czempiel, Ernst-Otto. *Friedensstrategien—Systemwandel durch Internationale Organisationen, Demokratisierung und Wirtschaft*. Paderborn, München, Wien, and Zürich: Ferdinand Schöningh, 1986.

De Bary, William Theodore, Tsunoda Ryûsaku, and Donald Keene. *Sources of Japanese Tradition*, two vols. New York and London: Columbia University Press, 1964 (1958).

Delassus, Jean Francois. *The Japanese: A Critical Evaluation of the Character and Culture of a People*. New York: Hart, 1972.

Delbrück, Jost, and Rüdiger Wolfrum. *Völkerrecht (begr. von Georg Dahm)*, vol. I/1, Die Grundlagen. Die Völkerrechtssubjekte. Berlin and New York: Walter de Gruyter, 1989.

Dewey, John. *Logic, the Theory of Enquiry*. New York: Irvington Publishers, 1982.

Dower, John. *Embracing Defeat: Japan in the Wake of World War II*. New York: W. W. Norton, 1999.

———. *Empire and Aftermath. Yoshida Shigeru and the Japanese Experience, 1878–1954*. Cambridge, Mass., and London: Council on East Asian Studies, Harvard University Press, 1988 (1979, Harvard East Asian Monographs, 84).

———. *Japan in War and Peace, Selected Essays*. New York: New Press, 1993.

———. *War without Mercy*. New York: Pantheon Books, 1986.

Drifte, Reinhard. *Japans Quest For A Permanent Security Council Seat: A Matter Of Pride Or Justice?* New York: St. Martin's Press, in association with St. Antony's College, Oxford, 2000.

Dülffer, Jost. *Regeln gegen den Krieg? Die Haager Friedenskonferenzen von 1899 und 1907 in der internationalen Politik*. Berlin, Frankfurt, and Wien: Ullstein, 1981.

Dumoulin, Heinrich (ed.). *Buddhismus der Gegenwart*. Freiburg i. Br.: Herder, 1970.

Dungen, Peter van den. *The Making of Peace: Jean de Bloch and the First Hague Peace Conference*. Los Angeles: Center for the Study of Armament and Disarmament, California State University at Los Angeles, 1983 (Occasional Papers Series, no.12).

Duus, Peter (ed.). *The Cambridge History of Japan*, six vols. Cambridge, Mass., New York, New Rochelle, Melbourne, and Sidney: Cambridge University Press, 1988.

————. *The Rise of Modern Japan*. Boston (Atlanta, Dallas, Geneva, Ill., Hopewell, N.J., Palo Alto, and London): Houghton Mifflin Co., 1976.

Einstein, Albert. *Über den Frieden: Weltordnung oder Weltuntergang*. Bern: Herbert Lang, 1975 (*Einstein on Peace*, ed. Otto Nathan and Heinz Norden, with foreword by Bertrand Russell; New York: Simon and Schuster, 1960).

Eisenstadt, S. N. *Japanese Civilization—A Comparative View*. Chicago and London: The University of Chicago Press, 1996.

———— (ed.). *Kulturen der Achsenzeit*, 2 Bde. Frankfurt: Suhrkamp, 1987.

———— (ed.). *Kulturen der Achsenzeit II—Die institutionelle und kulturelle Dynamik*, 3 Bde., Frankfurt: Suhrkamp, 1992.

Ellis, L. Ethan. *Frank B. Kellogg and American Foreign Relations, 1925–1929*. New Brunswick, N.J.: Rutgers University Press, 1961.

Eno, Robert. *The Confucian Creation of Heaven: Philosophy and the Defense of Ritual Mastery*. Albany: State University of New York, 1990.

Erzberger, Matthias. *The League of Nations: The Way to the World's Peace*, trans. Bernard Miall. New York: Henry Holt, 1919.

Eubel, Paul u.a. (ed.). *Das japanische Rechtssystem: Ein Grundriß mit Hinweisen und Materialien zum Studium des japanischen Rechts*. Frankfurt: Alfred Metzner, 1979 (Arbeiten zur Rechtsvergleichung; Schriftenreihe der Gesellschaft für Rechts vergleichung, 96).

Fairbank, John King, Edwin O. Reischauer, and Albert M. Craig. *East Asia, The Modern Transformation*. London: George Allen & Unwin, 1965 (A History of East Asian Civilization, vol. II).

Fieldhouse, David Kenneth. *The Colonial Empires: A Comparative Survey from the Eighteenth Century*. New York: Delacorte, 1967.

Finkelstein, Marina S., and Lawrence S. Finkelstein (eds.). *Collective Security*. San Francisco: Chandler, 1966 (Publications in Political Science, World Politics Series).

Fischer, Peter (ed.). *Buddhismus und Nationalismus im modernen Japan*. Bochum: Studienverlag Dr. N. Brockmeyer, 1979.

Foerster, Friedrich Wilhelm. *Europe and the German Question*. New York: Sheed & Ward, 1940.

————. *Mein Kampf gegen das militaristische und nationalistische Deutschland* (My fight against militaristic and nationalistic Germany). Stuttgart: Verlag Friede durch Recht, 1920.

Forke, A. *Geschichte der alten chinesischen Philosophie*. Hamburg: Kommissionsverlag L. Friederichsen & Co., 1927.

The Foreign Correspondents Club of Japan. *Foreign Correspondent in Japan: Reporting a Half Century of Upheavals: From 1945 to the Present*. Rutland, Vt., and Tokyo: Charles E. Tuttle, 1998.

Fortuna, Ursula. *Der Völkerbundgedanke in Deutschland während des Ersten Weltkrieges*. Diss., Zürich: Europa Verlag, 1974.

Fried, Alfred Hermann. *Handbuch der Friedensbewegung*. Berlin and Leipzig: Verlag der "Friedens-Warte," 1904 and 1911/1913 (reprint: New York, 1972).

Fujii, Masato. *Die Wahrheit über Japan, dritte Ergänzung: Frage an Dr. E. Naumann*. Tokyo: Japanisch-Deutsche Gesellschaft, 1982.

Fujimoto, Hiroshi (ed.). *Fifty Years of Light and Dark: The Hirohito Era*, by the Staff of the Mainichi Daily News. Tokyo: Mainichi Newspapers, 1975.

Fukase, Tadakazu, and Higuchi Yoichi. *Le constitutionnalisme et ses problèmes au Japon: une approche comparative*. Paris: Presses Universitaires de France, 1984.

Fukuzawa, Yukichi, *An Encouragement of Learning*, trans. David A. Dilworth and Umeyo Hirano. Tokyo: Sophia University Press, 1969.

———. *An Outline of a Theory of Civilization*. Tokyo: Sophia University, 1973 (A Monumenta Nipponica Monograph).

Gardner, Daniel K. *Chu Hsi and the "Ta Hsueh": Neo-Confucian Reflection on the Confucian Canon*. Cambridge, Mass., and London: Council on East Asian Studies (Harvard University Press), 1986.

Gayn, Mark J. *Japan Diary*. Rutland, Vt., and Tokyo: Tuttle, 1984.

———. *The Fight for the Pacific*. New York: William Morrow & Co., 1941.

Genoni, Maurizio A. M. *Die Notwehr im Völkerrecht*. Zürich: Schulthess Polygraphischer Verlag, 1987 (Schweizer Studien zum Internationalen Recht, vol. 48).

Gernet, Jaques. *A History of Chinese Civilization*, trans. J. R. Foster and Charles Hartmann. New York, Melbourne: Cambridge University Press, 1996 (Paris, 1972).

Gibney, Frank. *The Pacific Century: America and Asia in a Changing World*. New York: Charles Scribner's Sons, etc. (Maxwell Macmillan International, New York, Oxford, Singapore, Sydney), 1992.

Gneuss, Christian und Kocka, Jürgen (ed.). *Max Weber, Ein Symposium*. München: dtv, 1988.

Goodrich, Leland M., and Edvard Hambro. *Charter of the United Nations: Commentary and Documents*. Boston: World Peace Foundation, 1946.

Grahl-Madsen, Atle, and Jiri Toman (eds.). *The Spirit of Uppsala*. Berlin, New York: Walter de Gruyter, 1984 (Proceedings of the Joint UNITAR-Uppsala University Seminar on International Law and Organization for a New World Order [JUS 81], Uppsala 9–18 June 1981).

Grew, Joseph Clark. *Report from Tokyo: A Warning to the United Nations*. London: Hammond, 1943.

———. *Ten Years in Japan*. New York: Simon and Schuster, 1944 (reprint: Arno Press, 1972; German edition titled *Zehn Jahre in Japan*; Stuttgart: Mittelbach, 1947).

Grewe, Wilhelm G. *Antinomien des Föderalismus*. Schloß Bleckede a.d. Elbe: Otto Meissners Verlag, 1948 (Recht und Zeit, vol. 3).

———. *The Epochs of International Law*, trans. and rev. Michael Byers. Berlin and New York: Walter de Gruyter, 2000 (orig. German, *Epochen der Völkerrechtsgeschichte*; Baden-Baden: Nomos, 1984).

———. *Staat, Wirtschaft und Gesellschaft im heutigen Japan* (State, economy and society in contemporary Japan). Tübingen: J. C. B. Mohr, 1978.

———. *Verfassung und politische Realität im heutigen Japan*. Tokyo: Deutsche Gesellschaft für Natur- und Völkerkunde Ostasiens, 1978 (OAG-Aktuell).

Grimm, Tilemann. *Die weltpolitische Lage 1933-1935* (The world political situation 1933–1935). In Oswald Hauser (ed.), *Weltpolitik 1933-1939, 13 Vorträge* (World politics 1933–1939, thirteen lectures). Frankfurt and Zürich: Musterschmidt Göttingen, 1973.

Griswold, A. W. *The Far Eastern Policy of the United States.* New York: Harcourt, Brace & Co., 1938.

Grosser, Alfred. *Wider den Strom, Aufklärung als Friedenspolitik.* München: dtv, 1976.

Hall, John Whitney. *Das Japanische Kaiserreich.* Frankfurt: Fischer, 1968 (Fischer Weltgeschichte, vol. 20).

Hall, John Whitney et al. (eds.). *The Cambridge History of Japan.* Cambridge and New York: Cambridge University Press, 1988.

Hambro, Edvard. *Charter of the United Nations: Commentary and Documents.* Boston: World Peace Foundation, 1946.

Hammitzsch, Horst (ed.). *Japan Handbuch.* Wiesbaden: Franz Steiner Verlag, 1981.

———. *Die Entwicklung der Selbstverteidigungsstreitkräfte und Aspekte der zivilmilitärischen Beziehungen in Japan* (The Development of the Self-Defense Forces and aspects of civil-military relations in Japan). Diss., Bonn, 1985.

——— (ed.) *Von der Landesöffnung bis zur Meiji-Restauration.* Wiesbaden: Franz Steiner Verlag, 1976 (History of Japanese foreign relations by Dr. Morinosuke Kajima, edited in cooperation with the Kajima Peace Research Institute, vol. 1).

Hellegers, Dale M. *We, the Japanese People: World War II and the Origins of the Japanese Constitution,* two vols. Stanford, Calif.: Stanford University Press, 2001.

Henderson, Dan Fenno (ed.). *The Constitution of Japan—Its First Twenty Years, 1947–67.* Seattle and London: University of Washington Press, 1968.

Hilderbrand, Robert C. *Dumbarton Oaks: The Origins of the United Nations and the Search for Postwar Security.* Chapel Hill and London: The University of North Carolina Press, 1990.

Hinsley, Francis Harry. *Power and the Pursuit of Peace: Theory and Practice in the History of Relations Between States.* Cambridge: Cambridge University Press, 1963.

Hirsch, Felix. *Stresemann—Ein Lebensbild.* Göttingen, Frankfurt, and Zürich: Musterschmidt, 1978.

Holborn, Louise W. (ed.). *War and Peace Aims of the United Nations, Sptember 1, 1939–December 31, 1942.* Boston: World Peace Foundation, 1943.

———. *War and Peace Aims of the United Nations, January 1, From Casablanca to Tokyo Bay, 1943–September 1, 1945.* Boston: World Peace Foundation, 1948.

Holland, Harrison M. *Managing Diplomacy: The United States and Japan.* Stanford, Calif.: Hoover Institution Press, Stanford University, 1984 (also available in Japanese translation).

Hoover, Herbert. *The Memoirs of Herbert Hoover, The Cabinet and the Presidency 1920–1933.* New York: MacMillan, 1952.

———. *The Problems of lasting Peace* (H. H. & Hugh Gibson). Garden City, N.Y.: Doubleday, 1943.

Howes, John F. *Japan's Modern Prophet: Uchimura Kanzō, 1861–1930.* Vancouver, Toronto: University of Britich Columbia Press, 2005.

——— (ed.). *Nitobe Inazô—Japan's Bridge Across the Pacific.* Boulder, San Francisco, and Oxford: Westview Press, 1995.

Hu, Shi[h]. *The Development of the Logical Method in Ancient China.* New York: Paragon Book Reprint, 1963 (Shanghai, 1922).

Hudson, Manley O. *International Tribunals: Past and Future.* Washington, D.C.: Carnegie Endowment for International Peace and Brookings Institution, 1944

Hughes, Charles Evans. *The Pathway to Peace,* an address by the honorable Charles E. Hughes. Washington, D.C.: Government Printing Office, 1923.

Ike, Nobutaka. *Japan's Decision for War, Records of the 1941 Policy Conferences.* Stanford, Calif.: Stanford University Press, 1967.

Iriye, Akira. *After Imperialism: The Search for a New Order in the Far East, 1921–31.* Cambridge, Mass.: Harvard University Press, 1965.

————. *Cultural Internationalism and World Order.* Baltimore and London: The John Hopkins University Press, 1997.

———— (ed.). *The Chinese and the Japanese, Essays in Political and Cultural Interactions.* Princeton, N.J.: Princeton University Press, 1980.

Ishii, Kikujirô. *Diplomatic Commentaries,* trans. and ed. William R. Langdon. Baltimore: The John Hopkins Press/London: Humphrey Milford, Oxford University Press, 1936.

Jansen, Marius B. *Japan and China, From War to Peace, 1894–1972.* Chicago: Rand McNally College, 1975.

————. *The Japanese and Sun Yat-sen.* Cambridge, Mass.: Harvard University Press, 1954.

————. *The Making of Modern Japan.* Cambridge, Mass., and London: The Belknap Press of the Harvard University Press, 2002 (2000).

———— (ed.). *Changing Japanese Attitudes towards Modernization.* Princeton, N.J.: Princeton University Press, 1965.

Japan and the United Nations. *Report of a Study Group set up by the Japanese Association of International Law,* for the Carnegie Endowment for International Peace. Westport, Conn.: Greenwood Press/New York: Manhattan Publ. Co., 1958.

Jaspers, Karl. *The Origin and Goal of History,* trans. Michael Bullock. London: Routledge & Kegan Paul, 1953.

Jhering, Rudolf von. *Der Kampf ums Recht.* Wien and Leipzig: Manzsche Verlagsbuchhandlung, 1929 (twenty-second ed.) (1872) (Japanese trans.: Tokyo, 1890).

Johnson, Claudius Osborne. *Borah of Idaho.* New York and Toronto: Longman's, Green & Co., 1936.

Jones, Hazel J. *Live Machines—Hired Foreigners and Meiji Japan.* Vancouver: University of British Columbia Press, 1980.

Jordan, Donald A. *Chinese Boycotts versus Japanese Bombs—The Failure of China's "Revolutionary Diplomacy," 1931–32.* Ann Arbor: The University of Michigan Press, 1991.

Kagawa, Toyohiko. *Love, the Law of Life,* trans. J. Fullerton Gressit. Chicago: J. C. Winston, 1929.

Kaiser, Karl, and Hanns W. Maull (eds.). *Deutschlands neue Außenpolitik, Band 1: Grundlagen.* München: R. Oldenbourg, 1995 (Schriften des Forschungsinstituts der Deutschen Gesellschaft für Auswärtige Politik e.V., Bonn, Reihe: Internationale Politik und Wirtschaft, vol. 59).

Kaiser, Karl, Hanns W. Maull, and Pierre Lellouche (eds.). *Deutsch-Französische Sicherheitspolitik* (German-French security policy). Bonn: Europa-Union, 1986.

Kataoka, Tetsuya. *The Price of a Constitution: The Origin of Japan's Postwar Politics.* New York, Philadelphia, Washington, D.C., and London: Crane Russak, 1991.

Katō, Hiroyuki. *Der Kampf ums Recht des Stärkeren und seine Entwicklung* (The struggle for the right of the mightier and its development). Berlin: R. Friedländer & Sohn, 1894.

Kawai, Kazuo. *Japan's American Interlude.* Chicago: The University of Chicago Press, 1960.

Kawakami, K. K. *Japan's Pacific Policy—Especially in Relation to China, The Far East, and the Washington Conference.* New York: E. P. Dutton & Co., 1922.

————. *Japan and World Peace.* New York: The Macmillan Co., 1919.

Keene, Donald. *Appreciations of Japanese Culture.* Tokyo, New York, and London: Kôdansha, 1971.

————. *The Japanese Discovery of Europe,* revised ed. Stanford, Calif.: Stanford University Press, 1969.

Kelsen, Hans. *The Law of the United Nations: A Critical Analysis of its Fundamental Problems* (with supplements). New York: Praeger, 1951.

————. *The Legal Process and International Organization.* London: Constable & Co. 1935 (The New Commonwealth Institute Monographs).

————. *Peace through Law.* Chapel Hill: University of North Carolina Press, 1944.

Kennan, George F., and John Lukacs. *George F. Kennan and the Origins of Containment, 1944–1946: The Kennan-Lukacs Correspondence,* introduction by John Lukacs. Columbia: University of Missouri Press, 1997.

Kennedy, Malcolm D. *The Problem of Japan.* London: Nisbet & Co., 1935.

Kim, C. I., and Han-kyo. *Korea and the Politics of Imperialism, 1876–1910.* Berkeley: University of California Press, 1967.

Kôsaka, Masataka. *100 Million Japanese—The Postwar Experience.* Tokyo and Palo Alto: Kôdansha International, 1972.

Kracht, Klaus (ed.). *Japan nach 1945: Beiträge zur Kultur und Gesellschaft.* Wiesbaden: Otto Harassowitz, 1979.

Kreiner, Josef (ed.). *Japan und die Mittelmächte im Ersten Weltkrieg und in den Zwanziger Jahren.* Bonn: Bouvier Verlag Herbert Grundmann, 1986.

Krüger, Peter. *Die Außenpolitik der Republik von Weimar.* Darmstadt: Wissenschaftliche Buchgesellschaft, 1985.

Kurzmann, Dan. *Japan sucht neue Wege. Die politische und wirtschaftliche Entwicklung im 20. Jahrhundert.* München: C. H. Beck, 1961.

Ladd, William. *An Essay on a Congress of Nations, for the Adjustment of International Disputes without Resort to Arms.* New York: Oxford University Press, 1916 (repr. from the orig. ed. of 1840).

Lamotte, Étienne. *History of Indian Buddhism: From the Origins to the Saka era,* trans. Sara Webb-Boin. Louvain-La-Neuve: Université catholique de Louvain, Institut Orientaliste, 1988.

Lang-tan, Goat Koei. *Konfuzianische Auffassungen von Mitleid und Mitgefühl in der Neuen Literatur Chinas (1917–1942): Literaturtheorien, Erzählungen und Kunst-*

märchen der Republikzeit in Relation zur konfuzianischen Geistestradition. Bonn: Engelhard-NG Verlag, 1995.

Langdon, Frank C. *The Japanese Policy of Expansion in China 1917–1928*. Diss., Berkeley, University of California, 1953.

Langer, William Leonard. *The Diplomacy of Imperialism, 1890–1902*. New York: Alfred A. Knopf, 1935.

Latané, John H. (ed.). *Development of the League of Nations Idea: Documents and Correspondence of Theodore Marburg*. New York: Macmillan, 1932.

Lebra, Joyce C. *Ôkuma Shigenobu, Statesman of Meiji Japan*. Canberra: Australian National University, 1973.

LaFeber, Walter. *The Clash*. New York and London: W. W. Norton, 1997.

Lensen, George Alexander. *Balance of Intrigue—International Rivalry in Korea and Manchuria, 1884–1899*, vol. II. Tallahassee: University Press of Florida, 1982.

———. *The Damned Inheritance: The Soviet Union and the Manchurian Crisis 1924–1935*. Tallahassee, Fla.: The Diplomatic Press, 1974.

Linhart, Sepp (ed.). *40 Jahre modernes Japan—Politik, Wirtschaft, Gesellschaft*. Wien: Literas Universitätsverlag, 1986 (Schriftenreihe Japankunde).

Lippman, Walter. *The Cold War: A Study in US Foreign Policy*. New York: Harper, 1947.

———. *The Stakes of Diplomacy*. New York: Henry Holt, 1915.

———. *U.S. Foreign Policy and U.S. War Aims*. New York: Overseas Editions, 1944 (Boston: Little, Brown & Co., 1943).

MacArthur, Douglas. *Reminiscences*. New York: McGraw-Hill/London: Heinemann, 1964.

McCallum, R. B. *Public Opinion and the Last Peace*. London: Oxford University Press, 1944.

McEwan, J. R. *The Political Writings of Ogyû Sorai*. Cambridge: Cambridge University Press, 1962 (University of Cambridge Oriental Publications, 7).

McLaren, Walter Wallace. *Japanese Government Documents*, repr. Tokyo: Asiatic Society of Japan, 1979 (1914).

MacMurray, John V. A. (ed.). *Treaties and Agreements with and Concerning China 1894–1919*, two vols. Washington, D.C.: Carnegie Endowment for International Peace, 1921.

McNelly, Theodore H. *The Origins of Japan's Democratic Constitution*. Lanham, Md., New York, and Oxford: University Press of America, 2000.

———. *Sources in Modern East Asian History and Politics*. New York: Appleton-Century-Crofts, 1967.

Maddox, Robert James. *William E. Borah and American Foreign Policy*. Baton Rouge: Lousiana State University Press, 1969.

Maki, John M. *Japanese Militarism, Its Cause and Cure*. New York: Alfred A. Knopf, 1945.

——— (ed.). *Japan's Commission on the Constitution: The Final Report*. Seattle and London: University of Washington Press, 1980 (Asian Law Series).

Martin, Andrew. *A Commentary on the Charter of the United Nations*. London: Routledge, 1950.

————. *Collective Security. A Progress Report*. Paris: UNESCO, 1952.

Martin, Andrew, and John B. S. Edwards. *The Changing Charter: A Study in United Nations Reform*. London: Sylvan Press, 1955.

Martin, Bernd (ed.). *Japans Weg in die Moderne, Ein Sonderweg nach deutschem Vorbild?* Frankfurt and New York: Campus Verlag, 1987.

Maruyama, Masao. *Denken in Japan*. Frankfurt: Suhrkamp Edition, 1988.

————. *Studies in the Intellectual History of Tokugawa Japan*. Princeton, N.J., and Tokyo: Princeton and University of Tokyo Press, 1974.

————. *Thought and Behavior in Modern Japanese Politics*. London: Oxford University Press (expanded ed.), 1969.

Matsushita, Masatoshi. *Japan in the League of Nations*. New York: Ams Press (Columbia University Studies in the Social Sciences), 1968 (orig. 1929).

Maul, Heinz Eberhard (ed.). *Militärmacht Japan? Sicherheitspolitik und Streitkräfte*. München: Iudicium, 1991.

Maxon, Yale Candee. *Control of Japanese Foreign Policy: a Study of Civil-Military Rivalry, 1930–1945*. Berkeley: University of California Press, 1957 (University of California Publications in Political Science, vol. 5).

Mehren, Arthur Taylor van (ed.). *Law in Japan—The Legal Order in a Changing Society*. Cambridge, Mass.: Harvard University Press/Tokyo: Charles E. Tuttle, 1963.

Mei, Yi-Pao. *Motse, the Neglected Rival of Confucius*. London: Arthur Probsthain, 1934 (repr: Westport, Conn.: Greenwood Press, 1973).

Meulen, Jakob ter. *Der Gedanke der internationalen Organisation in seiner Entwicklung*, two vols. Den Haag: Nijhoff, 1917–1940.

Milatz, Alfred (ed.). *Otto von Bismarck: Werke in Auswahl*, vol. 5. Darmstadt: Wissenschaft liche Buchgesellschaft, 1973.

Minear, Richard H. *Japanese Tradition and Western Law—Emperor, State and Law in the Thought of Hozumi Yatsuka*. Cambridge, Mass.: Harvard University Press, 1970.

————. *Victor's Justice—The Tokyo War Crimes Trial*. Princeton, N.J.: Princeton University Press, 1971.

Minear, Richard H., and C. Hosoya, N. Andō, and Y. Ōnuma (eds.). *The Tokyo War Crimes Trial, An International Symposium*. Tokyo: Kodansha International, 1986.

Miwa, Kimitada. *Japan on the Periphery of both East and West: A Historical Interpretation of Japan's Conduct of International Affairs from Ancient to Recent Times*. Tokyo: Sophia University, Series A-34, 1979.

Miwa, Kimitada, and Takayanagi Shun'ichi. *Postwar Trends in Japan*. Tokyo: University of Tokyo Press, 1975.

Miyazaki, Tôten. *My Thirty-three Years Dream*, trans., with introduction, Etô Shinkichi and Marius B. Jansen. Princeton, N.J.: Princeton University Press, 1982.

Miyoshi, Masao. *As We Saw Them, The First Japanese Embassy to the United States (1860)*. Berkeley, Los Angeles, and London: University of California Press, 1979.

Mommsen, Wolfgang J. *Max Weber. Gesellschaft, Politik und Geschichte*. Frankfurt: Suhrkamp, 1982.

Moore, Frederick. *With Japan's Leaders—An Intimate Record of Fourteen Years as Councellor to the Japanese Government, Ending December 7, 1941*. New York: Charles Scribner's Sons, 1942.

Morley, James William (ed.). *Dilemmas of Growth in Prewar Japan*. Princeton, N.J.: Princeton University Press, 1971.

———— (ed.). *Japan Erupts—The London Naval Conference and the Manchurian Incident, 1928–1932*, translations from *Taiheiyô sensô e no michi: kaisen kaigo shi*. New York: Columbia University Press, 1984.

———— (ed.). *Japan's Foreign Policy, 1868–1941, A Research Guide*. New York and London: Columbia University Press, 1974 (Studies of the East Asia Institute).

————. *The Japanese Thrust into Siberia, 1918*. New York: Columbia University Press, 1957.

Morrison, Charles Clayton. *The Outlawry of War—A Constructive Policy for World Peace*. Chicago: Willett, Clark & Colby, 1927.

Morrison, Ian. *This War against Japan, Thoughts on the Present Conflict in the Far East*. London: Faber and Faber, 1943.

Mullins, Claud. *The Leipzig Trials, An Account of the War Criminals' Trials and a Study of German Mentality*. London: H. F. & G. Witherby, 1921.

Mutsu, Munemitsu. *Kenkenroku, A Diplomatic Record of the Sino Japanese War, 1894–95*. Princeton, N.J.: Princeton University Press and University of Tokyo Press, 1982.

Naberfeld, Emil. *Kurzgefaßte Geschichte Japans*. Tokyo: Deutsche Gesellschaft für Natur- und Völkerkunde Ostasiens, 1965 (Mitteilungen der Dt. Ges. f. Natur- und Völkerkunde Ostasiens, Supplementband XIX).

Najita, Tetsuo. *Japan—The Intellectual Foundations of Modern Japanese Politics*. Chicago and London: Phoenix edition, 1980 (orig. 1974, University of Chicago Press).

Nakamura, Hajime. *Ways of Thinking of Eastern Peoples*. Tokyo: Yûshôdô, 1988 (orig. Japanese ed. 1960).

Nelson, Melvin Frederick. *Korea and the Old Orders in East Asia*. New York: Russell & Russell, 1967.

Neumann, Reinhard. *Änderung und Wandlung der Japanischen Verfassung*. Köln, Berlin, Bonn, and München: Carl Heymanns, 1982 (Schriftenreihe, vol. 12: Japanisches Recht).

Nicolson, Harold George. *Diplomacy*, third ed. New York: Oxford University Press, 1963.

————. *The Evolution of Diplomatic Method*. Westport, Conn.: Greenwood Press, 1977 (orig. 1954).

Niebuhr, Reinhold. *The Children of Light and the Children of Darkness*. New York: Charles Scribner's Sons, 1944 (Prentice Hall, 1974; Macmillan, 1985).

Nippold, Otfried. *Die Wahrheit über die Ursachen des Europäischen Krieges* (The Truth About the Causes of the European War), ed. Harald Kleinschmidt, with an introduction by Akio Nakai. München: Iudicium, 2005.

Nish, Ian. *The Anglo-Japanese Alliance: The Diplomacy of Two Island Empires 1894–1907*. London and Dover, N.H.: The Athlone Press, 1985 (1966).

————. *Japanese Foreign Policy in the Interwar Period*. Westport, Conn.: Greenwood Press, 2002.

————. *Japanese Foreign Policy, 1869–1942, Kasumigaseki to Miyakezada*. London, Henley, and Boston: Routledge & Kegan Paul, 1977.

Nitobe, Inazō. *Bushido, The Soul of Japan*, revised and enlarged, with an introduction by William Elliot Griffith. Rutland, Vt., and Tokyo: Charles E. Tuttle 1969 (1900).

Norman, E. Herbert. *Japan's Emergence as a Modern State: Political and Economic Problems of the Meiji Period*. New York: Institute of Pacific Relations, 1948 (1946) (IPR Inquiry Series).

———. *Soldier and Peasant in Japan: The Origins of Conscription*. Westport, Conn.: Greenwood Press, 1973 (orig. 1943).

Oehler, Dietrich. *Internationales Strafrecht*. Köln, Berlin, Bonn, and München: Carl Heymanns, 1973.

Ogata, Sadako. *Defiance in Manchuria: The Making of Japanese Foreign Policy, 1931–1932*. Berkeley and Los Angeles: University of California Press, 1964.

Oka, Yoshitake. *Konoe Fumimarô, A Political Biography*. Tokyo: University of Tokyo Press, 1983.

Ôkuma, Shigenobu (ed.). *Fifty Years of New Japan (Kaikoku gojûnen-shi)*, two vols. London: Smith, Elders & Co., 1909/London: Neudruck, 1970.

Ozaki, Yukio. *Japan at Crossroads; an Outspoken Warning to the People of the World*. London: P.S. King, 1933.

———. *The Autobiography of Ozaki Yukio*, trans. Fujiko Hara, with a foreword by Marius B. Jansen. Princeton, N.J., and Oxford: Princeton University Press, 2001.

———. *The Voice of Japanese Democracy; being an Essay on Constitutional Loyalty*. Yokohama: Kelly and Walsh, 1918.

Passin, Herbert (ed.). *The United States and Japan*. Englewood Cliffs, N.J.: Prentice Hall, 1966 (Prentice Hall: The American Assembly, Colorado University).

Paul, Gregor. *Die Aktualität der klassischen chinesischen Philosophie*. München: Iudicium, 1987.

———. *Philosophie in Japan. Von den Anfängen bis zur Heian-Zeit, eine kritische Untersuchung*. München: Iudicium, 1993.

Pauly, Ulrich. *Ikkô-Ikki, Die Ikkô-Aufstände und ihre Entwicklung aus den Aufständen der bündischen Bauern und Provinzialen des japanischen Mittelalters* (diss.). Bonn: Rheinische Friedrich-Wilhelm-Universität Bonn, 1985.

Picht, Georg. *Hier und Jetzt: Philosophieren nach Auschwitz und Hiroshima*, two vols. Stuttgart: Klett-Cotta, 1980–1981.

———. *Mut zur Utopie: Die großen Zukunftsaufgaben* (Courageously embrace utopia: The great tasks for the future), twelve lectures. München: R. Piper, 1969.

Problems of the Pacific, 1927. Proceedings of the Second Conference of the Institute of Pacific Relations, Honolulu, Hawaii, 15–29 July 1927, ed. J. B. Condliffe. Chicago: University of Chicago Press, 1928.

Problems of the Pacific, 1933—Economic Conflict and Control. Proceedings of the Fifth Conference of the Institute of Pacific Relations, Banff, Canada, 14–16 August 1933, ed. Bruno Lasker and William L. Holland. Chicago: University of Chicago Press, 1934.

Rabl, Kurt. *Die Völkerrechtsgrundlagen der modernen Friedensordnung*. Teil I, "Geschichtliche Entwicklung," Hannover, 1967 (Schriftenreihe der Niedersächsischen Landeszentrale für Politische Bildung, Friedensprobleme, H.2).

Rao, M. V. Krishna. *Studies in Kautilya*. Delhi: Munshi Ram Manohar Lal, 1958.

Ratenhof, Gabriele. *Das Deutsche Reich und die internationale Krise um die Mandschurei, 1931–1933, Die deutsche Fernostpolitik als Spiegel und Instrument deutscher Revisionspolitik* (Diss. Freiburg). Frankfurt, Bern, and New York: Peter Lang, 1984 (Europäische Hochschulschriften, Reihe III, Bd. 215).

Ratenhof, Udo. *Die Chinapolitik des Deutschen Reiches, 1871 bis 1945*. Boppard am Rhein: Harald Boldt, 1987.

Reischauer, Edwin O. (trans.). *Ennin's Diary. The Record of a Pilgrimage to China in Search of the Law*. New York: Ronald Press, 1955.

———. *Japan—Past and Present*. London: Duckworth, 1947.

———. *The United States and Japan*. Cambridge, Mass.: Harvard University Press, 1950.

Reischauer, Edwin O., and Albert M. Craig. *Japan: Tradition and Transformation*. Tokyo: Charles E. Tuttle, 1978.

Reischauer, Edwin O., John K. Fairbank, and Albert M. Craig. *East Asia—The Modern Transformation*. London: George Allen & Unwin, 1965 (A History of East Asian Civilization, vol. II).

Reischauer, Haru Matsukata. *Samurai and Silk: A Japanese and American Heritage*. Cambridge, Mass.: Harvard University Press, 1986 (Charles E. Tuttle, 1987).

Reisen in Nippon—Berichte deutscher Forscher des 17. und 19. Jahrhunderts aus Japan, ausgew. und eingel. von Herbert Scurla. Berlin: Verlag der Nation, 1982 (1968).

Renouvin, Pierre. *World War II and its Origins. International Relations, 1929–1945*. New York, Evanston, and London: Harper & Row, 1969 (orig. French Paris: Librairie Hachette, 1958).

Richelson, Jeffrey T. *Foreign Intelligence Organizations*. Cambridge, Mass.: Ballinger Publishing Co., 1988.

Röhl, Wilhelm. *Fremde Einflüsse im modernen japanischen Recht*. Frankfurt and Berlin: Alfred Metzner Verlag, 1959.

———. *Die japanische Verfassung*. Frankfurt and Berlin: Alfred Metzner Verlag, 1963.

Röhrich, Wilfried. *Sozialgeschichte politischer Ideen—Die bürgerliche Gesellschaft*. Reinbek bei Hamburg: Rowohlt, 1979 (Rowohlts Deutsche Enzyklopädie).

Röpke, Wilhelm. *The German Question*, trans. E. W. Dickes. London: George Allen & Unwin, 1946.

Roetz, Heiner. *Confucian Ethics of the Axial Age*. Albany: State University of New York, 1993 (orig. Frankfurt 1992).

Rotblat, Joseph. *Scientists in the Quest for Peace, A History of the Pugwash Conferences*. Cambridge, Mass., and London: MIT Press, 1972.

Saitô, Hiros(h)i. *Japan's Policies and Purposes—Selection from Recent Addresses and Writings*. Boston: Marshall Jones Co., 1935.

Sansom, George. *A History of Japan*, three vols. Rutland, Vt., and Tokyo: Charles E. Tuttle, 1990 (Stanford University Press, 1958–1963).

———. *Japan, A Short Cultural History*, revised ed. Rutland, Vt., and Tokyo: Charles E. Tuttle, 1991 (1931).

———. *The Western World and Japan: A Study in the Interaction of European and Asiatic Cultures*. New York: Alfred A. Knopf, 1970.

Schaarschmidt, Siegfried (ed.). *Schrei nach Frieden: Japanische Zeugnisse gegen den Krieg.* Düsseldorf, Wien: Econ, 1984.

Schapiro, J. Salwyn. *Liberalism and the Challenge of Fascism.* New York: Octagon Books, 1964.

Scharfe, Hartmut. *Untersuchungen zur Staatsrechtslehre des Kautalya.* Wiesbaden: Otto Harrassowitz, 1968.

Scheler, Max. *Die Idee des Friedens und der Pazifismus,* aus dem Nachlaß ed. Berlin: Der Neue Geist Verlag, 1931.

Schlepple, Eberhard. *Das Verbrechen gegen den Frieden und seine Bestrafung.* Frankfurt and Bern: Peter Lang, 1983 (Europäische Hochschulschriften, Reihe III, Geschichte und ihre Hilfswissenschaften, Bd./vol.187).

Schlichtmann, Klaus. *Hausaufgaben—Eine Verfassungsbeschwerde gegen den Stationierungsbeschluss vom 22 November 1983* (Homework—a constitutional appeal against the decision on deployment [of medium-range missiles] of 22 November 1983). Kiel: Verlag Günter Hartmann, 1984.

Schlochauer, Hans-Jürgen. *Die Idee des Ewigen Friedens. Ein Überblick über die Entwicklung und Gestaltung des Friedensgedankens auf der Grundlage einer Quellenauswahl.* Bonn: Ludwig Röhrscheid, 1953.

Schmidt, Helmut. *Menschen und Mächte.* Hamburg: Hoffmann und Campe, 1988.

Schmitt, Carl. *Die Wendung zum diskriminierenden Kriegsbegriff.* München: Duncker & Humblot, 1939.

———. *Der Völkerbund und das politische Problem der Friedenssicherung.* Leipzig and Berlin: Teubner, 1930 (Teubners Quellensammlung für den Geschichtsunterricht, Reihe 4, H.13).

Schücking, Walther. *Der Bund der Völker—Studien und Vorträge zum organisatorischen Pazifismus.* Leipzig: Der Neue Geist Verlag, 1918.

———. *Das Genfer Protokoll* (The Geneva Protocol). Frankfurt: Societäts-Druckerei, 1924.

———. *The International Union of the Hague Peace Conferences.* Trans. Charles G. Fenwick. Oxford: Clarendon Press; London, Edinburgh, New York, Toronto, Melbourne, and Bombay: Humphrey Milford, 1918.

———. *Internationale Rechtsgarantien—Ausbau und Stärkung der zwischenstaatlichen Beziehungen.* Hamburg: Broschek & Co., 1918.

———. *Die Organisation der Welt.* Leipzig: Alfred Kröner, 1909.

———. *Der Weltfriedensbund und die Wiedergeburt des Völkerrechts* (The world peace league and the rebirth of international law). Leipzig: Verlag Naturwissenschaften, 1917.

Schwebell, Gertrude C. (ed.). *Die Geburt des modernen Japan in Augenzeugenberichten.* Düsseldorf: Karl Rauch Verlag, 1970 (dtv 1981).

Scott, James Brown. *The Hague Peace Conferences of 1899 and 1907,* two vols. Baltimore: The John Hopkins Press, 1909.

Sebald, Ambassador William J., and Russell Brines. *With MacArthur in Japan: A Personal History of the Occupation.* New York: W.W. Norton & Co., 1965.

Seidel, Anna. *Taoismus, die inoffizielle Hochreligion Chinas.* Tokyo: Deutsche Gesellschaft f. Natur- und Völkerkunde Ostasiens, 1990 (OAG Aktuell, Nr. 41).

Shigemitsu, Mamoru. *Japan and Her Destiny: My Struggle for Peace*, trans., with an introduction, Oswald White, ed., with an editor's note, F. S. G. Piggott Hutchinson. New York: E. Dutton, 1958.

Shillony, Ben-Ami. *The Jews and the Japanese. The Successful Outsiders*. Rutland, Vt., and Tokyo: Charles E. Tuttle, 1991.

Shimada, Kenji. *Die Neo-konfuzianistische Philosophie*. Berlin: Verlag von Dietrich Reimer, 1979 (Serie B: Asien, Bd.9).

Siebold, Alexander Freiherr von. *Der Eintritt Japans in das europäische Völkerrecht*. Berlin: Kisak Tamai, 1900.

Siemes, Johannes. *Die Gründung des modernen japanischen Staates und das deutsche Staats recht*. Berlin: Duncker & Humblot, 1975.

————. *Hermann Roesler and the Making of the Meiji State. An Examination of his Background and his Influence on the Founders of Modern Japan*. Rutland, Vt., and Tokyo: Sophia University in cooperation with Charles E. Tuttle, 1968.

Siegert, Karl. *Grundlinien des Völkerstrafprozeßrechts*. Göttingen: Musterschmidt, 1953 (Göttinger Beiträge für Gegenwartsfragen—Völkerrecht, Geschichte, Internationale Politik, Bd.8).

Simon, Edmund. *Natur und völkerrechtliche Tragweite des Urteils des Haager Permanenten Schiedsgerichtshofes vom 22. Mai 1904 betreffend die zeitlich unbegrenzte Ueberlassung von Grundstücken in Japan an Fremde*. Diss., Greifswald, 1908.

Singer, Kurt. *Mirror, Sword and Jewel*, ed., with an introduction, Richard Storry. New York: Routledge, 1997.

Sissons, D. C. S. (ed.). *Papers on Modern Japan—1968*. Canberra: Australian National University, 1968 (Department of International Relations).

Smith, Sarah. *The Manchurian Crisis 1931–1932: A Tragedy in International Relations*. New York: Columbia University Press, 1948 (repr. 1971).

Solf, Wilhelm H. *Kolonialpolitik, mein politisches Vermächtnis*. Berlin: Verlag von Reimar Hobbing, 1919.

————. *Wie kam es zum Konflikt im Fernen Osten?* (How did the conflict in the Far East come about?), a special supplement (Sonderabdruck) to the *Berliner Börsen-Zeitung* (Berlin Financial Paper), no. 143, 25 March 1932.

Steiner, Zara (ed.). *The Times Survey of Foreign Ministries of the World*. London: Times Books, 1982.

Stern, John Peter. *The Japanese Interpretation of the "Law of Nations," 1854–1874*. Princeton, N.J.: Princeton University Press, 1979.

Stimson, Harry L. *The Far Eastern Crisis*. New York: Harper & Brothers, 1936.

Storry, Richard. *Geschichte des modernen Japan*. München: Wilh. Goldmann, 1962 (English orig., Penguin, 1960).

Stoner, John E. *S.O. Levinson and the Pact of Paris, A Study in the Techniques of Influence*. Chicago: The University of Chicago Press, 1942 (diss., 1937).

Straelen, H. van. *The Far East must be Understood*. London: Luzac & Co., 1945.

————. *Yoshida Shôin, Forerunner of the Meiji Restoration, A Bibliographical Study*. Leiden: E. J. Brill, 1952.

Strauss, Lewis L. *Men and Decisions*. New York: (Doubleday) Popular Library, 1963.

Suzuki, Daisetz Teitarô. *A Brief History of Chinese Philosophy*. London: Probsthain, 1914.

Tagore, Rabindranath. *Der Geist Japans*. Leipzig: Der Neue Geist, n.d.

Takayanagi, Kenzô. *Comparative Study of Boycotts, Preliminary Considerations* (Contribution to the Fifth Biennial Conference, Banff, Canada, 1933), Part I—The Historical Development of the Chinese Boycott, Book I, 1834–1925; Part II—Economic Effects; Part III—Juridical Analysis. Tokyo: Japanese Council, Institute of Pacific Relations, 1933.

———. *The Tokio Trials and International Law—Answer to the Prosecution's Arguments on International Law Delivered at the International Military Tribunal for the Far East on 3 & 4 March 1948*. Tokyo: Yûhikaku, 1948.

Takemoto, Tôru. *Failure of Liberalism in Japan: Shidehara Kijûrô's Encounter with Anti-Liberals*. Washington, D.C.: University of America Press, 1978.

Takeuchi, Tatsuji. *War and Diplomacy in the Japanese Empire*. London: George Allen & Unwin, 1935.

Terasaki, Gwen. *Bridge to the Sun*. Tokyo: Charles E. Tuttle, 1981 (orig. 1957).

Terasaki, Taru. *W. Penn et la Paix*. Paris: A. Pedone, 1926.

Textor, Robert B. *Failure in Japan*. New York: John Day, 1951 (repr. Westport, Conn.: Greenwood Press, 1972).

Thapar, Romila. *Ashoka and the Decline of the Mauryas*. Bombay: Oxford University Press, 1961.

Thorne, Christopher G. *The Limits of Foreign Policy: The West, the League, and the Far Eastern Crisis of 1931–1933*. London: Hamish Hamilton, 1972.

Tiedemann, Arthur E. *The Hamaguchi Cabinet, first Phase July 1929—February 1930: A Study in Japanese Parliamentary Government*. Ann Arbor: University Microfilm Int., 1984 (1960).

Toby, Ronald P. *State and Diplomacy in Early Modern Japan, Asia in the Development of the Tokugawa Bakufu*. Princeton, N.J.: Princeton University Press, 1984.

Tokutomi, Iichirô (Sohô). *The Imperial Rescript Declaring War on the United States and British Empire*. Osaka: Osaka Mainichi, 1942.

Totman, Conrad D. *The Collapse of the Tokugawa Bakufu, 1862–1868*. Honolulu: University of Hawaii, 1980.

Toynbee, Arnold (ed.). *A Study of History*, vol. VIII. London, New York, and Toronto: Oxford University Press, 1955.

———. *An Historian's Approach to Religion*. London, New York, and Toronto: Oxford University Press, 1956 (Gifford Lectures, University of Edinburgh, 1952/1953).

——— (ed.). *Half the World*. London: Thames & Hudson, 1973.

Tsurumi, Shunsuke. *An Intellectual History of Wartime Japan, 1931–1945*. London, New York, Sidney, and Henley: KPI (Routledge & Kegan Paul Dist.), 1986 (Japanese orig., Iwanami Shoten, 1982).

Turnbull, S. R. *The Samurai, a Military History*. New York: Macmillan, 1977.

Uchimura Kanzô, *The Complete Works of*, with notes and comments by Tajiro Yamamoto and Yoichi Muto, vol. V (Essays and Editorials I, 1886–June 1897), vol. VII (Essays and Editorials III, June, 1898–1924). Tokyo: Kyôbunkwan, 1973.

Uhlig, Ralph. *Die Interparlamentarische Union 1889—1914: Friedenssicherungs-bemühungen im Zeitalter des Imperialismus.* Stuttgart: Franz Steiner, 1988 (Studien zur modernen Geschichte, Bd.39).

Upham, Frank K. *Law and Social Change in Postwar Japan.* Cambridge, Mass.: Harvard University Press, 1987.

Vahlefeld, Hans Wilhelm. *100 Millionen Außenseiter: Die neue Weltmacht Japan.* Düsseldorf and Wien: Econ, 1969.

Varley, H. Paul. *Japanese Culture,* third edition. Tokyo: Charles E. Tuttle, 1991 (1973)/ University of Hawaii, 1984.

———. *Warriors of Japan, as Portrayed in the War Tales.* Honolulu: University of Hawaii Press, 1994.

Varma, D. N. *India and the League of Nations.* Patna: Bharati Bhawan, 1968.

Vietsch, Eberhard. *Wilhelm Solf, Botschafter zwischen den Zeiten.* Tübingen: Rainer Wunderlich Verlag Hermann Leins, 1961.

Vining, Elisabeth Gray. *The Windows for the Crown Prince.* Philadelphia: J. B. Lippincott, 1952.

Vinson, John Chalmers. *The Parchment Peace: The United States and the Washington Conference 1921–1922.* Athens: The University of Georgia Press, 1955.

———. *William E. Borah and the Outlawry of War.* Athens: University of Georgia Press, 1957.

Waldecker, Ludwig. *Die Stellung der menschlichen Gesellschaft zum Völkerbund: Versuch einer Darstellung des Kampfes um die Weltorganisation.* Berlin: Carl Heymanns, 1931.

Waley, Arthur. *The Opium War Through Chinese Eyes.* London: Allen & Unwin, 1958.

Ward, Robert E. *Political Development in Modern Japan.* Princeton, N.J.: Princeton University Press, 1968.

Ward, Robert E., and Sakamoto Yoshikazu (eds.). *Democratizing Japan, The Allied Occupation.* Honolulu: University of Hawaii Press, 1987.

Watson, Burton. *Mo Tzu. Basic Writings.* New York and London: Columbia University Press, 1970 (1963).

Weber, Adolf. *Die neue Weltwirtschaft.* München: Richard Pflaum Verlag, 1948.

Weber, Max. *The Protestant Ethic and the "Spirit" of Capitalism and other Writings,* trans. and ed. Peter Baehr and Gordon C. Wells. New York: Penguin Classics, 2002.

———. *The Religion of India: The Sociology of Hinduism and Buddhism,* trans. and ed. Hans H. Gerth and Don Martindale. New Delhi: Munshiram Manoharlal, 1992 (orig. 1958 by The Free Press).

Wehberg, Hans. *The Outlawry of War,* a series of lectures delivered before the Academy of International Law at The Hague and in the Institut Universitaire de Hautes Etudes Internationales at Geneva. Washington, D.C.: Carnegie Endowment for International Peace (Pamphlet Series, Division of International Law No. 52), 1931 (orig. German ed., Berlin: Franz Vahlen, 1930).

———. *Die internationale Friedensbewegung.* M. Gladbach: Volksverein-Verlag, 1911 (Staatsbürger-Bibliothek Heft 22).

Wehler, Hans-Ulrich (ed.). *Imperialismus.* Königstein, Athenäum, and Düsseldorf: Droste, 1979 (überarb. Neudruck der Ausg. Kiepenheuer & Witsch, 1976).

Weinstein, Martin E. *Japan's Postwar Defense Policy, 1947–1968*. New York and London: Columbia University Press, 1971.

Weizsäcker, Carl Friedrich. *Der bedrohte Friede-heute*. München and Wien: Carl Hanser, 1994 (an expansion of the 1981 edition).

———. *Der Garten des Menschlichen—Beiträge zur geschichtlichen Anthropologie*. München: Carl Hanser, 1986.

———. *Die Verantwortung der Wissenschaft im Atomzeitalter*. Göttingen: Vandenhoeck & Ruprecht, 1963 (1957).

———. *Die Zeit drängt—Eine Weltversammlung der Christen für Gerechtigkeit, Frieden und die Bewahrung der Schöpfung*. München: Carl Hanser, 1986.

Weizsäcker, Ernst von. *Erinnerungen*, ed. Richard Von Weizsäker. München, Leipzig, and Freiburg: Paul List Verlag, 1950.

Wells, Herbert George. *Experiment in Autobiography*, two vols. London: Faber & Faber, 1984 (orig. London and Boston, 1934).

———. *The Outline of History, Being a Plain History of Life and Mankind by H.G. Wells*, revised and brought up to the end of the Second World War by Raymond Postgate. Garden City, N.Y.: Garden City Books, 1949 (1920).

———. *Phoenix: A Summary of the Inescapable Conditions of World Reorganisation*. London: Secker & Warburg, 1942.

———. *A Short History of the World*. New York: Penguin Books, 1970.

———. *Washington and the Riddle of Peace*. New York: Macmillan, 1922 (Dt. Übers., *Hoffnung auf Frieden*. München: K. Wolff, 1922).

———. *The War that Will End War*. London: F. & C. Palmer/New York: Duffield & Co., 1914.

Whitney, Courtney. *MacArthur: His Rendezvous with History*. New York: Alfred A. Knopf, 1956.

Wild, Adolf. *Baron d'Estournelles de Constant (1852–1924)—Das Wirken eines Friedensnobelpreisträgers für die deutsch-französische Verständigung und europäische Vereinigung*. Hamburg: Stiftung Europa Kolleg, 1973.

Wildes, Harry Emerson. *Social Currents in Japan—With Special Reference to the Press*. Chicago: The University of Chicago Press, 1927.

———. *Typhoon in Tokyo—The Occupation and Its Aftermath*. New York: Macmillan, 1954.

Wilhelm, Hellmut. *Gesellschaft und Staat in China: Zur Geschichte eines Weltreiches*. Reinbek b. Hamburg: Rowohlt, 1960 (orig. 1944).

Williams, Justin, Sr. *Japan's Political Revolution under MacArthur*. Tokyo: University of Tokyo Press, 1979.

Willoughby, Westel W. *The Sino-Japanese Controversy and the League of Nations*. Baltimore: The John Hopkins Press, 1935.

Wilson, George (ed.). *Crisis Politics in Pre-War Japan*. Tokyo: Sophia University Press, 1970.

———. *Nationalist in Japan: Kita Ikki, 1887–1937*. Cambridge, Mass.: Harvard University Press, 1969 (Harvard East Asian Studies, 37).

Yanaga, Chitoshi. *Japan since Perry*. New York: MacGraw-Hill, 1949.

Yardley, Herbert O. *The American Black Chamber*. Indianapolis: The Bobbs-Merrill Company, 1931.

Yoshida, Shigeru. *The Yoshida Memoirs: The Story of Japan in Crisis*, trans. Yoshida Kenichi. London: Heinemann, 1961.

Yoshitsu, Michael M. *Japan and the San Francisco Peace Settlement*. New York: Columbia University Press, 1982.

Young, A. Morgan. *Imperial Japan—1926–1938*. London: George Allen & Unwin Ltd., 1938.

———. *Japan under Taishô Tennô, 1912–1926*. London: George Allen & Unwin, 1928.

———. *Japan's War on China*. London: Fact, December 1937 (A monograph a month, number 9).

Zahl, Karl F. *Die politische Elite Japans nach dem 2. Weltkrieg (1945–1965)*. Wiesbaden: Otto Harassowitz, 1973 (vol. 34 of publications by the Institut für Asienkunde in Hamburg).

——— (ed.). *Japan ohne Mythos*. München: Iudicium, 1988.

Zitelmann, Ernst. *Die Möglichkeit eines Weltrechts*. München and Leipzig: Duncker & Humblot, 1916.

Zorn, Philipp. *Deutschland und die beiden Haager Friedenskonferenzen*. Stuttgart and Berlin: Deutsche Verlags-Anstalt, 1920.

Zürcher, Erik. *The Buddhist Conquest of China: The Spread and Adaptation of Buddhism in Early Medieval China*, phil. diss. Leiden: E. J. Brill, 1959.

2. Newspaper and Periodical Articles, Speeches, Papers, etc., in Western Languages

Abe, Teruya. "Betrachtungen zum Zusammenbruch der japanischen Meiji-Verfassung." In *Epirrhosis—Festgabe für Carl Schmitt*, ed. v. Hans Barion u.a., Bd.1. Berlin: Duncker & Humblot, 1968, 1–12.

Alles, Peter. "Zur Geschichte der Beziehungen zwischen Buddhismus, Nationalismus und Staat im modernen Japan." In Peter Fischer (ed.), *Buddhismus und Nationalismus im Modernen Japan*. Bochum: Studienverlag Dr. N. Brockmeyer, 1978, 1–27.

Antoni, Klaus. "Inoue Tetsujirô (1855–1944) und die Entwicklung der Staatsideologie in der zweiten Hälfte der Meiji-Zeit," *Oriens Extremus*, 33.Jg., H.1 (1990): 99–115.

———. "Kokutai, das 'Nationalwesen' als japanische Utopie." *Saeculum*, Heft 2–3. Freiburg and München, 1987, 266–282.

Asada Sadao. "Japan's 'Special Interests' and the Washington Conference, 1921–1922." *American Historical Review* LXVII (October 1961): 62–70.

Ballard, Melissa. "From Conciliation to Sanctions: US-Japan Relations, 1937–1939." *Drake Undergraduate Social Science Journal* (Spring 2003).

Baratta, Joseph Preston. "Was the Baruch Plan a Proposal of World Government?" *International History Review*, 7 November 1985, 592–621.

Basham, A. L. "Asoka." In Mircea Iliade (ed.), *The Encyclopedia of Religion*. New York: Macmillan (London: Collier MacMillan), 1987, vol. 1, 466–69.

Bennett, Neville. "Bitter Fruit: Japanese Migration and Anglo-Saxon Obstacles, 1890–1924." *Transactions of the Asiatic Society of Japan*, fourth series, no. 8 (1993): 67–83.

Bergsträsser, Arnold. "Diplomatie." *Wörterbuch des Völkerrechts*, Bd.1, 359 –378.

Bindschedler, Rudolf L. "Internationale Organisation (Grundlagen)." *Wörterbuch des Völkerrechts*, Bd.2, 70–89.

Bodard-Bailey, Beatrice M. "Tokugawa Tsunayoshi (1646–1709), a Weberian Analysis." *Asiatische Studien—Études Asiatiques* XLIII, no. 1 (1989): 5–27.

Borton, Hugh. "United States Occupation Policy in Japan since Surrender." *Political Science Quarterly* 62, no. 2 (June 1947): 250–57.

Boxer, C. R. "Notes on Early European Military Influence in Japan (1543–1853)." *Transactions of the Asiatic Society of Japan*, second series, vol. VIII (1931).

Brown, Sidney O. "Shidehara Kijûrô: The Diplomacy of the Yen." In Edward M. Bennett and Richard D. Burns (eds.), *Diplomats in Crisis*. Oxford and Santa Barbara: ABC-Clio Press, 1974, 201–25.

Burkman, Thomas W. "The Geneva Spirit." In John F. Howes (ed.), *Nitobe Inazô, Japan's Bridge across the Pacific*. Boulder, San Francisco, and Oxford, Westview Press, 1995, 177–214.

"Calogéropoulos-Stratis, La Souveraineté des États et les limitations au droit de guerre." *Revue Hellénique de Droit International*, avril-décembre (1949): 153 et ss.

Causey, Beverley D. "Why Germany Never Signed the Nine-Power Treaty." *The Far Eastern Quarterly* I (1941): 364–77.

Chelwood, Viscount Cecil of. "Peace through International Cooperation." *The Annals of the American Academy of Political and Social Science: When War Ends* (Addresses of the forty-forth Annual Meeting of the American Academy, 12–13 April 1940). Philadelphia (1940): 57–65.

Chemillier-Gendreau, Monique. "The International Court of Justice Between Politics and Law (Face aux etats souverains. La Cour internationale de justice entre politique et droit)." *Le Monde diplomatique*, Nr. 5079 (15 November 1996).

Cohen, Paul A. "Der erste Ansturm des Westens auf China und Japan." In Arnold Toynbee (ed.), *Der Ferne Osten—Geschichte und Kultur Chinas und Japans*. Braunschweig: Georg Westermann, 1974 (London, 1973), 263–92.

Conroy, F. H. "The Strange Diplomacy of Admiral Nomura." *Proceedings of the American Philosophical Society* 114, no. 3 (June 1970): 205–16.

Coox, Alvin D. "Evidences of Antimilitarism in Prewar and Wartime Japan." *Pacific Affairs* 46, no. 4 (Winter 1973–1974): 502–14.

Crowley, James B. "Japanese Army Factionalism in the Early 1930's." *Journal of Asian Studies* 21, no. 3 (May 1962).

Dicke, Klaus. "Gerechtigkeit schafft Frieden." In Max Müller (ed.), *Senfkorn, Handbuch für den katholischen Religionsunterricht* (Klassen 5–10) Bd.III/1. Stuttgart, 1987, 349–72.

Dionisopoulos, P. Allen. "The No-War Clause in the Japanese Constitution." *Indiana Law Journal* 31 (Summer 1956): 437–54.

Dore, Ronald. *Japan, Internationalism and the UN*. London and New York: Routledge, 1997.

Drifte, Reinhard. "Einige neue Gesichtspunkte zur Entstehungsgeschichte des Artikel 9 der Japanischen Verfassung." *Bochumer Jahrbuch für Ostasienforschung*, Bd. 1. Bochum, 1978, 438–55 (Studienverlag Dr. N. Brockmayer).

Dumoulin, Heinrich Zen. In Mircea Eliade (ed.), *The Encyclopedia of Religion*, vol. 15. New York and London: Macmillan, 1987, 561–68.

Eagleton, Clyde. "Peace means more than Political Adjustment." *The Annals of the American Academy of Political and Social Science: When War Ends* (Addresses of the forty-forth Annual Meeting of the American Academy, 12–13 April 1940). Philadelphia (1940): 35–24.

Egler, David G. "Pan-Asianism in Action and Reaction." In Harry Wray and Hilary Conroy (eds.), *Japan Examined, Perspectives on Modern Japanese History*. Honolulu: University of Hawaii Press, 1983, 229–36.

Enoki, Kazuo. "Dr. G. E. Morrison and the Tôyô Bunko: In Celebration of the Fiftieth Anniversary of the Transfer of Dr. G. E. Morrison Library to Baron Hisaya Iwasaki (1917–1967)." *East Asian Cultural Studies* VII, nos. 1–4 (March 1968): 1–57.

Erdmann, Karl Dietrich. "Toynbee—eine Zwischenbilanz." *Archiv für Kulturgeschichte* 23 (1951): 174–250.

Fan-Foo-ngai. "Das Lebensproblem in China und Europa." *Archiv für Geschichte der Philosophie,* XXXIV.Bd., Neue Folge. Berlin, 1922, 142–45.

Fischer, Peter. "Einige Überlegungen zur unterschiedlichen Behandlung von japanischem Buddhismus und Shintô zwischen den beiden Weltkriegen durch die Forschung bis heute nebst einer Bibliographie zum gegenwärtigen Stand der Forschung über die Beziehungen zwischen Buddhismus, Nationalismus und Staat im modernen Japan (1868–1945)." In Peter Fischer (ed.), *Buddhismus und Nationalismus im modernen Japan*. Bochum: Studienverlag Dr. N. Brockmeyer, 1979, 28–95.

Fried, Alfred H. "Die dritte Haager Konferenz." *Friedens-Warte*, 16.Jg., H.1, April 1914, 121–24.

Frobenius, Sebastian. "Hamano Teru: Gendai no mishingu rinku kara miru nihonkoku kempou to shin-sekai chitsujo." *Japanstudien* (Yearbook of the German Institute for Japanese Studies), vol. 8 (book review), 1996.

———. "Reflets japonais de symétries disparues." In *Albert Kahn, 1869–1940, réalités d'une utopie*. Boulogne: Musée Albert-Kahn, Département des Hauts-de-Seine, 1995.

Fukase, Tadakazu. "Les deux problèmes constitutionnels japonais d'aujourd'hui—La tradition et la paix." *Revue De La Recherche Juridique*, Droit prospectif N° XV, 42 (1990–1993): 482–505.

———. "Théorie et réalité de la formule constitutionnelle Japonaise de la rénonciation à la guerre." *Revue du droit public et de la science publique en France et à l'étranger*, 69, 1109 59 (November/December 1963).

Fukuzawa, Yukichi. "History of the Japanese Parliament." *Japan Weekly Mail*, 6 April 1889, 336–38. Abgedruckt in McLaren, *Japanese Government Documents*, 577–93.

Fussman, Gerald. "Central and Provincial Administration in Ancient India: The Problem of the Mauryan Empire." *The Indian Historical Review* XIV, nos. 1–2 (July 1987 and January 1988): 43–72.

Getreuer, Peter. "Die Sicherheits- und Verteidigungspolitik Japans." In Sepp Linhart (ed.), *40 Jahre modernes Japan—Politik, Wirtschaft, Gesellschaft*. Wien: Literas Universitätsverlag, 1986, 33–50.

Golzio, Karl-Heinz. "Max Weber on Japan: The Role of the Government and the Buddhist Sects." In Andreas Buss, *Max Weber and Asia, Contributions to the Sociology of Development*. München, Köln, and London: Weltforum Verlag, 1985, 90–101.

Groh, Dieter. "Imperialismus." *Geschichtliche Grundbegriffe, Historisches Lexikon zur politisch sozialen Sprache in Deutschland*, ed. von Otto Brunner, Werner Conze, and Reinhart Koselleck. Stuttgart: Klett-Cotta, 1982, 175–221.

Gross, Leo. "International Law and Peace." *The Japanese Annual of International Law*, no. 11 (1967): 1–14.

Hata, Ikuhiko. "Continental Expansion, 1905–1941." In Peter Duus (ed.), *The Cambridge History of Japan*, vol. 6: The Twentieth Century. Cambridge: Cambridge University Press, 1988.

Hayashi, Kentarô. "Japan and Germany in the Interwar Period." In James William Morley (ed.), *Dilemmas of Growth in Prewar Japan*. Princeton, N.J.: Princeton University Press, 1971, 461–88.

Heinemann, Robert K. "Tariki-Hongan und Jiriki: Erlösung durch Glauben und Selbstbefreiung durch Einsicht im Buddhismus Japans." In Heinz Bechert and Richard Gombrich, *Der Buddhismus, Geschichte und Gegenwart*. München: C. H. Beck, 1984.

Herold, Horst. "Innere Sicherheit: Organe, Zuständigkeiten, Aufbau." In *Deutschland, Portrait einer Nation*, vol. 2, "Gesellschaft, Staat, Recht." Gütersloh: Bertelsmann Lexikothek, 1985.

Hesselingk, Reinier. "The Assassination of Henry Heusken," *Monumenta Nipponica* 49, no. 3 (Autumn 1994).

Hook, Glenn D., and Gavan McCormack. *Japan's Contested Constitution—Documents and Analysis*. London and New York: Routledge, 2001.

Hunzinger, Kanso Utschimura. *Christenhilfe für die Welt*, Jg.46, Nr.7/8 (1930): 29–31.

Ikei, Masaru. "Ugaki Kazushige's View of China and his China Policy." In Iriye Akira (ed.), *The Chinese and the Japanese, Essays in Political and Cultural Interactions*. Princeton, N.J.: Princeton University Press, 1980, 199–219.

Inaba, Chiharu. "International Telecommunications during the Russo-Japanese War: The Development of the Telegraphic Service between Europe and Japan and the Russian Interception of Japanese Telegrams." *Kenkyu kiyô* 32 (Tôyô Eiwa Jogakuin Tanki Daigaku, 1993): 25–41.

Iriye, Keishirô. "The Principles of International Law in the Light of Confucian Doctrine." *Recueil des Courts*, Teil I, Leyden, 1967, 5–57.

Ishii, Yoneo. "Ayutthayam-Japanese Relations in the Pre-Modern Period: A Bibliographic Reflection." *The Transactions of the Asiatic Society of Japan*, fourth series, vol. 10 (1995): 1–9.

Jansen, Marius B. "Mutsu Munemitsu." In Albert M. Craig and Donald H. Shively (eds.), *Personality in Japanese History*. Berkeley: University of California Press, 1970, 309–34.

Jayatilleke, K. N. "The Principles of International Law in Buddhist Doctrine." *Recueil des Courts*, Part I, Leyden, 1967, 441–567.

Jessup, Philip. "Far Eastern Adjustments in the United States." *The Annals of the American Academy of Political and Social Science: When War Ends* (Addresses of the forty-forth Annual Meeting of the American Academy, 12–13 April 1940). Philadelphia (1940): 107–14.

———. "The Crime of Aggression and the Future of International Law." *Political Science Quarterly* 62, no. 1 (March 1947): 1–10.

Jung, Ernst. "Zur Entstehung des Kriegsverzichtsartikels in der Japanischen Verfassung 1946." In *Festschrift für Otto Riese aus Anlaß seines 70. Geburtstags*, ed. Bernhard C. H. Aubin. Karlsruhe: C. F. Müller, 1964, 259–76.

Kades, Charles L. "The American Role in Revising Japan's Imperial Constitution." *Political Science Quarterly* 104, no. 2 (1989): 215–47.

———. Discussion of Professor Theodore McNelly's Paper, "General Douglas MacArthur and the Constitutional Disarmament of Japan." *Transactions of the Asiatic Society of Japan* 17, no. 1 (October 1982): 35–52.

Katô, Shunsaku. "Postwar Japanese Security and Rearmament—With Special Reference to Japanese-American Relations." In D. C. S. Sissons (ed.), *Papers on Modern Japan—1968*. Canberra: Research School of Pacific Studies, Australian University, 1968, 62–78.

Kimminich, Otto. "Was heißt Kollektive Sicherheit? Völkerrechtliche Aspekte der Kollektiven Sicherheit in und für Europa." *Sicherheit und Frieden* 2, no. 1 (1984).

Kindermann, Karl. "Außenbeziehungen." In Horst Hammitzsch (ed.), *Japan-Handbuch*. Wiesbaden: Franz Steiner, 1984.

Kobayashi, Tatsuo. "The London Naval Treaty, 1930." In *Japan Erupts—The London Naval Conference and the Manchurian Incident, 1928–1932*, translations from *Taiheiyô sensô e no michi: kaisen kaigo shi*. New York: Columbia University Press, 1984, 11–117.

Kôsaka, Masataka. "Gedanken eines Realisten zum Frieden, II. Band, Heft 1 (1963/1964)," 14–16 (from *Chūō Kōron*, January 1963).

———. "Nach dem Tode Shigeru Yoshidas." *Kagami Zeitschriftenspiegel*, V. Band, Heft 2 (1967).

Krebs, Gerhard. "Das kaiserliche Militär—Aufstieg und Ende." In Heinz Eberhard Maull (ed.), *Militärmacht Japan? Sicherheitspolitik und Streitkräfte*. München: Iudicium, 1991 (eine Publikation der Gesellschaft für Natur- und Völkerkunde Ostasiens, Tokyo).

Krippendorf, Ekkehart. "Staatliche Organisation und Krieg." In Dieter Senghaas (ed.), *Friedensforschung und Gesellschaftskritik*. Frankfurt: Fischer, 1972 (1970), 23–36.

Krug, H. J. "Friedenspolitik." In Horst Hammitzsch (ed.), *Japan Handbuch*. Wiesbaden: Franz Steiner Verlag, 1981, 2017–18.

Kulke, Hermann. "Überlegungen zur Begegnung Europas und Asiens bis ins 19. Jahrhundert." *Oriens Extremus*, 33.Jg., H.1 (1990): 5–17.

Langdon, Frank, C. "Japan's Failure to Establish Friendly Relations with China in 1917–1918." *Pacific Historical Review* XXVI, no. 3 (August 1957).

Lee, T. S. "Japan: The Japanese Constitution, issued February 1973." In Albert Blaustein and Gisbert H. Flantz (eds.), *Constitutions of the Countries of the World*. New York: Oceana Publications, Inc. Dobbs Ferry. (April 1990).

Lin, Han-sheng. "A New Look at Chinese Nationalist 'Appeasers.'" In Alvin D. Coox and Hilary Conroy (eds.), *China and Japan, Search for Balance Since World War I*. Santa Barbara and Oxford: ABC-Clio, 1978.

Linck, Gudula. "'Gezwungen nur greift er zur Waffe'—Chinesische Gedichte für und wider den Krieg: Methodische Überlegungen zum Epochenvergleich." *Historische Anthropologie*, 3.Jg., H.2 (1995): 267–92.

Lummis, C. Douglas. "Japanese Pacifism under the U.S. War Machine." *Bulletin of Peace Proposals* 13, no. 1 (1982): 45ff.

McMullen, James. "Confucianism." *Encyclopedia of Japan*, vol. 2, 356.

McNelly, Theodore. "American Influence and Japan's No-war Constitution." *Political Science Quarterly* 67 (1952): 589–98.

———. "Constitutional Disarmament and the Global Abolition of War: The Meaning of the Japanese Experience." Paper presented at the Southeast Conference, Association for Asian Studies, Twentieth Annual Meeting, Washington and Lee University/Virginia Military Institute, 22–24 January 1981. *Southeast Review of Asian Studies*, Annals, vol. III.

———. "Disarmament and Civilian Control in Japan: A Constitutional Dilemma." *Bulletin of Peace Proposals* 13, no. 4 (1982).

———. "General Douglas MacArthur and the Constitutional Disarmament of Japan." *Transactions of the Asiatic Society of Japan*, Third Series, vol. 17 (October 1982): 1–33.

———. "'Induced Revolution,' The Policy and Process of Constitutional Reform in Occupied Japan." In Robert E. Ward and Sakamoto Yoshikazu (eds.), *Democratizing Japan, The Allied Occupation*. Honolulu: University of Hawaii Press, 1987, 76–106.

———. "Present Constitution." *Kodansha Encyclopedia of Japan*, vol. I, 3–7.

———. "The Renunciation of War in the Japanese Constitution." *Political Science Quarterly* 77 (1962): 350ff.

Maki, John M. "The Japanese Constitutional Style." In Dan Fenno Henderson (ed.), *The Constitution of Japan—Its First Twenty Years, 1947–67*. Seattle and London: University of Washington Press, 1968, 3ff.

———. "Renunciation of War." *Kodansha Encyclopedia of Japan*, vol. VI, 301.

Mangoldt, H. von. "Das Völkerrecht in den modernen Staatsverfassungen." *Jahrbuch für Internationales Recht*, Bd.3 (1950/1951): 11–25.

Martin, Bernd. "Japans Weg in die Moderne und das deutsche Vorbild: Historische Gemeinsam keiten zweier 'verspäteter Nationen' 1860–1960." In Bernd Martin (ed.), *Japans Weg in die Moderne, Ein Sonderweg nach deutschem Vorbild?* Frankfurt and New York: Campus Verlag, 1987, 17–44.

Maruyama, Masao. "Nationalismus in Japan—Theoretischer Hintergrund und Perspektiven." In Ulrich Menzel (ed.), *Im Schatten des Siegers: Japan*, Band 4: Weltwirtschaft und Weltpolitik. Frankfurt: Suhrkamp, 1989, 33–56.

———. "Some Reflections on Article IX of the Constitution." In Masao Maruyama (ed.), *Thought and Behaviour in Modern Japanese Politics*. London: Oxford University Press (expanded ed.), 1969, 290–320.

Matsushita, Masatoshi. "Japan's Role in the Asian Pacific Region." In *Emerging Asia—The Role of Japan* (by the Professors' World Peace Academy of Japan). Tokyo, 1981.

Mei, Yi-Pao. "Mo-ti." *Encyclopedia Britannica*, vol. 15. Chicago, London, Toronto, and Geneva, 1962, 848–49.

Minear, Richard. "Ogyû Sorai." *Kodansha Encyclopedia of Japan*, vol. 6, 73.

Mirkine-Guetzévitch, Boris. "Le droit constitutionnel et l'organisation de la paix (droit constitutionnel de la paix)." *Recueil des Cours*, III, 45 (1933): 676–773.

———. "La Renonciation à la Guerre dans le Droit Constitutionel moderne." *Révue Héllénique de Droit International* 4, 1951, 1–16.

Miwa, Kimitada. "Colonial Theories and Practices in Prewar Japan." In John F. Howes (ed.), *Nitobe Inazô, Japan's Bridge across the Pacific*. Boulder, San Francisco, and Oxford: Westview Press, 1995, 159–75.

———. "Fukuzawa Yukichi's 'Departure from Asia.'" *Monumenta Nipponica*, Special Issue: Centennial of the Meiji Restoration, ed. Edmund Skrzypczak. Tokyo: Sophia University and Charles E. Tuttle, 1968, 1–26.

———. "Japanese Opinions on Woodrow Wilson in War and Peace." *Monumenta Nipponica* XXII, nos. 3–4 (1967): 368–89.

Miyake, Masaki. "The Development of Russo-German Relations and Their Implications for Japan and East Asia 1870–1945." *The Bulletin of the Institute of Social Sciences*, Meiji University, vol. 14, no. 1 (1991).

———. "The Problem of Narrativity and Objectivity in Historical Writings, with Particular Reference to the Case of Japan." *The Bulletin of the Institute of Social Sciences*, Meiji University, vol. 18, no. 3 (1995).

Miyasaki, Shigeki. "Die Verfassung Japans und ihr Verhältnis zum Völkerrecht." *Archiv des Völkerrechts*, Bd.25 (1987): 1–23.

Mogami, Toshiki. "Normativity and Domestic and International Dimensions." *Peace and Change* 12, no. 3/4 (1987) (Kent State University, Ohio).

Mohs, Mayo. "Eying a grim Trade." *TIME*, 19 January 1981, 12.

Mühlmann, Wilhelm Emil. "Pacifism and Nonviolent Movements." *Encyclopedia Britannica*, vol. 13, fifteenth ed. (1980), 845–53.

Münch, Fritz. "Walther Schücking (1875–1935), Völkerrechtler und Politiker." In Ingeborg Schnack (ed.), *Marburger Gelehrte in der ersten Hälfte des 20. Jahrhunderts*. Marburg, 1977 (Lebensbilder aus Hessen Bd.1. Veröffentlichungen der Hist. Kommission für Hessen 35,1), 463–78 (separater Sonderdruck).

Najita, Tetsuo. "Die historische Entwicklung der kulturellen Identität im modernen Japan und die humanistische Herausforderung der Gegenwart." In Constantin von Barloewen and Kai Werhahn-Mees (ed.), *Japan und der Westen*, Bd.3, "Politik, Kultur, Gesellschaft." Frankfurt: Fischer, 1986, 176–92.

Nakamura, Hajime. "Suzuki Shôsan and the Spirit of Capitalism in Japanese Buddhism." *Monumenta Nipponica* XXII (Tokyo, 1967): 1–14.

Nakamura, Ken'ichi. "Militarization of Postwar Japan." *Bulletin of Peace Proposals* 13, no.1 (1982): 31–37.

Nakasone, Yasuhiro. "Réinterpréter la Constitution pour faire face aux urgences." *Cahiers du Japon*, 13e année, no. 47 (Spring 1991).

———. "Constitution must match the times." *The Daily Yomiuri*, 12 September 1994.

Nish, Ian H. "The Foreign Ministry." In Zara Steiner (ed.), *The Times Survey of Foreign Ministries of the World*. London: Times Books, 1982, 327–44.

————. "Japan's Policies towards Britain." In James William Morley (ed.), *Japan's Foreign Policy, 1868–1941* (A Research Guide). New York and London: Columbia University Press, 1974.

————. "Kato Takaaki, 1860–1929: Japanese Ambassador to London and Japanese Foreign Minister." In Hugh Cortazzi (ed.), *Britain and Japan: Biographical Portraits*, vol. IV. London: Japan Library, 2002.

Nitobe, Inazô. "The Influence of the West upon Japan." In Shigenobu Ôkuma (ed.), *Fifty Years of New Japan*, vol. II. London, 1910 (repr. London, 1970), 458–76.

Nomura, Kôichi. "Profile of Asian Minded Man II: Ikki Kita." *The Developing Economics* 4, no. 2 (June 1966).

Oda, Shigeru. "International Law in a Multi-Cultural World—Japan's Encounter with the Law of Nations in the Nineteenth Century." In Atle Grahl-Madsen and Jiri Toman (eds.), *The Spirit of Uppsala* (Proceedings of the Joint UNITAR-Uppsala University Seminar on International Law and Organizations for a New World Order [JUS 81], Uppsala 9–18 June 1981). Berlin and New York: Walter de Gruyter, 1984, 250–55.

Okamoto, Shumpei. "Meiji Imperialism: Pacific Emigration or Continental Expansionism?" In Harry Wray and Hilary Conroy (eds.), *Japan Examined, Perspectives on Modern Japanese History*. Honolulu: University of Hawaii Press, 1983, 141–48.

Oliver, Peter. "The French Constitution and the Treaty of Maastricht." *International and Comparative Law Quarterly* 43, part I (January 1994): 1–25.

Ômori, Minoru. "Die Hintergründe der japanischen Außenpolitik in dem vergangenen Jahrzehnt der staatlichen Selbständigkeit." *Kagami Zeitschriftenspiegel*, 3. Vierteljahr (1962): 1–25 (aus: *Chūō Kōron*, September 1962).

Ôta, Yûzô. "Kagawa Toyohiko: A Pacifist." In Bamba Nobuya and John F. Howes (eds.), *Pacifism in Japan: The Christian and the Socialist Tradition*. Kyoto: Minerva Press, 1978, 169–97.

Ottley, R. L. "Peace." In *Encyclopaedia of Religion and Ethics*, ed. James Hastings, vol. I. New York: Charles Scribner's Sons, 1951, 700.

Paauw, Douglas S. "The Kuomintang and Economic Stagnation, 1928–1937." *The Journal of Asian Studies* 2 (February 1957): 213–20.

Partsch, Karl Joseph. "International Law and Municipal Law." *Encyclopedia of Public International Law*, vol. 10, "States; Responsibility of States; International Law and Municipal Law." Amsterdam, New York, Oxford, and Tokyo, 1987, 238–57.

Patrick, Hugh T. "The Economic Muddle of the 1920's." In James William Morley (ed.), *Dilemmas of Growth in Prewar Japan*. Princeton, N.J.: Princeton University Press, 1971, 211–66.

Patterson, Earnest Minor. "Preface." *The Annals of the American Academy of Political and Social Science: When War Ends* (Addresses of the forty-fourth Annual Meeting of the American Academy). Philadelphia (1940): ix.

Paul, Gregor. "Die Anfänge der Philosophie in Japan, Die Rezeption chinesischer Kultur in vorbuddhistischer Zeit." *OAG Aktuell*, Nr. 47–54, Jg. 1991 (Tokyo, Dt. Ges. f. Natur- und Völkerkunde Ostasiens, 1992): 365–441.

Pauly, Ulrich. "Gedanken zum Bauch und zum Selbstmord in Japan." *Münchner Japanischer Anzeiger* 1 (1993): 20–36.

Picht, Georg. "Ist eine Weltordnung ohne Krieg Möglich?" In *Krieg oder Frieden? Wie lösen wir in Zukunft die politischen Konflikte? 12 Beiträge.* München: R. Piper, 1970, 203–21.

―――. "Philosophie und Völkerrecht." In Ders and Constanze Eisenbart (ed.), *Frieden und Völkerrecht.* Stuttgart: Ernst Klett Verlag, 1973 (Forschungen und Berichte der Evangelischen Studiengemeinschaft, Bd.27), 170–234.

Powles, Cyril H. "Abe Isoo: The Utility Man." In Bamba Nobuya and John F. Howes (eds.), *Pacifism in Japan: The Christian and the Socialist Tradition.* Kyoto: Minerva Press, 1978.

Ramsdall, David B. "Shidehara Kijûrô (1872–1951)." *Kôdansha Encyclopedia of Japan,* vol. VII, 88–89.

Rappard, William E. "Why Peace Failed." *The Annals of the American Academy of Political and Social Science: When War Ends* (Addresses of the forty-forth Annual Meeting of the American Academy, 12–13 April 1940). Philadelphia (1940): 1–6.

Reischauer, Edwin O. "The Sinic World in Perspective." *Foreign Affairs* 52 (1974): 341–48.

Röhl, Wilhelm. "Das japanische Verfassungsrecht." *Oriens Extremus*, 33.Jg., H.1 (1990): 19–36.

Romanov, B. A. "Rußlands 'friedliche Durchdringung' der Mandschurei." In Hans-Ulrich Wehler (ed.), *Imperialismus.* Königstein, Athenäum, and Düsseldorf: Droste, 1979 (überarb. Neudruck der Ausg. Kiepenheuer & Witsch, 1976), 351–86.

Rôyama, Masamichi. "Problems of Self-Defense." *The Annals of the American Academy of Political and Social Science*, vol. 308. Philadelphia, November 1956, 167–74.

Saitô, Yasuhiko. "International Law as a Law of the World Community—World Law as Reality and Methodology." In Atle Grahl-Madsen and Jiri Toman (eds.), *The Spirit of Uppsala* (Proceedings of the Joint UNITAR-Uppsala University Seminar on International Law and Organization for a New World Order [JUS 81], Uppsala 9–18 June 1981). Berlin and New York: Walter de Gruyter, 1984, 233–49.

Sakamoto, Yoshikazu. "Japan in Global Perspective." *Bulletin of Peace Proposals* (ed. International Peace Research Institute, Oslo), vol. 13, no. 1 (1982): 1–6.

Scheer, Matthias. "Verfassungsrecht." In Paul u.a. Eubel (ed.), *Das japanische Rechtssystem: Ein Grundriß mit Hinweisen und Materialien zum Studium des japanischen Rechts.* Frankfurt: Alfred Metzner, 1979 (Arbeiten zur Rechtsvergleichung; Schriftenreihe der Gesellschaft für Rechtsvergleichung, 96), 53–84.

Scheuner, Ulrich. "Die internationale Organisation der Staaten und die Friedenssicherung—Zum Werk Walther Schückings (1875–1935)." *Friedens-Warte*, Bd.58, H.1-2 (1975): 7–22.

Schlichtmann, Klaus. "Artikel 9 im Normenkontext der Staatsverfassungen—Souveränitätsbe schränkung und Kriegsverhütung im Verfassungsrecht des 20. Jahrhunderts." In *Gewollt oder Geworden?—Planung, Zufall, natürliche Entwicklung in Japan*, Referate des 4. Japanologentags der OAG, 17./18. März 1994, ed. von Werner Schaumann. München: Iudicium, 1996, 129–50.

―――. "Ein fernöstliches Locarno? Japanische Vorschlage für ein regionales Sicherheitsbündnis in den dreißiger Jahren (A Far-Eastern Locarno? Japanese proposals for a regional security pact in the nineteen-thirties)." *Japans Kultur der Reformen, Referate des 6. Japanologentages der OAG in Tokyo*, ed. Werner Schaumann. München: Iudicium, 1999, 103–15.

———. "The Ethics of Peace: Shidehara Kijūrō and Article 9." *Japan Forum*, April (Spring 1995): 43–67.

———. "A Draft on Security Council Reform." *Peace and Change* 24, no. 4 (October 1999): 505–35.

———. "Gandhi and the Quest for an Effective United Nations: The Stakes, 1917 to 1947." *Gandhi Marg* 26, no. 1 (April–June 2004): 55–79.

———. "H. G. Wells and Peace Education." *Journal of Peace Education* 4, no. 2 (September 2007): 193–206.

———. "The Ethics of Peace: Shidehara Kijûrô and Article 9." *Japan Forum*, April (Spring 1995): 43–67.

———. "Japan, Germany and the Idea of the two Hague Peace Conferences." *Journal of Peace Research* 40, no. 4 (2003): 377–94.

———. "Schweizerische Neutralität und japanischer Kriegsverzicht (Swiss neutrality and Japanese renunciation of war)," *friZ, Zeitschrift für Friedenspolitik* 1 (2007): 20–25.

———. "Shidehara Kijûrô, a Statesman for the Twenty-First Century?" *Transactions of the Asiatic Society of Japan*, fourth series, vol. 10 (1995): 33–67.

———. "Walther Schücking (1875–1935)—Völkerrechtler, Pazifist und Parlamentarier (Walther Schücking (1875–1935)—international jurist, pacifist and parliamentarian)." *Historische Mitteilungen* 15 (2002): 129–47.

———. "The West, Bengal Renaissance and Japanese Enlightenment: A Critical Inquiry into the History of the Organization of the World Around 1800." In Stephan Conermann and Jan Kusber (eds.), *Asien und Afrika* (Beiträge des Zentrums für Asiatische und Afrikanische Studien [ZAAS] der Christian-Albrechts-Universität zu Kiel, vol. 10), Studia Eurasiatica. Kieler Festschrift, Hermann Kulke for his 65th birthday. Schenefeld: EB-Verlag, 2003, 411–40.

Schlochauer, Hans-Jürgen. "Internationale Gerichtsbarkeit." *Wörterbuch des Völkerrechts*, Bd.2, 56–64.

———. *Das Problem der Friedenssicherung in seiner ideengeschichtlichen und völkerrechtlichen Entwicklung*. Antrittsvorlesung, Köln: K. E. Hoffmann Verlag, 1946 (Schriften zur Rechtslehre und Politik, Bd. 1).

———. "ßStändiger Internationaler Gerichtshof (Permanent International Court)." In *Wörterbuch des Völkerrechts*, vol. 3.

Schmidt-Glintzer, Helwig. "Intellektueller Imperialismus? Außereuropäische Religionen und Gesellschaften im Werk Max Webers." In Christian Gneuss and Jürgen Kocka (ed.), *Max Weber, Ein Symposium*. München: dtv, 1988.

Schmiegelow, Michèle. "How Japan affects the International System." *International Organization* 44, no. 4 (1990): 553–88.

Schmithausen, Lambert. "Buddhismus und Natur." In Raimundo Panikkar and Walter Strolz (ed.), *Die Verantwortung des Menschen für eine bewohnbare Welt im Christentum, Hinduismus und Buddhismus* (Schriftenreihe zur großen Ökumene) Bd.12, Herder 1985.

Schumpeter, Elisabeth Boody. "The Policy of the United States in the Far East." *The Annals of the American Academy of Political and Social Science: When War Ends* (Addresses of the forty-fourth Annual Meeting of the American Academy, 12–13 April 1940). Philadelphia (1940): 98–106.

Schwade, Arcadio. "Die staatliche Religionspolitik und der Einfluß der religiösen Gruppen." In Klaus Kracht (ed.), *Japan nach 1945—Beiträge zur Kultur und Gesellschaft.* Wiesbaden: Otto Harrassowitz, 1979, 56–69.

Scurla, Herbert. "Einführung." In *Reisen in Nippon—Berichte deutscher Forscher des 17. und 19. Jahrhunderts aus Japan.* Berlin: Verlag der Nation, 1982, 9–28.

Shimazu Naoko. "The Japanese Attempt to Secure Racial Equality in 1919." *Japan Forum* 1, no. 1 (April 1989).

Shimizu, Ikutarô. "Sorge um Japan: Nationale Verschiedenheiten der Friedensbewegung." *Kagami Zeitschriftenspiegel*, no. 4 (1962): 27–37 (originally published as "Heiwa undô no kokuseki," *Chūō Kōron*, October 1962).

Shotwell, James T. "International Organization." *The Annals of the American Academy of Politcal and Social Science: When War Ends* (Addresses of the forty-forth Annual Meeting of the American Academy, 12–13 April 1940). Philadelphia (1940): 19–23.

Sissons, David C. S. "The Pacifist Clause of the Japanese Constitution." *International Affairs* 37, no. 1 (January 1961): 45–48.

Solf, Wilhelm. "Das deutsche und das englische koloniale Kriegsziel" (The German and the English colonial war aim). Speech delivered at a celebration of the German Colonial Society in Leipzig, Berlin: Königl. Buchdruckerei v. E. S. Mittler & Sohn, 1917.

―――. "Wie kam es zum Konflikt im Fernen Osten?" *Berliner Börsenzeitung,* 25 March 1932.

Sumner, B. H. "Der russische Imperialismus in Ostasien und im Mittleren Osten 1880–1914." In Hans-Ulrich Wehler (ed.), *Imperialismus.* Königstein, Athenäum, and Düsseldorf: Droste, 321–50.

Swyngedouw, Jan. "Christliche Einflüsse auf die japanische Kultur." In Constantin von Barloewen and Kai Werhahn-Mees (ed.), *Japan und der Westen*, Bd.3: Politik, Kultur Gesell schaft. Frankfurt: Fischer TB, 1986, 201–29.

Tagami, Georg (Jôji). "Das Zustandekommen der japanischen Verfassung und Grenzen der Verfassungsänderung." In *Festschrift für Hermann Jahrreiß zum 80. Geburtstag, 19. August 1974.* Köln, Berlin, Bonn, and München: Heymann, 1974, 314ff.

Takayanagi, Kenzô. "A Century of Innovation: The Development of Japanese Law, 1868–1961," assisted by Thomas L. Blakemore. In Arthur Taylor von Mehren (ed.), *Law in Japan.* Cambridge, Mass.: Harvard University Press, 1963, 5–40.

―――. "The Conceptual Background of the Constitutional Revision Debate in the Constitution Investigation Commission." *Law in Japan*, An Annual, vol. 1 (1967): 1ff.

―――. "Für und wider die Verfassungsänderung." *Kagami Zeitschriftenspiegel*, II. Band, Heft 2 (1963/1964): 1–11.

―――. "Some Reminiscences of Japan's Commission on the Constitution." In Dan Fenno Henderson (ed.), *The Constitution of Japan, its First Twenty Years.* Seattle and London: University of Washington Press, 1968, 71ff.

————. "Whither goes International Law?" *Contemporary Japan* IX, no. 8 (August 1940): 1039–43 (originally published in Japanese in *Kaizô*, July, 1940).

Terajima, Jitsurô. "Wir, die Nachkriegsgeneration und 'Die Wolken über dem Hügel.'" *Kagami Zeitschriftenspiegel*, Neue Folge, Jg.VII, H.3 (1980): 3–29.

Thomas, Norman. "America's Contribution to an Enduring Peace." *The Annals of the American Academy of Political and Social Science: When War Ends* (Addresses of the forty-forth Annual Meeting of the American Academy, 12–13 April 1940). Philadelphia (1940): 43–49.

Thayer, Nathaniel B. "Japanese Attitudes toward the United States." *Annals of the American Academy of Political and Social Science*, vol. 497, Anti-Americanism: Origins and Context (May 1988), 89–104.

Tomkinson, L. "Chinese Historical Attitudes to Peace and War." *Journal of the North China Branch of the Royal Asiatic Society* LXXI (1940).

————. "The Social Teachings of Meh Tse." *Transactions of the Asiatic Society of Japan*, second series, vol. IV (December 1927).

Toynbee, Arnold. "The Third Biennial Conference of the Institute of Pacific Relations, Kyoto." *Journal of the Royal Institute of International Affairs* (London), vol. 9, no. 2 (March 1930): 189–201.

Toyoda, Toshiyuki. "Beyond the Mind-Set of Deterrence to Genuine Disarmament." *Japan Quarterly* (July–September 1992): 290–302.

Tsu(d)zuki, Keiroku. "Social Intercourse between Japanese and Occidentals." In Ôkuma Shigenobu (ed.), *Fifty Years of New Japan*, vol. II. London: Smith, Elder & Co., 1910 (Neudruck: London, 1970), 477–93.

Tsurumi, Yûsuke. "Japan's Internal Problems and Her Relationships with China, Russia, America, and the British Commonwealth." In *Problems of the Pacific, 1927*, Proceedings of the Second Conference of the Institute of Pacific Relations, Honolulu, Hawaii, 15–29 July 1927. Chicago: The University of Chicago Press, 1928, 496–502.

Ueda, Katsumi. "Tabata Shinobu: Defender of the Peace Constitution." In Bamba Nobuya and John F. Howes (eds.), *Pacifism in Japan: The Christian and the Socialist Tradition*. Kyoto: Minerva Press, 1978, 221–46.

Usui, Katsumi. "The Role of the Foreign Ministry." In Dorothy Borg and Okamoto Shumpei (eds.), *Pearl Harbor as History: Japanese Relations 1931–1941*. New York: Columbia University Press, 1973.

Varley, Paul. "Foreword." In S. R. Turnbull, *The Samurai, A Military History*. New York: Macmillan, 1977, vii–viii.

Ward, Robert E. "The Legacy of the Occupation." In Herbert Passin (ed.), *The United States and Japan*. Englewood Cliffs, N.J.: Spectrum Book, 1966 (The American Assembly, Columbia University), 29–56.

————. "The Origins of the Present Japanese Constitution." *The American Political Science Review* (Menasha, Wis.), vol. 50, no. 4 (1956): 980–1010.

Wehberg, Hans. "Der Völkerbund und der Mandschureikonflikt." *Ostasiatische Rundschau*, Jg.12. Nr.24 (1931): 599–600.

————. "Walther Schücking." *Friedens-Warte*, Jg.29 (March 1929): 65–76.

Weinstein, Lucie R. "Tôdaiji." *Kôdansha Encyclopedia of Japan*, vol. 8.

Weizsäcker, Carl Friedrich von. "Georg Picht als Philosoph." In Constanze Eisenbart (ed.), *Georg Picht: Philosophie der Verantwortung*. Stuttgart: Klett-Cotta, 1985, 46–57.

——. "Die reale Möglichkeit des Dritten Weltkrieges, Vortrag am 19.11.1984, Ringvorlesung 'PAX OPTIMA RERUM' der Universität Kiel." *Semester*, Nr. 29 (29 February 1985): 6–9.

——. "Westlicher und östlicher Geist (The spirit of East and West)." In C. F. von Weizsäcker, *Der bedrohte Friede—heute* (Threatened peace today). München and Wien: Carl Hanser 1994.

Wentz, Richard E. "The Prospective Eye of Interreligious Dialogue." *Japanese Journal of Religious Studies* 4, no. 1 (March 1987): 3–17.

Wildes, Harry Emerson. "Underground Politics in Post-War Japan (Symposium, 'Post-War Politics in Japan, II')." *The American Political Science Review* 42, no. 6 (December 1948): 1149–62.

Williams, Justin. "Making the Japanese Constitution: A Further Look." *The American Political Science Review* LIX (1965): 665–79.

——. "Party Politics in the New Japanese Diet (Symposium, 'Post-War Politics in Japan, II')." *The American Political Science Review* 42, no. 6 (December 1948).

Wippich, Rolf-Harald. "Deutschland und Japan am Scheideweg—Eine Skizze des deutsch japanischen Verhältnisses in den 1890er Jahren." In Josef Kreiner (ed.), *Japan und die Mittelmächte im Ersten Weltkrieg und in den zwanziger Jahren*. Bonn: Bouvier Verlag Herbert Grundmann, 1986, 15–55.

——. "The Beginnings of German Cultural Activities in Japan." *Sophia International Review* 15 (1993): 57–64.

Yokota, Kisaburô. "The Constitution of Japan and the Right of Self-Defense." *The Japan Annual of Law and Politics*, no. 1 (1952): 33–44.

——. "A Security Pact for the Pacific Area." *Contemporary Japan* II, no. 2 (September 1933): 409–25.

Zöllner, Reinhard. "Lorenz von Stein und *kokutai*." *Oriens Extremus*, 33.Jg., H.1 (1990): 65–76.

Index

Abe Isoo, 34, 38–40, 65n236, 65n237, 66n245
Abe Masahirō, 82
abolition: of the Anglo-Japanese Alliance, 254; of armaments, 39–40; of Buddhism (*haibutsu kishaku*), 28, 59n167; of class differences, 145n111; of extraterritoriality (consular jurisdiction), 19, 101, 117, 131; of *kazoku* institution, 247; of the nation-state, 19
abolition of war, xi, 5, 6, 8, 102, 103, 108, 109–10, 112, 165n267. *See also* outlawry of war
Achi, 14
Adachi Kinnosuke, 251, 300n429
Adachi Mineichiro, 127, 164n257, 296n387
Adams, William, 31, 60n185
Akiyama Yoshifuru, 283n222
Akizuki Satsuo (Akidzuki Satsuo), 220, 232, 291n316
Alcock, Sir Rutherford, 143, 149n140
Alexander II, 181, 193, 265n9, 271n86
Alexander III, 193
Alexieff (Alekseyev), Kuril, 185, 267n31
American Society for the Judicial Settlement of Disputes, 163n257

Anesaki Masaharu, 118
Angell, Norman, 39, 65n244
Anti-Oorlog Raad. *See* Netherlands Anti-War Council
Aoki Kon'yō, 77, 138n26
Aoki Shūzō, 131, 135, 157n202, 173n381, 175n405, 192, 195–97, 206, 214, 220, 267n33, 270n73, 271n82, 272n97, 272n99, 274n119, 274n121, 281n209, 282n212, 282n213, 286n250,
Arai Hakuseki, 77, 138n25
arbitration, international (obligatory), xi, 105–6, 107, 112, 118, 119, 134, 159n212, 162n245, 166n285, 177n420, 196–200, 216–18, 221, 227, 271n90, 273n114, 284n233, 284n236, 284n238; arbitration treaties, 185, 197, 211, 279n187, 284n234; boom (bilateral, multilateral), 106, 211; Hague Arbitration Convention, 273n115; house tax case, 284n238
arbitration court, 107, 159n212, 162n246, 188, 194, 197, 213
Ashoka, 23–27, 53nn114–15, 53nn120–21, 54n125, 54n129, 55nn131–32, 55n134
Ashoka mountain, 24, 53n121

About the Author

Klaus Schlichtmann was born in Hamburg, Germany, in 1944. Because of an early interest in Buddhism and Asian culture, he went to India, where he taught German from 1964 to 1966 at Benares Sanskrit University. Having worked as a jazz musician and a fine artist for some time, he later became a peace activist and locally participated in preparations for establishing Germany's Green Party. He was chairman of the (West) German branch of the World Federalist Movement from 1980 to 1992, during which time he took up studies at Kiel University in Schleswig Holstein, Germany, from where he obtained his MA in 1990 and in 1997 a PhD is in Asian history, political science, and international and public law.

ASIAWORLD

Series Editor: Mark Selden

This series charts the frontiers of Asia in global perspective. Central to its concerns are Asian interactions—political, economic, social, cultural, and historical—that are transnational and global, that cross and redefine borders and networks, including those of nation, region, ethnicity, gender, technology, and demography. It looks to multiple methodologies to chart the dynamics of a region that has been the home to major civilizations and is central to global processes of war, peace, and development in the new millennium.

Titles in the Series

China's Unequal Treaties: Narrating National History, by Dong Wang

The Culture of Fengshui in Korea: An Exploration of East Asian Geomancy, by Hong-Key Yoon

Precious Steppe: Mongolian Nomadic Pastoralists in Pursuit of the Market, by Ole Bruun

Managing God's Higher Learning: U.S.-China Cultural Encounter and Canton Christian College (Lingnan University), 1888–1952, by Dong Wang

Queer Voices from Japan: First Person Narratives from Japan's Sexual Minorities, edited by Mark McLelland, Katsuhiko Suganuma, and James Welker

Yōko Tawada: Voices from Everywhere, edited by Douglas Slaymaker

Modernity and Re-enchantment: Religion in Post-revolutionary Vietnam, edited by Philip Taylor

Water: The Looming Crisis in India, by Binayak Ray

Windows on the Chinese World: Reflections by Five Historians, by Clara Wing-chung Ho

Tommy's Sunset, by Hisako Tsurushima

Lake of Heaven: An Original Translation of the Japanese Novel by Ishimure Michiko, by Bruce Allen

Japan in the World: Shidehara Kijūrō, Pacifism, and the Abolition of War, Volumes I and II, by Klaus Schlichtmann